A LIFETIME
IN THE
EYE OF THE STORM

NGO DINH THI HIEP
A YOUNGER SISTER OF LATE
PRESIDENT NGO DINH DIEM

BY ANDRÉ NGUYỄN VĂN CHÂU

A Lifetime in the Eye of the Storm, 1st edition, Copyright @ Andre Nguyen Van Chau 2000, American Book Classics Publishing

ISBN 1-930586-55-8

A Lifetime in the Eye of the Storm, 2nd and revised edition, Copyright @ Andre Nguyen Van Chau 2015, Erin Go Bragh Publishing

ISBN 978-1-941345-51-1

eISBN 9781310563485

 AISN B00SBNWVKU

Library of Congress Cataloging in Publication Data
Main entry under title: A Lifetime in the Eye of the Storm
Library of Congress Control Number: 2015930391

ERIN GO BRAGH
Publishing

www.ErinGoBraghPublishing.com

PROLOGUE

I guess it was in January 1950, that I met her and her family for the first time. I remember that I was invited to stay at her home for a few days during the Lunar New Year celebrations. If I am not mistaken, it was the Year of the Tiger.

In her drawing room, dominating the sumptuously carved antique pieces of furniture stood the traditional blossomed branch of yellow ochna that sprang high from a large and tall blue Ming jar. The golden petals of the ochna blossoms symbolized prosperity and happiness.

It was *Tet*, the Lunar New Year, a time for joy and chatter, a time for family reunions, and visits of friends.

I sat there listening to the excited conversations between members of her family and visitors. So many visitors had arrived from far and near; each one came to greet her and her family and to offer the three traditional wishes of happiness, good fortune and longevity. Often, lowering their voices, the visitors respectfully inquired about her brother, the *Venerable Gentleman,* the *Prime Minister*.

Though he was only Prime Minister for a few months in 1933, a long time ago, the visitors seemed to believe that the Venerable Gentleman would soon come back to power. Strangely enough, they seemed to believe that he would come back to *save the country*. I listened to the inflection of their voices more than their words. Though still an adolescent, I recognized that the visitors were not referring to a man, but a legend.

That was how I first entered the life of the Ngo Dinh family and became acquainted with Ngo Dinh Thi Hiep and the future President, Ngo Dinh Diem.

I remember her smiling, humbly serving tea or passing around plates of cakes and fruit, or small saucers full of red-dyed watermelon seeds. I do not remember her participating in any serious discussion. I listened to her voice, soft and enchanting, with the particular accent of the people of Hue, modulating words of welcome and inquiring about members of the family of each visitor.

From what I saw and heard, she was endowed with a tremendous memory for names and places. As she chatted, the visitors seemed to be surprised and flattered that she remembered such or such insignificant incidents in their own personal lives.

I noticed how she looked confidently at the visitors with eager anticipation. Yet, even when she was engaged in an apparently engrossing chat with a visitor, I saw how her eyes discreetly followed every movement of her children and her husband with tenderness.

It was a long time ago. Today, almost fifty years later, I undertake to write the story of her life. In the interval, I have learned to know her better. At a certain time, after the great tragedy befell her family, I lived in a house belonging to her in Hue. Later, I used to go and see her quite frequently at her home in Saigon.

Over the years, her manners and her voice have enchanted me. I have admired her calm courage and her faith in men and women, in spite of every betrayal and disloyalty of which she and members of her family have been the victims.

I have always thought that one day I would sit down and write about her. At times, indeed, I have felt as if I have known her all my life and been a member of her family. At times, I have felt as if her children were all my brothers and sisters.

This book was initially had a narrower scope: it was to tell a story about her, not about her family, nor even about contemporary Vietnam. Longer and longer interviews with her and other members of her family, with her friends and relatives, have decided otherwise. In the end this book attempts to be the product of a collective memory from the time of her father to the day she died.

Everybody in Vietnam, and so many outside of her native country, know or pretend to know the history of her family. Dozens of foreign authors have written long stories about her father, her brothers and the crises that made of them tragic figures.

It is true that very few of those authors cared to know who the Ngo Dinh really were. Very few made a genuine effort to find out what their motives were, what goals inspired them, what their human weaknesses were that led them unerringly towards their final destiny.

Again, hundreds of foreign authors have written about contemporary Vietnam. Many of them are excellent, save for the fact that they have rarely given much importance to the Vietnamese perspective or shown much empathy with the suffering of the Vietnamese as a nation. A few of them, strangely enough, did not say anything at all about the Vietnamese, though obviously their subject was Vietnam.

This book was originally an intimate tale about a woman who, by no choice of her own, has found herself *in the eye of the storm* for nearly a century. It was about how this woman has lived through the terrible years that have torn to pieces the fabric of her country, and watched from her vantage point the drama that engulfed her people.

She saw with frightening vividness how millions of Vietnamese were tossed about, how they endured the horrors of wars. She had a larger share than most of them have, of the excitement and disillusionment of revolutions, the inhumanity and degradation of violence, war and terror.

She was a key witness of almost a hundred years of Vietnam's history. She, more than most of her fellow countrymen and women, experienced in her soul and in her flesh, the hopes and despair of her nation.

Her sensibility, sharpened by the tragedies that struck her directly, made her feel the impact of all the changes around her, with more acuity than that felt by most men and women in Vietnam.

This book was at first a simple tribute to her indomitable courage, and her unfailing loyalty to her faith, her ideals, her family, her friends and her country. In a certain way, it intended to be a tribute to all Vietnamese women, or rather, a tribute to all women.

This ordinary and yet extraordinary woman, showed to all those who had come to know her, that greatness is not to be found in what a person does or achieves but what he or she is. By simply living her life, she restored our confidence in human greatness.

I would not have completed this book without the generous assistance of hundreds of friends and collaborators besides the constant support of members of Ngo Dinh Thi Hiep's family, their relatives and their friends. To all of them especially her sons and daughters, I wish to offer my sincerest thanks.

The greatest encouragements and support for this book came from the late Cardinal Francis-Xavier Nguyen Van Thuan, the Servant of God, my friend, my spiritual brother, on whom I wrote the official biography, *The Miracle of Hope (2002).* At the time this revised edition of the book on his mother he is about to be beatified by the Catholic Church.

*

General comments about the second edition of *A Lifetime in the Eye of the Storm:*

After the first edition appeared, many wrote to me about the fact that I seemed to neglect to tell more about criticisms that had been leveled against Ngo Dinh Thi Hiep and her family, especially criticisms against her brothers, Ngo Dinh Diem, Ngo Dinh Nhu and Ngo Dinh Can. I was grateful for their critical remarks and told the writers that I had written the book completely based on what the Ngo Dinh's family members and friends had told me. I did not write a history book, not even a biography. In fact, I wrote a collective memoir.

If those who wrote to me -- and told me I had not addressed enough the Ngo Dinh's shortcomings and limitations -- read the book carefully, they would have found that all the members of the Ngo Dinh inner circle had leveled the harshest criticisms against their own foibles, shortcomings and errors or mistakes. Ngo Dinh Thi Hiep because of her special role, as the spokesperson of the late Ngo Dinh Kha was the bluntest of the critics and never hesitated to point out where and when her brothers (especially when they were in power) had made major blunders or acted too authoritatively.

In the years between the first edition of *In the Eye of the Storm* in 2000 and this second edition many new studies have been written by Vietnamese and foreigners on Ngo Dinh Diem and his brothers. They have brought new elements into the long debate about Diem's role in modern day Vietnam. The newly uncovered facts and documents tend to match the collective memory of the Ngo Dinh's family members that *In the Eye of the Storm* describes.

Note: See the two remarkable books by Mark Moyers, *Triumph Forsaken: the Vietnam War 1954-1964,* Cambridge University Press, New York, 2006 *and* Edward Miller, *Misalliance, Ngo Dinh Diem, the United States and the Fate of South Vietnam,* Harvard University Press, 2004.

I embrace with joy opinions and viewpoints that contradict the Ngo Dinh's opinions, points of view and their narrative, as the debate on Diem continues to be fueled constantly by newly uncovered documents. I respect the continued hostility towards the Ngo Dinh family. The viewpoints, judgments and narratives of those who continue to attack the Ngo Dinh family with vehemence are different than mine; but they may contribute to the debate in many ways. I do not have to respond to those in this book as they have found ample space elsewhere.

Like many Vietnamese, with passing days, I have found more and more reasons to admire the key members of the Ngo Dinh family, their indomitable personality, their certainty of purpose and their unvacillating faith in what they did in spite of their foibles and errors.

I hope that in the end the readers will find them quite human.

PART ONE

THE LEGACY OF NGO DINH KHA

CHAPTER ONE
FIRST RECOLLECTIONS

Her very first recollection, mixed with what older people in her family told her later, was about tigers and elephants. She was a tiny little girl when her mother took her to the Imperial Arena to see a fight that opposed elephants to tigers. It was an uncommon spectacle. It was in fact an imperial affair. The whole Imperial Court went to the Arena, seven miles southwest of the Palace, to attend the show.

It was a warm sunny day. She now remembers that she was at moments in her mother's arms and at others left standing on her feet. She was clutching at her mother's gown, all the while excited by what she saw around her.

The Imperial Arena was a very spacious place surrounded by a circular brick wall on top of which the spectators stood to watch. She remembers that an officer of the Imperial Guards had shown her mother and her to a spot on the raised section of the wall, next to the stand where the golden chair of the Emperor was set.

The Emperor was not there yet. Her mother and she spent their time looking at the colorful pennants and flags fluttering in the morning breeze and the red and blue parasols over the heads of dignitaries and mandarins.

She watched with awe and curiosity the two long lines of helmeted Imperial Guards standing still at regular intervals on the wall, as well as the noisy crowd of spectators. She had never seen such a large crowd of people before. Her mother said later on that she had expected the little girl to cry or become nervous at the sight of so many people. But, little Hiep did not cry; she was taking in all the sights and sounds around her, craning her neck this way and that way to get a better look at everything.

Then the rolling of drums and sharp sounds of trumpets were heard over the cacophony of the crowd. The spectators stopped talking, as the music of the five instruments came nearer. The clacking of ceremonial whips and the neighing of the horses of the Mounted Imperial Guards announced the arrival of the Emperor.

Her eyes wandered from golden parasol to glittering golden parasol carried by a horde of people around the Emperor. There was a hush when the Emperor, who had dismounted from his famous white horse, started walking towards the wall, ascended the steps and sat down on his golden chair.

The sun was already high, and his escort was brandishing long-stemmed golden parasols to keep him from the glare. From somewhere among the crowd, somebody shouted, "Long live the Emperor!" and everybody chanted in chorus, "Long live the Emperor!"

Her father, who had arrived with the Emperor, stood just one step behind the throne. He was dressed with simplicity a violet turban on his head and a violet satin gown over his immaculate white trousers. Violet was the color reserved for the rank of dukes, or Mandarins of the First Grade.

His gown was the most attuned to the Emperor's simple dress. Many of the mandarins who surrounded the Emperor were choking in the heat, dressed as they were in red, green, blue and violet brocaded court robes. The Emperor, by contrast, was wearing simply a silk yellow turban and a yellow satin gown.

Hiep found out much later that at that time her father was Minister of Rites and Commander of the Palace Guards and that he was the Tutor of the Emperor's brothers.

Little Hiep stared at the Emperor a minute, and then turned her eyes towards her father. He did not look in her direction, however, not even once. She made many attempts to attract his attention, but to no avail, and so she became a little restless.

Fortunately, right then, her mother said, "The fight's about to begin." Little Hiep forgot all about the Emperor, his suite and her father, and looked down into the arena. After three long rolls of the drums came the blare of trumpets, and the spectacle began.

A tiger was released into the arena from one of the tiger-cages built in the lower part of the wall. He looked so fierce that some spectators screamed in terror as he appeared on the scene.

Little Hiep was mesmerized by the way the tiger looked up at the Imperial Stand, as if he recognized the Emperor. He took a few steps, and then stopped, then beat the ground with his tail and roared. She would never forget that roar. In the bright sunlight, with his open jaws and his muscular and sinewy body bundled up, ready to spring forward, the tiger was quite a vision. The Emperor remarked in a loud voice, "What a beautiful beast!"

Suddenly the large ironclad gate on the Emperor's right opened, and an elephant entered the ring. At the sight of the tiger, the poor elephant stopped dead in his tracks, his gray white tufts of hair standing on end. Smelling his fear, the tiger raised a paw and roared again. The elephant, cringing with dismay, started backing away toward the gate through which he had just come in.

Elephant-herders ran into the arena with burning torches. They waved their torches and attempted to drive the elephant toward the tiger. Their repeated efforts remained fruitless. The elephant showed no desire to fight the king of the jungle.

The tiger kept roaring and, at each one of his louder and louder roars, the panic-stricken elephant shamelessly screamed and ran this way and that way, kicking up clouds of dust, his body covered with cold sweat. The crowd started laughing and jeering. The laughter and jeers of the spectators were in a way unforgivable, as spectators were expected to be firmly on the side of the elephant.

Indeed, the tamed elephant, little Hiep was to learn later on, symbolically represented the loyalty of the subjects to the Throne, and the wild and ferocious tiger represented the spirit of rebellion. But on that day, the spectacle was so funny that people could not help laughing.

Even the Emperor burst out laughing at first, and then his face showed disgust and displeasure. He shouted out an angry command, "Take that silly elephant out of there and bring in another."

While a guard hurriedly reopened the gate for the frightened elephant, a dozen elephant-herders were deployed in the arena to cover the risky rescue operation. Indeed, the victorious tiger, aware of his success, rushed about trying to cut off his enemy's retreat and threatened to attack both the elephant and the herders. The herders, with torches and javelins in their hands, formed a line and courageously fought the tiger back. Finally, the scared elephant managed to back safely out of the arena.

A few painful minutes passed and another elephant entered the ring, a female this time. She was colossal. The crowd, seeing how tall and voluminous she was, started cheering. Everybody in the crowd now seemed to be solidly behind the elephant.

She did not seem to need any encouragement. As soon as she entered the arena, she saw the tiger she stopped a second, but obviously not out of fear. Her eyes showed both indifference and contempt. She raised her trunk high in the air. With her large ears flapping wildly, she walked quickly, straight toward the tiger.

Seeing that the elephant was fearless, the Emperor was very pleased. He shouted his encouragement to her. At only a few paces from the Emperor, little Hiep distinctly heard his voice. It was the same voice she was used to hearing at home when, jumping down from his horse in her front yard, the Emperor called out to her father or her brothers.

She did not expect the fight to be so short and the outcome so horrifying. As the elephant approached, the tiger made a quick jump to the side, then, without warning, launched himself high into the air and landed right on the elephant's forehead.

The elephant screamed, shook her massive head and tried to throw the tiger to the ground. The tiger tore at the elephant's neck, without much effect. He attempted then to claw at her eyes. Enraged, the elephant suddenly ran to the brick wall and rammed her head against it.

To avoid being crushed against the wall, the tiger was forced to leave the elephant's eyes alone and jump down to the ground. Once on the ground, he started circling his enemy. He described narrower and narrower circles. Young as she was, little Hiep knew that the fight had come to a decisive moment. She watched intently as the tiger emitted a constant growl full of anger and scorn.

The crowd cheered as the larger animal succeeded in following the tiger's rapid movement. Turning almost constantly on herself, she faced him squarely eye to eye.

All of a sudden, the tiger jumped again, and once more landed on the elephant's head. He saw that the elephant was rushing to the brick wall again. But this time, throwing all caution to the wind, he kept slashing at her eyes with his claws, drawing blood. He seemed to be seized by frenzy at the sight of blood. He did not seem to notice that the elephant was rushing at full speed towards the brick wall. He crouched on her head and went on clawing at her eyes. The elephant rammed her head and the body of the tiger against the wall, crushing her enemy's backbone on the first thrust. But she did not stop; she went on ramming her head against the wall, over and over again.

The thudding sounds vibrated through the air and shook the screaming crowd. The whole brick wall trembled. Caught between the elephant's head and the brick wall, the tiger's body soon looked like a bag of blooded fur. The elephant threw off the dead tiger onto the ground and stamped repeatedly on his bloody and flattened body with her feet.

As the elephant banged her head against the wall to kill the tiger, the Emperor himself sat stone-faced, but as soon as the outcome became clear, he rose from his chair and signified that there would be no other fight that day. Apparently, he did not like such a gory sight. The spectacle ended abruptly.

Little Hiep had not enjoyed the sight either. She was not terrified by what she saw, but she felt like crying each time she remembered how the proud tiger had been transformed into a bag of bloody fur.

*

Why had such a memory haunted her for years? Why, even now, whenever she thought about the tiger, did she still feel like crying? Her father had told her on that day that the tiger was *the rebel* who had to be destroyed. He told her that the elephant represented loyalty to the Crown, and had to triumph over the tiger. But, she doggedly shook her head and wanted to keep a place in her heart for the poor rebel.

The next day, the Emperor, by edict, put an end to the Imperial Arena and the fights between tigers and elephants. When her father came home, he sat for hours in a chair that was placed on the balcony. Why was he so sad? His quiet sadness began on that very day. For months, he did not explain why he had lapsed into melancholy. For months he did not tell either his wife or his children that the Emperor had taken him into his study and told him on that day, with tears brimming in his eyes, "I *am* the tiger. I'm the rebel to be destroyed. Loyalty nowadays no longer means loyalty to the Crown. It means loyalty towards France. Sooner or later, my 'loyalty' towards France will run out. Then, I'll be crushed and trampled upon like the tiger was, yesterday. You will see, my dear friend, you will see."

But for months, the confidences of the Emperor were kept intact; his words were not repeated, even in the home of the Minister of Rites. For months, little Hiep did not know why, her father watching her sometimes playing in the garden, would mutter, "This little girl sees things that an adult fails to see."

Much later, at times Hiep wondered why her parents had wanted her to be at the Imperial Arena, to see that last fight between the tiger and the elephants. Was it because people of her parents' generation had been much tougher, less sensitive to pain and horror and the sight of blood? Was it because they did not know any better? She never judged her parents; yet she knew that she would never expose her own children to such a gory sight. Much later, she knew that the universe of her parents was sinking into oblivion, piece by piece. Old traditions were disappearing, like the fights between tigers and elephants that had ended for good with an imperial edict. Rituals and customs that had been there for hundreds of years faded away overnight.

Much later, she understood that she had been born in a period of transition, and that the world of the Emperors and the Court of Hue, the world of her parents, would soon be lost forever.

Ruins of the Imperial Arena

*

Note: Though later on Hiep and her children talked about this incident as Hiep's earliest memory, it cannot have been her own recollection. At the time she went to the Imperial Arena and witnessed the fight between the tiger and the elephant she was only one year old, though according to the Vietnamese way of counting she was two. Hiep apparently listened to the narrative given her by her father and mother and later came to believe that she remembered all the details of that eventful day.

*

Her next recollection was more vivid and more colorful. She was almost four years old at the time. She saw herself standing in the street at Ben Ngu, or the Imperial Landing, waiting for the Imperial Procession to come by.

She was there with her mother, her older sister and her brothers. They stood next to a beautiful altar that they had taken great pain to decorate. It was an altar set up in honor of the Emperor, the Son of Heaven. In the middle of the altar stood a heavy bronze incense-burner from which

7

escaped white whirls of fragrant incense. Four bronze candelabras remained lit in bright daylight. The altar was decked with brocade draperies, antique porcelain temple dogs, and long strings of minutely chiseled silver beads.

The nine Cannon-Gods guarding the Noon Gate, in front of the Imperial Palace had thundered half an hour earlier. So she guessed the Imperial Procession was about to approach her group and would soon be seen. She and her small party stood midway between the Palace and the Nam Giao Esplanade, the final destination of the Procession.

The Emperor was on his way to his tent that was pitched at the Nam Giao Esplanade. Confined to his tent, he would fast, pray and purify himself, in preparation for the next day when he was to offer abundant sacrifices to Heaven and Earth for the atonement of sins committed by his subjects and himself in the past three years. He also was to pray Heaven and Earth for good weather and good crops in the next three years.

Her father had explained to her that the Sacrifices to Heaven and Earth had been annual occurrences previously. Due to financial constraints, Emperor Thanh Thai had decided to perform the sacrifices only once every three years. Because they had become a rare occurrence, the crowd of participants in the ceremonies was expected to be much larger than in the past.

As she stood, silenced by her own excitement, she watched the face of her brother, Diem. He was her favorite, even though he intimidated her at times by his quiet and meditative eyes. She knew that somehow her father also had a soft spot for Diem. At six, he already showed extraordinary intelligence and a phenomenal memory. The Minister of Rites sometimes shook his head when he caught Diem writing complicated Chinese ideograms on banana leaves or on the dirt paths in the garden. She once asked Diem, "Why do you write Chinese characters on banana leaves and on the dirt?" Diem laughed, "Banana leaves and the dirt don't cost anything. Paper is expensive."

*

All of a sudden, the head of the Procession emerged on the far side of the long street. She heard the crowd chant in an uproar, "Long live the

Emperor! Long live the Emperor!" The vanguard of the Procession was approaching fast now.

It was led by a Commanding General who sat on an ornate chair covered with red velvet and firmly set on the back of a large elephant. He was followed by four others, all of about the same size and adorned in the same way.

Marching behind the elephants were the Imperial Guards in white uniforms, with red sashes around their waists. More than thirty flags representing the Five Primordial Elements, the Sun, the Moon and Constellations of Stars came next. The Imperial Orchestra followed closely behind the flag-bearers.

Having seen the Procession once every three years, her mother explained to her the meaning of what she saw. But then she stopped talking as the main body of the Parade approached.

The Emperor himself was only a hundred meters from them now. Mother and children took a good look of him, and then lowered their heads when the Emperor arrived at their level. Though on other occasions, especially during his visits to their home, it was all right to look directly at the Emperor, during solemn ceremonies, they were not supposed to see his face. He himself sat erect in his large gold and red palanquin decorated with dragons.

Dressed in a golden brocade Court robe, he looked quite different from his usual self. The little girl shouted, "Long live the Emperor!" Was there a faint smile on the Emperor's lips as he heard the child's voice? Her mother restrained her from other manifestations and, scared by her own unusual boldness; little Hiep turned, sat down and hid her face against her mother's knees.

A minute later, her brothers told her, "Stand up, here come Father's colleagues." She stood up quickly. Yes, there came her father's colleagues who walked and chatted, princes of the imperial blood and mandarins from the first to the fifth rank, all in their most colorful court robes. Some of the mandarins, recognizing them, smiled and waved. The little girl returned the smiles. She felt that they made up for her long wait in the street.

She turned and asked her mother, "Mom, where is Father?" Her mother explained to her, "Your father is a Christian. The Emperor doesn't want to force him to be part of the Imperial retinue for the Offerings at Nam Giao Esplanade. He has created for your father a new function, called *Luu Kinh Dai Than* (Keeper of the Capital). The title means that your father stays in the Citadel to protect the Imperial Palace while all the other high ranking mandarins are with the Emperor at the Esplanade."

The little girl asked, "Why does father prefer to stay away from the Nam Giao ceremonies, Mom?" Her mother knew that her little girl was beginning to see some contradictions in her little universe. She again explained patiently, "The Emperor and the mandarins will offer sacrifices to Heaven. That's all right for your father to participate in. In a way, Heaven means God for non-Christians. However, the Emperor and his retinue will also offer sacrifices to the Earth, and Constellations of Stars. Your father prefers not to participate in such rituals."

A big crowd of common people followed the Procession until it reached the approaches of the Nam Giao Esplanade. Little Hiep looked at the crowd and wanted to run into it and mingle with the people, but her mother put a strong restraining hand on her shoulder. "No little girl, you aren't getting into that crowd."

That evening, the family meal was taken without her father, who had to stay in the Citadel. She asked, "How many animals are they going to sacrifice, Mom?" Her mother was not sure of the number, "I don't know, girl, hundreds of them, of course. Lots of buffaloes, goats, pigs and birds! Why do you ask?" The little girl sounded quite sad, "You say, hundreds of them, huh, Mom? Poor animals!"

She jumped to another question, "I've heard that they don't allow women to be anywhere near the Nam Giao Esplanade. Why, Mom?" Her mother said, "It's true that they don't allow women to go near the Esplanade. Even the Emperor has to avoid the presence of women and purify himself before he is fit to go and offer the sacrifices to Heaven. That's why he left his palace this morning and sleeps alone in a tent tonight. They say women are impure."

Hiep asked, "I am a girl. Am I impure, Mom?" Her mother, taken by surprise, looked at her speechlessly for a moment then she fervently shook her head. "No, silly girl, of course you aren't impure."

10

The Nam Giao Esplanade (restored)

*

The fight between the tiger and the elephant, and the Imperial Procession stood out whenever she tried to recall her most distant memories. They stood out, with vivid colors and abundant detail. Why they and not other memories?

Years later, Hiep still wondered why. What significance had those two events had in her life? Weren't they simply pages torn out of an old history book? Were they important to her merely because they were the best gateway that led back to the imperial past of her nation?

Years later, Hiep would feel at times overwhelmed with nostalgia. Imperfect as it had been, the world of her childhood seemed to her to have been so secure, so peaceful and orderly. The absence of security, peace and orderliness that soon followed practically put an end to her childhood, when she was not yet five years old.

*

Soon, indeed, her father's life took a sharp turn and such an event propelled her almost instantaneously into maturity. After that dramatic change in her life, everything that happened to her and around her seemed to be carved in stone. There were no more gaps to be found in her extraordinary memory.

When she was born, on May 5, 1903, her father was at the apogee of his career. Ngo Dinh Kha cumulated many functions at the Court. He spent long hours every day at the Palace, as he was the Commander of the Palace Guards (*Thi Ve Dai Than*) and, as the Minister of Rites, was in charge of protocol at the Palace.

His title of *Thi Ve Dai Than* misled at least one French historian later into calling him the Head Eunuch. Hiep and her brothers and sisters laughed themselves silly whenever they found that reference in a French book.

It was a mistranslation of course. The Head Eunuch, like all the eunuchs at the Imperial Court, was emasculated and would have neither beard nor mustaches. Their father sported, apparently from a young age, a long beard of which he was very proud.

The title of Imperial Tutor (*Phu Dao Dai Than*) had been conferred upon him since 1898. As an Imperial Tutor, Ngo Dinh Kha was supposed to tutor the Emperor and his brothers in French language and French literature as well as Western philosophy. In fact, by the time Hiep was born, the Emperor was already quite fluent in French. By keeping her father as a Tutor, however, the Emperor gave himself a pretext to escape from the Palace from time to time, ride his horse to his Tutor's home in Phu Cam, and enjoy a couple of hours of relaxation.

To lend more prestige to her father, in 1902, the Emperor granted him the title of Great Scholar Assistant to the Throne (*Hiep Ta Dai Hoc Si*), which was the title given to mandarins with the permanent rank of Minister. His children knew the Emperor quite well, as he used to ride to their home at least once a week, whether he needed a chat, or a lesson in French, or simply a nap in the parlor of his Tutor's home.

Ngo Dinh Kha's home was quite large. It was built, according to his detailed instructions, at the foot of the hill on which stood the Cathedral of Hue. Various kinds of hardwoods found only in the mountains of Central Vietnam were used for the construction. The house had two floors with traditional four-panel carved doors and moon-shaped windows.

It was surrounded by a very large garden. Later on, parts of that garden were turned into a small zoo, while the rest continued to be an orchard with lots of litchi and longane trees.

Visitors, most of them mandarins of the Court and French functionaries or missionaries, but also occasionally some neighbors, were offered the choice between the parlor and the garden. During the hot summers, most visitors chose the garden.

Notes: Many enemies of the Ngo Dinh have expressed doubts about Ngo Dinh Kha's career as mandarin, suggesting that he was a minor figure in the Imperial Court. Those should spend some time reading the Annals presented by the History Department of the Nguyen Dynasty, especially the 6th Supplemental Period covering the 28 years of the reign of Emperors Thanh Thai and Duy Tan from 1889 to 1916. The mandarin career of Ngo Dinh Kha was recorded in detail from the time he started as an interpreter to the time he became Minister of Rites, Marshal of the Palace and Imperial Tutor. The official Annals confirmed every detail of Kha's ascent and the moment he was fired and exiled by the French following the forced abdication of Emperor Thanh Thai. They show that the Ngo Dinh family has not created a myth concerning Kha's loyalty to the Emperor and the French hostility toward Kha.

*

Hiep, as soon as she was able to walk, was allowed into the company of the most powerful men of her time. She played around them and was rarely intimidated by their presence.

It was in that small universe that she lived, taking for granted that her father would always be just a step behind the throne. But she was wrong. That universe was suddenly shattered when she was only four years old. It was then, that Emperor Thanh Thai was forced by the French officials to abdicate.

Her father was the only Vietnamese mandarin who resisted the French authorities and voiced his opposition against the moves to force the Emperor to abdicate, and then to exile him.

He was loyal to the Emperor to the very bitter end, and consequently, paid a heavy price for his courage. The French colonial administration stripped him of all his titles and functions and sent him back to Phu Cam as a commoner, forcing him to eke out a living as a poor farmer.

That was the first misfortune that struck the Ngo Dinh family. The humiliation that the French colonial authorities wanted to inflict upon the family did not, however, have the desired effect. Ngo Dinh Kha and his children would regard that moment of disgrace as one of the proudest moments in the family's history. The people of Hue immortalized Kha's courageous behavior in a folk song, which also honored his friend and classmate, Nguyen Huu Bai, *"Kha was not among those who exiled the Emperor. Bai was not among those who acquiesced to the profanation of the Imperial Tomb."*

Note: These lines were recorded in the Imperial Annals. They are not invented by the two allied families like some critics said.

It may be a bit exaggerated to say that Hiep became mature overnight, but the memories of that turn of events were engraved in her memory. It is to be noted that memory was the prime and sometimes the only educational tool for Vietnamese children in her day. Books were rare and expensive. Lessons were to be memorized.

At the age of four, most of the Vietnamese children of the educated elite, started to memorize the three thousand Chinese ideograms in the primer called *San Qian Zi* or *Tam Thien Tu*. After they had memorized the three thousand words of the primer, they would start memorizing five thousands ideograms, using another glossary called *Wu Qian Zi* or *Ngu Thien Tu*. At the age of thirteen, many of them would have to learn by heart not only the texts but also the commentaries of the *Ming Xin Bao Jian* or *Precious Mirrors to Enlighten the Heart (Minh Tam Bao Giam)*, and the *Lun Yu* or Kongzi's *Analects (Luan Ngu)*.

Developing a child's memory at an early age was a natural preoccupation of parents and teachers as Hiep grew up.

大南成泰

TOQ ANNAM - Hué - Empereur d'Annam et Soutane de Ceur

Emperor Thanh Thai

*

Until today, she remembers every little detail of the tragedy that struck her nation and her family in 1907. As her parents and her older brothers continued to talk about that event for many years, things that she had not understood, or only half understood at the time, became clearer with time.

The pain endured by the little girl of four as she registered the gamut of her father's feelings - anger, bitterness, revolt and helplessness – remained in her mind, for the longest time, as real and fresh as if the events had only taken place yesterday.

*

When she was four, Hiep's parents wanted her to see and understand the contradictions around her. She was a Christian, but she stood next to an altar decorated to honor an Emperor, who claimed to be the Son of Heaven. She believed in one God, yet the Emperor and his mandarins went to Nam Giao Esplanade and offered sacrifices to Heaven, the Earth, the Moon and the Stars and hundreds of other divinities. She even knew the names of the Cannon-Gods who defended the Noon Gate, all of them made divinities of the first rank by Imperial Decrees.

Before she started asking too many questions, her mother took the time to explain everything to her. She would remember those early religious lessons all her life. Her mother did not simply ask her to learn by heart the questions and answers found in the Book of Catechism. Though Hiep quickly memorized the first chapters of the book, her mother taught her how to think for herself.

One day when she was barely four years old, the Minister of Rites, testing his wife's instruction, asked Hiep, "Can God be called Heaven, Hiep?" The little girl responded quickly, "We Christians call him God, non-Christians call him Heaven." He took her tiny hand. There was surprise in his eyes. He asked, "Is the Emperor the Son of Heaven?"

Hiep hesitated for a second, and then took the plunge, "Yes. He calls himself the Son of Heaven, because he's the High Priest of the non-Christians. He offers sacrifices to Heaven at the Nam Giao Esplanade, on behalf of the people."

Her father pushed harder, "Is it a sin to set up an altar in honor of the Emperor, who claims to be the Son of Heaven?"

Hiep shook her head, showing him that she was aware she could have her way with him, "Father, you ask me too many questions. You make my head swim."

She looked at her father and saw that, at least for this time, he did not relent. She said, finally, "The Emperor is our father and mother; he should be honored, not worshipped. We set up altars in honor of our ancestors, but we do not worship them. So we can set up altars in honor of the Emperor in the same way. He calls himself the Son of Heaven. We shouldn't quarrel with that title. It shows the Emperor's submission to Heaven."

From that day, the Grand Chamberlain took delight in asking Hiep increasingly difficult questions. Whenever she could not answer, she claimed that she had a headache. Then, she would run to her mother or her elder brothers or sister to ask for help. Eventually, she would come back with the right answer.

Her memory was phenomenal. She learned her catechism by heart and loved to recite it.

"Question: Who is God?"

"Answer: God is the Creator of Heaven and Earth."

"Question: How many persons are there within God?"

"Answer: "Within God, there are three persons. The first person is the Father, the second person is the Son and the third person is the Holy Spirit. The three persons are of the same nature. The three persons are the same God."

Ngo Dinh Kha's predilection for her grew with every passing day. He spent an inordinate time with her, chatting like he had never done with his other children. The little girl, however, would rather listen to him. She did not like to talk when her father was around. For her, the greatest pleasure was to listen to him in the quiet of the parlor.

He, who had traveled as far as Penang, Malaya, and had read hundreds of Chinese, French and Latin books, was, for her, the best teacher in the world.

Whenever she saw him in a good mood, she would come and sit at his feet. Sooner or later he would start talking to her about something he had experienced or some book he had read. She would make herself more comfortable on the floor and urge him on with her large and bright eyes. She did not understand everything he said, but she remembered his words.

One day, while her father was explaining something quite complicated to her, her mother intervened, "Don't you think that she's still a bit too young to understand all that?"

Her father smiled and turning to Hiep, he ordered her, "Little child, repeat what I've just said." Without hesitation, she repeated word for word what he had told her. He then turned to her mother and said with confidence, "She may not understand all of that now, but she'll remember my words. Someday, she'll understand it all."

That period of grace was soon to be interrupted by a series of events the significance of which she could not understand at first.

*

For several weeks in a row, Emperor Thanh Thai did not make a single visit to Ngo Dinh Kha's home in Phu Cam. Hiep noticed that her father was more somber than usual. Once, she summoned her courage and asked, "Father, why the Emperor doesn't come to visit us anymore?"

Her father took her face in his two hands and said, "Little one, you have to pray hard for him. He's in trouble."

She found that his hands pressed her too hard around the jaws but managed to ask, twisting her mouth, "But Father, how can the Emperor be in trouble? Isn't he the Emperor?"

The Commander of the Palace Guards pondered for a moment and finally confessed, "You see, my little girl, the Emperor is no longer the Supreme Ruler. It's been a while since the Vietnamese Emperor stopped being the Supreme Ruler. The French are *above* the Emperor, and *they* don't like him."

She was devastated. She had always thought that the Emperor, the Son of Heaven, was the highest authority in her country. Didn't he offer the sacrifices to Heaven and Earth every three years? Hadn't she helped set up an altar in his honor in front of her home?

While chatting with her brothers, sometimes she overheard the Emperor say to one of them, "Look, don't be brash young man, or I will have your head chopped off." He said that as a joke of course (she even burst out laughing every time he used those words), but she had never entertained any doubt about the Emperor's power to chop off the head of *just anybody, at any time*. Does he, or doesn't he have such a power, she wanted to know now.

Then, little by little what her father had told her started sinking into her mind, "The French are *above* the Emperor," he had said. Even though she was only a child of four, she understood that if the French were above the Emperor, they were above her father, and above all Vietnamese. She did not know why such a notion gave her excruciating pain.

In the next few days, as the great drama at the Imperial Court unfolded, her father came home in the evening more and more taciturn. The little girl of four knew that things had gone awfully wrong for the Emperor and that her own life would soon undergo dramatic changes.

Andre Nguyen Van Chau

20

CHAPTER TWO
THE MINISTER AND THE EMPEROR

The little girl – that was what her parents always called her --stopped to look at the large portrait of the Emperor, displayed in the place of honor on the wall of the parlor.

It was a photograph of Emperor Thanh Thai taken on his Inauguration Day: the Child-Emperor, with his Nine-Dragon Crown, his golden Court Robe and his white jade belt, looked a little bewildered.

He had never expected to be Emperor, as he was the seventh son of a deposed Emperor. There he was, nonetheless, serious-looking, with all the imperial paraphernalia, sitting on the throne with his booted feet wide apart, each foot resting on the head of a dragon flanking the base of the throne.

Whenever she looked at the photo, she was saddened by the expression of his face. It was still a childish face, but the eyes and the mouth gave away memories of the pain and bitterness that he had experienced. There was also anger in his face, she decided.

The little girl now looked at the portrait and wondered. As a child, the Emperor had gone through hell and now he seemed to be heading that way again. She remembered bits and pieces of his life as recounted to her by her father. Her father used to tell her everything. Wasn't she the apple of his eye? As soon as she could pipe up childish questions at him, he took real pleasure in giving her the answers.

Once she asked, "Was the Emperor a happy child?" He pulled her into his arms and said, "No, little girl. He was not a happy child. You see his father was made Emperor after the death of the mighty Emperor Tu Duc.

21

But immediately, he was entrapped by powerful and cruel mandarins and was deposed *after a reign of only three days*. Emperor Thanh Thai who was then a tiny four-year old prince, like you today, was sent to prison with the deposed Emperor. A year later, his father was transferred to another prison and starved to death."

Hiep urged him on, "What happened to him next, Father?" The Grand Chamberlain had a sad smile as he went on, "The little prince was sent away to the village of his mother. He lived there in exile with her, deprived of everything. But then, his grandfather (on his mother's side), Regent Phan Dinh Binh, a powerful mandarin, wanted to have a hand in the choice of emperors… He apparently didn't know how dangerous a game it was."

"What happened to his grandfather?"

"Emperor Dong Khanh, whom the old Regent wanted to discard, was crowned, despite of all of Binh's efforts. Once he was crowned, the new Emperor condemned the old man to death. Before his execution, Binh succeeded in hanging himself in his prison cell. At that time, the future Emperor Thanh Thai was nine years old. He was taken back to the capital, with his mother and put under house arrest. You see why he couldn't be a happy child?"

Hiep nodded. Her eyes were so bright that, for a second, the Minister of Rites thought she was crying. He pursued, "Well, hardly a year passed, and Emperor Dong Khanh himself died. Without rhyme or reason, the young prince, who had only known unhappiness, was made Emperor."

*

The short history lesson made the little girl's head swim, but she still wanted to know more. She asked, "Was he happy to become Emperor?" Her father shook his head, "No, not at all. A delegation was sent to his home to tell him that he had been chosen to be the next Emperor. The young prince was terrified. Though he was only a child of ten, he knew enough about the treachery and the cruelty of the mandarins at the Imperial Court. He certainly didn't want to be Emperor, at least not at first."

The little girl pointed to the photo on the wall and said, "He seemed all right on Inauguration Day." Again, her father shook his head, "No, my dear, no. He was both frightened and angry. You see that photo was taken right at the moment he ascended the throne. His old attendants, who were there in the service of the Emperor before me, told me that just before he came into the Throne Hall several disastrous incidents had taken place."

Seeing that her father was in a talkative mood, the little girl sat down on the floor at his feet. He went on: "First, when he was about to go to the inauguration ceremony, a eunuch brought him a cup of tea on a jade tray. He froze, and looked at the cup fixedly, without saying a word. The head eunuch finally understood, picked up the cup, took a sip from the cup and returned it to the tray. Only then did the Emperor drink the rest of the tea in the cup."

The girl had a little laugh that delighted her father. "So, she understood the funny side of the story," he thought. He stroked her long hair and said: "My little girl, as you know, he was only a child of ten, yet he was already so suspicious. I don't blame him; but he saw poison and assassins everywhere. That day, he was angry with himself for showing his suspicion so plainly. Even as a child he knew that *to show suspicion was to invite disloyalty*. That was the first incident which spoiled the day for him."

Something in her father's tone made her heart jump. "*To show suspicion is to invite disloyalty.*" She would remember that little sentence all her life.

"What was the second incident, Father? You said several disastrous incidents had occurred before the photo was taken." She pressed on. Her father's eyes became steely all of a sudden. The girl was a little nervous, because she knew that his eyes looked that way only when he was very angry. She touched his arm, in a childish attempt to calm him.

As if he awoke at her touch, he tried to smile and replied, "The other incidents? One day, little girl, one day you will understand the importance of all this." Controlling his voice, he said, "Another incident took place the day before, right on the Lunar New Year. That day, the French Resident Superior came to the Court to solemnly announce that France had no objection to the prince becoming Emperor of *An Nam*."

At first the little girl did not understand why her father's intonation had changed. He had to repeat, *"France has no objection,"* in exaggerated pomposity, to help her understand. Then, she laughed and repeated, *"Oh, France has no objection!"*

Her father said, "Even now, whenever the Emperor talks about that visit of French Resident Superior Rheinart, he's still angry. Once he raged as he described the scene, 'It was the Lunar New Year's Day, the first day of the Year of the Buffalo. That arrogant Frenchman came to the Imperial Palace when I still was under the shock of being chosen, only a few hours earlier, as the new Emperor. He came when I still was in mourning.'"

Ngo Dinh Kha stopped. He saw that little question mark in his daughter's eyes. He explained, "Yes, as soon as he became the new Emperor, he had to mourn his predecessor who had died a few days earlier. The young emperor was in mourning, because he was Emperor Dong Khanh's successor, therefore his heir."

"So the young Emperor was angry because the Resident Superior entered the Imperial Palace on the first day of the Lunar New Year, and he was angry because the Resident Superior intruded upon his mourning?"

"Yes, the Emperor once said: "Can you imagine the arrogance and the impudence of that Frenchman? He, a foreigner, came to see me on *the first day of the year*, uninvited, unannounced, as if the whole purpose of the visit was to remind me that he was more important than I. Of course, I knew that without him I would still be an obscure prince. As an obscure prince, anybody could insult me. But I was Emperor and I knew that as soon as I became Emperor, even the French officials had to show me some respect.'"

Hiep objected, "The Emperor, at that time, was only a child of ten. How did he know so much?" Her father had, at the beginning of his friendship with the Emperor, wondered about that himself. Yet, over the years, he had seen how intelligent the Emperor was, and guessed that as a young prince he had suffered so much that his sensibility and intelligence had developed precociously.

He said, "The young emperor was very precocious. He knew much more than did other princes in his age group. But listen to what the Emperor told me about that visit of the Resident Superior." Hiep had resumed the attitude of an entranced listener. Her father pursued, "The Emperor said: 'His walking into the Imperial Palace as if it were his own home, showed a complete lack of respect for the Throne. I thanked him rather curtly and offered him tea. The man didn't enjoy tea. So he took a sip, stood up and wished me a good year, a good reign, and was about to leave when he stopped and told me that *he* had selected the next day for Coronation Day. I could hardly contain my anger. I knew that the Imperial Astrological Bureau had chosen the same date. Our astrologers had chosen the date, not *he*. Yet he claimed that he had made the decision, just to taunt me. Seeing how he smirked, I considered my Coronation Day already spoiled irremediably.'"

The girl was a little confused. She knew that, according to tradition, only close relatives and close friends might mutually pay a visit on the first day of the Lunar New Year. She understood that the French Resident Superior had committed a *faux pas* when he showed up at the Imperial Palace on that day.

She could not understand, however, the significance of the French official's claiming that *he himself* had set a date for the Coronation. She recognized that she had no way of knowing how grown-ups played games, but she could feel that what the Resident Superior had done, had given enormous pain to the Child-Emperor and to her own father.

Ngo Dinh Kha's eyes were as cold as steel again. He went on, "Now, are you ready for the most disastrous incident? Well, it took place early in the morning of the Inauguration Day. The Emperor was stunned when he heard that the Resident Superior had come into the Imperial Palace with a large detachment of French soldiers armed with rifles and with two batteries of artillery."

The little girl exclaimed, "Rifles and cannon?" Her father nodded confirmation, "The French soldiers had marched into the Palace through the lateral doors of the Noon Gate. When he first heard about it, the Emperor laughed and exclaimed ironically: 'Thank Heaven, at least the French soldiers did not use the central door.' (Only the Emperor was to use the Central Door of the Noon Gate). The soldiers crossed the Middle Way Bridge over the Thai Dich Lake and lined up on two sides of the Audience Hall. The first soldiers stopped only a few paces from the Steps to the Throne."

Kha looked at his daughter and saw that she was flushed as if with anger. He was a little surprised but went on with his story, "The presence of armed French soldiers in the Audience Hall was too much for the young Emperor. You must notice his angry look in that photo, little one. As I said, the photo was taken as soon as he had walked up the steps and sat down on the throne. It was taken as he looked out and saw the two lines of armed French soldiers."

Hiep looked up at the photo, "He must have been angry." Ngo Dinh Kha nodded, "To the further amazement of the Emperor, right then the French cannon fired several salvoes. Resident Superior Rheinart walked straight toward the throne and stopped only two feet away from the young monarch. With a barely perceptible inclination of his head, the Frenchman proclaimed him Emperor of *An Nam* and greeted him as a loyal friend of France." Hiep cried out, "Poor Emperor!"

Her father was watching her as he concluded, "By then, the Emperor's face was scarlet. Even the most obtuse mandarins present sensed his anger. The Resident Superior himself, seeing how hard the Child-Emperor had to fight for self-control, decided to step aside and let the real coronation ceremony begin."

The Minister of Rites stooped down and pulled his daughter up. Holding the little girl in his arms, he said, "The days of an independent Vietnam are gone, little girl. They are gone." His strong body shook as he fought back angry tears. She was frightened by the violence of his grief. Many years later, she still remembered the moment when she felt the strong body of her father shake with anger and sorrow.

*

Another day, she asked, "When did you first meet the Emperor?" Not in a talkative mood, Ngo Dinh Kha walking away from her, shrugged, "A long time ago." The little girl, patient and confident, pressed on, "When, Father?" He turned and smiled, as if he had forgotten all his worries, "It was a hot summer day. I was resting in my hammock in the orchard when I heard a commotion at the gate. I was in my white cotton tunic and was in no condition to receive anyone. But the voice calling from outside the gate was quite peremptory, 'May I come in?' it said."

The little girl laughed: "He did not say please?" Her father smiled, "No, the voice did not say please. I left my shaded refuge and went to the front yard. A young man on horseback, accompanied by a small retinue, looked straight at me and did not make a move. I knew he waited for me to bow first, and instantaneously I realized that I was standing in front of the Emperor."

The little girl wanted to know, "Why were you so sure he was the Emperor?" Her father waved his hand, "Of course, I'd seen pictures of him. But even without the pictures I would still have recognized him because of the way he deported himself. He was dressed simply in blue silk. Yet, there was so much majesty in his mien and his poise that anybody would recognize him to be the Emperor."

Sensing that she was awakening in him happy memories – and she knew *that* was good for him - she asked, "What did the Emperor tell you, Father, in your first meeting with him?" For a moment, her father looked genuinely happy. He said, "I opened the gate and invited him in. He dismounted and followed me into the parlor. He asked me not to observe any ceremony and so I called for tea and we sat down to talk. He brought up the matter immediately. He said he wanted me to build and head a National Institute *(Quoc Hoc)* that would combine Eastern and Western studies. I was enthused, as I had dreamt about such a project myself for quite a long time."

She took his hand, "You accepted immediately, didn't you?" Her father shook his head "I hesitated. As if he didn't see my hesitation, the Emperor went on explaining what he wanted, 'We should never forget about our own culture and traditions. So in this Institute, we should give an important role to the Chinese Classics, Chinese philosophy, and Vietnamese literature and culture. But we also have to opt for progress. That is why we need to have a curriculum which gives major importance to the study of French language, Western philosophy, sciences and mathematics.'"

The little girl was curious, "I don't understand. You had always dreamt about building a school yourself. The Emperor came and offered to you the means to build a National Institute. Why did you hesitate?" The Grand Chamberlain sighed. He would like to see her go through life with such simplicity. He said, "I was very flattered but I had to know why he came to me instead of somebody else. I was young and arrogant, but I was not stupid. I knew that there were at least a dozen people better qualified than me to head such an Institute. So I asked, 'Sire, I am forever in your debt for having thought I could serve your purpose, but may I be bold enough to ask why you come to me?'

She smiled, "You were quite blunt with the Emperor, Father. What was his answer? I hope he was not angry with you." Ngo Dinh Kha shook his head, "On the contrary, the Emperor seemed pleased that I asked the question. He said without hesitation, as if he had rehearsed his response, 'I chose you for two good reasons: One, you are a man of two worlds. You know the Chinese Classics as well as any of the Doctors who successfully passed all the sessions of the Imperial Exams, but you are also versed in Latin, French and Western philosophy, having spent several years in Penang, Malaya, and studied under the French missionaries. Two, you don't care about ranks and titles. You don't seek the favors of the Court. I know you served for a while as a military command advisor (*Tham bien*) under my predecessor, Emperor Dong Khanh. Yet, in the middle of a successful campaign, you left everything and went home to take care of your ailing mother.'"

The little girl was a little perplexed. She asked, "People keep telling me that you lost all your family when the *Van Than* militia surrounded the church of your parish and burned it down, killing everybody inside. Did grandmother survive the fire?"

Her father shivered, remembering the terrifying moment when, in Penang, he was told of the massacre of his family. He shook his head, "Fortunately, your grandmother was not there in Dai Phong Parish when the massacre took place."

He shrugged as if to chase away a very painful memory then pursued, "The Emperor said, 'Yes, I know everything about you. After your mother passed away, you went into a long period of mourning. You didn't go back to the Court. Few people today are like you. I am literally surrounded by flatterers and professional courtiers. Now that I have told you, without embellishment, the reasons of my choice, will you accept my offer?' I still hesitated. I knew how envious people were of any imperial favor. I wanted to stay away from the Court."

She asked, "What made you decide then?" "The Emperor saw my hesitation", her father said. "His eyes holding mine, he said: '*Your* Emperor is asking you to build this National Institute and run it for him. *Your* Emperor believes that this Institute will one day help us liberate our country from French domination.' The Emperor had said enough. He had said more than enough. What he had just said, if reported, would cause him no end of trouble. The fact that he said it meant that he did not want a courtier. What he wanted was a trusted friend to the throne. At our first meeting, he had placed his life in my hands, intentionally committing a most dangerous indiscretion when he talked about liberating the country from the French. With tears in my eyes, I bowed my head and did obeisance three times to him. A bond was created, and for my part, it will only end when I die."

The little girl knew what had happened next. The National Institute (*Quoc Hoc*) was born out of that bond. Ngo Dinh Kha as the Principal, and Nguyen Van Mai (who later on also became a Minister) as Director of Chinese Studies, built the Institute.

In the first academic year, the Emperor wanted the candidates to be screened and re-screened. Out of two hundred candidates, only fifty were finally admitted. They were graduates from the Imperial Institute (*Quoc Tu Giam*), graduates of four full sessions at the Provincial Exams (*Cu Nhan*) and princes of the royal blood.

For the second year, however, the Emperor decided that any young student of proven talents be he prince or commoner should be admitted. Ngo Dinh Kha was glad to comply.

The National Institute quickly grew from its humble origins and soon enough provided Vietnam with generations of leaders. Pham Van Dong, the future Prime Minister of North Vietnam and Vo Nguyen Giap, the future victor of Dien Bien Phu studied at the Institute.

After two years of hard work at the Institute as its *Chuong Giao* or Principal, and having turned one of the Emperor's most cherished dreams into reality, Ngo Dinh Kha was called to the Palace and started assuming additional responsibilities near the Emperor.

The little girl asked, "You were so enthused with the National Institute. If you agreed to be a mandarin at the Imperial Court, you must have had very strong reasons for doing so. What made you leave the Institute, Father?" Her father knew that his answer would be too complicated for her. He told her that some day he would tell her the reasons why.

As she walked away, he said to himself: "She's right. I was so happy with my work at the National Institute. Why did I go to the Imperial Court?" The main reason why he had agreed to become a courtier once again was his desire to stand by the Emperor's side, and to re-negotiate the treaties that tied Vietnam to France. Yes, he sincerely hoped that with patience and skill, the Emperor would be able to take back from the French some *autonomy* for Vietnam. Independence was so much of a fantasy that he discarded it from his mind for the time being.

As soon as the French knew that the Emperor wanted them to loosen their grip on Vietnam, they decided to get rid of him.

Sensing the danger, the Emperor played dumb. He wanted the French to believe he was a selfish playboy. The French knew better than that. They knew he was no playboy. They saw through his artifice.

For decades, they had been studying *Sunzi* and *the thirty-six stratagems*. One of the ruses that they learned pleased them: *'Use the enemy's ruse against himself.'* The Emperor wanted them to think he was a stupid playboy? Fine, they took advantage of the Emperor's ruse to spread horrible rumors about his behavior with women.

The Emperor was frightened by the rumors spread by the French and their spies at the Imperial Court. He released hundreds of Court maids from the Palace and reduced the number of his concubines. But stories about his debauchery continued to be circulated. Ngo Dinh Kha was horrified as he saw that the Emperor was unable to get rid of a reputation that he had originally wanted to create for himself.

The Emperor then started pretending that he was a little crazy. He thought that the French would no longer consider him to be politically dangerous, if they thought him to be mentally weak. He was wrong. The French again used the Emperor's ruse to spread the rumor that he was a dangerous mental case. By 1906, Ngo Dinh Kha realized that he could no longer do much to help the Emperor.

As their spies, placed at the most vital positions in the Imperial Court, reported every one of the Emperor's moves to French officials, the Emperor was overcome by irrational suspicion. He was again that little boy of ten who refused to drink a cup of tea because he thought people were trying to poison him. Little by little, he discarded many loyal friends who could have offered him good advice.

Though the Emperor never suspected Ngo Dinh Kha of betraying him, the latter, seeing how suspicious the Emperor had become once again, did not impose himself on the Emperor and only answered whenever he was asked a question.

Note: Many Vietnamese and foreign writers have decided to espouse the French administration line and called Thanh Thai a crazy and debauched monarch. But the Imperial Annals kept reporting on the Emperor's wisdom in his decisions until the end.

The Emperor still rode to Ngo Dinh Kha's home once in a while, but now they talked about inconsequential matters. The Emperor tried to fool himself by saying that idle chat was what he needed. But Ngo Dinh Kha knew that betrayals committed by others had embittered the Emperor and cast a shadow on their friendship.

At times, he longed to break the silence and ask the Emperor to confide in him. At times, he wanted to ask the Emperor to discuss important issues with him during those visits. Being a shy and proud man, however, he could never bring himself to tell the Emperor that what he needed was not a chat or relaxation but frank discussions with somebody he trusted.

The ranks of those who betrayed the Emperor grew steadily. The French colonial authorities controlled the lists of promotions of mandarins and therefore, any courtier who wanted to advance in rank and title had to be submissive to them.

The Emperor finally understood that it was only a matter of weeks or even days before the French authorities would strike. Yet, he was not about to surrender without a fight. He made two other attempts in self-defense. They both failed and only served to hasten his downfall.

CHAPTER THREE
THE ABDICATION OF AN EMPEROR

Hiep looked at the photo of the Emperor and felt sad for him The Emperor whom she knew was no longer that melancholy Child-Emperor in the picture. When Hiep was born, he was already twenty-four and in 1907, the Emperor was a twenty-eight years old man whom the French had decided to eliminate.

Her father, with a great deal of reluctance, told her about what was going on with the Emperor's improvised schemes.

The Emperor did not want to surrender without a fight. Only a few months earlier, the French administration had further reduced the size of the Battalion of the Imperial Guards.

Now, the Emperor sent his people out to recruit young girls who were willing to become new court maids. Once they were in the Forbidden City, however, he personally trained them to be amazons and sharpshooters. French officials were appalled: they understood that the Emperor was trying to keep about his own person and in the Forbidden City a small army loyal only to himself.

"Is he preparing a *rebellion*?" they wondered. Laughable and outrageous as it seemed; an army of amazons might be a dangerous toy in the hands of the Emperor.

The Commander of the Palace Guards was blamed for that folly. Was he not the man in charge of all the Imperial Guards? Why did he let the Emperor organize his own guards using women? To all the French officials' questions on the subject, Ngo Dinh Kha answered curtly that court maids were not under his jurisdiction. Then he added that behind the

Purple Walls, in the private residential area of the Emperor, his Imperial Consort and Concubines, the Emperor could do anything he liked.

French officials came to Ngo Dinh Kha's home to press him to disband the women guards, but he kept insisting that he had no authority inside the Purple Walls.

Mandarins who worked for the French administration then spread terrifying rumors about the Emperor. They said that the Emperor in one of his fits of madness had maimed and killed some of his amazons.

Ngo Dinh Kha requested a private audience with the Emperor. Thanh Thai, trying to avoid a confrontation, kept saying that the Commander of the Palace Guards did not need an audience to see him. But Kha insisted. They finally met at the Can Chanh Palace.

Kha said, "Sire, all your armed court maids come from noble families. We know that you did not bring them to the Court to make of them your concubines. There are, however, widespread rumors accusing you of committing sadistic atrocities on them. Now, their families are in an uproar. Though they may not believe the rumors, they are angry because you have inconsiderately risked the reputation of their daughters."

The Emperor was silent for a moment, and then he inquired, "Is it true that the French went to see you at your home precisely about this issue?"

Sensing that he was treading on dangerous ground, Ngo Dinh Kha replied, "Yes Sire, they did. But I had no problem answering their criticisms on this matter. I will have a much greater problem discussing this with the parents of your amazons."

The Emperor insisted, "So, French officials *did* go to your home and talk to you on this matter?"

Sensing the suspicion of the Emperor, Ngo Dinh Kha felt a surge of anger within him. He tried to control his voice as he replied, "Yes Sire, *I said yes*. They came and asked me why I didn't stop you. I told them that what you did within the Purple Walls was your business, and that I didn't have jurisdiction over the people residing in the Forbidden City."

All of a sudden, the Emperor burst out laughing. His laughter rang true. He was happy. He said, "When you told me you needed to see me in private audience, I was afraid *you would come with a message from the French*."

The words of Ngo Dinh Kha put the Emperor to shame, "You should have known better, Sire. I'll never be a messenger for the French." The Emperor nodded, "Yes, I should have known that."

He added, lowering his head, "You are right. I'm sending those damsels back to their families. You see my intention was to train them fifty at a time and create a whole army of women. But as soon as the first fifty came, the French started a campaign to stop the whole process."

Kha said, "Sire, you don't need to tell me your original intention. Why do you tell me?" The Emperor put a hand on his friend's arm and said, "I tell you my original intention, because I want to trust somebody. I want to prove to myself that I can still afford to trust somebody."

At the end of their meeting, the new court maids were asked to leave the palace. The dream of an army of amazons evaporated. There was only one thing left for the Emperor to do.

The Emperor thought that he should flee. *To flee is the last of the thirty-six stratagems*. When nothing else works, one has to flee. The Emperor thought that he should flee to China, then to Japan, possibly, to join the Rebel Prince Cuong De.

He didn't bring Ngo Dinh Kha into his confidence in advance on that scheme either. He knew that what he wanted to do was so harebrained that Kha would surely oppose it.

He asked the French authorities to let him go north to visit Thanh Hoa, the native province of the founders of the Dynasty. He wanted to go and pray on the tombs of his ancestors, he said.

Thanh Hoa is only a few hundred miles north of Hue. He needed to go farther north, closer to the Chinese border. So while he asked the French authorities to allow him to visit Thanh Hoa, he suggested that he would like to visit North Vietnam too. He thought that once in North Vietnam, he would find an opportunity to escape French surveillance and flee to China.

*

At that time, North Vietnam was called *Tonkin* and was under the firm control of French officials. It was a Protectorate in name only; in fact, it was almost a French colony. Indeed, though treaty after treaty affirmed that Tonkin was only a Protectorate, French officials directly administered the region and Vietnamese mandarins sent there by the Imperial Court had practically no power at all.

The French colonial authorities questioned the Emperor's wish to visit *Tonkin*. The Emperor said he wanted to visit the people in *Tonkin* because they had recently been suffering from widespread famine.

French officials repeatedly questioned Ngo Dinh Kha: "Why does the Emperor want to go north? Does he want to revive the feeling of loyalty toward the monarchy among the people of the North? Does he want to arouse their hostility against France, especially in this time of famine?"

Kha patiently explained to French officials that the Emperor's visit to Thanh Hoa was necessary, as he had not done his duties by his ancestors so far. He went on to say that the visit to *Tonkin* would be of benefit to both the French and the Vietnamese administration, as the Emperor wanted to exhort his mandarins to collaborate more effectively with the French. As he was not in the confidence of the Emperor and knew nothing about the latter's intention to escape to China; Kha genuinely believed what he said.

He also told French officials that the Emperor was moved by what he had heard about the famine in *Tonkin*, and that he simply wanted to be with the people in their time of hardship.

His arguments did not convince the French authorities. As they controlled the Treasury, they refused to pay for the trip. The Emperor insisted that he would pay for it from his own budget. Still the French refused to let him go any farther north than Thanh Hoa. So the Emperor and a small retinue went to Thanh Hoa where he dutifully paid his respects to his distant ancestors.

His companions said that they saw him cry. It was the first and perhaps the last time the Emperor, as an adult, was seen crying. While in Thanh Hoa, the Emperor again made a request to visit *Tonkin*. But the responses from Levecque, the French chargé d'affaires in Hue, were firmer and firmer. Finally, the French official told the Emperor that he must return to

Hue without delay. The tone of the message showed it was an ultimatum. The Emperor knew then that the fight was over and that the French held all the cards.

The Emperor's improvised plan to escape to China was discovered by the French secret service. An investigation was conducted, but without substantive evidence, the French could not convict the Emperor for attempted desertion. The fate of the Emperor was, however, practically sealed.

After the Emperor had returned to Hue, Levecque asked him to refrain from leaving the Palace without advising him in advance. The Emperor understood that he had become a prisoner in his own palace. That was the reason why, for weeks on end, the little girl did not see the Emperor come to her home.

According to her father, the fall of the Emperor could occur in a matter of days now. Hiep looked at the photo on the wall then went back to her bedroom, closed the door, knelt down and prayed hard for the Emperor. Though she had prayed for many things, this time, she knew she was asking God for a miracle. Her mother, who had taught her how to pray, had warned her once, "Though God is always listening, don't ask him for too many miracles." Hiep whispered, "I am not asking for a miracle, but dear God, save the Emperor from his enemies, please."

*

Among those who spied the most openly and shamelessly on the Emperor and reported everything to the French was a prince, the Head of the Bureau of the Imperial Clan. As the Imperial Clan numbered thousands of members, the Bureau was one of the highest instances of the Imperial Court, and as the Head of the Bureau he was one of the highest-ranking mandarins. The Emperor felt physical revulsion whenever the man came near him.

That day, the Emperor was cleaning his pistol when the man entered the room. The Emperor was not alone - he rarely was. Seeing him come in, the Emperor asked, "Tell me, what have you got today to report to your masters?" Bowing obsequiously, the prince said, "Sire, you're my only master and I've really nothing to report today. I simply come to inquire about your Majesty's health."

The Emperor, having finished cleaning his gun, started loading it, one bullet at a time. The prince, sensing danger, suggested, "Maybe I should leave now." The Emperor raised a hand: "No, prince, don't leave right away. Let me ask you. What's the penalty for betraying the Emperor?" The Prince stared helplessly at the loaded gun and started sweating profusely. The Emperor laughed, "You seem to be very perturbed, Prince. Suppose I've found out who the biggest, stinkiest rat in the Empire is, suppose I've found out who the most vicious of the spies in this Court is and suppose I've a loaded gun in my hand. What should I do?"

The man was pale with fear now. He stammered, "Your Majesty should not…."The Emperor cut him off, "Prince, beware." He leveled his pistol, took careful aim at the man, then swung the weapon far to the right and fired into a large mirror behind the prince. The mirror crashed down, sending splinters of broken glass all over the hall. The man fell on his knees as the Emperor laughed and threw away his pistol, saying unrepentantly, "Poor bastard, do you really think I would waste my time killing a worm like you?"

Within a matter of hours, French officials were apprised of the incident. They summoned the pro-French ministers to a meeting and the French chargé d'affaires told the ministers that the Emperor had really gone berserk, and that he should be tried for attempted murder.

The Vietnamese mandarins timorously observed that the Emperor had not really aimed at the prince. The French chargé d'affaires looked at them and asked with a touch of contempt in his voice, "What do you say? My God, even after this madness, you still try to protect him. Wait until he kills some of you with his gun!"

The French chargé d'affaires went to Ngo Dinh Kha's home in the evening and asked him what he thought about the incident. Kha told him that it would be absurd to think that the Emperor had wanted to shoot to kill and missed his mark.

He said, "Look, the Emperor is one of the best marksmen in Vietnam and perhaps in the whole world. Do you think he could possibly miss a man, and a fat man at that, standing just three steps away from him?"

The chargé d'affaires became very frustrated. He said, "I don't think that you understand the situation. The Emperor clearly shows that he's a lunatic. It's the responsibility of the colonial authorities to put an end to his rule. You should distance yourself from him, or you will not survive his fall." Ngo Dinh Kha smiled, "Dear Mr. Levecque, if it's true that our Emperor is to be deposed, I don't wish to survive his fall."

Levecque became threatening, "I know your code of mandarins, but maybe you should be a little more careful. If you don't cooperate with us you may find yourself in jail, not as a political prisoner, but as a common criminal." Ngo Dinh Kha laughed, "You're scaring me. Tell me what have you found in my public or private life that could land me in jail as a criminal?"

The French chargé d'affaires could no longer contain his anger. He snarled, "The French secret services have documented the fact that you built a church in the Citadel. Don't you know that the construction of a Catholic church in the Citadel is completely illegal? By successive ordinances, the Emperors have always categorically forbidden the erection of Buddhist pagodas, Taoist temples and Christian churches in the Citadel. Don't you know that the Emperor is the only 'god' that is to be worshipped in the Citadel? The French administration is seriously considering taking you to court. Do you want to have your own day in court?"

Ngo Dinh Kha replied sarcastically, "So, you have become an expert in Vietnamese law as well? Let me tell you that the Emperor himself authorized the church to be built. He does not believe that he is a 'god'. I have in my possession the authorization written and signed by the Emperor himself."

It was the Frenchman's turn to be sarcastic, "Oh, your Emperor! Wait and see how much longer he will remain an Emperor!"

Kha was calm as he said: "You have *the power of the guns*, so you can dictate everything in this country. You can kill our Emperor, but you should know that, in that case, we would mourn his death. You can depose him, but you should know that, in that case, he would remain, in our hearts, our Emperor forever."

Before he left, the French official said, "I will give your Emperor a last chance. Tell him to show loyalty to France, and his throne will be safe again." Ngo Dinh Kha did not say a word as he silently accompanied his uninvited visitor to the gate.

He was silent because he understood what Levecque meant by 'loyalty to France.' It didn't simply mean submission to France but also total submission to him, *to Levecque personally*. The French chargé d'affaires wanted to see Emperor Thanh Thai come to him on his knees and to ask for mercy.

As Levecque was about to leave Hue for Hanoi to report on the situation at the Court to the Governor-General, he sent word to the Emperor that he expected *'His Imperial Highness'* to come to his residence and wish him God's speed. He told his messengers to make it plain to the Emperor that he was ready to forgive and forget if the Emperor showed him respect.

While Ngo Dinh Kha was amazed at the little man's arrogance and thirst for power, the Emperor was really annoyed. He took Kha aside and said, with sorrow in his voice, "I've landed myself in this horrible situation and I know I cannot save anything…anything at all, except my honor and my pride. I'm not going to humiliate myself in front of that Frenchman. He can take away everything else from me, but not my pride."

As his own mandarins pressed him to pay a courtesy visit to the French *'Resident Superior'*, the Emperor asked for his horse to be brought to him. He left the Court, on horseback, despite the Frenchman's warning against any such outing. By afternoon, he had returned to his palace. When he dismounted, he walked with a limp. He told his attendants that he had fallen and twisted his ankle.

The court physician was summoned, and soon enough the Emperor's leg was wrapped in layers of bandages. To the mandarins who came to inquire about his health, the Emperor pointed at his leg and said mirthlessly that they should go and tell the French official that having twisted his ankle, the Emperor regretfully could not pay him the courtesy visit he had intended to do.

Levecque, upon hearing about the mishap, started screaming, "Childish! Childish! What a stupid game he's playing! He's finished!"

He left for Hanoi where he reported to the Governor-General that the poor Emperor had really lost his marbles and should be deposed immediately.

Subtler, the Governor-General suggested that a list of promotions be presented to the Emperor with only the names of pro-French mandarins on it. They both laughed, as they knew what the reaction of the Emperor would be.

The trap was set. French officials, who had outmaneuvered the Emperor so many times, were about to outsmart him again. They knew his character. They could foretell, at any moment, what the Emperor's reaction would be.

They had not begun their chess game with the Emperor very well, but the pro-French mandarins had been coaching them. They were quick-witted and they had the advantage of knowing every word spoken by the Emperor, and every one of the moves he made, thanks to their network of spies.

On his part, the Emperor would not have been so easily outsmarted by the French if only he could rely on his mandarins and if he could go to them with his problems and ask for advice. But he couldn't. By nature, he was suspicious, and by experience, he knew that many of them would betray him to please the French authorities. No tactical or strategic discussion with his courtiers was possible.

There remained, of course, Ngo Dinh Kha in whom he trusted. But he knew now that he had to be careful: He should not come too close to his trusted friend. He had to keep him in power, even after he was gone. He had to make sure that Kha would survive his own downfall. But he had not counted on his friend's integrity.

Ngo Dinh Kha came home gloomier every evening. That night, his wife pushed the little girl forward. Only *she* could make him smile. Only she made him forget his worries, even if only momentarily.

The little girl asked, "Why do you hate the French so much, Father?" The question startled her father. He was stunned for a moment. Then he shook his head and said, "No, little girl, *I don't hate the French*. Where did you get that idea? I've so many good French friends, Father Allys, for example. I'd be ready to give my life for him. I've a great admiration for the French professors who taught me in Penang."

He seemed lost in his thoughts again, but not for long. He took her by the hand and asked, "Have you heard that the French authorities are about to get rid of the Emperor? I'll stand by him. French officials will not forgive me for my continued loyalty to the Emperor. You all will suffer as a consequence. But you know, my little girl, I cannot live without honor."

Her father knew he was saying things intended for his older children who were standing close to him as if they were drawing a protective circle around him. He knew that very likely the little girl could not begin to understand what he was saying. Her older brothers listened in silence. They were amazed at the facility with which their little sister made their father talk. Kha himself was more than once amazed at his daughter's questions, and at his own answers.

He loved her not because she was the brightest of his children - she was not, but because he felt that she was the most sensitive. She seemed to have the strange ability to empathize even when she could not understand other people's feelings. She seemed to have the ability to put salve on fresh wounds, and her eyes seemed to see through the maze of people's subterfuge and pretense.

She also had a ravenous thirst for understanding. Now she asked, "What is honor, Father?" Was it a *faux pas*? Did the little girl go too far this time? Her mother approached, and wanted to take her away. She thought her husband had no time for such a question now. But with a quiet glance at her, he signified that it was all right. He mused a little, then said: "Honor, for me, little girl, is *the courage of being yourself.* You don't understand what I've just said now, and it's all right. Later in your life, if you remember the words I spoke today, you will understand them."

She shook her head, trying to file *that* in her memory then returned to her first question, "Do you hate the French Resident Superior?" He saw that she was looking at him intently, so he said, "Mr. Silvain Levecque is *not* the Resident Superior, not yet, and maybe not ever. He is a *chargé d'affaires*. That means he takes care of current affairs while the French Government is pondering on the issue of whom it should appoint as the next Resident Superior. He does not have either the privileges or the responsibilities of a Resident Superior. Yet, Mr. Levecque conducts himself as if he were God Almighty. May God have pity on Vietnam, *and France and Mr. Levecque himself*! I do not hate the chargé d'affaires, I am sure that he will live to regret the insults and injuries he has been inflicting on our country."

He turned to his older sons Khoi, Thuc and Diem, who had been listening in silence, and said, *"Beware of chargés d'affaires. They are transition men who strive for permanence, or men pressed by time to achieve the unachievable."*

She did not remember that last remark for a long time. Then one day, many decades later, the voice of her father boomed back from that evening and resonated in her ears, *"Beware of chargés d'affaires."* At that time, the Ngo Dinh family was again approaching total disaster and the name of the American chargé d'affaires was *William Trueheart.*

On that evening, the little girl felt like crying. Her father's anger could only mean that he was feeling helpless. Neither she nor her older brothers and sisters could help him in any way. They were just a bunch of children. She looked at her mother. Her mother tried to avoid her eyes. Hiep knew that her mother could only share her father's pain, but could not give him either advice or solace.

For years, her mother's helplessness at that time would haunt Hiep. Was it the fate of women to watch the men they loved fight, struggle and fall, to feel the blows that hit them, to bleed through their wounds, to stagger along with them, but to remain helplessly on the sidelines?

Years later, when given the opportunity to play an active role in politics, she was tempted to step into the breach to fight with her brothers. The memory of the helplessness of her mother at the most critical moment of her father's political life urged her on. But then, the knowledge of her own limitations steered her away from such temptation. She knew she, like her mother, was not prepared for the world outside her home.

The standard education that her brothers received as a natural birth right with other boys their age was not forthcoming for her and her sisters. They, like most young girls at that time, received a few years of schooling, learnt how to read and write, and a little French, and then stayed home to learn how to run a household.

At four, Hiep did not understand all of that yet. What she saw was the pain in her mother's eyes, the pain of somebody *things were done to*, the pain of somebody who wanted to help but couldn't.

Hiep went to her mother. Mrs. Kha attempted to smile. She said: "Both the Emperor and your father will be all right, you will see." But Hiep knew better. She knew that the sky was falling, and that the end of her childhood world was near.

*

The promotion list was presented to the Emperor for his signature. All his ministers had signed, so the final approval of the Emperor should be a mere formality. But the Emperor did not see it that way.

He looked at the list and realized that all the names on the list were pro-French elements in his Court. He asked, "Who made the recommendations?" There was no answer. He raised his voice, "Who gave this promotion list to the Cabinet?" A timid answer came from one of his attendants, "It appears that the list came from Mr. Levecque." The Emperor's face flushed with anger. He pushed away the tray on which the promotion list was presented and thundered, "Then let Mr. Levecque sign it."

Minister Nguyen Huu Bai intervened, "Your Majesty, please understand that this is a trap. Do not fall for it. If you do not sign the list, the French will declare that you refuse to collaborate with them." The Emperor was so angry that he spoke caustically to a man he usually respected: "Your Excellency, I don't wish to collaborate with the French, if they, on their part, don't wish to collaborate with me."

Note: Nguyen Huu Bai, Ngo Dinh Kha's classmate at the seminary when both of them studied for priesthood entered the madarin world as a junior to Kha. He climbed up quickly the steps to the highest ranks. He was finally made Duke, while Kha was only once nominated for the title of baronet (nam tuoc).

The Minister stood his ground, "Your Majesty, please accept your loss on this one and live to win another day." The Emperor looked at Ngo Dinh Kha and said: "Your friend seems so sure that this is a trap. Do you agree with him? Is it a trap? Or is it merely a test? Yes, suppose that this is a test. Suppose they want to know how weak I am feeling at this moment. If this is a test, and I show weakness, they will move in for the kill."

With great sorrow in his voice, Kha said, "They know you are weak, Your Majesty. They do not need to test your strength. This is definitely a trap."

The Emperor hesitated. He now began to understand the French game plan. But other ministers weighed in. They pleaded for loyal collaboration with the French. Their plea, as innocent as it sounded, had the desired effect on the Emperor. He screamed at them, "You want loyal collaboration with the French? What do you mean by loyal collaboration, total submission to their demands? Never! Go tell them that as long as I am on the throne, I will not give in to their unreasonable demands. You are dismissed! "

The trap had snapped shut. The ruse had worked, and the Emperor was the one who had sprung the trap on himself.

*

The Cabinet was convened for an urgent consultation with the French chargé d'affaires. Levecque was to the point. He said, "Excellencies, you all know by now that the Emperor has rejected the promotion list recommended by the French administration. By the power conferred upon me by the Governor-General of French Indochina, I declare that the Emperor has demonstrated a complete lack of collaboration with the Colonial Power. I therefore ask you, Excellencies, to make all the decisions on affairs of the Crown by yourselves from now on, without consultation with the Emperor. Is this clear to all of you?"

He spoke in French, and the Ministers spoke in Vietnamese. What they said was translated back and forth by several interpreters. Some of the Ministers were fluent in French, but they preferred to speak in Vietnamese, and glared at the interpreters whenever the translation was not adequate.

One of the Ministers asked, "What will happen to the Emperor?" Levecque cleared his throat and replied, "You can go and tell the Emperor, Excellencies, that he should consider himself under house arrest. Also tell him that Mr. Sogny, our Director of Security, is assigned the responsibility from now on, of looking after the security of His Majesty. We don't want anything unfortunate to happen to him, do we?"

Minister Nguyen Huu Bai asked, "Is he still the Emperor?" A cruel smile curled the thin lips of the Frenchman; "He still is the Emperor until he signs an Edict of Abdication. But from now on he is confined to the Can Thanh Palace, his private residence." After a short silence, he added, "Perhaps in the future, I will assign to him a more appropriate abode. He often says that he is a paper emperor, a clown-emperor, especially when he wants to infer that France has not given him enough power. We will soon give him the Imperial Theater (*Duyet Thi Duong*) as his residence. There he will really be at home, as a clown-emperor."

He looked around the table. Nobody said anything in defense of the Emperor. Three of the ministers had tears in their eyes. They were ashamed of their helplessness. The other ministers, having plotted with the French from the very beginning, pretended to look sorrowful.

The French official said, "I am waiting for clear instructions from France. As soon as I receive them, you will be the first to know." With that, he said good-bye to the Ministers.

*

Upon learning of his misfortune, the Emperor had a disarming smile. He simply inquired about the Ministers, and was glad that those loyal to him had not spoken out in his favor. He did not want them to sacrifice themselves uselessly for him.

Ngo Dinh Kha approached the Emperor, but the monarch put his hand out, "No, my friend, go home and rest. I am finished, but you still have the interests of the country to defend. Stay away from me. I want you to survive my fall." Ngo Dinh Kha protested, "I don't want to survive your fall." But with sorrow in his eyes, the Emperor raised his hand, and said, "Please understand your Emperor." He turned and walked away.

*

Two days later another consultation took place. The chargé d'affaires told the Ministers that considering the mental health of the Emperor, it was in the best interests of the country and the Emperor's that he abdicated.

Minister Nguyen Huu Bai asked, "Who will succeed the Emperor?" He was stunned when the Frenchman said, "There will be no need of a new emperor." Now, the other two loyal ministers protested, "We are a vanquished nation. We've accepted the protection of France. But, we've accepted it on the condition that we would be able to preserve dynastic continuity and to keep alive the Nguyen Dynasty, symbol of our sovereignty. You cannot take that away from us."

The French official had not expected such a vehement protest. He said, "This is what France recommends: a Council of Regents is to be set up, chaired by the French Resident Superior. The Council of Regents will make all the decisions concerning state affairs."

Minister Nguyen Huu Bai said, "A Council of Regents can only be set up to take care of current affairs when an Emperor is too young to rule. We cannot accept such a recommendation."

Even the pro-French Ministers had some qualms about putting an end to the monarchy. Levecque knew when to cut his losses. He said, "I will ask for new instructions. For the moment, Excellencies, the abdication must be carried out smoothly. You are to draft an edict of abdication in the name of the Emperor. Once I have reviewed it, you will submit it to the Emperor for his signature. I guess the best thing to do is to attach to the draft edict a petition signed by all the highest ranking mandarins at the Court, requesting Thanh Thai to abdicate."

A Minister sighed, "Not all will sign the petition." Levecque was displeased. He said, "I should point out to you, Excellencies, that the signing of the petition will be considered as evidence of your loyalty to France. Please advise your colleagues that not signing the petition will be considered a demonstration of hostility towards French policies and an act of rebellion."

Minister Nguyen Huu Bai said, "Ngo Dinh Kha will never sign it." Levecque was angry now. He said, "Excellency, please tell your friend the Commander of the Palace Guards that our patience has its limits. Tell him that he should not pit himself against the power of France."

On that threatening note, the meeting came to an end.

*

Ngo Dinh Kha, as expected, did not sign the petition that asked the Emperor to abdicate. For many years, he had been soft-spoken, discreet and patient. Now, as his colleagues pressed him to sign the document, he looked at them angrily and his disparaging responses to their entreaties made them angry with him for the first time. But he did not care. Looking at his colleagues and the princes of the blood around him, he still recognized some friends, but he saw that the rest of them hated him for doing something that they themselves were not ready to do, that is, stand up for what they believed in.

They all knew that the Emperor was not a madman. They knew that he was neither a mental case nor a man given to debauchery. They believed that the Emperor was a patriot, whose only mistake was in not being patient enough to wait for the right moment before confronting the French.

Now, Ngo Dinh Kha stood tall among them, the professional courtiers. They saw in him an interloper, a man who had come from nowhere, an upstart, a first generation mandarin, who lashed at them with his words and his eyes. The more he played the hero, the more they felt ashamed of the miserable role they themselves played. For that, they swore they would never forgive him. They turned and went to see the French Resident Superior, with the draft edict of abdication and the signed petition…with Ngo Dinh Kha's signature missing. The Frenchman congratulated them for the draft edict and for the content and style of the petition. He congratulated them for the signatures they had collected for the petition. Then, suddenly, with fury, he turned against them, "Where, Excellencies, is the signature of Ngo Dinh Kha?"

The mandarins and the princes tried to calm him down, "It is just one signature missing," they said. But the French official was not to be pacified. He paced the large office in which they had gathered, "Yes, one signature missing! You know what *that* means? It means that we don't have unanimity. Had he signed the petition, he would have to keep his mouth shut. But as it is, I can already see him penning hundreds of articles for the French press here and in France - yes, even in France! - to protest against the forced abdication of that lunatic. And you know, Excellencies; a lot of people in France will read his articles and agree with him."

Minister Nguyen Huu Bai pointed out, "Perhaps the shabby way in which the Emperor is dismissed, has created this impasse. If you show some respect for the Emperor, if you give him an honorable way out, maybe Ngo Dinh Kha will not be so adamant. I for one know that even my friend understands that the Emperor has to go."

Levecque glared at Nguyen Huu Bai. He raised his voice, "Excellency, you and Ngo Dinh Kha are birds of a feather. How do you dare tell me I am shabby in my treatment of that lunatic whom you continue to call Emperor? We have tried for a long time, to overlook his weaknesses, his crimes and his lack of collaboration with us. To offer him an honorable exit now would merely encourage future rebellions."

He swung around and told all those present, "Look, we have a major problem here which you will have to help me resolve. Please go to Ngo Dinh Kha's home tonight and insist that he sign the petition. You, Mr. Prime Minister, and you Minister Bai, I will hold you responsible for this."

Minister Nguyen Huu Bai replied, "I am Ngo Dinh Kha's friend, but I am not his conscience; therefore, I cannot ask him to reverse his decision. I am not his father. I cannot order him to do something against his will. I already know what his answer will be. So, *Mr. Prime Minister*, with your permission, I wish to offer my resignation effective right now."

Levecque was pale with rage. He registered well the implied challenge to his authority when Nguyen Huu Bai offered his resignation *to the Prime Minister*, and not to him.

While Truong Nhu Cuong, the Prime Minister, tried to placate Nguyen Huu Bai, the French official struggled to regain his composure. In his calculating mind, he knew he had to dispose of Ngo Dinh Kha. He had no doubt about it. But if Nguyen Huu Bai were to leave at the same time, he would have a tremendous problem on his hands.

The two of them were the only Catholics in the Imperial Court. If he made both of them leave at the same time, then even his superiors, as ardent anti-Catholic Freemasons as he was, would have to disown him. They were certainly not prepared at the moment to fight all the Catholic forces in France. No, he must keep Nguyen Huu Bai in the Cabinet at any cost.

He cut short Truong Nhu Cuong, who was trying to placate Bai, saying, "Look, Excellencies, no resignation may be tendered or accepted at this moment. We are in a major transition. We are all of us, in the same boat. We have to work out a smooth transition. The Commander of the Palace Guards, unfortunately, doesn't seem to like our team. He may have to go, but it's up to him. His Excellency Nguyen Huu Bai is the person who among us has the most influence on him. We want you, Minister Bai, to try once more to convince your friend to show some good judgment by signing the petition. Please, all of you accompany Minister Bai to Ngo Dinh Kha's home and tell him that if he signs the petition, his membership in the Council of Regents is assured."

*

They went to Ngo Dinh Kha's home that evening. They sat down and sipped tea and tried not to get into the matter at hand immediately.

Minister Bai called his old friend's children to come into the parlor and told his colleagues something about each one of them. He was quite fond of his friend's eldest son, Ngo Dinh Khoi, who was fifteen, and his godsons Thuc and Diem who were respectively ten and six.

He also knew how to mollify Ngo Dinh Kha by praising his friend's favorite daughter. Even when all the other children had left the room, he still held little Hiep's hand and he asked her to stay and sit next to him on the sofa.

Prime Minister Truong Nhu Cuong began, "We are sorry that we have come here so late in the evening and disturbed your well-deserved rest, but we need to talk to you. We all agree with you that the Emperor is neither a madman nor a playboy, and under ordinary circumstances, none of us would suggest he should go. But these are not normal times; the French have all the power, and the Imperial Court has none. Now the French want the Emperor to abdicate. We do not want to let the people know that the measure comes from the French. That would be a loss of face for all of us, and a great dishonor to the Emperor. That is why we wrote this petition to ask the Emperor to abdicate. We are petitioning the Emperor. We are not forcing him to abdicate. Nobody loses face…"

Ngo Dinh Kha had heard enough. "Excellencies, I've seen the petition. I've seen your signatures on it. I've tried to understand why you've written and signed such a terrible document. Now, with the Prime Minister's explanation, I understand your motivation and your intention.

The Emperor will certainly be forever grateful for such an attempt to save his face."

Though the tone was not very mocking, the words lashed at them mercilessly. Ngo Dinh Kha paused a second, then added, "But we are not living in the world of intentions. We are living in a world of actions and facts. What are we doing here? Even if our intentions were, in some odd way, honorable, our action would still speak louder: what we are doing here is dismissing our Emperor. Yes, *our* Emperor, Excellencies. When we were children, we were taught to honor the Emperor more than our own parents. Can children dismiss their parents?"

Nobody wanted to respond to Ngo Dinh Kha's terse tirade. He went on, "The Prime Minister said that if the French were seen as the authors of this palace coup, the Emperor would suffer dishonor. It would not be the first time. The French have time after time dishonored him and all of us, and our nation as a whole. So, what's new? But if we disown him, the Emperor will be dishonored by his own people, and by the mandarins he has personally elevated to high offices."

Prime Minister Truong Nhu Cuong sat stone-faced for a while, and then he stood up and said, "We're sorry we have bothered you. We came here to entreat you, for the sake of solidarity among colleagues, to sign the petition. We've not come here to listen to sermons. Nothing that we, or you, do or don't do will change the situation or save the Emperor."

Ngo Dinh Kha replied, softly but firmly, "I agree with you there, but what we do and don't do at this critical time will determine whether we can or cannot look at ourselves in the mirror, every morning, for the rest of our lives."

One by one, the mandarins and the princes said good-bye and Ngo Dinh Kha accompanied them to the gate. At the last minute, Minister Nguyen Huu Bai said: "I still need to talk to you." Ngo Dinh Kha nodded and returned to the parlor with him. Standing at the door, the little girl who had heard everything was still trembling over the confrontation between her father and the visitors. Again, Nguyen Huu Bai took her by the hand and sat her next to him.

Ngo Dinh Kha opened up immediately, "You should not have stayed behind. They suspect you enough already." Minister Bai said, "Well, my dear friend, they are past suspicion now. They *know* that I am with you all the way. But this afternoon at Levecque's office, I realized that they were afraid to let both you and me go at the same time. They don't want to be accused of being anti-Catholic. If they are perceived as ardent anti-Catholics who are deliberately eliminating all Catholic presence at the Imperial Court, that will cause some reaction in Paris."

Ngo Dinh Kha still felt uneasy, "I heard that you submitted your resignation this afternoon. That was not a smart move." Minister Bai laughed, "I see that even the walls at the Resident Superior's office have ears. So you heard about my resignation? I wanted to know whether the anti-Catholic Freemason in Levecque had really overpowered his political judgment. If that were the case, he would have been more than pleased to see me go. But I think that his calculating mind is still functioning pretty well."

He added after a pause, "Levecque offers you membership in the Council of Regents if you agree to sign the petition. Nobody mentioned it tonight, because they knew that the offer would not change your mind."

He hesitated a while and then added, "Look, I know the Emperor wants you to stay in power; he also wants me to stay in power. You disobey the Emperor and look like a hero while I obey the Emperor and feel like a worm. But in spirit, I am with you. Here is an article I wrote to protest the forced abdication of the Emperor. If you like it, sign it with your name. Publish it here or in France, as you like."

Ngo Dinh Kha walked to a writing table in the corner of the parlor. He opened a drawer and took out a few sheets of paper, "Thank you, but I have already written two articles here, one for the local newspapers, and the other for the press in France."

Minister Bai insisted, "Take a few ideas from my article, incorporate them into yours. It will make me feel a little better." Ngo Dinh Kha smiled, "Oh, in that case, yes. I will use some of your ideas."

Minister Bai asked the little girl, "Have you heard anything that we said? Have you witnessed a conspiracy?" The little girl shook her head and was quick to respond, "I have heard nothing, nothing at all." The Minister and Ngo Dinh Kha laughed until tears came to their eyes.

*

The Ministers reported to Levecque the next morning. Truong Nhu Cuong suggested that Ngo Dinh Kha should be fired immediately, but Levecque was cautious. He said that the fate of the *troublemaker* could wait.

Indeed, he now had new instructions. The instructions were so vague and confusing that he would have to improvise and take the blame if the plan would not work out. He knew that before long, he could possibly be the fall guy, and kept repeating to himself, *"Prudence, mon cher, prudence!"*

Though the instructions he had received now gave him the authority to leave the monarchy intact, he did not want to make such a major concession to the Vietnamese mandarins without making them sweat a little first. He told the ministers that his mind was made up and that the new instructions recommended that he eliminated the monarchy once and for all.

Several ministers said that they would resign if the monarchy were to be abolished. Levecque made lengthy protests, and then left the room saying that as they were all so bent on preserving the monarchy, he needed to take a few minutes to think things over.

He came back a short time later and with a gracious smile, said he admired the Ministers' loyalty to the Throne. He admitted that the instructions he had received left a little flexibility for him to maneuver. Saying that the long friendship each one of them had shown him deserved to be rewarded, he agreed to leave intact the monarchy.

He announced then that, even though what he was about to do might endanger his own career; he would allow the Council of Regents to choose a successor to Emperor Thanh Thai, on the condition that the Emperor Thanh Thai's sons would not be considered. He also asked the ministers to propose a few suitable candidates as soon as possible.

Minister Bai immediately objected, "A stable monarchy demands that a son succeed his father on the throne. The successor must be one of the Emperor Thanh Thai's sons." Levecque was displeased; he said, "It is not in the best interests of your country to have a loony prince succeed a crazy emperor. I believe that all of Thanh Thai's sons are mental cases; therefore, let us rule out Thanh Thai's breed."

Seeing that Minister Bai seemed to be preparing to speak again in favor of Emperor Thanh Thai's sons, Levecque quickly put an end to the discussion, "Gentlemen, please think it over. We will talk about the succession in our next meeting. In the meantime, I want Thanh Thai to sign the Edict of Abdication."

Minister Bai raised another question; "There is a blank in the draft edict. The Edict says, 'The Emperor abdicates in favor of…', then there is a blank. Should we ask him to sign a document with a blank in it?" Levecque was losing patience. He replied, "Yes, let's not procrastinate. He must sign the Edict today. On the day we find a successor, he will be given the pleasure of filling in the name of the chosen one." Minister Nguyen Huu Bai sighed. He knew that he had another uphill battle ahead of him.

*

The Emperor took the petition from the hands of the Prime Minister and read it carefully. He did not show any emotion as he read it and when he had finished, he said very slowly, as if weighing every word he uttered, "Mr. Prime Minister, I congratulate you for the style you have used for this very important historical document. Your children and grand-children will one day enjoy reading it."

He laughed and added: "May I, however, make a very slight reproach to this document that, in every other way, is a true literary pearl? I regret that even a casual reader may find this document a little *too clear*. Or let us say, even a casual reader may sense that a *Cartesian* editor has reviewed it. Yes, even a casual reader may see the hand of a Frenchman here."

Note: The French are proud of their "crystal clear language". René Descartes' Discours de la méthode shows how ideas can be developed with an economy of words and with strict logic. The French are normally proud to be called "Cartésien".

The face of the Prime Minister was scarlet. He bowed his head, then raised it up and looking straight into the Emperor's face, his eyes full of defiance and hatred, he said, "Thank you very much, Your Majesty, for your comment on the style. But the signatories of this petition, who include every high-ranking mandarin of the Court, are suggesting that Your Majesty abdicate. What is your decision, please?"

The Emperor smiled suavely and remarked, "I notice that the signature of His Excellency Ngo Dinh Kha is missing. Have you, Excellencies, intentionally omitted presenting this petition to him for his signature? Or have you already demoted him?"

Many of the ministers talked at the same time, "Your Majesty, we did show him the petition and entreated him to sign it, but he refused." The Emperor shook his head, "I have asked him to cooperate with all of you in every way. He has disobeyed me then, but I'm cannot blame him. Would you blame him, Excellencies, if you were in my shoes?" None of those present said anything, as the Emperor's question was merely rhetorical and he did not expect them to answer.

The Emperor took a few steps and, by doing so, forced everybody to move along with him. He stopped and faced the Prime Minster, "You ask me what my decision is? Do I have a decision to make? Hasn't the decision been made for me already? Mr. Prime Minister, let me ask you: How many decisions have you made, since I was made a prisoner in my own Palace?" The Prime Minister blushed and said nothing.

With a sigh, the Emperor said, "Please forgive me. Why should I make you all feel miserable? Give me the Abdication Edict. I am ready to sign it." But he took his time to read the edict. He read it very carefully, noticed the blank, smiled and with a wave of his hand ordered his writing tablet and his brushes to be brought to him. He sat down and copied the edict, word by word, leaving a blank where the name of his successor would be written, and then he signed it.

As he finished signing, the mandarins knelt down to thank him for his decision and to bid him farewell. He dismissed them, saying: "Please don't do that. I am no longer your Emperor."

He turned to walk away, but stopped and said, "The Imperial Seal is in my office. The Edict needs to bear the mark of the seal. Yet, that seal of mine, symbol of the continuity of the Nguyen Dynasty, is a fake. The true seal, the one handed down by Emperor Minh Mang, was taken, as you may already know, by one of my courageous predecessors, Emperor Ham Nghi, to the jungle after he had failed in his *rebellion* against the French.

The French captured him, in the end, but the Imperial Seal was lost in the jungle and was never recovered. Gentlemen, dynastic continuity is just an empty word nowadays. May Heaven help you in the days ahead!"

*

The two friends met in the afternoon. Ngo Dinh Kha had sent his articles to the local and the French press. It would be only a matter of hours or days now before Levecque read the articles, confronted him with his handiwork, and asked him to resign. Kha's future was not the issue at hand.

What they needed to do together that afternoon was to design a strategy whereby one of the sons of Emperor Thanh Thai might succeed his father on the throne, in spite of Levecque's objection. The friends lamented that there had been no Crown Prince. Had there been a Crown Prince, it would have been much easier for them to put him on the throne.

The first Emperors of the Nguyen, jealous of their absolute power had instituted the *Rule of the Five No's.* They decreed that there would be *no* Empress, *no* Crown Prince, *no* Prime Minister, *no* granting of the title of Prince to anyone except to members of the Imperial family, and *no* First Laureate at the Imperial Exams.

Three *No*'s had been easy to live with. So, there had been no Crown Prince, and no First Laureate. Nobody outside of the Imperial Family had been made prince. But how could the Emperor live without an Empress? Soon enough, the title of Imperial Consort (*Hoang Quy Phi*) was invented to replace that of Empress. A country could not function without a Prime Minister, so the Minister of Government and of the Interior (*Lai Bo Thuong Thu*) acted in lieu of the Prime Minister.

The absence of a Crown Prince at that critical moment made the nomination of one of Emperor Thanh Thai's sons extremely difficult. Kha and Bai knew that. They sat and sipped tea for a long time, and then Ngo Dinh Kha asked, "When he knew that he had to allow the monarchy to survive, did Levecque announce it immediately?" Minister Nguyen Huu Bai, not knowing where his friend's question was leading, answered with the same tone, as if they were playing a game when they were young classmates, "He did not. He made us sweat first. He kept saying that he was for the abolition of monarchy."

Ngo Dinh Kha, pointing to the obvious, asked, "What did he want to get as concession from you, before he said he would allow the monarchy to go on?" Minister Nguyen Huu Bai shrugged: "He wanted us to rule out the Emperor Thanh Thai's sons as candidates."

Kha said, *"Then we will also adopt his tactics*. You will suggest names that throw fear into his heart, and then back down and let him think that the Emperor's sons are not so bad after all." The Minister laughed, "I understand what you mean."

The two men did not have to mention names. They knew which names would horrify the French the most. Ngo Dinh Kha leaned over and told his friend, "Tell the Frenchman that a very young prince surrounded by a large number of Regents would mean *no trouble* for many years. He would like your idea. He might even change his opinion about you."

Minister Nguyen Huu Bai sighed, "Easy to say, my friend. To succeed in this, I will need a miracle." Kha answered optimistically, "Then I will pray for a miracle." The Minister shook his head, "I will need a *big* miracle." His friend laughed, "I will pray for a *big* miracle."

*

Kha told his wife and children, "This evening, we will all pray for His Excellency Nguyen Huu Bai and for the family of the Emperor." They went to the cathedral across the street and chanted the evening prayers with the other parishioners. When the evening prayers were over and the other parishioners had left, they stayed behind.

The little girl was amazed at her father's power of concentration when he prayed. He might be chatting, making jokes outside of the cathedral, but as soon as he passed the threshold of the cathedral, he would genuflect, and then become completely oblivious to kin and friends with whom he had just been chatting with outside. Now, praying for his friend and the Emperor, he was completely insensitive to the hordes of mosquitoes that had invaded the cathedral. To the little girl it seemed as if he was in a trance, with tears brimming over his eyes.

As soon as they were back home, she asked her father, "Why didn't we pray for you this evening?" Her father said, "Pray for me every morning and evening, I need your prayers. Tonight, however, we prayed especially for the Emperor's family and Minister Bai because tomorrow a major decision will be made, and if it's God's will, a son of the Emperor will succeed him on the throne."

With a little smile, Ngo Dinh Kha looked intently at his daughter and said, "But you know all of that, because you heard my conversation with Minister Bai this afternoon, didn't you? I saw your little hand over the door jamb of the parlor while I was talking to him."

The little girl laughed, "Yes, I was there, behind the door." She looked at her father, saw that he was in a good mood, so she laughed again and said: "But, I didn't hear a thing. Not a thing, Father." Her mother was amazed at the way the little girl had her father wrapped around her little finger. She knew that soon enough her husband would be dismissed from the Court and she hoped that the girl would continue to entertain him the way she had always done. "He will need a lot of support from his family in the future," she thought, "whether he will admit it or not."

*

They all knew that the meeting would be stormy. From the very start, Levecque insisted: "Emperor Thanh Thai's sons should not be considered as potential candidates to succeed their father."

He stood up and made a long speech, recalling every mistake, real or imaginary, ever made by Emperor Thanh Thai during his eighteen-year rule. He concluded that the Emperor was a madman. Then he went on to describe Thanh Thai's sons. He had a thick dossier on each and every one of the nineteen princes. He did not see any one of them fit to rule. He said repeatedly: "They are all mental cases just like their father."

He transfixed Minister Bai with his eyes. He knew that the opposition would come from Bai. He was a little taken aback when he noticed that Bai listened to him with obvious interest. When he had finished, Bai's reaction took him by surprise. Bai did not offer a frontal opposition to what had just been said. On the contrary, the Minister even smiled at him and stated that he agreed with most of what Levecque had just said, although he was not sure he could subscribe to Levecque's statement that Thanh Thai's sons were all lunatics.

As Levecque was about to respond, Bai held his hand out, asking for permission to finish speaking. To Levecque's complete surprise, he said that, in order to save time, he would like to propose other candidates.

Levecque and the pro-French ministers breathed a little easier. They thought, "Nguyen Huu Bai is abandoning Thanh Thai's brood, after all." Their relief was short-lived. Bai, with very little hedging, announced, "I wish to propose Prince Cuong De as successor to the deposed Emperor."

A big hush followed his proposal. Now, Prince Cuong De was *the rebel Prince*, the one who had left Vietnam for Japan in the company of the great patriot, Phan Boi Chau, where both were striving to obtain Japanese military and political support to put an end to French domination in Vietnam.

Months earlier, in one of his reports to his government in France, Levecque had precisely mentioned that in case Emperor Thanh Thai had to go, Prince Cuong De, though popular, should never be allowed to become a Pretender. Now the French chargé d'affaires hit the table with his clenched fist, "Excellency, are you out of your mind? Prince Cuong De is a nothing but a rabble-rouser, a troublemaker who has no claim to the throne. None at all! At this time he is in Japan, blasting at France three times a day. And you want him to be the new Emperor?"

Minister Bai put up a hand and explained, "Excellencies, so many things have gone wrong in the last fifty years with the Nguyen Dynasty and with the French-Vietnamese relations. Why? I believe that the founder of the Dynasty was at fault. If he had stuck with the children of his eldest son, Crown Prince Canh, whom he had sent to France to obtain assistance for his struggling armies, we would not have gone to war against France, and experienced all the tragedies of the past fifty years."

As they did not know what Bai was driving at, they had to wait for him to finish speaking. Bai went on, "The greatest tragedy began when Emperor Gia Long did not obey the ancestral rules, and forgot the right of primogeniture. In Catholic terminology, we would say, that this was the original sin of this Dynasty. By placing Emperor Minh Mang on the throne, he invited trouble. Emperor Minh Mang did give the throne to his eldest son who became Emperor Thieu Tri. But Emperor Thieu Tri again ignored the right of primogeniture and left his throne to Emperor Tu Duc. Emperor Tu Duc, having no children of his own, left his throne to one of his nephews whom he had adopted, Emperor Duc Duc, the father of Emperor Thanh Thai."

Clearly, Bai was enjoying every word he said. But those who listened to him still did not know what his conclusion would be, after so long a speech. Bai smiled as he added, "You all know what happened after that; three Emperors in four months: that was what we had. Since Emperor Minh Mang, French-Vietnamese relations went from bad to worse, and under Emperor Tu Duc we had the big war against the French. From 1883 to this day, just over twenty-four years, we have had six Emperors. After Emperor Thieu Tri, we have never had the eldest son of an Emperor succeed his father. What country could survive such chaos?"

Bai suddenly said with emphasis, "Today we have a chance to erase the original sin and the troubles which have been its evil consequences. Let us put back on the throne a descendant of Crown Prince Canh. Mr. Resident Superior, I pray you to consider my proposal, not as a whimsical thought, but as a serious plea. Who among Emperor Gia Long's sons was the most loyal friend of France? It was Crown Prince Canh. Isn't it time for his stem to be rewarded for his loyal friendship to France? Prince Cuong De descends directly from Crown Prince Canh. You say Prince Cuong De is a rabble-rouser. I know that no commoner has even heard of his name. Didn't you say that he is in Japan, making speeches? What can a Pretender do, except make speeches? If his speeches are not exactly what we want to hear, we can see that they have been quite harmless, so far."

Levecque was really annoyed. But French officials and historians had been so full of praise when they talked about Crown Prince Canh that the mention of his name in relation with Prince Cuong De could not be taken lightly.

He finally answered, "Look, Excellency, I now understand that you have considered Prince Cuong De seriously and not facetiously. I also think that maybe someday, we should do justice by the stem of Crown Prince Canh. But perhaps you do not know all the facts about Prince Cuong De. My services can give you evidence that there was collusion between Thanh Thai and the Prince. At the moment of his departure for Japan, the Prince received several secret messages from Thanh Thai, who wanted to make of him his secret envoy to Japan. Their scheme was to ask for assistance from Japan to overthrow the French administration in Indochina. That is treason. So let us not talk about Cuong De anymore."

Nguyen Huu Bai said humbly, "You are right. I was not aware of the secret ties between Emperor Thanh Thai and Prince Cuong De. In the past few weeks, I was led to believe that the Emperor was being forced to abdicate due to mental illness. But from what you have just said, he is not really insane then, because apparently he is able to go on conducting secret plots against France."

Levecque was livid with anger, but he succeeded in controlling his voice. He replied curtly, "I assume that you want to make this process as unpleasant as possible." Nguyen Huu Bai smiled and waved his hand, "It certainly is an unpleasant process. It is not every day that mandarins are required to force their own Emperor to abdicate. But from what you have just said I need to assume that Emperor Thanh Thai is not really insane, after all. Once we know that he is not insane, it seems extravagant to assume that all his sons are mental cases. If the father is not really insane, what is the rationale for assuming that all his sons are insane?"

Seeing that Levecque was again about to explode, Nguyen Huu Bai said, "All right, if you do not want the Emperor's sons, that is all right with me. But whom do we chose now, if Prince Cuong De does not appeal to you either?" He shook his head, then suggested, "How about calling Emperor Ham Nghi back from exile?"

There ensued a heavy silence. Finally Levecque replied, "Emperor Ham Nghi led a rebellion against France, in 1885, failed in his attempt and was exiled for his crime. Why do you mention his name now?"

Nguyen Huu Bai said: "In 1885, Emperor Ham Nghi was fourteen years old. He did not lead the *rebellion*. His regents were responsible for the assault on the French garrisons in Hue. The Emperor has been punished long enough for an attack on a few French garrisons, an attack that he could not have prevented due to his young age. Since he began his exile in Algeria, he has learnt to speak French, and has even married a French lady. He has not spoken against France. He has led a quiet life as a painter. Don't you think that eighteen years of exile are long enough?"

Levecque shook his head. He said, "I do not know where we are heading with this discussion. If the candidates you propose are all like those already named, a son of Thanh Thai might not be so bad, after all." He started sweating; the name of Ham Nghi was also on the list of people he had ruled out, in his report to Paris. How did this man know?"

Nguyen Huu Bai, humbly apologizing, said, "I am really sorry if I have inadvertently said something wrong. If you are absolutely against Emperor Ham Nghi, then let us propose somebody else." Levecque asked suspiciously, "You have another proposal?" The Minister looked at the Frenchman a long time before answering, "Yes, I do. Let us then have Prince Ung Nguy." This time, Levecque knew! Ung Nguy was his own candidate. But in his report to his superiors in Paris, he had not dared hide the fact that the prince was addicted to opium, and so Paris had told him to forget it.

Now he realized that all the names that appeared on his report had been communicated to the Minister. Stating one name after another, the Minister showed that he was an insider, and that he was able to get all the information he needed. The French official wondered, "Who is the spy in my services? No, nobody here in Hue would dare spy on me for the *Annamites*. But then, who in Paris is keeping this man informed?"

He stared at the inscrutable face of the Vietnamese mandarin, and threw in the towel, "All right, Excellency, you want a son of Thanh Thai as the new Emperor. Everybody here in this room understands that point. But how can we be sure that the son will not cause us headaches like the father has done?"

Nguyen Huu Bai said, "We all know that you, Mr. Resident Superior, still have a soft spot for Emperor Thanh Thai. We know that despite all your tough talk, you still want to avoid punishing his children. Let me suggest that we choose a very young prince from among them. We will educate the young prince and make of him a loyal friend of France. Anyway, a very young Child-Emperor cannot cause trouble for many years."

Levecque seemed to be somewhat placated, but he asked with a hint of disdain in his voice, "Will you do that, your Excellency? I mean will you educate him to be a loyal friend of France?" Holding the Frenchman's eyes, Nguyen Huu Bai assured him, "Yes, he will be as loyal a friend to France as I have always been."

Levecque replied, "Then fine. But I will not agree to permit *you* to choose among Thanh Thai's children. *We, the French Administration,* will do it ourselves. Please make sure all the princes are present for the selection tomorrow morning. I will be at the Imperial Palace, accompanied by my staff, and a medical doctor." With that the Ministers were dismissed.

*

The little girl followed her father into the garden. He was in a pensive mood and paced the orchard, with his hands joined behind his back. The little girl walked behind him until he noticed her and stood still. She walked over to him and holding on to one of his fingers, she inquired, "Father, are you satisfied?" Her father nodded, "Yes, I am satisfied. The new Emperor will take the reign name of Duy Tan. He is the fifth son of Emperor Thanh Thai. Our prayers have been answered."

The little girl knew that he was not telling her everything. She pressed on, "You say you are satisfied, but this afternoon, after Minister Bai's visit, you were quite disturbed. You went into your study and hit your head against the wall. Why were you so angry, Father?"

Her mother was also in the garden. Overhearing what the girl had said, she was worried. She hurried over to where father and daughter stood and scolded, "Girl, don't bother your father now! And since when have you been going around spying on your father like that?"

Her father shook his head and told his wife, "Please let her be. She does not bother me at all." He took the little girl by the hand and said, "This morning, Mr. Levecque and a group of French officials went to the palace and talked to all of the princes. There was a medical doctor in the group."

She wanted to know, "Why a medical doctor, Father?" He patiently explained: "The French pretended that the princes might all have some kind of mental illness, so a doctor came along to see to it that the prince they chose was not insane."

The girl asked, "Do the princes have any kind of mental illness?" He shook his head and said emphatically, "Of course not." He was not only emphatic, he was angry. But the little girl did not seem to be worried at all. She looked at him, waiting for him to resume his narrative.

After a pause, he went on, "The medical doctor kept saying: 'This one looks weird to me. Oh, this one is definitely a mental case, and this one looks exactly like his father. He will grow up to be a loony.' At each one of his remarks, the group of French officials laughed uproariously. Finally, the head of the French Secret Services, a Mr. Sogny, took a very young prince by the ear and dragged him to where Mr. Levecque stood, saying, 'This guy has got big ears. He will be a good emperor!' Levecque and his followers laughed and they all agreed on the spot that the young prince with the big ears would do. That was how they selected our new Emperor, little girl. That's why I was angry."

She said, "I too am angry, Father. They should not have treated our future Emperor like that." He looked at her; he was genuinely surprised. He had always thought that the little girl never got angry. She was standing there two feet from him breathing hard, her face a little flushed. He had never felt so much love for her.

He said, "Anger is neither a good nor a bad emotion. But anger cannot solve anything." She smiled and took hold of one of his fingers again.

After a while she asked, "Do you think that the new Emperor will be a good Emperor?" Her father looked up at the sky for a long moment as if he was reading some sign in the white clouds, then he nodded, "Yes, the new Emperor will be a good Emperor. He is the brightest among Emperor Thanh Thai's sons. The French do not know whom they have chosen."

Hiep was no longer a child. She had acquired the capacity to understand and empathize with adults' pain. She had been projected into a world of intrigues and plots, betrayals and hypocrisy. She had seen the arrogance of the French and the humiliations inflicted upon her people. She had seen how her father tried to endure the ordeal without losing his pride, his faith in God and without hating the representatives of the colonial administration.

She would grow up treasuring the memories of moments she had spent with her father and the simple lessons he had tried to teach her. Soon enough, he would spend more time with Diem than with her. He would place all his hopes on Diem. But she would remain until the day he died, his favorite child, the one to whom he would talk without reservation about his deepest thoughts.

Emperor Duy Tan, the Child Emperor

CHAPTER FOUR
THE COMMONER

The whole family assembled downstairs as Ngo Dinh Kha threw a few clothes into a small suitcase. He had learned that the French were sending the Emperor into exile. He was prepared to share the Emperor's fate. Thanks to his sources of information, he knew which train would leave Hue with the Emperor. He had bought a ticket for the same train.

Though they did not know how long he would be absent, neither his wife nor his older children were crying. Only the little girl who stood in a corner of the parlor facing the wall was shaking uncontrollably. But she did not cry either.

Kha did not like long farewells. When he came downstairs he simply said to his eldest son, "Khoi, please take good care of your mother." Then he turned to his wife and said, "Please take good care of the children." He was about to leave when he noticed the little girl in a corner of the parlor. He stopped and said, "Make sure you pray for me morning and evening." The little girl said, "I will pray for your return." With that, the Grand Chamberlain walked to the front yard where a rickshaw was waiting for him.

It took only about ten minutes to get to the railway station. He asked the rickshaw man to slow down. He did not want to arrive too early for fear that the French would spot him on the platform while he would be waiting for the train.

He arrived at the station right on the dot. French security agents were everywhere and seemed to be waiting. The Emperor had not arrived. Ngo Dinh Kha sat down on a bench, pulled a Chinese book out of his suitcase and hid his face behind it, pretending to read.

A few minutes passed, and then there was a commotion at the double door of the main building. A man all bundled up in a large shawl was half pushed, half dragged towards a carriage. Ngo Dinh Kha looked up and saw no other passengers in that carriage except a few guards. He knew the Emperor had arrived. He immediately boarded the train himself, but the train did not start moving. French policemen entered each carriage, examining each of the passengers.

Ngo Dinh Kha hoped that somehow the policemen would not recognize him. Futile hope! They had been looking for nobody else but him! When they spotted him, they dragged him from the train and took him to the commanding officer.

The man was actually Sogny, the head of the Secret Services, who in the past few weeks, had served as the jailer of the deposed Emperor. Sogny said, *"Vous êtes fini, Cher Monsieur le Ministre, bien fini!* "

Ngo Dinh Kha did not seem to hear him. He was looking up at the window of the carriage where the Emperor was. At that moment, the Emperor leaned out of the window and waved to him. Kha stared at his sovereign but did not find any word to say. It was the Emperor who, raising his voice above the noise of the departing train, shouted, "Don't worry about me, I will be all right."

As he sat sadly in the same rickshaw, going through the same streets to return to his home, Kha thought, "Little girl, you said you would pray for my return. Well, your prayers have been answered too soon."

*

The Imperial Court did not take long to deliberate. The Council of Regents presided by Levecque was quick to deliver the sentence: Ngo Dinh Kha was to be stripped of all his ranks, functions and honors. He was to be sent back to his native village in Le Thuy, in the province of Quang Binh, a hundred miles north of Hue, with the express order not to leave that province.

Everybody expected Regent Nguyen Huu Bai to put up a fight for his friend. But he lowered his head and did not say anything at all. Nobody knew that he had promised his friend that he would keep silent when the Council debated his case.

Now, hearing that his friend was to be banished to Quang Binh, he stood up and pleaded, "Let him be in Phu Cam, his current parish of residence." Levecque nodded agreement, but he was adamant on the next point: Ngo Dinh Kha would not receive the pension to which he was entitled as an official of permanent Minister Rank.

Note: Kha had served continuously for 22 years, and was 51 years old. Normally, pensions were paid only to mandarins with 30 years of continuous service and who retire at 60 or at a more advanced age. A few of his colleagues did plead for him saying that he had rendered outstanding services to the Crown. Leveque nodded assent during the meeting, but afterwards told the mandarins that the pension should not be paid.

Portrait of Ngo Dinh Kha

*

So, in September 1907, Ngo Dinh Kha, the commoner, started his life as a farmer at the age of fifty-one, and a *poor* farmer at that.

For Hiep, being the daughter of a commoner had at least one advantage: her father, who had worked long hours in the Palace, was now at home most of the time, at least in the first weeks But she saw that he was worried. He worried about the church he had helped build in the Citadel of Hue. Now that Emperor Thanh Thai was gone, his decree authorizing the construction was revoked. Soon enough, the church would be pulled down.

Ngo Dinh Kha often went to the site and looked at the piles of lumber, bricks and tiles, the remnants of what had been a beautiful church, and came home looking quite disconsolate. (1)

Then of course, he worried about the family's livelihood. As an honest mandarin he had never been able to save anything, and now without a salary, and without a pension, he would have to depend on the crops he produced on three hectares of rice paddy near his home.

His wife and children were ready to help, but his eldest son was only fifteen, and his second son only ten. He was not discouraged though. During school-breaks, and the summer holidays his older sons went out to the field with him, after going with him to Mass, and worked beside him all day. His wife and his twelve-year-old daughter brought lunch to the field at noontime. He never went home before dark.

Ngo Dinh Kha and his children did not work alone in the rice paddy. He hired a few farm hands. But he insisted that whenever they could, his sons would work with him, as hard as the farm hands.

In the lean years after his forced retirement, Ngo Dinh Kha discovered in his wife who was born of farmers, a tremendous ally. Not only did she cook and carry lunches to the rice field for her family members and farm hands, she also planted and tended her own vegetable patch, then spent her remaining time raising pigs and taking care of the poultry. She worked from dawn to dark without uttering a single word of complaint. Until the day he died, Ngo Dinh Kha always showed great respect for her and told his children that without her he would have panicked when he suddenly became a poor farmer.

Note: As a concession to Kha's loyal colleagues, Levecque allowed the Court to pay compensation to Kha for the rebuilding of the Church in Tien Non, west of the Citadel. Here again the collective memory of the Ngo Dinh family place this event at the wrong time. The event actually took place in the 18th year of the Thanh Thai reign. The embattled emperor could not protect Kha anymore and Leveque ordered the destruction of the church in the Citadel.

Soon enough, a few events happened which made the life of the household less precarious. First, the neighbors in Phu Cam realized that the former Minister, Commander of the Palace Guards was really poor. They had suspected his poverty but had never expected him to be penniless. Now they knew.

They dispatched some rich farmers who came to see him one evening and proposed a deal. They said that they had plenty of land, and would like to lease some of it to the Minister. They proposed that he leased ten hectares. They said that he did not need to start paying rent immediately as they could wait until he grew a few good crops.

Ngo Dinh Kha at first refused to accept such a thinly disguised favor, but seeing how sincerely they wanted to help him and his family, he finally accepted. He and his children would never forget that favor.

Then his colleagues at the Imperial Court began to send him part of their salaries. Again he protested, but they continued to send their contribution every month. He realized that he still had good friends at the Imperial Court, after all.

Though the secrecy with which they acted in his favor did not please him too much, he knew that they needed to be discreet about their friendship with him. The French administration would make their life miserable if it learnt about their solidarity with him.

Each time he received money from his friends; he would call his children in, show it to them and ask them to remember his friends' generosity. They would remember those debts as long as they lived.

*

The years of hardship passed by, though not too quickly and Ngo Dinh Thi Hiep, at the age of seven was still the daughter of a poor farmer; one who had expensive needs such as French newspapers and magazines.

She remembers now how her father asked his French friends to keep their reading materials for him after they had done with them, then he would send his children to go and collect them. She remembers distinctly, she and her younger sister Hoang going once a week to Father Allys' house to pick up magazines and newspapers for their father.

Wearing their only presentable gowns, one red and one violet, they came to his house, as regular as clockwork. The priest, seeing them week after week wearing the same gowns, exclaimed once, "Why am I to be honored this way? How come every week a cardinal (in red) and a bishop (in violet) come to visit me in my humble abode?" The girls laughed as they had already heard similar jokes from their father about their being bishop and cardinal.

At seven, Hiep also accompanied her mother and her older sister Giao to the field, bringing lunch at noon and snacks in the afternoon for her father, brothers and the hired hands. There were more workers on the rice paddy now. Her father, as he farmed on larger and larger fields, needed to hire more farm hands. Even at the age of nine, her brother Diem, the future President, was required to work in the muddy rice fields whenever he was out of school.

Soon enough, her two oldest brothers deserted the family rice paddy. First, her eldest brother, Khoi, became a mandarin and began his career at the Ministry of Defense. Then her brother, Thuc, left home to join the Minor Seminary in An Ninh, seventy miles north of Hue.

With the older sons gone, Ngo Dinh Kha put his younger children to work on the field. When they complained, he told them that only by being good farmers would they come to understand the essence of their country.

He drove them hard in the field and taught them to loath waste and luxury. He personally supervised their education and tutored them in the evening. The children responded well to the treatment and became as hard-working as their father.

*

For over six years Ngo Dinh Kha did not want to hear anything about the Imperial Court. Even Regent Nguyen Huu Bai, Minister of Public Works, and Minister of Defense had to promise he would not talk politics when they met.

This self-exile from politics did not stem from his disgust with the Court. It came from his deference to the Emperor he had served. The former Emperor, exiled to Cape Saint-Jacques in South Vietnam, had kept an obstinate silence after his departure from Hue. He wanted his son Duy Tan, Emperor at the age of seven, to succeed. He believed that by keeping his mouth shut, he would give his son a better chance with the French.

The former Minister, Commander of the Palace Guards imitated his sovereign's silence. After the new Emperor was crowned and after the former Emperor was sent into exile in the South, he never made a single political statement. He and the members of his family prayed every day for the former Emperor and the new Child-Emperor, but neither in public, nor in private, did he allow himself to make a political comment.

Hiep knew instinctively that he was missing the intrigues of the Court, and the running battles with the French. She came to him every evening and asked him questions about the past. As long as he only had to reminisce, he felt himself on firm ground, and he was pleased to give long answers to her questions.

On a Sunday afternoon, Hiep and her father were crossing the Truong Tien Bridge, a silvery work of art spanning the Perfume River. She asked him, "Who built this bridge?" He answered without thinking, "Emperor Thanh Thai built it in 1897." Then, seeing her incredulity, he corrected himself: "Well, the bridge was built under Emperor Thanh Thai, but the design and the engineering came from France." He slowed his pace and asked, "Do you want to hear a story?" She said, "Of course, I do."

He smiled, wondering whether one day she would know how much the hardships that he endured were made so much lighter by her mere presence. He said, "At first, the bridge was named after the Emperor. It was called The Thanh Thai Bridge. On the day the bridge was inaugurated, the French Resident Superior gave endless praise to the French genius and technology. The Emperor said, "We don't know yet how French technology will fare under the assaults of our typhoons." The French official was perplexed. He said to the Emperor, "Sire, the day this bridge collapses under the gusts of a typhoon, we will abrogate our Protectorate and hand over the rule of the country to Your Majesty."

"Four years later, the Big Typhoon of the Year of the Dragon occurred and the bridge collapsed. As they walked among the debris and looked down on the broken, twisted spans of the bridge, half immersed in muddy water, the Emperor informed the Resident Superior, "The bridge has collapsed." The French official pretended not to understand, so the Emperor reminded him of their conversation at the inauguration. But of course, Vietnam did not regain its independence. The Emperor, by reminding the Resident Superior of his foolish words, only succeeded in making an enemy."

As he was talking about the typhoon, Hiep, who had often heard her mother describe the devastation caused by it, asked: "Will you tell me more about the Big Typhoon? "Her father said, "If you want to hear about the Big Typhoon of the Year of the Dragon, let's go and sit on that bench over there and rest our weary feet."

They had finished crossing the bridge and were walking among the flower gardens in the Thuong Bac public park. His daughter knew that when her father said 'our weary feet,' he actually meant her weary feet, as he never tired of walking. She sat down on the bench with him and they gazed at the river, upstream and downstream.

It was a beautiful summer day. The riverbanks were lined with flowering flame trees. The red masses of heavy flame tree blossoms reflected on the crystal blue of the water. Downstream hundreds of fishing boats and sampans plied the crowded channels near the wharves of the Dong Ba Central Market.

Ngo Dinh Kha said, "The Big Typhoon of the Year of the Dragon came a few months after you were born. I remember that Emperor Thanh Thai was about to celebrate his mother's elevation to the distinction of *Pious-Enlightened-Generous* Empress-Mother. The Emperor revered his mother. He had seen her suffer when her husband, Emperor Duc Duc, was starved to death, then again when her own father, Regent Phan Dinh Binh hanged himself in a prison cell. The Emperor had prayed that the celebrations would be memorable, but he hadn't considered that the weather would cause any problems.

"For several months, the whole country had been devastated by a terrible drought. All the crops had been destroyed, and. most of the wells had dried up. Buddhist pagodas, Christian churches and Taoist temples were full of crowds praying for rain.

"The Emperor humbled himself and wrote a beautiful edict, accusing himself of lack of virtue and publicly recognized his grievous sins. In the same edict, he asked the mandarins of all levels to practice virtues, redeem their sins, and pray hard for forgiveness and for rain. The Emperor fasted and prayed continuously, and the whole country prayed and fasted with him.

"Then the prayers were answered and the rain came. It rained for thirty days without interruption. The Perfume River rose by more than three meters. The whole Citadel was under water. In the Imperial Palace, only high structures emerged from the muddy water, like small islands in a lake. The ceremony planned to honor the Empress-Mother had to be postponed.

"Just as the rain stopped and the big flood was about to subside, the Big Typhoon arrived. It destroyed wooden and steel bridges alike. The air was thick with whole thatched roofs flying about like heavy broken wings of monstrous birds. In our parish the flood had not done much damage, as we were located at the foot of the mountains, but the typhoon destroyed most of the houses. Parishioners fled toward the church for protection. The church was a beautiful, solid building. It had been inaugurated only two years earlier and seemed like a good refuge.

"Unfortunately, on the way to the church, many were killed by flying debris. The most horrible death was for men and women whose long hair was caught in the branches of swaying bamboo. Imagine the strong gusts of wind, bending the tips of the bamboo canes to the ground, catching the long hair of men and women. Then imagine that in the lull between the gusts, the bamboo canes jerked back straight up. After the Typhoon ended, many bodies were seen hanging from bamboo branches. What a terrifying sight!" He still shuddered as he recalled the scene he had seen years earlier.

Hiep looked at her father. His long hair was tied into a chignon that rested at the back of his turban. He had never wanted to cut his hair short, though even the Emperor, who had done so, kept urging him to follow his example. No, though he was very fond of the Emperor, he would never follow him in that little matter.

She asked, "Is the former Emperor a religious man? "He responded, "Not exactly. As a child, he was horribly affected by the murder of his father. He grew up to be a little boy with problems. On his Inauguration day, he received four Regents who watched over him like hawks. Three years after he was made Emperor, he showed more turpitude than virtue, so the Regents confined him on a small islet in Serenity Park (*Ho Tinh Tam*). There he meditated and read, and repented. He wrote to the Empress-Mother asking for forgiveness and promised to be a better person. He was taken back to the Palace by all the courtiers, dressed in their ceremonial Court robes, who wholeheartedly congratulated him for having achieved maturity."

He mused a little, and then added, "There was something nobody needed to teach him, and that was filial piety. He was a pious son. As soon as he became Emperor, he immediately started the construction of an Imperial Tomb for his father, who had been buried hurriedly by the side of a dirt road near our village. Four years later, he honored his mother, by granting her a series of 'Honorary Qualifiers' to be attached to her title of Empress-Mother."

Little Hiep knew that the wound in her father had not healed. She saw that he still grieved for the Emperor. Sensing her melancholy and thinking that she was simply tired, he told her they had better go home.

*

By the time she was ten, her family was no longer impoverished. Several good harvests gave back to Ngo Dinh Kha his former lifestyle. He stopped going to the rice paddy and no longer demanded that his own sons worked the fields during their holidays. His wife and daughters no longer carried lunches to the rice field for the farm hands. But the years of relative indigence had given them habits of thrift and hard work, which would remain permanent traits of their character.

As the financial situation of the family improved, Ngo Dinh Kha spent more time educating his children. Khoi, his eldest son, and Diem, his third son received the most attention. Thuc, his second son, had by that time

76

been admitted to the minor seminary of An Ninh, where Kha himself had studied in his childhood and early youth.

Among his three daughters, Kha spent time mostly with Hiep. Diem, the future President, and Hiep were his favorite companions for long walks in the city, in the Citadel, and to the Mount Ngu Binh behind their house.

One day, when they were in the Citadel, in front of the Noon Gate, the most elaborate entrance to the Imperial Palace, Hiep asked her father about life inside the Palace. With his children, he climbed up the steps of the Flag Monument until they could see parts of the trees and roofs inside the Palace grounds behind high walls. In a good mood, he humored Hiep by telling her about the life of the Emperor and his Consorts and Concubines inside the Forbidden City.

In her French class, several girls her age had told her that Emperor Thanh Thai had several hundred Consorts and Concubines and thousands of children. Hiep asked her father whether that was true.

The former Minister, Commander of the Palace Guards laughed, "Emperor Minh Mang who reigned from 1820 to 1840, was the one who, among our Emperors, had the largest number of children: seventy-eight princes and sixty-four princesses, one hundred and forty-two children in all. He had forty-three Consorts and Concubines."

To Hiep's disappointment, her father added, "As for Emperor Thanh Thai, I don't know exactly how many Consorts and Concubines he married, but he has only fathered nineteen princes and twenty-six princesses. Yes, he has only forty-five children." Hiep protested, "That's not what people say!"

Their father said, "People don't understand. Beside the consorts and concubines there are a number of palace maids, who serve the Emperor and his wives. But their number has also been limited. Our Emperors have never had resources similar to the Chinese Emperors, so they could never keep too many ladies in the Palace. People tend to exaggerate, especially about things they don't understand."

Seeing that Diem blushed as he always did at the mere mention of women, Hiep teasingly continued to asked her father, "Father tell us then about the Three Palaces and the Six Residences."

Ngo Dinh Kha noticed Diem's embarrassment. He asked him, "Do you want to know about the Three Palaces and the Six Residences?" Diem, red-faced, shook his head, "I don't see why we need to know so much about the Emperor's private life."

His father was not of that opinion. He said, "You should be interested in everything that is part of our culture. The life of our Emperor is a matter of culture. Listen, the *Long Life (Trang Sanh)* Palace houses the Emperor's grandmother. If the grandmother has passed away, the Palace is the place where her soul is honored. The *Longevity (Dien Tho)* Palace is where the Emperor's mother lives. The *Khon Thai* Palace is the residence of the Empress, called the Imperial Consort during her lifetime, and Empress after she dies. The Imperial Consort shares her palace with up to three other consorts of the first rank. Their titles are *Precious Consort, Gentle Consort, and Spiritual Consort.*"

Hiep urged her father on, "What about the Six Residences?" Ngo Dinh Kha replied, "The First Residence is reserved for the three Consorts of the second rank. Their titles are *Virtuous Consort, Obedient Consort* and *Wise Consort.* In the Second Residence live the six Concubines of the third and fourth ranks, called *Precious Concubine, Gentle Concubine* and *Dignified Concubine, Beautiful Concubine, Peaceful Concubine* and *Sweet Concubine.*"

Hiep asked, "After the Concubines are there other ranks?" Her father thought for a moment, then continued "So far, the number of Consorts and Concubines has been limited: the most you have is twelve or thirteen. They are very high-ranking ladies. Even the *Tiep du* or Concubines of the Fifth Rank who live in the Third Residence are as high ranking as Ministers. The ladies who live in the Fourth Residence are called *Precious Ladies*, those in the Fifth Residence are the *Beautiful Ladies* and the lowest ranking ladies are called the *Talented Ladies* and they live in the Sixth Residence."

Kha asked his two children to turn and look at the Imperial Palace from where they stood and showed them, "There, in direct line, straight from the Noon Gate you see the *Can Chanh* Palace. Can Chanh means Diligent Governance. It is the Office of the Emperor, his workplace. Right behind it is the Emperor's Residence or *Can Thanh* Palace. Behind the Emperor's Residence is the Empress' Residence or *Khon Thai* Palace. *Can* stands for

Heaven or the Male Principle, while *Khon* stands for Earth and the Female Principle."

He then took them to another point on the left side of the Flag Monument and showed them the rest of the Imperial Palace. "There, on this side facing us, you have the Long Life and Longevity Palaces, housing the Emperor's mother and grandmother. Behind those Palaces, are the Six Residences."

He turned to Diem and asked, "Have you learned anything from what I have said?" Hiep smiled. "So, this is a test after all," she thought, hoping that Diem had listened. Diem answered, "From what you said, the Emperors have been very pious. They offered the best palaces to their mother and grandmother. All the Consorts and Concubines are placed in a strict hierarchy. The ladies of first five ranks are honored more than Ministers of the Court."

Ngo Dinh Kha turned to his daughter and asked, "And you, what have you learned?" Hiep sighed, "You talked so fast, I did not have a chance to understand it all. But I wonder why, with the Palaces of the Emperor, being in the middle, they place the palaces of his mother and grandmother on his right? Father, is not the right *lesser* than the left?"

Her father frowned, "From ancient times, men have been placed on the left and the women on the right." Hiep giggled, "I know, but that means men have always been seen as more important than women." The Grand Chamberlain laughed, "Oh, I see, do you want to change the traditional order of things?" Hiep did not respond. Her father asked, "What else have you noticed?"

Hiep said, "The titles of the Consorts and Concubines emphasize only the virtues considered by the Emperors to be most feminine: Sweet, Peaceful, Gentle, Obedient and Dignified. There are no titles such as Brave Consort, Intelligent Consort, Vigorous Consort, Valiant Consort…"

Both her father and her brother laughed, encouraging her to continue. "What else?" Hiep sighed, "Even the Empress has to share her Palace with three other Consorts. It is not that fantastic to be an Empress, then! Furthermore, she and all the other ladies have to live all their entire lives within the Forbidden City. What a terrible fate! "

Though Kha knew that the ladies of the Court were permitted a few outings every year, he did not want to contradict his daughter. He knew that the life of the Imperial Concubines was dreadful indeed.

He thought with relief that because Emperor Duy Tan was only in his early teens, there was no harem in the Imperial Palace at the time. "So much the better," he thought.

Why did that lesson about life behind the Purple Walls stand out in her memory for so long? Hiep did not know. It is a fact that the secret life of the Emperors interested the people in Hue considerably. Even the common people talked about it incessantly, repeating rumors and false legends.

The life of the Imperial Consorts and Concubines seemed to Hiep, a long and painful tragedy. How could women be reduced to such a life? She shuddered when she thought about them.

She was glad that Emperor Duy Tan, being a Child-Emperor had no need of an Imperial Harem.

Imperial Palace in Hue

*

Ngo Dinh Kha's self-exile from politics ended in late 1912. Hiep was then ten years old. Since Khoi, his eldest son, had started working at the Ministry of Defense under Minister Nguyen Huu Bai, in 1910, he found it hard not to respond to his son's questions on how to deal with certain issues.

In 1912, Khoi was engaged to Nguyen Thi Hoa, Minister Bai's eldest daughter. The preparations for their wedding made the two families even closer than before. Ngo Dinh Kha could no longer turn a deaf ear to his friend's political concerns.

The young Emperor was now thirteen years old and had become quite difficult to restrain. No doubt, he was as patriotic as his father was. But he was showing too much impatience. Regent Nguyen Huu Bai, whom he trusted and respected, could no longer prevent his outbursts of rage against the French, in front of mandarins who obviously spied on him. New reports were sent to French officials every day. The French Secret Services and the French Resident Superior constantly harassed Regent Nguyen Huu Bai who had promised to educate the Emperor to be a loyal friend of France.

Both Ngo Dinh Kha and Nguyen Huu Bai wanted a patriotic Emperor. But both of them knew that any hasty move by the young Emperor would only jeopardize the chances of achieving national autonomy. They had hoped that the young Emperor could be trained to be a tough, mature sovereign who would use his intelligence and the prestige of the throne to slowly regain through negotiation, some freedom for the country.

For years, they had thought that negotiations would bring back more power to the Imperial Court, and that some day, when the monarchy was strong enough, other negotiations might restore autonomy. Indeed, *autonomy* was their goal. In their wildest dreams, they did not envision *national independence* as a possibility, at least in the foreseeable future.

That entire dream of autonomy was for naught, if the young Emperor let the French see too soon that he wanted them out of Vietnam. The two friends became more and more afraid that Duy Tan would soon face the same fate that had befallen his father.

Seeing the imminence of danger, Ngo Dinh Kha broke his vow of silence, and began to have weekly meetings with Regent Nguyen Huu Bai, and frequent discussions with Regent Cao Xuan Duc. Together, they devised strategies to deal with the French and the Imperial Court. But they soon discovered that only the Emperor could save himself.

*

Hiep was very excited. She followed her mother everywhere, trying to help. The wedding of her Brother Khoi to Hoa, Regent Nguyen Huu Bai's daughter, was to take place the next month, and the house was in turmoil. People were saying that it promised to be one of the biggest events in the capital that year.

The French administration was concerned: alliances among the influential families in Vietnam had been methodically discouraged. This marriage would put the official seal on the friendship between the Nguyen Huu and the Ngo Dinh families. There had been enough evidence of their alliance before, when Nguyen Huu Bai became the godfather of Thuc and Diem, the second and third sons of Ngo Dinh Kha. Now, with Khoi marrying Hoa, the two families would almost be one.

Hiep was not preoccupied with the political alliance of the two families. To see her brother, Khoi, and Hoa show so much happiness on their faces really intrigued her. They were literally radiant with joy. "So," she wondered, "is this what grown-ups call love?"

In the back of her mind, she also remembered her own sister Giao, then sixteen, crying as she talked to her mother. She had heard rumors about Truong Dinh Tung, a young man who wanted to get engaged to Giao, but feared a refusal from her parents. She said to herself, "So, love means joy and unhappiness, smiles and tears."

That morning, following her mother, who apparently wanted to remodel the entire house, both upstairs and down, Hiep wanted to know more about the mysteries of adult life. But then she heard the distinct noise of Regent Nguyen Huu Bai's car outside and she ran to open the gate for him.

The Regent was in a hurry. He smiled at her and asked whether her father was at home. Of course, Ngo Dinh Kha was at home. Unless he went to church or took a long walk with his sons or daughters, he never left home. He spent most of his time reading and writing, and chatting with his children.

She ran upstairs to call her father, and he came downstairs and asked her to get tea. Now that she was ten, she could not play the little girl anymore and she knew she should leave the room as soon as she had served tea. But more often than not, either her father or the Regent would ask her to stay. She never guessed that her presence had something to do with their serious conversations, until one day her father said, "Having you between us is not a bad idea. Your presence makes us talk more politely, our arguments are less strident, and our discussions better organized. But you must continue to be the silent observer. The day you open your mouth, your presence will no longer be tolerated."

The rules were spelled out for her. She didn't want to lose that role of silent observer for anything in the world. She did not know that the adults would soon change the rules and that they would ask her more questions than she cared to answer.

*

That day, the Regent had no time for small talk and began immediately, "Mahé is at it again! This time he is excavating Emperor Tu Duc's Tomb for gold." Ngo Dinh Kha laughed uproariously, "Here we are fighting another Acting Resident Superior. He must be in a hurry, I've heard that they are about to transfer him."

Nguyen Huu Bai nodded his head thoughtfully, "You have always been right about chargés d'affaires and acting officials. They are pressed for time. They have to finish what they want to do, quickly. This morning he sent his handyman to the tomb with Minister Huynh Con, to start excavating."

Ngo Dinh Kha sighed, "The poor Minister is way over his head. But you're the Minister of Public Works, aren't you? Excavating Imperial Tombs obviously falls under your jurisdiction. You should be over there with them right now, *excavating*." Nguyen Huu Bai shrugged, "Stop kidding. Tell me, what I should do?" Ngo Dinh Kha replied, "Tell me what you plan to do. I no longer work in the government. You know that I cannot give you advice. What do you have in mind?"

Nguyen Huu Bai took a few sips of jasmine tea before he said, "This is the second time Mahé has gone after buried gold. The first time, he did some digging right in the Imperial Palace. It panned out. There actually was some gold buried in the palace. The gold had been buried when Emperor Ham Nghi fled into the mountains in 1885. When he heard about the excavation, our young Emperor was enraged. He blamed me for failing to prevent it from happening. Unfortunately, I am not the Commander of the Palace Guards. As I told the Emperor, I have no jurisdiction over the Imperial Palace. We all know who allowed it to happen. Mahé now wants to go after the big treasure buried with the body of Emperor Tu Duc. I know, I know. The Tomb is immense; he may have to dig for a hundred years before he finds the Emperor's coffin and the treasure buried with him. But this is a real sacrilege. I intend to write to Governor-General Albert Sarraut, and to the press."

Ngo Dinh Kha said, "I understand that Governor General Albert Sarraut is coming to Hue in a couple of days. That is good. On the other hand, you have to tell the Emperor about this today." Nguyen Huu Bai shook his head; "I don't want to tell him about this. He will explode and say something he shouldn't about Mahé."

The Regent looked thoroughly miserable, and his friend let a moment pass before he pressed on, "Sooner or later he will know. I think that the best thing to do is to tell him about this in private, so that his reactions will not be seen or heard by anybody except you."

The Regent again shook his head, "You don't have to live and work at the Court now, so you don't understand. The French have established a rule by which, two by two, the Ministers take turns standing at the Emperor's side. I have the good fortune of being paired off with Huynh Con, who reports everything to the French."

For a moment Ngo Dinh Kha's eyes were clouded, but he controlled his anger and said, "From what you say, I presume that we are living in the last days of another reign."

Nguyen Huu Bai pondered for a moment and replied, "We are witnessing the unfolding of yet another dynastic tragedy. But the Emperor is not facing any immediate danger. Not yet, unless he provokes Mahé unnecessarily. Sarraut still seems to see the Emperor as just a child, and will be tolerant. Eberhardt, the Imperial Tutor, writes hundreds of good reports on the Emperor. But we know that ultimately the only reports that really count are those written by the French Security Services. You and I know that those reports are not favorable; therefore, one day, without warning, those reports have said enough to convince the Resident Superior or the Governor-General to move in for the kill."

Ngo Dinh Kha proposed, "You should not be the only one who writes to the press, to Hanoi and Paris about this sacrilege. We will all write letters and articles. You should focus on the Emperor. Try to keep him calm."

Though he agreed with his friend, the Regent was not sure he could keep the young Emperor subdued.

After the Regent had gone, Ngo Dinh Kha turned to his daughter who sat in a corner of the parlor, and asked, "Do you feel as if we were reliving the days before Emperor Thanh Thai was forced to abdicate?"

The young girl shivered She came to the low table and served her father another cup of tea, then she said softly, "When I was a little girl, I thought the Emperor was all-mighty. I could not imagine who might have the power to bend him or destroy him. Now I realize that the Emperor is just a toy in the hands of the French. They can break him at any time. Yes, I feel as if we were reliving the days when Emperor Thanh Thai was about to be deposed. I feel afraid and ashamed."

The former Minister and Commander of the Palace Guards looked at his daughter for a long time. Somehow the young girl expressed his feelings exactly. He should not feel responsible for whatever was happening at the Imperial Court, now that he was merely a commoner. Yet, he too intensely felt fear and shame.

*

The scandal of the Imperial Tomb hit the French Governor-General in full force on the first day of his short visit to Hue. Albert Sarraut spread the newspapers in front of him. All of them, whether they were published in Hanoi, Saigon or Hue, were running headlines about the sacrilege committed against Emperor Tu Duc. Other headlines directly pointed to the monstrous greed of somebody in the French Administration.

Even Sarraut himself was dragged into the scandal. Did he know about the excavation? If he knew, why didn't he prevent it? And if he didn't know about it, he must be a fool.

At the center of the storm was Nguen Huu Bai who stridently condemned the excavation as a vulgar expression of unbridled greed, a profanation, and a sacrilege. Other leading Catholics joined the chorus. Sarraut thought irritably, "Damn Bai! Damn the Catholics!"

Even before he had arrived in Hue, he had already heard the folk song, which had been picked up by the population *"Kha said no to the exile of the Emperor, Bai says no to the excavation of the Tomb."* The people were marrying their names, even before their children were married at the altar, Sarraut thought bitterly. Yes, even Paris was concerned about the joining of the two families, Paris that he missed so terribly. "Damn Kha! Damn Bai!" Sarraut cursed silently.

He had several stormy meetings with Mahé, who pretended that he had done all the excavating for France, and who demanded that he be allowed to fire Regent Nguyen Huu Bai. He had a confrontation with the young Emperor who became ever more incoherent as his anger mounted. Another tumultuous meeting took place with the Regents, for whom finger pointing seemed to be the favorite sport. And now he had to meet with Minister Huynh Con, whom everybody on the Vietnamese side blamed for playing the main role in the excavation of the Tomb, and who had offered to resign.

Sarraut stared fixedly at the Vietnamese mandarin who seemed to shrink physically with fear. "Is this the quintessence of Vietnamese intellectuality?" he wondered. He had seen the likes of Huynh Con before. The man somehow had the weird notion that he was serving his country by spying for France. He talked about his duties. He was a name-dropper. But the names he dropped, those of low and middle-level French officials were not familiar to Sarraut's ears.

Sarraut was stunned by the fact that a Vietnamese Minister was quoting a French assistant-chief of service for his defense. He became more attentive; however, when the man said he had consulted with Prime Minister Truong Nhu Cuong, President of the Council of Regents before the excavation had begun at Tu Duc Tomb.

"Truong Nhu Cuong who goes along with anything a Resident Superior wants! Truong Nhu Cuong who had turned in full fury against Emperor Thanh Thai! They are all alike," Sarraut said to himself. He considered, "My aides have insisted that I visit this man and encourage him to stay on as Minister, as a loyal friend of France. I have come, and I am disgusted."

He said, "Excellency, your services to the colonial government are priceless. You are an essential element in the Council of Regents. Please do not resign."

Having received the fawning gratitude of the mandarin, he was about to leave when he turned and asked brusquely, "What do you think of His Excellency Nguyen Huu Bai?" The mandarin replied quickly, "He is most loyal to the Emperor."

"Do I smell poison here? What does he mean by "loyal to the Emperor"? Does he mean disloyal to France?" Sarraut wondered. He asked, "And what do you think of the Emperor himself?" The mandarin thanked him for asking, but he narrowed his eyes and only offered his advice, "About the Emperor, Your Excellency may want to have a long talk with His Excellency Nguyen Huu Bai. He knows the Emperor better than any of us in the Council of Regents."

Regent Nguyen Huu Bai

*

Sarraut wondered what the French establishment would say if he paid a visit to Ngo Dinh Kha. He toyed with the idea for a minute, and then shrugged, "Nay, I am going to see Nguyen Huu Bai, his *alter ego*. Isn't it enough for one day?" Regent Nguyen Huu Bai's home faced the An Cuu River, on the opposite bank from where Ngo Dinh Kha lived. He wondered whether his meeting with Nguyen Huu Bai at the Regent's home was a good idea.

Nguyen Huu Bai was not obsequious. His French was perfectly fluent. After a few moments spent in civilities, Sarraut abruptly asked, "I have heard, Your Excellency, that the Emperor wants a revision of the peace treaties signed with France. Is that true?"

Nguyen Huu Bai looked a little annoyed. He was silent for a long moment, and the French official was about to rephrase his question when the Regent shrugged and replied, "Your security services are usually reliable. You don't need me to confirm the information you have received. There are others who can offer you that kind of service. The Emperor is young, and needs to learn about everything before he dissolves this Council of Regents. Is learning about history a crime? Isn't he supposed to know all about the terms of the treaties signed with France, so that he is aware of the limits of his power?"

Sarraut was pleasantly surprised. *"So, there are still Vietnamese with whom I can talk equal to equal."* He felt a little relieved, but he was not going to make it easy for his interlocutor, "Excellency, you and I both know that the Emperor claims that we, the French, have not fulfilled our end of the bargain and that we have not honored certain terms of the treaties. According to our information, he is not simply learning about the treaties, he wants to discuss the implementation of the treaties. Is our information correct?"

The Regent responded candidly, "If he intends to discuss certain terms of the treaties with the colonial administration, he has the right to do so. Discussing the implementation of a treaty is within the prerogatives of the signatories. In view of his young age however, the matter may better be postponed until he reaches maturity."

The French official smiled, "That would mean that we would have to wait another five years. Will the Emperor have the patience to wait that long? You, Excellency, are patient. You can wait. But the Emperor is not patient, and may I add, *neither are we.*"

Nguyen Huu Bai smarted under the implied threat, but he pretended not to be aware of it. Sarraut said, "You and your Catholic allies have done a great deal of writing recently, I've heard." The regent shrugged, "Catholics, Buddhists, Confucians... does it matter if those who wrote the letters and articles worship God, the Buddha, or honor the Sage of Sages? What matters is whether they are right in denouncing the profanation of the sacred ground of an Imperial Tomb, a sacrilege which saddens all of us."

Sarraut smiled, "Then, there is only one more thing left for me to say: my sincere congratulations and best wishes for the wedding of your daughter and the son of the former Minister and Commander of the Palace Guards."

Nguyen Huu Bai thanked him and accompanied him to the gate. There, Sarraut turned and asked, "Do you wish to see the last of Mr. Mahé?" Earnestly, Nguyen Huu Bai replied, "Mr. Mahé has a savoir-faire which is quite astounding. I would like him to remain in Hue with us for long years to come."

Sarraut laughed, "You want him to go, but you know that if you asked me to fire him, I would do exactly the opposite. So you say you want him to stay. Yes, I have at least learned that language." It was now Nguyen Huu Bai's turn to laugh. Sarraut, seated in his car, felt elated. *"Now, it is clear,"* he said to himself, *"Mahé has to go."*

And so, after the chargé d'affaires Henri Sestier came the Acting Resident Superior Georges Mahé. After Mahé, came the chargé d'affaires Joseph Labbé, and only after Labbé, came a true Resident Superior, Jean Charles. Four men were at the helm of the French administration in Central Vietnam within a period of only one year.

Older Vietnamese in those days remembered that thirty years earlier there had been a time when Vietnam had successively, three Emperors within four months. Some said that if the period of Four- Months Three-Emperors were disastrous for Vietnam, then the successive change of men in charge of the French administration would also spell disaster for France.

As Europe was engulfed in World War I, many Vietnamese, Emperor Duy Tan included, thought that the moment for national liberation was at hand. As the French were forced to levy heavier and heavier taxes on the population, and as they were forced to recruit young Vietnamese to go and fight ten thousand miles away from their own country, popular discontent grew. The Emperor thought that he could tap into the people's anger to launch an armed rebellion.

He forgot that he was a young boy of fourteen, that he was surrounded by dangerous spies, and that the monarchy had been cut off from the people for many decades.

The French did not take him seriously. They knew he hated them, but they also knew that he was helpless. They believed that the Emperor whom they had put in a golden cage could be silenced, sent away, or even eliminated at any time.

Surrounded by the Council of Regents, kept tied and bound in the Imperial Palace, the rebel monarch represented only a danger to himself and the people loyal to him. With exceptional skill, the French Security Services made him into a decoy to lure patriots and revolutionaries into the open.

It was in that political landscape that every Sunday after Mass, the two friends, Regent Nguyen Huu Bai and former Grand Chamberlain Ngo Dinh Kha, met to discuss strategies, to map out plans of action, to figure out the worst-case scenarios, and to express their hope for the future.

They were used to seeing the young girl who served them tea and who sat down in a corner to listen attentively to what was said. Having held her on their knee when she was a small child, they were familiar with her constant presence near them. The young girl was their silent companion. They did not know how much their discussions hastened her maturity. They never suspected that their debates had given her the rare ability to understand things half-said, foresee conclusions before others, and intuitively arrive at judgments about people and events.

She did not realize it at the time either. She only knew that it gave her tremendous pleasure to listen to her father and his friend. She knew that what she was learning from them was far more interesting than what she learned from Sister Marie, who taught her French.

In their shadow she grew up, happy and ready. She had come to believe that nothing would change in her little world. But the world, including her country, was already caught in a maelstrom of change. Soon enough, very little of her childhood universe would remain intact.

CHAPTER FIVE
THE YEAR OF THE DRAGON

In 1916, Hiep was fourteen. It was another Year of the Dragon. Like the year, decades earlier, when the legendary typhoon had struck the Imperial City, this Year of the Dragon also left the country devastated, not from a natural disaster but from a series of miscalculations made by Emperor Duy Tan.

The Emperor was sixteen and he was becoming extremely impatient with the Regency. He wanted to be treated like an adult, not a child. He resented being advised by dignitaries whom he did not respect.

Nguyen Huu Bai was becoming more frustrated with the Emperor. He told the former Grand Chamberlain about the time he had recently spent with the young monarch on the beach of Cua Tung, a hundred kilometers north of Hue. He was not there alone with the Emperor. No, his nemesis, Huynh Con, the Minister of Rites, was with them as well.

One day, the Emperor had started running and challenged them to catch up with him. Nguyen Huu Bai who was vigorous and knew the beach well - with Kha, he had studied at the An Ninh Minor Seminary, a mere two miles from there -, had no problem keeping up with the young man. Huynh Con, on the other hand, almost had a heart attack. In the eyes of the Minister of Rites, Bai saw fear. Sure enough, Huynh Con suspected that the Emperor and Bai had run far ahead of him in order to have a private talk.

The Emperor chided his Minister of Rites, "If you are in such poor physical condition, how will you be able to endure hardships with me when the time comes?" '*The time*' plainly meant the time of rebellion.

Bai knew that his colleague would certainly report this conservation to the French. He said, "Physical condition should be required from military officers. We are only a couple of old civilians." With a long look at the Emperor he added: *"We are not fit for any military action."*

The Emperor understood him well; he became moody, and after that day the walks on the beach were unpleasant exercises where each of them pursued their own separate thoughts in silence.

Nguyen Huu Bai also told his friend about another incident that had taken place at the Imperial Palace. On that day, the Emperor had screamed at the mandarins attending him, "Every one of you treats me like a child! I want you to obey me! I want you to help me restore national independence!"

These were reckless words, indeed. Did the young Emperor, out of desperation, wanted to commit suicide? Bai had entered the room just as the Emperor had finished speaking. He squarely faced the Emperor and retorted, "All right, Sire, you want us to fight the French? Great idea! Then show us, Sire, where is your treasury? Where are your troops?"

The Emperor was pale with rage and humiliation; he shouted at Nguyen Huu Bai, "You are like all the others. Don't you see that France is in trouble in Europe? Don't you see that they have withdrawn their best units from our territory? Don't you see that our people are waiting for a sign from their sovereign to march against the French?"

Nguyen Huu Bai trembled with fear for his Emperor. He spoke softly, "I know Your Majesty must be joking. I know it because Your Majesty, like *most of us* here, are loyal friends of France." The Emperor shuddered. Suddenly he realized who had been listening to his imprudent words. He stood up abruptly and left the room.

*

Right before the new Lunar New Year, the Capital City and the Imperial Palace were brightly decorated with flowers and bright lights, to celebrate the marriage of the Emperor to the Imperial Consort Mai Thi Vang, daughter of his Tutor (in Chinese Studies). French officials and Vietnamese mandarins were elated. Now the Emperor will settle down, they thought.

There was a false note during the wedding: a three-meter long roll of firecrackers was ignited at the moment the Imperial Bride was leaving her home, but after a few bursts, the fuse stopped burning and the firecrackers went silent. Those present at the wedding considered that to be a very bad omen.

The marriage of the Emperor had a strange side effect. Until then, every mistake the Emperor made was blamed on his young age, and more and more often on the unfulfilled sex drive of an adolescent. His Tutor Eberhardt, a Frenchman of German origin, kept saying that one should not hold the Emperor responsible for his transgressions. He conceded that the Emperor occasionally acted and talked wildly, but he declared that such behavior was merely caused by his *âge bête*, and that there was nothing wrong with him that marriage could not cure. Now, unfortunately, the Emperor was married and there was no longer room for such easy excuses.

*

Nguyen Huu Bai and Ngo Dinh Kha knew that the impulsive young man could no longer be restrained. They knew that the French had started looking openly for alternatives. One day, in the company of Minister Huynh Con, French officials made a round of visits and spoke with all of the Emperor's brothers. At the end of the visits, they ominously informed the Minister that none of the princes seemed like a good alternative. *"They all look very much like the Emperor,"* they said disdainfully.

In the meantime, revolutionaries of all kinds were attempting to plan an armed uprising. The plots centered on the person of the young monarch. None of the conspirators was a good organizer. Few of them could see the difference between dreams and reality.

A small group of military men were involved; the highest ranking among those was a sergeant. There were claims that three thousand new Vietnamese recruits waiting to be shipped to France, and a number of French officers of German origin, were ready to rise up, but those claims were unverifiable.

The fact that German troops had crossed the Aisne and were surrounding Paris had generated all kinds of rumors. It was generally suspected that the Imperial Tutor, Eberhardt, who was of German origin, was involved in the uprising and encouraged French soldiers of German origin like him, to turn against the French Administration. Whether Eberhardt was involved, or how effective he was could never be determined.

The rumor that German troops would land in Da Nang to lend a hand to the uprising was false. Also untrue was the rumor having it that the German Government was giving moral and financial support to the undertaking.

The uprising of May 3, 1916, never really took place. It ended before it began. The Emperor did leave the Palace as planned, but everything else went wrong. An hour after he had left the Palace, the Emperor knew that the uprising had failed.

The next day the French were told where he had taken refuge. They soon came to take him back to the Capital. He was then confined in the Mang Ca Fortress. Curiously enough, the French were quite gracious with him. They tried to persuade him to stay on as Emperor. Perhaps they thought that the Emperor had learned a good lesson and would be ready now to serve as a pawn in their hands.

The young monarch, however, refused to bend. He demanded, as conditions to his return to the throne, that the Council of Regents be dissolved immediately, and that the implementation of peace treaties with France be reviewed.

The Council of Regents, in furious response, called for the Emperor to be removed, and demoted to his previous rank of prince. As for Eberhardt, the French sent him back to France.

*

Once again, there were rumors circulating in the Capital that the French were about to put an end to the monarchy. Nguyen Huu Bai and Ngo Dinh Kha met for hours at the former Grand Chamberlain's home in Phu Cam. They decided to begin a vigorous letter-writing campaign.

They wrote to every French politician they knew. At the same time, under various pseudonyms, their articles appeared in the local and the Parisian press. Their French friends were mobilized: Yes, they admitted, the experience with Thanh Thai and his son had not been very satisfactory.

But there were many stems in the Imperial Clan and a good choice outside of Emperor Thanh Thai's offspring might be made.

At a meeting of the Board of Regents, presided by the French Resident Superior, Regent Ton That Han, who was almost in tears, pleaded with the French, "How can we live even one day without an Emperor?"

Other Regents argued that while World War I was still raging, and while France still faced so many difficulties in Europe, it was absurd for the French to take the unpopular measure of ending the monarchy.

Once more, the French conceded that it might not be the best time to destroy the monarchy in Vietnam, and told the Vietnamese to choose a successor to Emperor Duy Tan.

*

It was the first time Hiep had seen her father this angry with Nguyen Huu Bai. Glaring across the tea table, her father barely controlled his temper.

He punctuated his words as if he were talking to somebody that was hard of hearing, or to a half-witted boy, "So you have proposed the son of Emperor Dong Khanh as our new Emperor, and nobody opposed your proposal? Of course, nobody wants a new Emperor who will stand up to the French. So you have proposed a compulsive gambler for the job, a man with no dignity!"

Minister Bai put a finger to his lips, "Yes, I know he is a gambler." Ngo Dinh Kha grumbled, "But maybe you don't know what kind of a gambler he is. Haven't you heard that he gambled away three out of his five guards?"

Nguyen Huu Bai nodded, "Yes, I did hear something like that." Ngo Dinh Kha shook his head, "He's an inveterate, compulsive gambler who doesn't care if he is indebted to just anyone in the Capital! Do you know that he has even borrowed money from fishmongers in the market and hawkers in the street?" Minister Bai laughed: "Maybe under the guise of a gambler, you will find a patriot." Ngo Dinh Kha growled, "Don't say that! His father was a weakling, and he will be a weakling. Don't you remember how his father, Emperor Dong Khanh was?"

Bai reminded his friend, "Yet you served Dong Khanh." Ngo Dinh Kha nodded, "Yes I did serve under him for four months. I resigned quickly, however." The Minister smiled, "Only because your mother was ailing and you wanted to go home and take care of her."

Kha lowered his head reminiscing then he argued: "I never returned to serve Dong Khanh, even after my mother died." Bai agreed, "Yes, you never went back. You did not want to brush elbows with the *Prince Protector* De Courcy and the *Duke Protector* De Champeaux. Emperor Dong Khanh did give grand titles to the Governor-General and the Resident Superior, didn't he?"

The former Grand Chamberlain was not easily placated with the old memories; he said, "It was a long time ago. We both were very young. Yet, we saw that the Emperor was totally submissive to the French. He scandalized us. Now, you are a respected Regent, a senior minister, and you chose his son as our next Emperor?"

Minister Bai said, "Please listen to me. Do you know that the Emperor-Elect helped Prince Cuong De in his escape to Japan? Since then he has spent substantive amounts of money every year to assist the Rebel Prince's family. Did you know that? Did you know that many times, he visited Kang You Wei and Liang Kai Chao, when the two Chinese reformers were banished from China and took refuge in Hue?"

Kha was stunned. He said, "No, all of that is new to me. But if you know, then the French also know. Why then didn't they oppose your proposal?" Nguyen Huu Bai shook his head, "Perhaps because they think that the new Emperor can be bent. Maybe they hope that I am making a mistake." Ngo Dinh Kha sighed, "How many mistakes can we afford to make? I hope that you know what you are doing."

*

Though the French did not oppose Minister Bai's choice, the Office of the Imperial Clan was enraged. At first, the reasons for the displeasure of the Imperial Clan were not disclosed.

Then their rationale became known: the members of the Family Clan claimed that the Emperor-Elect, whose reign name would be Khai Dinh, was impotent and would be childless. According to them, this was not a wise choice, as there would be another succession crisis when he died. Their claim obviously was belied by the fact that he *did* have a son. Everybody including the French was drawn into endless arguments about the legitimacy of the birth of Khai Dinh's son.

Before he even began his reign, the new Emperor already seemed inadequate. Ngo Dinh Kha was again angry with his friend. He said, "You know that the French are trying hard to do away with the monarchy. Now, look at what you have done! You invite them to denounce the Emperor's son's illegitimacy and abolish the monarchy as soon as Khai Dinh dies."

Bai answered remorsefully, "My God, I did not foresee this scandal. How would I know that they would declare Khai Dinh impotent? How could I know that they would call his son illegitimate? It is too late to change now. But let me promise you my friend, I will fight to preserve the monarchy the day Khai Dinh dies. May he live a very long life!"

*

Immediately after the Coronation of Emperor Khai Dinh, Emperor Thanh Thai and his son, Emperor Duy Tan, were sent into exile on the French island colony of La Reunion. Ngo Dinh Kha despaired. He knew that he would never see his sovereign again in his lifetime.

Emperor Khai Dinh

For weeks on end he moped around, and Hiep tried hard to shake his depression by asking all kinds of questions about the former Emperor. Though she was not totally successful in drawing him out of his depression, she learned countless little details about the Emperor from him.

Later on, the information she acquired during those weeks helped her understand her elder brothers, who consciously or unconsciously imitated the Emperor in their taste, their sports, and their likes and dislikes. For example, their fondness of white horses, their predilection for 'Dragon-eyed' goldfish, their passion for hunting, especially big game hunting, their quotations from Chinese classics were Emperor Thanh Thai's passions, too.

She knew that loyalty towards Emperor Thanh Thai would never end in her family. Long after her father's death, her brothers would continue to keep alive in their heart the memories of their 'Martyred Emperor.'

CHAPTER SIX
PHOENIX RISING

During 1914, something happened to the former Grand Chamberlain. Ngo Dinh Diem, his third son, began to dominate his thoughts. Somehow, gradually, the studious, headstrong and irascible young boy came to represent in his father's eyes, the great hope for his country. The boy was only thirteen; yet, his father treated him like an adult. On him, he started pouring the treasure of his experience, knowledge and wisdom.

Hiep was surprised by Ngo Dinh Khoi's reaction. Her eldest brother, once he saw the solicitude shown by his father to Diem, immediately adopted the same attitude towards his younger brother. He did not show any sign of jealousy. He accepted his father's judgment. With his father, he believed that one day Diem would become the leader of their country. Hiep was amazed, because Khoi was not in any way less intelligent, less hard working, or less sensitive than Diem.

Moreover, Khoi was already a mandarin, with strong support from his father-in-law, who was one of the most powerful men at the Imperial Court. Without a second thought, he decided to build up his young brother, rather than work selfishly for his own promotion.

Regent Nguyen Huu Bai, after some hesitation, decided to go along with his friend's preference. He did not hesitate to put Diem, who was his godson, before Khoi, his son-in-law.

Why they made that choice, Hiep had no way to determine, at the beginning. But once Diem had become the 'chosen' she carefully observed his manners and his character. In time, she discovered that their decision had not been arbitrary at all.

One day, the former Grand Chamberlain asked Diem to write an essay about himself. Diem, taken by surprise, stood there looking at his father, trying to figure out what his father expected from him. Seeing his hesitation, his father said, "All right, I will narrow down the subject and make it easier for you. Take this subject: 'I am Ngo Dinh Diem. I am an irascible boy. What is wrong with me?' Now, will you write the essay first in Vietnamese, then translate it into Chinese, and finally into French?"

Diem smiled and complied. He did not argue that he was not irascible. He sat down and wrote a thoughtful essay on one of his major shortcomings. With care, he translated his essay into Chinese and French, then gave all the copies to his father, saying, "I will remember this lesson."

Diem was extremely headstrong, and apparently nothing could make him change. In 1915, when Diem was fourteen and about to finish his studies at Pellerin Institute, his father decided to take drastic measures to eliminate that unfortunate trait from his son's character. One evening after supper, he asked Diem, "Are you satisfied with the way the Brothers are teaching you at Pellerin Institute?" Diem replied, "They are good teachers. Yes, I am satisfied."

His father then informed him, "I have made arrangements with the Brother Superior to keep you after hours at the school." Diem protested this time, "But, Father, the school does not offer room and board. It is not a boarding school." His father replied, "I know, but it has a novitiate. You can stay with the novices there, after school." Diem mused, and after a moment, firmly rejected the idea, "I don't want to become a brother. Why should I stay in a novitiate?"

Now, the whole family was watching them. Ngo Dinh Kha said, "You are obstinate and headstrong. You have to learn how to be humble and obedient. You will stay in the novitiate for as long as necessary. I do not intend to make a friar of you, but I want you to learn from the novices how to behave humbly and obediently. When you have learnt how to behave yourself, send me word, and I will come to take you home."

Diem, trying to control his anger, did not say anything in response. Ngo Dinh Kha explained, "Remember, you will be the judge. You will know when you have learned enough. So, I will wait for you to decide when you have your obstinacy and your hardheadedness under control."

Diem was so angry that his whole body shook. But when he talked, he used mild words, "Father, I believe that I am the victim of an injustice here. I know I have to obey you, but I do protest against this injustice. To leave no doubt over that point, I am not going to bed tonight. I will stand on this spot from now to sunrise. If by then, you do not change your mind, I will be ready to go to the novitiate."

Ngo Dinh Kha did not demand that his son go to bed. He knew his son better than that. So Diem stood in the same spot all night long, and only when the sun rose did he go to his room and throw a few clothes into a small suitcase. Descending the stairs, he told his father that he was ready to go.

Six months later, Diem showed up at the door, one evening He said he had not had any supper and asked his mother whether there was any leftovers. Then he turned and faced his father.

In silence, his father watched him. Diem finally said softly, "Father, I have improved." He did not say how much. His father, however, was so pleased that his son was back that instead of grilling him, he simply nodded and whispered, "Welcome home, prodigal son!"

It was during that short period when Diem was forced to live with novices that gave rise later on to the legend that Diem had wanted to become a religious in his youth.

*

As Diem was always far ahead in his classes, his father decided that something should be done to allow him to start his career earlier than his classmates. He declared his son to have been born in early 1897, while in fact Diem had been born four years later. On certain birth certificates it appeared that Diem was older than was his brother Ngo Dinh Thuc who was born in late 1897.

So in 1916, at the age of fifteen, but with papers stating that he was nineteen, Diem entered the Hau Bo Institute, an elite school in Hue that specialized in training future mandarins. All the trainees were considered as Imperial interns and after three years there were appointed as mandarins.

When he was eighteen, Diem had already begun his career as a young mandarin. At nineteen, he was made Chief of District. At twenty-four, he was Head of a Prefecture and at twenty-six; he was appointed Chief of Province. At the age of thirty-two, he was made Prime Minister.

Hiep understood gradually, why her father, her brother Khoi and Regent Nguyen Huu Bai had chosen Diem, since his early teens, to be a future leader, why they had placed all their hopes on the shoulders of a little boy of fourteen.

Yet, with her critical eyes, she saw all of Diem's shortcomings as well as his qualities. She saw that he was as thrifty as their father, as pious as their mother, as studious as Big Brother Khoi. But she also saw that he was still headstrong and irascible. There seemed to be no remedy for those major shortcomings of his.

Over time, Diem had become *the man* at home, as their father spent more and more time at church and Khoi was a full time mandarin. Disciplining the younger children was Diem's duty. He hated it when he was called upon to discipline his brother, Luyen, the youngest of the family.

Indeed, whenever he was at home, Diem was usually found upstairs with a book. He hated it when his mother interrupted his reading by calling out, "Diem, where are you? Go look at what your little brother has done in the parlor."

Mrs. Ngo Dinh Kha usually called out from her kitchen, only when little Luyen had broken an old vase or an antique mirror in the parlor, or done something equally naughty. Whenever his mother called out to him, Diem would rush downstairs like a whirlwind.

He would catch the little culprit and angrily gave him a spanking. But the little tot was never afraid of him and would laugh when his older brother spanked him. Diem, his anger gone, would stop his hand in mid-air, knowing that he would soon hear his mother say: "That is enough." He would gladly leave little Luyen and run back upstairs to his books.

One day, however, the child did something that Diem could not forgive so easily. Diem kept a dozen beautiful dragon-eyed goldfish in a large fish tank. Probably he did that because Emperor Thanh Thai, as a young man, had also kept a huge fish tank filled with the same variety of goldfish near his bedroom in the Imperial Palace. Diem was very fond of his goldfish.

On that day, little Luyen stealthily took out all the goldfish from the tank, put them in a bag and carried them to the orchard where he displayed them on the dirt, and pretended to be a fishmonger. Noticing the unusual silence downstairs, Diem wondered what the child was doing to be so quiet.

He went downstairs, found his fish tank empty and half guessing what had happened, he let out a bloodcurdling scream that made Mrs. Ngo Dinh Kha leave her kitchen quickly and run to the parlor to see what had happened.

She immediately saw the empty fish tank and Diem standing in front of it yanking at his own hair in despair. Guessing correctly who the culprit was, she ran to the orchard, grabbed the child and went like a flash to a neighbor's house. There she left the child for several days, waiting for Diem to calm down. Though Diem calmed down, and the child came home without incurring bodily harm, it took Diem several weeks to forgive him.

Hiep found the incident funny. Yet, it reinforced her opinion that Diem still had much to do in order to control his anger. Along with her father and her brother Khoi, she believed that Diem would have to overcome all his defects if he were to one day become the leader they all expected him to be.

*

One day in the fall of 1919, Ngo Dinh Kha was summoned to the Imperial Palace. For weeks he had felt that something was about to happen, as his friend, Nguyen Huu Bai, kept smiling in a certain way. When Nguyen Huu Bai finally told him what the surprise was, there ensued another big argument between the two old friends. Bai had to use all of his skills to persuade the former Grand Chamberlain to accept the honors that the Imperial Court had prepared for him.

After showing a great deal of reluctance, Ngo Dinh Kha went to the Imperial Palace. Walking through the Hien Nhon Gate, Kha remembered the time when he had been the Governor of the Palace, when every day he came and tried to serve an Emperor who had the courage to stand up to the French.

Emperor Khai Dinh received him ceremoniously at the Can Chanh Palace and told him that he had decided, upon recommendations from most of his Ministers, to restore to him his title of Great Scholar Assistant to the Throne with the permanent rank of Minister. The Emperor also told him that his decision was made retroactively so that the former Grand Chamberlain would receive the uncollected payments of his pension starting from the date of his departure from the Imperial Court in 1907. Suddenly, Ngo Dinh Kha had become a rich man.

Hiep was sixteen at the time. The next day, her father called all the children in and asked them to stand around a table on which he had spread all the money he had just collected from the Imperial Treasury, back payments of twelve years of pension. He said, "We are rich now. But rich or poor, I want you to always remember *one* thing. *Do everything according to your conscience*, then one day, in this life or the next, God will do justice to you." Years later, Hiep's brothers still remembered that scene and the lesson that they had learned from it.

CHAPTER SEVEN
THE LAST BLESSINGS

In the summer of 1924, Nguyen Van Dieu, young Nguyen Van Am's father, after long hesitation, went to see the former Grand Chamberlain at his home. He wanted to ask Hiep's hand in marriage for his son.

Nguyen van Dieu was a wealthy businessman. His prosperous construction company was steadily expanding, and Am worked for him as his principal assistant. Dieu belonged to a well-respected family in Phu Cam. His father, Nguyen van Vong, headed the parish council, after years of work as a lay missionary.

Most everybody in Hue knew the beautiful story of Vong's legendary childhood. Vong, over the years, had become the model of filial piety. From the time he was he was a boy of fourteen, Vong had to run twelve miles every morning, to bring food to his starving father. He did this for several years.

Emperor Tu Duc had signed an Imperial Edict in 1860, aimed at destroying Christianity in Vietnam, once and for all. The Emperor's Edict announced his most devilish policy called *phan sap,* or 'separate and integrate.' It was based on separating the Christian heads of family from their dependents. Christian men were sent to work on farms owned by non-Christians: it was recommended that they be fed poorly, and not be paid for their labor. Meanwhile, the Christian women and children were taken into non-Christian families to work as menial helpers and to live like non-Christians.

The objectives were clear. The men would be starved to death, while their families, deprived of the main breadwinners, would become destitute and sooner or later, would forsake their Christian faith.

Vong's father, Nguyen van Danh, was separated from his family, and forced to work without payment, in a village six miles away from where his wife and children were.

With the consent of his boss, a devout Buddhist and a compassionate man, Vong was allowed to take food to his father every day. Vong got up when it was still dark, to prepare a daily ration of food for his father, and then he started running, to bring the food to him. He had six miles to go, and then six miles back. Not wanting to take advantage of his boss' good will, Vong made a point of being back by sunrise to work in the paddy field. Vong continued to do this, day after day, until the Emperor revoked the edict.

Nguyen van Danh was finally reunited with his family. Vong no longer had to run twelve miles a day. He decided to move to Phu Cam, and married a young girl there.

In Phu Cam Parish he met Father Joseph Eugene Allys, known by the Vietnamese as Father Ly. He was so impressed with the priest that he volunteered to serve as a lay missionary. Father Ly had by that time, a new scheme for evangelization. He brought good Catholic families that he recruited in Phu Cam parish, to the areas of Cau Hai and Nuoc Ngot, forty miles South of Hue. A missionary family was provided a small house and a small plot of land. The evangelizers were not to preach. They were asked to lead a virtuous and exemplary life. They were to convert non-Christian around them merely by their example.

The concept was beautiful, yet its implementation was not quite that simple. Vong spent fifteen years of his life converting people to Christianity. When he was forty, Father Ly told him that he had sacrificed more than enough, and that it was time now for him to take better care of his family. Vong went back to Phu Cam and prospered as a farmer. He served in the parish council and soon became its chairman. In his old age, Vong enjoyed great respect and admiration from the Catholic communities in Hue.

Though Am, his grandson, was a promising young man and his family was among the wealthiest in the parish, his father, Nguyen van Dieu, hesitated a long time when Am pleaded with him to go and ask for Hiep's hand.

Dieu hesitated because he had heard that she was the apple of her father's eye. People said that Ngo Dinh Kha would surely try to keep her near him for as long as possible and that he would not let her go easily.

Dieu counted Ngo Dinh Kha among his friends. He had served as godfather for two of Kha's sons, Nhu and Luyen. Between friends, no go-betweens could be used. Dieu himself had to go and ask Hiep's hand for his son. This was another reason for Dieu's reluctance.

The former Grand Chamberlain himself came out and opened the gate for him. Dieu walked in, rehearsing for the last time what he planned to say. He could not use his prepared speech. Kha asked him simply what was on his mind. Reluctantly, he had to go right into the subject - contrary to all the rules - and ask the Grand Chamberlain to consider with indulgence his young son's humble merits and accord him Hiep's hand.

Ngo Dinh Kha was stunned. He had never thought that one-day he would be asked to give his *little* daughter away in marriage. Dieu, seeing Ngo Dinh Kha's expression of surprise, was ready to make a tactical retreat. He said that he had in fact hesitated for a long time. He said that maybe the Grand Chamberlain was not ready to be separated from his favorite daughter.

Recovering from his surprise, Ngo Dinh Kha exclaimed, "You should know that I am quite fond of young Am. You should also know that I have a very deep respect for you and your father. But, I cannot give away my daughter in marriage just like that. I will have to ask her first."

It was Dieu's turn to be stunned. Parents arranged marriages at that time. The young people, especially the daughters had little to say. Everybody knew how conservative the former Grand Chamberlain was. Dieu could not figure out what Ngo Dinh Kha was doing, by bringing up the strange necessity of consulting with his daughter. He said to himself, "He pretends he wants to ask for his daughter's opinion first. That clearly means he wants to find a nice way to refuse." Once more, Dieu was ready to accept defeat.

The former Grand Chamberlain totally confused Dieu when he said, "Wait for me here. I will go inside and talk to my daughter and my wife. Then I will come back to tell you how it goes."

Dieu resigned himself to a long wait. He thought, "All of this to save my face? Well, at least the Grand Chamberlain did not show me to the door immediately. He certainly will tell me that his daughter or his wife has some objection. Surely if he wanted the match, he would not invent all these useless excuses."

He did not have to wait for long. Hiep, upon hearing her father's direct question, blushed and answered shyly, "I will accept your decision, Father." Ngo Dinh Kha smiled and said, "It is a *yes* then. You cannot be clearer than that." He turned to his wife, and she inclined her head, smiling.

Ngo Dinh Kha was back in the parlor in no time. He said, "Please let me say this: Out of my deep respect for your father and yourself, I have no hesitation whatsoever in giving my daughter in marriage to your son. I will not pose any unusual demands for the engagement and the marriage. Please, let us organize these ceremonies nicely but simply."

It was as simple as that. The young people were so happy! The engagement ceremonies followed closely and the fiancés expected to be married in the spring of the following year.

Ngo Dinh Thi Hiep on the day of her engagement to Nguyen Van Am.
Standing next to her is her sister Ngo Dinh Thi Hoang

*

Ngo Dinh Kha's health, however, became a serious problem. During the winter of 1924, he began to seriously prepare himself for death. He had never failed to go to Mass or to read the Office of the Blessed Virgin every day. He had also written several books of devotion. Now, he spent long hours meditating and praying and he worked to settle every unresolved issue concerning the family. Little changed in his life style outwardly, however, and he continued to hold weekly meetings with his friend, Nguyen Huu Bai.

In January 1925, a few days before the celebrations of the Lunar New Year, Ngo Dinh Kha suddenly began to run a high fever and cough ceaselessly. Taken to the hospital, he was soon diagnosed as having severe pneumonia with complications. He had great difficulty breathing and was distraught at having to be in the hospital. The doctors told his family that his case was hopeless. He then asked the doctors to let him leave the hospital so he could die at home. The doctors had no objection. Ngo Dinh Kha was taken back to his home on the eve of the New Year.

*

There were no festive celebrations in the family that year. On the third day of the Lunar New Year, Ngo Dinh Kha's life was about to be extinguished.

Having received the Sacrament of the Sick, Ngo Dinh Kha called his family to his deathbed. With his wife standing at the head of the bed, the children came in and lined up by the bedside. Khoi, freshly promoted Deputy Governor of the Province of Binh Dinh came in with his wife. Giao, his oldest daughter, and her husband followed them. Diem, recently appointed Head of the Prefecture of Hai Lang, came in next. Hiep and her fiancé followed, and then came the younger children, Hoang, Nhu, Can and Luyen. Of all his nine children, only Thuc, who was studying in Rome, was absent.

Looking in silence at his children for a while, Ngo Dinh Kha raised his hand and said, "You should not cry. I am well prepared for death. I hope that by now God has forgiven all my sins. Death is just a part of life. It delivers the soul from the weaknesses of the body. You will join me one day in death, so there is no loss and no farewell here. I called you in to tell you that I am ready to give you my blessings. But, one of you must ask. Who will come forward to ask for my blessings?"

The children pushed Khoi forward. Khoi hesitated. Though he was the eldest son, he was not sure whether he or Diem should step forward. He knew that his father had chosen Diem to lead. But Diem shook his head and said, "You are the eldest brother."

Khoi, pale with emotion, stepped forward. But the old statesman put up a hand, "Not you Khoi. You are my eldest son. You will have heavy responsibilities. I am most proud of you but to ask for my blessings, choose someone else."

Khoi was relieved. He looked at Diem. Diem tried to avoid his eyes and would not step forward. Khoi took Diem by the hand and pulled him closer to the bedside. Their father's eyes were filled with amusement as he said, "Khoi, my son, you are not Esau and Diem is not Jacob. Why do you think he should represent my children instead of you?" Now all the children were surprised and a little alarmed.

They did not know whom their father wanted. Khoi humbly asked, "Father, tell us." Ngo Dinh Kha did not say anything for a moment, and then he pointed his finger at Hiep and said, "This one must ask for my blessings."

The children, quite relieved, said, "Father wants you, Hiep. Please step forward." Hiep sobbed uncontrollably. Pushed forward by everyone, she stammered, "Father, please bless us all." He slowly raised his hand, touched her chin and said, "Why do you cry? You who have more courage than any one of your brothers, why do you cry? I called you out, because my other children have made me proud, but you have given me joy."

Solemnly, he placed his hands on her head, "Now I call God's blessings, through you, upon all my children and my grandchildren. May He grant all of you the strength and the perseverance to accomplish His will, endure all hardships in His name, and fulfill your destiny."

He looked at his children one more time and nodded, "Every year, on the anniversary of my death, Hiep has the right to speak out and tell you what she thinks about your deeds and words of the past year. Please listen to her. Listen to her, who has listened so patiently to me all these years." All the children answered in a chorus, "We will listen to her, Father."

Kha's children came closer to his bed. Over each of them he slowly made the Sign of the Cross. When he had finished blessing them, he turned to Khoi and said, "Khoi, promise me that you will take good care of your Mother." Khoi nodded, "Father, I will take good care of Mother as long as I live." His father said, "That is good. You must also promise me that you will make arrangements to send little Luyen away to France for studies. He is the youngest, and I guess both your Mother and I have been spoiling him too much. In order for him to be stronger in character, he must be separated from your mother."

Khoi looked at his mother, and knew that she would suffer deeply from such a separation, but he also knew that he could not refuse to obey his dying father's wish. With a lump in his throat, Khoi managed to say, "As you wish, Father."

Ngo Dinh Kha smiled contentedly, "Now, I have a more pleasant task for you: Do not let my death delay your sister's marriage. I want her marriage to take place this year, according to the plans." Hiep protested, "But Father, I want to mourn your death appropriately. I want to wait another three years. Am and I are young, we can wait." Her father took her hand and asked, "Wait for what, girl? Be happy when you are still young." Khoi again promised, "It will be done as you wish."

The dying man surprised them then by saying; "I want your brother Thuc, who is in Rome now, to do something for me. I want him to go and give my respects to the Emperor in La Reunion. Tell him not to return to Vietnam until he makes that pilgrimage." Even on his deathbed, the Grand Chamberlain still thought about his sovereign. With tears in his eyes, Khoi said, "I will make sure that my brother Thuc visits the Emperor as you wish."

Ngo Dinh Kha turned to Diem, "You are born to be a leader, so lead. You and your brothers and sisters will all have to fight for national liberation. Unfortunately, liberating our country will not be an easy task. You have everything it takes to be a good leader, but you also have shortcomings that may destroy you and all of your undertakings. Do not let your anger overwhelm you. Do not be headstrong. Seek advice. Be patient. I have made many mistakes in my life. My generation has been so fearful of French power that the most I and many of my contemporaries could dream of for our country was *autonomy*. Autonomy could be the first step, but your goal must be for *total independence*, do you hear me?" He was completely exhausted. Diem replied, "I hear you, Father. With your blessings, I will try to accomplish what you are expecting of me."

The Grand Chamberlain made a great effort and said distinctly: "Nobody will restore Vietnam's independence easily. You will have to fight for it. If necessary, you will have to accept armed struggle as a means to liberate your country, do you hear me?" Diem was sobbing uncontrollably; he struggled and managed to answer, "I hear you, father."

The old man nodded. He bade Hiep to come closer. He whispered, "Pray for my soul. Pray for your brothers and sisters, morning and evening. Don't forget."

*

The former Grand Chamberlain died in peace, without fear and without regret, on January 27, 1925, or the third day of the Lunar New Year, in the Year of the Buffalo. His body was buried in the family vault in Phu Cam Cemetery. The vault was built exactly like the tombs used by Jews in Jesus' times. His coffin was placed in a small cavern dug into a rocky mound. A large stone was rolled over to block the entrance, which was then sealed with mortar.

Every year, whenever possible, his children returned to Hue to commemorate the anniversary of his death on the third day of the Lunar New Year, after presenting their wishes to their mother on the preceding days. At each annual ceremony, Hiep was asked to speak.

Usually known by her brothers as too conciliatory and too kind, every year, Hiep rose to the occasion and spoke on that day with a frankness and toughness that surprised them all. They listened to her remarks in silence.

In those moments, the children seemed to hear their father's voice again, and they bent their heads. Decades after he died, the presence of the Grand Chamberlain among them was almost physical. Their reverence for him never waned.

PART TWO

BEFORE THE CATACLYSM

CHAPTER EIGHT
A YOUNG WOMAN'S JOYS AND SORROWS

Nguyen Van Am and Ngo Dinh Thi Hiep on their wedding day flanking
Am's parents

*

Diem took a long walk between his sister and her husband, after they had prayed together for an hour in the La Vang Sanctuary. It was a Sunday afternoon in late November 1925, only a few days after Hiep and Am

117

were married. Diem was glad that they had chosen to spend a few days of their honeymoon with him in his own Prefecture.

The Sanctuary of La Vang, hidden behind lush and thick vegetation, was unusually quiet. Recent rains had made the air a little chilly, and that day, in the quiet afternoon, the leaves in the jungle around the sanctuary grounds, freshly washed by the rain, shone like sheets of dark green jade. The path they took was clearly marked, but new branches and fast growing creepers on both sides of the path had again begun to form arches above it here and there.

Diem and Hiep talked about their father's death. Ten months had passed since he had died, but their sense of loss had not subsided. In the first months after he was gone, their sorrow was so great that they could not even talk about him. Slowly though, they had ventured a remark, an allusion, until finally they reminisced more and more together about his physical presence, his voice, his mannerisms, his long conversations with them. In that quiet afternoon, as they walked, again they reminisced. Both were afraid that some of the lessons their father had wanted to teach them would be forgotten. As neither of them kept a diary, they felt the need to compare mental notes, to check out the detail of their memories. The walk was long and their reminiscences endless.

After a while, Hiep returned with determination to the present. She wanted to know how her brother had been organizing his life in his Prefecture. Hai Lang Prefecture extended over a hundred and eighty villages and included the Sanctuary of La Vang. Vietnamese Catholics firmly believed that the Blessed Lady had appeared to their fathers and grandfathers who had taken refuge there, during the worst periods of religious persecution by the Emperors.

Because Hai Lang was an important Prefecture, her brother was becoming the envy of his colleagues. Indeed, he was only twenty-four and traditionally Hai Lang Prefecture, because of its size, and its relative closeness to the Imperial City, had been the envied prize for older mandarins.

Hiep, at the moment, was not interested in either the size or the importance of the Prefecture, but wanted to know the practical details of Diem's life there. She asked with a note of concern in her voice, "Who cooks for you here?" Diem was a little embarrassed. He would blush whenever somebody inquired about his personal life.

He looked at his sister with an air of mild reproach and said, "I have an old soldier detailed to serve as my adjutant. He is very clean, honest and loyal. He is not much of a cook, but as you know, I am not a great connoisseur of fine food. As long as the old man knows how to cook rice porridge and salted fish for my breakfast, vegetable soup and vegetable dishes for lunch and dinner, I am satisfied. In fact, occasionally, he even manages to roast a chicken." Hiep laughed.

She remembered him sitting at table as a child. He used to say: "Oh, this is good, this is very good." Even in the dark days of 1907, when their daily diet was appallingly poor he never complained about the food that was served. Now, she was concerned. She said half-scolding, "You must eat well if you want to work hard. Apparently, you are not eating well." Diem waved his hand and dismissed the subject, "Maybe, but I have time to exercise a lot here. I can assure you that I am in the best physical condition. Actually, I ride for hours every day."

Yes, Hiep had heard that sometimes, for weeks on ends, he was on horseback from dawn to dark, riding up the mountains and down the valleys, visiting every village to acquaint himself with every topographic detail of the territory that was under his jurisdiction.

She asked, "What do you do when you arrive in a village, during your riding exercises?" Diem smiled, "I stop and ask people questions, all kinds of questions. I now know thirty varieties of rice, twenty varieties of corn, and just about all the names of the trees that grow in my prefecture."

Diem sounded happy and proud, no doubt about that. Hiep measured her words when she said, "I hear that the district chiefs in your prefecture are quite nervous. They think that you go to each village to find out whether they are taking bribes." Diem laughed heartily now, "Oh, I don't need to investigate. As I am everywhere, all over the prefecture, the district chiefs hold their breath, and I think none of them has the courage to take bribes at the moment."

They walked in silence for a while. Then she asked with a note of concern in her voice, "Are you *still* trying to convert people to Christianity?" Though sensing a little irony here, Diem did not become irritated. He shook his head and gave her a straight answer, "Maybe nothing is equal to saving a soul. But I am not supposed to do the job of missionaries who are in the business of saving souls. I am a mandarin who has been assigned a fairly large prefecture. I have to deal with everyone in my prefecture on the same footing, whether they are Christians, Buddhists or Confucians."

Hiep stopped walking and answered, "That is not what people say in Huong Thuy, where you were district chief just four years ago." At first, Diem was silent. He knew that she had been angling toward *that* incident which had taken place four years earlier. Showing no irritation, he raised his eyes, faced her squarely and admitted, "Once in Huong Thuy, I tried to convert a man who had been condemned to be beheaded." He took a few steps before he continued: "Yes. I admit that. I was fresh out of school, and I thought I could work miracles. Upon my arrival in Huong Thuy, I found in the district jail a man who had been condemned to death. I spent time with him, because nobody else wanted to talk to him. *He had killed his own father.*" Diem was lost in thought, as if he were reliving the episode. He went on after a while, "You certainly remember the case. It was reported widely in the newspapers at the time. A parricide! It is one of those crimes that have always been listed as one of the ten unforgivable crimes, according to our traditions. The perpetrator of such an inhuman atrocity must be a monster. The first time I met him in his cell, he already knew that soon he would be taken to An Hoa and would be beheaded publicly."

"To my great surprise," Diem continued, "I found a tormented young man who was not afraid to die. What tormented him, he said, was his crime. He did not understand how he could, even in a moment of frenzy, kill his own father. He wanted to understand why he had done it. In my mind, I can still see that poor young man walking in circles in his cell asking himself, and me, 'Why did I kill my own father? How could I?'"

Hiep was impressed. She remembered how her father constantly reminded Diem, "To care for the people, but not to care for a person, is absolute hypocrisy."

Diem continued, "I was not much help to him. All I could do was to visit him from time to time. In the end, I asked him whether he would like to see a Buddhist monk or a priest. He decided that he would like to see a Buddhist monk, and why not, a priest as well."

Seeing Hiep's smile, Diem said, "I went home that day gloomily, thinking that the young man was betting on both the Buddha and Christ. Two weeks later, he was baptized. A priest stood at his side when he was executed."

Hiep nodded. She avoided Diem's eyes, knowing that he was remembering a crucial moment of his life. Diem seemed to be overcome by his emotions. It was only a moment later that he said, his voice a little altered: "I was walking on clouds for weeks. *I thought I had saved a soul.* Soon enough, however, I realized that only Christ could save a soul, not I, not anyone. I was merely a little road sign to point the young man in a certain direction. I was depressed for many days. I realized that saving a soul was not humanly possible. I also realized that building a chapel, a church or even a large cathedral meant very little. God cannot be bought with gifts, even immense gifts. So, Sister, give me the credit of a little wisdom. I am a mandarin, not a missionary. I am not in the business of saving souls. *I am not going to try to convert anyone.*"

Again, they walked in silence for a while, then Am, Hiep's husband brought up a new subject, "You are already twenty-four. When will you finally decide to get married?" Diem blushed profusely. He answered with a self-deprecating smile, "Not everyone has the good luck of finding an ideal spouse. I am not as handsome as Brother Khoi, or Brother Nhu. None of the eligible women would take a second look at me. So, I am likely destined to a life of solitude."

His sister laughed and told him, "Do not underestimate yourself. In Huong Thuy, lots of young girls found you eligible. I heard that there was a landing in front of your district headquarters, and that many beautiful young ladies in the neighborhood came there every day to wash their feet, hoping that you would notice them."

Diem shrugged, "Little girls, teenagers who wanted simply to tease me. Why do you want to talk about them?" Hiep went on: "Let us not talk about those young damsels then. So many of my young friends in Hue came to our home, pretending to see Mother, or me, while in fact all they wanted was a chat with you. Why did you always run upstairs whenever some young girl turned up at our home?"

Diem hesitated, then, looking more and more pensive, he said, "Sister, I am trying not to be melodramatic, but let me say this: you know what

121

Father's dream was. It was nothing less than the independence of our country. You heard him say it when he was dying. How can I think of love and marriage when I have not done anything yet to begin to turn his dream into reality?"

Dark clouds were fast gathering overhead. Gusts of chilly winds made the young woman shiver. Diem, turning to his sister, said, "I guess tonight I will taste some good food, with you doing the cooking." He was really happy, for though he was not a connoisseur of good food, Diem did enjoy the cuisine of his mother and his sisters. Hiep was not thinking at all of dinner. She was genuinely concerned: she saw her brother all wrapped up in his dream of liberating the country, without a friend or companion, rejecting in advance all attempts to alleviate his solitude. "If only he falls in love!" She knew that he would never, never fall in love though. *She knew that such would be his destiny.*

*

At table, Diem showed how much he appreciated Hiep's culinary talents by eating enough for two. Hiep admired his appetite. It had been like that when he was at home. He never missed a meal, never left a dish untouched.

She remembered how hard her mother had worked, to teach her daughters the sophisticated cuisine of Hue. A farmer's daughter herself, her mother did not know at first, how to fix a twelve-course dinner. Yet she knew she had to learn. The high society in Hue was quite exacting in matters of cuisine. The Emperors gave the example to their mandarins. Even when they ate alone, the Imperial Kitchen served no fewer than thirty courses or entries at each meal. The Imperial *Yen* or Grand Dinners, when a large number of guests were invited, were elaborate affairs with up to sixty-.four entries served at each table.

The cuisine of Hue catered not only to the palate. The dishes had to address all of the human senses. Flavor had to be accompanied by aroma and fragrance. Sometimes the taste buds played second fiddle to the eyes, as the beauty of food arrangement, the artistic combination of colors and shapes, dominated a tray of food. Drawing from the menus of various emperors, three hundred complicated dishes were taught the young ladies in Hue, besides the common people's specialties. Those specialties, simple as they were, however, served as a standard to measure a young lady's culinary talent As many aristocrats in Hue ended up becoming Buddhist monks or nuns in their old age and adopting a vegetarian diet, one hundred and thirty vegetarian dishes, almost as complicated as the imperial dishes, were added to the culinary lessons given the ladies in Hue. The vegetarian dishes tended to imitate meat and fish. The skillfulness in the use of soybean paste skin for such imitations was pushed to the limit.

Not only Buddhists but also Christians enjoyed a vegetarian diet. Hiep and her sisters spent months perfecting their vegetarian cuisine, under the watchful eyes of their mother. Then, there were lessons on pastries. Salted and sweet pastries completed the register of the cuisine of Hue. They were as demanding as the dishes.

As a young girl, Hiep had learned everything she could learn from her mother. She admired the latter for her intuitive respect for harmony and balance when she was playing with spices and foodstuff, and her constant rejection of excess and waste even when she was working on the most elaborate menus.

She had watched her mother when she approached some lady visitor for a secret recipe. How tactful she was, and how grateful when the recipe was given! How hard she worked on the new dish until it tasted, smelled and looked just the way it should.

She looked at Diem and thought, "He will never enjoy real food. He will go on allowing his old soldiers and adjutants to serve him salted fish and pickled cabbage every day." She knew, however, that she could do nothing to ever change that. He was an ascetic young man, not by nature, but out of necessity. *That was his destiny.*

*

Prime Minister Nguyen Huu Bai sat at a low table, with Khoi, Diem and Hiep facing him. The table was small and square, the type of table which was called a 'Four-Immortal Table.' A large one would have been called an 'Eight-Immortal Table.' In the Imperial Tomb, where they were, pavilions were furnished with those marble and wood tables and chairs. Sitting around those tables, one had the impression of being Immortals enjoying an endless game of chess.

Bai had written to Hiep's brothers inviting them to come to Hue on official business. Only a year had passed since the Grand Chamberlain's death and all of his children were still wearing the white robes of mourning. They were sitting in the Xung Khiem Pavilion facing the Luu Khiem Lake at Emperor Tu Duc's Tomb.

The Prime Minister seemed to be lost in thought. At times, the young people thought he was about to improvise a seven-word and eight-line poem. They respected his silence and gazed around them. From where they were, sitting right at the side of the lake, they took in the beauty and fragrance of thousands of white and red lotus flowers and emerald-green lotus leaves. To their right, two little wooden bridges spanned the lake leading to the Khiem Cung Gate, and massive structures behind it. A little behind them, also on their right, was where the grave of the Emperor should be. But *no one knew* whether the coffin containing his remains and an invaluable treasure of gold and precious stones was actually buried there or at another spot in the tomb. No one knew including Resident Superior Mahé who twelve years earlier had tried to excavate the tomb in search of the treasures buried with the Emperor.

The one Regent who had opposed the sacrilegious excavation was sitting in front of them now, with his eyes half closed.

They enjoyed the perfect peace around them. The pine trees murmured, discreet waterfalls whispered, a single cicada started brushing its wings somewhere in the distance. They appreciated that the Prime Minister had invited them there that day, but they knew they were not on a sightseeing trip. The Prime Minister had something very important to tell them.

Finally, Nguyen Huu Bai began, "Eighteen years ago, when Emperor Thanh Thai was about to abdicate, and your late father was about to be dismissed, I offered Prime Minister Truong Nhu Cuong my resignation. Twelve years ago, when Mr. Mahé excavated this tomb, I opposed him and he wanted my head on a plate. Nine years ago, your late father and I had our first serious quarrel when I chose Emperor Khai Dinh to be the successor of Emperor Duy Tan. Now we have an absentee Emperor and I have to decide about almost everything."

He shook his head and asked, "You have certainly followed closely the trial of Phan Boi Chau, the Great Patriot, haven't you? "They nodded but did not say anything. They knew that without Nguyen Huu Bai's direct intervention, the Great Patriot might have lost his life. By saving the great man's life, however, Nguyen Huu Bai, once more, had put his career in jeopardy. Phan Boi Chau had opted for the Pretender, Prince Cuong De. To defend the Great Patriot, Nguyen Huu Bai had indicated his disenchantment with the ruling stem of the Nguyen Dynasty.

Hiep and her brothers remembered that at the time Emperor Thanh Thai was forced to abdicate, Nguyen Huu Bai had defiantly recommended to the French that they choose Prince Cuong De as Thanh Thai's successor. They wondered now, "Was it merely a tactical move or was he already in contact with Phan Boi Chau's revolutionary group at the time?" The three young people had never asked Nguyen Huu Bai questions about his secret contacts. They waited for the Prime Minister to explain himself.

Nguyen Huu Bai pursued his thoughts, "The Nguyen Dynasty has come to an irreversible decline. I was wrong in selecting Khai Dinh for Emperor, and your father was right when he quarreled with me about my choice. In 1916, I took my dream as reality. I thought, "Both Emperors Thanh Thai and Duy Tan were too obviously patriotic, and the French were too astute not to see the danger that they both represented for their colonial rule. Both of them ended in exile. I have to do better this time." I tried to find a prince who outwardly was a good-for-nothing, but who in his heart was a patriot. A few incidents, secretly reported to me, seemed to point to Khai Dinh as the right man. I gambled on him and I was wrong!"

He stopped a moment before continuing; "At least he did justice to your late father and gave back to him all his titles and ranks." He hesitated a moment before he said, "There is something I need to tell you now: your late father, who had opposed from the beginning the choice of Khai Dinh as Emperor, was not at all happy about receiving a favor from him. I had to talk him into accepting. I had to convince him that getting back his titles and rank was a matter of justice. I also had to remind him that by giving back his titles and rank, the Imperial Court was in effect acting against the will of the French, who wanted him to be buried and forgotten. But what persuaded him to accept the restitution of his rank was *your* future. I told him that by recovering his status, his name would help to advance your careers more rapidly. After I had said that, he no longer objected."

Kha's children bent their heads, reminiscing. Nguyen Huu Bai continued, "I was wrong when I helped to put Emperor Khai Dinh on the throne. He was completely dependent on the French and was consequently treated with contempt by them. He tried so hard to please the French that he left the education of his son, the Crown Prince, to Mr. Charles, the former Resident Superior: You all knew Mr. Charles when he was in Hue, a decent man, but uniquely focused on the interests of his country. It was in the hands of such a man that Khai Dinh left his son. Then he died when his son was only thirteen. His son now believes he must finish his studies in France." The three young people did not say anything. They, like everybody else, had been concerned with Emperor Bao Dai's continued stay in France. Hearing the Prime Minister mention it, however, made them more concerned.

Nguyen Huu Bai looked at the lake. A swarm of black and green dragonflies were dancing in the air then dipping, one after another, onto the surface of the lake where the water was free of lotus leaves, while red-orange damselflies flew aimlessly in the sunlight.

Hiep watched Bai a moment, then turned and looked at Diem. He was following with his eyes, some large butterflies with shining blue wings dotted with light yellow and reddish circles, - between the two of them, they used to call them *'Peacock Butterflies'*. The butterflies fluttered from flower to flower on the grassy banks of the lake. Hiep knew how fond Diem was of butterflies. They reminded him of the transient nature of life and the fragility of beauty, he had told her.

The Prime Minister resumed his monologue, "Your father died on the third day of the Lunar New Year, that is I remember, on February 27 last year. Emperor Khai Dinh died less than nine months later. I was still grieving over your father's death, and Khai Dinh's body still lay in state when the Council of Ministers was asked to endorse new demands from the French."

The Prime Minister smiled wryly. "Prime Minister Ton that Han and I opposed their scheme as much as we possibly could. But, the French said they would not let us bury the Emperor unless we agreed to the new demands, which would take away practically all the power of the Imperial Court."

Bai smiled bitterly and added: "I, for one, declared, 'Let the dead bury the dead. I don't care.' But the French were using their trump card. They announced that they could prove that the late Emperor was impotent and that the Crown prince was illegitimate. They threatened to divulge the secret and decree that the Nguyen Dynasty had ended with Emperor Khai Dinh."

The three young people did not react. They had heard the rumors before. The Prime Minister went on, "Whether they were telling the truth or not was not important. But the French could have fatally damaged the survival of the Dynasty if they revealed the so-called secret. So we had to sign on to the new Convention on November 6, 1925. Prime Minister Ton That Han and I succeeded in changing a few words here and there, but not the main purpose of the Convention. "

There was more than sadness in the Prime Minister's face. He looked at the young people in front of him for a long time, but they did not offer any comment. So he said, "With the Emperor still in France, and we do not know for how much longer, I think that it is time we revise our strategy."

Diem said, "Before he died, my father said he had been wrong to strive for the *autonomy* of the country, as the main goal. He said we should be striving instead for *total independence*. He said that we would have to accept the option of armed conflict in order to liberate the country."

The Prime Minister nodded, "Yes, we had come to that conclusion while Emperor Duy Tan was chasing his wild dream of getting the people behind him to drive the French out of our country. Duy Tan was right on two points: one, what we should fight for is *total independence*, not *autonomy*, and two, the people, the whole people must be mobilized to fight the French. He was wrong, however, on one major point: *This monarchy* can no longer mobilize the people. To use the old expression, we may say that this dynasty has lost *Heaven's Mandate*."

Khoi asked, "Where do we start?" The Prime Minister looked at him and Diem, then waving his hand, he said: "First we have to abandon all our erroneous concepts. Your late father and I were wrong in two main points. We limited our goal to autonomy; and, and we believed that negotiations with the French would help us to achieve our goal. We spent long years trying to convince the Emperors to wait for the right time to negotiate with the French, in order to regain more power for our court and our people. That should no longer be our strategy."

His eyes shining with determination, the Prime Minister declared, "Now you will have to use revolutionary means to reach our goal of total independence. You will have to face armed struggle against the French. The people will have to be mobilized, so you will have to organize a revolutionary party of your own, an underground party of course. This party will need to take roots in all classes of the people. You also will need to coordinate your action with other revolutionary groups and parties."

Khoi inquired, "Why have you changed so drastically?" Nguyen Huu Bai shook his head, "It is not only I who have changed. Your father had come to the same conclusion before he died."

Diem asked, "What about the timing? Is now the right time to take action in that direction?" The Prime Minister replied, "The time is now! You saw the popular movements last year when the Great Patriot, Phan Boi Chau, was put on trial by the French. In the last few months, you have witnessed the popular movements honoring the Patriot Phan Chu Trinh's death. Spontaneous mass movements like those indicate that the people are no longer afraid of the French. The people are ready." He sighed and the words he uttered were almost inaudible, "Unfortunately *you* are not ready yet."

Bai kept a long silence and allowed the young men to absorb his cruel words in their regards, and then he said, "Even in your careers as mandarins, you are not prominent enough for the people to recognize your names. I must move more rapidly. During this very year, Khoi, I will make you Province Chief of Quang Ngai. Next year, Diem, you will be the Province Chief of Ninh Thuan."

Both Khoi and Diem protested, "Sir, you should not do that. We are too close to you. If you promote us that way, people may rightly criticize you for favoring your son-in-law and your godson." The Prime Minister grimly acknowledged that such would be the case. He was, however, adamant in his decision. He said, "Look around you. Who among the mandarins you know have the talent, the decency, the dedication and the integrity you two have. I will answer only to my conscience; I will not listen to words of envy."

Diem objected, "Sir, you have to protect your reputation." Bai smiled bitterly, "What reputation? Tell me, Diem. Tell me truthfully, what have you heard people say about me?" Diem hesitated. Finally, he replied, "There are people who say good things about you, and others who criticize you. But, few people understand you."

Bai nodded, "There are people who say I am too close to the French and that I would sell out the interests of my country. They say I am a loyal collaborator of the French, and that I am a traitor. You, who know me, do you think that I have at any point in my career, betrayed our country?" The young people responded in chorus, "Never, Sir."

Bai looked at them a long time, and then went on, "I am no longer a young man. Neither you nor I can wait any longer. We have wasted too much time already. In a very short time, you must be promoted to Governors, even Ministers so that the people will recognize your names."

Hiep, as well as her brothers, were stunned by the way the conversation was going. She was the first to recover her composure. She asked, "Sir, do you mean that all these career promotions will be only a means to an end? Do you want my brothers to move up the ladder simply for name-recognition among the people?"

The Prime Minister looked at her and thought, "How much like her father! Right to the point! She's blunter than her brothers are, when bluntness is called for." He did not answer her immediately though. She went on, "In that case, you may want them to create a public scandal, a *really big scandal* against the French. Their names would then be recognized instantaneously by the people."

Nguyen Huu Bai looked at her again. He thought, "*This time*, she is wrong. Her father created quite an uproar when he opposed the Emperor Thanh Thai's forced abdication. I myself created quite a stir when I opposed the excavation of Emperor Tu Duc's Tomb. We were, however, among the highest ranking mandarins when we created the 'scandals'. We were already well known before we took a stand publicly against the French.

Hiep's words rang again in Bai's mind, *"A really big scandal,"* she had said. Suddenly, he understood her: Her brothers' career should not end in a protest against an isolated act like the forced abdication of Thanh Thai,

129

or the excavation of Tu Duc's tomb. The scandal should be greater than that. They should end their career by denouncing French rule, by condemning French domination.

Bai thought, "How much she learned from my late friend! Of course, that must be her line of thought. How could I think, even for a moment, that she was wrong?"

He shivered as if the shadow of his friend had just brushed against him. *"Their career as mandarins should end with a public scandal, a really big scandal,"* he said to himself. Hiep had fallen back into the attitude of a listener. "At the highest point of their careers, they must stand up against the French and denounce French rule. Only by doing that will they truly attain name recognition."

Turning to Hiep's brothers, he said, "Yes, all of your future career promotions will serve only as a means to an end. You should not attach any importance to them. Use your leadership roles to become known by the people." He paused a minute, then went on: "Do not waste your time writing reports. I will not read them. Spend your time with the people. Do not be afraid of controversy. Get your names recognized! Make friends. Make enemies. Make the French love you. Make them hate you. You do not have much time ahead of you. Once people widely recognize your names, you can begin to organize your revolutionary party." There was so much in what he said they could agree with immediately. There was also much that they needed time to digest.

Hiep did not know whether she felt happy with the outing any longer. The day had started out so well. Now, she no longer felt the calm and peace of the tomb within herself. She looked at her brothers. They both gazed at the lake crowded with lotus flowers; their young bodies seemed to be weighed down with a heavy burden.

She looked at them again. They were both good horsemen. They were continuously visiting their territories. "Have they been talking with the people? Have the people recognized them as leaders, or just mandarins? Have they learned to know what the people's day-to-day concerns are? Have they learned how hungry, poor, and angry most of the Vietnamese are?" She wondered, "They have been educated to be mandarins. Who will teach them to be revolutionaries?"

As if he had read her mind, Khoi, turning to the Prime Minister, said, "You have asked from my brother and me even more than my father ever did. I hope you are right in presuming that we are strong enough for the roles you are asking us to perform."

Nguyen Huu Bai stood up, to signify that the meeting was over. Walking towards the gate of the tomb where his car was, he turned to Hiep and said: "Do not worry. Your brothers know exactly, their capabilities and their limitations."

Hiep nodded and looked up at the sky. There was no relief. Not a single wisp of cloud was in view. The springtime was gone; summer had set in for good. They walked between lines of large temple trees with fragrant white and yellow blossoms. The pine trees sang farewell. A hidden gecko from somewhere in the wood structures of the gate let out a series of loud and strangled shrikes.

Hiep looked at her brothers. Mandarins of their age should be enjoying their envied life, but here they were, burdened beyond redemption by the trust of the aging Prime Minister, and the dream of their late father. They walked side by side. Their resemblance was striking. They seemed to draw strength from one another. Hiep thought, "As long as they are together, nothing can stop them." She remembered the verse in the *Proverbs*, '*A brother is a better defense than a strong city.*' Yet she knew that the forces aligned against their dream were more than considerable. Again she looked up to the sky trying to find a sign, a good omen. There was no sign, no good omen in the summer sky. High, very high up in the air, a white heron flew past. Its lonely shrikes found no echo in the deserted and cloudless immensity.

*

Hiep was happy each time her father-in-law came home. He was a quiet man, almost taciturn. She knew that he liked to talk with her. She had appreciated him ever since that day, that happiest day of her life, her wedding day.

The groom's family had come to the Grand Chamberlain's home to escort her and the groom to their new home. According to tradition, on the wedding day the bride would leave her parents' house without too much of a farewell. At her new house, she and the groom would kneel down and

131

do obeisance to the groom's parents. Tradition allowed that only on the following day would the bride return home with the groom, to prostrate themselves in front of her parents.

The clear priority given to the parents of the groom was intended to show that the bride recognized her husband's parents as her own, and that having adopted her husband's name, she was no longer a member of her own family.

Hiep, as well as her recently widowed mother and her brothers and sisters, were stunned when Nguyen Van Dieu, breaking from the tradition, asked his son and his new daughter-in-law to prostrate themselves in front of her mother, on their wedding day. He explained his gesture by saying, "I want her to remember that she always is a Ngo Dinh, and that she has not left her family by marrying into ours." Oh, she remembered the commotion that such a gesture had caused. Nguyen Van Dieu was unrepentant. He encouraged her to go and visit her mother every day.

When her son, Xuan, was born a year later, her father-in-law placed her on a pedestal. She could do no wrong. Nothing was good enough for her and the little baby. He would abandon his work and come running to her home if he heard that the baby had fever or did not sleep at night. She wondered how he could do that, as his construction company continued to expand incessantly. Her husband, Am, who still worked for him - though he knew he would soon have his own business-, was also ordered to leave the job he was doing to accompany his father home.

One day, her husband came home early and told her that his father was going to arrive in a moment. She dressed the baby and went out to the parlor with her husband to wait for his father. While waiting for him, she thought that she should tell her husband the news.

This time was not any easier than the last. She wrung her hands until he decided to ask, "Another baby is on the way?" She blushed and nodded. She was amazed that he guessed so quickly. She inquired, "How did you guess?" He smiled: "I did not guess. I only had to remember. You acted exactly the same way when you wanted to tell me about Xuan." She was flabbergasted, "Am I so transparent?" He was about to answer her when the doorbell rang.

Nguyen van Dieu came in with a handful of little toys, as usual. He never wrapped them. He preferred to give the toys to his grandson one at a time and to show the boy how to play with each one of them. After he had played with the boy for half an hour, he was ready to talk with his daughter-in-law.

She asked, "What's new today, Father?" He shook his head, "There is really nothing new at work but I already told your husband. Be careful with the baby these days. I heard that there has been an epidemic of cholera south of the city." At the hint that some danger might threaten her baby, Hiep paled. She said, "The baby is strong and healthy, Father. Nothing will happen to him."

Her father-in-law replied quickly, "I am sure of that." He looked at the young couple and added, "Both of you are strong and healthy, too. When are you going to give me another grandchild?" Seeing that they simply blushed and did not respond, he laughed happily, "Oh my God, are you expecting again?"

He declared with pleasure, "This call for celebration! Your mother will cook her best dishes for the occasion. Tomorrow evening at six, then?" Hiep and Am nodded, the happiest couple in the world.

*

By the next day, they no longer had cause for celebration. The whole household was busy tending to the sick baby. It was soon obvious that Xuan was another victim of the cholera epidemic. One doctor after another was sent for. No one could really do anything for the baby.

It was at the time when cholera killed. With all their science, there was nothing they could think of to save the life of a child suffering with cholera. Year after year, in the summer, tens of thousands of people in Vietnam died of cholera. The annual epidemics struck in the cities and in the villages and both traditional and modern medicines proved to be useless.

The doctors could only watch their little patient die. For three days, the little baby fought valiantly against the shadow of death. Exhausted, he still looked fixedly with his big eyes at his anguished parents, as if he wanted to comfort them.

A priest came, anointed the child, and stayed to pray with the family. Everyone watched the baby, as if he himself had the power to decide whether to die or to live. Sometimes his mouth moved as if he wanted to smile or to say something. At the end he closed his eyes and stopped struggling. His long eyelashes still seemed to move from time to time, though. Then a doctor stepped forward and took his wrist, trying for a moment to find his pulse. He turned around and said in a whisper, "He is gone."

*

"They have laid him on a little bed draped with white satin," Hiep thought sadly. "They have placed hundreds of red, pink and white roses around his little body. He looks so calm, so handsome. Only when my fingers touch his cheeks and I feel how cold they are, am I reminded that he is no longer alive."

"So this is death," she thought in sorrow. "This is how somebody you love more than yourself, is gone, gone, forever. I will never see him smile, hear him laugh, help him walk, ever again."

"So many dreams were woven around you, my son," she wept, "and so many hopes are now shattered. Yet tonight, in so many families in Hue and all over the country, how many mothers are grieving, each one entombed it her own sense of loss, grieving for her dreams that the epidemic has extinguished?"

She turned around and found her husband standing there looking at her with eyes which made her sob uncontrollably, and which at the same time seemed to put salve on her soul. She buried her head on her husband's shoulder and cried, her whole body shaking with tremors, which came from deep inside her. She said to herself: "God has taken my baby away. It is His will. For some reason known only to Him, God has taken away my baby and allowed him into His presence, now, not later. I should not cry. But my God isn't there another way?"

Only three days earlier, her son had been the picture of good health. Three days earlier, he had been testing her patience with his pranks and laughing heartily when she pretended to be angry.

"How long will a mother mourn the death of her son?" she asked herself. "How long? I know, you will mourn for him until your very last day on earth," her heart replied.

*

Seven months later, her second son was born. She and her husband named him Thuan. Xuan had meant springtime. His death marked the end of a season in her life. After him, the springtime was gone. She had grown into a woman whose eyes had seen death face to face. Her former vulnerability was gone. She felt both strength, which helped her to overcome her grief, and resignation to God's will, which tempered her greatest moments of joy with a certain melancholy.

Thuan means submission to a higher authority, submission to God's will. The name summed up the deepest feelings of his parents in those days. They felt that dreams and plans for the future were not matters under man's control. "The future is in the hands of providence," they said to themselves.

The new baby looked almost exactly like Xuan. Bending her head over his cradle, Hiep prayed morning and evening: "God, please let me keep this child. God, keep him safe from dangers, which are lurking all around him. Only you can protect him from harm."

Her pain was under control most of the time, but still she mourned. There were moments when, while walking about in her beautiful garden full of flowers, she had to stop and try to breathe: she felt as if she were walking with half of herself missing, and the gaping wound had not healed.

She was fully aware now of human frailty and the limitation of the human condition. While in her childhood and her youth she had spontaneously opened herself to God's grace, now she knew that she needed to abide by His will. She had become a stronger Christian.

*

Thuc was taking a walk with Hiep in her garden. Two years had passed since Xuan's death and her brother Thuc, now Father Thuc, had returned to Hue. He was talking to her about his years of studies in Rome, the people he met there, the beauty of Rome and the historical monuments he had seen there, when she interrupted him and asked, "Did you go to Reunion Island to see Emperor Thanh Thai in his exile?" Thuc nodded and smiled, "Brother Khoi kept reminding me of that 'pilgrimage', until I finally went."

Brother and sister walked in silence for a while. Hiep was reminiscing about the Emperor she had known when she still was a child. Thuc volunteered, "The Emperor told me that he was very sad when he heard about Father's death but very encouraged to know that Khoi and Diem are doing so well in their careers."

Hiep asked, "Did he say he missed the country?" Thuc nodded, "He kept repeating that the only wish he had was to be allowed to come back to Vietnam and die in his native land. But he knows that the French will never let that happen."

She wanted to know more, "Did he have any idea of what is going on in Vietnam?" Thuc was a little surprised at his sister's curiosity. He said, "He reads the newspapers. He knows what is going on here. He said that he regretted not being able to accomplish much during his reign of eighteen years."

Hiep protested vehemently, "Did you tell him that many Vietnamese still honor him for what he had done, and find his continued exile unjustified?" Again, Thuc was surprised by the emotion he sensed in his sister.

A maid was playing with Thuan in the garden, a little distance away from where they were. Following Thuc's eyes, Hiep laughed, "He is quite a darling, isn't he? After Xuan's death, I would have gone crazy if it weren't for him." Thuc shook his head, "I've heard that you were very strong, very courageous, and that you accepted God's will with dignity."

Hiep smiled, "It is easy to keep a brave face. Part of me died with Xuan, though. You know when Xuan was here with us, Am and I made all kinds of plans for his future. Thuan is now two years old, yet neither Am nor do I dare talk about his future."

Sensing the pain in his sister, Thuc replied, "Then I need to tell you something about Thuan's future. He will grow to be a great man." Thuc laughed, and her pain assuaged, Hiep smiled back at him.

CHAPTER NINE
PORTRAIT OF TWO YOUNG MANDARINS

In the summer of 1932, Hiep and her family went to Hoi An, about a hundred miles south of Hue. Hoi An, was the capital of the Province of Quang Nam, where her brother Khoi was Governor. Diem, who was then Province Chief of Binh Thuan, farther to the South, also met them there.

One afternoon she was walking with her husband near Khoi's beach house. She saw from afar, Diem's horse galloping at full speed towards them. Diem was holding Thuan, her son, in front of him. Both of the riders were laughing happily as they drew near. They sped past her and her husband, and then stopped. Diem dismounted and took the boy down from the saddle. He turned and said to her, "This child is not afraid of horses. See how he laughs!"

It was rare to see Diem in such a happy mood, so she said, "We should have family reunions more often." Diem lowered his head and replied, "I know. The problem is time. How do you find more time for happy moments like these? You know that we are dealing with growing unrest everywhere. The hardest problem today is dealing with Communists. The French think we should catch them and put them all in prison, or send them to the Prison Island of Poulo Condore. *That* will not solve the problem. Those in prisons will believe more fervently in what they have done, while the people will see them as martyrs, and there will be more converts."

Hiep remembered. Twelve months had passed since the day Prime Minister Nguyen Huu Bai had called all the heads of provinces back to Hue to discuss with them ways to deal with Communism. Diem and Khoi came home looking grimmer each day during that long consultation. They argued about methodology. Diem maintained that heavy penalties for Communist actions would not help. He said only patient education and genuine compassion would win them over.

Hiep listened to her brothers' arguments. Khoi wanted to be convinced by Diem, but he doubted that Diem's methods would work. As she listened to them, Hiep once again understood why her father had chosen Diem, and not Khoi to be the leader. Diem spoke with his heart, acted with his heart. Khoi was more rational and pragmatic. Hiep saw that they complemented one another. She also saw that Diem was the better of the two.

A guard from the beach house had come to take the reins of the horse from Diem's hand and he led the magnificent animal away. Diem sat down on the sand. Hiep and her husband followed his example. She had heard stories about his long monologues. Now she feared that one was coming. She knew that he had acquired that habit only after he left home and lived a solitary life as a mandarin.

Diem went on, "I am not dealing with them that way in my province. I have our people penetrate their groups, identify them, and then catch them. I am not keeping them in jail. I let them go home, but make them go to classes to study Marxism. Most of them heard very little about Marxism when they served in Communist groups. We tell them what Communism is all about."

Her husband, with a twinkle in his eyes, asked, "Any of them die of boredom yet?" Diem laughed, but quickly resumed his seriousness, "Many of them are now working with me to reconvert former comrades."

The ocean was blue and calm. All the turmoil seemed so distant, so remote to her at the moment. She said, "I heard rumors about what you did to the mandarins in your province." Diem looked a little embarrassed. He was about to answer when they noticed Khoi walking briskly towards them.

Khoi was seven years older than Diem, but somehow managed to look like Diem's twin brother. It was only their ways of walking that differed. Diem walked very fast and from afar, he seemed to be jogging. Khoi walked in long, dignified strides. Since Ngo Dinh Kha had died, Khoi took his role as his brother's mentor very seriously. He was quick to point out Diem's mistakes, but always with great courtesy.

Hiep was nine years younger than Khoi. She did not talk with Khoi as freely as she did with Diem. When she still was a baby, Khoi had often carried her in his arms, and later on his back. But since she was four, he had been awed by the skill with which she communicated with their father. In the parlor of their home, she was the one who posed questions to the Grand Chamberlain, and the older sons smiled and listened in silence to the long responses given by their father. She sometimes triggered his laughter, sometimes made him pensive, and Khoi, Thuc, and Diem, knew that they could never elicit such spontaneous responses from their father.

Then Khoi was eighteen and his father began to spend more time with him. He was for a while, his father's hope and pride: Thuc had gone to the seminary and Diem still was a brooding boy of eleven, so Khoi had been the first one to embrace a career as a mandarin. He needed advice and his father had never failed him.

Three or four years later, however, he knew that his father had seen in Diem a rising star, the hope not only of his family, but also of the whole country. Surprised at first by his father's choice, he soon accepted it, and without envy, without jealousy, decided to work to build up his younger brother's potential, often at his own detriment. He could not do otherwise. He venerated his father too much to question the latter's dreams. Diem did not disappoint him.

Now approaching his sister and Diem, Khoi had a vivid flashback and saw the Grand Chamberlain on his deathbed. He, and Diem and Hiep had been uppermost in their father's mind at that timeless moment. The three of them were bound together by that death scene, until each one of them had accomplished his or her destiny. He knew it. He felt it.

He had left his office a little early that afternoon. In his pocket were two handwritten letters sent him, one signed by members of the family of a former Minister of Defense and the other from the Minister of Education. Both letters were threatening.

He smiled at everybody in the small group, bent down and asked his nephew, Thuan, "Did you have a good ride today with Uncle Diem?" The little boy looked up, not intimidated at all by his Big Uncle, "Well, riding with both of you is much more fun." Khoi laughed, "Of course, but while all of you are on vacation, I have to work. I can ride with both of you only during the weekends." Hiep noticed that whenever both her brothers could ride together, they would disappear for hours with Thuan, and come back tanned and radiant as if the long rides never tired them.

But today even while Khoi laughed, Hiep saw that her eldest brother was preoccupied. She asked, "Is something the matter?" Khoi never lied to her, so he straightened himself up and said, "Yes, trouble is brewing."

He turned to Diem; "The families of the late Minister Hue and Minister Trung are not very happy with what you did in Binh Thuan. I guess you know what you are doing. They are furious because you arrested some of their family members."

Diem did not respond immediately. He looked at the ocean for a while, then at Hiep and finally said, "Before you arrived, our sister had already started grilling me about the arrest of those *Tri Phu* (Heads of Prefecture). I knew the late Minister Than Trong Hue quite well and was fond of him. I also know Minister Ho Dac Trung. I have a great deal of respect for their families.

"You know that I'd hate to hurt their feelings. But the *Tri Phu* of Hoa Da, the nephew of late Minister Hue, is a corrupt mandarin and I cannot ignore the evidence of his corruption."

He again looked at the ocean. His eyes followed the seagulls that circled over the blue water. He lowered his voice so that Khoi, Am, and Hiep had to strain their ears to hear him, "It's the same thing with the *Tri Phu* of Ham Thuan. I know his uncle, Minister Ho Dac Trung, who is quite powerful in Hue. But I cannot ignore his wrongdoing."

Khoi sat down on the sand. He knew that he could not blame Diem, but he wondered how many powerful enemies Diem had created for himself over the past few years. This time, Diem was 'touching the tiger's whiskers.'

The Than Trong and Ho Dac families were well-respected families in Hue. They would never forgive Diem for this affront. He said to his brother who had lay down next to him on the sand, "You've just begun your long voyage. Don't burden yourself so heavily. You have your whole life to make enemies. Why are you in such a hurry?"

Diem shook his head, "I know that you are merely playing the devil's advocate. You remember as well as I do what Father said, '*Do everything according to your conscience!'* Khoi shook his head, and then admitted thoughtfully, "No. Really, for a moment I did forget. You're right. We have to do what Father asked us to do. The rest will take care of itself."

He knew that the rest would not take care of itself. He asked, "What will I say to the Hue family?" Diem shrugged, "Tell them that I do what I have to do, and that if they show understanding now, one day I'll repay my debt of gratitude to them."

Little did they know how much the Than Trong family would weigh on the destiny of the Ngo Dinh family! Only ten years after that afternoon on the beach, one of the Ngo Dinh brothers, Ngo Dinh Nhu married Than Trong, Hue's granddaughter.

Hue's granddaughter was to be a historical personage, known all over the world. Her real name was Tran Thi Le Xuan, but to the outside world, she was *Madame Nhu*, the Dragon Lady. She was to play a pivotal role in Ngo Dinh Diem's Presidential Palace; she was even called *the First Lady*. Her qualities and shortcomings, in large measure, contributed to some of the achievements of Diem's presidency, and to the acceleration of events, which brought down the President and tragically ended the lives of three of the Ngo Dinh brothers.

Tran Thi Le Xuan

*

Khoi watched his younger brother. Prime Minister Nguyen Huu Bai had kept his end of the deal. Both Khoi and Diem had received several promotions. Did Diem create the scandal because he followed the advice of the Prime Minister to the letter? Khoi remembered each word pronounced by his father-in-law that day, seven years earlier, at Emperor Tu Duc's Tomb, "Do not be afraid to be controversial. *Make friends, make enemies!*"

*

Hiep studied her brothers. They were so much alike, and yet so different. Khoi was definitely more decisive than Diem, yet he was less trenchant. He acted faster than Diem did; yet he was more tolerant of human weakness. Diem would brood for days before he made a decision, but by the time he decided, compromises, allowances for human errors, and every other consideration had been discarded from his mind. Then, no one could make him deviate from the course of action that he had adopted.

Hiep felt that she should look at things from another perspective Khoi was more tolerant, not because he had more compassion than Diem, but because he was more rational. Diem was less decisive, because he could see all the consequences of his acts. Diem never went back on a decision simply because before he made it, he had thought everything through and had already accepted the consequences.

Watching them, Hiep sighed: She had long ago stopped wondering whether Khoi should have been built up as the leader, instead of Diem. She knew that none of her father's children would dare alter the terms of his political testament. Diem was the leader, and all the others were the followers. They could disagree with him, they could criticize him, they could even scream at him, but when all was said and done, whatever Diem decided would be regarded as their collective decision. They would have to live with it, and if necessary, die for it. Hiep sighed, *"This is our destiny.* Father determined that we would proceed in this way. There is no turning back."

She watched the beautiful sunset and the screaming seagulls circling over their heads. One after another, the seagulls plunged into the waves crested with golden foam. The graceful birds, so light in their flight, suddenly dropped like heavy stones into the sea. Upon hitting the water, however, they managed to penetrate the waves softly, without a splash. She wondered whether there was some lesson to learn from the seagulls.

Looking at Diem, she saw him narrow his eyes, watching the birds so intensely that he did not hear his brother's repeated suggestions to walk back home for supper. She felt a little pain inside: "Yes, my poor brother Diem, you would like to be as free as those birds, but your life is tied to the promise you gave to Father. You will never be free of that promise. You can watch the birds and dream, but you will never be free like them, until you die."

Thuan was playing with his father a short distance away from them. He was laughing heartily as his father ran after him and pretended he was unable to catch him. Hiep said to herself: "This is the picture of happiness. I should feel contented, fulfilled, yet, why do I feel as if a storm were brewing, as if behind this quiet and beautiful twilight, an angry seascape is hidden, with ominous dark clouds battling over a seething ocean?"

Khoi turned to her and asked with obvious concern, "Are you cold, Sister? Why are you shivering?"

*

The dinner prepared by Khoi's wife, Hoa, was elaborate. Hiep had vainly insisted on giving Hoa a hand, but she had been sent off to the beach. Hiep had protested and said that she should stay home with Niem, her baby daughter. But, Hoa assured her that a maid would take care of Niem and firmly showed her and Am to the door.

Gathered around the dinner table were Khoi, Hoa and Huan, their sixteen years old son, Diem, Am, Hiep and Thuan. The conversation was lively at first, as they talked about the sea, the city of Hoi An, and the beautiful weather.

Then, Hoa suddenly announced, "My father wants to resign." The old Prime Minister wanted to resign? There were expressions of disbelief and concern around the table. Even Khoi had not been told. Hoa looked at her husband as if to reassure him that she had not intended to hide the information from him or surprise him.

She told him, "When you came home, you gave me my father's letter. I opened it and there it was! He said that the Emperor had completed his studies in France and plans to return to Vietnam this summer. My father said that as soon as the Emperor is settled, that is, sometimes before the end of the year, he would resign and go back to Phuoc Mon."

Diem was stunned, "Back to Phuoc Mon? Impossible!" All the adults at the table understood his terse exclamation. Even if he wanted to resign, he could not retire to that far-off mountain hideout. Even after his resignation, the young Emperor, who had never reigned, and who had been staying in France to complete his studies, would still need his advice. He should stay in Hue even if he resigned.

 Hoa smiled, "Look, he has been Prime Minster for the last nine years. He is really tired. He wants to forget all about the worries and the intrigues of the Imperial Court, and enjoy a long retreat before he dies."

Khoi nodded in agreement, "In Phuoc Mon, he has built a beautiful estate. Oh, it's nothing really fancy, but he has planted all kinds of trees and flowers around the house. He has also built his own tomb, a round shaped brick wall, which encloses a thatched hut. The hut is also round and completely open, no walls and no door. Within the hut, in the middle of the floor, there is a little dirt mound. That will be his tomb. I once asked him why the tomb was without stone or cement slab. He laughed and said that a dirt mound was a better idea. He said that buried that way, on Resurrection Day, he would not have to break through a stone or cement slab to get out when he awakened from the dead."

Hoa volunteered again, "He would like to see Brother Diem succeed him." Khoi asked, "Did he say that in his letter?" Hoa shook her head, "No, he didn't, but you all know his wish. He has continued at his post for such a long time simply because he wanted to wait until Brother Diem is ready to replace him."

Hiep said, "Brother Diem *is not* ready." Everybody was startled. Diem did not say anything. Hiep had spoken in such a matter-of-fact manner that either they had to contradict her, or agree. They remained silent and waited for her to explain her thoughts.

Instead, Hiep asked Diem, "Do you think you are ready?" Diem laughed and replied, "I am *not* ready. In fact, I'm just a *Tuan Vu*, Chief of a medium-size province. I'm not even a Governor like Brother Khoi. If I become Prime Minister next year, that would create a lot of envy. So, Hiep is right. I'm not ready. Looking at the other side of the equation, I would say that the situation is not ready for me either."

Khoi said, "There will never be an ideal situation. If you want to wait until all the ideal conditions are there, then you'll die waiting." Diem waved his hand, "I know, but if none of the necessary conditions is there, it would be foolhardy to consider jumping into the situation with both feet."

*

Once alone in their room, after rocking Niem to sleep, Am asked his wife, "Why were you so direct at table? Bother Diem must resent what you said." Hiep nodded, "He would have resented what I said, if he were an ordinary man. However, he is not supposed to be an ordinary man. Our father has built him up to be a leader. If he cannot accept frank advice, then our poor father wasted his efforts."

Am was fascinated by his wife's firmness when it came to dealing with Diem. He was intrigued by the way Diem's brothers and sisters had pinned their hopes on him. Curiously enough, they were never afraid to be tough with him in order to make him see all his little shortcomings, to draw his attention to the details, to prevent him from confusing dreams with realities.

He was also amazed at the way Diem was willing to play the game according to such set rules. Diem seemed to feel quite comfortable with his brothers and sisters shooting holes into his ideas, testing his character constantly, and playing the devil's advocates with his plans. Yet, none of them showed him disrespect. Every one of them genuinely believed that someday, he would become the leader of the country.

Am had never wanted to play a role in politics. He was at times, concerned with his wife's involvement in her brothers' plans. But he knew that he could not change an iota in the course of events which was unfolding before his very eyes and which one day might take his wife's family to unimaginable heights, or plunge it into an unfathomable abyss.

He said to himself, "They can't help living their collective dream. There is nothing that can stop them from going to that rendezvous with their own destiny."

CHAPTER TEN
PRIME MINISTER FOR SEVENTY DAYS

In the summer of 1932, as Prime Minister Nguyen Huu Bai and the Imperial Court waited impatiently, Emperor Bao Dai seemed reluctant to leave Paris. His return had been postponed a number of times. Finally in the fall, the young monarch returned with great pomp to Vietnam. Bao Dai, who was now twenty years old, was to proclaim, with the French colonial administration, the Great Reform announced by Governor-General Pierre Pasquier. Upon his return, the Emperor spoke fervently about the beginning of a new era of cooperation between France and Vietnam.

A few weeks after his return, Bao Dai, with the French placidly looking on, announced the abrogation of the Convention of November 6, 1925, which had been forced upon the Imperial Court immediately after the death of his father, Emperor Khai Dinh.

The abrogation of the Convention was in the end a joke. Bao Dai agreed that the French Resident Superior in Hue could veto every one of his decisions, however unimportant they were.

During several quick meetings at his residence or at Ngo Dinh Kha's home, Prime Minister Nguyen Huu Bai and Khoi and Diem, discussed this new 'reform song and dance.' They did not believe in Pasquier's good will. They saw the Great Reform as a big trap. They had already been told of Bao Dai's lack of focus, and that the young Emperor tired easily of his new toys. They wondered when Bao Dai would stop playing his new game of reform.

Diem enjoyed the short stays in Hue when he was called back for meetings. After the necessary meetings with Bai, he would make an excursion to a pagoda, an Imperial Tomb or a temple. Sometimes Hiep came along with him with him but more often, he went with Thuan, taking lots of pictures. Hiep never asked him about politics anymore. She knew that he had to think things through by himself. At times he would ask her questions and she surprised him often with her answers. On many occasions, she seemed to have guessed what his questions would be, and answered concisely and bluntly, challenging him to go deeper into the matter at hand.

Upon hearing that Bao Dai had promised, with French support, to modernize the administrative, educational and the judiciary systems, Nguyen Huu Bai convened his protégés to yet another meeting.

After they had met, Diem took both Hiep and Thuan to the Quoc An Pagoda. There, in the shade of a centenary banyan tree, Diem expounded his own view regarding the modernization of the system of mandarins. Then he asked Hiep, "What do you think about the Emperor's proposed reform?"

Hiep answered, "The idea did not come from the Emperor, it came from Pasquier. He wants to change the mandarin system because he hates to receive official documents from the Imperial Court written in Chinese. He wants to read the documents in the original, not the translated French version. He wants the Imperial Court to employ only mandarins who can speak and write French fluently. You and Brother Khoi will be all right, but the Prime Minister himself will not be spared. Though he speaks and writes French perfectly, he always writes his officials reports and comments in Chinese. Pasquier hates that!"

Diem was astonished. He asked her, "How do you come to such a conclusion? This morning, when we talked with the Prime Minister, he did not say anything about Pasquier not liking him."

Hiep did not answer until Diem pressed her "The Prime Minster is always making jokes about Pasquier's *grandiose* Reforms. Do you think that those jokes haven't been reported to the Governor General? I have talked with many of the mid-level Vietnamese officials who work at the Resident Superior's Office. Many times they have told me that the Prime Minister's days are numbered."

Diem was very concerned now. He asked her, "Emperor Bao Dai owes a lot to the Prime Minister. Do you think that he will forget his debts so easily?" Hiep shook her head, "No, not very easily, but he will not endanger his own security for the sake of the Prime Minister. Diem asked, "Have you mentioned this to him?" Hiep smiled, "Of course, I have, many times, but he just keeps saying, "They will ask me to resign one day, but not now, not yet."

Diem watched her. She did not seem to be too tense. She talked about the danger incurred by Nguyen Huu Bai without any expression of urgency. But if what she said proved to be correct, the implementation of the plans they had been developing for the past two years was in jeopardy. Diem asked her: "How is it that you know people at the Residence Superior's Office?"

Hiep smiled again, and her voice contained a veiled reproach, "In Father's time, Vietnamese officials who worked there gave him plenty of information. That's why he was always one step ahead of the French. Even after his retirement, he maintained those contacts. That's why he was effective in his collaboration with Nguyen Huu Bai in various moments of crisis, when Bai was still the Minister. These people, many of whom come from very good families, even from the Imperial Clan, are not at ease with you. They remember that you forced the French Resident in Phan Thiet to fire his top Vietnamese assistants there. They do not have anything against me, so, they talk to me."

Diem shrugged, "I remember the Phan Thiet case. The people who worked for the French administration were very corrupt. I could not fire the corrupt Vietnamese mandarins in my province and allow the officials working for the French administration to think that they were immune." Hiep nodded but did not comment on what Diem had said.

An uneasy silence lingered until Diem muttered: "The French have allowed the Emperor to visit many of the provinces of Central and North Vietnam, as well as those of the Central Highlands. That will help the young Emperor to begin to see the different aspects of our country. He will learn to love his country."

Hiep sighed, "He has the freedom to visit any province he cares to see because the French trust him. Do you remember how difficult it was for Emperor Thanh Thai to go anywhere? I recall Father saying, 'We are in a horrible situation; we are forced to mistrust whomever the French trust. *May God forgive us for being so mistrustful*!' Do you remember?"

Diem nodded. He replied, "So far, the young Emperor appears to be a miracle worker and a capable monarch who is making the French loosen their stranglehold on the entire country. Yet, we do not know when the miracles will stop. We certainly don't expect this to continue for much longer."

The big bell of the pagoda started ringing. Listening to the pure and melancholy sounds of the bell, Diem seemed perfectly serene and relaxed. But, when the bell stopped, he turned to scold his sister; "You have kept too many things to yourself. We need to hear much more from you in the future."

Hiep shook her head energetically, "No, Brother Diem, Father asked me to talk only once a year. Please, do not ask me for more. I have a husband and two children to tend to. I don't want to get too involved in your plans. Now that Brother Thuc is back, please get him involved, instead of me." Diem smiled, "He is a priest. He must dedicate all of his time to the service of God. We should not bother him with worldly matters."

They strolled about in the large gardens of the pagoda. In the peace of the late afternoon, the old pagoda, a perfect jewel of traditional architecture, seemed to remind brother and sister of the vanity of all human undertakings.

As they walked, Diem wondered whether his brother, Thuc, had not chosen the best thing in life: to serve God. The rest is vanity, Diem said to himself. He remembered the poem pronounced by the Venerable Hanh Doan, the Founder of the pagoda, a moment before his death in 1728. He recited it to the delight of his sister:

> *"Silent is the mirror without reflection,*
>
> *Radiant, the jade without form,*
>
> *Clearly the object is no-object,*
>
> *Immense is nothingness which is not nothingness."*

Hiep asked Diem, "Do you really appreciate that kind of poem?" Diem pondered for a moment before he answered, "I do not comprehend the depth of the poem. But, it affects me in a strange way. I feel sad when I recite it. Then I feel exhilarated by it. In the end, I simply feel peaceful."

Hiep laughed, "I can tell that you love the poem. It is completely different from the poems written by Prime Minister Nguyen Huu Bai." Diem shook his head, "I don't think so. Outwardly, the Prime Minister's poems seem to indicate his predilection for action. If you read them carefully, however, you will begin to realize that he too, is reluctant to give undue consideration to the physical world. His poems frequently paraphrase the Ecclesiastes, 'Vanity of vanities; all things are vanity'."

Hiep asked, "Since your childhood, you have frequently gone to pagodas and meditated there. Why do they appeal to you so much? If you were not Catholic, would you want to be a Buddhist?"

Diem replied, "I have never imagined myself without my Christian faith. But, I understand why so many of our famous mandarins who were great Confucians during their working life, found their way to a Buddhist temple at the end of their life. My godfather, Prince Huong Thuyen, was such a monk before he was converted to Christianity. I have always been inspired to meditate, whenever I have come to a pagoda ground."

Years later, when Diem was accused of discrimination against Buddhists, Hiep remembered that afternoon, when Diem had shown her his great appreciation of a poem composed by a great Buddhist monk.

*

Prime Minister Nguyen Huu Bai was concerned. Only two months after his return, and having implemented some minor changes under the guidance of Pierre Pasquier, Bao Dai decided to appoint, as Chancellor of the Imperial Secretariat, a journalist named Pham Quynh.

For the longest time, Pham Quynh had been a protégé of Louis Marty, the feared Head of the French Directorate of Political and Indigenous Affairs. By accepting the advice of Governor-General Pasquier to appoint Pham Quynh as the Chancellor, Bao Dai had demonstrated that he would always be cooperative and loyal to the French.

Both Khoi and Diem were in Hue to celebrate Thuc's birthday, when Prime Minister Nguyen Huu Bai came to their father's home to announce the news. Before long, he, Khoi and Diem escaped from the celebrations and went out into the garden to talk.

Nguyen Huu Bai declared, "This new development means that I will no longer have total access to the Emperor, and my discussions with him will not be as frequent as before. Furthermore, each one of my visits to the Emperor will be reported. I submitted my resignation some time ago, but the Emperor refused to let me resign. I understand that he has made me Duke of Phuoc Mon. But, from now on Pham Quynh's power will increase significantly. We have to move much more rapidly. I think that a new cabinet will be brought in by next September. This gives us barely ten months to impress upon the French and the Emperor that you, Diem, should be the next Prime Minister."

Khoi said, "We are pressed for time. Pasquier is an old hand. Before he became Governor-General he was the Resident Superior in Hue for five years. We cannot play too many tricks with him. He has never recognized what you, Father, did for Emperor Khai Dinh. He thinks of himself as the one who put Bao Dai on the throne."

Diem said, "As the Resident Superior, he was the one who forced the Convention of 1925 down our throats, after Khai Dinh's death. Now, he is the Governor-General and he generously allows Bao Dai to abrogate the Convention. In 1925, it was he who threatened to use the rumors about the illegitimate birth of Bao Dai. Now, he appears as a father to Bao Dai. He is a dangerous man. At times, it seems that he wants to play God."

Khoi added, "Let's play the card of Yves Châtel, the Resident Superior. He understands the Vietnamese, and is always ready to listen." Prime Minister Bai nodded, "Yes, Châtel is always ready to listen. Unfortunately, I have more bad news for you: It seems that Yves Châtel will soon be transferred. I am not discouraged though. We have to work on Bao Dai and Pasquier. I will work on them as much as I possibly can. I believe that within ten months, you will be able to replace me as Prime Minister, Diem." The timing of the Prime Minister was off by five months. Events evolved much more rapidly than he had predicted.

By late April 1933, sensing that he had miscalculated the timing of his retirement, Nguyen Huu Bai sent in another letter of resignation. It was too late. A palace coup was already in the making. On May 2, 1933, the 'massacre' took place.

*

Two days before the young Emperor fired Prime Minster Nguyen Huu Bai together with four of his colleagues there was a lengthy meeting at Ngo Dinh Kha's home.

As usual, Hiep had come to see her mother in the morning and stayed to talk with her until eleven. She was about to leave when there was a commotion at the gate, and the servants ran to the house to announce: "The Governor is here!"

Hiep went into the parlor to welcome Khoi. Seeing her, he nodded and said, "Your presence here is a good omen. Diem will arrive in a couple of hours. Please stay and have lunch with us. Send someone to tell your husband that you will stay here with us until dark." Just by looking at him, she knew that something very important was about to happen. But of course, he first had to go in and talk privately with their mother.

He emerged from the meeting with their mother; more pensive than when he had first arrived. Hiep served tea and sat down facing him. He knew that she would not ask him what was going on, even though she was bursting with curiosity. She had acted like that with their father. When he had been reluctant to talk, she would ask pointed questions, but when she knew that he was ready to talk anyway, she would just sit in front of him, calmly waiting for him to begin.

It had been a long time ago, yet the image of Hiep, the little girl, was pervasive in the parlor. He said, "Diem and I are here to discuss the Emperor's offer. He wants to appoint Diem as Prime Minister. It has already been decided that all the old Ministers including my father-in-law, will be dismissed." She said softly, "In all your plans, the Prime Minister was to resign, not to get fired."

Khoi admitted, "I'm afraid that he acted a little too late. His letter of resignation was delivered to the Emperor a few days ago. The Emperor, however, wants the cabinet's fall to appear to be his own palace coup, so he will not publicize my father-in-law's letter of resignation. As compensation, the Emperor has promised to retain him as the Imperial

Advisor. As well, he has offered the position of Prime Minister to Brother Diem."

That was news of great consequence, yet Khoi noticed that Hiep did not seem very enthusiastic. He wondered, "Why do both Mother and Hiep show such lack of enthusiasm for this?" He challenged her by asking; "You don't see how Diem can succeed as Prime Minister in the present situation, do you?"

She was too astute to answer his question directly. Years of listening to their father had taught her to look at a situation from various angles. She startled him by asking him frankly, "What are the advantages or disadvantages of a Prime Minister using his resignation as a sign of protest?"

"Oh, how much like Father!" Khoi was dumbfounded for a moment. So she had come to the same conclusion they had reached after so much soul searching! He asked, "Who is talking about resignation?" She shrugged and smiled; "Don't play games with me, Big Brother! This debate is not about accepting or rejecting the offer. The three of you have already decided that Brother Diem should become the next Prime Minister. What you want to debate today is how and when he should resign in protest."

He had never felt so much love for her. She brought back so many memories of his father. The memories were so vivid that his eyes burned and brimmed with tears. He turned away to hide his emotions, but he could not help saying, "I wish Father were here."

"But, at least you are here, Sister," he said to himself; "at least you are here."

*

Duke Nguyen Huu Bai arrived before Diem did. He was not surprised to see Hiep in the parlor. He sensed immediately that Khoi and Hiep had been having a serious discussion and that both of them were more concerned than excited. He went to greet Mrs. Ngo Dinh Kha, a routine he had established for each visit he had made after his friend died. Even if Diem or Khoi was there, the first person he talked to was Mrs. Kha.

When he came back to the parlor, he asked Hiep, "You've heard about the Emperor's offer, I guess?" Hiep nodded. He continued, "You don't seem to like the idea very much, do you?" Hiep shook her head. It was a ritual between the two of them for so long that it came back almost automatically: She was to be the silent listener. If her father or Nguyen Huu Bai asked her something, she would simply nod or shake her head. Only on rare occasions did she would she give a quick answer.

Now, seeing how troubled she was, Bai wanted to hear her objections. But, just as he was about to focus on her concerns, Diem arrived. Diem also went to greet his mother before going to the parlor. Hiep stood up and said, "You will discuss strategies without me." They insisted that she stay, but she smiled and walked out of the room.

*

She was right. They had no delusions at all. The former Prime Minister was blunt: Diem had to accept the offer, not out of loyalty to the Crown, but to achieve national name recognition. He would soon have to find his way out, an honorable way out!

Diem said, "If I understand the situation, you want me to become Prime Minister, then to begin making both reasonable and unreasonable demands to the French. If, for any inconceivable reason, the French accept all of my proposals, I should stay on and then begin to make even more unreasonable demands. When the French reject my demands, I will resign from the post, using French interference as my pretext. Do I understand you correctly?" The Duke nodded, "Yes, that is exactly what I want you to do"

Khoi allowed a moment to pass then asked, "As a consequence, in a few months Brother Diem will no longer be a Prime Minister. Probably he won't be a mandarin, either. Is this what you want, Father?"

Bai had a sad smile, "Do you want him to go on being as a mandarin all his life? Do you want to remain a mandarin all your life? Look at me: I have spent my life as a mandarin, more precisely forty-eight years under five Emperors, and another ten years as Prime Minister. Have I achieved anything? Do you want to follow my poor example? I was perfectly clear with both of you seven years ago when I said, that day at Emperor Tu Duc's Tomb that I would build you up. I also told you that you should use your career of mandarins merely as a means to an end. Have you forgotten?"

Khoi did not bristle at the implied reproach, but answered the question, as his father would have done, "This means that he will antagonize not only the Emperor and the Imperial Court, but also the French. He will obviously offend the French when he resigns. He will be cast away, probably as a commoner." The Duke nodded, "You are right again. But if Diem becomes a commoner, so will I. Do you think that if Bao Dai does not forgive him, he will forgive me, who recommended him as Prime Minister? If the French hate him for his actions, will they love me? No, they will make us both commoners, exactly like what happened to your father twenty-six years ago."

Khoi pursued his line of questioning, "Then will I also resign?" Nguyen Huu Bai shook his head, "No, it would be a useless sacrifice. Your resignation would pass unnoticed. No, you have to stay to be our channel of communication with the mandarins." Khoi did not argue. He simply said, "I don't think that the Emperor and the French will let me stay anyway, if they come down hard on both of you." The Duke replied, "That may be the case. But we will have to try and keep you where you are."

Khoi asked his last question, "Brother Diem will in all probability achieve national recognition after he resigns. But, what will he do after that?" Nguyen Huu Bai was blunt, "He will have to be a revolutionary. He will have no other option. *We will have destroyed all the bridges behind him.*"

*

Khoi felt a need to talk with his sister. He left his car in front of his mother's home and walked briskly towards Hiep's house. Upon entering her garden, he saw her tending to her flowers. She did not hear him coming and was startled by his voice, "Sister, Brother Diem has accepted the offer to become the next Prime Minister." She nodded as if to say that was no news to her.

She placed her small watering can down on the ground and faced him, "It will be a short mandate?" Khoi replied, "Yes, Brother Diem is expected to make it as short as possible, within the limits of decency." Hiep laughed and Khoi also burst out laughing. Hiep asked again, "Brother Diem is expected to confront the French, then step down?" Khoi nodded. Hiep asked Khoi to come in, but he said he had to go back to their mother's home to discuss the detailed strategies.

She sensed the tension in her brother. She said softly, "You seem to be perturbed. But we agreed to this strategy seven years ago." He nodded again. "Why is she so attuned to each one of us like this?" Khoi wondered. He had hardly needed to talk. She again sensed his tension, and looking him in the eyes, she asked, "What will be the extent of the damage?" He was relieved that she had asked the question. His tension eased up.

He admitted, "The damage will be extensive. Brother Diem and my father-in-law will likely end up as commoners. I will stay, if the French and the Emperor will allow it." He watched for her reaction. There was none. She had clearly measured the consequences of the big gamble.

She hesitated for a long moment before she decided to speak out, "What you have decided may be the right thing to do. I only have two points of concern: First of all, the timing for the Duke's second letter of resignation was wrong. He should have sent it in some time ago. None of us thought that the young Emperor would sack him, even under pressure from the French. But the Emperor has decided to make this resignation look like a dismissal."

Khoi muttered, "Very callous!" Hiep nodded, "That is the point. It is a very callous thing to do to the man who helped put his own father on the throne, to say, "Sorry, but I will have to fire you and four of your colleagues. I cannot allow you to resign according to your own schedule. As compensation, I will have Ngo Dinh Diem, your protégé, as Prime Minister. Please go away quietly, and I will keep my end of the bargain. I will even give you the title of Imperial Advisor." We have misjudged Bao Dai. Are we sure that there are not more serious errors in the rest of our plans?"

Khoi nodded and said, "I never thought that Bao Dai would consider dismissing my father-in-law after granting him the dukedom. Yes, we have been a bit too complacent. What is your second point of concern?"

Again, Hiep mused a long time before she replied, "Brother Diem has been educated to be a mandarin. He was continuously taught to show respect to traditions and the law. He was taught to be obedient. Father punished him each time he rebelled. We all criticized him when he was headstrong. Now, all of the sudden, he has to become a revolutionary. He is now expected to break away from rules and traditions, to fight the monarchy and the aristocracy. Who will teach him to organize an underground party and to mobilize the people?"

Khoi was pensive for a while. Then he said, "My father-in-law will help." She had been afraid that he would say that. She had heard reports of the Prime Minister's poor health. She believed that her brother, Khoi was just as capable as the Duke, so she simply asked him, "Will you help Brother Diem become a good revolutionary?"

Her question was as unnecessary as his own had been. "Will you pray for us?" Walking out of her garden, on the way back to his mother's house, he felt that somehow the burden in his heart had become much lighter.

*

The Emperor had decreed earlier that there would not be any kow-towing in front of him. So, the new Cabinet members, along with Ho Dinh Khai, who was the only survivor of the *May 2 Massacre*, went early in the morning to the Palace of Supreme Harmony (*Thai Hoa*) and did their obeisance to the empty Throne. Then they went to the Palace of Diligent Governance (Can *Chanh*) to meet with the Emperor.

Young Emperor Bao Dai

*

Pham Quynh who was Chancellor of the Imperial Secretariat and new Minister of Education, showed off by acquainting the new Cabinet members with the rituals to follow, the protocol to observe, and the way to address the Emperor.

It was Nguyen De, the new Private Secretary, who accompanied the Emperor. Pham Quynh frowned at him, as Nguyen De was a very close friend of Ngo Dinh Diem.

Diem spoke on behalf of his colleagues. He thanked the Emperor for his trust in them and said that he would implement the Emperor's vision of a Great Reform which would give the Imperial Court far more autonomy than before and have the French less directly involved with the administration of the country.

Though Diem's discourse was mild and his intentions vague, it was not well received. His colleagues sensed that he would soon start asking for reforms that the French were not ready to approve. The Emperor himself urged Diem to solve the administrative problems at hand before embarking on reform issues.

Diem seemed to be impervious to the concern felt by his colleagues who were more reluctant to confront the French. He continued to talk about reforms, reminding them that he had not only been appointed Prime Minister, but also the Secretary of the Joint Commission on Reform.

The Emperor, seeing that he could hardly stop Diem, became quite blunt and told Diem that any decision made by the Cabinet should be a collective decision. At that stage, Pham Quynh felt that it was necessary to warn Diem that reform measures should not be taken lightly and that advance consultation with the French was advisable.

Having tested the Emperor and the Cabinet members and seeing where they stood, Diem smiled and said he was sorry that he had led them into a tactical discussion while strategies had not yet been settled. He announced that he had talked with Leon Thibaudeau, and had been encouraged to submit a master plan for upcoming reforms as soon as possible.

With that he stood up, thanked the Emperor once more for the trust he had shown by choosing him as Prime Minister and on behalf of his colleagues bade farewell to his Majesty.

*

It was a long drive. Highway 1 was a paved highway and its maintenance was not bad, but it took them more than four hours to reach their destination, which was only a hundred kilometers north of Hue. They had decided to make an overnight stop at Cua Tung Beach after a visit to the seminary.

The An Ninh Seminary occupied more than a hundred acres of land. Tall and thick hedges of bamboo surrounded it. The two cars followed a long alley leading to the main buildings.

As their visit was unannounced, it took a few minutes before Father Superior Urutia came out to greet them. Thuc, in the meantime, had already begun showing them around. Diem and Can, as well as Hiep and Hoang had never been to the Seminary before and they were seized with fervent emotions. It was here that Ngo Dinh Kha, their father had studied. So many times they had heard their father tell stories about the place. It was also here that Thuc and Nhu had studied for years. It had been a mysterious place for the four of them who had never set foot there, until that moment.

Father Urutia was extremely pleased. Yet, he kept wondering what brought the new Prime Minster and his brothers and sisters here. Diem laughed, "Oh, this is an old tradition. You see, a new mandarin is supposed to go back to his village in his brocaded robe and celebrate with the villagers the honors newly conferred upon him by the Emperor. So we are on our way to Dai Phong, our village in Quang Binh. But we wanted to see together the place where our father, as well as our brothers, Thuc and Nhu had studied. That is why we decided to stop here."

Father Urutia smiled, "I will be honored to show you around, Your Excellency, but I understand that new mandarins usually announce their homecoming, days in advance. Have you announced your homecoming to anyone?" Again, Diem laughed, "To none, Father. I want to surprise everybody."

Hiep and Hoang looked at each other, thinking, "So. This is another of dear Brother Diem's pranks. Hiep remembered that all of the *boys*, Diem, as well as all her younger brothers Nhu, Can and Luyen, had been fond of playing all sorts of pranks as young children. She thought, "The villagers will be very upset because they have not been forewarned. Oh, they would love to make this homecoming the biggest event of their life! But he would not let them. Then what about the mandarins? They will be aghast." She had thought, when she got into the car that morning, that Diem had made the necessary announcements. Now she knew that he had done nothing of the kind.

She wondered if she should be angry with him. Then she smiled and said to herself, "If he had his homecoming in the usual way, people would forget about it after a few years, but this unusual, unannounced homecoming will be remembered forever."

They were invited into the parlor. Father Urutia pointed at the portraits on the wall and said, "I guess you recognize these two gentlemen." With affection, they looked at the large photos of their father and Nguyen Huu Bai.

They sipped tea and then were shown the immense orchards around the buildings, the various flower gardens, and the chapels hidden behind tall camellia trees, the large libraries containing precious collections of books that had been brought and left there by generations of missionaries.

They walked around the seminary, looking at the thick bamboo windbreaks. In many places, the windbreaks were a hundred feet thick. It was that wall of bamboo windbreaks that forty-seven years earlier had protected the seminarians and the Christians who had taken refuge there, against the attacks of *Van Than* militia. The militia could not, even after a three months' siege, enter the place and finally had to leave the seminarians and Christians alone.

*

Diem laughed happily. So many old memories came back to him as he watched the waves run from the deep blue sea towards the shore. The wind sang in the willows around them. Diem said, "We could have stayed at the seminary tonight, but our sisters would have been sent to the Sisters' House, which does not seem to be very comfortable. The Government guest houses are much more suitable."

Hoang immediately asked, "Why do the Sisters have to work so hard, and live in such discomfort? Why are seminarians treated better than the Sisters?" None of her brothers could give an answer.

Hoang went on, "Why should I be speaking of comfort, anyway? What does Brother Diem know about comfort? I've heard that you slept on a straw mat when you were Chief of the Province of Binh Thuan. Is it true?" Diem looked up and blushed, as he never wanted anybody to look into his ascetic lifestyle. He protested, "I never slept on a straw mat spread right on the floor." Hoang laughed, "So, you slept on a hard wooden bed covered with a straw mat, right?" Diem nodded, but added, "Look here, I tell you that hard beds are good for your back." Everybody laughed.

Hiep thought about a popular saying that prescribed, "Eat Chinese food, sleep in a French bed and marry a Japanese wife." French beds, with springs, mattresses and white cotton sheets had been around for quite some time. But of course, Diem had never tried the rich Chinese dishes nor did he adopt a French bed. He certainly was not about to marry a Japanese wife.

In the afternoon, Diem insisted on visiting the botanical garden, next to the Di Luan Church, created by Father Cadière, the famous biologist and scholar, and a close friend of Ngo Dinh Kha. They walked on endless paths where the French scientist and scholar had accumulated thousands of botanical species and varieties, until their clothes were drenched with the hot and moist air, their skins covered by the fragrance of weeds, herbs and flowers.

The sun had set now and the moon hung pale behind the willows. They enjoyed the exquisite beauty of the twilight. Hiep, looking at the golden sand and the deep purple sea, was afraid to move as if even a slight movement on her part would break the magic of the moment.

She knew that more trying times were coming and that between the major decisions her brothers would have to make; this moment was the only haven, the only respite. Pulling on her silk kerchief, looking up in the pale sky, she prayed fervently, "Some more moments like this one, please, a few more moments like this, for my brothers."

*

Diem stepped down from his car. Though it was early in the morning he had to find a refuge from the sun. His brothers and sisters followed him to the shade of a tall cotton tree by the roadside. At first, only a few children came, gathered around and looked at them with curiosity. Then some adults came to welcome the three gentlemen and the two ladies. They made inquiries as to what the gentlemen wanted. Diem said that he was the new Prime Minister, and that he and his brothers and sisters simply wanted to come back and see the village of their ancestors.

They knew that it was not a joke because they saw the golden badge hung on his brocade robe. Some of them had seen badges like that one worn by the district chief or the Chief of Province, during their official visits. But their badges had been made of ivory.

One, then two, then three of the adults finally understood and they started down the village shouting: "The Prime Minister is here! The Prime Minister is here!" Soon enough half the population of the village was in the street. Cousins and relatives stepped forward and introduced themselves. Then the mayor of the village invited the Prime Minister and his brothers and sisters to visit his humble abode.

Everybody in the village was tremendously excited. They could hardly believe that the Prime Minister had come home to his village without an escort. Some told the others anecdotes about Diem, concluding that he would be Prime Minister for the next thirty years.

While Diem and his group were sipping tea, the mayor sent for the head of Canton, who sent for the District Chief who in turn, sent for the Head of Prefecture. In a couple of hours everybody, including all of the hierarchy at the provincial level, had shown up. No one blamed Diem for arriving there unannounced. Everybody took his breach of protocol quite nicely.

Tents were set up in the mayor's garden first, then in front of the community hall. In a dazzle, the villagers organized the biggest feast of their lives. The chaotic movement of people, the din of drums, cymbals, gongs and human voices created an atmosphere of spontaneous festivity while long-stemmed parasols of all colors appeared from out of nowhere and surrounded the Prime Minster.

Diem was beaming with good humor. He had found his native village kind and generous to him. The villagers did not fear him. They were proud of welcoming a Prime Minister whose first thought had been for his village. The local dignitaries were also in festive mood. They did not see Diem's sudden foray into their territory as a threat, but rather as a promise. They hoped that Diem would give priority to his native province in the future.

After the long lunch, Diem and his brothers and sisters, accompanied by all those present, walked to the cemetery, up on the hills at a distance from the village. There rested the remains of most of the Ngo Dinh family members who had been killed in 1885. They had fled into the church during a raid of the *Van Than* militia. The militia had set fire to the church and more than three hundred Christians had perished.

Years later, Ngo Dinh Kha built a tomb for his father. He wanted his father to be buried like the Jews in Jesus' times. A large hole was dug into a rocky mound, and the coffin with the remains of his father was placed into the hole.

Standing in front of her grandfather's tomb with the graves of martyred Christians all around it, Hiep sadly remembered the stories of two centuries of religious persecution during which more than a hundred thousand Christians had been killed. She turned to look at her brothers and Hoang. There was also great sadness on their faces.

Walking away from the cemetery, Diem told her, "Without the help of the Buddhists, there would have been even more deaths among the Christians." Hiep nodded. She had heard stories told by Aunt Lien, one of the survivors of that fateful night in 1885.

It was during the time when Ngo Dinh Kha, her father, was studying in Penang at the major seminary there. In 1885, the mandarins in the Imperial Court decided to attack the French garrisons in Hue. The attack failed and they fled to the jungle, taking with them the Child-Emperor, Ham Nghi.

The *Can Vuong* movement was created with the mission to assist the Emperor in flight. The *van than* movement spontaneously emerged. *Van than* meant the *literati* and dignitaries. The *van than* movement included the most patriotic elements of the educated elite, leaders of local communities, and also the worst elements in a troubled society.

Both movements, without any valid reason, blamed the Christians for the failure in the attack against the French. Pushed by the worst elements among its membership, the *van than* militia organized murderous raids against the Christians. Dai Phong parish was the victim of such a raid.

On that fateful day, the parishioners, sensing danger, had taken refuge in the church. The militia placed haystacks around the church and set fire. The priest standing at the altar encouraged the people to pray, until he fainted.

Aunt Lien was only ten years old at the time. Adults threw children out of the church. Many were seen by the militia and thrown back into the blaze. But in the confusion and the smoke, some of the children rolled themselves into the surrounding darkness and ran for their lives. Lien ran to the home of a Buddhist family. They hid her for days until the militia was gone and she was safe.

Many of the Christians owed their lives to generous Buddhists during that fateful night. At the time of Diem's visit to Dai Phong, most of the remaining Ngo Dinh clan members were Buddhists.

On that joyful day in Dai Phong, Hiep never suspected that, only three decades later, her brothers would be accused of persecuting the Buddhists. She never suspected that one day many people would see political advantages in fueling a conflict between Buddhists and Christians.

On the way back, Thuc suggested that they make a side trip to Phuoc Mon, to see Duke Nguyen Huu Bai. Both Diem and Hiep shook their heads. For tactical reasons, it was better for Diem not to be seen with the old lion, unless a meeting was an absolute necessity.

*

Diem was very frustrated. He walked back and forth in the parlor, stopping from time to time to look at his sister, waiting for some reaction from her. Hiep knew that Diem needed Khoi's or Bai's advice, not hers. She recognized one of Diem's weaknesses. He needed a sounding board whenever he had to deal with a difficult problem. He needed a person who reacted to what he said and who clearly pointed out where he was right and where he was wrong.

She was concerned, because she knew that Diem would have to act alone sometimes. She knew that there would be times when he wouldn't be able to consult those he trusted, before he had to make a decision.

Now, Diem was confronted with a new set of problems: How should he proceed with the plans, when unexpected complications kept cropping up. First of all, Diem confessed, "I have not been skillful enough to avoid constant arguments with Pham Quynh, the Minister of Education, at the Council of Ministers meetings."

Hiep had heard about that. She looked at her brother quizzically for a while and said finally, "The reaction of the Vietnamese Ministers should not be the issue. Why do you have to argue so frequently with Minister Quynh? The plans are for you to submit to the French both reasonable and unreasonable demands. The reasonable demands may help ease up some of the French controls, if they are accepted. The unreasonable demands are to draw the French into an open conflict with you. The plans don't call for your acrimonious conflict with Minister Quynh or Minister Ho Dac Khai."

Diem considered what Hiep had said; he shrugged, "Who says I *want* to fight with them? Every time I open my mouth, they jump on me. They know how to get me irritated. They merely have to mention the need to give the French advance notice on whatever we want to discuss, and my blood starts boiling."

Hiep smiled, "Precisely! They know how to get you angry and forget your objective. Why are you so transparent? Why should you give importance to that childish game? Keep your mind clear for the drafting of the reform proposals."

Diem again showed his frustration, "I wanted the drafting of the proposal to be a dragged-out process, involving more and more public controversy, with leaks to the press, letter-writing campaigns and so on. But Leon Thibaudeau, the Acting Resident Superior, wants me to deliver a full draft of all the reform proposals as soon as possible. I guess, if I go that way, within a week, the draft will have been submitted and rejected and I will have to resign without even the possibility of making the public aware of what reforms I have been proposing and what the French have rejected."

Hiep knew that Diem simply wanted her to react to his own guessing game, she complied, "Look, put yourself in Mr. Thibaudeau's shoes. You would do exactly the same thing he is doing. By now, he has sensed what you are up to. He won't make matters easier for you."

Diem seemed to be surprised, "What did you say? You think that Thibaudeau has figured out *our* game plan?" Hiep nodded, "Even if you believe he hasn't, you must still operate as if he knows." Diem mumbled something to himself and sat down on the sofa.

Hiep inquired, "Did you give Thibaudeau any hint as to the major points of your reform proposals?" Diem nodded, "I had to. You see, I had no alternative but to give him a summary of my planned proposals."

He reluctantly added, "During our last meeting, after a few minutes spent on civilities, we sat for a quarter of an hour looking at each other in silence. He did not say a word to me, hoping to see me lose my calm. Probably, he was saying to himself, "If I stare at him in silence for a few more minutes, he will start sweating and give away all his plans." I kept calm, thinking that if I sat there saying nothing, he, as a Westerner, would feel the situation awkward, and would feel the need to say something to break the long silence. But neither of us said anything for fifteen minutes." Hiep laughed, "Fifteen minutes? You have found your equal there. What happened finally?"

Diem also laughed, "We were not alone, you know. The attendants on both sides, seeing that we were apparently struck by a fit of silent madness, were so nervous that I could distinctly hear their tense breathing. Finally a Frenchman said, "Maybe we should meet another day, when both sides are more ready to talk?" Hiep laughed until her ribs hurt.

Diem added, "I replied that there was no need to meet another day. I said I was ready to give my ideas in a nutshell." Thibaudeau frowned and replied, "What we need is an extensive briefing on your reform proposals but if you are not ready for such a briefing, then please proceed." I told him, "Reform proposals will be done in writing and will take time. I will have to consult with a great many people, before I can couch anything on paper. I understand that the process of drafting the proposal is to be a collective, collegial process." Thibaudeau nodded, and I went on, "I have a few basic ideas that I would like you to reflect on, and discuss with your superiors."

Hiep prodded him on, "What did you tell him?" Diem said, "I told him that I would propose that we endow the Joint Assembly of Representatives with real power. I said I would propose putting North and Central Vietnam together and that one single Resident Superior, not two, might be assigned to the united Vietnam. He looked on impassively as I told him I would recommend that the Imperial Court should have its own budget, independent from the French Indochina's budget, and that the French should observe the Treaty of 1885 and forgo any pretension of administrating directly any part of the united Vietnam."

Hiep was silent for a while. She knew that there was no way that the French would accept reforms based on such demands. The French would surely angrily reject the demands. She asked, "What did Thibaudeau say?" "Diem replied, "He listened attentively. He even took notes. After I finished, he thanked me for my basic concepts, promised that he would report back to Governor-General Pasquier then accompanied me and my attendants to the door."

Hiep again felt that the Frenchman was a respectable chess player. She wanted to warn Diem, to ask him to be cautious. But she knew that prudence or no prudence, both sides were limited in their possible moves, and that confrontation was inevitable.

Diem stood up and said, "I see that I need to move faster than I have planned. I think I should to go to Phuoc Mon and meet with the Duke immediately. I will write the reform proposals with him in Phuoc Mon. "

Hiep reminded him, "That will mean that you openly involve the Duke. When the French find out, and I know they will find out immediately, the Prime Minister will be completely identified with you and your reform proposals. Your fall will also be his fall."

Diem nodded, "I know. But haven't we agreed on that point already? I believe he wants to be identified with what I am going to propose. *Our reform proposals will be his swan's song.*"

Hiep again reminded Diem, "How do you plan for the conflict to be made public?" Diem laughed, "I will make a short trip to Saigon to talk to journalists there as soon as I send in my resignation, by mid-July."

Hiep sighed, "All my prayers are for your success. Please do not presume too much. There may be surprises on the way." Diem laughed, "There may always be surprises. I may die in the next hour. But trust me, Sister; everything we have planned for will work out all right. All we need are your prayers."

*

Nguyen Huu Bai watched Diem intently. So, all of his and his friend's hopes were resting squarely on the shoulders of this young man of thirty-two. Before Diem arrived, the Duke had received updated information about the French plans.

By then, Governor-General Pierre Pasquier had seen the extent of their folly when they accepted Diem as the Prime Minister. He told Thibaudeau, "Diem is a dangerous man, perhaps the most dangerous man among the *Annamites,* these days. *We have to destroy him.*"

Pasquier was engineering a plan to keep Diem busy with criticisms leveled against him by his own Vietnamese colleagues in the Cabinet. Diem's reform proposals could then be watered down until they looked ridiculous. Diem was to be kept in his position long enough, a couple of years perhaps, during which time, every one of his serious undertakings would be boycotted, so that he appeared at the end to be completely ineffective and even foolish in the eyes of the Vietnamese.

The Duke did not completely believe in his sources. He thought, "Maybe Pasquier knows our game plan in and out. Maybe he knows that Diem is about to resign. His planned strategy may have been invented, merely for our own confusion."

Looking across the table at Diem, for the first time, Nguyen Huu Bai felt very sad for Diem. "This is a young man, whose only goal in life is to gain the independence of his country," he thought. He mused on, "Yet the aim of his pursuit is so elusive, the success so improbable, that he could have tried to find the moon at the bottom of a water bucket, with the same result." He shook his head and tried to be optimistic. With effort, he joyously called out to the servants, "The Prime Minister will stay with us for the next three days. I want him to be well-fed and well cared for."

He told Diem, "We have already discussed everything in the minutest detail. Take your time to write down what we have discussed. Write only an hour at a time. When you are not writing, we will take a walk in my plantation. We will not discuss the draft of your reform proposals but instead we will make our plans for after your resignation. Do you agree?" Diem nodded. Once again, he felt that Nguyen Huu Bai was trying his best to take the place of his late father. He was moved and recognized that without the Duke, he would be feeling like an orphan indeed.

*

Governor-General Pierre Pasquier was more than annoyed. Diem did not engage in quarrels with his Vietnamese colleagues in the cabinet anymore. Whenever they started quarreling with him, he merely smiled and said that in spite of apparent differences, they were fundamentally in agreement. When they asked him to refer one matter or another to the French, he accepted their advice immediately.

Besides Diem's reform draft proposals, referrals for decisions, and his requests for advance approval piled up on Thibaudeau's desk. Thibaudeau threw up his hands; "I cannot understand the man anymore. He seems to be even more pliable than Pham Quynh is! The only problem comes from the reform draft proposals." Pasquier nodded, "What he is asking for amounts to more than mere autonomy. We have to stop him now!"

Thibaudeau replied, "We have to make a decision on how we are going to handle these reform proposals. They have been sitting here on my desk collecting dust." Pasquier said, "On all other matters, Diem seems to be more than ready to cooperate with us. Maybe we should persuade him to amend his reform proposals." Thibaudeau protested, "Do you think that I haven't already tried that?"

Pasquier answered, "Then it's my turn to try to persuade him." Thibaudeau again protested, "You are the Governor-General. You talk to the Emperor, not to the Prime Minister. Look at what happened when Governor-General Albert Sarraut talked to Nguyen Huu Bai." Pasquier smiled, "If I remember it well, Bai wasn't even the Prime Minister yet. In the end, Mahé was fired. Mahé was an Acting Resident Superior like you." His smile broadened, and he laughed with unconcealed merriment, "Are you afraid that after I meet with Diem, I'll fire you?"

Thibaudeau did not find the question funny. He said earnestly, "You want to persuade him to withdraw his reform proposals. What arguments do you plan to use to win him over?" Pasquier laughed, "His family has a real attachment to the monarchy. I'll talk about the need for his young monarch to be guided by a man with his integrity and prestige. I also know that he venerates his mother. I'll talk about his mother's old age and her need of comfort and costly medication. I hear that the man is vain. I'll flatter him."

Thibaudeau replied, with a trace of skepticism in his voice, "You may be right, sir."

*

It was raining cats and dogs. Pasquier, who had spent many years in Hue knew that it could go on raining for the next thirty days. He hated the persistent rain in Hue. Even those born in Hue complained about 'the rain that made the earth rot'. He stepped out of his car, and escorted by his chauffeur armed with a large umbrella, he walked to the gate of Ngo Dinh Kha's home and rang the bell.

From inside the house, Diem had seen the Governor-General's car arrive, with his flag flying. He asked his adjutant to go and open the gate. He himself came out to the verandah and waited for Pasquier.

The Governor-General shook hands with Diem and followed him inside. He insisted on offering his greetings to Mrs. Ngo Dinh Kha and sat down only after she had come and gone.

Diem said he was grateful for the respect the Governor-General had shown his mother. Pasquier explained that, like Albert Sarraut, he had a great respect for the late Grand Chamberlain. He said that in the long line of Governor-Generals, only Paul Beau who had been there when Emperor Thanh Thai was forced abdicate, and who had a hand in forcing the Grand Chamberlain to retire, did not understand the nobility of such a man. Diem did not know what to say, but he already begun to understand Pasquier's motive in visiting him now.

Playing for time, he undertook to describe his father's friendship with so many outstanding Frenchmen. He described his brothers' enthusiasm for the French culture, and confessed his own admiration for Joan of Arc,

Pascal and Marie Curie. Pasquier thanked Diem and expressed the wish to have Diem visit *la belle France.*

He was feeling quite confident now. He turned to the matter at hand. He said, "You know my desire to begin, with Emperor Bao Dai, a new era of cooperation between France and *Annam.* You are a man of integrity. You are incorruptible and visionary. We need you to help make our common dream a reality. I want reforms, the Emperor wants reforms, and you want reforms. Let us work together for the prosperity of *Annam* and the glory of France."

Diem answered, "That is the point I wish to raise with you. We all want reforms. Yet, my draft reform proposals have been sitting somewhere collecting dust for the last month. Please tell me when I am to receive a response."

Pasquier smiled charmingly. He looked Diem in the eyes and assured him, "Let me say that I have no objection to any of your reform proposals." Diem was stunned. He took a few sips of tea while watching the face of the Governor-General. Pasquier exuded good will. He went on, "Your Excellency, you have found the way to my heart. Each one of your proposals responds to one of my secret wishes."

Diem tried hard not to show astonishment. Pasquier asked him, "If I promise to accept all the reforms you recommend, will you consider me as a friend?" Sensing a trap, but not knowing what else to say, Diem conceded, "If you accept my reform proposals, I will be eternally indebted to you." Pasquier extended his hand and asked, "Are we friends?" Diem was totally confused. He had never refused to shake a hand extended to him. He shook hands with Pasquier but did not respond otherwise. He knew Pasquier was playing a cat and mouse game with him.

The Governor-General stood up as if he was ready to leave, and said, "I totally agree with your proposals. Let us work on their implementation together. I really believe that we can carry them all out. As a friend, however, let me say that I am a little worried about the scope of the work ahead of us. All the reforms will take at least five years to be implemented, possibly more. But you can count on my solid support. Please come to Hanoi next week. We will discuss the timetable. As long as the implementation lasts, you will be Prime Minister, and the first artisan of the reforms."

Now Diem fully understood how Pasquier had tricked him. He said, "Your Excellency has forgotten only one little detail. We Vietnamese can no longer wait. Five years, ten years are nothing in the course of our long history. But no Vietnamese today can wait that long to see the dawn of their freedom."

Pasquier sat down again. He saw that Diem was angry. He shook his head and told Diem, "People have told me that you are headstrong and over proud. You can see as clearly as I, that all the things you have proposed will take time to materialize. You want an independent budget for the Imperial Court? Fine, it will take a couple of years for you and me to figure out how to do it right. You want to put *Tonkin* back into the *Greater Annam?* Fine, but it will take at least a couple of years for us to unite the two regions. The French colonial administration has done what it could for *Annam.* Maybe we have gone too far in directly administrating the provinces. You want us to change that? Fine, but it will take time to train Vietnamese civil servants to replace French counterparts. Logically, reforms take time. We are no miracle workers, your Excellency, we are ordinary people."

Diem shrugged, "We want the reforms now, not later." Pasquier replied, "I am beginning to believe people who have been telling me that you are not at all interested in the reforms. They say you plan to confront us and make of your resignation as big a scandal as possible. I have dismissed those reports, until now."

Diem smiled, "If you approve those reforms I've proposed immediately, you will see whether I am genuinely interested in them or not."

Governor General Pasquier considered for a moment then his expression hardened. He put on another face as he said threateningly, stressing every word, "You should know that unless you withdraw your ridiculous claim for Vietnamese autonomy and other unacceptable demands, you will lose your position and your old mother will be without help."

Diem looked at him with incredulity in his eyes. He replied: "If I lose my honor, what good will I be for my mother? I must follow the instructions of my father who taught his children to do everything according to their conscience."

Over the next few days, Diem prepared articles and letters to be published in both the local press and the press in Paris. He was ready then to resign.

*

It was hardly five in the morning and the whole Citadel was still asleep. Diem was driven in his Citroen to the Citadel. From Phu Cam, the car crossed the An Cuu River into the French city. Diem wondered how long it would take the French Resident Superior to be advised of his resignation. The car now started to cross the Truong Tien Bridge. On the river, Diem saw oil lamps burning in the small boats of shrimpers. They had been working all night long, trying to catch shrimps in their small black nets.

The car veered now to the left and headed towards the Southeast Gate of the Citadel. In the early morning, the ramparts of the Citadel loomed tall and large, formidable defenses built *à la Vauban.* Again after entering the Citadel, the car turned left, towards the Imperial City. He stopped the car at the Hien Nhon Gate on the East Side of the Palace. There, Cao Xuan Tao, his Chief of Staff was waiting for him.

They walked together across the bridge that spanned a fairly large moat. The moat, which followed the crooks and nooks of the wall surrounding the Palace, had been originally designed as an additional feature of the Palace defense system. For decades, though, the moat had lost all of its military value. In the still water under the bridge, lotus flowers blossomed and the morning breeze carried wisps of their chaste and pervasive fragrance.

They walked past the Hien Nhon Gate. The half-awakened Imperial guards were quite surprised to see the Prime Minister arrive at that time in the morning A brief order was called out and two guards came running. They preceded Diem and his assistant, carrying two lit lanterns. In the weak light of the lantern, trees, pavilions, and palaces seemed to move and undulate in the dense mist around them. Diem knew the graveled road well and did not stumble, even though he did not watch where he put his feet as he walked. They headed straight towards the Audience Ground in front of the Thai Hoa Palace (Palace of the Greater Peace). The Palace was indeed peaceful at that time of the morning. It seemed completely deserted.

Diem asked his Chief of Staff to give him the round-shaped lacquered box that the latter had been keeping under his arm. Cao Xuan Tao ceremoniously handed the box over to the Prime Minister. He whispered, "I really don't know whether this is proper." It was perhaps the thirteenth time he had repeated the same remark. Diem smiled and said, "Don't worry. This is the best way."

Diem walked towards the Steps of the Throne. He bent down and laid the lacquered box containing his own official seal, his golden badge and his letter of resignation on the last step in front of the empty throne. He backed out into the Audience Ground and kneeling down, made obeisance three times in the direction of the empty throne. His assistant did the same. Then, they turned around and walked out of the Palace.

*

Nguyen De, the Private Secretary to His Majesty, smiled bitterly. He had known that sooner or later Diem would resign, but he had never thought that Diem would return the seal of the Prime Minster to an empty throne, like that. Diem knew the ancient ritual, of course! One used such a ritual, however, only when one wanted to show defiance. In ancient times, angry and defiant mandarins who resigned hung their seals on the flagpole in front of their offices, and left. Rarely, very rarely indeed, had a Minister used Diem's ritual of leaving his seal on the Steps to the Throne.

He was packing when the Emperor walked in. Surprised by Nguyen De's untidy office, the Emperor asked, "Are you going to move your office somewhere else?" Nguyen De replied, as calmly as he could, "No, Sire. I am packing, because I have to resign." The Emperor was intrigued. He looked at his Private Secretary in silence, waiting for an explanation. Finally Nguyen De told him about Ngo Dinh Diem's foray into the Imperial Palace earlier that morning to leave his Prime Minister's seal on the Steps to the Throne.

It took the young Emperor a moment to figure out what had happened. When he did, he angrily screamed at Nguyen De, "He is your friend. You are so proud of him. Look at the way he has insulted me! You are fired!" Softly but defiantly Nguyen De replied, "Too late, Sire, you will find my letter of resignation on your desk."

Bao Dai felt as if he had been slapped. He stormed out of his secretary's office and into his own. There on his desk, he found Nguyen De's letter: Out of loyalty to his friend, Ngo Dinh Diem, Nguyen De's letter said, he regretted that he had to submit his own resignation to the Emperor.

Bao Dai sat down heavily, feeling tired. After a while, he called Nguyen De in and calmly told him, "Listen, go and ask Diem to come to see me one last time. We cannot act this way, like characters in a tragedy. We have to be reasonable." Nguyen De indicated that he would comply. He said, "Before I go, would your Majesty read Diem's resignation letter first?"

The letter was in the same lacquered box, which also contained Diem's seal and his golden badge. Bao Dai broke the seal of the letter and read. The more he read, the more he was moved by the tone. Diem was not defiant. He said that he was resigning because his nature and character did not agree with the times and because conditions were not there for him to effectively serve his Emperor and his country.

Turning to Nguyen De, he urged, "Please, go and get him to come today. This is all a terrible misunderstanding." Nguyen De said, "It is no misunderstanding, Sire. The Prime Minister cannot work without the full support of Your Majesty. He knows that he does not have your full support."

Irritated, Bao Dai replied, "He can tell me, face to face."

*

The meeting was longer than Diem expected. The young Emperor genuinely wanted him to stay on as Prime Minister. He tried to convince Diem to be more patient and willing to accept compromises.

Diem did not want to hurt the Emperor's feelings anymore than he had already done. He wanted, however, to make the Emperor understand that his decision to resign was irrevocable. The Emperor tried everything. He analyzed the situation in France, and the liberal trends in French politics that were favorable to the colonies' liberation.

He analyzed the composition of Diem's Cabinet and said that its members were not fundamentally opposed to Diem. He said that they were afraid of

Diem's impetuosity, that even people like Minister Pham Quynh were ready to collaborate with him, if only he would show more flexibility.

Diem finally stood up and said, "The times are not favorable to my plans. I do not blame anybody, least of all Your Majesty. I appreciate your friendship, but my conscience dictates what I have to do. It tells me I have to go. You are not free to do what you would like to do. Even if you wanted to give my reforms your full support you would not be allowed to do that. If you really supported me, both of us would end up in exile. No, really, I have to find other ways to serve our country."

Bao Dai asked, "Some people say that if I fired Minister Pham Quynh, you would stay. Is that the case?" Diem shook his head, "No, Sire, you have been misled there. Indeed, Minister Pham Quynh and I have gotten into many arguments. But he is not my chief concern. The problem we have, both you and I, is the French rule, not differences we may have with our fellow-countrymen."

Bao Dai nodded and said, "I regret that I have failed to convince you to stay. Take good care of yourself. A man with your integrity is rare in our time. Remember that some day, when the situation is right, your Emperor may once again call on you."

*

Diem had no idea of what was to happen next. His last meeting with the Emperor had been so friendly that he was lulled into a false sense of security. He even feared that his resignation would not be a scandal at all.

He did not expect the Emperor's decree demoting him to commoner, stripping him of all his ranks and titles and banning him to the province of Quang Binh. Surprised as he was, he did not need any explanation for the harshness of Bao Dai's measures.

He knew that the young Emperor got his orders from Governor- General Pasquier who had read countless articles in the local and Parisian press describing the thwarted reforms, criticizing him for his lack of good will, and calling for his demotion or transfer. Other articles recommended the return of Varenne as Governor-General and Yves Châtel as Resident Superior. The Governor-General guessed with good reason, that the articles had either been written by Diem or at least inspired by him.

Nguyen Huu Bai smiled without bitterness when he also received an Imperial Decree stripping him of the functions of an Imperial Advisor, all his ranks and titles, taking away all his medals and honors and confining him to the province of Quang Tri.

Nguyen De did not escape the ax either. A proud man, De declared that he was honored to have received the same treatment as Diem and Bai.

Khoi survived the disaster. But he was firmly advised not to go to Hue, Quang Tri, or Quang Binh to confer with his brother or his father-in-law.

For months, the scandal caused by the resignation of Prime Minister Ngo Dinh Diem would not die, and the vengeance wrought on him and his friends by the French only helped to make martyrs of them.

Even the Great Patriot, Phan Boi Chau, sent Diem a poem praising his courage and integrity. Using the simplest terms, Phan Boi Chau wrote:

Under the skies of Vietnam, there is such a man, nobody knew,

Suddenly one hears a shattering blast like the explosion of thunder,

A thousand teals of gold are for him as light as wild geese feathers,

The highest position for him is no more valuable than an old sandal,

He has showed to heaven his luminous courage,

To the world of darkness, he has showed his contempt.

If one day, he achieves his destiny,

I will be happy to follow him as his horse groom.

Various groups of patriots now were ready to rally to Diem. Nguyen Huu Bai's scheme had worked perfectly. Diem was riding high in public opinion and the French officials who had forced Diem to resign, understood in the end that they were the losers in the contest.

*

Nobody foresaw that only two months later, Governor-General Pasquier would die in a plane crash near Paris. The new Governor General René

Robin and the new Resident Superior, Maurice Graffeuil, agreed to restore Nguyen Huu Bai's and Ngo Dinh Diem's ranks and titles.

Neither Bai nor Diem gave much attention to the French officials' new decision. They had accepted becoming known as commoners and the ranks and titles that had been taken away and now given back to them, were not what they were after.

Nguyen De also recovered his rank. Contrary to popular belief, De did not break away from Diem; though the French tried to convince De that Diem did not deserve his loyalty. They told De that while he had acted in good faith and in all sincerity with Diem, the latter had betrayed him by excluding him from his plot. They pointed out to him that Diem had never shared with him any of his secret plans.

De continued to be Diem's friend. Four years after Diem had resigned as Prime Minister, De became a Christian. All the Ngo Dinh brothers, Khoi, Thuc and Diem stood at the baptismal font and became godfathers of De's sons.

It was much later that De became very involved with French financiers and plantation owners. He became a trusted friend of the French elite in Indochina and regained favor with Emperor Bao Dai. After being one of Diem's closest friends, he gradually drifted away from him.

Yet, even after an unhappy episode when Ngo Dinh Nhu broke up with De's sister and married Tran Thi Le Xuan instead, and after De declared that he had had enough of the Ngo Dinh family, both De and Diem knew that their friendship had never ended. Neither De nor Diem knew that their old friendship would again emerge, in spite of everything, and affect in a major way, their diverging lives and their country.

*

Diem retired to Phu Cam and by all appearances, led the quiet life of a retired Prime Minister. He was not forced to return to the life of a farmer, like his father had twenty-six years earlier, as he benefited from a full pension. He had the means and the time to read, to take photography as a serious hobby, to practice horticulture for enjoyment, and to take long walks to the mountains, the Imperial Tombs, the churches and pagodas, and to the Citadel.

The quiet former Prime Minister was, however, a revolutionary. He made frequent visits to the Duke of Phuoc Mon. The Duke and Diem took long walks together in the plantation in Phuoc Mon. Diem was happier than ever before. He knew no stress. He had the best mentor in the world and both of them took pleasure in the solitude of the Duke's retirement home. Leisurely, they developed their work plan.

The Duke whose intervention in the trial of Phan Boi Chau, back in 1925, was decisive in saving the life of the Great Patriot, knew many discreet ways to communicate with him, though Phan Boi Chau was watched day and night by a horde of spies. He gave his contacts to Diem, who had also greatly impressed the Great Patriot with his resounding resignation. Phan Boi Chau was sincere in his admiration for Diem, as testified to by the poem that he gave Diem in July 1933.

Being watched by the French Secret Service, the Great Patriot knew he could not personally do much for Prince Cuong De, whom he represented in Vietnam. He was more than happy to shift the burden to Diem; therefore, soon after his resignation, Diem became the official representative of the Rebel Prince in Vietnam.

Various revolutionary elements in the country recognized Prince Cuong De as their *minh chu,* or enlightened leader. Diem, over the years, very discreetly entered into contacts with all of them. At the Imperial Court, now that he was no longer a competitor, his former colleagues gave him the benefit of the doubt and became friendlier with him and his family. With only a few exceptions, the aristocracy in Hue, the rich landlords in the South and members of the Northern elite, were no longer fighting him, but tried to find ways to help him. He was in an enviable position indeed.

*

One year after Diem had resigned; an event shook the Catholic community in Vietnam. Emperor Bao Dai married Jeanne-Mariette Nguyen Huu Thi Lan, and named her Empress Nam Phuong (*Perfume of the South*), breaking the most entrenched taboo of the Nguyen Dynasty.

Empress Nam Phuong

*

Indeed, no Nguyen Emperor had ever named an Empress, among their living wives. Jealous of their power, the Emperors did not want to have a somewhat equal consort. Moreover, they, like all the Chinese and Vietnamese Emperors before them, feared the influence of the Empress' relatives.

Throughout Vietnam's history, in too many instances, relatives of an Empress had become so powerful that they oppressed the Emperor or eliminated him. To make sure that no such dire eventualities took place, the Nguyen Dynasty had said 'No Empress.' Such a title could only be bestowed after either the Emperor or the Empress had died.

Emperor Bao Dai broke another dynastic taboo by elevating an uncle of the Empress to the rank of Prince. Le Phat An, the Empress' uncle was made Prince of An Dinh.

Before it took place, the projected marriage between the Emperor and the future Empress had created a major controversy. The Office of the Imperial Clan formally opposed the marriage, claiming that it might someday put on the throne a Catholic prince.

The Vatican, unwilling to allow a mixed marriage that would not guarantee the baptism of the couple's children, was adamant in its demand that the Emperor sign an assurance guaranteeing that all his children would be baptized.

For the Imperial couple, it was love at first sight. The Emperor was ready to sign anything in order to receive permission to marry his imperial fiancée. A compromise was made, in the end. The religious wedding ceremony was celebrated in secret and the assurances given by the Emperor were also put under the seal of secrecy.

But the people knew. The Catholic Empress charmed everyone who came near her and the imperial couple won the admiration and the affection of most of the people. However, there were always critics who pointed out the fact that if a male infant was born from that union, he might one day become the first Catholic Emperor in Vietnam's history.

In January 1936, a son was born. He was baptized secretly. Three years later, breaking another taboo of the Nguyen Dynasty, Emperor Bao Dai made Bao Long the Crown Prince.

The Empress shocked the conservatives in the country by her simple manners and her straight talk. She went to Mass every Sunday at the Phu Cam Cathedral and did not hesitate to mingle with the people at the end of the Mass. In years when the crops failed, she personally went to the hungry people. She organized lunches and dinners to feed them in her presence.

What irritated the conservatives the most were her frequent talks about women's rights, women's needs and women's education. Unlike the Emperor, who during his years of studies in France forgot how to speak Vietnamese fluently, the Empress, who had returned to Vietnam every summer during her years of overseas education, spoke Vietnamese elegantly and charmed most of her audiences, old and young.

Soon, it was known in the Capital that among the written assurances given by the Emperor was his pledge to allow the Empress to advise him on State affairs and to take an active role in ruling the country. She did not seem too eager to take advantage of those prerogatives, yet she liked to make speeches.

She visited girls' colleges, calling on them to stand up and fight for their rights, to demand equality in education, and the right to have a public life. Response to her pleas varied, but without a doubt, she deserved to be recognized as one of the first feminists in Vietnam's modern history.

Sometimes, after the Sunday mass, the Empress dropped by to see Mrs. Ngo Dinh Kha. She never stayed long. She rarely talked to Diem, though he was always there. They were great nodding acquaintances. Her kind words to his mother during those years made Diem her admirer for life.

Diem, who had been a diehard conservative, was mesmerized by her feminism. She broadened his horizon and made him aware of the great potential of Vietnamese women. Slowly, Diem became open to more liberal ideas and attitudes. Years later, he recognized the influence that the Empress' endeavors had on him. When Tran Thi Le Xuan, or *Madame Nhu*, introduced feminist legislation and scandalized her male colleagues in the Parliament, Diem stood by her, partly because of that influence from the Empress.

*

In July 1935, the Duke of Phuoc Mon gave a big dinner at his mountain retreat, to celebrate the Episcopal Ordination of Bishop Ho Ngoc Can, the second Vietnamese priest to be named Bishop. The Duke was particularly happy because he had been most instrumental in the creation of a Vietnamese hierarchy. In 1922, during his visit to the Vatican, Bai had pleaded with the Pope for the appointment of Vietnamese Bishops. Eleven years later, Nguyen Ba Tong was the first Vietnamese priest to become

Bishop. Ho Ngoc Can's appointment followed Tong's closely. The Duke of Phuoc Mon was exhausted by the preparations for the celebrations and caught cold during the dinner. He soon became seriously ill and was transported to the Central Hospital in Hue. Diem was at his bedside most of the time. The Duke decided not to call back his son who was studying in France. He said that Diem was the one he wanted to have at his bedside.

The Duke felt that he did not have too much time left. He spent all his waking hours telling Diem what he knew about people and places, books he had read, ideas he had come by, and stratagems he had tested. Laboriously, he transferred to Diem's memory all his lifetime's experience.

He passed away peacefully on July 28, 1935, at the age of seventy-two, and Diem mourned for him like a son mourns for a father. The Emperor decreed a day of national mourning and ordered the flags to be flown at half-mast, including the one on the Flag Monument in front of the Noon Gate. At his funeral, Prime Minister Thai van Toan and Resident Superior Graffeuil read two separate funeral speeches, extolling the Duke's virtues and achievements. Bishop Chabanon said a solemn funeral Mass at the Phu Cam Cathedral. Then a convoy took the remains of the Duke to Phuoc Mon. The next day, after another blessing by Bishop Ho Ngoc Can at the Phuoc Mon Parish Church, the Duke was buried on a hill next to his residence.

*

It had been a long day. Now they all sat a few meters away from the fresh grave. They were on the grass inside the encircling wall of the tomb site. None of them wanted to talk while the last sunlight was slowly fading way. A maid had come to light the four lanterns nearby in the pavilion, which sheltered the grave. As dusk descended, the light from the lanterns became brighter.

The fragrance of ylang-ylang and magnolia surrounded them. Finally Khoi said, "He was a wonderful man." Hoa, still with swollen red eyes, echoed her husband's remark, "Yes, he was a wonderful man. But like your father he was all eaten up inside with hidden anger. How could he not be angry when he felt so helpless in the face of the misery of the people and the shame of the country?"

Diem said pensively, "He died so peacefully, though. I remember how Emperor Khai Dinh died. You know, at the time I was Head of the Prefecture of Hai Lang. One day I received a visit from a eunuch. He wanted me to go with him to offer a big gift to Our Blessed Lady of La Vang, in the name of the Emperor who was very sick at the time. We went together to the Sanctuary to pray."

"The eunuch asked me to light candles for the Emperor in front of the statue of the Virgin. We lit seven candles together. But then, a cold gust of wind blew past us and extinguished all seven candles. The eunuch trembled and said, 'What a terrible omen!' He asked me, 'How should I report to His Majesty?' I said, 'Tell His Majesty that we did pray for him and we lit seven candles.' A few days later, the Emperor died in terrible convulsions. The offerings at pagodas, temples and churches did not give him a peaceful death."

Few of the men who were there that night would die peacefully. They did not know what their future held. Only Ngo Dinh Thuc and Ngo Dinh Luyen died in their beds. Khoi, Diem, Nhu and Can, as well as Khoi's son, Huan, were all to suffer a violent death.

In the silence that followed Diem's words, they sat watching the shadows move around them as the lanterns swayed in the light breeze. Hiep remembered all the times she had spent with Nguyen Huu Bai from the time she was a baby. Those were precious moments when Bai and her father had allowed her to listen to all their conversations. She had been their silent partner, their silent listener.

Even after her father's death, Nguyen Huu Bai never tried to exclude her from his meetings with Diem and Khoi. On the contrary, sometimes he expressly asked her to be present. For more than thirty years, she had felt Bai's eyes on her. She had learned so much from him, almost as much as she had learned from her own father.

Nguyen Thi Tai, the Duke's youngest daughter, suddenly broke the spell and said, "Father enjoyed all kinds of honors and had a meaningful life. Yet, he was never happy. I've thought about this for a long time. I am going to enter the Order of the Carmelites."

Enter the Order of the Carmelites! All of them were stunned. She was so beautiful, so accomplished in everything. Now she was telling them that she wanted to live in a cloister where the most severe discipline was observed!

For years, there had been rumors that the Duke had wanted Diem and her to marry. All of them turned and looked at Diem. He frowned and his eyes became sadder than usual, but he did not say anything. A moment passed. The first star appeared in the dark sky. They all saw Diem and Tai look up at the star in at the same time, then turn to look at each other.

Hiep closed her eyes and said a quick prayer, which was never answered.

*

The tall priest came in unannounced. He was the son of the late Minister Nguyen van Mai, the one who had, with the encouragement and support of Emperor Thanh Thai, built the National Institute with Ngo Dinh Kha. Father Nguyen Van Thich was a convert, a late convert. He had discovered Christianity as an adult, and though his father was a fervent Buddhist, he had decided to change his religion.

He had become a priest by sheer will power. Now he was Diem's confidant and his trusted link with the Great Patriot Phan Boi Chau. The priest, who was more than six feet tall, had gained the favor of the French who saw him as a talented poet and calligrapher. They never suspected that he was the liaison between Phan Boi Chau and Diem.

Diem, who was disconsolate after the death of the Duke of Phuoc Mon, was dealt another harsh blow when Bishop Allys, a friend of the family, died only a few months later. Bishop Eugene Allys, whom the Vietnamese affectionately called Father Ly, had been blind for a couple of years. But even his blindness did not stop him from being one of Diem's most valuable advisers. Diem had gone to see the retired bishop almost every day. They talked about the past and about the future. The bishop believed that Europe was going to experience another big war, and told Diem that the future European conflict would give the Vietnamese the best opportunity to reclaim their independence.

Though honored by the colonial administration in many ways, Bishop Allys had become an ardent advocate for Vietnamese freedom. His death, like Nguyen Huu Bai's was a devastating blow to Diem.

Now he hurried to meet with Father Thich. The priest looked at Diem, sensing his grief. He asked, "Are you going to be all right?" Diem was embarrassed that his emotional state was so apparent. But, Father Thich was a very close friend, so he replied without too much reticence, "Except for the fact that I haven't been able to eat or sleep for the last couple of days, I think I'm alright."

Father Thich was concerned. He shrugged and said, "Everybody dies, you know, including you. I have something here that may warm your heart." He pulled a piece of paper out of the pocket of his cassock. Diem was curious now. He asked, "What's that?"

Father Thich replied, "A poem written by the Old Man in Ben Ngu. That was what the priest used to call Phan Boi Chau. Diem asked again, more intrigued: "What is the poem about?" Father Thich unfolded the paper and showed it to Diem, a poem entitled 'Mourning Old Father Ly (Allys)'."

Diem held the poem in his hand. Only a man like Phan Boi Chau would do something so audacious! The Great Patriot was a pure Confucian. To write a poem to mourn for a Christian Bishop was already out of the ordinary. But the Bishop he mourned was also a Frenchman, and the French had kept Phan Boi Chau under house arrest for the last eleven years.

Diem asked, "What are we to do with the poem?" Father Thich said, "The Old Man in Ben Ngu said he wished you to read it at the funeral, and have it published it afterwards."

Diem thought for a while and said, as if to himself, "Phan Boi Chau wants all of the Vietnamese to know that he does not hate the French. He does not want the Vietnamese to hate the French either. He also wants to say that it does not matter if one is Confucian or Buddhist or Christian. A good man is a good man; an evil man is an evil man regardless of his race or his religion." Father Thich smiled, happy that Diem had understood the point of the poem.

Diem went on, "Please go and tell the Great Patriot that I will be honored to read his poem at the funeral of Father Allys and that we will publish it in all the papers we know."

A little later, Diem showed the poem to his sister. Hiep read it and said that the poem was perfect for the occasion. She was worried though, when Diem said he was to recite the poem at the funeral. Though she knew that Diem wrote poetry, she also knew that he would have a hard time reciting a poem properly. Even in his leisure, when he recited a poem to her, she thought that the poem would improve markedly if somebody else recited it.

Now, at the funeral of Father Allys, Diem would be struggling with his emotions. He would simply 'massacre' the poem of the Great Patriot. She sat down and asked Diem to practice reading it. Slowly, Diem improved his recitation. Embarrassed at times, laughing at his mistakes, he learned to recite it almost correctly. Before she left, Hiep told him, "You still need to practice some more." Diem threw up his hands and confessed, "I have tried my best. Now I understand why you have asked me not to read my poems to you."

Hiep walked away relieved. Diem was no longer as depressed as he had been during the last few days. Sadly she remembered the times she had spent with the old Bishop. She smiled to herself as she recalled what the French priest had said to her and her sister, Hoang, a long, long time ago. Pointing at their red and violet gowns, he had said, "How come I, a mere parish pastor, have the honor of receiving, week after week, the visit of a cardinal and a bishop?" As far as a cardinal, there was nothing in view yet, but, what about bishops? Her brother, Thuc, was about to become one.

CHAPTER ELEVEN
THUC BECAME A BISHOP

On January 6, 1938, on the Feast of Epiphany, Ngo Dinh Thuc was appointed Bishop of Vinh Long.

For the family, his elevation in the Church had an extraordinary meaning. The Ngo Dinh family had now achieved both political and spiritual leadership. Though two other Vietnamese had been appointed as Bishops before Thuc, they were elevated to the rank of Bishop as coadjutors, that is, as potential successors of a European Bishop.

Thuc was the first Vietnamese Bishop to be appointed to a vacant see, to immediately administer his own diocese. The family rejoiced with all the Church in Vietnam. Hiep spent hours with her mother, watching the radiant joy on her face. Diem became loquacious. He talked to Hiep about the future with renewed enthusiasm, as if he saw in Thuc's appointment, encouragement from God for what he was attempting to do

One day, Hiep and Hoang were talking in the garden of their mother's home, when Thuc came in. He saw them and waved, signifying that he wanted to come and talk with them where they were.

Hiep observed him as he was approaching. Thuc looked physically different. He had aged overnight. He was radiant and yet, he looked a little tired and bewildered, like he had just returned from a long journey. Hoang asked him, "When are you going to be ordained Bishop?"

It was a simple question, yet Thuc did not answer immediately. He started walking with his two sisters under the shade of the fruit trees. Finally, he answered, "According to current practice, a bishop is to be ordained only on Sundays or on the feasts of Apostles. I have asked for an exception to

191

the rule, *an exemption*." He stopped, searching for words. His sisters were silent. As he had started his little speech with some strong emotion, they did not want to interrupt him, though they could not guess the reason for his emotion. They waited for him to tell them about the exemption.

After a while, Thuc went on, "We all venerate Mother. *She is a saint.* All of us can bear witness to her simplicity, her modesty, and her immense faith in God. She raised nine children, at times in the worst situations. Yet, each one of us has received from her the best care, the best religious instruction." He smiled and added; "I have always seen her as a saint and myself as a sinner. I have drawn a parallel between us and St. Monica and St. Augustine before his conversion."

Hiep intervened, "Please do not exaggerate. I cannot imagine that you have sinned the way St. Augustine did in his youth." Thuc laughed then shook his head, "No, I have not sinned like he did and certainly I will not be a saint like he was afterwards. What I mean is, I always have a strong feeling that without Mother's constant prayers for me, I would have ended badly. That is why I have asked for an exemption. I want to receive my Episcopal ordination on the feast of St. Monica, or May 4, in honor of Mother."

Hiep looked at her brother for a long moment. She had not been very close to Thuc during their childhood. Her father had drawn her into a small circle with Khoi and Diem and had talked to them more and more separately from the rest of the children. Thuc himself left the family home at the age of thirteen to enter the seminary. She had not known Thuc very well.

It was only after his return from Rome, when she needed to talk about Xuan's death and about Thuan's future that she had become closer to him. But even then, she felt that he was different from her and from her brothers, Khoi and Diem.

Now, he was not talking about himself, but about their mother; she felt as if for the first time, they had really connected. She was struck by the fact that all of them, brothers and sisters, thought and felt pretty much the same way and even looked very much alike physically.

All of a sudden she had an unfounded premonition that Thuc, for better or for worse, would play a major role in the political fortune of their family.

She tried to forget that ridiculous thought. "Come on", she said to herself, "a Bishop in politics?"

*

The celebrations were elaborate. Knowing that Diem was not a man for detail, Thuc looked after everything himself. Khoi was to make only a short appearance on the day of the ordination. The French *advice* for him to stay away from Diem was still valid.

Giao, their eldest sister, Hiep and Hoang were there to help, but it was Thuc who looked after every little detail. Hiep watched as Thuc made the plans for the ceremonies, checked on the invitation lists, tried on the vestments, and discussed the menus. Hiep regretted that Khoi could not be there to organize the celebrations. He would be as decisive as Thuc, but he would not let himself be bothered with every minute detail, like Thuc was.

Everything went well, however, including the ordination itself, presided over by the Apostolic Delegate Anton Drapier. The family, so highly honored on the political front, could now also be proud of Thuc's elevation on the religious scene. Hiep looked on. Something was bothering her. "It is too much", she realized finally. "My family has received too many blessings from God. Will we some day, have to pay the price for so much solicitude?"

Throughout the celebrations, Hiep watched her mother who glowed with joy and pride. She showed her pride without any reservation. Even when Diem was made Prime Minister, she had not been as proud.

During his speech at the banquet at the Providence Institute, Thuc repeatedly called Mrs. Ngo Dinh Kha *'my holy mother'*, with tears in his eyes. Once his mother leaned on Hiep and whispered, "Now, I can die without regret." Hiep was startled by her mother's words, but she understood well what her mother was feeling.

Even Hiep's father had wanted to be a priest. Only the massacre of his family in 1885 by the *van than* militia, and the urgings of his professors in Penang prompted him to leave the seminary and found a family. Nhu had been at the seminary for eight years before he abandoned the priesthood. Only Thuc persisted to the end and became a priest.

His elevation to bishop was also a matter of national pride. The new Vietnamese Bishops were ending the long centuries of having only French and foreign bishops in Vietnam.

Watching her mother's joy and pride, Hiep wished her father were there. Then she corrected herself. "Of course, Father is right here with us today," she thought, and her eyes filled with a mist of tears.

*

After the public ceremonies, the family assembled. Ngo Dinh Nhu, who had recently graduated from the prestigious *Ecole des Chartes* in Paris, had finally returned to Hue. He missed the Episcopal ordination, but was there for the final family photo session. Nhu's arrival added another note of joy He was the first Vietnamese to have graduated from that elite school. For the first time in years, all nine children of Ngo Dinh Kha were together again.

With Nhu's arrival, Mrs. Ngo Dinh Kha could barely contain her joy. She remembered how she had cried the day Luyen, the youngest of her children, had graduated as an engineer from the *Ecole Centrale des Arts et Manufactures* in Paris and had returned home, only two years earlier.

Luyen had been so spoiled by her that on his deathbed, Ngo Dinh Kha had asked Khoi to swear that he would send the eleven-year-old boy to France, as soon as possible.

The day Luyen came back from France, his mother could still see the baby in him. With all the joy he brought back to her with his return, she could still feel the agony of the moment he had left for France. Holding his hands, she remembered the sleepless nights that she had spent in her bed, wondering how a twelve-year-old boy could possibly survive in a foreign land without his family. She remembered the emptiness that weighed on her for the longest time after he was gone.

Now, Nhu was back, strong and handsome. Nhu did not seem to have been as Europeanized as his younger brother had. While Luyen constantly stunned his brothers and sisters with his words and his thoughts, constantly challenging them to think and act like *modern persons*, Nhu appeared more comfortable with the traditional way of life.

To his mother, and his brothers and sisters, Khoi offered a treat: He had produced a color movie of his Quang Nam Province and wanted to show it to them.

Hiep sat in the dark and watched her eldest brother on the screen. The color was not fantastic, but it was the first time she had seen a movie in color. She smiled as she watched Khoi ride past on horseback, with a large straw hat on his head. He was at that time still the Governor of Quang Nam, but he had also been named Viceroy of all of the south-central provinces. As she watched him, she remembered the happy days that she had spent with his family and Diem in Hoi An. She wondered when she would make a trip to Hoi An again.

*

She was not to go to Quang Nam but instead traveled to Vinh Long. Her mother wanted her and Hoang to go and have a look at the arrangements that had been made for Thuc in his diocese. She had also heard about a certain good party for Luyen in Cho Lon, the Chinatown of Saigon, and asked her daughters to go and visit with the young lady's family, to see whether it would be a good match.

Hiep and Hoang were very happy to go to Vinh Long. They were not so sure about the mission in Cho Lon. *Modernized* as he was, Luyen would not be willing to accept an arranged marriage, they thought.

Yet, Luyen had constantly surprised everybody. Having graduated from one of the *grandes écoles in* France, and being a close friend of Emperor Bao Dai since childhood, Luyen could acquire any position he liked, if he waited a little for a good opening. Luyen did not wait. He took a decent, but not terribly important job at the Land Survey Service. He astonished everybody by displaying an incredible enthusiasm for his work. He spent days in torrid sunshine, or in the rain, mapping a hill, surveying the course of a river, and spending all of his time in the open.

Europeanized as he was, he was very shy with women. When Hiep and Hoang told him about Lucie Nguyen Thi Danh in Cho Lon, he turned red and would not say anything. His sisters understood then that he would not object to his marriage being arranged. They kept teasing him until he admitted that he would appreciate very much if his sisters would go and have a look at Lucie. In September, Hiep and Hoang went south on their delicate mission.

*

It was the first time Hiep and Hoang had traveled so far from home. They traveled by train from Hue, and enjoyed the scenic route the train followed. They had heard Diem and Khoi talk about the emerald sea. Now for the first time they saw the enchanting gulfs and bays of the south central provinces, the dark rocky promontories, the white sand beaches and the primeval jungles that touched the train at every turn.

Hiep and Hoang had grown up together. Hiep was only two years older than Hoang, who had married one of Am's cousins. It was an opportunity for them to relive their childhood together, reminiscing about the time when the family was poor and they each had only one dress. Hoang was more assertive than Hiep. She ran her household. She kept the purse strings at home, and was capable of advising her husband on his business deals. Hiep had no such ambition. She ran her household but would not consider being the household treasurer. She never gave advice to her husband in his prosperous construction business.

Hoang, however, said that she would play second fiddle on their mission south. She said that Hiep would have to play the main role and report back to their mother. So, it was with some trepidation that Hiep went to the Bishop's house in Vinh Long and then to Cho Lon, to make sure about the young lady who could possibly become her sister-in-law.

In Vinh Long, the Catholics of the diocese were still in a festive mood, when the two sisters arrived. Thuc was the first Vietnamese Bishop they had seen; in fact, he was only the third Vietnamese to be appointed bishop nation-wide. It was with national pride that they celebrated his arrival.

Rich landlords and poor tenant farmers alike wanted to show the new pastor their pride and contentment, even though he was not a Cochinchinois or Southerner. Hiep and her sister were favorably impressed by the arrangements that had been made for the new bishop's comfort. After a few days spent in Thuc's company, they were ready to go on to Saigon-Cholon.

Hiep told Hoang, "In Hue, we use the phrase *'fields over which a stork can fully stretch its wings'* to describe large estates. Actually we have never seen such an estate in all Central Vietnam. Here, in South Vietnam, especially in the Mekong River deltas, the fields stretch endlessly. I never thought that I would one day see such immense fields."

Hoang became thoughtful, she replied, "Maybe all the people in Hue should come here to have a look at these immense estates. The small size of our estates may contribute to the narrow-mindedness of so many of our people in Hue." Hiep was not in complete agreement with Hoang, but she understood what Hoang was trying to say. Some Hueans, conditioned by their continual struggle for survival in a relatively difficult environment, tended to be envious and narrow-minded.

For the first time, Hiep had continuous contact with the Vietnamese of the South. She found them simple, open-minded, generous and forthright. It was quite refreshing for her, coming from Hue where people were complicated, provincial, refined to the point of accepting hypocrisy and polite to the point of embracing flattery.

In Hue people smiled, but in Saigon people laughed. In Hue people hid their tears, in Saigon people cried openly.

At first, the Southern accent confused her. She misunderstood simple statements. Slowly, she learned to recognize the sounds and eventually she could converse with the southerners without any difficulty.

At that time, Saigon was not yet a bustling city of three million people. Yet, in Hiep's and her sister's eyes, it was a huge city. Hiep tried hard not to let the noise of the city disturb the contentment she was feeling.

Lucie was a very accomplished young lady, even though she was only sixteen years old! She was so simple and good-natured, so candid and yet so charming. Father Huong, the Vietnamese priest who was in charge of a parish in Cho Lon, and who had played go-between originally, was also very happy. Hiep and Hoang couldn't praise Lucie Nguyen Thi Danh's family enough. They kept thanking the priest for having found the perfect match for Luyen.

Hiep told Hoang, "Mother will be so happy! And Luyen, too!" But she knew that her mother would not be perfectly happy. Three of her sons were still bachelors: Diem would likely never get married. But what about Nhu, and Can? Khoi had once told her that he was worried about Nhu and Can. He wanted them to get married soon, not after the French had uncovered Diem's revolutionary activities.

*

On the trip home, although she still enjoyed the passing scenery with her sister, Hiep began to dream about the possibilities for her family.

Thuc was now in Vinh Long, soon Luyen would be married to the young lady from Cho Lon, and her family was no longer Central Vietnam bound. They were about to take roots in the south, too.

There was no doubt in her mind that Thuc had already won the hearts of the Catholic landlords and the poor farmers in the south. Members of the Empress' family, especially *Prince An Dinh*, her uncle, swore they would not let the new Bishop lack in anything.

Certain things that Hiep saw puzzled her. In the south, she had noticed a strong republicanism that was nowhere to be found in Central Vietnam. The south, Hiep discerned, was more progressive and more aware of the changes occurring in the world outside of Vietnam.

Though Diem had gone south many times and had a few political friends there, Hiep decided that she would try to persuade him to spend some time in Saigon and in the Mekong Delta, to learn more about the southerners' way of thought. She wanted him to learn more about the new religions that had emerged there recently: Hoa Hao Buddhism and Caodaism. The new religions had been captivating both the imagination and the patriotism of the southerners, and Hiep saw that they were new forces to be reckoned with.

*

Hiep was fully aware that Diem had started his underground network. There was not much risk of being betrayed by the nucleus of handpicked revolutionaries he had gathered around him.

They were all conscious that the French Secret Services were watching them and they acted accordingly. The risks existed only when they had to contact sympathizers in Hanoi and Saigon. Traveling with revolutionary documents hidden in one's luggage was never safe, and the French had succeeded in planting their spies among the sympathizers.

Prince Cuong De and the Patriot, Phan Boi Chau, had worked hard, and Diem now had to coordinate a large network of isolated cells, not only in Central Vietnam, but also in the South and in North Vietnam.

The cells were autonomous and could operate for years without being contacted by the higher coordinating layers of command. Yet, the nature of such a structure, dictated by the need for secrecy, gave rise to a horde of problems such as difficulty of training and retraining, lack of common direction and perspectives, and lack of mutual support.

Diem knew that he could not sacrifice safety for sake of party discipline. Even the name of the party was left open. Diem referred to and the organization that he directed as *The National Revolutionary Movement*, or *Phong Trao Cach Mang Quoc Gia,* but soon enough autonomous groups took other names, while recognizing Diem as their leader.

Hiep made it a point never to discuss with Diem, his secret efforts. Only at their father's birthday each year, would she say a few words to encourage him in his *difficult and dangerous pursuit*. She was inspired by Diem's fearless comportment. He and his loyal followers knew that if they made the slightest slip, they would end up in jail, or worse.

She was concerned as she saw Diem working alone, without the help of his brothers. Khoi, for tactical reasons, had to stay away from Diem. The younger brothers, Nhu and Luyen, were in their apprenticeship days. Diem wanted them to learn more about Vietnam before he assigned them to serious tasks.

Diem closely followed Nhu's progress as an archivist, and Luyen's career as a land surveyor. While Nhu immersed himself in old documents, retaining with his extraordinary memory, the names, dates and locations of past events, Luyen covered the country with his footsteps. He even spent a year in Cambodia, mapping the mountains and the plains of the kingdom.

Diem definitely eliminated Thuc from any political role, saying that he should dedicate all of his efforts to the service of God and the Church. There remained Ngo Dinh Can, who was near Diem, day and night, in their mother's home.

Can's extraordinary memory of faces and names, and his attention to detail, often amazed Diem. But Can had, from an early age, developed heart and lung problems and was not the least bit interested in politics.

For years, since he had resigned as Prime Minister, Diem had worked alone, aided very discreetly by Khoi. Even that discreet help was to put Khoi's career in jeopardy and would eventually force him to resign in 1943.

*

As World War II swept over Europe, many Vietnamese thought the time had come for the liberation of their country from French domination.

In February 1939, Prince Cuong De was in Hong Kong to implement the Alliance for National Restoration. A year later, he organized the first units of the *Kien quoc quan* (National Rebuilding Army). In September 1940, elements of the *Kien quoc* forces entered Lang Son in North Vietnam. Contrary to the Prince's expectation, the Japanese signed a truce with the French, and accepted continued French rule in Vietnam. They also demanded that the *Kien Quoc Quan* units, which had entered Vietnam, withdraw into China. Elements of the *Kien Quoc Quan* that refused to comply were rapidly encircled and pitilessly massacred by the French, while the Japanese stood by.

The duplicity of the Japanese leaders in 1940, in their dealing with Prince Cuong De and his troops, was to determine one of the most important decisions Diem would have to make in 1945.

In 1940, the French colonial administration accepted the presence of Japanese troops in Indochina, and in return, the Japanese assured the French that they would not interfere with the established French colonial rule.

Diem, though he continued to expand his Japanese contacts, knew that he should not count on them as reliable allies to help achieve his dream of national liberation.

CHAPTER TWELVE
LOVE AND POLITICS

It was in the spring of 1943, a few days after Lunar New Year. The Ngo Dinh family council was gathered in the absence of Thuc and Giao. For once, it was presided over by Mrs. Ngo Dinh Kha herself. At issue was Nhu's wish to get married to Tran Thi Le Xuan.

Hiep had never seen so grim a family reunion. There was electricity in the air. Mrs. Ngo Dinh Kha had not spoken, but everybody in the room knew that she would be tough.

Nhu looked very unhappy. He said, "I know what you all think about the family of Mr. Tran van Chuong. But I love Le Xuan, his daughter, and I want to get married to her. Father and all of you wanted me to go to study in France, so I went and I studied very hard. What you and I did not foresee was that I was bound to change. My character has changed. My perspectives have changed. I cannot accept a marriage arranged by my family. I want to marry somebody I love."

Mrs. Ngo Dinh Kha nodded as if she approved of what he said, but when she spoke, her tone was almost harsh, "So, you have changed. I have only two objections to the marriage you are contemplating. First of all, I want you to think first about what is good for your soul. We are Christians. We believe in God. *They* do not believe in anything, not even in the Buddha." She paused, looking to see whether Nhu would react, but he did not utter a word.

She went on, "You say that she is ready to convert. I have seen good converts in my life. Father Thich is an example. Before him, I can cite the example of Prince Huong Thuyen, your brother Diem's godfather. But they converted to Christianity out of conviction, not out of love."

201

She stopped, allowing time for Nhu to see her point, then added, "You want to marry a young lady who is virtuous, but not a Christian. She will be converted, but out of love for you, not out of conviction. Are you so sure of *your* faith now? How strong is your faith? Will it be strong enough for the two of you? Or will it wither at the daily contact with a wife who does not have much room for God in her life?"

Khoi, Diem, Can, Luyen, Hiep and Hoang were stunned by her words. She had never said so much. They looked at Nhu. His face was ashen. He seemed to be on the verge of crying.

Mrs. Kha also looked at him. Her eyes were much softer than her words. She went on, "My second objection comes from my view of her family. An old proverb says, 'When you want to buy a pig, you look at the sow first. When you buy a wife, you look at her family first.' We no longer buy a wife these days but the old proverb still is valid. I am not going to judge her family. I am not going to repeat the rumors about Le Xuan's mother. I only want you to ask yourself whether the lifestyle of her mother did not put her reputation in jeopardy."

Nhu cried out painfully, "But I love Le Xuan and she loves me." There was pain in the eyes of Mrs. Kha now. She replied, "I don't doubt that is true."

Nhu turned to his brothers and pleaded, "My life will be completely ruined if I cannot marry Le Xuan. I will die if I cannot marry her." Khoi asked, "Are you threatening to commit suicide if you are not allowed to marry her?" Nhu clenched his fists, "I don't think of suicide. I am a Christian. But I know that if I cannot marry her, my heart will break and I will die."

They did not know how to handle the situation anymore. That Nhu would talk about his feelings so freely shocked them. At the same time, they saw how deeply and passionately he was in love.

Hiep stood up and said, "We are at an impasse. I do not think that brother Nhu will ever change. He loves the young lady, and she loves him. What can we do, except approve this marriage?" Having opposed her mother's verdict, Hiep waited for Mrs. Kha to lash out at her. But her mother merely looked at her with neither objection nor approval in her eyes.

Khoi was also afraid that his mother would lash out at his sister, so he said quickly, "Let us look at the difference in age. Brother Nhu is thirty-four, she is eighteen. Nhu, don't you see that she is too young for you?" Nhu lowered his head, but did not respond to Khoi's question.

In the silence that followed, Can spoke, "I cannot see how Sister Hiep can arrive at a conclusion like that. We have to stop this foolishness. Please think of Mrs. Tran Van Chuong. We have little knowledge of the merits of Mr. Chuong, but we have heard plenty about Mrs. Chuong. To ally ourselves with that family would be a terrible mistake."

Diem asked, "Don't we hear that though Le Xuan is modern and a little rebellious, she is quite an eligible young lady? We cannot reasonably blame her for her mother's reputation. Anyway, how much credence should we give to the rumors about Mrs. Chuong?"

He looked apologetically at Mrs. Kha and went on, "Le Xuan's mother, Than Thi Nam Tran, is the daughter of the late Minister Than Trong Hue. You know I hurt the feelings of the Than Trong family when I put one of the Minister's nephews in jail. But they were, in the end, quite kind to me. They did not consider me as an enemy. The Than Trong family is an honorable family. The grandmother of Le Xuan was Princess Nhu Phien, who was the sister of Emperors Kien Phuoc, Ham Nghi and Dong Khanh, and an aunt of Emperor Khai Dinh."

Diem stopped to see whether his mother would speak, but as she remained silent, he went on, "You have asked us to look at her family, Mother. I can tell you that Tran Van Chuong, her father, was also the son of the late Governor Tran van Thong. We know her family on both her father's and her mother's side. I do not take lightly the fact that there are many bad rumors about Mrs. Chuong, but even if we were to believe the rumors, it would not mean that her whole family is bad."

Can said: "*Telle mère telle fille.* She will not be different than her mother." Luyen frowned, "How can you say such a thing? It is unjust! Neither Brother Diem nor I believe in the nonsensical rumors people have spread about Mrs. Chuong. But, as Brother Diem said, even if the rumors prove to be true, we cannot blame the daughter for what her mother does."

Can was about to respond, but Hiep shook her head, and looked at Can until he felt embarrassed and turned away, then she said, "My marriage seems to have been an exception. Both my sisters, Giao and Hoang, had problems when they wanted to get married with the ones they loved. For fair or unfair reasons, their marriages were opposed until our parents and our older brothers relented. In the meantime, for months, my sisters suffered. Mother, please excuse me for saying so, but people outside our family say we are too demanding, too exacting, and even too arrogant whenever we talk about alliances with other families."

Mrs. Ngo Dinh Kha did not reply. In her eyes, there was a trace of reproach but she knew Hiep was right. Suddenly, Khoi raised his hand, as a signal for everybody to stop talking. He had come to a decision. He turned to Nhu and said, "I want to make this clear once and for all. Our family has made a lot of sacrifices for the national cause, and we will make more sacrifices for the cause in the future. We live our father's dream. We cannot do anything which may jeopardize our set goal. We cannot place our personal happiness above the cause."

He shook his head in disapproval and went on, "From what I have heard, Brother Nhu definitely wants to get married to Le Xuan. Brothers Diem and Luyen, as well as Sister Hiep, do not oppose such a marriage. Mother, Brother Can and I have serious reservations about it. Sister Hoang has not said a word during this entire meeting. Sister Giao has never attended family meetings and Brother Thuc cannot be prevailed on to leave his diocese for a few days. How shall we decide about this matter? I will ask permission from our mother to allow me to make this decision."

Mrs. Ngo Dinh Kha nodded, knowing that she had lost. Khoi said, "I will accept this marriage." Nhu looked like a dying man who had received a reprieve. He smiled and said, "Oh, thank you, Brother Khoi."

Khoi did not smile. He went on, stressing every word he said: "But, you will no longer be involved in the common cause of this family. You will have to stay away from politics. You will not need to know what we plan, or what we do. You and your future wife will not try to find out about our plans and our activities." Nhu was aghast. His whole body shaking with indignation and frustration, he asked, "Am I cast away from this family?"

Khoi said as softly as he could, "Certainly not. We love you as much as ever. I will go to Hanoi and ask Le Xuan's hand in marriage for you. But, to protect your personal happiness, which means so much to you, we will not bother you with our work. On the other hand, as we are not at all sure of the political role your future father-in-law wants to play in our country, it is safer for you and Le Xuan not to know anything about our plans."

Nhu asked, his voice cracking "Is this decision irrevocable?" Khoi threw up his hands and said, "Who knows what will happen ten years from now? But if you ask whether it will hold true in the foreseeable future, then yes. Until I say otherwise, please do not get involved. Do you agree?"

Nhu looked at everybody present in the room. All of them held his eyes and saw his despair, but none of them wavered and came to his side. He turned to Khoi and nodded. Khoi prodded him on, "I want you to say it clearly to all of us that you agree." Nhu cleared his throat and with anguish painted all over his face, he said, "I agree."

*

A few days after that incredibly disturbing scene, Khoi took the train to Hanoi. The French, who did not know how much turmoil the planned marriage had caused the Ngo Dinh family, were worried. The Resident Superior Grandjean was so alarmed that he fired several cables to his superiors, reporting the dangerous alliance between the two powerful Vietnamese families.

Hiep was disconsolate. She remembered how she had watched Nhu grow up and how she had laughed at his continual pranks. He had always been different from his brothers. As a child, he was the only one who complained about the food, when the family was poor. At times he had made her mother cry. At times, he had made her father angry enough to leave the table and go to the parlor in search of the disciplinary whip. Nhu had always been fast enough to escape punishment, though.

Hiep remembered how passionate a football player Nhu was. In the evening some kids always brought a football to the Cathedral ground, next to their home and started kicking. Nhu, who had been ordered to go to bed early, would sneak out of his room and join the game. His laughter, however, was very distinct, and sooner or later their father would get up and go to check to see if Nhu was still in his room.

Hiep remembered that one of Nhu's tricks was to put the cat under a conic hat and cover the hat with his blanket. In the semidarkness of his room, the movements of the cat made her father think Nhu was still in bed. But one night, the cat moved too much and her father, suspicious, stepped into the room, walked to the bed and found that he had been tricked. Nhu got a spanking that he remembered a long time.

Now that young boy was gone. Nhu had come back from France a tense young man who seemed to live in his own dream world, as much as he enjoyed reality. He did not talk much. He was pensive most often, and then suddenly would burst into feverish activity.

Hiep knew that Nhu wanted to live their father's dream as much as any one of them and that he took the exclusion dictated by Khoi very, very hard. Yet Hiep also understood why Khoi had made such a decision. Nhu's future wife was the cousin of Emperor Bao Dai, a man they had learned to mistrust. Nhu's future mother-in-law had caused the rumors about herself to be persistent. Such constant rumors were enough to endanger Diem and Khoi's political reputation, if Nhu was too close to them, politically.

Hiep sighed. She thought that if her family were not so dedicated to their one political cause, there would not have been any need to make a fuss about whom Nhu wanted to marry.

She did not know then that soon enough, Nhu would be called upon to play a role in the family battle plan and that at the end he would play a most sensitive part in the family's drama, together with his beautiful wife.

Ngo Dinh Nhu and Tran Le Xuan

*

"Is this a trap?" Khoi was not sure, but he had to act quickly. Two of Diem's most valuable collaborators were about to be arrested by the French Secret Services. Affiliated with Prince Cuong De's network, the two Caodaists who had fled from South Vietnam found temporary refuge in Quang Nam.

For years, Diem had placed his Caodaist affiliates at the center of the battle plan for South Vietnam. There were then at least one million followers of the new religion, and the majority of them were responding to the call for national liberation. Many of them had been pro-Japanese.

Their alliance with the Japanese was easy to understand. It was a temporary alliance. Caodaist patriots needed weapons and financial resources that only the Japanese could provide. Caodaist militia units were organized and trained by Japanese officers, while the *Kampetai* or Japanese military police provided the Caodaists with vital information about French moves.

The French were very concerned. The alliance between the Caodaists and the Japanese dated back a long time. Prince Cuong De, who had overtly courted the Japanese and asked the Japanese to help him and his followers to liberate Vietnam from French rule, had made inroads among the Caodaist population. They were afraid that the Caodaists would soon spread their pro-Japanese network into Central Vietnam. That was why they were so upset to learn that two prominent Caodaists of the Cuong De network had found their way to Quang Nam.

The French had discovered where the two Caodaists had taken refuge and were about to seize them. Khoi did not hesitate. He sent a messenger to warn them of the danger and help them to escape.

*

Resident Superior Grandjean was not happy. He had come half way to meet with Khoi, but Khoi did not seem to appreciate his gesture. For Grandjean, who only wanted to deal with Prime Minister Pham Quynh and Emperor Bao Dai, to be dragged out of Hue to deal with a mere Governor was almost inconceivable.

He admitted that Khoi was more than a mere Governor. Khoi had been made Viceroy of the South Central Provinces, but the title of Viceroy was more nominal than operational, and Khoi had no real supervisory power over the other heads of provinces of his region.

Khoi had made this arrangement. They were to meet at the border of his province, right on the Hai Van Pass. "Ridiculous!" Grandjean snorted. "He acts as if the provinces south of the Pass are his, and that I have to come to see him at the border to discuss *disagreements* between two states. He does not seem to understand that I can have him fired at any moment for what he has done with the Caodaists."

When he saw Khoi, his anger boiled. The Vietnamese Viceroy arrived, tall and handsome, extending his hand in greeting, as if they were equals. Before he had been appointed Resident Superior in Hue, Grandjean had served for long years in the French Secret Services. He had learned all about the Vietnamese.

The archives of the secret police showed that Khoi had entertained certain contacts with Phan Boi Chau and Prince Cuong De's network, together with his father-in-law, the late Duke of Phuoc Mon. The archives also showed that Khoi had laughed at the orders of some of the Governor-Generals who wanted to see incense altars set up on their way, during their tours in the provinces, and that Khoi had never complied.

Khoi had patiently explained to the irritated Governor-Generals that incense altars were set up on the Emperor's path because of the ancient notion that pretended that the Emperor was the Son of Heaven. He explained that though he personally did not believe in such pretension, he could not go against tradition, and that was why he continued to have incense altars set up for the Emperor.

He then asked, "Do you, Excellency, believe that you are the *Son of God*? If you don't, then why do you want incense altars set up on your way?" So Khoi had his way.

Grandjean shook hands with Khoi, and then bluntly remarked, "This is an odd place for a rendezvous. Did you always ask my predecessor to meet with you here? Anyway, why do you wear a white tunic for this meeting? I understand that Vietnamese mandarins only wear a white tunic when they deal with commoners, and that they wear more appropriate dress when they meet with people to whom they want to show respect."

He thought he had caught Khoi off guard. But Khoi, with pretended sadness in his eyes, simply said, "Two years ago, I had the sad honor, as the personal envoy of our Emperor, of accompanying your predecessor to his final rest in the Phu Cam Cemetery. Resident Superior Graffeuil was a great man and my heart still grieves for him. That is why I still wear white, as a sign of mourning."

Grandjean was taken aback by Khoi's quick response. He knew that Graffeuil had not been Khoi's friend in his lifetime. When he died, the French decided they would play a trick on Khoi by asking Emperor Bao Dai to assign Khoi as the representative of the Imperial Court at the funeral. Khoi, imperturbable during the ceremony, delivered a more than decent eulogy praising Graffeuil's virtues.

Among other things, Khoi had talked about Graffeuil's love for Vietnam. He said Graffeuil loved Vietnam so much that he had wanted his remains to be buried in the land he loved. Grandjean, who had seen the text of the eulogy, had snorted: Of course Khoi knew that Graffeuil's body could not be repatriated, simply because France was at war at the time.

Now Khoi went on, "Resident Superior Graffeuil and I had no problem communicating with each other."

Grandjean was becoming more infuriated. "This insolent *Annamite* is again mocking us. He will pay dearly for his insolence," Grandjean promised to himself. He knew that Khoi was doomed. The evidence he had against Khoi was indisputable. All of that could be forgotten if only Khoi humiliated himself and pleaded for clemency. Yet now, only a few minutes after they had shaken hands, Grandjean knew that Khoi would never do such a thing.

All smiles now, Grandjean began, "I also have a great reverence for my predecessor. It is good to hear that you had so much affection for him. I am here because of the long friendship between you and the colonial administration. We appreciate such a long and loyal friendship, and we will not be quick to condemn what you have done recently with regard to the two Caodaists our services want to interrogate."

Khoi did not react immediately. He knew that his career as a mandarin was about to end. He had no regrets. Yet, he knew he had to be careful with Grandjean. Any slip now and hundreds of people could be adversely affected. He finally said, "I know whom you are talking about. My services were also interested in what they had to say. We wanted to arrest them, but they escaped before we could lay our hands on them."

Grandjean smiled ironically, "The men you wanted to arrest belong to Prince Cuong De's network, the same network which was secretly supported by the late Duke of Phuoc Mon, your father-in-law. So, out of loyalty to France, you were about to arrest those men?"

Khoi shrugged, "First of all, I think you should not talk about the late Duke now. He cannot defend himself from any kind of accusation, now that he had passed away. If he worked against the interests of France, he should have been stopped when he lived. As for those men who entered my territory without my knowledge and seemed to be secretive about their activities, it was my duty, as Governor, to have my security services ask them a few questions."

Grandjean again smiled, "It is known to our services that your brother, Diem, the former Prime Minister, is involved with the Cuong De network. I assume that those two men work with or for your brother."

Khoi responded quickly, "Once your services have decreed that my late father-in-law was involved with Prince Cuong De's network, being Cartesian, they would conclude that my brother is also involved. I will not respond to any accusations against the Duke of Phuoc Mon, but I can tell you that in my brother's case, your services are committing a terrible blunder."

Grandjean threw his hands up, "Mistakes are made by the most intelligent people. You warned those two Caodaists before our services could capture them. We have all the evidence to prove that fact. Before I came here, I had hoped that somehow we would find a terrain *d'entente*. I had hoped that we would find together, something which would spare me the pain of having to announce to you that your Emperor has agreed with us to thank you for your good services to the throne and wish you success in your next career."

Khoi kept his calm and simply replied, "My Emperor and I can communicate without an intermediary. I know that you have the power to dictate certain things to the Imperial Court, but in order to keep up appearances, please act with the strictest courtesy towards our Emperor. I do not think we have anything else to say to each other, so farewell."

He rose to go. Grandjean said, "Normally, you would have the rank of *Hiep Ta Dai Hoc Si* or permanent rank of Minister when you leave, but considering the circumstances of your retirement, I think His Majesty will be reluctant to grant you that honor. Farewell."

Khoi turned to look at the Resident a minute, but left without saying another word. He was tempted to say that his father, his brother and even the Duke of Phuoc Mon had been stripped of all their ranks and titles, the day they left the Imperial Court, but instead he decided to walk away in silence.

*

Nhu hated himself for the role he played. He had to play deaf and dumb, because he had been condemned by Khoi and his brothers to stay out of politics. He had abandoned his position of Senior Librarian at the National Library in Hanoi and taken the job of Chief Archivist at the Resident Superior's Headquarters in Hue. He now lived in Hue with his wife, in a little house near Providence Institute.

Every day he walked to his office, though his wife often fumed at him for not using her private rickshaw. The black rickshaw adorned with fine brass work, completely distinct from the ordinary rickshaws for hire, was a present from his in-laws. He never used it. Tiny problems like that one had quickly injected themselves between him and his wife. He did not understand his wife's homesickness for Hanoi, and her dislike for Hue. He did not understand why she could not see and appreciate the greatness in Diem and the integrity in Khoi. In short, he was unhappy at home, though he loved his wife, and by all appearances, she also loved him.

At work, he was faced with a multitude of problems. He supervised the work of a large number of men and women. Most of them came from the royal clan or families of high-ranking mandarins. He noticed that some of his employees showed too much servility to the French.

He tried to stiffen their backs. He encouraged them to see Frenchmen and women as their equals. His efforts were in vain. They continued to act as if the French were all gods and goddesses. They resented his remarks and spurned his efforts. They saw in him a dangerous example: his father and his brothers had all been fired because they had not submitted to the French. How long would Nhu himself last in his position, if he continued to talk to French men and women the way he did, they wondered.

Nhu also noticed that many of them came from families who were opposed to the French rule. Two among them stood out. Trang Dinh and Trang Liet were sons of Prince Cuong De, the Rebel Pretender. That the French allowed them to work at the Resident Superior's Headquarters was beyond Nhu's comprehension at first. Then he understood the reasons why. The French wanted them there so that they could observe them at all times. They also wanted them there to show to other Vietnamese how generous they were, even with their enemies.

Nhu knew that Prince Cuong De's sons were off limits to him. Besides common civilities, he talked to them only when he needed to give them instructions for their work as assistant archivists.

He also noticed that they discreetly came to his mother's home to see Brother Diem. Remembering Khoi's stern warnings excluding him from political activities, he was even more careful in his behavior towards Prince Cuong De's sons.

Nhu sighed. When he was in France, life had been so simple. He had taken freedom for granted. Now back in his own country, he found that even the most innocent contact with people around him could have the direst consequences. He wondered when this intolerable situation would come to an end.

*

Diem was not really surprised. Since 1933, he had lived with the premise that, sooner or later, the French Secret Services would learn about his underground activities.

It was July 7, 1944. A Dr. Chi, who had extensive contacts with middle-level employees at the Resident Superior's Headquarters, was the first to tell Diem of the imminent raid by the French Secret Services. Diem thanked him and asked him to leave the scene immediately. Then he sat down to think.

He did not have lists to burn or documents to take away with him. His memory was his filing system. If the French descended on his mother's home, the only thing Diem feared was that they would cause his mother some anxiety. But he could not tell her anything. He could not even say goodbye to her. The less she knew, the better it would be for her.

Can was, so far, uninvolved, so he would not have anything interesting to tell the French, if interrogated.

Diem's remaining questions were where to go, and what to do to protect his network. The network was organized in such a way that it would survive without him. Diem did not know the extent of the information the French had gathered. He did not know how many names the French had gotten. Quickly, he wrote a few cryptic messages and sent An, his trusted butler, to warn his Brother Khoi and the leaders of the Movement.

The gate bell rang. Diem went out to open the gate. He was surprised to see standing there, Nguyen De's trusted secretary. Diem led the way back to his parlor. De's secretary presented with both hands, a letter from De. Diem opened it. The letter had been written hurriedly. It told Diem about the French secret police's discovery of his network, and the impending raid on Diem's mother's house. De warned Diem to escape as quickly as possible. He said the French intended to send him away to a prison in Laos.

Diem was moved to tears. So, his former friend had not forgotten their past friendship, after all. He noticed that De had not even asked him to burn the letter after he had read it. Knowing De's prudent nature, Diem appreciated that omission. It meant that De had wanted to say that he did not care for himself, when his friend's safety was at stake.

Diem struck a match, burned the letter on an ashtray, then went outside and emptied the ashes around a plant. He came back to the parlor and having taken paper and a pen from his desk, sat down to write a long letter to De. De's man was nervous. He interrupted Diem, "Sir, you have to leave now."

Diem looked at him and said, "Mr. Nguyen De risked everything to send this letter to me. Don't you think that I should tell him that I appreciate his friendship?" He finished the letter, sealed it and gave it to the young man.

As he accompanied the messenger to the gate, he saw hurrying towards his home, a nephew of Minister Pham Quynh.

Minister Pham Quynh

*

As his friend's secretary slipped out, Diem stood at the gate waiting. Pham Quynh's nephew said, "Please let me in." Diem shook his head, he said, "I am sorry, but I am busy." The young man pleaded, "I have here a confidential message from my uncle. Please let me in."

This time Diem was really stunned. He stood aside and allowed the young man to enter. In the parlor, Diem opened Pham Quynh's letter. It was also a message warning him to escape quickly. The man who had opposed him

214

when he was Prime Minister, the most powerful man in the Imperial Court who had waged a running battle with his Brother Khoi all these years, was also risking everything to save his life.

Diem said to Pham Quynh's nephew, "Please tell Minister Pham Quynh that his gesture in my favor at this moment will never be forgotten."

The young man said, "I noticed at least two Vietnamese who work for the secret police walking in the street in front of your home. Please, be careful." Diem nodded and replied, "I have taken a few measures. Please tell your uncle I will be safe."

Pham Quynh's nephew was gone now. Diem smiled, "Even those *they* trusted the most, would not let me down. The French rule is certainly about to come to an end."

It was dark now. Diem asked his butler to go out and watch. Ngo Dinh Kha's garden had three entrances. Secret police guarded all of them now. Diem said, "They will enter the house only in the morning. Keep watching." An kept watch. By midnight, nobody was at any of the gates. Apparently there was a break between two shifts.

Diem called Phuc, his rickshaw man. The rickshaw left the place without any problem. In ten minutes, Diem was at the gate of the Japanese Consulate. The next day, a Japanese plane took him to Da Nang. Then another Japanese plane took him to Saigon.

In Hue, the French made a useless raid on his mother's home. Diem had escaped them, though the operation had been planned in the strictest secrecy. For a long time, the French suspected every Vietnamese working around them, except those who had actually warned Diem of the danger.

An, the butler, was left unharmed by the French, while Phuc, Diem's rickshaw man, was interrogated repeatedly by the French Secret Services, then sent to jail until 1945, when the Japanese released him. Both An and Phuc served later on in Diem's household after Diem came back to power in 1954.

*

The French had discovered more than Diem realized. They knew the names of the leaders of one section of Diem's network. They had somehow obtained all ninety names of the cell of his network known as the Restoration of the Greater Vietnam Party *(Dai Viet Phuc Hung Dang)*.

They arrested a few dozen people and sent them to distant mountain prisons. They wanted to arrest more, but many members of Diem's network belonged to the most aristocratic families in Vietnam. Vietnamese Ministers protected many others. Some of the Japanese counterparts of the French officials indicated that they would not sit still and allow the waves of arrests to go on, without interfering.

In the end, Governor-General Decoux, who had been forced to cooperate with the Japanese, decided that only top leaders of Diem's party members should be kept in jail. In the meantime, in a clean sweep, all of Diem's sympathizers among the mandarins were either demoted or given a stern warning.

One of the leaders of the Restoration of the Greater Vietnam Party was Tran van Ly, Province Chief of Ha Tinh. As his wife was a close relative of Empress Nam Phuong, he was given a warning and reassigned to another province. Tran van Ly was to play a major role in Diem's network over the next two decades.

*

In Hue, both Mrs. Ngo Dinh Kha and Can were interrogated by the French secret police. As they did not know anything about his activities and were completely ignorant as to his whereabouts, French officials decided not to arrest them. They did not arrest Nhu either. Though they spent time trying to badger him into saying what they wanted to hear. Unfortunately for them, Nhu had been kept totally in the dark concerning Diem's political activities and intentions.

As for Hiep, unsuspected by anybody, including Can and Hoang, she continued corresponding with Luyen, who was in Saigon, through trusted messengers. She was constantly aware of Diem's whereabouts, and through Luyen's subtle hints, was kept updated on Diem's activities.

*

Diem, for his part, found safety in Saigon, where he was beginning to have a large following. Assisted openly by the Japanese now, Diem was becoming increasingly concerned about that patronage. He had seen the duplicity of the Japanese leaders in their dealings with Cuong De. The Prince had been expelled from Japan when the Japanese thought it convenient to do so. He had seen the *Kien Quoc Quan*; the Prince's army, enter Lang Son on the wake of the Japanese victory over the French in 1941, only to be pushed back into China by the Japanese themselves. He had seen Japanese officials collaborate with the French to destroy the elements of the *Kien Quoc Quan* that remained in Vietnam. Diem had also seen the cruelty of the Japanese troops when they sacked Nanjing. He had heard reports of Japanese atrocities in Korea, Malaya and the Philippines.

Though originally, due to Prince Cuong De's influence, Diem had thought that somehow he could one day convince the Japanese to help Vietnamese patriots combat the French, he had gradually come to abandon such a vision.

Over the years, he had developed close friendship with many Japanese. He had trusted them implicitly. Now, he realized that he should not rely on such personal friendships, for the mission he had assigned himself. He realized that his Japanese friends would sacrifice themselves to save his life, but they would not help him liberate Vietnam from the French.

When he arrived in Saigon, the future victors and vanquished of World War II had already been clearly determined. The forces of the Axis were being defeated and pushed back everywhere. The final defeat of Germany and Japan was only a question of time.

Japanese patronage at that time was not an advantage. Diem had come to see that such patronage might even represent an unacceptable risk for his future plans.

Diem sometimes stayed with Luyen at his home, and occasionally with Father Huong, in Cholon. He altogether avoided meeting with his Japanese friends. He received visits from many. Southern patriots, Caodaists and Hoa Hao Buddhists, and sent word to Khoi in Hue, to establish a coalition of all Vietnamese revolutionary parties.

Khoi immediately succeeded in contacting various political leaders in Central Vietnam. He took over the leadership left by Diem there. Everybody who worked with Khoi during that period described him as imaginative, decisive and trustworthy.

It was then that the Japanese, needing to have a free hand in Vietnam, decided to launch the *Meigo* operation, known as the Japanese *coup de force* of March 9, 1945.

*

Though details of Diem's activities in that period were only made known to Hiep much later, she was able to follow the general line of his progress through messengers and friends who traveled from Hue to Saigon. She understood Diem's stance in regard to the Japanese, and was not surprised by Diem's decision not to assume power after the Japanese ended the French colonial rule.

PART THREE

WHEN WIND AND DUST ROSE

CHAPTER THIRTEEN
A SEMBLANCE OF INDEPENDENCE

It was the coldest winter in decades. On the Lunar New Year Day, the temperature dropped to six degrees at noontime in Hue. People told Hiep that in Hanoi, it was even colder. She had been used to having all of her brothers and sisters gathered for the family reunion on the third day of the Lunar New Year.

In that Year of the Rooster, however, only Khoi and Can were there with her sister Hoang and herself. Her sister, Giao, had been recurrently ill lately, and had excused herself. Khoi was quite cheerful in spite of the fact that he had been forced to retire, and in spite of Diem's uncertain future.

They attended Mass together for the peace of their father's soul then sat down to go over the situation. Khoi said that the Japanese were about to launch an attack on the French garrisons in Indochina and put an end to the French rule in Vietnam, Laos and Cambodia. Though such an attack had been expected for a while, Khoi's confirmation of its imminence took them by surprise. Khoi had apparently obtained the information from the highest authorities among the Japanese military and civilian leaders in Indochina.

He talked quite excitedly for a while, describing the inevitability of the outcome. The French would surely be defeated within the first few hours. The French rule would finally end. Then Khoi stopped. He looked up at the large portrait of the late Grand Chamberlain that hung on the wall. It was a portrait recently framed. Ngo Dinh Kha looked both proud and jovial in his court robes with all his insignias and medals.

In silence, Hiep addressed her father, "You see, Father, the time has come. The French will no longer rule over us."

Khoi's voice trembled with emotion as he picked up where he left off. He seemed to be giving a warning, "Even though the French rule is about to end, unless the Vietnamese act quickly and effectively, our chance of recovering national independence will be wasted. The Japanese may not be worse masters than the French, but surely they are not going to get rid of the French only to give back full independence to Vietnam."

Hoang asked, "Haven't they extolled every day since 1940 the need for solidarity among the Asians and the building of Greater East Asia? Don't you think that they will have to keep some of their promises?"

Khoi laughed, "I do. They *will* keep some of their promises. They will give us nominal independence. They cannot, however, in view of the precarious situation they are facing, turn over the reins of the government to the Vietnamese. They need to have a free hand in making decisions in and for Vietnam. They want total control over the axes of communication. They want to keep fighting the Allies on our territory for as long as possible. Holding the line here in Vietnam would give them time to put up a more effective defense system for the final battle in Japan."

Hiep asked, "Then, what should the Vietnamese do?" Khoi replied, "Our government has to seize this opportunity. Unfortunately, Emperor Bao Dai and Pham Quynh won't be able to do that. Bao Dai will most likely call upon Brother Diem to head a new Cabinet."

Hiep smiled a little sadly and commented, "In view of the situation and Brother Diem's contacts with the Japanese military and civilian leaders, you are right to predict that the Emperor will call on him. But should Brother Diem agree to head the government at this time when the Japanese, are about to lose the war at the hands of the Americans?"

Khoi answered, "You certainly ask the right question. It seems that Brother Diem has been in touch with you. In the latest message he sent, he told me that he does not want to accept any offer from Bao Dai in the near future. He says he does not want to be looked upon by the Allies as a man propped up by the Japanese." Hiep told Khoi, "I have not received any communication from him, for quite a while, but I guessed that he would have thought that way."

Khoi thought a while then said, "I disagree with both you and Diem. The Allies will have little to say until they have defeated the Japanese in

Indochina. By the time of their arrival, if we have succeeded in forming a stable and effective government, they would not blame Brother Diem for accepting an offer, not from the Japanese, but from his Emperor."

Hiep asked, "What about Prince Cuong De? Is he not the first choice of the Japanese if they take over from the French?" Khoi replied, "From my conversations with Japanese diplomats and military commanders, Prince Cuong De seems too old to most of them. In fact, if the Japanese had taken over a few years ago from the French, they would have put him on the throne. At this moment, however, they do not have time to dethrone Bao Dai and to replace him with a new Emperor. They actually told me: 'We cannot afford to change horses in midstream now.' The Prince, on the other hand, would make a good Emperor, but he definitely would not make a good Prime Minister."

Hiep asked, "What has the Prince told Brother Diem to do?" Khoi shrugged, "If, or rather, when the Japanese take over, the Prince may want to return home and assume whatever role he may be offered. He has been too long overseas and misses the country. But he cannot come back as the new Emperor, and he cannot be a Prime Minister under Bao Dai, either. That is why I do not think he should come home right now."

Hiep insisted, "Brother Diem cannot and should not compete with the Prince, who has been his *minh Chu* (enlightened Prince) for so long. If the Prince wants to come back, Brother Diem should assist him in every way possible."

Khoi exclaimed, "That is exactly what Diem said!" Once again Khoi was amazed at the way Hiep related to Diem. He had said that he disagreed with both of them, yet he understood their point of view. Khoi had felt in the last few months a fire burning within him. He had a compelling urge to do something now, before it was too late. He looked up at the portrait of his father again.

In the portrait, the Grand Chamberlain was almost smiling. He seemed to be saying to him, "Do not worry, my son, Diem knows what he is doing."

He turned to Hiep and found her with her head bent in contemplation. Hiep knew that Diem was always more prudent than Khoi and that Khoi was always more decisive than Diem. Over the years, Diem had talked to her about his Japanese friends, especially about Mitsushiro Matsushita, the

Director of the Greater Vietnam Company, Kiyoshi Komatsu, Senior Advisor of the Japanese Cultural Institute, and Masayuki Yokoyama, the Japanese Ambassador. Diem told her that originally he had cultivated Japanese friendships as a means to ward off the French Secret Services. He had thought that the French, 'in bed' with the Japanese after 1941, would not venture to put him in prison, when they saw him so close to the Japanese establishment.

Diem admitted later, that his friendship with certain Japanese was no longer politically motivated. He was genuinely fond of them. He liked to discuss poetry and Chinese classics with them. He liked their patriotism, their pride, and their sense of duty and honor. He discovered in Komatsu a poet, and in Yokoyama, a vast and balanced knowledge that spanned East and West.

As they became genuine friends, he also began to have tremendous reservations about the Japanese ambitions. He knew that his friends were doomed. He knew that Japan would have to pay a terrible price for having entered the war against the Allies.

His close links with the Japanese did not prevent Admiral Decoux, the French Governor General, from ordering his arrest in 1944. Though the Japanese had facilitated his escape from Hue, Diem realized that any future ties with them would only create complications for his future role in Vietnam.

In Saigon, he distanced himself more and more from his great friend, Matsushita. He stayed at his brother Luyen's home or at Father. Huong's rectory in Cho Lon and he made frequent trips to Vinh Long to see Bishop Thuc.

Hiep continued to correspond with her other brothers, but rarely wrote to Diem. She knew that he was going through a lot of soul searching, as he stood on the sidelines, watching World War II come to an end, and anticipating the Japanese defeat. Hiep did not see why Diem should agree to serve in a Japanese supported government now. Finally, Hiep concluded, "It is up to Brother Diem now to make the decision. I hope that he will not venture into the muddy waters of Japanese politics."

And muddy they were. There were persistent rumors that Mrs. Tran van Chuong entertained intimate relations with Yokoyama, the Japanese

Ambassador, whose French wife appeared to be having an affair with Emperor Bao Dai. That represented another complication. Diem had to preserve his reputation of integrity and purity. Any suspicion that he received Japanese political support from Yokoyama now would be a stain on his mantle.

After the meeting was over, Hiep lingered on. When they were finally alone, she asked, "Is something bothering you, Brother Khoi?" Khoi shook his head, "Nothing should be bothering me. Yet, it is true, I often feel as if I were approaching an abyss, walking on shifting and brittle gravel, slipping closer and closer to the edge. In my dreams and even in my waking hours, the nightmarish feeling is always with me. I want to accomplish something, to finish something before a tragedy strikes me."

Hiep exclaimed, "Nothing bad will happen to you! Nothing!" Khoi looked at her with fondness, but she saw in his eyes excitement and sadness, light and darkness. Khoi shrugged and smiled, "This is not the time to be worrying about the state of my mind."

*

During the night of March 8, deafening explosions shook the City of Hue. From midnight onwards, gunfire was heard mainly around the French garrison near the Resident Superior's headquarters and the Mang Ca Fortress, northeast of the Citadel. Heavy cannon were being used, along with all kinds of lighter weapons.

Hiep woke up and asked Am, anxiously, "What is happening?" Am tried to reassure her, "There's nothing to worry about. The French may have started a military maneuver." But Hiep knew better than that. She knew that the Japanese were attacking the French garrisons and that the attack was heralding the end of French rule. She went to the chapel and lit a candle. She sat there in contemplation. She knew that the outcome was clear. The Japanese would have no difficulty in defeating the French. She had seen the weaponry displayed by the Japanese. She knew what kinds of weapons the French were still using. The French forces were definitely no match for the Japanese.

She felt it strange that she was not overjoyed with that knowledge. The French, who had dominated her country for more than sixty years, were about to be defeated. The French, who had humiliated her nation, exiled three of her Emperors, stripped her father of his rank, and forced her brothers, Diem and Khoi, to resign, were about to be defeated. Yet all she felt was compassion for the French soldiers who were facing a much stronger and better-equipped enemy!

She could not bring herself to go back to bed. She wondered, "If Father still lived, what would he say?" He would not be overjoyed either. She was certain of that. 'Independence is not a gift. You will have to fight for it,' she remembered him saying. Yet, he would also proclaim 'Seize the opportunity!' like Brother Khoi said. "But what Brother Khoi says and what I say are only idle words. Only what Brother Diem says will matter. What will his decision be now?" She went on musing.

The gunfire subsided in early morning. By noon the next day, the fighting was over. It was over in the entire territory of Indochina. The French rule had come to an end.

*

On March 11, 1945, Emperor Bao Dai announced the independence of the 'Empire of Greater Vietnam', the termination of all treaties with France, and the alliance with the Japanese for the establishment of Greater East Asia.

Soon enough it was clear that within the newly independent state, the power was held not by the Emperor, but by General Tsuchihashi, the Commander-in-Chief of the Japanese Imperial Forces in Indochina. He was named Governor-General to make the point clearer for those Vietnamese who still refused to acknowledge the new reality. Yokoyama, the Japanese Ambassador, became the Emperor's Supreme Advisor, for the same reason.

"It is a mere illusion, this independence that has been offered by the Japanese," Hiep said to herself. "The Japanese are substituting themselves for the French, that is all." She felt herself even more committed to Diem's way of thinking. No, if the Emperor offered him the position of Prime Minister, he should decline.

Emperor Bao Dai sent word to Diem, officially inviting him to form a new cabinet. When, after two requests, Diem did not respond, the Emperor asked Supreme Advisor Yokoyama to convince Diem to return to Hue.

The Japanese official promised to do his utmost. A few days later, pressed by Bao Dai, he reported that Diem had received the letters the Emperor had sent him. He added that the Japanese had also been in touch with Diem, but regrettably Diem was very ill, and was in no condition to - return to Hue for the time being.

Ngo Dinh Khoi was becoming edgy and frustrated. Meeting Hiep one day at their mother's home, he again argued, "Diem must assume power now. The Allies will not be here for quite some time, and between now and then, the Communists will have taken over. Diem has to return to Hue to help the Emperor deal with the Communists, and assemble a stable government. By the time the Allies arrive, they will not be able to find fault with Diem's accomplishments." Hiep listened to Khoi but could not bring herself to agree with him.

The Emperor, having fired Pham Quynh and his entire Cabinet on March 19, was a toy in the hands of the Japanese. They suggested that, as Diem was not available, he should appoint Tran Trong Kim, a pro-Japanese scholar, to be his Prime Minister.

In the meantime, the Emperor, playing with fire, continued his intimate relationship with Yokoyama's French wife. Pretty, fond of hunting and adventure, the French lady and the Emperor were seen escaping from the Imperial City and traveling together to the jungle for long hunting trips.

The Empress, still as beautiful as ever, had known for years of Bao Dai's frequent infidelity but she had suffered in silence. This time, it was different. Bao Dai's indiscretion could easily get him into serious trouble. She pleaded with him again and again. The Emperor defiantly declared that there was nothing more than pure friendship between him and the pretty huntress.

Empress Nam Phuong

*

Soon enough, on April 17, Prime Minister Tran Trong Kim presented his Cabinet. Among the members, was Tran Van Chuong, the Minister of Foreign Affairs. Evil rumors hinted that Mrs. Tran Van Chuong had not been indifferent to Yokohama's charm, and that her husband had her to thank for his elevation. Soon enough, even though Tran Trong Kim did not like Tran van Chuong at all, the Foreign Minister succeeded in becoming Vice-Premier.

Hiep was glad that Diem was not involved in the muddy waters of Japanese politics.

*

Tuyen, Hiep's second son, came home from school quite disturbed. His class at Pellerin Institute had been cruelly torn apart. Where his French and Eurasian friends had sat, there were now empty seats. The Vietnamese children were distraught. War had been all around them for years. Yet, only now did they experience personally its bitter taste. Even more than the experience of war, what struck them hardest was the realization that there were differences among them.

They had not been completely unaware of those differences. Indeed, when they fought, they used racial insults. French and Eurasian schoolboys had called Vietnamese classmates *sales annamites,* when they fought. Vietnamese schoolboys had in turn called their French classmates *sales mangeurs de grenouilles*, and their Eurasian classmates s*ales métisses*, but only when they fought. They had never envisaged that someday those differences would land some of them in a concentration camp, leaving the rest outside.

Overnight, all the French and Eurasian men, along with their families had been assembled and sent 'for their own security' to the Providence Institute and other large buildings in the French Quarter. They had become refugees. There were mostly children and women at the new refugee sites. The men were sent to the Mang Ca Fortress where it was reported that many of them were tortured or beaten badly.

Tuyen went to the Providence Institute every day before he came home from school. He stood outside the fences and talked to his friends inside. He and other Vietnamese classmates brought their captive friends what they could find at home: sugar, matches, and salt, wax candles, thread and needles. Famine had begun in North Vietnam and was progressing southward. Tuyen was really scared for his French and Eurasian friends and their families. If the people outside the fences were near starvation, what would happen to those inside?

Soon the Japanese sent the former French military men to the south. They went south, marching. The Japanese did not allow their wives and children to say goodbye to them or even to steal a last glimpse of them. In Hue, few people believed that the French male prisoners would arrive in Saigon alive.

In the meantime, planes of the Allies bombed Hue more and more frequently. It was fortunate that the Americans never bombed the Imperial Palace or Hue's historical sites, but the bridges on the Perfume River became their choice targets. Pellerin Institute was quite close to the White Tiger Bridge, one of the targets of the planes. Hiep cringed at the sounds of sirens announcing the approach of the planes, thinking about Tuyen who would be sitting in a bomb shelter at his school, only a few hundred meters from the bridge.

Tuyen was impervious to the danger of the bombers. What shook him was what he saw on the streets bordering the Providence Institute. He said he saw Japanese soldiers harassing and threatening the French women and children.

Hiep sighed. Since the French had surrendered, she had heard stories about their plight and had prayed hard for them. Once she came close to the Providence Institute and watched the women and children inside the fences. She did not see any Japanese threatening or ill-treating them, but she saw the vacant eyes and the weariness of the French refugees. From then on, she lit a candle every night for them in her chapel, under the statue of the Virgin Mary. Now that the French were no longer the masters of the land, she only remembered the good things about them, the French friends of the family, Bishop Allys, Father Cadiere, and Father Urutia. She forgot about the fact that her family had been in and out of favor with the French authorities and that they had treated her father and her brothers pitilessly.

*

Hiep took the letter from Khoi's hand. Diem's handwriting remained as simple and regular as when he was a young boy. The rounds were round; the vertical and horizontal lines were straight, without any artifice. The letter was long and covered many pages. The sheets were neatly numbered.

It was mid-May. The weather was perfect. Khoi had driven up to the Ngu Binh Mountain and now they could look down and see the whole panorama of the City of Hue. There was no haze, no mist. Their eyes could see miles and miles away.

Diem had entrusted the uncoded message to a friend, who had found the means to bring the letter back to Hue within three days. Diem had written it from Da Lat, the resort city in the mountains.

Governor Tran van Ly hosted Diem at that time and he was staying at one of the luxurious guesthouses near the center of the city. The French had deprived Tran van Ly, a loyal friend of Diem, of any promotion since he had been involved in Diem's Restoration of the Greater Vietnam Party in 1933. Tran Trong Kim had recently made him Governor of four provinces.

In his letter, Diem once again explained to Khoi the reasons why he could not accept Bao Dai's invitation to form a cabinet. He explained that he saw too much duplicity in the Japanese policy in Indochina, and knew that very soon Japan would have to abandon Indochina. He argued that in view of the imminent defeat of the Japanese, he should not get involved with a government supported by them.

The letter went on to describe General Tshuchihashi's hostile attitude towards Prince Cuong De. He did not see what Prince Cuong De's role would be anyway, even if the Prince were allowed to return He said the Japanese were not going to waste their time changing horse in midstream, now that they needed every minute to strengthen their defenses in Indochina.

He related his meeting with Tran Trong Kim in Saigon, when the Japanese flew Kim back from Bangkok to Vietnam. He said that in the meeting with Kim, he told the soon-to-be Prime Minister, that he had declined the offer, not because he did not want to collaborate with the Emperor, but because he saw that the conditions of work in 1945 similar to those in 1933. He asked the Emperor to wait until the Japanese were defeated. Then he would gladly come to the Emperor's summon.

Diem said that his conversation with Tran Trong Kim had a strange effect on the old historian. Kim realized that he would only be Prime Minister for the transition. He realized that he would have to go when the Japanese were defeated. He also understood more clearly after talking with Diem, that national independence was merely nominal and that the country was firmly under Japanese rule.

Diem said that he admired Tran Trong Kim, who told him that, having listened carefully to Diem, he would focus in his short mandate on the reunification of the three regions of Vietnam under the nominal rule of the Emperor.

The letter went on with the promise that Diem would find his way back to Hue, as soon as the Japanese were defeated. At the end of the letter, Diem said that he had consulted frequently with Luyen in Saigon, and Thuc in Vinh Long. He said that he had even talked with Nhu, even though he remembered Khoi's interdict. He said that as long as Nhu was not told anything about the party structures, he did not see why they couldn't discuss the present military and political situation. He said that Governor Tran van Ly was the most attentive host, and that he would never forget the warm hospitality shown him by the Governor.

*

By the time they had received Diem's letter, Germany had surrendered. Khoi now agreed with Diem. He said that they would have to wait until the Japanese were defeated.

In the light breeze of the late afternoon, Khoi could see the red and yellow flag, which flew miles away on the top of the Flag Monument, in front of the Noon Gate. The pine trees swayed and sang softly. Over the years, each pine tree had been planted on the Ngu Binh Mountain by a recently appointed mandarin. From the ninth rank to the first rank, each mandarin had, generation after generation, contributed to the beauty of the mountain by planting his own pine tree.

According to *feng shui* or the art of geomancy, the Ngu Binh Mountain was the Imperial Screen, standing guard against enemies coming from the south. The pine trees made the Imperial Screen look like a slumbering jade green mountain god.

In their childhood, Khoi and Hiep and their other brothers and sisters had enjoyed the mountain beauty close up or at a distance, day in and day out. Their home was less than a mile away from the foot of the mountain.

Khoi said, "I agree that Brother Diem should agree to be Prime Minister only after the Japanese are no longer part of the equation, but don't you think that he should have returned to Hue by now?"

Looking up at Khoi's eyes full of torment, Hiep agreed, "Yes, I would like him to be here. There are so many preparations to be made. Here, he will have you as adviser. In Saigon, he hasn't anybody to talk to. Brother Thuc is a bishop, not a statesman, and Brother Luyen only knows the geography of our country."

Khoi nodded and added, "Nhu knows a lot; however, we cannot tell him anything important. Hiep realized that Khoi had been hearing rumors about Mrs. Tran van Chuong again. She sighed, "In time, we will need to review that situation with Nhu. He is too precious an asset to leave on the sidelines forever."

The brother and sister listened to the murmur of the pine trees that sounded as sad as their own sighs.

*

The radio told them the horrible news about the new weapon that the Americans had used on Hiroshima. As the information came in, Hiep was devastated. She cried without shame. She felt as if the world were collapsing around her. What had happened was beyond her understanding, beyond her imagination. It was impossible for her to comprehend such madness created by human kind. She ran to the chapel and cried. The chapel offered her no relief this time.

"How many people have died? Close to a hundred thousand, the radio said. So, we have the modern age, with the power of mass destruction," she sadly lamented.

Hiroshima was a name that was burned into her soul. For a long time, she woke at night in a cold sweat, trying to shake off the terrible visions of her nightmare: thousands upon thousands of bodies caught in the whirlwind of fire. The visions haunted her. From that time onward, she could not bear the thought of war. Hiroshima had transformed her, whose nature was already predisposed to reject war, any kind of war, into an articulate advocate for peace.

To her brothers, she would in future years, impart her abhorrence of war. She would ask them to consider all other options before they resorted to armed forces. Yet, unbeknownst to her, her country was already slipping into one of the longest wars in its history. She did not know that her brothers would not be able to prevent the use of armed forces.

After Hiroshima, Vietnam was to experience thirty years of devastating war that would only end when Hiep herself became a refugee exiled in a foreign land with no hope of seeing her country ever again.

*

After Hiroshima came Nagasaki. Hiep had known Nasgasaki as a Christian city through her reading of many narratives written by missionaries. The day Nagasaki was bombed, Hiep felt the same as if the bomb had been dropped on Phat Diem in her own country, destroying most of its Christian population.

The mighty armies of the Mikado could not defend their country from such a terrible weapon. The war had now become utterly senseless. Hiep prayed that the Japanese Emperor would stop the useless bloodshed.

She did not know what she felt exactly, the day the Mikado surrendered. "In the long history of Japan," Hiep said to herself, "this is the first time its territory will be occupied by foreign troops." Soon she learned that the Mikado had been forced to humble himself and visit the American Commander-in-Chief at the latter's headquarters. Soon, she saw the proud sons of the Sun Goddess vanquished and the dream of Great East Asia destroyed.

The Second World War had effectively ended. But what was to become of Vietnam? The Tran Trong Kim Cabinet had resigned twenty-four hours before the first atom bomb was dropped on Hiroshima. The Prime Minister was unable to form another cabinet.

"It is time for Brother Diem to be back here in Hue. Where is he?" Hiep heard the throbbing question in her mind, day and night.

Diem had left Saigon and was on his way to Hue. He did not know that he would never reach his destination on that fateful trip, and that he would have to wait until 1947 before he would see his family in Hue again.

*

Tuyen had gone to see the Japanese standing on the walls of the Mang Ca Fortress, singing to the setting sun. He had come home with tears in his eyes.

Hiep decided to go and see for herself. It was a beautiful afternoon, and the setting sun was glorious, cushioned against the large masses of red clouds. Facing out, the whole garrison of Japanese soldiers and officers stood on the top of the ramparts of the Fortress and sang. The voices of a thousand men filled the air with moving sadness. The soldiers, in military uniforms, but without their weapons, sang with tears in their eyes to the Sun Goddess and to the Fatherland they had failed to defend. Children of neighboring villages, who day after day had heard the songs, joined in with their high-pitched voices and the Vietnamese who stood under the ramparts cried with the soldiers they had learned to hate earlier.

"How quickly human feelings and emotions change," Hiep thought. "Only a few days ago, the Japanese were seen as the cruel victors; now they are defeated and people feel only compassion for them."

Hiep knew that she would never forget the tears of Japanese soldiers singing in the sunset. She began to understand that human suffering, besides whatever intrinsic value it might have, was often a powerful means of communication, a bridge to mend past enmities, a basis of renewed mutual understanding.

"Are there among them some who participated in the massacre of three hundred thousand Chinese in Nanjing eight years ago? Are there among them some that recently killed with bayonets, famished peasants crazed by hunger, who tried to steal rice bags from the Japanese military convoys in North Vietnam? Are there among them those who recently kicked and beat French prisoners right there inside those walls?" Hiep wondered, her heart going out to them, the vanquished, the proud and sad singers on the ramparts of Mang Ca Fortress.

"Have they been punished enough? Has their nation been punished enough for the excesses and the crimes that they committed in their victorious days?" Hiep asked herself.

Soon the sun went down. It went down like so many of the proud Japanese battleships, like their mother country thousands of miles away. The Japanese soldiers continued to sing until their faces no longer glittered in the twilight, until their shapes became uncertain. The thousand voices went on echoing over the walls of Hue, until Hiep found in the darkness, a safe refugee for her tears.

CHAPTER FOURTEEN
YELLOW STAR ON A RED FLAG

One morning, as the Citadel woke up, people noticed a few strings of red flags hung over the streets. Where did the red flags with a yellow star in the middle come from? At first nobody seemed to know. The Marshal, Protector of the Citadel on his horse ordered his guards to pull them down. By noontime, however, everybody in the Imperial City of Hue knew that the Viet Minh had hung the red flags, and that their agents had arrived in the city.

Note: In 1945 the Marshal Protector of the Citadel (Ho Thanh Do Doc) no longer commanded regular troops. All he had under his command was a platoon of militiamen used as his own bodyguards and as a police force.

An unreasonable fear seized the people. Parents made their children stay home and only a handful of adults ventured into the streets. For a while, very few people in Hue knew much about the Viet Minh, their organization and their ambition.

Only a few officials in Hue heard the news: The Viet Minh had seized the control of Hanoi. The information remained though for a couple of days sketchy and confusing. People waited anxiously for the Emperor to tell them what he knew and what he would do about the Viet Minh. They waited in vain.

*

Khoi was allowed to be brought to the study of the Emperor.

Bao Dai looked at the former Governor in silence for a moment. On a little chair next to them sat the Chancellor of the Imperial Secretariat.

Khoi said, "With your permission, Sire, I would like to talk to you privately." The Emperor waved his hand, "You know that I share everything with Mr. Pham Khac Hoe. You can speak confidentially in his presence."

Khoi insisted, "Sire, I trust your Chancellor as much as you do, but I need to talk to you in private." Pham Khac Hoe stood up and said, "Sire, the Governor will not speak if I stay. Please allow me to go." Emperor Bao Dai was irritated but waved his hand to dismiss his Chancellor.

Khoi didn't think the Emperor would listen to him, but he had to speak out, before it was too late. He asked, "I understand that Your Majesty intends to surrender to the Viet Minh. Is that true?"

Bao Dai frowned, "I am not *surrendering* to anybody, but I do not see how I can resist the Viet Minh. It appears that I have no troops and no officers. It turns out that the Vanguard Youths that Minister Phan Anh has been training recently in Hue are all Viet Minh infiltrators."

Khoi shook his head, "Sire, what you have said is only half true. Units of the National Guards are ready to fight. You have military units and police units ready to fight for you. The Viet Minh has only a small rag-tag army which could hardly defend Ha Noi from a serious attack."

The Emperor asked, "Where would I get the weapons and the ammunition?" Khoi replied, "I have talked with the Japanese authorities. They are ready to supply Your Majesty with sufficient weapons and ammunition if you decide to make a stand against the Viet Minh."

Bao Dai hesitated, "I do not trust the Tran Trong Kim Cabinet. I need a strong Prime Minister. Will you agree to be the new Prime Minister now?" Khoi replied, "Sire, I thank you for having asked me that question before. I told you then that I thought only my brother, Diem, could fill that position. I have not changed my mind. My brother, Diem, is on the way here, to meet with Your Majesty. Please wait for him."

The Emperor complained, "Twice, I offered him the position of Prime Minister and he never responded. If he had been here, we would not be in this horrible situation now. Do you really believe that he will agree to be Prime Minister now?" Khoi nodded, "Yes, Sire. Now that the Japanese have surrendered, it can no longer be said that the Japanese chose him for the position. He will be seen as chosen by you, and you alone."

Bao Dai was pleased. He said, "I'm not ready to give up without a fight. But my chancellor has advised me to abdicate. He says that I don't have a chance against the Viet Minh."

Khoi shrugged, "It is important for Your Majesty, during this critical time, to know where to obtain good advice. I hate to say it behind his back, but your chancellor is on your enemies' side. Sire, be cautious."

But the Emperor kept changing his mind. His view was constantly the one that was held by the person he had last talked to. He hoped that Diem would arrive soon, and take over the responsibility of having to decide whether or not the monarchy should surrender to the Viet Minh. Instead there came the unfortunate news of Diem's capture by Viet Minh agents at Tuy Hoa.

Note: Pham Khac Hoe, was to join the Viet Minh, and later became Chancellor of the Ministry of Interior in Hanoi. He also penned the Abdication Edict that Emperor Bao Dai read as he surrender the Imperial Seal and Sword to Ho Chi Minh's representatives. See his Memoirs: "From the Court of Hue to the Northern Battle Zone "(1983).

*

Diem walked quickly and had no problem in keeping up with the small group that was his captors. They traveled on byroads, as the Viet Minh agents did not want to run the risk of Diem being recognized by the people he had governed earlier. That would be disastrous. The peasants might even try to liberate the prisoner. From Tuy Hoa, where they had arrested him, to Quang Binh, they would have to stay alert, as both Diem and Khoi had left their mark in all the coastal provinces.

They could not fathom the reasons behind the orders that they had received.

By stages, the orders were to take Diem further and further to the North.

In August it rained ceaselessly and the dirt roads became muddier and muddier. They also became more and more slippery. They caught a ride here and there on rusted and crowded busses and trucks, but most of the time they had to walk. Their prisoner walked steadily, without any complaint. He even seemed to enjoy the march under the torrential rain. They had given him a straw hat and a straw raincoat, and he had put them on, as if he had been used to them since childhood. At meal stops, Diem ate like a trencherman. He ate everything they served him and ate a lot. Gradually, they began to appreciate his company. He told them stories about places he had been to. He talked about rice, trees and fish. He never mentioned names. He never mentioned his family or his past career as a mandarin. He explained to them how to recognize a bird by its song, how to catch small crabs in a rice-paddy, and how to catch fish with bare hands in a mountain stream.

The young men listened with growing respect. By the time they arrived in Quang Binh, they had begun to wonder whether they would have the courage to shoot at him if he ever tried to escape.

But instead of running for his life, he started to suffer from bouts of malaria, which sometimes made him shiver for hours while his skin burned with fever. His illness slowed them down considerably. They had counted on arriving in North Vietnam by mid-September, yet by early October they had not left Northern Central Vietnam.

Now because they were afraid to see him die, they started becoming far more authoritative while dealing with the people. For short hauls, they commandeered trucks, jeeps and busses, any type of vehicle with four wheels they could lay their hands on. They had to get their prisoner to the nearest hospital, and allow him to rest.

In Hanoi, North Vietnam, they were not relayed by other personnel. No, they were ordered to take the sick man to the Chinese border. They protested that the prisoner would die if he had to make that long and arduous trip. No matter, he was to be taken to a tribal village in Lang Son.

The guards protested that they would not be able to accomplish their mission unless they were assigned a truck, with sufficient ration slips for gasoline. In the end, they got what they asked for, though the trip to the mountainous region of the Northern provinces in the winter was not exactly a pleasure trip. The old, rusty, smoky truck labored up the slightest slope at a snail's pace. The roads were rutty and the vehicle was constantly getting stuck in a large and deep hole. The guards had to push, and push, with onlookers jumping in to help. But they would not let the prisoner push.

They did not know why they felt like crying when they left the prisoner in the tribal village, which was their final destination. They shook hands with him and wished him good luck. They told him to take good care of himself. On their way back to Hanoi, they rarely talked about him, but when they did, they agreed that the prisoner would not survive the winter.

*

Nobody in the tribe, not even the tribal village chief, knew in advance that they would receive a prisoner. But the chief was used to the foolishness of the French, and now he was sure he could stand some foolishness from the *Vietnamese of the lowlands (dân Kinh)*.

He asked Diem who he was, and where he came from. Diem knew that he should not lie to the tribal chief. He said, "I am Ngo Dinh Diem, a former Prime Minister." The village chief was stunned. He said, "I have heard about you, not as a Prime Minister, but as a district chief, then as head of a prefecture, and then as province chief. Wherever you went, you treated the tribal people correctly, kindly. I have always wanted to meet you."

The tribal village soon showed a new face. It was feast time. A buffalo was killed for the occasion. All the tribesmen presented Diem with personal gifts. Diem felt dizzy and said, "I enjoy celebrations, but I am really sick. I cannot sit up for long." The village chief laughed, "Do not think much about your sickness. By tomorrow we will take care of that. We will cure you."

*

Over lunch at the residence of the late Duke of Phuoc Mon, Ngo Dinh Khoi was discussing with Vo Nhu Nguyen and Phan Thuc Huynh, his closest colleagues, various ways to put pressure on the Emperor to stand firm and to fight the Viet Minh. Khoi advised Vo Nhu Nguyen, who was an aide to Tran Dinh Nam, the Minister of the Interior in Tran Trong Kim's Cabinet, to make sure Bao Dai did not yield to the Viet Minh.

Unexpectedly, at about 2:30 in the afternoon, they heard voices outside. They went to the window and saw a group of Vanguard Youths demonstrating noisily in the street against Khoi. They watched the young men for a while, from behind curtained windows, and then returned to their discussion. Khoi was calm and his friends listened to him attentively. They ignored the growing clamor outside.

Another half-hour passed and then there was a knock on the door. Huan, Khoi's son, opened it. Standing outside was a young man they knew. He was Dang van Viet, the son of Dang van Huong, a friend and colleague of Ngo Dinh Khoi.

Viet politely asked whether Khoi would agree to follow him to the headquarters of the local Provisional Administrative Committee and meet with the Viet Minh leaders. Khoi had known the young man for a long time. Viet's presence was reassuring yet Khoi sensed the danger. Clearly this was a trap. He looked at his wife and son; he saw the futility of any resistance. He faced the young man and asked him to wait for him to get dressed properly. He soon came out of his bedroom, dressed in a black tunic and wearing a black turban. Huan sensing the danger insisted on accompanying his father. Khoi hesitated a moment then nodded, and Huan followed him outside.

As soon as Khoi was in the street, the Vanguard Youths who were demonstrating outside the gate, poured into the garden, blocked the gate and the doors of the house, and advised Khoi's wife, his friends and the servants that they should not attempt to leave the house.

On the same day, the Viet Minh also arrested former Minister Pham Quynh, who for more than a decade had been the most powerful man at the Imperial Court.

*

As soon as she heard about the demonstration in front of Khoi's home, Hiep got dressed and prepared to go and see what was happening. Am asked her to let him go instead. Hiep looked worriedly at her husband. He was not interested in politics but he would do anything to help her and her brothers whenever they needed him. That afternoon, Hiep was not so sure that she wanted Am to go in her place. She was worried and thought that Am might have trouble with the demonstrators. She feared that Am would get into an argument with the demonstrators: She knew that Am was no hero but he would not fail to say what was on his mind when he saw foolishness.

After a while, Am returned. With deep concern in his voice, he said, "They took Brother Khoi and Huan away." He could not hide his distress. Hiep asked, "Where is Sister Hoa? Did you talk to her?" Am shook his head, "The Vanguard Youths have surrounded the place. They are guarding the gate, and groups of them stood in the garden. They would not allow me to go in. Apparently, they have also forbidden everyone inside the house to come out."

Hiep couldn't endure waiting helplessly any longer. She said, "I have to try. I'll go to Brother Khoi's home. They may let me go in." Am took his wife's hand and tried to reason with her, "I have tried everything, Hiep. I assure you that I tried everything with the Vanguard Youths. There were nice kids among them, too. But they have received formal orders not to let anybody in."

Hiep knew that Am was right, but to imagine Hoa all by herself at that moment was unbearable. She turned to Am and asked, "What do you think they will do to Brother Khoi and Huan?" Am tried to be reassuring, "According to the youths, Huan was not involved. He simply volunteered to accompany his father. Brother Khoi was summoned to a meeting with the Viet Minh leaders. I expect that they will be back soon."

Hiep shook her head, "You don't believe a word of what you've just said. They were arrested. They will be...jailed? Executed?" Hiep watched her husband's face, and read there the same fear she was feeling in her own heart.

*

Hiep entered her mother's house. She saw that both Can and her mother already knew what had happened. There was sadness in Mrs. Ngo Dinh Kha's expression, but when she talked, her voice did not tremble, "We have to pray for them. Their fate is in God's hands."

Hiep sat down and bent her head. She still had much to learn from her mother. She remembered when the family was devastated after her father's forced retirement in 1907. Her mother had been as solid as a rock.

She had worked from dawn to dark and not a single complaint came from her lips.

Now in the darkened parlor, her mother again showed her indomitable spirit. Hiep and Can who had been worrying about their mother now drew comfort from her. The woman, who rarely spoke, started to talk about Khoi, her first-born child, her pride for so many years.

Listening to her, Hiep shivered. Her mother was talking about Khoi as if he were already gone, as if she expected never to see him again.

*

It was only two days later, when the Vanguard Youths had left the residence of the Duke of Phuoc Mon that Hiep could go in and see Hoa. Hoa was tending to her garden when Hiep arrived.

Obviously, Hoa had been crying. Her eyes were all red and swollen. But like Mrs. Ngo Dinh Kha, Hoa tried not to show how distressed she was. Her conversation was first directed to the birth of Le Thuy, which had taken place that very day. She said, "Le Xuan must be very happy, I am sure. Poor Nhu, he is in Ha Noi. The conversation drifted towards politics, and Hoa commented without a trace of resentment, "So, the Emperor has abdicated. You know, my husband tried so hard to persuade the Emperor not to surrender to the Viet Minh. He even put his life in jeopardy to give Bao Dai that advice."

Hiep shrugged, "The Emperor was surrounded by people who thought that the Viet Minh had won and that nobody could stop them from taking over the country." Hoa managed to smile, "Nobody except Brother Diem. Where is he anyway?" Now that the question was out in the open, both of them feared the answer. Hoa asked, "Do you think that Brother Diem also encountered problems on his way here?" Hiep nodded sadly, "If he hadn't, he should have been here by now."

The two women walked in silence for a while. The collective dream had rested on Diem and Khoi. Now, all that was left was senseless hope. They drew courage and fortitude from the lessons learned from their fathers and mothers, and from their faith in God. But they knew that the days ahead would be even darker. Hoa commented, "Men do things, while we women can only suffer the consequences of their acts." Hiep knew better than that. Neither Hoa, nor she was a non-participant. They had always been involved with what the men in their families did.

*

It was a splendid day in August. The sun shone bright. White clouds built up castles far in the west while the rest of the sky was an immense blue field. Hiep said: "Somehow, I feel that Khoi and Diem and Huan are safe."

Hoa smiled, "I hope so." Then she shook her head and said, "For Huan, I have no fear. They are not going to kill him. But I fear for my husband. He has been firmly opposed to the Emperor's intention to surrender. The Viet Minh will not forgive him for that. As for Brother Diem, I think that Ho Chi Minh may even want him to join his government."

Hiep disagreed, "Brother Diem has also been opposed to the Emperor's intention to surrender. He is as much at risk as Brother Khoi. But I hope that for the sake of national unity, the Viet Minh leaders will let them go free."

The water of the An Cuu River, fronting the Duke's residence, shimmered in the sunlight. The two women looked at the calm beauty surrounding them and tried to imagine what the future held for them. They did not know that the future would reveal itself to be even more devastating than anything they could imagine at that moment.

*

In Hue, it rained endlessly. In the presence of tens of thousands of sad-faced Hueans assembled in the park in front of the Imperial Palace and surrounded by Vanguard Youths, Emperor Bao Dai surrendered the symbols of his power to the Viet Minh representatives. Among them were the heavy Imperial Seal in solid gold, and the sword that had been handled down to successive Nguyen Emperors from the time of Gia Long, the founder of the dynasty.

One of the Viet Minh representatives callously drew the sword out of its jeweled sheath, held it high in the air and taunted the crowd, "This damned sword is rusty. The symbol of the Imperial power is rusty!"

Note: The Seal was not the Dynastic Seal. He did not know that the original Seal had been lost in the mountains of Quang Binh in 1885, when Emperor Ham Nghi became a fugitive there.

Dai read the Edict of Abdication written by his Chancellor Pham Khac Hoe that contains the quotable sentence: "I prefer to be a citizen of an independent country, rather than the Emperor of an enslaved nation."

Events took place quickly after that in Hue. Within a week, the Emperor, who became Citizen Vinh Thuy, was invited by Ho Chi Minh to join his government as Supreme Advisor. The Japanese in Hue and elsewhere decided to surrender their weapons to Ho Chi Minh's army before the arrival of the victorious Allied troops to disarm them, according to the terms of Japanese capitulation.

*

Over lunch at the residence of the late Duke of Phuoc Mon, on the next day Ngo Dinh Khoi was discussing with Vo Nhu Nguyen and Phan Thuc Huynh, his closest colleagues, various ways to face the new situation after the public abdication of the Emperor. Khoi still believed that the Vietminh did not have strong support among the people and that with the arsenal of weaponry that he could get from the Japanese; there was still a chance to chase the Viet Minh out of Central Vietnam.

Unexpectedly, at about 2:30 in the afternoon, they heard voices outside. A group of Vanguard Youths was demonstrating noisily in the street against Khoi. They watched the young men for a while, from behind curtained windows, and then returned to their discussion. Khoi was calm and his friends listened to him attentively. They ignored the noise coming from outside.

Another half-hour passed and then there was a knock at the door. Huan, Khoi's son, opened it. Standing outside was a young man they knew. He was Dang van Viet, the son of Dang van Huong, a friend and colleague of Ngo Dinh Khoi.

Viet politely asked whether Khoi would agree to follow him to the headquarters of the local Provisional Administrative Committee to meet with the Viet Minh leaders. Khoi had known the young man for a long time. Viet's presence was reassuring yet Khoi sensed the danger. Clearly this was a trap. He looked at his wife and son; he saw the futility of any resistance. He faced the young man and asked him to wait while he went to get dressed. He soon came out of his bedroom, dressed in a black tunic and wearing a black turban. Huan sensed the danger and insisted on accompanying his father. Governor Khoi nodded, and Huan followed him outside.

As soon as Khoi was in the street, the Vanguard Youths who were demonstrating outside the gate, poured into the garden, blocked the gate and the doors of the house, and advised Khoi's wife, his friends and the servants that they were confined to the house.

On the same day, the Viet Minh also arrested former Minister Pham Quynh, who for more than a decade had been the most powerful man at the Imperial Court.

*

As soon as she heard about the demonstration in front of Khoi's home, Hiep quickly got dressed and was ready to go and see what was happening. Am told her that he would go instead. Hiep looked anxiously at her husband. He was not the least bit interested in politics. But he would do anything to help her and her brothers whenever they needed him. That afternoon, Hiep was not so sure that she wanted Am to go in her place. She was worried and thought that Am might have trouble with the demonstrators. Am was no hero, but he never failed to say what was on his mind when he saw foolishness.

After a while, Am returned. With deep concern in his voice, he said, "They took Brother Khoi and Huan away." He could not hide his distress. Hiep asked, "Where is Sister Hoa? Did you talk to her?" Am shook his head, "The Vanguard Youths have surrounded the place. They are guarding the gate, and groups of them stood in the garden. They would not allow me to go in. Apparently, they have also forbidden everyone inside the house to come out."

Hiep couldn't endure waiting helplessly any longer. She said, "I have to try. I'll go to Brother Khoi's home. They may let me go in." Am took his wife's hand and tried to reason with her, "I have tried everything, Hiep. I assure you that I tried everything with the Vanguard Youths. There were nice kids among them, too. But they have received formal orders not to let anybody in."

Hiep knew that Am was right, but to imagine Hoa all by herself at that moment was unbearable. She turned to Am and asked, "What do you think they will do to Brother Khoi and Huan?" Am tried to be reassuring, "According to the youths, Huan was not involved. He simply volunteered to accompany his father. Brother Khoi was summoned to a meeting with the Viet Minh leaders. I expect that they will be back soon."

Hiep shook her head, "You don't believe a word of what you've just said. They were arrested. They will be…jailed? Executed?" Hiep watched her husband's face, and read there the same fear she was feeling in her own heart.

*

Hiep entered her mother's house. She saw that both Can and her mother already knew what had happened. There was sadness in Mrs. Ngo Dinh Kha's expression, but when she talked, her voice did not tremble, "We have to pray for them. Their fate is in God's hands."

Hiep sat down and bent her head. She still had much to learn from her mother. She remembered when the family was devastated after her father's forced retirement in 1907. Her mother had been as solid as a rock. She had worked from dawn to dark and not a single complaint came from her.

Now in the darkened parlor, her mother again showed her indomitable spirit. Hiep and Can who had been worrying about their mother now drew comfort from her. The woman, who rarely spoke, started to talk about Khoi, her first-born child, her pride for so many years.

Listening to her, Hiep shivered. Her mother was talking about Khoi as if he were already gone, as if she never expected to see him again.

*

It was only two days later, when the Vanguard Youths had left the residence of the Duke of Phuoc Mon, that Hiep could go and see Hoa, her sister-in-law. Hoa was tending to her garden when Hiep arrived. They took a stroll around the garden.

Obviously, Hoa had been crying. Her eyes were all red and swollen. But like Mrs. Ngo Dinh Kha, Hoa tried not to show how distressed she was. Her conversation was first directed to the birth of Le Thuy, which had taken place that very day. She said, "Le Xuan must be very happy, I am sure. Poor Nhu, he is in Ha Noi. The conversation drifted towards politics, and Hoa commented without a trace of resentment, "So, the Emperor has abdicated. You know, my husband tried so hard to persuade the Emperor not to surrender to the Viet Minh. He even put his life in jeopardy to give Bao Dai that advice."

Hiep shrugged, "The Emperor was surrounded by people who thought that the Viet Minh had won and that nobody could stop them from taking over the country." Hoa managed to smile, "Nobody except Brother Diem. Where is he anyway?" Now that the question was out in the open, both of them feared the answer. Hoa asked, "Do you think that Brother Diem also encountered problems on his way here?" Hiep nodded sadly, "If he hadn't, he should have been here by now."

The two women walked in silence for a while. The collective dream had rested on Diem and Khoi. Now, all that was left was senseless hope. They drew courage and fortitude from the lessons learned from their fathers and mothers, and from their faith in God. But they knew that the days ahead would be even darker. Hoa commented, "Men do things, while we women can only suffer the consequences of their acts." Hiep knew better than that. Neither Hoa, nor she was a non-participant. They had always been involved with what the men in their families did.

*

It was a splendid day in August. The sun shone bright. White clouds built up castles far in the west while the rest of the sky was an immense blue field. Hiep said: "Somehow, I feel that Khoi and Diem and Huan are safe."

Hoa smiled, "I hope so." Then she shook her head and said, "For Huan, I have no fear. They are not going to kill him. But I fear for my husband. He has been firmly opposed to the Emperor's intention to surrender. The Viet Minh will not forgive him for that. As for Brother Diem, I think that Ho Chi Minh may even want him to join the "revolutionary" government."

Hiep disagreed, "Bother Diem has also been opposed to the Emperor's intention to surrender. He is as much at risk as Brother Khoi. But I hope that for the sake of national unity the Viet Minh leaders will let the go free."

The water of the An Cuu River, fronting the Duke's residence, shimmered in the sunlight. The two women looked at the calm beauty surrounding them and tried to imagine what the future held for them. They did not know that the future would reveal itself to be even more devastating than anything they could imagine at that moment.

CHAPTER FIFTEEN
THE END OF MANY ILLUSIONS

On September 2, Ho Chi Minh proclaimed national independence in Hanoi. Three days later, in Hue, Hiep held in her hands, the text of the proclamation, which read:

'All men are created equal. The Creator has endowed them with certain unalienable rights; among them are Life, Liberty and the Pursuit of Happiness. They are unalienable rights.

'Nevertheless, for more than eighty years, the French imperialists, abusing the standards of Liberty, Equality and Fraternity, have violated our Fatherland and oppressed our fellow citizens. Their acts are the opposite of the ideals of humanity and justice.

'In the field of politics, they deprived us of all liberties. They have enforced inhuman laws...they have built more prisons than schools. They have mercilessly slain our patriots; they have drowned our uprisings in rivers of blood.

'We are convinced that the Allies who have recognized the principles of equality of all people at the Conferences of Teheran and San Francisco must recognize the independence of Vietnam...

'Vietnam has the right to be a free and independent country, and in fact is so already...'

Hiep's hands trembled. So the independence that her father had dreamt of, that her brothers had been fighting for, had been proclaimed. A free and independent Vietnam! Yet, she knew that what was proclaimed was not, in fact, her father's dream. It was not what her brothers had been fighting for.

Her brothers Khoi and Diem had been arrested. Their lives were in jeopardy. If what had been proclaimed was indeed national independence, then both of them should be recognized as heroes. All the people around her should be overjoyed. There should be no fear, no anxiety among the people.

Bitterly, Hiep said to herself, "This is not freedom. This is not independence. We are still far from being there. There will be a long and hazardous road ahead of us, before we finally get there."

She did not know then, that within a couple of days after Ho Chi Minh's proclamation of independence in Hanoi, both her brother, Khoi, and his son, Huan, would be executed, along with Pham Quynh, Khoi's lifelong nemesis, at the border of the Black Panther Forest, sixteen miles north of Hue.

On the day that Hiep sat at home, reading and rereading the proclamation of independence, the people in Phu Cam already knew what to expect from the Viet Minh. Many started going into hiding at night, fearing arbitrary arrest. Those who had at first adhered to the Viet Minh began to distance themselves.

That very day the local Viet Minh, having received orders from *On-High,* condemned Ngo Dinh Khoi, Ngo Dinh Huan and Pham Quynh to death. Their execution followed the next day.

The place chosen for their execution was a clearing near the Black Panther Forest, not very far from the town of Hien Si. As they were taken to the site, they saw a freshly dug hole. It was not a deep hole, but fairly large. They knew that their bodies would be piled up in that hole. Khoi and Huan had prayed during the march. Now the three of them were given some water, and an officer decided that they should be untied. With his hands free, Pham Quynh straightened his eyeglasses on his nose. Ngo Dinh Khoi rearranged the turban on his head.

Khoi looked at his son and saw that the young man was calm and defiant. He turned to look at Pham Quynh who smiled awkwardly and said, "We did not know that one day we would die together, did we?" "Khoi replied,

"That is the irony of life. We acted like enemies, then in the end, we share the same fate."

The Viet Minh officer read their death sentences, ceremoniously, laboriously. The three listened to the sentences and looked at the shallow grave in front of them. They did not react until they were asked, "Do you have any last words to say?" Pham Quynh shook his head, then as an afterthought, he said, "For the last two months, I have been tending to my chrysanthemums. I hope they flower well. I also hope that the revolution you have started will not be soiled by too much blood."

Khoi looked affectionately at his son and said, "You are killing my son whom you have not even found guilty of a misdemeanor. You are killing him because you are afraid that he would tell the world how your system of people's tribunal works." Khoi asked his son, "Are you afraid of dying?" Huan said, "No, Father, I am not afraid." Khoi smiled and went on, "You are killing me not because of any crime I have committed, but because you cannot tolerate any valid opponent. May our country be governed by more tolerant people some day." He turned to his son again, "Do you want to say anything, Huan?" "Huan said, "No, Father." Khoi turned his face to the sky and prayed: "Dear God, please receive the souls of your children."

The first shot was for Khoi. He fell to the bottom of the grave. Pham Quynh was killed next, and his executioners rolled him over and threw him on top of Khoi's body. The third shot was for Huan, who was shoved on top of Pham Quynh. Nobody bothered to see whether they were dead or not. Their bodies were covered with a thin layer of dirt. Then their executioners turned and marched away. A newsletter published by the local Viet Minh announced the execution, and a week later their families learned about their deaths.

But what the victims had said at the last moment, and the location of their execution were only known eleven years later. Two of the Viet Minh soldiers who had witnessed the execution related the details of the event to their parents. The parents later reported to the Ngo Dinh family what their sons had witnessed. This information not only helped the Ngo Dinh family to retrieve Khoi's and Huan's remains, but also helped somewhat to humanize the terrible tragedy.

*

Vo Nhu Nguyen, who had taken lunch with Ngo Dinh Khoi just before his arrest, was also the one who found a copy of the newsletter that announced Khoi and Huan's execution.

After he had left Khoi's home in August, Nguyen was himself arrested and jailed for over a month. On the day he was released he went to see Mrs. Ngo Dinh Khoi, but on his way there, a friend of his stopped him and gave him the copy of the newsletter.

Blinded with tears, Nguyen ran to Khoi's house and showed the announcement to Khoi's wife. Hoa sat down and read the terse announcement several times. The announcement was accompanied by warnings to those who betrayed the country and the revolution like Khoi, Quynh and Huan. Tears ran down her face but she did not sob. She did not make a sound. She did not say a word.

Nguyen sat and watched her, slowly realizing the serious mistake he had made in showing her the newsletter just like that, without any preparation. But he had been crazed with pain too. He didn't think about what he was doing. It was Hoa who, still in a daze, found words of comfort for him. It was she who called for tea to be brought in. Then they sat and exchanged memories, as if death had struck many, many years ago.

Hiep arrived and surprised them, sitting there chatting. The tears and the newsletter were in view though. Hiep immediately understood what had happened. She called the maids and asked them to take Hoa to her room. She accompanied Nguyen to the gate. Then she returned to the house and went to Hoa's room.

It was only then that Hoa, her body shaking uncontrollably, began to sob. Hoa struggled with her grief, until she could talk again. What she said devastated Hiep. There was so much love, so much anger, and so much despair in her words, that Hiep knew she should not say anything. Hiep bent her head over Hoa and listened.

Each of Hoa's words hurt. Hiep knew she would never, ever fathom the depth of Hoa's despair. Once she had witnessed the death of her first-born son. But at the moment Xuan died, devastated as she was, she still had inside her the stirring of the baby she was carrying and she was still had her husband's shoulder.

Hoa had lost both her husband and their only son. Her lineage had stopped. Her life had become a barren desert. Hiep and Hoa knelt to pray silently. Then Hiep began the *De Profundis* in a whisper. Hoa joined in, and they allowed their God to bear a part of their terrible burden.

*

Can cried like a child. Hiep had never imagined that Can would cry like that. The more she tried to comfort him, the more frenzied he became. Am and Hoang stood helplessly while Mrs. Ngo Dinh Kha sat staring vacantly, her eyes almost tearless.

Suddenly, Can stopped crying and wailing. He turned and said, with fear in his voice, "Without Brother Khoi to help him, Brother Diem can never succeed." Hiep noticed first the fear. The intrusion of such an emotion in the general feeling of despair was so unexpected that Hiep was also seized by irrational fear. What Can had said, Hiep dismissed at first, as babbling madness, but a split second later, she was shaken by the truth of Can's tremulous statement.

Can, whose face equally expressed pain and fear, pleaded to Hiep, "Tell them, Sister Hiep, tell them. Without Brother Khoi, Brother Diem will fail." Hiep started sobbing now. "Oh, how true what Can has said! Without Khoi, Diem will be completely vulnerable, even if he survives his present ordeal. But will he even survive?" She heard the scream inside her, "Will he survive? Will they spare him when they did not give Brother Khoi a chance, and when even Huan's life was not spared?"

Hiep looked up at the portrait of her father, flanked now by the newly framed portrait of Khoi. She said to her father in thought, "Father, Brother Khoi is dead. We don't know where Brother Diem is, or if he is still alive. But even if he survives, how can he succeed now that Brother Khoi is gone?" She felt so much pain that she had to close her eyes.

When she opened them, Can was by her side. He said, "I have never been interested in politics. I have stayed away from it, intentionally. But I swear to God, from now on I will try to compensate for the loss of Brother Khoi. If Brother Diem comes out of his ordeal alive, he can count on me."

Hiep looked at him. She had never understood Can. Now she understood him even less. But she realized how important it was for Can's sanity that she agree with him now. So, she nodded.

Can seemed somewhat calmed down. He came and sat near Mrs. Ngo Dinh Kha who asked, "You know how far your Brother Khoi surpassed you in everything?" Can replied meekly, "Yes, Mother, I know it full well." His mother again asked pointedly, "So, what is this talk about compensating for your Brother Khoi?"

Can looked strangely calm now. He held his mother's eyes and answered, "Only partially, Mother, only partially." Mrs. Kha nodded and turning to Giao, Hiep, Hoang, Hoa and Am, she said, "You should never underestimate your brother Can, do you hear?" "All of them nodded. She half closed her eyes and said, "Let him play at least a part of the role that was assigned to your brother, Khoi." Again they nodded.

Daylight was fast fading now. In the parlor huddled around the frail but unbroken matriarch, Giao, Can, Hiep, Hoa and Hoang wept softly. Am stood at a little distance, watching the group of mourners. Even as they mourned, their minds, numbed by the loss of the man who had for twenty years, stood as head of the family, numbed also by fear for Diem's life, still planned ahead, seeking other options. Diminished, defeated, grief-stricken, the small group showed more clearly than ever to Am's eyes, the indomitable will they had inherited from Ngo Dinh Kha.

It was then that Mrs. Ngo Dinh Kha cried out, "Why, God, do you let me see the sun of the morning? Why didn't you let me die before my son?" Can stood up and helped the grieving woman to her room.

*

The Lunar New Year fell on February 2 that year. It was the Year of the Dog. The government had decreed that the people should celebrate the New Year not with their family, but with their community. Few people knew how to implement such an order. In the end, people did not pop firecrackers or cook the traditional festive meals but instead huddled around their fires, because the winter was quite harsh that year.

Hiep went to see her mother on the first of the year. Mrs. Kha told her that she had dreamt a terrible dream the night before. She said she had seen the whole country at war. She said she had seen big battles right in Hue.

Of course the war had already been going on since the previous September, in South Vietnam. The French prisoners of war, released and armed by the British, had started their rampages in Saigon. Then the Viet Minh retaliated. There had been massacres of civilians on both sides. General Leclerc had landed with his troops and fought to reclaim South Vietnam. A sense of *déjà vu*! Eighty years earlier, the French had started their invasion in the same way.

On the third day of the Lunar New Year, Mrs. Kha presided over the family reunion that followed the commemorative ceremonies in honor of her husband.

She began by asking Can to analyze the general situation. Can knew that his mother was giving him the chance to prove his worth in front of his three sisters. Without any hesitation, he began, "At this moment, the Ngo Dinh family is at the lowest point of its history. Brother Khoi is no longer with us. The Viet Minh have presumably captured Brother Thuc and Brother Diem. There remain to carry out Father's dream: Brother Nhu, who is more dedicated to his wife than to the common good, myself, and the three of you."

He looked at his sisters a long moment, and then went on, "I was never interested in politics, until we learned of Brother Khoi's death. Sister Giao, you are the free spirit of the family. You are perhaps the best of us all, but you are like I was in the past. You still don't care for politics. Sister Hiep and Sister Hoang, I know you will both be important for future plans, Sister Hiep especially.

"I have taken over Brother Khoi's interrupted work and gone on with his efforts to develop a national coalition of political parties. I have also taken over Brother Diem's National Revolution Movement. The leaders of the Movement have no objection to my leadership. The French decimated the Movement for a time, in 1944. Fortunately all of its captured leaders have been released from prison.

"The problem is the national coalition. You know that the Viet Minh has continued to harass all the non-Communist parties. Many of the non-

Communists leaders have been kidnapped and murdered. In Hanoi, the war between the Viet Minh and various Nationalist parties is raging on. Governor Tran Van Ly, who is now back in Hue, is working closely with me to form a monarchist coalition. We have come to the conclusion that as Emperor Bao Dai has chosen to become the Supreme Advisor of the Viet Minh government; the *minh Chu* should be Crown Prince Bao Long. Empress Nam Phuong does not seem to oppose such an alternative."

He stopped and waited for comments. Hoang asked, "Do we have any idea of Brother Diem's whereabouts?" Can nodded, "We have been able to track down the place where he was arrested by the Viet Minh in late August last year. From Tuy Hoa to Hanoi, we have learned of his ordeal, from the words of his captors. Also, we know that he is somewhere near the Chinese border, in a Tho tribal village. I have asked Bishop Nguyen Huu Tu of the diocese of Phat Diem, who is the second Supreme Adviser to Ho Chi Minh, to intervene in his favor. The northern chapters of Brother Diem's network are working on Vo Nguyen Giap, who knows of Brother Diem. We hope to have him released within the next thirty days."

Hiep and Hoang already knew the details. What Hoang wanted to know was Can's opinion of the chances of Diem's release. As Can seemed quite optimistic, Mrs. Kha and Can's sisters took pleasure in the thought of Diem's release. They sat in silence for a while, imagining their joy when Diem was finally freed.

Can said, "According to some reliable sources in Hanoi, Ho Chi Minh is about to offer Brother Diem any portfolio of his choice in the Cabinet." It was good news indeed. But none of them thought that Diem would agree to sit with the people who were responsible for Khoi's death.

Hiep startled Can by asking, "How is your relationship with Governor Tran van Ly? "Can looked at his sister, trying to figure out how much Hiep knew. He shrugged and stated casually, "I think we are close friends. He is the apparent standard bearer. I advise him"

He knew that he would not get away so easily with Hiep. He prepared himself for the next question. Hiep continued with her questioning, "Governor Ly is the leader, for now. I do not think we question that point. Brother Diem is absent. Governor Ly stands in for him. Do you agree?"

Can, a bit irritated, reluctantly agreed, "Yes, I will not dispute his leadership in external affairs. I still have to maintain and develop the structures. So I am in charge of internal affairs." Hiep was not to be disarmed. She asked, "What are the potential areas of conflict between you and the Governor?"

Can sighed. So he would have to come clean then. He answered, "The idea of a monarchist party came from the Governor. I am reluctant to commit us to monarchism at this point. Emperor Bao Dai's rule was a disaster. His ambiguity may have been the major cause for our Brother Khoi's death. If he had opposed the Communists, Brother Khoi would not have had to die, and he himself would not have had to accept this farcical role of Supreme Advisor."

Hiep was not in agreement. She said softly, but firmly, "We are not here to distribute blame for Brother Khoi's death. I believe that the people responsible for his death are the people who killed him."

Can remained calm; he went on, "All right, forget what I have just said. I am convinced, however, that we have to keep our options open. Prince Cuong De is still alive. He has never claimed the throne for himself. He has never wanted to be an Emperor, even of a constitutional monarchy. Brother Khoi and Brother Diem had worked on a certain scenario: With the Prince as a Regent, a transition government could be installed. A constitutional Assembly would be convened, so that finally we would have a republic, instead of a monarchy."

He waited for a reaction. There was none, so he continued, "Governor Ly is entirely committed to the Bao Long option. The Crown Prince is only ten years old. So, Governor Ly has proposed that we commit ourselves to a Regency, with Empress Nam Phuong as Regent... he also concedes, though with some reluctance, to Prince Cuong De's role as a Co-Regent."

Hiep asked, "According to you, what is wrong with that option?" Can replied, "I have many objections to such a plan, the first and the most important objection being that all this smells like a Catholic plot. The Empress is a Catholic, the Crown Prince was baptized and has been educated as a Catholic, and we are all Catholics. The non-Christians will find this unacceptable."

Hiep looked at Can. She said, "Earlier, you said that both you and Governor Ly were working on the Bao Long solution. Now, it seems that you are really opposed to that solution. Can you tell us in plain language, what you are for and what you are against?"

Can nodded, "All right, in order to preserve unity within our ranks, I have gone along with the Bao Long solution. But it is the wrong solution. We will have to back out of this commitment, sooner or later."

Hiep agreed, "The sooner the better, I think. We all revere the Empress, but that does not mean that we should support Bao Long as a Pretender and her as the future Regent."

Can seemed surprised by her blunt talk. Then he remembered that she had always been blunt on the anniversary of their father's death. Hiep went on, "So this is a serious conflict on policy. Is there also a personality conflict?" Can shook his head, "No, so far I do not think there is a personality conflict. I have great respect for the Governor, and he knows that."

Hiep said, "I think we all must show the Empress great respect. She has shown tremendous courage since the Emperor was taken to Hanoi to serve in the Viet Minh government. I admire her sincerity with the common people when she attends Mass at the Redeemer Monastery, or here in the Cathedral."

Can agreed that he had only admiration for the Empress, but added that in view of the situation, in view of the fact that the Catholics represented less than ten percent of the population, a regime with only Catholics at the top should not be considered an option.

Hiep would remember that discussion for the rest of her life. Can, like all her brothers, knew instinctively that they should never try to build a regime with only Catholics in the top command, and that they should be sensitive to the followers of the other religions in Vietnam.

Years later, when a Buddhist movement described Diem's regime as discriminatory and anti-Buddhist, Hiep had only to remember all the words and deeds of her brothers, to know that they were being accused maliciously. Can, who would later be branded as a murderer of Buddhists, was adamant against any action that might be construed as insensitive to other religions.

The meeting was frequently interrupted by Giao's bouts of asthma. Giao had been living in stark poverty in recent months. Her husband had died, leaving nothing except a large house that had been assigned to him and his family, by the government. At any time now, the government could reclaim it. Though her eldest son bravely worked day and night to feed the family, there was not enough food to go around. With the revolution, there was no more medicine in public hospitals and Giao was too destitute to afford care in a private clinic.

Hiep looked at her helplessly. Both she and Hoang had offered to help, but Giao adamantly refused. Giao knew that both Hoang and Hiep had gone bankrupt. In peacetime, their construction businesses had been prosperous. But in 1945, their businesses had collapsed. Their clients had refused to pay for the work already done, and there were no new construction projects. Hiep, like Hoang, had also advanced large amounts of money to needy relatives who were now unable to pay back.

Hiep thought, "Even if I had millions now, she would still refuse help. Giao is proud and headstrong like most of the members of our family. The only difference has been her determination to lead a life totally independent of her clan, and her lack of interest in politics." Looking at Giao, listening to her labored breathing, Hiep was seized with fear. "No, not another death in the family. No, not now, right after Khoi and Huan's death." Hiep's fear was not groundless. Only a couple of months later, Giao, the free spirit of the family, was gone.

*

Diem was celebrating the Lunar New Year with the *Tho* tribesmen. After a month in the tribal village, Diem's malaria was gone. He did not know whether the herbal concoctions had anything to do with the miracle. What he did know was that the friendship of the people in the village was a constant encouragement for him to cling to life and to get well.

He took long walks in the forest with the villagers, went on hunting trips with them, and learned to use their bows and arrows and blow-darts. He loved the Tho cuisine, and the villagers were both surprised and delighted that he could consume so much of their food.

With his hunting and fishing skills he did his part in putting food on the table. In his spare time, he called the children to him, and taught them how to read and write. For a while he forgot all about the outside world, and the *people of the plain.* Apparently, they had not forgotten him. Some of the Viet Minh leaders, who had sent him there, thought that he would die of hunger, cold, or malaria. But he did not die. Now, some others thought that he should be recruited to enhance the image of a national coalition government, before Ho Chi Minh started a series of talks with the French. One day in March, a truck came to take him away from his new friends. His destination was the North Vietnam Government Office Building in Hanoi.

*

They arrived early in the afternoon. Vo Nguyen Giap was waiting for him. In his youth, Giap had studied at Quoc Hoc, the school that Diem's father had founded. He knew and admired the Grand Chamberlain. Later, he also admired Diem for his integrity and his resounding resignation in 1933. Giap was born in An Xa, a village in Le Thuy District, located across the river from Dai Phong, the birthplace of the Ngo Dinh family.

Giap told Diem that Ho Chi Minh was in his best mood, and that he would see Diem a little later in the afternoon. He asked whether Diem would mind spending some time with him first. Diem looked at Giap. How many bitter experiences he had gone through! Diem knew about the terrible death of Gaip's wife in a French prison some years earlier. Giap talked softly about her, still nursing his pain. Diem was moved by Giap's sincerity.

Giap was not at all reluctant to answer Diem's questions. Finally, Diem said, "Tell me everything. You know that I have been secluded up in the mountains while important events have taken place in the country." Giap smiled, "Are you still angry with us?" Diem shook his head, "No, I know that many people have been detained. I don't like that, but I understand."

Diem was cautious. He did not know what had happened since his arrest seven months earlier. Though he had talked with the men who escorted him during the ride from his mountain refuge to Hanoi, they had been quite laconic in their answers, and were not willing to give him any specific information.

He asked Giap to brief him on the situation. Giap gave Diem lengthy descriptions of the difficulties that were being encountered by the Viet Minh government. He sounded frank. His briefing was comprehensive. He did not try to hide the problems. Yet, Diem had the feeling that Giap's words had all been rehearsed. He interrupted Giap. He was anxious to know if Giap had any news about his family. Giap looked embarrassed. After a short silence, he told him that Khoi, and his son had been killed at the beginning of the revolution.

Diem gasped. Then, with extreme effort, he controlled himself and asked for more details about Khoi's death. Giap did not know much, but he shared with Diem the little that he did know. Giap concluded by saying, "Chairman Ho wanted me to tell you what happened to your brother Khoi first, before you meet with him. He is going to offer you a portfolio in the next cabinet. He wants you to make the decision, in full knowledge of your brother, Khoi's death. It was a terrible mistake."

Diem excused himself and Giap, understanding his distress, showed him to a fairly large room in the building, saying, "You can use this room for as long as you want. Chairman Ho desires that you agree to work and live here, right in the Government Office Building."

Diem thanked Giap and said that he would like to be alone a moment. When left alone, Diem knelt down on the floor and prayed, tears streaming down his face. For a while, he could not remember any prayer. Then the words of the *De Profundis* came back to him.

He wondered how he could possibly work there; in that building where he had first learned that his brother had been pitilessly killed, along with his innocent, young nephew. He would have to confront Ho Chi Minh himself over their unnecessary deaths.

Then, he bent his head, remembering. His brother had given him so much since their father's death and even before then. How many times had Khoi, even though dreading Diem's reaction, asked him to be a little more patient, more moderate and more humane!

Now Khoi was dead. "What will I do now, without your guidance, Brother Khoi?" In his anguish, he thought again that he should drop everything, flee to a tribal village and live there for the rest of his life, educating the children, hunting and fishing with the adults. But he knew that he would not do that. Khoi had paid the ultimate price with his life. He had to go on with the struggle. Khoi's death should not be in vain. Diem rose up; he was ready to meet with Ho Chi Minh.

*

Ho Chi Minh was not at all unhappy that Giap had told Diem about the death of his brother. He told Diem that at the beginnings of a revolution there were always a few mistakes made. Diem, with a baleful look, did not make any comment.

They were both chain smokers. They talked haltingly, and there were often long silences. Ho Chi Minh assured him that he did not take the murders of Ngo Dinh Khoi and his son lightly. There had been investigations, and those responsible would be punished.

Diem listened, his head, and his heart, still aching. The Communist leader went on to talk about the problems he was facing. Diem recognized the pattern. Ho Chi Minh was giving him the same version of what Giap had said earlier. That was the Communists' trademark. He had dealt with them before, in Phan Rang and Tuy Hoa, when he was Province Chief. He had learned how the Communists rehearsed their phrases to be used with outsiders.

"The country is now facing external and internal problems," the rehearsed text said, with Ho Chi Minh's voice, "Externally; the world is slow in recognizing the government of Vietnam. The Americans remain silent, while the British give the French every means to return to Vietnam. The British have gone as far as to allow the French to replace them south of the Sixteenth Parallel.

"The French are now authorized to be present everywhere south of the Sixteenth Parallel, in order to disarm the Japanese. Taking advantage of their official mandate, the French have completed their reclamation of Southern Vietnam and they are now occupying the cities in South Central Vietnam. China may soon follow the British example and permit the French to replace them north of the Sixteenth Parallel.

"Internally, the Nationalist Parties have joined forces against the government, even though their leaders have been made Ministers in the Cabinet. They are receiving support from the Chinese who came to disarm the Japanese troops. The Treasury is practically empty. The government has been forced to re-institute the taxes that were eliminated earlier.

"It is now time to create a genuine national coalition government to negotiate with the French, first in Dalat, and then in France."

It was an exact repetition of Giap's earlier briefing. Diem was horrified that leaders of a country would submit themselves to such collective control. They obviously were not allowed to think or speak out independently, at least when they were acting in their official capacity.

Chain-smoking and sipping tea, Ho talked as if he was chatting with an old friend. Diem recognized the studied simplicity, the rehearsed pauses and hesitations. In the end, Diem asked, "What do you want of me?"

Ho looked at Diem as if he was distressed at such abruptness. He replied, "We are reshuffling the Cabinet, within a couple of days. I would like you to be a member of the new Cabinet. I want to give you the choice of your portfolio. Tell me what ministry you want, and I will be glad to entrust it to you."

Diem smiled sardonically, "Suppose I want to be Prime Minister, would you accept?" Ho laughed. He said, "I did not offer to let you to lead the Cabinet." Strangely enough, Ho went on, "It is not fun to be the Prime Minister, not at this moment. Only last week, I told former Emperor Bao Dai that I would like him to replace me as Prime Minister."

Diem had the clear impression that Ho was not lying. He asked, "What was the Emperor's response?" Ho did not seem to hear the question. Diem leaned back in his chair and waited. Ho crushed the butt of his cigarette in the ashtray and said with a sigh, "He said that he needed a few days to think about it. In fact, two days later, he came back and told me that he accepted."

Diem laughed, "But you still are Prime Minister. So, what did you tell him, when he said he accepted?" Ho said, "It is not what you think. I had sincerely wanted to quit. But certain comrades insisted that I stay on." There was a note of sincerity in Ho's voice; however, Diem suspected that Ho was merely acting. Diem wondered how clever Ho was at acting. He felt uneasy. He did not want to prolong the conversation. He said, "I sincerely thank you for pulling me out of the northern mountains. I would have died without the generous help of the tribesmen. Now you offer me a post in your Cabinet. I appreciate that. But let's not waste time with small talk. I cannot accept a position in your Cabinet. I cannot do that, not only because your men have killed my brother and my nephew, but because I recognize your government as a Communist government, whatever adornments you use to try to cover that fact."

Ho Chi Minh protested, "There is no longer a Communist Party in Indochina. We have decided to disband the Party in order to better serve the country." Diem said bluntly, "I would prefer that the Communist Party remain visible, and that the Communist Party members be recognized as such. People may now say that you are disbanding the Indochina Communist Party in order to hide the fact that its members are holding the key posts in the government."

Ho insisted, "You know that is not true! Many key positions are in the hands of the Nationalist Parties, who act as if they were nations within the nation. You, on the other hand, have the reputation of integrity and selfless patriotism. I sincerely want you in my government." Diem replied, "I'm sorry, but I have to decline the honor."

Ho Chi Minh remained friendly, "Please do not say no in such a hurry. You are welcome to stay in this Government Office Building, like all the comrades in the Cabinet who wish to do so. You are welcome to stay for as long as you wish, even if in the end, you cannot be convinced to be part of the Cabinet."

Diem stood up and asked, "Am I a free man, or am I still a prisoner?" Ho also stood up. He smiled courteously, "You are free, of course." Diem asked again, "That means I can leave, and go anywhere I want?" Ho nodded as he remarked, "I don't think that Hanoi is very safe at this moment. Be careful if you do not know the city well."

Sensing a threat, Diem replied, "Don't worry about me. I am not a child." Ho nodded again, but laughed as if he had just remembered, "It is dark now. It is better that you stay here tonight. As a matter of fact, we have ordered an elaborate dinner in your honor tonight. Please join us for the dinner. "

Exhausted by the three-day ride from the mountains, and the news of Khoi's death, Diem was rather reluctant to accept the invitation, but years of self-discipline enabled him to seem strong that evening. He thanked Ho and said that he would stay for dinner.

*

He had heard that the former Emperor had been appointed Supreme Advisor and hoped that he would see Bao Dai at dinner. He was disappointed when he saw that Bao Dai was not among the people gathered around the table that evening.

Besides Ho Chi Minh and Vo Nguyen Giap, there were only Nguyen Luong Bang, Tran Huy Lieu and Hoang Minh Giam, all of them Communist leaders. Diem looked at them, observing their mannerisms. He had known all about Vo Nguyen Giap and Hoang Minh Giam. He had also known about Nguyen Luong Bang, a diehard Communist, whose two separate escapes from the French jail had made him famous.

Diem learned that Nguyen Luong Bang and Tran Huy Lieu had been present at the abdication of Emperor Bao Dai in Hue, in August 1945.

Bao Dai had abdicated one day before Khoi and Huan were arrested. Diem asked pointed questions about his brother's arrest and murder. Both Lieu and Bang were evasive. They assured Diem that they had not known anything at the time. It was a mistake made by the lower echelons.

Diem asked them about the strategy that they intended to use, to deal with the French. Ho looked at his colleagues in embarrassment. Apparently, no definite strategy had been planned. Finally, Vo Nguyen Giap said, "What we can do is wage guerrilla warfare in the zones that the French have occupied. The French have started to wonder whether they can sustain casualties every day, every night, while trying to hold on to the territory they have recaptured." Diem nodded, "Guerrilla warfare is the only option. We do not have the weapons the French have. It is also the only way we will be able to keep our casualties low."

Giap went on, "In the meantime, we need to negotiate with the French. We have to be able to restore peace." Diem asked, "What do you have to offer the French, to obtain peace?" They all looked at Diem, uncomprehending. Diem explained his question, "What concessions are you ready to offer the French, so that they call a halt to further attacks?"

Again Ho and his colleagues looked at one another. They had, apparently, not considered what they would offer the French. Diem was perplexed. "How do they function? What are their mechanisms for decision-making?"

Ho informed Diem, "The French are about to land in Haiphong. We have asked General Lu Han, the Chinese Commander-in-Chief, to temporize as long as possible. Lu Han has written to the French advising that, although China has agreed to be replaced by the French north of the Sixteenth Parallel, General McArthur, the Allied Commander-in-Chief, must first approve such an agreement before it can be implemented." Diem replied tersely, "There is no doubt in my mind that McArthur will approve the agreement between the French and the Chinese." Diem asked, "Then, what do you plan do next?"

Ho shrugged, "I think that then it will be time to negotiate with the French, permitting them to land in Northern Vietnam." Diem asked, "Is that your only concession to the French?" Ho asked, "What else do you think the French want?"

Diem reflected for a short time, and then replied, "The French will tell you first, what concessions *they* are ready to make. They will say that they are ready to declare that Vietnam is an independent state." Ho and his colleagues exclaimed, "That would be incredible!" Diem shook his head, "They will add that Vietnam will be independent within the Indochinese Federation, and perhaps also within a kind of French Union, along with other former colonies."

They were eager to hear more. Diem told them, "The problem is that they will want you to give South Vietnam to them. They will tell you they want the old *Cochinchina* back." Vo Nguyen Giap cried out, "Never! We cannot accept a truncated Vietnam." Ho waved his hands, "Mr. Diem has put his finger right on the sore spot. Suppose that is what the French will ask. What do you suggest that we do?" Diem smiled, "You have to negotiate, even when the French ask for unacceptable concessions. You need to be patient. You have to tire them out. In the end, those who tire out first will have to make the biggest concessions." Ho nodded, "I understand you, perfectly; however, time may be working against us." Diem looked at Ho and said sadly, "Then you are already on the losing side at the negotiating table."

Ho sighed, "We need you on our team. We thought for a while that Bao Dai, in view of his familiarity with the French, could assist us in our negotiations with the French. We realize now, that familiarity with the French is not all that we require in a negotiator." Vo Nguyen Giap added, "We have many sympathizers among the French. Our French friends will help us in our negotiations, too. We definitively need somebody like you on our team."

Diem replied firmly, "I'm sorry, but I cannot bring myself to work with you after what happened to my brother. As for French friends, I would like to offer you a word of caution. Friends are friends. Vietnamese or French, Japanese or Chinese, all friends are invaluable. They are invaluable to us personally. They are, however, not our political allies, nor our comrades. In the end, like ourselves, our friends have also to look after the interests of their own country."

Ho nodded agreement. Vo Nguyen Giap again offered courteously, "You are our guest for as long as you want to stay. You are free to go anywhere, anytime."

The next morning, after a good night's rest at the North Vietnam Government Office Building, Diem walked out of the gate. No one asked him any questions. He was a free man again.

*

The first thought Diem had was to find the few friends he knew in Hanoi. He abandoned the idea as he walked. He was afraid that he was being followed, and that any friend he visited would be in trouble with the government. He decided finally to find temporary refuge at St. Paul's Hospital.

Sister Françoise was thrilled to see him. Quickly she made arrangements to provide him with a safe room. Diem told her that he yearned to see Nhu, whom he knew to be in Hanoi. Within an hour, Nhu arrived.

Nhu could not contain his joy at seeing Diem. He exclaimed, "How is it, that you are here? I thought you were dead!" Diem laughed, but at the thought of Khoi, his laughter ended. He asked Nhu, "Do you know about Brother Khoi and Huan?" Nhu sadly nodded. Joy suddenly disappeared from his face.

They went down into the courtyard and walked. Nhu asked, "Have you accepted?" Diem was at first surprised by the question. Then he realized that only *he* had been lost in the northern mountains and that in the cities, rumor mills continued to function as usual. He smiled and asked, "Have I accepted what?" Nhu laughed, "We have been expecting you for the last two weeks. Bishop Le Huu Tu, the Supreme Advisor of the government, has been telling everybody that he has obtained your release. Everybody in town knows that Ho Chi Minh needs you in his government."

Diem shrugged, "Maybe. But I don't need to be in his government. What did you expect? Did you expect that I would agree to serve in a government that ordered the killing of Brother Khoi?" Nhu shook his head, "Of course not. The order to kill Brother Khoi might, however, have come from lower echelons." Diem nodded but was not easily placated. He asked Nhu, "Do you have other news about the family?" Nhu pulled Diem to a bench in the shade of a large plane tree and undertook to tell Diem all that he knew.

"Mother is all right, after the initial shock. She is not alone. Can, Hoang and Hiep are constantly at her side. They are all right, too. I am here because I was assigned, just before the revolution, to the National Museum in Hanoi."

Nhu sighed, "I came here, thinking that Le Xuan would be able to join me right away. But, because of the revolution, we have remained separated. Le Xuan has given birth to our first child. Her name is Le Thuy, named after our native district in Quang Binh." Diem smiled, "At least in the naming of your first child, you have won the argument against your wife."

He blushed, as he was not good with jokes. Nhu went on, "I heard that Sister Giao's asthma has taken a turn for the worse. My in-laws are here, in Hanoi. They are afraid of being arrested by the Viet Minh at any time now. They have hoped that you would agree to be in the government. That would save them from a lot of trouble."

Diem thirsted for more information. He asked, "What about Emperor Bao Dai? What happened? I understand he is now the Supreme Advisor." Nhu shrugged, "He is here in Hanoi. I have met him a couple of times. He is the same Bao Dai, always chasing women, dragging Ho Chi Minh along with him now." Diem exclaimed, "That's impossible! Ho Chi Minh, a partner in Bao Dai's pleasures parties? Come on, you are kidding!" Nhu looked serious, "That was what Bao Dai said. He said he has given Ho rides home many times, when Ho was dead drunk."

Diem shook his head. He was not happy to hear these allegations about Ho's nightlife with Bao Dai. He said, "I don't know if these rumors about Ho are true or not, and you don't either. The Emperor may have told you stories to make himself seem more interesting. I don't want you to repeat these stories about Ho."

Nhu threw up his arms, "I didn't know that you were a secret admirer of Ho!" Diem again shook his head, "No, I am not. I don't admire anybody who allows murders to be committed, and does not take responsibility for them. However, there have always been too many evil rumors going around in our country. Even when you are not assassinated, your reputation is."

Nhu had to agree. He had seen the many evil rumors spread around, about his mother-in-law. He said, "Don't worry. I am not going to repeat those stories about Ho to anybody. There are too many secret service agents around." He laughed again, showing his strong teeth. He was indeed one of the most handsome men in Hanoi, in those days.

Diem told Nhu, "Yesterday, while I talked with Ho Chi Minh, he told me that only a week ago he had asked Bao Dai to replace him as Prime Minister. I thought it was only a trick to make the Emperor look ridiculous." Nhu confirmed the fact, "Bao Dai told us the whole story. He said that Ho was sincere when he made his offer. Ho apparently was quite depressed and really wanted to quit. Two days later, when Bao Dai said he accepted, Ho's mood had changed. He told Bao Dai that he had reconsidered and found that being a Prime Minister did have its advantages."

Diem asked, "How is the Emperor? He doesn't live at the Government Office Building. He must have independent means. Who provides for him? I don't think that the government can afford to pay him much."

Nhu laughed, "Don't worry about him. He told me that the Empress sends him money from time to time. He also receives money from his mistresses here. Excuse me; I know that I should not mention that to you. His main source of revenue comes from our old friend, Mai Van Ham, the millionaire. Ham has given the Emperor a house, a car and everything else he needs."

Diem said, "I don't want their secret police to spot you with me. I am going to disappear for a while." Diem was happy to see Nhu. Yet, he found Nhu too flippant and too casual for his taste. He was not about to divulge his immediate plans to Nhu. Diem had, indeed, while he was talking to Nhu, reflected upon a plan of action and was about to carry it out. He did not ask for help from Nhu, even though he was penniless.

Not wanting to be bothered with Tran van Chuong, Diem told Nhu that he would disappear in a couple of days, and that Nhu should not try to contact him. Nhu felt a little hurt, but he did not question his brother's decision. He knew that the decision that Khoi had made earlier in 1943 was still valid, and that he should not attempt to intrude into the political activities of his brother.

*

The first person that came to his assistance, after the Sisters of St. Paul's Hospital, was the same Mai Van Ham who had been financing Bao Dai. A devout Catholic, Mai Van Ham had entertained tenuous, though real, ties with Diem's network in North Vietnam. An indiscretion of a Sister at the Hospital made Ham aware of Diem's presence there. He immediately came to see Diem and advised him to seek better refuge. He also provided Diem with a substantive war chest that allowed Diem to carry out his organizational work around Hanoi.

In agreement with Ham and other leaders of his northern network, Diem soon took refuge at the *Redeemer Monastery* at Ap Thai Ha. From there he made frequent trips to the villages around Hanoi, to recruit membership for his newest creation, the National Solidarity Front *(Mat Tran Quoc Gia Doan Ket)*. The name appealed to him as he was witnessing the daily confrontations between the Communists and the Nationalists. He was horrified by the assassinations, bombings and kidnappings practiced by both sides in what appeared to be an unending struggle for power. After the assassinations and the skirmishes, came frontal assaults against well-defended targets. Then whole armies were deployed and launched against one another in a bitter civil war.

As the Nationalist Parties relied heavily on the support of the Chinese armies, their days were numbered, after the Chinese agreed to withdraw from Vietnam, north of the Sixteenth Parallel, allowing the French to come in to disarm the Japanese troops.

In the end, the Viet Minh made temporary peace with the French. The Viet Minh troops turned their full fury on the Nationalist forces and destroyed most of them in bloody battles. The remnants of the Nationalist units regrouped themselves in Southern China.

Diem studied the conflict closely, though he was horrified by it. For the first time, Diem saw what a civil war looked like. He would bear the mental scars of that bloody war for the rest of his life. He also learned many lessons from it. He learned not to underestimate Vo Nguyen Giap and his under-equipped troops. The civil war also showed him that there would be no way to co-exist with the Communists. They had not, and never would learn to share power.

It was in his daily contact with the common people, in his efforts to organize small cells and chapters of the National Union Front, that Diem found his joy. He also came to understand the difference between the immense reservoir of patriotism among the people, and the small political factions that disputed among themselves, and that claimed to best represent the will of the people. The National Solidarity Front that Diem tried to create reflected what Khoi, his brother, had done in Hue. It was an earnest attempt to have people unite themselves against the splinter groups that exploited them, and failed to represent them.

From that time on, Diem always believed in the possibility of creating an organization large enough and flexible enough to include all the political tendencies in the country. Such an organization would prevent political struggle and armed conflicts among the people. Bent on seeing only the benefits of such an organization, he failed to see that such a concept would lead to the permanence of monopartism. He also failed to see that to give himself the right to determine when the people were mature enough, was a capricious and authoritarian concept.

Working alone in the most precarious environment, seeing with his own eyes the horrors of civil war, which had resulted from partisan thirst for power and partisan intolerance, Diem came to include in his mind a major erroneous concept in his political philosophy.

*

In Hue, the news of Diem's release galvanized Tran Van Ly, Ngo Dinh Can and the Empress into action. It was then that the Empress, departing from her usual reservation, told Tran van Ly that she was ready to commit herself to the 'Crown Prince' solution.

From time to time, after Mass at the cathedral, the Empress still dropped by to see Mrs. Ngo Dinh Kha. She could do it, now that Diem was no longer officially a suspect of the regime. But she never stayed long. A Viet Minh official was never too far behind her.

In the meantime, French troops under the command of Lt. Colonel de Crèvecoeur arrived in Hue on March 29, 1946. As the column of tanks and armored cars arrived from Laos, the French refugees in Hue, consisting mainly of women and children, lined up the streets in the French Quarter to welcome the troops.

The Viet Minh troops posted around the French Quarter started a real siege, and for the first time, the inhabitants of Hue prepared themselves for a long war. The atmosphere of war was omnipresent, even though on March 6, in Dalat, the Viet Minh had signed the Preliminary Accords with the French. According to the terms of the Accords, France would recognize the Republic of Vietnam as a free state, within the Indochinese Federation and within the French Union.

The Viet Minh was ready to accept major concessions in order to preserve peace, but Ho Chi Minh and his colleagues would not agree to leave South Vietnam under French rule. The French, on the other hand, knew that they could push Viet Minh troops into the mountains at any time; therefore, they did not see any reason to give South Vietnam back to the Viet Minh.

*

Hiep lived in complete uncertainty. At night, Am left their home and went to sleep in his friends' homes, never two consecutive nights in one place. Can did the same. One night, he showed up at Hiep's house. Hiep almost burst laughing, as she had just a moment earlier, seen Am off to a safer home.

Life in such a precarious environment was not favorable to long-term planning. Yet, with all the uncertainties in their life, Can, Hiep and Hoang often huddled around a small table and talked about the future. They knew that war between the French and the Viet Minh was inevitable. They also knew that in such a war, the Viet Minh troops would lose on the first round and would withdraw to the mountains and the jungles of Vietnam.

The French would rule over the plains and the cities, unless a government could fill the vacuum of power. While Tran Van Ly was becoming a more ardent monarchist, and definitely supported the Crown Prince solution, Can and his sisters questioned the wisdom of such a choice. Emperor Bao Dai had of his own accord, stepped down from the throne. They did not think that he should be made Emperor again. Prince Bao Long, with the Empress as Regent was attractive at first as an option, but it was clearly impossible for Can and his sisters to envision a regime with a Catholic Emperor and a Catholic Regent.

They thought that the time had come to forget about monarchy. Soon enough, they were the first republicans in the family. As well, though agreeing on the surface with Governor Tran Van Ly' s monarchist views, Can saw that eventually he would be drawn into an unpleasant conflict with his brother, Diem's, best friend.

Can sighed. Two years earlier Tran Van Ly could have been put in jail after he had been found to be one of the leaders of Diem's National Restoration Party. His wife, who was very close to the Empress, had gone to her and asked for help. The Empress had intervened effectively. Ly was simply transferred to another province, keeping his rank and function as Chief of Province. Under Tran Trong Kim, through the intervention of the Empress once again, he was made Governor of four provinces in Southern Central Vietnam.

Can sighed again, "No favor given, will be forgotten. In the end, every favor carries its price tag." He would prefer Governor Tran van Ly to distance himself a little from the Empress. Then again, Can could not be sure of Diem's opinion on the matter. "Maybe Brother Diem would like me to commit myself to the service of the Empress. He has such admiration for her!" Can would have liked to see his brother in Hue. But Diem, last seen in Hanoi, had disappeared into thin air. Can didn't know at the time that Diem, disguised as a priest of the Redeemer Monastery, and escorted by Canadian priests, had boarded a French plane and flown south to Saigon.

*

Diplomacy and revolution did not mix well. The revolutionaries had not yet learned the art of bargaining.

After the disaster in Dalat, where the Preliminary Accords had not accomplished anything for Vietnam, but had allowed the French to land safely and comfortably in North Vietnam, Ho Chi Minh himself went to France for the Conference of Fontainebleau. The Conference went nowhere, when the Vietnamese delegation learned that the French had created the Autonomous State of Cochinchina.

In a last ditch effort, Ho achieved the signing of a 'modus vivendi', which recognized the independence of Vietnam within the Indochinese Federation and the French Union. The 'modus vivendi' also authorized the French to establish their presence in the entire Vietnamese territory. Furthermore, it postponed the discussions on the 'Autonomous State of Cochinchina', for a future time.

Whatever propaganda efforts the Viet Minh deployed to make of the 'modus vivendi', as a diplomatic success, the average Vietnamese understood that Ho Chi Minh had been *had*. After such a diplomatic *success*, the only option for the Viet Minh was to prepare for war. The French also knew that war had become inevitable and prepared to attack first.

*

On December 20, 1946, Vo Nguyen Giap launched his General Offensive against the French. But in Hue, for weeks before the General Offensive was declared, Hiep was aware of all the preparations. Units of regular troops and the self-defense militia started digging foxholes and trenches in her gardens. Meter-thick concrete and dirt barriers were erected in the streets. Militiamen armed with swords and sharpened bamboo sticks ran this way and that way, commanded by platoon commanders who may have been even more ignorant than the men they commanded.

Two batteries of 75-mm cannon were pushed through Phu Cam, on their way to the Ngu Binh Mountain. Two Japanese, who had deserted from the Imperial Army when Japan surrendered to the Allies, commanded the batteries. They were served by a horde of militiamen. These were the only modern weapons of the rag-tag army, which lay siege to the French quarter in Hue.

Hiep was troubled as she watched the regular army units go by with their rifles of World War I vintage. How could they fight against the well-armed French garrison? The militiamen had no firearms. They were armed with broad-bladed knives, swords of all shapes and sizes, and bamboo sticks.

Hiep wondered how they could hope to win against three hundred French men armed with submachine guns, heavy machine guns and mortars. In the weeks preceding the siege she had seen the French display their weaponry, as if they hoped to convince the local Viet Minh not to launch an attack against them.

On the night of December 21, that year, the first assaults were launched. The self-defense militia was ordered to attack and secure the strongest French defenses, at the Morin Hotel. This hotel was a sizable complex, with two-story buildings surrounding a large rectangular inner court. The walls of the building were remarkably strong, in fact, at some places, the walls were more than a meter thick.

Having received the order *from On High,* the militiamen swam across the Perfume River. Most of them survived the swim, except for a few who were not good swimmers. At midstream, where the water was the coldest, they suffered severe cramps, and drowned. The survivors arrived on the Right Bank and followed the underground sewage system until they emerged into the inner court of the Hotel.

The French had decided not to defend the ground floor, but they had seen the arrival of the militiamen and from the windows of the second floor, a heavy crossfire caught the attackers as they emerged into the inner court. Militiamen tried to rush to the arches of the ground floor, leaving behind hundreds of dead and injured. Once inside the ground floor, their fate was not enviable either.

The French had withdrawn to the second floor and only needed to defend the staircases. The attempts by the militiamen to rush the stairs were futile and costly. From time to time, the French men at the top of the stairs sprayed the hapless militiamen with a hail of bullets.

A few militiamen had homemade hand grenades, but they were of no use against the French. Most of the time they exploded too soon, causing unfortunate casualties among the attackers themselves. All night long, the militiamen sustained casualties without any hope of inflicting damage to the French occupying the upper floor. Finally, in the early dawn, they received the order to withdraw. The swim back to the left bank in the bleak morning light proved to be far deadlier than the swim across the night before. French sharpshooters leisurely picked one target after another among the swimmers, and carelessly sent them to the bottom of the river.

The regular units did not fare any better in their attacks against the Providence College, the Dai Cang Temple, and the former Resident Superior's Headquarters. Their primitive weapons were useless against an enemy who had surrounded their defense perimeter with multiple barriers of barbed wire.

The same wanton ritual was repeated, night after night. Casualties among the militiamen were extremely high, while there was almost none on the French side. The French had procured searchlights, which they put to good use. The searchlights made the swimmers in the Perfume River and around the French defense perimeters easy targets, as they were spotted long before they came within firing range. The massacre went on for almost two months.

Hiep listened to the horror stories told by young militiamen who had managed to survive. She saw them shivering with fear and cold and wondered if there was any justification to that battle of Hue. She came to the conclusion that there was no rationalization to any type of war.

*

Hiep never thought that her life was in danger while she stayed in Phu Cam. She was very worried about the fate of her mother, Can, and her sister, Hoang. She did not know where they were, after the General Offensive was launched. She guessed that they had joined Le Xuan at her house near the Monastery of the Redeemer. But then people told her that the whole household had moved. She did not know that Can and her mother, together with Hoang and her daughter Hoang Anh, Le Xuan and her daughter, Le Thuy had been 'forcibly moved to safety' to Lai An village, northeast of Hue.

Can considered Nhu's villa near the Monastery of the Redeemer, to be a safer place than Ngo Dinh Kha's home in Phu Cam. He thought that his household could easily dash into the Monastery and find refuge there if it became necessary. Unfortunately, the villa was located right on the battle line between the French and the Viet Minh troops. So, after the first night of fighting, the Communists came knocking at the door and commanded the household to follow them.

They were forced to walk from there to various locations specified by the Viet Minh authorities. At most resting places, they were sheltered in a barn. Mrs. Ngo Dinh Kha was always provided with a straw mat for the night. The others were shown where they could find straw, which they put on the floor to make their own beds.

The Viet Minh officials were not intentionally hostile towards them, but the long marches through muddy paddies had become extremely exhausting for Mrs. Ngo Dinh Kha. The terrible diet provided by the Viet Minh further endangered her health.

Can finally demanded that they be allowed to stay in one place, long enough to recuperate. So, for the last weeks of the battle for Hue, they stayed at Lai An village, a small place near the sea, about twenty miles north east of Hue.

*

After numerous pieces of artillery and ample supplies of ammunition had been parachuted to the French, the chaos of daily battle became unbearable.

Hiep had insisted on staying in Hue, even after stray bullets pockmarked the walls of her home and mortar shells rained on her garden. Now her husband convinced her that they had to leave, for the sake of the children. Her mother-in-law, Mrs. Nguyen van Dieu, also had to be considered, and Hiep finally agreed to leave home.

Now they had to cope with the uncertainty of being refugees. Am decided to take the longest, but safest route to their destination. They left Phu Cam and went west into the mountains, with Mrs. Nguyen van Dieu and the children.

Far into the mountains, Am led his family east southward toward the sea. He had rightly chosen the safest route, and they had managed to avoid being at any moment, close to the battle line. After three days' march, they arrived safely in Hoa Da. The march had taken its toll on the children, but they soon forgot about the ordeal, as life in Hoa Da, where they owned a small farm, was not without some charm.

Hiep liked the sights around her, the smell of the sea in the air, the sound of the waves that could be heard at night. But the abysmal news the villagers received on a daily basis appalled her. Few families did not have a husband, a son, a brother, or a relative that was not injured or killed in the battle of Hue. She prayed day and night for those who had died and those who would soon die. She was horrified by the war.

She understood why her husband announced that they would not celebrate the Lunar New Year that year. Instead of celebrations, they had a day of prayer. No toys, no firecrackers, no traditional delicacies! Cold drizzle started on New Year's Eve and continued for the first three days of the year. Hiep and her family experienced one of the bleakest Lunar New Years of their lives.

In late February, French reinforcements landed in Da Nang and were rushed to Hue. They broke open the siege of Hue. The rag-tag army, which had lay siege to the French for more than two months, received an order *from On High*, and fled to the mountains. The battle of Hue was finally over.

As the last units of the National Defense Army retreated out of Hue, they burned down the Imperial Palace. Hiep watched the dense smoke billowing from the Palace. She cried out helplessly, "They are burning down two hundred years of history."

The Viet Minh had come and gone. Hue, much sadder and poorer, having seen its cultural treasures of two hundred years obliterated, and its imperial days reduced to regrets and memories, stood forlorn in the spring drizzle, most of its pride gone. Among the people, few illusions were left.

The high tide of the revolution had come and gone, and the people of Hue were left stranded in a landscape they could hardly recognize as their native city.

CHAPTER SIXTEEN
A TIME FOR INDECISIONS

The battle of Hue had lasted two months. It started with Giap's order to launch a general offensive all over Vietnam on December 19, 1946, and ended when General Burgonde's reinforcement column arrived in Hue on February 7, 1947.

When the noise of battle subsided, Hiep and Am had to make one of the most difficult decisions of their life. Being cut off from Hue, they had scant information about what was happening. On the faith of reports gathered from people who said they had gone to Hue and found the city completely quiet and safe, they decided to leave their refuge of Hoa Da and move their family back to Hue.

On their way home, they saw the charred bodies of Viet Minh soldiers on the highway. French military jeeps and trucks crowded with heavily armed soldiers, sped past them and the columns of refugees, in both directions. They wondered at times whether they had made a wise decision. As it turned out, when they arrived, they found Hue quiet and safe.

A few days after Hiep had arrived home, Mrs. Ngo Dinh Kha and her group showed up in Hue. The Viet Minh officials had forgotten about them, when the French reinforcement arrived from Da Nang. Can immediately decided to return to Hue, as Mrs. Ngo Dinh Kha's health was rapidly declining.

When they arrived in Hue, Mrs. Ngo Dinh Kha found that she no longer had the use of her legs. She struggled for a long time, trying to regain the use of her limbs, but finally she had to accept the fact that she was no longer able to walk.

The joy of their reunion was marred by the sudden infirmity of the matriarch. Hiep spent more and more time with her mother, relieving Can whenever she could, by their mother's bedside. Hoang, who had shared the two-month ordeal with her mother, became very close and visited her mother daily.

Le Xuan heard no news from her husband for a few weeks, after she returned with her baby in Hue. She thought he still was in Hanoi. In fact, he was making a long trek through the jungle of Laos to Saigon.

*

A month later, Nhu appeared at Hiep's door. He was still emaciated. He had walked in the jungle for three weeks and the two months' rest in Saigon had not helped him to regain his strength. Hiep froze and stared at him for a long moment, overwhelmed by her joy. Finally, Nhu laughed and said, "Come and touch me, I am not a ghost."

He was back, with his booming voice and his infectious laughter. Hiep couldn't help crying as Nhu calmly told them about his long ordeal in the jungle. Hiep and her family were amazed that Nhu had risked his life by walking several hundred kilometers on jungle trails.

Actually, Nhu did not have any other alternative. By June 1946, his in-laws had been placed under house arrest. As Tran van Chuong was not exactly a model of bravery, and as Mrs. Chuong could no longer stand to live within the confines of her home, they had rendered life impossible for Nhu, who had been staying as a guest there. By December, Nhu decided to flee and seek refuge in the Phat Diem diocese.

Bishop Le Huu Tu was no longer the Supreme Advisor of the government. The Catholic self-defense units created by the Bishop had declared the diocese an 'autonomous zone' and had repelled the Viet Minh's attempts to overrun it.

Nhu decided to go there. The Chuong's wanted to join him in his flight. Nhu did not like the idea, as the Chuong's would represent more trouble than he could afford. He could not leave them behind, though. In December, the three of them fled. When they arrived in Phat Diem, Nhu was not very confident in the capabilities of the Catholic self-defense militia there. He decided to move farther south. Bishop Le Huu Tu sent him off with guides who took him to Thanh Hoa Province. From there they went due west until they reached the Laotian border on the Lunar New Year. At the border the guides said good bye to Nhu, and with an old map, he fought his way through the jungles and finally arrived in Xiang Khoang three weeks later.

Nhu described the rainy days when tiny leeches launched themselves from wet leaves on to every part of his body and feasted on his blood. He talked about digging out roots, and catching fish in the mountain streams, for food. He talked about fever, and fear of tigers, of encounters with snakes and boas.

Listening to him, Hiep was moved to tears. Her brother had come back, not with long jeremiads, but with refreshing stories about human capabilities and faith in providence. Nhu's eyes shone with tremendous joy and pride at having survived his precarious ordeal.

Nhu recounted his flight to Phat Diem with his in-laws, imitating the shrill, fearful voice of his father-in-law. While her children laughed, Hiep wondered why her brother had to relate this unsavory detail about his in-laws. Had he become even more disappointed in his relations with them?

Then Nhu told her that he had seen his wife and their daughter, Le Thuy. His eyes softened and his voice softened to a whisper. Hiep could see how much he loved them. She wondered if he and Le Xuan would find more peace and happiness together now, after both of them had gone through so much. In her heart, she prayed that the ordeal they had each endured alone had made them both wiser and happier. Nhu seemed confident that his life with his wife in Dalat would be marvelous. Nhu talked about the villa owned by Tran van Chuong in that resort city and said that Le Xuan and he had decided to go there, and spend a few years in tranquility.

*

The battle of Hue lasted much longer than the one that took place in Hanoi. There, Vo Nguyen Giap had some crack units he could use for the defense of the city. Yet, from the very beginning Giap wondered whether he could afford to squander units of his main force, to make a stand in Hanoi.

The outcome was clear from the outset. Ho Chi Minh and Vo Nguyen Giap knew that they would lose the battle for Hanoi in a matter of days, if they did not engage all of the crack units in the defense of the capital. Both Ho and Giap saw that the capability of waging guerilla warfare in the future depended very much on their ability to keep their main force intact and to avoid the risk of its being encircled.

On the French side, storming the Viet Minh defenses in Hanoi was not the primary goal. The French knew they had to destroy Giap's crack units, pursue them if necessary into the jungle, and destroy them as soon as possible.

After some hesitation, Giap decided to cut his losses and ordered his troops to withdraw from Hanoi, with the French in hot pursuit. His main force was not annihilated, and quickly reached safe zones in the mountains.

*

Sitting in his tiny room in Cho Lon, Diem was aware of what was going in the minds of the military leaders on both sides. He concluded that the war would go on, with the Viet Minh playing hide and seek in the countryside and the French occupying the cities. He knew that soon the French would come to him for advice. He knew that Admiral Thierry d'Argenlieu, a monk turned Commander-in-Chief of the South Asian theater of operations, would soon come and ask him to lead Vietnam.

The fighting went on in the mountains of the North and in the marshlands of the South. Diem sat and looked out of his window. Outside, sparrows were flying this way and that way, chased by Chinese children who laughed heartily. The children did not seem to notice that a war was going on.

Diem suddenly remembered another innocent face he had seen in Hanoi, the young Redeemer Brother who had served him with devotion for several months when he was there. He wondered why such an intelligent and sensitive young man found nothing else to do besides serve him.

Marcel Van, the young man did pray and meditate. But, when he was not praying or meditating, he was Diem's full-time assistant. The Canadian

Father Superior did not seem to find it strange that Marcel Van spent so much time with Diem.

In time, Diem had wondered whether he was dispensing his wisdom on the young man or if, in fact, Marcel Van's words and thoughts were shaping his own transformation. The daily contact with Van made Diem feel stronger than ever before. It made him believe more firmly that he had a mission to accomplish, and that somehow he now knew the way to accomplish it. Talking with Van made him eager to ensure that innocent children and youths lived in freedom and in peace.

Now, Van was only a memory. Diem sat and watched the Chinese children outside of his window. He said to himself, "I have to assume power soon, if I am to save the innocence of these children, if I am to deliver them from disaster." Yet, he also knew that he could not collaborate with the French who seemed determined to re-conquer Indochina at any cost. He knew that he must be patient.

Marcel Van

Note: Marcel Van or Joachim Nguyen Tan Van is in the process of being beatified by the Vatican like Cardinal F.X. Nguyen Van Thuan.

*

In March 1947, Tran van Ly succeeded in setting up the Governing Council of Central Vietnam, of which he was president. He became, *de facto,* the Governor of Central Vietnam. The French appreciated his collaboration, and soon Ly became a force to be reckoned with in Vietnam.

He also organized an army and a police force. Because he had to set up everything quickly, he relied on the people he knew best, and that meant, the Catholics. Can was adamantly opposed to that practical approach. He saw that Ly might create, by leaning on Catholics alone, a situation that would adversely affect the relations between Catholics and Buddhists, in the long term. That was to be the origin of all the problems that would arise between the Ngo Dinh and Tran van Ly in the future.

Bishop Thaddeus Le Huu Tu, another Supreme Advisor of the "Revolutionary" Government

*

It was in April 1947, that Hiep saw Diem again. Diem had aged considerably. Before 1945, Diem had looked like a young man, with a ready smile and an almost childish face. That was how Hiep had remembered him in the interval, since he had left hurriedly in 1944. Now, three years later, Diem looked completely different. He still appeared to be younger than his age, but there was a great deal of melancholy in his eyes, and his gestures were slower and more ponderous. Even his voice had changed; it had become deeper and more controlled.

Diem was on his way to Saigon and did not plan to stay too long in Hue, but he wanted to spend a few hours with Hiep. She suggested that they walk to the Ngu Binh Mountain, where she had read Diem's letter to Khoi, a few days before Khoi' s arrest.

Diem was grateful for the suggestion. They walked and talked, while Tuyen, her fourteen-year-old boy followed them at a short distance. They did not know that it would be the last time they could go to the mountain and see the pine-trees around them. Soon, the French, thinking that the trees could give cover to the Viet Minh guerrillas, decided to cut all of them down. The barren mountain would stand forlorn for the next three decades.

Hiep asked, "Have you been contacted by the French?" Diem nodded, "As soon as the guns went silent in Hanoi, French officials came to ask for me. There were three of them, one colonel in uniform, and two civilians. They said that they were all close assistants of Admiral Thierry d'Argenlieu... According to them, the Admiral, High Commissioner for Indochina, and Commander of the French Land, Naval and Air forces, wanted to know whether I was ready to assume the responsibility of setting up a government."

Hiep laughed, "Knowing you, I can guess that you told the French that they had asked the wrong question." Diem was delighted; he exclaimed, "That was exactly what I told them. I told them that the question should be: What kind of Vietnam are the French ready to accept?"

Midway between their parish and the foot of the mountain, they stopped for a moment and looked around them. It was springtime. The tender green of the rice fields contrasted with the dark green of the grass on the slopes of the hills around the mountain, while the pine trees, only a short distance away, looked almost blue. It was a picture of peace. They knew, however, that peace was an illusion. At night, Viet Minh guerrillas had been spotted near the mountain.

Diem said, "I told the French that I would like to present them with a plan for the future of Viet Nam, if they would wait for a few days. They said they had all the time in the world. After they left I sat down and wrote a comprehensive plan: how to phase in a Vietnamese government to replace the French administration, how to set up a Vietnamese army, a national police, a national treasury, a diplomatic corps…"

Hiep laughed again, "You expected immediate and total independence! D'Argenlieu then told you that not only did he ask the wrong question, but he also asked the wrong man, didn't he?" This time, Diem also burst laughing, "Precisely!"

Hiep said, "I have heard that d'Argenlieu firmly believes that Vietnam should not gain independence until at least thirty years from now. You scared him. However, I also heard that he really cares for Empress Nam Phuong, and has a great deal of admiration for you."

Diem nodded, "That is true. Now, what about the Empress? I heard from Can that he, Hoang and you have agreed that she should not be a regent, if Crown Prince Bao Long becomes the head of state. Is that true?"

Hiep shook her head, "You know me. I never entertain any such definite opinion. I am a listener. I do not make political decisions. I do not propose or reject options. I listened to what Brother Can had to say about the issue. I told him to wait for your decision. You certainly know by now that Governor Tran van Ly is all for the 'Bao Long solution.' Brother Can conveyed a note of caution. He does not want the whole affair to look like a Catholic plot."

Diem looked up to the sky and sighed, "You know I really admire the Empress. From what I have heard, she behaved perfectly during the battle of Hue. She made decisions for the survival of her children, with amazing courage. If the Bao Long option becomes the reality some day, she should be one of the regents, but I appreciate Can's reservation. We are Catholics, a small minority in our country. We need to be careful."

They were climbing up the slope of the mountain. Diem was walking quickly, and from time to time he would stop to help either Hiep or Tuyen. When they arrived at the top of the mountain, it was already late in the afternoon. Hiep asked, "What do you think about the Catholics and politics?" Diem seemed to have pondered the question for long months. He said, "When Father was close to Emperor Thanh Thai, some people said, 'Be careful, the Catholics are becoming too powerful.' When the late Duke of Phuoc Mon became Prime Minister, some people also said: 'Look, be careful, the Catholics are now too powerful.' When I became Prime Minster, the same people said: 'Now the Catholics are taking over.' When Bao Dai got married to Empress Nam Phuong, again the same people objected."

Diem paused a moment before he went on: "We have to be sensitive to the people of the other religions, but we should not be paralyzed by the criticism of a small group. If we listened too much to them, we would stop being involved with politics, and that means we would be marginalized. We should not let that happen. At the same time, I should never attempt to monopolize political power. We should always remember that we are a minority."

Hiep asked, "What are your plans now? "Diem shrugged, "From what I have seen, the French know they cannot govern Vietnam the way they did before 1945. In 1933, to talk about autonomy was an act of rebellion. Today, to talk about independence is altogether natural. The French can only restrict our independence in three ways. They can postpone the date of total independence; they can offer independence within the French Union or, they can offer partial independence. That is, they can offer independence while keeping for themselves certain areas of national sovereignty such as the diplomacy and the treasury."

Hiep asked, "Knowing all that, what will be your strategy? "Diem was sad when he answered, "The French are not ready to abandon Vietnam without a fight. As long as they think that they can keep Vietnam somehow within the French Union, they will not need me. But they will come to me when they are tired of fighting a guerrilla war, when they lose patience, when the Viet Minh troops have inflicted on them, unacceptable losses in human lives."

Hiep, seeing Diem's sadness, did not want to pursue her questioning. It was Diem who broke the silence after a while. He smiled and said, "That will probably take another ten years. I have plenty of time to prepare myself for the occasion."

Hiep asked, "Why ten years?" Diem had a ready answer for that question, "It will take Giap at least five years to build up his army. After that, he will launch mobile warfare to inflict as much damage as possible, on the French. Unfortunately, by that time, France will have recovered from the devastation of World War II. The French will use more and more modern weapons, and may succeed in wiping out Giap's larger units. The war will escalate until the French tire out." Hiep asked again, "You do not expect to see the French come out of the war as the winners, do you?" Diem shook his head. "No," he said.

Hiep stood up, "Maybe we should go back to the village, now." Diem nodded. For a moment, they looked in the direction of the sea. Three fighters-bombers came out of the dark red clouds of the sunset. They veered left towards the jungles in the west. Their silver wings shone briefly in the sunlight, and then they were lost behind the rising darkness above the Truong Son mountain ranges. On the road at the feet of the mountain two armored vehicles rumbled past, waving their long and curved antennas. Emerging from the village, a platoon of foot soldiers was heading towards the hills for their night patrol.

Hiep and Diem looked at each other. The long, long war was unfolding before their very eyes. Diem said, "We will live to see the return to peace, one day, Sister. Trust me, we will."

*

Diem did not wish to stay idle. He wanted to assist in the process of negotiating with the French to slowly regain independence.

The French soon showed that they preferred to play the *Bao Dai option* once more. Though Diem, by now, had become completely disappointed with the former Emperor, he was ready to help him. He did not want, however, to be too prominent in Bao Dai's team.

Diem made three separate trips to Hong Kong where Bao Dai was staying. He convinced Bao Dai to present the Vietnamese aspirations to the

French: these included total independence, and national unity. Soon enough, the terminology became familiar even to French leaders' ears.

Tran Van Ly, who had set up and presided over the Provisional Government in Central Vietnam, accompanied Diem twice on his trips. Their friendship remained strong, even though ideologically, they differed more and more.

During his trips to Hong Kong and Along Bay where he met with the French, Bao Dai and others, Diem managed to spend a great deal of time with Nguyen van Xuan, Prime Minister of the Autonomous State of Cochinchina. He persuaded Xuan to accept the concept of national unity.

Xuan was not too reluctant, and soon enough a National Council for National Safety was set up with participation of the leaders of North, Central and South Vietnam. The French, seeing that they had not succeeded in separating Southern Vietnam from the rest of the country, finally accepted the *fait accompli.*

*

The year 1948 came and went without much change in Diem's situation and position. He was consulted frequently by Bao Dai, but would not commit himself. Most of the time, he stayed in Saigon, but made frequent trips to Hanoi, Dalat (where Nhu was) and Vinh Long, where he discoursed freely with Thuc on most every subject under heaven.

He was caught by surprise; however, when without prior consultation with him, Thuc approved and gave support to a new Party founded by Tran van Ly, the Christian Social Party.

*

Until then, Diem's relations with Thuc had been without a cloud. Diem did not know how to tell Thuc that he disapproved of Thuc's hasty decision. Khoi, Diem, or Can had never, at any time, organized anything they called Christian. The simple reason for that was their acute awareness of the minority position of the Christian population in Vietnam.

Having distanced himself from Tran van Ly's monarchist views, Diem was even more concerned that a member of his family was involved with a Christian party founded and led by Governor Tran van Ly.

293

Diem was not amused. He exclaimed, "This is my year! The Year of the Rat!" Though not superstitious, he could not totally discard the traditional belief that someone born in the Year of the Rat, should be careful when another Year of the Rat turned up.

It bothered Diem that his brother had not consulted with him on the Christian Social Party, even though he had met with Thuc several times that year. It also upset him that Tran van Ly had turned to Thuc, knowing that he would have no chance at all of obtaining patronage, if he approached Diem or Can about his Party.

Thuc was not merely a member of Diem's family. He was the eldest brother in the family. After Khoi's death, Thuc stood in for Khoi and the late Grand Chamberlain, as the head of the family. By committing himself to Ly's Party, Thuc had committed the whole clan.

Diem did not know how to redress the situation. He decided to take it up at the next family reunion, which was to take place on February 12, 1949.

CHAPTER SEVENTEEN
RETURN TO AN EMPTY THRONE

Hiep knew that something was wrong. Whenever Diem was very angry, he had that look. He kept smiling but his eyes did not smile. With his index finger, he kept brushing his thick eyebrows. He did not answer simple questions, but kept smiling as if to say: "Don't bother me with those kinds of questions right now."

Nhu had tried to excuse himself, but Diem with a wave of his hand, indicated that Nhu should no longer be excluded from the family council meetings. Nhu insisted, "When you discuss politics, I will leave." Diem shook his head, "We are not going to discuss *political secrets*. Please stay until the end." Nhu was grateful. He took a seat far from Diem and Thuc, making himself as unobtrusive as possible.

Can knew what the meeting was about. He took it upon himself to start delving into the issue at hand. He said, "Nine months ago, Brother Thuc, you gave support to the Christian Social Party, without consulting any one of us." It was a statement of fact. Thuc turned to his young brother and said, "So what? Do I have to ask your opinion whenever I want to do something?"

Can knew that Thuc was in trouble, because Diem was so angry that he did not even speak. Can knew the risks if he continued to take Thuc on, all by himself. He turned to Hoang and Hiep and said, "You too have lived difficult moments with me, in Hue. We have discussed the merits of Catholic solutions. Please tell Monseigneur."

Diem raised his hands, "Please don't drag Sister Hiep into this dispute. I can talk about the disadvantages of Catholic Parties, myself." Thuc, seeing the effort Diem made to control his anger, suddenly realized that he might have done something wrong. He exclaimed, "This happened nine months ago. If you did not like what I did, why didn't you tell me when you came to see me in Vinh Long?"

Diem stared in front of him and said, "In Vinh Long, I was your guest. Today it is different. We meet once a year under the eyes of our late father, to review what we have done during the past year, and what was right, what was wrong in our actions. I do not think that I need to tell you all the reasons why we do not approve of the formation of a Christian party in Vietnam."

Thuc was as intelligent as any of his brothers and sisters. Seeing the unanimous condemnation of what he had done, he immediately understood what their reasons were. He said, "I realize that I was hasty. I have seen Christian Democrats in Europe..." Diem cut him off, "Why do you say that? You know that the situation in Vietnam is completely different than that of certain countries in Europe. It is not a good excuse."

Hiep asked, "What can we do now that the mistake has been made? Brother Thuc will have to tell Governor Tran Van Ly that he can no longer give support to the Christian Social Party. When he does that, our political alliance with him will come to an end. He will blame Brother Can for having incited you to break with him. A campaign of verbal attack on Brother Can is inevitable. As Brother Thuc is the head of the clan, Governor Ly will take it as an affront, coming from the whole clan. What do you propose?"

Diem said, "Thank you very much, Sister Hiep. You have correctly summed up the situation. What I hate in all this is that we will look like a bunch of ungrateful people. I owe Governor Ly a debt. He was one of the leaders of my original network. He was punished for having belonged to it. Even after that, he has extended to me the greatest courtesy in Dalat, and here in Hue. To break up with him like this is unthinkable. Yet, our clan cannot commit itself to a Christian party."

Thuc said, "It is all my fault. I will go and meet with the Governor tomorrow and try to make him understand the situation. Maybe he will listen to me." Diem shook his head, "He will not listen to you. Bao Dai has again asked me to be his Prime Minister. You go and tell Governor Ly now that we are withdrawing our support, and he will conclude that we have dropped him as soon as I was given the opportunity to become Prime Minister."

Hiep said, "I will go and meet with him, then." Diem exclaimed, "Oh no! The mistake is not yours. Brother Thuc will have to meet with Governor Ly, but not tomorrow. He will go, perhaps in a couple of months, when it is clear that I will not be the next Prime Minister. I hope that we do not make too many mistakes of this kind."

Nhu watched his brothers and sisters, not understanding at first. Then he saw why they had kept him away from such meetings until now. For a few hours each year, the clan met and all his brothers and sisters acted as one single being, even when they had come in the meeting originally with opposite views. He also saw in the quandary they had gone through in front of him, that they were good at learning from their mistakes and that they could be extremely hard on one another. He noticed that even during moments of high tension, they never failed to show their true love for one another.

He recognized that he had not been ready for such an experience. He had lived too much outside of their circle and had kept to himself. While he watched them, he was moved to tears. He realized that he was changing, and that he had always wanted in. Now he was on the threshold of a world from which he had been excluded for many years.

*

Hiep did go to meet with Governor Ly, accompanied by Am. She did not go in defiance of Diem's decision. She knew that Thuc had not been successful in convincing Ly that the creation of a Christian party was a bad idea. After the civilities and a few cups of tea, Governor Ly asked Am why they had come to visit him.

Am smiled. Ly, familiar with the Ngo Dinh clan, should have known better. He said, "I am here simply because it would be against our code of behavior if my wife came here by herself. The initiative is hers. She will tell you what she has in mind."

The Governor looked a little embarrassed. He apologized to Hiep and turned to her indicating that he was ready to listen to her. He was not alien to women's role in politics. His wife had played an important part in his own political life. For many years now, his political model had not been a man, but a woman, the Empress herself.

He had never heard that Hiep was an active participant in her clan's activities. Having chosen to come during his office hours, Hiep must certainly have a political message to deliver. Ly was glad he finally had the chance to gauge the intelligence of the women in the Ngo Dinh clan. He had had plenty of opportunities to observe Khoi, Thuc, Diem and Can. He was, he thought, about to see the weaker side of the clan.

Hiep began, "I understand that you had a good conversation with my brother, Thuc. He reported that you and he had reached an agreement about how to proceed with the Christian Social Party."

Ly looked up. The woman had observed all the rules of diplomacy. He decided to be blunt, "Look, let us not fool ourselves with words. *Monseigneur* Thuc wanted me to dissolve the Party. I intend to go on with it. That is the extent of our agreement."

The Governor's irony did not catch Hiep by surprise. She understood his bitterness. She asked, "From what you say, I assume that you now plan to go it alone. It is a pity, because I know that my brother, Diem, has always highly appreciated you as a friend and a comrade-in-arms. It is a pity, because my brother still wants to support you in all your other activities."

Ly was irritated. He replied, "I really do not need any help. I have everything I need. I have an army, an administration, and a territory. I am more than a Viceroy here in Central Vietnam. I don't need your brothers to tell me when I am right, or wrong."

Hiep smiled, "We have always supported you; therefore, if you are wrong, we are wrong as well. If the founding of the Christian Social Party was wrong, we made the mistake together with you."

The Governor looked at Hiep, surprised. The woman, with all her sweetness, knew how to rebuke him. He had followed Diem for so long that he really did not want to part ways with him now. Yet, Diem had turned Thuc against him. Thuc had reneged on his promise to support his Party. He was angry and confused. He asked, "Isn't it true that your brother, Can, slandered me when your brothers, Diem and Thuc were here for the Lunar New Year?"

Hiep put up her hand and said, "No, it is not true. A difference of views does exist between you and my brothers. It did not start with the creation of the Christian Social Party. It started with the Bao Long solution."

Ly sat back and frowned. Now she was telling him something he did not know. Hiep went on, "Of course, like you, my brothers are all admirers of the Empress, and they would be happy to see Prince Bao Long on the throne, with the Empress as the Regent. They would be happy, if the Prince and the Empress were not what they are."

The Governor chided her, "Now I don't understand you anymore. Please explain." Hiep replied, "They are Catholics. The country is not ready yet for a Catholic Emperor. If, in addition, you have a Catholic Empress as Regent, there will be enormous protests. Again, if such a solution is adopted and either you or my brother Diem becomes Prime Minister, a Catholic Prime Minister, then the country will be in an uproar."

Thuc had said something similar to this, but Ly had not really wanted to listen to him. Or perhaps Thuc had not used the words that Hiep now used. Ly sat up and said, "I see your point. If Can did not agree with me then, why didn't he tell me anything?" Hiep said, "Can is by many years your junior. He could not presume to talk to you that way." Ly smiled, "I see."

Hiep said, "If my brothers have some reservations about the Bao Long solution, those are minor compared to the creation of a Christian party." Ly objected, *"Monseigneur* Thuc did not have any reservations until recently." Hiep replied, "He has acknowledged that he was wrong."

Ly asked, "Are there any other things on which they disagree with me?" Hiep nodded, "Yes, one more thing. When you first organized the National Guards, you recruited primarily Catholic soldiers and officers. In some of your private and public conversations you have praised the fighting spirit of the Catholic soldiers. My brothers think that the National Guards should reflect the ratio of Christians and non-Christians in the general population, and the Catholic soldiers should not be seen as the better soldiers."

Ly again objected, *"Monseigneur* Thuc shares my view that a Catholic soldier is a better soldier in the face of Communism." Hiep shook her head, "He might have. I know he does not share that view now." Hiep stood up and asked, "Will my brother, Diem, find a friend in you the next time he comes back to Hue?" Ly smiled, "A friend is a friend forever. Please tell your brother that I am looking forward to his next visit." As he accompanied Hiep to the door, he asked her, "Do you think that your brother will agree this time, to become Prime Minister?" Hiep shook her head; "The situation has not changed much since he last declined the honor. I sincerely do not believe that he will accept."

Ly told Hiep, "Thank you for being straightforward with me. I hope that I have other opportunities to converse with you in the future." As he rode back with Hiep, Am turned to her in the car and said, "You did a good job. The Governor and Brother Diem, however, cannot be allies for much longer. Their views are too far apart."

Hiep nodded agreement, "Yes, I see that. The Governor knows he draws strong support from the Catholics and will not let go of that support so easily. If they cannot be allies, let us hope they can at least remain friends."

*

The people of Hue had come en masse to attend the abdication of Emperor Bao Dai in August 1945. They had witnessed his surrender of the Imperial Seal and the Dynastic Sword to representatives of the Viet Minh. Under the rain they had stood and cheered as he proclaimed, "I prefer to be a citizen of an independent country than to be the Emperor of an enslaved nation."

Now, in May 1949, the people of Hue also came massively to acclaim the return of Bao Dai as the Chief of State. Few of them knew that a French initiative had made him the Emperor again: They had carved out of Vietnam a large region, the Central Highlands, and called it 'The Imperial Domain'. In that domain, Bao Dai remained the Emperor.

*

In September that year, Diem returned to live in Hue. Hiep found it amusing that Diem reclaimed his place at his mother's house and acted as if he had never left. He recovered his room that was never used by Can. He also recovered his Chinese and French books, his photo lab and his rose garden.

For two months, Can surrendered the direction of his network to Diem's control. Every day, Diem held several meetings with party members and talked to them about the National Union Front, asking them to work for a broader coalition with members of other political parties.

It was a time when Diem was totally relaxed. All of the politicians in the country knew about the recent offer from Bao Dai. That he rejected Bao Dai's invitation to become Prime Minister so off-handedly only gave him more prestige among them. Diem knew now that he had the luxury of waiting for the right time.

Diem read, trimmed the roses, developed films in his photo lab, and every day he went to a different quiet site, in or outside of the city, to sit and think. Often he asked Hiep to accompany him with one of her children.

One day, when they were walking around, visiting the various buildings of the Thien Mu Pagoda, Hiep suggested that Diem should go overseas. Diem stopped walking. He looked at Hiep as if in anger. He asked, "Do you believe I should go abroad to learn how to think?"

Hiep shook her head. She looked up the tall Phuoc Duyen Tower and asked Diem, "How many floors are there in the tower?" Surprised, Diem answered all the same, "Seven floors." Hiep asked, "Where are you now? On what floor?"

Diem blushed. The game had begun, and he had to continue, "I am on the fifth floor." Hiep smiled, "What have you seen going through the first five floors?" Diem improvised, "On the first floor, I saw our people in chains. On the second floor I saw the missed opportunities. On the third floor, I saw myself incapable of decisions. On the fourth floor, I saw our country at war and our people divided, and on the fifth floor, I saw myself surrounded by darkness and ignorance."

Hiep laughed, "On the sixth and the seventh floors there are golden statues of the Buddha. That is why the stairs stop at the fifth floor. To go up to them you use the wooden ladder that the monks from above slide down to you. To see the golden statues of Buddha the Enlightened, you have to be humble and ask the monks to give you access."

Diem asked, "What is the point?" Hiep explained, "You have never gone up to the sixth and the seventh floors. You have never asked the monks upstairs to slide down the wooden ladder. Up on the seventh floor, you can stand and look out of the windows on all four sides. You see miles and miles around you. No one will try to interfere with your meditation up there. You will see things that you have never seen before."

Diem laughed now. He realized what she was trying to tell him. "I know I need to expand my knowledge. The only question is: Do I have time now? I have to keep my ear to the ground, right here, in Vietnam." Hiep did not react to his objection. Diem finally said, "All right, I will think about it."

In front of the Thien Mu Pagoda, the Perfume River made a slight curve, which caused the water to dig into the hillside. The riverbed was quite deep, and the water here was clearer and greener than most any part of the stream. The shadows of the centenary trees and the beams of the autumn sun played on the surface of the water creating thousands of shapes and hues.

Diem asked, "Will I see anything as beautiful as this overseas?" Hiep smiled, "You are asking the wrong person. I have never gone anywhere. You also asked the wrong question. What you need to see overseas is people, how they think, how they act, how they feel, what makes them tick. Of course, you will also see beautiful landscapes, and proud monuments made by human hands."

Diem said as if to himself, "I have seen French people, I have seen Japanese, Chinese, Americans..."Hiep stopped him, "Yes, but you have not seen them in their natural environment. You have not seen a Parisian in Paris, a Japanese in Tokyo, a Chinese in Pekin, an American in Washington DC."

Diem sighed, "When I am with my brothers and sisters my strength is multiplied. I think well, I talk better, I feel better... I even breathe better. I will be really lonely if I am to travel overseas alone." Hiep nodded, but she cautioned him, "Your family, your clan can be an asset to you, at times; but don't be completely dependent on us. Your family, your clan may also cause you irremediable harm some day."

Diem nodded agreement. He had seen how Thuc and Nhu had adversely affected his plans. He sighed, "Only Brother Khoi and you have never created any problem for me since our childhood." As Hiep did not say anything, Diem added, "Yes, some day in the future I will go up to the sixth and the seventh floors of the Tower."

*

It was the twenty-fifth anniversary of Ngo Dinh Kha's death. All the children were there to commemorate. Diem was about to make some major decisions. Nhu expected that Diem would assign him a role. Can expected that Diem would talk about building up a popular base in Central Vietnam. Thuc thought it was time for Diem to collaborate with Bao Dai.

When they assembled in Hue, on Lunar New Year's Day, however, Diem's own intelligence network uncovered evidence of a Viet Minh plot to assassinate him there. The plot surprised neither Diem, nor his brothers and sisters. Diem had seen so many Nationalist leaders assassinated by the Viet Minh that he was surprised not to have been a target before that time.

Thuc, who presided at the family gathering, on the third day of the New Year, said to Diem, "It is absolutely necessary for you to go overseas for a while." Diem objected, "I am not going to run away just because *they* threaten to kill me." Thuc insisted, "Let us not make a show of bravery here. I told the French about the plot yesterday and asked them to give you police protection."

Diem did not say anything. His anger mounted visibly. Everybody, except Thuc, could see how angry he was. He looked like he was about to explode. Finally, he managed to smile and say, "Brother Thuc, even if at times you think of yourself as my guardian angel, please let me take care of my own security." Thuc finally became aware of Diem's anger. He exclaimed, "You are my brother. Your security is a concern to all of us. I do not see why you should be angry with me for taking some precautions to protect you."

Diem was livid. His hands trembled as he said, "So you do not see why. I will tell you why I cannot accept your interference. You go to the French to ask for police protection. What have I done to deserve such protection? Please tell me." Thuc, seeing Diem shaking with fury, raised a hand, trying to calm him down, "Look, where do I turn to, if not to the French? The Vietnamese police force is at its infancy. How can I trust it?"

Luyen saw that Thuc was aggravating the situation. He intervened, "Brother Thuc, you listened to Brother Diem's words, but you refuse to listen to their meaning. We all agree with Brother Diem that by reporting the plot to the French, you have done a disservice to our cause. Brother Diem prefers to die rather than to ask for protection from the French." Nhu added, "The French do not like Brother Diem. They never have, and they never will! They will never give him protection."

Thuc sat there, not knowing what to say. Diem asked, "What did the French tell you?" Thuc replied reluctantly, "They said that they did not have enough resources to follow up on this plot." Diem laughed bitterly, "That was the result of your intervention. Now, if all the assistance I got from my brothers and sisters were of that nature, I would be better off working alone."

There followed a long and heavy silence. In the end, Can suggested, "Brother Thuc has committed a terrible mistake by going to the French. He did that, however, out of love for Brother Diem. Are we going to sit here for the rest of the day or are we going to discuss a strategy to preserve Brother Diem's life?"

Hoang said, "So far there have been three attempts on Brother Diem's life: once when he was still Chief of Province in Binh Thuan, the second time, when he was captured in Tuy Hoa, and the third time, here in Hue. The orders all seem to have come from local Viet Minh initiatives. That means he has Viet Minh enemies in Central and South Vietnam. Maybe it is safer for him to live in the Central Highlands or in North Vietnam. The best solution for him would be to go overseas for a while."

The other people in the room were surprised to see Diem smile and nod. Diem did not associate his departure from Vietnam with *running away* anymore. Thuc, seeing that Diem was not reluctant to go overseas said, "Maybe it is a sign from God. Brother Diem, this year is the Holy Year. I really want you to be in Rome to celebrate it with the Holy Father. I will accompany you if you want."

Diem nodded. He told everybody, "I will go to Japan to meet with Prince Cuong De. Then I will go to Rome for the Holy Year. I want to be standing in St. Peter's Square at night, listening, like you said, Brother Thuc, to the heartbeats of the Universal Church. After that, I want to go to the United States. Without a good understanding of that country, I will be a blind leader. I will also want to see France. I want to correct my views about France, by seeing the French in their natural environment."

Diem dismissed his brothers and sisters saying that their lives would not be safe if he stayed around. Intended to be the longest one in years, the meeting of the Year of the Tiger was the shortest.

Saying good-bye to Hiep, Diem said, "I am going up the sixth and seventh floors of the Phuoc Duyen Tower." His brothers and Hoang did not understand what he meant. Thuc exclaimed, "You are not going to visit the Thien Mu Pagoda at this dangerous time, are you?" Diem shook his head and laughed, "No, certainly not."

*

Hiep saw Diem once again before he left for Japan. In July 1950, upon receiving news that his mother was ill, Diem hurried back to Hue. But it was merely a false alarm, and Mrs. Ngo Dinh Kha, more emphatically than anybody else, insisted that Diem not abandon his plans to go abroad for a while.

After two weeks spent in Hue, Diem and Thuc left for Saigon, on their way to Japan, Rome and the United States. Diem met with Cuong De in Tokyo in August 1950. He was alarmed by the look of the Prince. Diem did not know that the first time he met the Prince would also be the last.

Strangely enough, it was during that trip that for the first time, Diem told Thuc all about his political philosophy. Thuc listened eagerly to Diem's explanations of his past behavior and plans for the future. Thuc was humbled by the experience. He learned to ask questions, to play the devil's advocate, to discuss both politely and bluntly. He was amazed to see how his own father had shaped Diem's thoughts and behavior. He began to understand for the first time, why his father had chosen Diem instead of Khoi to lead.

He started thinking about how he could use his own talents to help Diem in the future. He laughed at his own mistakes in the past. He knew that he would have to learn fast, to catch up with all his brothers and sisters, who had shown an instinctive understanding of Diem's thinking and feelings.

Diem was amazed at what he saw on that trip. Arriving in the United States, he told Thuc that he wanted to stay there a couple of years to learn about the American way of thinking. Having made some useful introductions, Thuc left Diem and went back to his diocese of Vinh Long.

*

Ngo Dinh Thi Hiep with her youngest daughter,
Nguyen Thi Thu Hong in 1951

*

Hiep decided that she would not say anything that year at the commemorative ceremony of her father's anniversary. It was a Year of the Hare. It was traditionally believed that if you were born in the year of the Hare, every year of the Hare in your life would only bring disaster to you.

Hiep was not suspicious, but the notion of doing less, not more, during the year named after her birth year was so much a matter of culture, that she decided she should stay out of the limelight that year. She remembered that the latest Year of the Hare, 1939, was when World War II began, not a very propitious year indeed.

As usual, Thuc returned to Hue on the first day of the Lunar New Year, and together with his brothers and sisters, wished their mother good health and much happiness in the coming year. Then, two days later, an elaborate ceremony commemorating their father's death was held.

After they prayed together for the repose of Ngo Dinh Kha's soul, Thuc began by saying that he had decided to ask Nhu to participate actively in the clan's political activities. Hoang asked, "Don't you remember that Brother Khoi excluded Brother Nhu from any political role, at least inside our family?"

Thuc nodded. He replied, "Diem told me about that matter a long time ago. Brother Khoi made the decision in 1943; we are now in 1951. In the meantime, eight years have elapsed. New developments have made such exclusion unthinkable. Brother Khoi is no longer with us, but I think he would agree with me if he were still with us."

Can intervened, "I have changed since Brother Khoi died. Before his death, I wanted to stay out of politics. Since his death, I have committed myself to help Brother Diem, and to compensate with my poor talents for the loss of Brother Khoi's contribution."

He paused, and then went on, "I still do not understand why Brother Nhu should be brought into politics. The reasons for his exclusion are still as valid today as they were eight years ago. Those reasons have been even aggravated, especially during the Japanese interregnum. We, like everybody else, should have grave reservations about Tran Van Chuong's

307

and his wife's role during that time. I have nothing against Brother Nhu, but I do not think that he should participate in our collective work."

Thuc was not very pleased that he had been contradicted. He looked at Can with mild reproach in his eyes, but Can held his gaze, pretending not to see Thuc's displeasure. Thuc turned and asked Luyen, "You have to speak your mind now, Luyen, what do you think?" Luyen shrugged, "I am not going to be the arbiter in this silly matter. Brother Khoi wanted to punish brother Nhu for not obeying Mother. His exclusion, which was intended to be temporary, was a lesson he wanted to give Brother Nhu. He wanted Brother Nhu to be less selfish, less focused on his own sentiments, and to think more about the family. He did not want to make Brother Nhu a pariah for life. If I remember correctly, when Brother Nhu asked him, if the exclusion was irrevocable, Brother Khoi said, 'Who knows what will happen, ten years from now'... Am I right, Sister Hiep?"

Hiep nodded but did not say anything. Thuc turned to her and asked, "Hiep, can't you say something today, when we need your advice most?" Hiep looked at Nhu, who had been chain smoking since the meeting started. She finally decided to talk, "This is the Year of the Hare. *My year*! I wanted to keep my mouth shut this time; however, I see that I am not going to be allowed to do so. I agree with Luyen. He was correct to assume that Brother Khoi merely wanted to give Brother Nhu a lesson in 1943. Two years later, however, Brother Diem went to Da Lat to consult with Nhu during the Japanese interregnum, when he had to decide whether or not he should accept the request to become Prime Minister."

Nhu shook his head and corrected her, "It was not exactly like that. Brother Diem merely needed a sounding board, somebody that would react to his thoughts. He did not need my advice, and I did not offer any."

More than anybody else in the room, Hiep understood what Nhu had just said. Diem depended on his brothers and sisters to serve as sounding board. She thought, "What will he do when he has to work alone?" Hiep argued, "I know that to be true, but Brother Diem did find in you what he needed. You did give him the assistance he was looking for. Those days in Dalat broke the exclusion."

She turned to Hoang and her other brothers and concluded, "I think that we should no longer discuss Brother Khoi's interdict eight years ago. I understand that in 1947, 1949 and even this year, Brother Diem stayed with Nhu for long periods in Dalat, and that he discussed politics with him. He has not seen it necessary to continue with the exclusion. "

Ngo Dinh Thi Hoang, Hiep's younger sister and her staunchest ally in all family discussions

*

Can objected, "It appears to me that Brother Diem could not make up his mind concerning Brother Nhu during the stays he made in Dalat. I will ask Brother Nhu a blunt question: Can you tell us why he does not trust you one hundred percent and why he has still not given you access to the network of his followers?" Nhu sighed, "My wife, of course. He blames her for being Bao Dai's cousin."

Hiep, seeing Nhu's pain, intervened quickly, "All right, now we know. Brother Diem, whether he is right or wrong, thinks that Bao Dai should not be trusted. He and Brother Thuc have gone so far as to promote the alternative of putting Crown Prince Bao Long on the throne, with Prince Cuong De and Empress Nam Phuong as Regents. In this case, anyone close to Bao Dai, with the sole exception of Empress Nam Phuong, cannot be trusted."

Thuc nodded, "During our recent trip to Japan, Rome and the United States, Brother Diem and I frequently discussed that option not only between ourselves, but tested it on many ... Yes, he continues to mistrust the Emperor and Bao Dai's entourage. So, Hiep, how do you vote?"

Hiep was very pensive when she replied, "There will be no ideal solution here. We all trust Nhu. We all know that he would never do anything harmful to Brother Diem. I propose that Nhu participate in the political activities of our family. But, I do not know whether we should let Nhu take over the network."

Thuc showed some anxiety when he said, "Diem wants Nhu to take over the network during his absence. Diem's absence may be long and somebody has to take over the network in North and South Vietnam. He knows that Can is doing quite well with the network in Central Vietnam, but he wants Nhu to supervise what Can is doing. He wants a unified party, not an assemblage of autonomous groups. He wants Nhu to head the new party."

Can was about to protest, but Thuc holding up his hand, went on: "However, he expects Nhu to make some major sacrifices: he wants Nhu to move to Saigon and put some distance between his family and Emperor Bao Dai. He also wants Nhu to keep certain secrets from his wife. It will be painful for you, Nhu, to leave Le Xuan out of this, but I know nobody here would agree to give all the secrets of the networks to her."

Nhu looked very unhappy. He said, "My wife is not going to betray us! For God's sake, what are you talking about?" Everybody kept a stubborn silence and finally, Nhu managed to smile and go on, "I have not asked for this. I may as well walk out of here and say that I am not interested. The fact is, I cannot do that. Like any of you, maybe more than most of you, I want to live Father's dream. I want to help Brother Diem accomplish Father's wishes." He shrugged, "One of these days, you will see that Le Xuan more than deserves your trust. You will see how valuable she is for the cause we are fighting for. For now, I agree to move my family to Saigon, and to keep my wife out of my political activities."

Everybody sighed with relief, except Nhu. With smoke billowing around him, he sat there looking into the void, looking into his broken marriage, feeling more than ever before how much he loved his wife, and how unendurable his life had been. Now that he had to go back and tell his wife about the family's decision, Le Xuan would certainly be more than humiliated. She would make him pay for what his family had done to her.

Watching Nhu, Hiep felt helpless. Here they were, giving him additional pain. Having known only love and tenderness from her husband, she knew she would never understand how love could be cruel and how two people in love could be so unhappy together. Nhu caught her eyes. He turned away. He did not want the only member of his family who was really happy, to share his despair. As the meeting drew to an end, he stood up, walked resolutely to Hiep and said, "Don't you worry about me, Sister Hiep, I will be all right."

*

Nhu sat in the armchair in his small office on Rue Pyres, in Saigon. He had gone over the details of the transformation of the Christian Social Movement with Tran Trung Dung and Le Quang Luat. The Movement had been created back in 1947, by the two northern leaders, and had taken root among the Catholics in North Vietnam. Over the years, in spite of the name, a large number of non-Christians had joined the Movement.

Dung and Luat agreed with Nhu that the name should be changed. They discussed various names and finally decided on 'The United Popular Front.' They spent the rest of the day discussing strategy, focusing on the questions of how to deal with the French, the Viet Minh and Bao Dai.

They also discussed ways to coordinate the Front in the North with the National Revolutionary Movement in Central Vietnam and the *Tinh than* (Spirit) Group in the South. In Central Vietnam, the hard-core elements of the Movement, who had been recruited as early as 1933, were under the leadership of Ngo Dinh Can, while the *Tinh Than* group, founded in 1947, was led by Dr. Tran van Do and Nguyen Tang Nguyen.

Only the National Revolutionary Movement in Central Vietnam and the Front in the North were of a revolutionary nature. The *Tinh than* group included intellectuals who were moderate reformers.

Now, alone in his small office, Nhu was concerned by the inconsistency among those allied organizations. He knew it would take time for them to work together. His long discussions with Dung and Luat showed that they had an incredible faith in Diem. Earlier talks with Tran Quoc Buu yielded the same impression. Buu was finely attuned to Diem's thinking. Nhu turned his attention now to the *Tinh than* group. Dr. Tran van Do was his wife's uncle and Tran van Chuong's brother. Nhu knew, however, that he must handle Do carefully. He knew that the moderate nature of the Tinh than Group would tend to put a break on the revolutionary activities of the other components.

Nhu sighed. He would have to direct the *Tinh than* group himself. He would have to create a newspaper with the group, but with the participation of the other structures. He knew that it would take him a year or two before a unified party emerged.

Thuc had given him *carte blanche*. But Thuc had insisted that, while he whipped all the diverse groups who sympathized with Diem into a unique party, Nhu would also have to continue the work started by Ngo Dinh Khoi in 1943. That meant the building of a national coalition of all the parties, with the exclusion of the Viet Minh.

Within a few months after he was settled in Saigon, Nhu had begun establishing his contacts with Caodaists and Hoa Hao's, as well as independent patriots in Saigon. He knew that he had years of work ahead of him.

"C'est la mer à boire," said Nhu to himself. He should go home now, but he did not want to. He sat there nursing his pain, knowing that the terrible tension between his wife and himself would never end, and that they

would never be happy together. Yet he had never stopped loving her, and was aware that she loved him. "It is my family, and her family," he said to himself. "There is too much difference between the two. Now that Le Xuan cannot even tolerate the mention of my family any more, what will become of us?"

Once again, Nhu bent his head over the dossier of the *Tinh than* group and tried to forget his family problems.

*

In the month of June, Paris was almost deserted. Nguyen De looked at his watch. He was late for the meeting with Diem. He hated to go and see Diem where he was living. For months, Diem had been staying with Ton That Can, the son of late Prime Minister Ton That Han, who owned a small villa in Paris. De had been told that Diem was staying there with a large staff. Diem's staff had rejected De's offer to hold the meeting at a hotel.

De hated his own reputation, which followed him everywhere. The reputation was that he was the smartest man in Vietnam, a reputation he earned first as a banker, after his graduation from the School of Commerce in Paris. In 1933, he was the Chancellor of the Imperial Secretariat, when Diem was Prime Minister. It was the only time that people said he made a blunder. He had trusted Diem, and resigned when Diem resigned, only to learn that Diem had not trusted him at all.

He became a banker again, a businessman, and a shrewd investor. He thought he had severed all ties with Diem. Yet, in 1943, knowing that Diem was making a series of mistakes when he was approached by Prince Cuong De's bumbling aide in Hanoi, Nguyen De intervened and got Diem out of there intact.

He hated himself for wasting his time with Diem. Yet in 1944, when he learned from his own network that the French were about to arrest Diem, he immediately, at the risk of his own safety, sent a message to urge Diem to escape. Why did a man with a reputation of being the smartest man in Vietnam, play so dumb every time he had to deal with Diem?

He smiled, thinking about the times people had called him *too clever*. He knew that Bao Dai had refused to make him a Minister in the Tran Trong

Kim Cabinet in 1945, because both Bao Dai and Tran Trong Kim judged him to be *too clever*! In 1946, he was asked by Ho Chi Minh to assist in the negotiations with the French. Yet soon enough, Ho's entourage discarded him, again because he was too clever.

Now, looking again at his watch, De wondered why he wanted to meet with Diem once again. His mission in Paris was simple. The Emperor, vacationing in Cannes, had told him, 'Do not come back to Cannes without a new Prime Minister.' Originally, he had told himself, "Diem is not in the race. Diem is not in the race. Diem is not in the race!" Now, in his limousine rushing through the almost deserted streets of Paris, De said to himself, "I am a fool, I am a fool. Suppose he agrees to be Prime Minister. My life will be hell!"

*

The outcome was clear after five minutes' talk. Diem agreed to go to Cannes to meet with the Emperor, but with a face that did not show any enthusiasm. De tried to reason with Diem. Diem hardly listened to him. At the end of the meeting, however, Diem smiled and said, "The timing is wrong for now. Please come back...next year." He surprised De by accompanying him to the gate. As they shook hands, Diem said, "Fate has bound us together, in spite of ourselves! Do not worry about me. We will meet again."

*

That evening, De called the Emperor on the phone, "Sire," he said, "You may want to make your cousin, Prince Buu Loc, your next Prime Minister. In a couple of days, you will receive a visit from my old friend, Ngo Dinh Diem. Do not offer him the position. He will not accept it, anyway." Bao Dai was irritated, "I have no intention of offering him anything. Why in the hell do you bring up his name? Have you met with him?" De replied, "Yes, Sire, like a fool, I did meet with him."

*

In 1953, Nhu regrouped all the separate entities he and his brothers had organized into one single party. He called it The Farmers and Workers Party. Contrary to what he had expected, he found that the diverse groups joined forces with incredible enthusiasm.

Within a few months the Farmers and Workers Party saw its memberships in the three regions of Vietnam soar, with the enlisting of former members of the Confederation of Christian Workers in the South, the National Revolutionary Movement in Central Vietnam and the Christian Social Movement in North Vietnam.

The leaders of the old entities became executives of the new party and assisted Nhu, not only in expanding the membership, training and retraining the members, but also in planning and implementing strategic alliances with political and religious forces in Vietnam.

The membership of the Farmers and Workers Party would in the future play the most important role in the forming of the *Can Lao* Party, once Diem returned to power in 1954.

On that day, lighting another cigarette, and looking out from his crowded office, Nhu told himself, "Everything is ready now, except for the leader. I should have given him the nickname of 'Diem the Unready.' He wants a perfect, an ideal situation before he walks in to assume power. The strange thing is, he believes that such a situation will arise."

Over the past few years, Nhu had changed his lifestyle. He was now as ascetic as Diem was. He prayed day and night like Diem. He worked tirelessly like Diem. He talked with union leaders, farmers, Hoa Hao's in the Delta and Caodaists in Tay Ninh. He was Mr. Coalition and Mr. Labor Union. He was everywhere; he tried to understand everything.

Nhu raised his eyes to the ceiling, praying, "God, please tell my brother that we cannot wait forever." He had received a short letter from Diem. The letter indicated that once again he had declined to serve as the next Prime Minister. Nhu hit the desk with his clenched fists: "You are not a politician, Brother Diem. You should spend your life working on your sainthood!"

When he calmed down, he managed to smile and said to himself, "I wonder why people keep coming back to you, and ask you to play a leadership role, even your enemies."

*

In Hue, Hiep and Am celebrated their eldest son's ordination as priest. They did not know at the time that Thuan would become someday a Bishop, then an Archbishop and finally a Cardinal. They did not know that in the intervening years Thuan was to go through thirteen years of imprisonment, and that those painful years was to make of him a saint.

Thuan on the day of his ordination: besides his parents and his siblings the picture shows Mrs. Ngo Dinh Kha, Bishop Ngo Dinh Thuc, Ngo Dinh Thi Hoang and Ngo Dinh Can

(June 11, 1953)

PART FOUR

A MANDATE TO LEAD

CHAPTER EIGHTEEN
IN THE FULLNESS OF TIME

Hiep held the letter in her hand and looked out into the garden. Diem had told her to keep a secret. She could not tell anybody, at least, not for now. On January 1, 1954, Diem had become an Oblate of the Order of St. Benedict. Wasn't that to be expected, though, Hiep thought. Nhu had so often called Diem 'the monk'. His ascetic way of life, his love of privacy, his meditative nature, and his great faith in God had for years pointed to this final decision.

He had taken the vows at the Abbey of St. Andrew in Bruges, Belgium. Hiep read and reread the copy of Diem's vows, "Peace, in the name of Our Lord Jesus-Christ, Amen. I, Brother John the Baptist, Odilo, Ngo Dinh Diem, offer myself to God Almighty, Our Blessed Virgin Mary, and Our Saint Benedict at the Abbey of St. Andrew, and promise to convert my way of life according to the spirit of the Order of Saint Benedict and according to the statutes of the Oblates, in the presence of God and all the Saints."

Diem explained that he had taken the religious name of Odilo in honor of the Saint whose feast fell on the first day of January. Odilo was so unknown in Vietnam that Hiep could not figure out at first why Diem had chosen him for his patron saint.

Diem's letter was long and elaborate. He talked about St. Odilo who lived in the Tenth Century. Hiep tried to understand the points made by Diem. Why was Diem so suddenly attached to that French abbot who lived so long ago in Paris? It was much later that Hiep understood the implications.

319

It was only after Diem died that Hiep finally realized that Diem's choice of Odilo as his religious name was an act of prophecy.

Saint Odilo practiced severe austerity. Diem himself led an extremely austere lifestyle. The saint sold church properties to feed the poor during a period of famine. Hiep could see how much Diem would approve of such a Christian gesture. Saint Odilo obtained from the Kings of France and the nobility, their acceptance of the 'Truce of God', that guaranteed the 'inviolability of the sanctuary' given to people who sought refuge in a church. Later on Hiep saw how much Diem cared for the hundreds of thousands of refugees from North Vietnam.

Like Saint Odilo, Diem was devoted to the Blessed Virgin Mary. Finally, Saint Odilo had established November 2, as All Souls' Day, a day to commemorate all the faithful departed.

It was only when Diem at the last minute took refuge in a church, then was killed on November 2, 1963, that Hiep called out to him, "Odilo, Odilo, where are you?" It was later, when all those faithful to Diem's memory, chose November 2 to commemorate him, that Hiep completely understood the prophecy.

*

The letter went on to explain to Hiep that Diem, while taking the vows to become a Lay Brother, did not renounce his political potential. He said that he was as impatient as ever to return to Vietnam and assume leadership responsibilities.

He joined to the letter his poem, which read:

With a sword and a guitar on my back, I wait to cross the river,

At the landing, no trace of a boat, or a boatman.

What a pity to see a war-horse pulling a heavy salt chariot.

What a regret to see the wild geese disappear in the cloudy sky.

Still a large crowd at the market of honors and profits!

In rain and sunshine I follow the ups and downs of the world,

A long pole in my hand, I wait.

When will the river water be limpid again?

Hiep suddenly realized that she was crying. So much loneliness, why? All his life, he had been a lonely man. And now, in a cell at the Abbey of St. Andrew, he was waiting, waiting, believing and disbelieving that his hour would come one day. Hiep exclaimed, "Father, it is so hard to live your dream! It is so hard for Brother Diem to turn your dream into reality!"

*

The chapel was her refuge. Her father-in-law had built it with love. Over the years, Am had expanded it, and now twenty people could attend Mass or pray comfortably in it. At moments of crisis in her life, Hiep went there to pray and to think. It was there that, before he was taken sick, Thuan, her son who had been ordained a priest, came from time to time to say mass for the whole family.

At present, Thuan was seriously ill. He might become handicapped for life. The French doctors at Grall Hospital in Saigon, with all their modern science, had decreed that they would soon have to remove large parts of his lungs. Hiep could not stand the thought of seeing her son crippled for life. After Xuan's death, she had placed all her hopes on Thuan. She had not dared to make plans for him, like she had done with Xuan. She had watched him grow up, trembling at the thought that something could happen to him. She had let him go to the seminary. She had accepted that he had dedicated his life to the priesthood. Anything, anything, provided he lived.

And now, he was lying in a bed in Grall Hospital, waiting the doctors' verdict. She sat in the darkening chapel, unable to pray, with too much pain in her heart. Thuan in the hospital, Diem in a lonely cell in Belgium, then Emperor Thanh Thai… Hiep had just heard on the radio that Emperor Thanh Thai had passed away.

Emperor Bao Dai and Ex-Emperor Thanh Thai in Dalat 1951

*

Sitting in the semi-darkness of the chapel she reminisced, trying hard to draw all the lessons from the Emperor's life. The French had, until the end, punished him. They had allowed him to go back to Hue for a few weeks to visit the tombs of his parents. Then, they had confined him in Saigon. They had kept him under house arrest since his return to Vietnam in 1947.

All the bitterness of a child of five, watching the Emperor's and her father's fall came back. She thought of her father and the changes that had come after the Emperor had abdicated, and of the way those changes had determined the rest of her father's life.

Without the Emperor's tragic fate, their fate would have been different: her own life, the life of her whole family. "Now you are gone and the country has not been freed from French domination" She addressed herself to Thanh Thai, "Your dream, like my father's dream, has not become a reality."

The passing of the Emperor created a feeling of emptiness in Hiep. She had been expecting the news for quite a while; yet, when it came, she found that she was not ready for it. A large part of her universe had faded away. She remembered how she had identified the fortune of her family with those of the Emperor, how she had cried when he was dethroned and sent into exile. She remembered how her father had reacted to the humiliations endured by the Emperor, how he had revered the martyred Emperor until his dying day. She reiterated mournfully, "Now, the Emperor is dead, and his country is still under French rule." She felt the pain swell within her, like immense sea waves during a big storm.

The French doctors who treated Thuan at Grall Hospital had said that it would take a miracle for them to save Thuan's lungs. As Hiep was mourning for the death of Emperor Thanh Thai, she wondered whether such a miracle would occur for Thuan.

Then Hiep remonstrated herself. Wasn't her life already a miracle? She remembered herself growing up under the watchful eyes of her parents, a little girl, already pensive and curious, finding her place in her large family, among her sisters and her brothers. Her life had been a miracle. With her husband and her children around her, she could not have dreamt of a better, happier life.

She still was unable to pray. Her son in a hospital, Diem in a cold and solitary cell and Emperor Thanh Thai lay in a common casket -- her mind drifted from the 'Magnificat' to the 'De Profundis', from pain to hope, then back again.

*

The pain did not leave her for many days. Then it was her forty-first birthday. She never really wanted to celebrate her birthday, unless pushed by the desire of others in her family to mark the date, to do something different, to show her their love and their respect. She would then spend time combing her long hair, put on her best clothes and come out of her room to wait for her husband and the children.

That year, she had to make an extra effort to come out of her room. As she came out into the parlor, she felt that there was more joy in the faces of her husband and her children than the circumstances warranted. After all, Thuan was fighting for his life in the hospital. Surprised, she asked, "What is it?"

Am laughed and said, "What is what? This is your birthday. We just want to wish you the best birthday in your life." There was so much joy in his eyes that she knew. She asked, "Good news about Thuan?" Am took her hands, "Better than good news. It's a miracle! Read this letter from Thuan. He was leaving the hospital, when he wrote. He may arrive, any moment now." Trembling, she took the letter from Am's hand. Tears of joy welled up in her eyes. How was it possible?

The miracle did happen. Only a moment before Thuan was to have large parts of his lungs taken out, and become handicapped for life, his French doctors discovered in the last minute X-ray film that somehow, his lungs had cleared up. They walked back and forth discussing his case, shaking their heads. Finally, they came to Thuan, and said to the young priest, "It is incredible, but your lungs have cleared up. Completely cleared up! *You will live to see many of us die.*"

Was it a promise or a prophecy? Thuan and she did not know. But, Thuan would live on and see so many of those dear to him die. He would live on to suffer together with her, in their souls and in their flesh, the terrible tragedy of their family and their country.

*

It was May 7, 1954; two days after her birthday; Hiep and her family were celebrating Thuan's return to good health. They spent much time, however, around the radio. As the day progressed, it became ever more apparent that Dien Bien Phu had fallen to Communist hands, and the French had suffered their biggest single defeat of their long war in Vietnam.

For the last three months, the outcome had been clear to everyone. The Dien Bien Phu garrison, with its complex defense system, was engineered as bait to lure all of the large Vo Nguyen Giap units into the open. Then, the French generals thought, their general reserves, their air squadrons, their armored columns, their paratroopers and their artillery regiments would converge on Giap's forces and smash them into oblivion.

Diem Bien Phu was a narrow valley. Over time, Giap's artillery units, the very existence of which the French intelligence had not known, were installed neatly on the slopes of the mountains encircling the valley.

Soon enough, rain and fog rendered the French air force ineffective. Their paratroopers landed on death grounds. Their rescue armor columns were beaten back before they came near Dien Bien Phu. Before long, the runways at the Dien Bien Phu airports were damaged beyond repair by Communist artillery pieces.

As his heavy guns thundered day and night, blowing up cement blockhouses and human limbs, Vo Nguyen Giap launched wave after human wave, which washed over the strong points and communication trenches.

French soldiers mired in putrid mud, pushed back, again and again, the nightmarish human waves. Bodies of the injured and the dead served as ramparts for the survivors. Acts of heroism on both sides were countless.

In the end, the French acknowledged that they were defeated, and surrendered. For the disheartened French generals, the battle at Dien Bien Phu was the 'Waterloo' of modern times. Vo Nguyen Giap, who had never gone to a military academy, was crowned a military genius.

For days, Hiep had been numbed at the thought of so many casualties. She had been praying for the killing to stop, for the battle to end. Then, at last, the battle ended.

*

Hiep was aware that from now on, the French would no longer care about whom would take over in Vietnam. She knew that they would have only one wish: to get out of Vietnam at any cost and as soon as possible. The eventual departure of the French from Vietnam filled her with joy. It also filled her with sadness: all the French soldiers, who had died during the war, had died in vain.

For a moment, she took herself to the French side. She wanted to feel, for a moment, the bitterness of so many Frenchmen who had thought their war against the Viet Minh to be a *just* war. She tried to imagine the sorrow of the families of French soldiers who had died in Vietnam and that of the brave French soldiers who had surrendered in Dien Bien Phu a few hours earlier. She wondered what would become of them.

At the same time, she was troubled. The victory of the Communists and their imminent takeover of all Vietnam would not mean happiness for all the Vietnamese. Those who had opposed Communism and those who continued to reject Communism would have nowhere to go. They would most likely rot in Communist jails.

The war, which had opposed not only the French against the Viet Minh, but also brothers against brothers, would not end immediately with reconciliation. There would be much retribution. There would be retaliation.

"Where is Brother Diem?" she wondered. "Is it too late for him to do anything significant now? Is it too late to salvage anything?"

"Would he agree to be Prime Minister now?" she asked herself. "A few months from now, people have predicted that the country will be firmly under Communist control. Would Diem agree to become Prime Minister, just for a few months? Then in all probability he would be blamed for the final disaster?" No, she could not believe that. Her brother, Can, assured her that Diem would find a way to save the country. "That would be a really big miracle, indeed," she thought.

*

Luyen looked at his cup of tea, then at his untouched cup of rice wine. He had raised the cup several times, saying *ganbei,* but knew that the rice wine would go to his head. Zhou Enlai, the Chinese Premier, smiled and said, "We have heard that your brother, Diem, will soon become Prime Minister." Luyen smiled back, but did not confirm his host's announcement, "Our Emperor is still in consultation. He has not made up his mind yet."

Sitting across the table, facing Zhou-Enlai, was Pham van Dong, who listened absent-mindedly to the conversation around the table but did not say anything. Dong was wondering why the Chinese Premier gave so much attention to the Special Envoy of Emperor Bao Dai. "Isn't it a waste of time, to talk to the representative of a dying regime? In a few days, the French will abandon their Vietnamese allies to their fate," he thought.

The joy and pride he had felt for the victory at Dien Bien Phu had not subsided yet. In his heart there was a song. 'And we will march through Central and South Vietnam. We will dip our helmet into the Perfume River and drink from it. We will wash our dusty uniforms in the Mekong River. We will celebrate our victory in all the cities and villages in all Vietnam…'

Dong stopped dreaming and listened attentively to Zhou. The Chinese Premier said, "Please tell your brother we will be happy to see him in Beijing." "What? Still talking about Diem? Who is Diem? A vagabond! A man who has a past, but no present and no future!" Dong thought.

Suddenly Dong was concerned, "What if the Chinese betray us now, when total victory is in view?" Bitterly, Dong reminded himself, "They will never accept the idea of a unified and strong Vietnam." Emaciated, his large forehead with a receding hairline making him look more like a philosopher than a politician, Dong looked around the table and foresaw disaster.

Zhou Enlai said to Luyen, "We want the war to stop for good. But in order for it to end, we will have to separate the Vietnamese regimes that apparently cannot live together. We will have to separate the people who do not want to live under the same regime. We may have to draw a dividing line across Vietnam." Pham van Dong raised his hand and protested, "Partition? Never!" Zhou Enlai smiled and waved his hand, "Oh, just an idea, Comrade, just an idea!"

It was mid-June. A cold front had moved in and the heat had subsided temporarily in Geneva. Out of the window, in the dark night, Luyen saw the dark Lake of Leman whipped up by gusts of strong winds. The winds pushed white crested waves towards the shore. The rain hit hard against the deserted wharves and the asphalt streets.

Both Luyen and Dong shivered. Only that morning, the sun had shone brightly and they had taken a walk along the lakeshore under the willow trees. They had bumped into each other, not far from where they were sitting now. Luyen had stopped, and raised his hat, and Dong had greeted him with the greatest courtesy.

Dong had thought, "We will have to learn to live together, *we* and *they*." He had wanted to say something nice to Luyen, the Special Envoy of the puppet emperor. Luyen had also seemed to be about to say something, but in the end, they had parted ways with a long look at each other, and a smile, which might have been interpreted as friendly or hostile.

Now both were contemplating the winds and the rain out of the window, trying to absorb what they had just heard. The dinner was not gratuitous. The Chinese Premier had not spoken in vain. It was not merely an idea. But how could they be reconciled with such a plan? Partitioning their country? Isn't there another way? They wondered.

*

Diem faced Nguyen De, his old friend, and the old enemy. Both Diem and De were ill at ease. De was still hurting as he remembered the moment when five years after Diem had resigned as a Prime Minister, he was shown evidence that Diem's move had been premeditated and that before he had accepted the appointment, Diem had already planned for his resignation. For a long moment, De stood there, his mind in a whirlwind. So Diem had not trusted him. He had been left in the dark. He had sacrificed his career for a man who had not trusted him.

De was hurt so badly that he had refused to meet with Diem for years. Out of bitterness towards Diem, he had, for years, gone to the French, not just any Frenchman, no, he had gone to the Frenchmen who hated Diem most and collaborated with them. De had become a very wealthy man.

In 1942, De thought he and Diem would be friends again. It was the time when Nhu courted De's sister. De thought that Nhu would be married to her soon. But in the end, Nhu married Le Xuan instead. That left a far more bitter taste in his mouth than any other grudge he had had against Diem previously.

Yet, friendship never died. In 1944, only one year after Nhu's marriage to Le Xuan, when the French were about to raid Diem's home and capture him, De got wind of it and immediately sent an aide to warn Diem of the imminent danger. Diem, on his part, responded appropriately, that time. He had sat down and took the time to write a long letter to De, thanking him for the warning, but most of all, for finding in the depth of his heart, the memories of their old friendship.

De had kept the letter for a long time. He had opened and read it many times over the years, remembering his youth, and the old friendship he had shared with a man who had not trusted him enough.

A year earlier, in 1953, De had reluctantly gone to Diem and asked him to meet with Bao Dai, who was seeking a new Prime Minister. The meeting between him and Diem, as well as the one between Diem and Bao Dai, were pure disasters. Diem spent time blaming De for selling himself to the French. Then in his meeting with Bao Dai, he expressed his doubt about the Emperor's character and the French good will. The Emperor was furious. He told De never to talk to him about Diem ever again.

Two days earlier, De had struggled with himself: No, he was not going to recommend Ngo Dinh Diem once more to the Emperor. Not this time.

Ngo Dinh Nhu and his National Solidarity Movement had caused so much strife in Saigon that nobody else besides Diem would have a chance in succeeding to form a viable Cabinet. In Paris, and in Cannes, so many people had come and asked him to intervene for Diem. Most of the men who came to talk to him were never-ending in their praise for Diem.

De exclaimed, "The fools, they do not even know that their leader has become a monk." De had his own sources of information and had learned that Diem had become an Oblate of the Order of St. Benedict. De paced back and forth in his spacious office. He knew, like Bao Dai, that only Diem might have a tiny, a very tiny chance of success. He mumbled to himself, "Any other candidate, if named Prime Minister, would simply sit by and watch the Communists take over the whole country. Only *he* would try to stop the Communists."

This time, the choice of the Prime Minister depended only on De. Bao Dai had said, "I have made so many bad choices lately. This time, I will let you make the choice. Tell me the name, and I will make any man you choose my next Prime Minister."

De also knew that Diem, as engrossed as he presently was with his recent religious vows, had been waiting for *the right situation* for years, for the situation to be really desperate, to assume power.

De struggled with himself for hours, pacing back and forth in his office, feeling lonelier than he had ever felt in his whole life. The night did not bring in any relief. The morning came and without even a thought about the consequences, he walked up to Bao Dai and said, "You know I am no longer a friend of Ngo Dinh Diem's. But I believe that *only he* can save the day now."

Bao Dai shook his head, "Diem is the only one man who can make you lose your mind. Have you talked with him? Have you told him that if I made an offer to him this time, it would be because you asked me to do so? No, I guess not. My dear friend, I am not blind. You have allowed your old friendship to awaken again. Will Diem ever know how much he owes you?"

De shrugged, "I have not talked with him about this. Anyway, I cannot say that he owes me anything if you offer him the job." Bao Dai looked at De quizzically, "Do you know how many times that arrogant man has refused my offers?" De's voice was calm, "He will accept this time. I know he will." Bao Dai mused and said: "Strange friendship! How strange! Our life will be topsy-turvy with him around. Have you thought of that?"

Nguyen De simply reminded Bao Dai, "You promised that I would make the choice this time." Bao Dai nodded, "Yes, I did. I am not going to forget my promise. But to live with that man! My God, may Heaven save us from all the incorruptible and the saints!"

The Emperor pondered a moment, and then said, "You are right in saying that he is the only man who can save the situation. I am not fond of him, but I will survive." De smiled, "You don't have to live near him. He will be in Saigon, and you will be here in Cannes." The Emperor sighed and told De, "I will tell him that *this is your choice*." De shook his head, "No, Sire. Please do not tell him that. The Emperor makes the decisions, not the Chief of Staff."

*

On the phone, De argued a long time before Diem said yes. Diem was stunned when he found out that De knew about his secret vows at the Abbey of St. Andrew. De showed his respect for Diem's devotion to God, but reminded Diem that he also had to be devoted to his people.

He overcame Diem's reluctance in the end. De felt that Diem was struggling against himself all the while they were speaking. Somehow, De felt that he had taken advantage of Diem. He knew that Diem's mission was impossible, and that he might be sending his friend into a *death ground*. He asked Diem to come to Cannes immediately. Diem laughed, "I travel light. I don't need much time to pack my only suitcase." De said, "Please be here tomorrow. The Emperor is waiting impatiently for you." And then he hung up.

*

But Diem knew. He knew that both Bao Dai and Nguyen De made the decision together. The Emperor had already abandoned all hope. Left to himself, he would have chosen a caretaker, somebody who would not make waves, somebody who would sign the death certificate for the State of Vietnam, and walk away without remorse. Left to himself Bao Dai would not try to convince him, of all people, to assume power.

So Diem had asked to see Nguyen De before his appointment with Bao Dai. Now that they were face to face, neither could say anything. They stood, looking at each other. The years had left their marks on both of them. Yet, twenty years seemed to have dissolved for a moment, leaving them standing in the mist of their youth. Finally, Nguyen De said, "I know that whatever you do, it will be done out of your love of our country." Diem struggling with his own emotion, replied, "You and I are worlds apart now; yet we remember!" Nguyen De rejoined him, his voice soft and young, "Yes, we remember."

Diem said, "One day, people will say that the French made me Prime Minister, or the Emperor made me Prime Minister, or even, the Americans were responsible. Only you and I know, the offer came from your friendship for me."

Nguyen De put up a hand; he said, "Few people will know that you also wanted to reject the offer this time. Few people will know that I succeeded in making you see how desperate the situation is and convinced you to assume power." Walking to the heavy door, he turned and said, "Please, go in. The Emperor is waiting for you."

*

Bao Dai was blunt and to the point. Years of being shown obsequious respect by people who had no respect for him, and who said plenty of appalling things about him once his back was turned, had stiffened his demeanor. He told Diem, "In 1933, I told you that one day your Emperor would call on you again. You promised me that you would be ready to respond to my call. You weren't. I called you twice in 1945; you did not even care to give me an answer. After that year, how many times have I turned to you? But you chose to ignore my extended hand. Now, will you tell me why have you accepted?"

Diem listened calmly to Bao Dai's reproaches. He chose not to give any excuse for his repeated rejections of Bao Dai's past offers. He simply said, "I accept this time, because the situation is desperate." Bao Dai couldn't help being sarcastic, "Yes, the situation is desperate, but I need a Prime Minister, not a Joan of Arc."

Diem looked at the Emperor until Bao Dai felt uneasy and corrected himself, "I do not want to be irreverent, but please don't feel that you have to sacrifice yourself." Diem did not wish to let the Emperor get off so easily. He argued, "You recognize that the situation is desperate. Do you think that I am arrogant enough to believe that I, a mere human, can make miracle by my own power? Only God can make miracles, not you or I, Sire."

That was what Bao Dai hated the most about Diem. His former Prime Minister had so much faith in his God that he sounded like an *'enlightened prince'* who wrapped the Mandate of Heaven around himself like a mantle. Bao Dai was both amused and afraid of Diem's faith. "He believes that he can force God to make miracles for him any time, just like that!" Bao Dai thought. Yet he, more than anybody else around him, knew how desperate the situation was and he understood Diem's logic.

He asked Diem, "Besides your faith in God, what do you have to offer?" Diem pondered a moment and replied, "For years, I have reflected on the most enigmatic advice my father gave me, *'Any leader knows how to exploit his advantages; a great leader knows how to take advantage of his own weaknesses';* now I finally understand it. Bao Dai nodded and repeated words of the sentence. His voice was much softer when he told Diem, "Yes, we only have weaknesses now. May Heaven show you how to take advantage of them!"

He turned to Nguyen De, who had attended the meeting without saying a word, reminding him, "Have you asked the Empress to come over?" As

Nguyen De nodded, the inner door was pushed open and Empress Nam Phuong walked in. Diem stood up and bowed. She was as beautiful as ever. Diem who would blush whenever he was in the presence of a woman felt at ease with the Empress. It was her gift, he thought, to make people feel so comfortable around her.

The Empress inquired graciously about the health of Diem's mother. She then asked Diem quite directly, "Do you think that the situation is irreversible?" Diem shook his head, "Your Majesty, if I thought that way, I would not have accepted the Emperor's gracious offer."

The Empress looked at Diem a long time, then said at last, "What do you intend to do? The French will abandon us to our fate. Mendes-France will be made Prime Minister in a couple of days. He has recently boasted he could get France out of Vietnam in no time. What can you do to stop the Communists from taking over right after the French leave?"

Diem held Nam Phuong's eyes, and he replied, "The Chinese are maneuvering against their Vietnamese comrades. We have to exploit such a rift, which is our best opportunity to salvage what we can in the short term. The French are confused and frightened. Mendes-France may want to get out of Vietnam as soon as possible. But the French generals in Vietnam still want to make life as difficult as possible for the Communists. We have to exploit such a desire for vengeance. The Americans are standing on the sidelines now. But they believe they are far cleverer than the French. They believe that they could have defeated the Communists. We have to exploit such a belief."

Diem looked at Bao Dai now, as he went on: "The Communists believe that they have practically won the war, and that all of Vietnam will come under their rule very soon. We have to take advantage of such foolish optimism. The people who don't like Communism in Vietnam know that it is now or never, to unite and fight. We may be able to tap on that sense of urgency. With God's help, we will build on what remains under our control, after the Geneva Conference is over. Besides divine intervention, I will need the unfailing support of Your Majesties, to succeed in my mission."

Nam Phuong said with restrained emotion, "You once had problems with the Emperor. I have always regretted that you two were so different in your outlook, and that you had not become friends. This is a critical time, however. Please be *faithful to the mission* the Emperor has entrusted to you, and I will do my best to have him support you unfailingly. Difficulties are innumerable on your way. Think of your Empress, think of my son, Crown Prince Bao Long, whenever you are not satisfied with your Emperor's entourage."

Diem bowed his head. He knew that the Empress would do her utmost to support him. Bao Dai, sensing he had been pushed to the background, said, "Before you came in, he told me something very interesting. He said that he would exploit the existing weaknesses of our situation and transform them into advantages."

Emperor Bao Dai and Empress Nam Phuong

*

The Empress made a sign for the attendant, who wanted to pour some more tea for Diem, to leave it to her. With queenly grace, she poured tea for her husband, and for Nguyen De, Diem and herself. All the while she seemed to be pondering on what Bao Dai had said.

Then she asked Diem, "Was that one of the teachings you learned from the late Grand Chamberlain?" Both Diem and Bao Dai were surprised by her remark. Bao Dai was surprised because he had never thought that the

Empress knew anything about Ngo Dinh Kha, Diem was surprised because of the accuracy of her guess.

She smiled sadly and said, "What else do we have at this moment to exploit, besides own weaknesses? But I also understand that it will not be easy to put that concept into practice."

Diem knew now why he had always preferred to deal with her rather than with Bao Dai. But he also knew that in the coming months, he would hurt Bao Dai, and by doing so, he would hurt her. He sighed and said, "I appreciate Your Majesty's understanding of the difficulty."

CHAPTER NINETEEN
DIFFICULT BEGINNINGS

Diem repeated for the hundredth time, "*C'est la mer à boire.*" Standing on the balcony of his mother's house in Phu Cam, he was contemplating the orchard surrounding the house. Hue and Phu Cam were in a festive mood. Tens of thousands had assembled at Phu Van Lau that morning, to welcome him back.

The people of Hue were celebrating the victorious return of one of Hue's most illustrious sons. Diem gave the occasion the proper appreciation. He noticed Phan Van Giao's efforts in organizing it.

Giao, the Governor of Central Vietnam, whom Diem was ready to fire, had gone to all kinds of trouble to make the reception imperial. But Diem was not impressed with the extravagance. He did not need people like Giao, who for years had exploited the population of Central Vietnam.

Diem was pensive and a little restless. After a few days in Saigon, Diem departed for Hue. He returned, not to bask in his glory, not to enjoy the popular support he knew he had there, but to go and lay a wreath at his father's tomb, and to tell his mother how much he had missed her.

He had wished to spend time with his brother Can, and his sisters, Hiep and Hoang. But his schedule had been so full and he could only tell Hiep at the last minute, "I will come back in a couple of weeks. Then, we will talk."

*

Prime Minister Ngo Dinh Diem

*

He had gone to North Vietnam and seen the extent of chaos there, then back to Saigon where he announced the composition of his cabinet. Then he hurried back to Hue, where all his brothers and sisters were to meet with him.

He spent some time receiving well wishers. He was surprised by the confidence they expressed in him. Most of them believed that he would soon find a solution to every problem facing the country. They were not flatterers. They were, simply taking their wishes for realities. They needed a miracle-worker, so they believed him to be one. He, on the other hand, needed men and women who were willing to face hard realities, not dreamers.

After the visits and dozens of cups of tea, he was at last left alone with his brothers and sisters, to try to sort out the many trends of thought, to set priorities, and deal with a multitude of issues, all at the same time. Before he met with them, he needed to have a few minutes for himself. He wanted to see a little more clearly, how he would chart his course for the next twelve months. Now, on the balcony where his father used to stand, looking at the cathedral across the street and praying, Diem said to himself, "To draw advantage of one's own weakness! Easy to say, easy to say." He remembered what the Empress had told him just a few weeks earlier, "It will not be easy to put that concept into practice." How right she was.

*

All his brothers and sisters were present, including Luyen who had arrived hurriedly from Geneva. Diem presided over the meeting, but it was clear that he did not say anything without looking at Nhu for approval or backup.

Luyen reported on the Geneva Conference, "When Dr. Tran Van Do arrived in Geneva; he met immediately with Pham Van Dong, according to your wishes." Diem nodded his approval, "Nhu correctly suggested to me that Dr. Do is the right choice for the Foreign Affairs spot. He was a friend of Pham Van Dong in his youth. How did the conversations go?" Luyen shrugged, "You have seen his report on the meetings with Dong. Though Dong still treats him like an old friend, Dr. Do could not make a breakthrough with him on any issue."

Diem asked Luyen, "What about the Chinese?" Luyen smiled, "You received a standing invitation to Beijing, to meet with Zhou-Enlai. He kept smiling at me as if we shared some secret. It was quite disturbing. Once, he took me by the elbow, steered me to a corner, and suggested that once the Geneva Conference ended, he would like to talk with us about exchanging embassies."

Diem nodded, "That's good. But what is the general direction of the talks at the present?" Luyen was noticeably tense as he said, "I have the impression that the Chinese and the French have already agreed together on many issues, and what they have to deal with now, is how to convince everyone else to agree to their peace plan."

Diem frowned and asked, "Do you have any idea about the general lines of the French and Chinese peace plan?" Luyen smiled, "We have an advantage over the Viet Minh delegation. They are running around trying to figure out what both the Chinese and the French want. We are privy to good information on both French and Chinese intentions. We are so weak, and so marginal, yet we are quite well-informed."

He paused a moment before he went on, "Basically, the Chinese are working against the Viet Minh in Geneva. They aren't going to allow the

Viet Minh to exploit to the fullest, their military victories. They aren't allowing Pham van Dong to translate Vo Nguyen Giap's successes on the battlefield into political advantages at the conference table. They want the partition of Vietnam. Mendes-France has agreed with them. They also want to keep the Americans out of Vietnam. So, their common strategy with the French is to keep the French troops south of a demarcation line which is still to be determined by the military experts."

Diem argued, "No Vietnamese would like to see our country partitioned, even temporarily. Are the Chinese and the French discussing modality for the reunification of the two zones?"

Luyen laughed, "Yes, they've been quite elaborate about the procedures for reunification. They will pay lip service to a popular referendum to be worked out between the two Vietnamese 'sides'. But neither the Chinese, nor the French expect that such a referendum will ever take place."

Diem asked, "What do the Americans say?" Luyen shrugged, "The Americans stand on the sidelines. They haven't offered any new ideas. They have no initiative. Of course, they want to have a presence in Vietnam now, to contain Chinese expansion, and they don't really want the continued presence of French troops south of the demarcation line. But, they haven't suggested any alternative."

Diem then proceeded to talk about the new cabinet he had announced in Saigon. There was an uneasy silence following his briefing. The composition of his cabinet was not extraordinary. It did not include any name that added weight to the Prime Minister.

Can asked Diem, "Why did you make Tran Van Chuong the Minister of State? I understand why you appointed his brother, Dr. Tran van Do, as Foreign Minister, because he led the *Tinh than* Group for several years and has been a loyal friend for so long. But why Chuong?"

As Diem hesitated to respond, Can went on, "His only title to glory is his few months as Foreign Minister under Tran Trong Kim, in 1945. In fact, Tran Trong Kim, in the end, did not at all appreciate diplomatic talents. Here you are, making him the Minister of State. His name came right after yours, on the list of cabinet members. For goodness' sake! People will talk about nepotism now, with good reason. He is Nhu's father-in-law, or have you forgotten that?"

Diem was irritated. He talked quietly though, "Look, Can, we are here to discuss general strategy, not appointments. If you are unhappy about the appointments, we can talk about that later."

Can saw just by looking at those around him, that not everybody disapproved of his questioning Diem about Chuong's appointment, so he pressed on: "No strategy will work without appropriate human resources. Recognize that appointing Chuong is a mistake! There are many who would be a better choice for that position."

Both Nhu and Diem were embarrassed. Can was right, of course. Diem had appointed Chuong upon Nhu's recommendation. Nhu had recommended Chuong upon his wife's insistence. Diem had understood that, unless he appointed Chuong, Nhu's life would be hell. Now, he did not have any good argument for his own defense.

As Diem did not say anything, Can angrily continued, "Eleven years ago, Brother Khoi cried as he boarded the train to go and seal the alliance between our family and Chuong's. He did that after he clearly pronounced the exclusion of Brother Nhu from any political involvement. Now, do you see how right he was?"

Nobody responded, so Can went on, "Since Brother Khoi's death, many things have changed. Brother Nhu has now become almost as important a player as Brother Diem. He has done well with his organizational skills, and his coordinating skills. We are happy with his work. We have admiration for his skills. But he is the hostage of his wife's whims, and through him, we are all her hostages. If we do not want Brother Nhu to be unhappy, we have to march to her tune. Am I correct? If that is the case, and I think it is the case, then Brother Diem, you should resign now. Now, before you cause further damage to our family reputation."

They were all shocked by Can's vehemence. Most of what he said was correct. He exaggerated of course, but he was not far from the truth. Thuc rose up and said; "I think we should have a pause now. I think we need to discuss Nhu's family matters in another setting. I propose that we take a tea break."

*

They all stood up. Hiep took Hoang aside in the room, but when they saw their brothers milling around, too close to them, they went out into the garden. Hiep said, "I am very concerned. Appointments seem to me very important. I will never intervene in favor of any candidate, but I am concerned with the process. Lots of the 'old friends' from Central Vietnam, people who have been sympathizers from the first hour, have come to me and expressed their surprise. They said that Brother Diem ignored all of them. None of them were consulted or interviewed before he announced his cabinet."

Hoang replied, "I have never been interested in politics. But I am a businesswoman. I make decisions about whom to hire and whom to fire. I always hire the best for a job. The best! I do not want to know who his father is, whether he is Christian or Buddhist. The cabinet that Brother Diem has announced includes two Tinh Than Group leaders, a few intellectuals he recently met in France, and a mixture of people from a variety of political parties. He has definitely not chosen the best, maybe because he had limited freedom in choosing. Perhaps he is trying to project the image of a broad coalition."

Hiep asked, "What about the choice of Tran van Chuong?" Hoang laughed, "I knew what was really on your mind, when you took me away from the men. You really want to know my view on Mr. Chuong as a Minister of State? For the people, few would object to such an appointment. Chuong is not a household name, but some people know him to be a wealthy lawyer. Some remember his days as a Foreign Minister, under Tran Trong Kim, and some even know that the Viet Minh put him under house arrest. He has adequate credentials to be a Minister of State."

Hiep asked, "Then, you approve the appointment?" Hoang took Hiep by the elbow and steered her to a fig tree. She plucked a fig from the tree, extended her hand and let the white sap drip, drop by drop, to the ground. Watching her, Hiep remembered. Hoang's gesture was so familiar and so timeless, that Hiep was overwhelmed with a flood of childhood memories.

Hoang threw the fig away and answered her sister, "No, I do not approve. Brother Diem wanting to create a national coalition accepted to appoints inept people from various political parties. But we know he does not have a good reason for appointing Mr. Chuong. He has to preserve his integrity; that is the most precious virtue he has."

342

Hiep looked at Hoang. So, she was not alien to politics after all. The little girl who had always followed her like a shadow, and who had grown up to be a much feared and independent business woman, could be as sharp, as trenchant as anybody in their family, when it came to making a political judgment. Hiep did not worry about showing her anxiety any more. She told Hoang, "Can's remarks hurt Diem's and Nhu's feelings. His reference to Le Xuan was exaggerated. What can we do to preserve our family harmony?"

Hoang shrugged, "Our brothers, because they have to be blunt with each other, in order to see the issues more clearly and more quickly, will continue to hurt each other's feelings. But, they will survive. I don't like Nhu's plan to move his family into the Palace with Brother Diem, either. Nhu is a good and competent aide. But if he moves too close to the center of power, Le Xuan will be tempted to rule. If that happens, all of this will end in tragedy!"

Hiep shivered in the shade of the large litchi trees. The music of cicadas was raucous. Hiep said, "I am fond of Le Xuan, and I am very fond of their daughter, Le Thuy. Why don't we have a heart to heart conversation with Le Xuan. We may find some way to help solve the problem." Hoang sighed, "I have tried many times. Each time, I went away feeling that I had accomplished something significant. Then I started feeling that I had been a fool."

Hiep protested, "But Le Xuan does have many outstanding qualities!" Hoang nodded in agreement, "She does. Unfortunately, she is probably twenty years ahead of her time. She was born too soon, before her time. All of the things she wants women to do at this moment; other women will do in another twenty years. Then, besides her incontestable qualities, she also has obvious shortcomings."

Hiep was overcome by an immense wave of sadness. She said, "I wish that I could just sit down here under this litchi tree and never go back to the meeting." But already Nhu's strong voice was heard calling them back to the house.

*

Am had come with Hiep and stayed for a little while, but then he had gone home. Le Xuan, on the other hand, had nowhere to go and had to wait for the family gathering to end. She found the procedure deplorable. How could they meet and keep her shut out like a stranger? But she had noticed that Am did not protest. He even seemed to be relieved at not having to stay. Le Xuan decided to go down to the kitchen and help prepare the lunch. But she found her presence there unnecessary and unwelcome.

She went back to the garden and found Hoang and Hiep discussing her father's appointment. She walked away quickly, not wanting to spy on them. She felt so lonely that she wanted to cry. She found a large grapefruit tree and sat down by it, trying to sort out her thoughts. She knew that what she and Nhu had done was for their own peace of mind. She knew that her parents would not give her and Nhu any respite until he got a major appointment. Either they gave her father the appointment he sought, or they would have constant disputes with her parents. She could not afford to have any more tension in her family, just at that moment.

Their marriage, always fragile, was on the rocks since Nhu and she had come to live in Saigon, because he dedicated all his time to the Party, and the *Tinh Than* Group, and the *Xa Hoi* (Society) Magazine. Nhu no longer hid the fact that he did not like her life style. She no longer hid the fact that his obsession with saving the country was boring her to death. Her parents did not seem to understand that she was going through hell with her husband. "Don't they see that we are walking on glass?" She thought, "Don't they see that we are walking on a tightrope, Nhu and I?"

On Nhu's side of the family, it was not any better. Nhu's brothers and sisters seemed to be interested in only one thing: the dream of their father. In the last few weeks, since Diem was about to become Prime Minister, the situation had gotten far worse. Nhu was never there for her. He immersed himself in his preparations, negotiations, consultations, trying to do the work of a whole army all by himself.

One day, she had foolishly challenged Nhu and said, "You and your brothers and sisters should relax more. You have received no mandate from God to save the country. Your father never expected all of you to forget everything and consume yourselves with this obsession about saving the country." He had turned away from her, as if she had committed a sacrilege. She cried out "Listen to me, Nhu, listen to me…"But he left without even saying goodbye.

344

Now, bitterly, she clenched her fists, "He will never listen to me. They will never listen to me, especially from now on. I have made a big mistake by insisting that my father should be appointed Minister of State. They will never forgive me for that. And they are right. His appointment has jeopardized my role in this family, maybe forever."

She heard footsteps coming her way. Hiep stopped and asked with a note of concern in her voice, "Why are you sitting out here all by yourself? Why don't you come in and talk with Mother?" Le Xuan shook her head, "She is fast asleep." Hoang suggested, "Why don't you let my daughter, Hoang Anh, take you to the Imperial Palace or to an Imperial Tomb while you wait for us to finish our foolish meeting?"

Le Xuan waved her hand to dismiss the suggestion. She asked bluntly, "You have discussed my father's appointment, haven't you?" Her sisters-in-law nodded. Le Xuan frowned and said, "It was either that, or my husband and I will have to deal with my parents' pressure, day and night. Things are not going well between Nhu and me lately. We hoped that by keeping my parents quiet and happy for a time, we might have a better chance to put our house in order. But, we were wrong. We were wrong to put pressure on Brother Diem. He was wrong to have listened to us. I am really sorry."

Hiep was stunned by Le Xuan's candor. She said, "Both your father and your Uncle Do have received the highest appointments. In Saigon, people talk about Brother Nhu as the Co-Prime Minister. The problem is not going to go away easily. I think that both you and Nhu will have to do a lot of soul-searching and try to find a way to assist Brother Diem and put a little distance between him and you."

Le Xuan looked unhappy. She nodded and said, "The men are waiting for you. Hurry up before they also exclude you from their meetings." Both her sisters-in-law laughed and hurried back to the house.

Left alone, Le Xuan thought, "They are both capable women. Yet they march to the tunes of the men, without ever questioning men's power. When will women escape from such dependence?" She had originally thought of her sisters-in-law as insignificant, yet a brush with them, and she began to think differently. Now, she vaguely dreamt of them as her allies, fighting alongside with her for more female participation in politics. Finally, she shook her head and told herself, "That will never happen!"

*

Diem asked tersely, "Who thinks I made a bad decision, when I appointed Mr. Chuong?" Can raised his hand. Hoang followed his example, then Hiep, then Luyen. Diem turned to Thuc and asked, "Do you think that my decision was good?" Thuc shook his head, admitting, "No, I agree with the others."

Grimly, Diem stated, "We have unanimity then, because Nhu and I also recognize now that we made a terrible mistake." Can commented, "I am not going to ask you to dismiss him, but in your next cabinet reshuffle, please make sure that he is no longer Minister of State, even better, make sure that you send him overseas." Diem nodded. Can went on, "What continues to worry me is your statement, '*We made a terrible mistake.*' I would be more at ease if you had said; 'I made a terrible mistake.' Brother Nhu may make recommendations, but only you make the decisions. Or is it true that Brother Nhu has become the Co-Prime Minister?"

Nhu was really annoyed, and he retorted, "Please do not twist Brother Diem's words. Whatever words he used are not important. What he meant was that both he and I made a mistake, I, because I made the recommendation, and he because he made the decision. I am not the Co-Prime Minister nor do I want to be one. The first mistake we made shows us how easy it is for us to err. It helps us to be humble. I pray that you don't show hostility towards Le Xuan because of our mistake."

Luyen said, "It's easy to make mistakes. Fine! But what cannot be excused is the way *you two* made the mistake. You cannot make decisions for the good or the convenience of the family. Brother Diem, you have *carte blanche* from Bao Dai. It does not follow that you can do anything you want. On the contrary, because you have full power, you have to use it for the benefit of all your fellow-countrymen; you have to use it in the best interests of the nation. Brother Nhu, you are officially Brother Diem's adviser. You have the responsibility of helping him to walk straight. It was you, however, who led him astray."

Diem and Nhu lowered their heads. Luyen said, "I am the youngest in the family. I should not be talking like I have been, but neither Brother Thuc nor sister Hiep have said anything. I am disturbed. Brother Thuc, you are the eldest brother, after Brother Khoi died. You are also a bishop, a spiritual leader. Yet you have not said anything. Sister Hiep, I was a child when father died. But I remember he told us that you were to speak out in his name. You have also kept your silence."

Thuc looked at Hiep. Hiep said, "I don't know what criterium was used for the selection of the members of the cabinet, this time. I don't have full knowledge of Mr. Chuong's past achievements. I am certain that had it not been the fact that he is Brother Nhu's father-in-law, none of us would have objected to his selection. Mr. Chuong is not any worse a man than most of the other Ministers.

"Yet we have all recognized that his appointment, because of the way it was done, was a serious mistake. Brother Diem's integrity is in question here. He cannot mix public and family interests. When public and family interests are at odds, he has to sacrifice the family interests. I do not know what else to say. Maybe, our sense of family has been too strong. It should not interfere with Brother Diem's mission, though."

While she was speaking, Diem looked at her in silence, apparently trying to hear another voice, one that had shaped his life and his character as he grew up. The silence went on after she stopped speaking, until Diem broke the spell, and said, "Thank you, Sister Hiep, we will remember your words." Everybody nodded. The presence of the Grand Chamberlain seemed to fill the room.

In the end, Luyen said, "As long as this case is merely an isolated incident, I am ready to move that we begin to discuss other issues."

How different Luyen was from her other brothers. Hiep thought. He was serious, prudent and thorough, but he seemed so carefree. He moved from issue to issue and never let a problem take more of his time that it should. Hiep would like to see Luyen take more heart in what Diem was doing and provide Diem with his 'scientific' perspective.

*

Diem took control of the meeting again. He said, "The goal is clear for us. That helps us to have a good strategy. Our goal is total independence for our country. That was our father's dream. Now, let us look at the present situation: We are losing control of a large portion of our country to the Communists. The Geneva Conference will soon decree the partition of our country into North and South Vietnam."

Diem stopped and looked at his brothers and sisters a moment before he went on, "The destiny of North Vietnam will not be affected by us in any significant way, in the next few years. Whether it will achieve total independence or not remains to be seen, but even if it is totally independent, still the people living in Vietnam will not be free. You and I do not see the merits of national independence when the people are not free. Someday, we will have to deal with that part of our country."

Again Diem stopped. He took a cigarette and slowly lit it. Then he said: "What we will have to deal with in the present and in the near future is the part of Vietnam located south of the future demarcation line. We are facing tremendous problems. We still have French troops occupying our territory. These troops have to leave our land. That is our first major objective."

Diem puffed at his cigarette, waved it in the air and went on, "The territory south of the future demarcation line is splintered: The South Central Highlands form the Imperial Domain, a country within the country, where the French under the name of the Emperor are training tribal Vietnamese against the central authority. It has to be returned to the nation. That is our second major objective."

"In the Southern Provinces, we have politico-religious sects whose generals occupy large domains. They are real warlords, some good, and some bad. We have to reintegrate those fiefdoms, and place all of the territory under the national government. That is our third major objective."

"In Saigon and Cho Lon, a gang of bandits has been allowed to take over gambling dens and prostitution centers, as well as the National Police Force, itself. We have to destroy its power and place the National Police under the control of the government. That is our fourth major objective."

"We have an army commanded by officers, the majority of whom prefer to receive orders from the French, rather than from their own government. We have to place the army firmly under government control. That is our fifth major objective."

"Our administration from the national level, down to the village level, is overflowing with ineffective and corrupt officials. We have to reorganize all the structures and put in place more effective and honest officials. That is our sixth major objective."

"We still depend on the French for all our expenditures, as the French still control our National Bank and our Treasury. We have to have our own Treasury. That is our seventh major objective."

Diem stopped, then laughed and said, "I can go on, with another seven, with another seventy objectives. But I think that if by this time next year, we have made significant progress on all these seven major objectives, we will have done a great service to the nation, and we will be encouraged to go on working until our final goal is achieved."

As her brothers began to ask questions, and as Diem answered them with precision and confidence, Hiep sat back and thought, "What a difference! Diem today is no longer the Diem I knew, in 1933. This time around he is ready to assume power, and shows that he has the answers to most of the important questions."

Diem looked at her and addressed his question to her directly, "You are not saying anything, Sister Hiep. What is the weakest point of my plan?" Challenged, Hiep reverted to the familiar game of questions and answers, "Your weakest point, Brother Diem, is the lack of any means to achieve your seven objectives. But again, *that* may also be your strongest point." Diem smiled with secret understanding while the others, less familiar with Ngo Dinh Kha's teachings, were not sure they had heard her correctly.

*

After lunch, Diem asked Hiep to take a walk with him in the garden. The litchi season always came late in Hue. They had a few litchi fruit in their hands, and as they walked, they managed to peel the rough skins, and taste the marvelous translucent flesh inside. The fruit not only tasted good, but the flavor lasted for hours in their mouths.

Diem asked, "Explain to me what you said earlier at the meeting." Hiep shook her head and laughed, "You understood me at the meeting. If you did not understand me, you would have asked questions right then." Diem mockingly joined his hands on his chest in an attitude of prayer, "Please tell me."

Hiep sat down on a bench and Diem stood over her, waiting. Hiep said, "You mentioned seven major objectives, but your objectives are already, by the force of events, half achieved." Diem frowned, showing his objection to what she had just said, but he did not utter a word.

Hiep went on, "You have nothing you can call your own. You don't have an army, you don't have a treasury, you don't have a reliable ally, and you are faced with the Communists who have won the war, with the French who still occupy our territory and control our treasury and our army, with the warlords who have well garnished their coffers and their arsenal for many years, with river bandits who have control of your own National Police. You do not own anything. You are totally vulnerable."

Diem smiled sadly. "That much I already know. Why do you want to rub salt in my wounds?" Hiep shook her head, "You have used the wrong words. I do not rub salt in your wounds, for the simple reason that the knowledge of your weaknesses does not really bother you."

Diem nodded, "You are right. Such knowledge does not bother me." Hiep went on, "You are faced with the Communists. They are strong enemies. But precisely because they have shown how strong they are, everybody including the Chinese wants to weaken them. Because they are too strong, they will see their allies of yesterday turn to help you today.

"You talked about the French presence as if such a presence could be permanent. Of course there is a risk of that happening. But if you play your cards right, the Americans, seeing that you have no means to get rid of the French presence, will step in and help you throw the French troops out. They will not do that because they like you, but because they themselves want to have a certain presence in Vietnam.

"If the French troops are no longer here, or if the Americans succeed in reducing the French power in Vietnam, your army will be yours, your treasury will be yours, and the Imperial Domain will no longer be French.

"As for the sects, you look so weak that many of the warlords do not see you as the greatest threat. They are ready to ally with you, to face other warlords whom they think to be their most dangerous enemies. Anyway, Nhu has been diligent in entertaining contacts with all the sects. That will help.

"The river bandits represent the worst danger for you. They can kill you any time now. But because they are so sure they can kill you at any time, they are not going to do it right away, and they will give you time to establish your own loyal battalions. And when they see what you are up to, it will be too late for them."

Diem sat down next to Hiep. She never traveled anywhere, had never read a book on strategy, never met one single warlord, never spoke with one single French general, yet she had summed up his thoughts in a second. He said, "Father taught you too much. If the Communists knew how much you learned from Father, they would have eliminated you when they still controlled Hue."

Hiep stood up. She said, "Nhu is your strength, and your weakness. Le Xuan is an asset, yet she can turn everything you build into ashes. Be close to her, help her to achieve her dreams, but don't be soft with her. Don't be soft with Nhu either."

Diem asked, "What about Can?" Hiep bent her head in thought for a while before she replied, "Can has more intelligence than the rest of us put together. But he was devastated by Brother Khoi's death. There is too much pain, too much rage in him. You can never control him. But he loves you and he will work day and night for you."

Diem shook his head, "I can never understand him. He is like a force of nature. He can hurt himself and people close to him, easily. At the same time, he has a big heart, and is so sensitive, that anything we say to him can really wound him severely. What are we going to do with him?"

Hiep walked away without answering Diem's question.

*

In the afternoon, Diem wanted his brothers and sisters to focus on what was to be done quickly, within the next hundred days.

Diem told Ngo Dinh Luyen, "Please take the first flight to Geneva and tell Dr. Do to denounce vehemently, the partition of our country. He must also denounce any part of the Accords, which the French have agreed to without any serious consultation with us. He will denounce the modalities set up for the reunification of the two zones."

Luyen replied, "You know that such denunciation will not stop the signing of the Accords." Diem nodded, "If we refuse to sign the Accords, I understand *they* will still sign them. But if we do not sign the Accords, they will not legally bind us. That will allow us to have more flexibility to maneuver in the future."

He turned to Nhu, "You go back to Saigon this evening. Make sure that the arrangements to welcome and assist the refugees from north of the demarcation zone, are ready." Nhu asked, "How many refugees do you expect? "Diem pondered, and then said, "I expect many will vote with their feet. I think at least three hundred thousand will arrive from the north."

Thuc said, "From the looks of it, a large number of Catholics in the north will go south." Diem nodded, "Then, the number of refugees could easily reach half a million."

Nhu shook his head, "Then, their number will overwhelm our capabilities." Diem agreed, "Yes, I expect that we will be overwhelmed. But the plight of those refugees will be such that the international community will have to react." Nhu asked, "With the problem of refugees, when will we have time to work on your seven objectives?"

Diem seemed to have already thought through the issue. He waved his hand, "I will appoint a General Commissioner for Refugees. He will have the rank of Minister, and he will also be the Chairman of the Inter-Ministry Coordinating Board. We will give him *carte blanche*. That will help free us from the problem of refugee reception and resettlement and allow us to work on other national priorities."

He reflected a moment then went on, "Nhu, you have to start consultations with all the sects and the warlords. We will reshuffle the cabinet in a couple of months and expand it, making of it a coalition cabinet. After that, unfortunately, it will include potential enemies. Decisions will not be made at cabinet meetings. Can was right. We cannot keep Mr. Chuong as Minister of State. I think you should prepare the ground for him to be sent to Washington as our Ambassador." Nhu nodded. He looked relieved.

Diem said, "Many things will depend on the American attitude now. We do not want to be freed from the French, only to become dominated by the Americans. From the start, we have to make it clear to the Americans that we are ready to welcome an alliance with them, but will not tolerate any attempt at domination from them. Nhu, you work closely with Lansdale. He can be trusted. I like him."

Diem wrapped up quickly and said: "While Bothers Thuc, Luyen and Nhu have to go back to Saigon today, I will stay here another day. I want to hear more from Can and our sisters."

*

The next day Diem spent time with Can, trying to understand him. Can continued to amaze Diem with his encyclopedic memory. Diem knew his life depended largely on Can's preparations. Can had secretly recruited officers and non-commissioned officers of at least two battalions that could be moved quickly to Saigon. That was Diem's secret weapon. Those two battalions, that none of Diem's enemies knew existed, would make a significant difference.

They spent time working on the logistics of moving the battalions: transportation, weapons and ammunition. Can assured Diem, "By the time you need protection and a strike force, we will have at least four battalions ready." Diem looked at Can. His younger brother was never boastful. He would accomplish what he promised. He had worked steadily, building up this military force without any help. Diem shook his head, as he told Can, "You should be the Prime Minister, not I."

Can ignored Diem's remark. He said, "It appears to me that Sister Hiep unsettled you a bit, yesterday afternoon." Diem nodded. All afternoon, while he talked, his eyes kept going back to her, seeking her approval, seeking her questions. She sat there, listening intently, but she did not say anything.

Can asked, "Did she explain to you what she meant by saying that your weakest point is also your strongest point?" Diem nodded. Can mused and said as if to himself, "At times, I have the impression that Father talks through her. Even her gestures at those moments are like his." Diem nodded again. Can told Diem, "Then, go and see her again. I understand that Father Thuan, is at her house right now. It has been a long time since you last saw him." Diem did not need more encouragement than that. He took his hat and walked out into the bright sunlight.

Though only two hundred meters separated his mother's and Hiep's home, he was preceded and followed by a large number of aides and bodyguards. When he was Prime Minister in 1933, he had been assigned two guards and a driver. What a difference! He walked quickly, forcing some members of his escort to run to keep up with him.

Hiep was waiting for him at her gate, warned by telephone that he would soon arrive. Diem laughed, finding that he could not surprise her with his visit. He threw up his arms, "That is modern life for you. I intended to surprise you, but my aides found it more appropriate to use the telephone and tell you I was coming."

Am and Thuan were at the door, while the younger children were waiting for Diem inside. Diem, who was used to having Nhu's children around him, felt a little remorse for having spent no time with Hiep's children all these years. He sat down, and calling each of his nephews and nieces correctly by their name, he asked them about their schooling and their friends. When the younger children were gone, Diem stayed to chat with Thuan and Niem, Hiep's eldest children.

Diem had great respect for Thuan, and invited him to come to Saigon from time to time to say mass for him at the Palace. Diem, who had not seen Niem for the last four years, said that he would like Niem to come and spend some time with him in Saigon. Both accepted his invitation.

Am suddenly said: "I think Uncle Diem and your mother need to talk. We should leave them now." Diem waved his hand in protest, "No, I have no secrets from my family. You three stay here with us, please." He turned to Hiep and commented; "You did not say anything in the afternoon session, yesterday."

Hiep smiled, "I was overwhelmed by the scope of the work ahead of you. Half a million refugees to welcome and resettle will require billions of piasters. As you said, the international community, especially the Americans and the French will help. But where do you resettle them? Where do you find land for the rural refugees? Where do you find jobs for the urban refugees? There are tremendous differences between the North and the South. How will the refugees fit into the southern communities? Will there be conflicts between the refugees and the local residents?"

Diem looked at her, lost in his own thoughts. Hiep went on, "In the end, however, they may represent the greatest asset for you. They will appreciate everything you do for them, they will be grateful, and will constitute one of your popular bases. You will need them, as you now have only the people of Hue and Vinh Long solidly behind you."

Diem nodded, "In Hue, thanks to Can's work, and in Vinh Long, thanks to Brother Thuc's prestige. But I have almost no support in Saigon, the capital." Hiep asked, "That is why you have decided to resettle the bulk of refugees near Saigon?" Diem looked up. Of course, she was right again. Where could he resettle half a million people, if not in the jungle stretching from Xuan Loc to Ho Nai, at the gate of Saigon?

He asked, "Yesterday, in the garden, you mentioned the river pirates, the Binh Xuyen, as the most imminent danger. According to you, what are the other dangers?" Hiep shrugged, "You know all of them better that I do. Any of your enemies may soon throw the first stone at you, and then the others will follow. Politicians are slow to act, but military commanders and warlords are not patient. Father said, 'You can do lots of things with bayonets, except sit on them.'"

Diem laughed, finding the image funny. He thought a moment before he said, "Among those who are the most impatient are General Le van Vien, the Binh Xuyen leader, then General Nguyen van Hinh, my own Army Chief of Staff."

Hiep commented, "General Hinh does not know what he wants. He is the most powerful among your enemies, yet, he is not sure whether he should submit himself to you, or fight you. He is a man who is easy to confuse. You will need to go on confusing him, keeping him off balance, making him vacillate until you find the best way to remove him. General Le van Vien, on the other hand, is ready to fight you from day one. He has to fight you, because he knows that you are virtuous and he is the head of an empire of vices. He has to fight you because he knows you want the national police, now under his control, to fight vices, not to protect them."

Diem said, "From what you say, a war against General Vien and his river pirates is inevitable." Hiep nodded in agreement. Diem frowned and pondered a moment then cried out in anguish, "I do not want bloodshed. I cannot tolerate bloodshed."

Hiep looked at him, feeling sorry for him, and wished she could predict a more peaceful resolution of the Binh Xuyen problem. Finally, she said, "I cannot tolerate the idea of bloodshed either. But then, I have stayed away from politics."

Diem looked sad. He reminisced, "Father kept reminding me of Sunzi, 'To win one hundred victories in one hundred battles is not the acme of skill. To subdue the enemy without fighting is the acme of skill.' Yesterday, you sounded as if you thought all could be won without fighting."

Hiep shook her head, "No, I said you had already won half of the battle against all the enemies, without fighting. But you may be forced to fight; first the river pirates then certain warlords before it is all over. Of course, I know you will do your utmost to avoid battle and to limit casualties. But when you accepted the offer from the Emperor to assume power, didn't you foresee the possibility of having to use armed force?"

Diem lowered his head. He said, "At the last minute, before father died, for the first time in his life, he considered armed struggle for the liberation of our country. Armed struggle means casualties on both sides. Fighting the French, when no other alternative was available, was thinkable. Now, I may have to use armed force against my own fellow-countrymen."

Hiep asked bluntly, "Then, when you and Brother Khoi decided to convince Emperor Bao Dai to fight the Viet Minh, did you not agree to fight against other Vietnamese?" Diem paled. He looked stunned. He cried out in protest, "No, it was not like that, at all. Both Brother Khoi and I myself thought that with all the regular troops, the National Guards, the police force, well armed with Japanese weapons, Emperor Bao Dai could force the Viet Minh to recognize their military inferiority and negotiate with him."

Hiep felt sorry for her brother. He was now the leader of a country, with a tattered territory. Armed bands claimed larger and larger fiefdoms and his police force was under the control of a corrupt empire. He wanted to re-establish order and national integrity, and yet he was not ready to overcome his reluctance to shed even a drop of blood.

Hiep could already see the outcome. Surely, he would soon be forced by his advisers to take military action. Each time he had to use armed force, however, he would do it with extreme anguish. In the end, his enemies would learn how to exploit his fear of bloodshed.

She herself was that way, like their father before them. Her brothers all acted as if they could go to any bloody war, when necessary, but they were never really ready for that. In wartime, she saw, their enemies would soon see that gaping hole in their armor, and would take advantage of it.

Hiep wondered if Diem was thinking along the same line. She saw him become more preoccupied as she talked. Now he sat there, brooding. He came out of his silence and told Hiep, "We have made plans for the next hundred days. After that period has lapsed, I would like you to be in Saigon to review the results and evaluate the progress with all of us."

Hiep shook her head, "No, Bother Diem. I am not going to Saigon. My place is here with my family, and with Mother. You will have the advice of Thuc, Nhu, Luyen and Le Xuan. That is enough family around you already."

Diem did not accept her refusal. He said, "We will see. My invitation still stands for you, and Am too, of course." Nodding at Thuan and Niem, he said, "That invitation goes for you two, as well, and your younger brothers and sisters." As she accompanied Diem to the gate Hiep said, "Your strength is in your prayers and your faith. Do not let the problems of the moment discourage you. God will show you the way." Diem smiled fondly at his sister. He insisted, "I am looking forward to welcoming you in Saigon." Hiep smiled but did not say anything, one way or the other. Again Diem felt at peace with himself. He looked at the blue cloudless sky and he walked briskly back to his mother's home, amid his large escort.

CHAPTER TWENTY
A TIME FOR DECISION

The Geneva Ceasefire Agreements were signed on April 20, 1954. They divided Vietnam into two zones and set a demarcation line at the Seventeenth Parallel. They set deadlines for the withdrawal of the opposing forces to their respective zones, and allowed the free movement of the population between the two zones, within the next three hundred days. In the Joint Declaration, which was attached to the Agreements, it was stated that general elections would be organized by July 1956, to reunify the two zones.

Diem called the date *A Day of Shame,* while in Geneva Dr. Tran van Do protested against the abandonment of the territories still occupied by the National Army, to the Communists, and the announcement, without prior consultation with the Vietnamese delegation, of the planned general elections in July 1956.

Authorized by Diem, he declared that South Vietnam welcomed peace initiatives and would not use its armed forces to oppose the application of the Agreements, even though the Agreements did not respond to the aspirations of the Vietnamese people.

In Geneva, Zhou Enlai invited Luyen to dinner again on April 22, along with Pham van Dong, two days after the Geneva Agreements were signed. This time, Zhou Enlai, in the presence of Pham van Dong, told Luyen that he was permitted to officially invite South Vietnam to set up an Embassy in Beijing, at any time in the near future.

Diem, when told about the invitation, judged that American friendship was more important than the Chinese courtship. Had he accepted the invitation to open an Embassy in Beijing and exploit the rift between

Communist China and North Vietnam, history might have taken quite a different turn.

*

Perhaps because of the strong emotions she had experienced over the past few weeks, Mrs. Ngo Dinh Kha was not feeling well. Hiep and Hoang spent long hours with their mother, and from time to time, came out of her bedroom to have a chat together. Hoang was excited for Diem and Nhu, but was concerned with Diem's vulnerability.

Hiep had never talked politics with Hoang until recently. She regretted that she had not done so earlier. Hoang made her laugh, even when she talked about the most serious subjects. She was irreverent, almost as irreverent as Giao; their eldest sister had been in her lifetime.

Since Diem's visit, Can had been working hard. He met with civilian and military leaders every day. He sat with them, holding discussions far into the night. Hoang commented, "With all their astuteness, Brothers Diem and Nhu would not survive without Can." The two sisters avoided Can, not wanting to distract him from his work. But Can always popped in to greet them and to assure them that everything was going according to the plans.

Once, Can seemed to have some free time. He stopped to talk with his sisters. He said, "When Brother Diem arrived in Saigon, Nhu had already arranged for his father-in-law to go to Washington. To sweeten the pill, he offered Mrs. Chuong the position of Permanent Observer to the United Nations, in New York."

He waited for a reaction that did not come. He had to offer his own comment, "Just like that, Madame Nam Tran, oh, forgive me, Mme. Chuong, who was made Senator of the French Union last February, along with a number of pro-French elements, has now become our Representative at the United Nations. I tell you, I don't trust Brother Nhu any more, when it comes to dealing with Le Xuan's family"

He turned to go, but out of a sense of fairness, he added, "On other matters, he has been doing quite well. He and Lansdale have started negotiations with warlords and the sects. Brother Diem needs them to be quiet for now, as he wants to deal with General Nguyen van Hinh first."

Hiep asked, "What about the Emperor? Is he solidly behind Brother Diem?" Can shrugged: "You know Bao Dai. He will never give Brother Diem his full support. General Hinh was his Military Adjutant earlier. He is also the son of former Prime Minister Nguyen van Tam, still one of Bao Dai's confidants. The French are backing Hinh to the hilt. In view of all that, if Bao Dai is called upon to choose between Hinh and Brother Diem, he will choose Hinh without a doubt."

Hiep said, "I heard that Empress Nam Phuong has promised Brother Diem her full support." Can nodded, "Yes, for sure. But at this moment, she cannot bring herself to see the Emperor. Bao Dai is living more and more openly with his Imperial Concubine, Mong Diep."

Hiep wanted to understand the situation better, so she pressed on, "According to what you say, I presume that the greatest danger facing Brother Diem does not come from General Hinh, but from the Emperor himself."

Can shook his head, "If Brother Diem is doing well in Vietnam, if he has the situation under control, the Emperor cannot fire him. The absentee Chief of State cannot claim to have more power than the Prime Minster to whom he has given full power. But if General Le van Vien joins forces with General Hinh, then the situation may become very dangerous."

Can hesitated a minute, then added, "You see, though the Emperor receives a monthly payment from the French, probably more than five million piasters a month, he depends very much on the largesse of General Le van Vien, who makes tremendous amounts of money with his gambling casinos, his opium dens and his prostitution centers. When Brother Diem attacks General Vien, he will be ruining a major source of Emperor's revenue."

Hiep said, "Danger or no danger, Brother Diem must put an end to this terrible shame." Both Hoang and Can nodded their approval. Hiep asked, "Does Brother Diem face any imminent danger at this moment?" Can smiled, "You ask questions even when you already know the answers, just like Father. Of course, his life is in danger. That is why I am working my tail off, to make sure that he survives."

*

Three days before their wedding anniversary that year, Hiep and Am received a phone call from Diem, who insisted that they come to Saigon and celebrate it with him.

Hiep cautiously said that she was not going to come to the Independence Palace to participate in any review of Diem's first hundred days in power. Diem laughed and said that he had been in power for more than four months, and the review of the first hundred days had already been done.

Hiep and Am agreed to go to Saigon for a couple of days but said they would stay at Nhu's house, outside of the Palace. Diem agreed. He said, "Everybody will be here in Saigon, to celebrate with you, except for Can. He said he regretted it, but he has too much to do right now. I know that you will excuse him. But Brothers Thuc and Luyen will be here for the occasion, and of course the Nhu's and I will be here."

*

On the day of their arrival in Saigon, they found that General Nguyen van Hinh had left for France. That was the first major victory for Diem. In spite of all her reservations, Hiep wanted to know more about the conflict between her brother and the young general, and its final outcome.

After having half unpacked at Nhu's villa, Hiep and Am went directly to the Independence Palace in the car that Diem had provided for them.

The Palace, formerly known as the *Palais Norodom*, used for so many decades by French Governor-Generals, had been restored to Diem in September. Diem had renamed it Independence Palace. When Am and Hiep arrived, Diem was already on the lawn, waiting impatiently for them.

Diem looked happy and did not show any sign of depression. Hiep was surprised, as she had heard reports about his anguish in late October. Several people who visited Diem in early November, had told her that Diem was so saddened by the situation that he wanted to resign.

Diem toured Hiep and Am around, showing them all the different floors and wings in the Palace, awkwardly playing host. He apologized, saying, "Normally, Sister Nhu plays hostess. But she has been very depressed since the unhappy incident in October. You will see her later, at dinner." Hiep nodded but did not say anything. Diem looked at her quizzically,

"You know all about the incident?" Hiep shook her head, but admitted, "Brother Can did mention it to me briefly, but he did not know what your reaction was to the deaths."

Diem led them back down to the garden, and as they walked Diem sighed and said, "It was Sister Nhu's fault. She organized that big demonstration, without telling me in advance. Why did she do that? Why did she think we needed to demonstrate against the French then? The objective of the demonstration was so vague. Was it against the French only? Was it against General Hinh and the French support for him? Was it against the Binh Xuyen river pirates? …. The mass of demonstrators had arrived at the Saigon Central Market Square when the police, under the orders of the Binh Xuyen, opened fire. Six demonstrators were killed, several more injured. The first dead under my administration…"

Diem looked distraught now. Hiep asked him, "Do you feel responsible for those deaths?" Diem clenched his fists and replied, "Of course I do!" Hiep asked him again, "Do you believe that you were the primary cause of those deaths?" Diem looked at her a long time. Then he lowered his head and said in a whisper, "I am responsible." Hiep shook her head, "As long as you continue to think that you are the primary cause of those deaths, you will not make enough effort to find those who were the murderers."

Diem cried out, "Those demonstrators were out there shouting slogans in my favor. They were not told in advance that they would be exposed to any danger. Then the shots were fired and they died." Hiep shook her head, "While you and Le Xuan blame yourself for their deaths, gnawing at your own hearts, their murderers go free."

Diem said almost angrily, "That is Nhu speaking, not you." Hiep spoke as softly as possible, "Look, you invited Am and me here for our anniversary, promising us that we would not talk politics… But what we are discussing now is not about politics, it is about you. It is about putting things in their proper perspective. I will ask you a few questions. If the questions are too hard for you, do not answer. After that, we will talk about the menu of tonight's dinner."

Diem smiled, "Please, ask me the questions." Hiep asked the first question, "Do you see the incident as a skirmish, the first deadly skirmish in the war you will have to wage against the Binh Xuyen?" Diem said, " Yes, I saw those deaths as the first of many more to come."

Hiep reminded him, "In Hue, you showed anguish when I told you that you would have to face battles and bloodshed. Are you now more ready than you were before, to accept violence and casualties?"

Diem replied, "Right after the incident, I told myself that I did not have the right stuff to lead people into battle and see some of them die. That was why I seriously considered resigning."

Hiep looked at Diem a minute, then turned away and said, "I hate bloodshed, maybe a hundred times more than you do, so I am not going to ask you to stay on and fight. I simply want you to see clearly within yourself, before you make an irrevocable decision. I have asked you a question, and you have not answered it yet."

Diem shook his head, "No, Hiep, I am no more ready now than when we spoke in Hue, four months ago. I am still uncertain. I guess that if, because of me, a major slaughter takes place tonight, by tomorrow I may have resigned. "

Hiep felt like crying as she said, "Then I will give you another reason to resign: By now, everyone among your enemies both inside the country and outside, knows that you are incapable of seeing your followers, or even your enemies die. They will use that knowledge against you. You are already doomed if you stay on."

Diem did not say anything for a long moment. The bright lights over the Palace grounds went on in the darkening dusk. They kept walking, until Diem stopped and said, "If I leave, what happens then?" Hiep laughed, "That is my question. You have no right to ask questions tonight. Please answer." Diem said, "If I leave now, the country will go on rotting, maybe it will rot even faster than before. The French will continue to occupy our territory, then by July 1956, that is to say within two years from now, the whole country will be placed under Communist control."

Hiep asked, "How many will lose their lives in the wars among the warlords between now and July 1956?" Diem shrugged, "Thousands, tens of thousands, maybe." Hiep pressed on, "People who voted with their feet, those who came here from the North, and the people who opposed, those who will continue to oppose Communism, how many of them will die in 1956?"Diem said, "Many. The rest will rot in Communist jails."

Hiep continued to ask, "Do you think that if you stay, you will reduce the misery of the people and the number of dead and prisoners?" Diem admitted, "Yes, I would be able to reduce the number of deaths. Yes, I would be able to reduce the misery of the people." Hiep persisted, "Then, do you think you should stay?" Diem again shook his head and said, "Maybe." Hiep did not relent; she asked, "If you stay, do you think you are doing it because you have embraced a good cause?" Diem nodded.

Hiep concluded, "Then, you will have to resign!" Diem and Am were stunned. Diem protested, "I don't understand your conclusion." Hiep admonished him, "No, it's not true, Brother Diem. You understand me very clearly. At this moment, you have not resolved whether you can face going into battle with your troops, and causing casualties on both sides. You have not resolved that problem, even when you have seen that by staying and fighting you may save lives and reduce misery. You place the salvation of your soul far above political considerations. That is good. That is what Father taught us. But that also makes you unfit to govern at this moment. Please resign."

Diem did not respond. What Hiep had said was so accurate that Diem was overwhelmed with pain and frustration. But like a large wave, the pain and frustration soon subsided and he only felt a great peace inside of himself. Finally, he asked Hiep, "Do you really believe that I must resign?" Hiep, as blunt as she could manage to be, replied, "Yes, I really believe that you must resign, unless you can come to terms with the demands of your responsibilities."

The night was hot and moist. Even in November, Saigon was as hot as an oven. But Diem suddenly felt that he knew what he would have to do now. He felt as if a heavy weight had been lifted from his chest. He could breathe easier now. With real pleasure, he turned to Am and Hiep, and suggested, "Now, let us go in and have dinner."

*

Hiep and Am did not know that Thuc had already arrived. He was to say mass the next day, for the renewal of their wedding vows. But he had not shown up until Diem, Am and she arrived at the dining room.

Luyen, who had returned from Paris, had popped his head out of the office to greet them when Diem had shown them around in the afternoon. Hiep had insisted on spending some time with him, asking him about his children and Marie. Hiep had never seen Marie, Luyen's new wife and the sister of his late wife, Lucie. He had married her three years earlier. The mention of Marie's name brought radiant joy to Luyen's face.

Lucie had died in Paris five years earlier, and Luyen thought he would go crazy. Marie, who was Lucie's sister, nursed Luyen back to life. Hiep had heard about Marie's simplicity and her strong character. She was very impatient to have the chance to get to know her new sister-in-law.

Luyen promised he would ask Marie to return to Vietnam sometime in the next few months. Diem had to drag Hiep out of Luyen's office, telling her that he had given Luyen something urgent to finish.

Am and Hiep had not seen Nhu and Le Xuan all afternoon. So, it was in the dining room that they all finally met together. Hiep noticed that Le Xuan was extremely depressed, while Nhu looked anxiously at her from time to time without saying anything. At table, Thuc did most of the talking, while Diem, Nhu, Luyen, and Hiep and Am listened. Le Xuan did not even pretend to listen to what Thuc was saying.

Hiep had the impression that Thuc was trying to fill a vacuum with his voice, apparently afraid that if he stopped talking, there would be little conversation around the table. Now, Hiep could see that not only Nhu but also Thuc and Diem from time to time, cast a worried glance in Le Xuan's direction.

After the dinner was over, the men went downstairs to visit in Diem's office, and Hiep followed Le Xuan to her room in the left wing of the Palace. As soon as they arrived in her room and she had closed the door behind them, Le Xuan threw herself on a sofa and began to cry. Hiep stood there watching helplessly. "Le Xuan studied in a French school, when she was a child," Hiep thought "She may expect me to come over, hold her in my arms and comfort her." But Hiep could never do that. Her upbringing had taught her to be in control of her feelings, and to restrain her emotions. So she stood there, trying to imagine Nhu's problems with his wife. She knew that Nhu would have the same reluctance to show his feelings and his emotions. That alone would suffice to create inordinate problems between the two of them.

After a while, Le Xuan stopped crying and as she dabbed at her eyes with her handkerchief, she asked, "You know what happened with the demonstration I organized last month?" Hiep nodded. Le Xuan understood that she must have already discussed the details with Diem, so she asked, "Do you blame me for the deaths?"

Hiep shook her head, "Brother Diem blamed you for not telling him in advance about the demonstration, and for not discussing with him the objectives and the necessity of such a demonstration, but he does not blame you for the deaths. He has been blaming himself."

Le Xuan wailed, "By blaming himself, he condemns me. Don't you see? I was the one who was directly responsible." She stood up and started pacing the room, saying, "Since Hue, I knew that I had not made a good impression when my father was appointed as Minister of State; therefore, as soon as we were back in Saigon, with Brother Diem's prior approval, Nhu and I proposed to my father that he take the Embassy in Washington. My father was not very eager to go overseas. His idea of importance was to have daily access to the Palace. He said he would lose out by going to Washington."

Le Xuan quickened her nervous pacing, waving her sandalwood fan, though the room was perfectly cool. She went on, "Brother Diem then had a bright idea: why not give my mother something to do in New York. The post of Permanent Observer in New York, when South Vietnam has no membership in any UN agencies, was not the grand dream of my mother. But it appealed to her. So she convinced my father to go to Washington. They left only a few days after we came back from Hue."

Le Xuan sat down heavily and said, "I thought that the departure of my parents would placate Brother Can. But not at all, he sent a cable to Nhu, saying that he no longer trusted Nhu's promises. He said that by appointing my mother to the New York post, we had shown to the world that in reality, it was the Tran family that was in the saddle, and that Brother Diem had no real power. You can imagine how terribly angry Nhu was with me. For days he would not even say a word to me."

Hiep intervened, "Can was angry because he did not know that the idea of appointing your mother came from Brother Diem. Why didn't Nhu tell Can?" Le Xuan shook her head, "Do you think that if Nhu had told Can where the idea had come from, that Can would have believed him? Of course not! That would have made Can even angrier at Nhu and me."

Hiep urged her on, "What happened next?" Le Xuan smiled: "While we were dealing with that family conflict, General Hinh, with French backing, used the Army Radio to abuse Brother Diem and Nhu and me day and night. He sent his tanks to parade, only two hundred yards in front of the Palace. Like a hooligan, he rode his motorbike around the Palace saying that he wanted to scare us to death.

"He even planned a coup d'état. Nhu and Lansdale foiled it. But Hinh and the Army Radio continued to insult Brother Diem. The French went, more and more openly, to General Hinh's side.

"I wanted to do something to help. I wanted to prove my worth to all of you. I wanted to prove that I deserved your love and respect. I organized a very large demonstration. It was well organized, with the participation of tens of thousands of people. Then, the shots were fired at the Central Market Square, and I was proven wrong again."

Hiep asked, "The demonstrators were for Brother Diem, and against the French and General Hinh, not against General Le van Vien or the Binh Xuyen. Yet, the people who fired on them were assault policemen under the orders of the Binh Xuyen, weren't they? Can you tell me why the Binh Xuyen got involved?"

Le Xuan shrugged, "General Le van Vien knew full well that if General Hinh was defeated, he would be weakened. He knew that it was vital for him to keep General Hinh in power. Also, he needed to show he was loyal to the French who were being heckled by the demonstrators. He knew he would need French support in the days ahead."

Hiep asked, "Since the demonstration ended in bloodshed, on the surface nothing has changed. Why did General Hinh decide to leave? Why did he accept defeat so easily?" Le Xuan replied, "The four battalions from Hue had arrived, and two other battalions from South Central Vietnam were on their way to Saigon. They are all loyal troops, led by officers who have taken an oath of loyalty to Brother Diem. General Hinh was an officer of the French Air Force. He had never commanded any ground troops before. Faced with a real army, he was frightened. In fact, the balance of forces had shifted towards Brother Diem. Emperor Bao Dai and the French saw that too. In a hurry, the French demanded that the Emperor summoned General Hinh to Paris. Hinh left yesterday. He knew that if he went, he could never come back, but he went any way. He no longer represents a danger for Brother Diem."

Hiep said, "That is Brother Diem's first victory." She weighed her words carefully, then said, "I want you to know this. I do not blame you for what happened at the Central Market Square. After the shooting, Brother Diem wanted to resign because he saw that if he stayed in power, he would feel responsible for more deaths in the future. That thought has not left him."

Le Xuan cried out, "I began to understand the problem when I came back from the demonstration. He looked at me as if I were a stranger."

Hiep went on, "I do not know whether you are aware of it or not, but Brother Thuc, your husband and Luyen feel the same way. I have not talked with any of them, but I am sure they have had the same concern."

Hiep came closer to Le Xuan and added, "We were brought up by our parents with certain principles. My father, even when he commanded the imperial troops in Quang Binh in 1886, did not want to shed blood. He sent food and supplies to the Can Vuong militia who were entrenched in the mountains, asking them to return to the plains. In 1930, after Prime Minister Nguyen Huu Bai launched the campaign to eliminate Communist insurgents, while the French and other mandarins were using military might to fight and kill the Communists, my brothers Khoi and Diem used peaceful methods to make peace in their provinces."

Le Xuan exclaimed, "Then how can your brother, Diem, take control of the present situation? People are out there waiting to kill him. His enemies are not reluctant to shed blood."

Hiep nodded, "For many years, we had accepted the idea of armed struggle, yet until last month, we had not seen any corpses. What happened was a wake-up call. I hope that now whether he decides to go or to remain, Brother Diem will make his decision with his eyes wide open. "

Le Xuan took a long look at Hiep. She had not really seen Hiep until the last meeting in Hue. She was aware of Hiep's strength now. She asked, "Will Brother Diem decide to stay, or will he resign?" Hiep shook her head and replied, "At the end of my conversation with him earlier this afternoon, he was still undecided. Yet, somehow, I feel that he will stay."

Moved by a sudden impulse, Le Xuan said, "I would like to have you as an ally, a comrade-in-arms." Hiep stared at her sister-in-law in astonishment, "I am not merely an ally. I am your sister-in-law. We are family."

Le Xuan explained, "I understand that, and please believe me, I appreciate that very much. I saw in Hue that you …that you were at least the equal of your brothers. When we came back to Saigon, I asked Nhu about you. For the first time, he told me about your childhood, and how much you had learned from your father. I was amazed. Forgive me for saying that. I never suspected that you were Brother Diem's favorite confidant, that he frequently sought your advice."

Hiep waved her hand, "Look, Le Xuan, I understand now what you are driving at. I am not, definitely not interested in politics. I have made that decision, not because I am a woman, but because I was not brought up to be a politician. I have no inclination to be one. Brother Diem sometimes talks to me, using me as a sounding board, not because I know anything about politics, but because I played the game of questions and answers with my father, with the Duke of Phuoc Mon, Nguyen Huu Bai, and with him, as a child. I have never given advice to Brother Diem. I help him see what he wants more clearly, that is all."

Hiep hesitated before she added, "You, on the other hand, have all the attributes and the upbringing to be a politician, and a very good one at that. But maybe you are a little bit ahead of your time."

Hiep smiled to herself. She had not been afraid of restating her sister, Hoang's opinion. She had thought about Hoang's remark for months. She believed that Le Xuan was definitely ahead of her time. She said good night to Le Xuan, and without any more worries about her sister-in-law, she went downstairs, straight to Diem's office to meet with the men.

*

As Hiep walked in, the men awkwardly stood up. To stand up for a woman was not usual in the code of Vietnamese behavior. Am, out of his love for her more than his desire to conform to modern mores, had gradually acquired that habit. Nhu had learned to do so in France, and with his wife. Luyen acted naturally like a French man, but Thuc and Diem were not at all adept at the European courtesy to women, even though both of them had been overseas. To stand up when a woman walked in, still seemed to cost them an effort. As both of them hesitated, Am, Nhu and Luyen copied their attitude, and only when both Diem and Thuc rose up did they get to their feet, as well.

Hiep smiled and took one of the rather uncomfortable carved and lacquered wooden chairs, like all the others. Diem had disregarded the ornate and more comfortable chair behind his large desk, to sit with the others. Diem served tea himself. He waited for Hiep to finish taking the first sip before asking her, "How is Sister Nhu?"

She looked up and noticed Nhu looking at her intently. How much he loves her, Hiep thought. She shook her head and said, "You and other people told me she was depressed, but I didn't see any sign of depression. She has been blamed for the outcome of the demonstration, and feels that she has been treated unfairly. But what is really distressing her is the fact that you haven't decided whether or not to go on fighting."

Diem smiled, "You have been upstairs explaining our behavior to her, haven't you?" Hiep did not respond. Out of the corner of her eye she noticed that Nhu's face had brightened up. He asked, "What did you two discuss?" There was an odd note of urgency in his voice. Hiep answered candidly, "The demonstration of course, the reasons why she organized it, the outcome. We also discussed General Hinh; or rather she briefed me on what happened with General Hinh. She said that the new balance of forces was in your favor and that Hinh had no alternative other than to accept exile."

Nhu exclaimed, "She, who has not put two words together since the demonstration, talked about all that with you?" He and Diem were both genuinely surprised. It was Hiep's turn to ask, "Do you mean that this is the first time she has talked since the incident?" Both Nhu and Diem nodded. Even Thuc confirmed, "She put walls around herself after the shooting. When you followed her to her room, we didn't think she would talk to you either."

Hiep replied, "But she did talk. I am happy that she has broken her silence. Now, tell me what you discussed, while I was upstairs." Diem declared, "Within a week's time, I will unilaterally announce a deadline for the evacuation of all French troops from our territory."

Hiep was moved to tears. She thought, Father would be so happy now. The French troops will no longer occupy our country. What a daring thing to do! She asked Diem, "What will you do if the French reject your deadline? What if they respond by using their military to take over all the Vietnamese government buildings, capture you, and send you to France?"

Diem answered confidently, "That will not happen. They will not capture me alive. My battalions will fight to the death. Other units will join in the fight, as well."

For a moment, Hiep was genuinely amazed. She thought, "Is this the man who only two hours ago, was agonizing over the thought of bloodshed?" Then she reminded herself that Diem had long ago come to terms with the possibility of armed struggle against the French.

She objected, "To use Le Xuan's terminology, in any confrontation against the French, the balance of forces will weigh heavily in favor of the French. They still have 200,000 well-armed, battle-trained troops in Vietnam. For the time being, you can only count on six battalions at most."

Diem nodded. As he talked, his face became somber, "Yes, you are correct. The French would, in the case of armed confrontation, outnumber us by at least ten to one. But there will not be any armed confrontation. After Dien Bien Phu, the French Army will, for a long time, only be good for parades, maneuvers and bluff shows of force. No general would dare use it for real combat right now, and they know I'm aware of their situation."

Hiep replied, "So, you are counting on another victory without doing battle?" Diem affirmed, "Yes. Unfortunately, we will not be able to achieve the same kind of victory over the Binh Xuyen."

Hiep waited for Diem to expand, but he had stopped speaking. Thuc joined in, "Brother Diem is now faced with the moral and practical question of whether he is willing to accept the responsibility of a civil war." Hiep remarked, "He is still having difficulty making a decision, isn't he? Yet, if he does not decide very soon, events will make the decision for him."

Nhu replied, "You are right. We are swiftly sliding into civil war. I foresee major fighting within a couple of weeks, at the latest. I want to know whether we are going to prepare for battle, or we are going to allow ourselves to be surprised by the Binh Xuyen. The only other option is for Brother Diem to resign right now."

Diem seemed to be deep in thought, as he listened absent-mindedly to what the others were saying. Finally, he said, "I am not going to resign. There is national independence to achieve. There is national unity and integrity to recover. We will not allow ourselves to be surprised by the Binh Xuyen. We will prepare for battle, immediately."

There was a long silence after he finished speaking. In the stillness, Hiep felt that everybody in the room was saying a prayer. She knew that together, they had just lived one of the most important moments of their lives.

*

It was two days after their wedding anniversary. Hiep and Am went to the Independence Palace to say good-bye to the Nhu's and Diem, before they took a flight back to Hue. Both Thuc and Luyen had gone back to their work, Thuc in Vinh Long, and Luyen in Paris.

After seeing Nhu and Le Xuan, they went downstairs to wait, as Diem was in conference with General Ely, the French Commander-in-Chief and High Commissioner, and General Lawton Collins, the new American envoy, President Eisenhower's personal emissary.

After a while, the visitors left, and Diem invited them into his office. He said, "Please excuse me for having to make you wait. I had to see those two Sisters of Charity." Hiep was surprised. She asked, "What Sisters of Charity? I only saw two generals come out of your office. Your staff told me they were General Ely and General Collins." Diem laughed, "I called them Sisters of Charity because they always come together, just like the sisters. They talked to me gently, insisting that they were only making proposals for my own good, like the sisters. They preached, like the sisters. But they are not going to be charitable. They want to me to go along with their proposals, and if I resist, they threaten me with dire consequences."

Hiep was concerned, "I understand that you cannot count on the French. But from what you say, I have to presume that you cannot count on the Americans, either." Diem smiled a little bitterly, "The Americans have extended their economic aid to Vietnam, but they still work very closely with the French. Even Ambassador Heath went to see the Emperor in France, and then came back here to force me to take General Nguyen van Xuan into my cabinet. He came here with General Ely and would not leave until I agreed to his demand."

Diem stopped, and took some time to light another cigarette. Then he went on, "Now the situation is worse. General Lawton Collins and General Ely are old friends. They came here to pressure me to once again broaden my Cabinet. If I listen to them, I will have forty Ministers. I am not going to accept their recommendations this time."

Hiep asked, "Do you see major problems ahead, with the Americans?" Diem nodded, "Both Ely and Collins want to dictate the choice of my next Army Chief of Staff. I told them that the choice would be mine."

Hiep commented, "You have learned to resist the French, and I believe that you can also handle the American pressure." Diem shook his head, "Until we stop requiring American assistance, I am still at risk. The donor will find many hands ready to receive assistance in the name of Vietnam." Hiep stood up; "I need to go home now to pack. Tomorrow we will return to Hue, early in the morning."

Diem also stood up and said, "In three months we will meet again in Hue, on the thirtieth anniversary of Father's death. I want that anniversary to be organized solemnly. We will honor Father and talk about what remains to be done. Everybody will be there. From now on, Am and Le Xuan will be invited to all our family meetings. Will you accept the invitation, Am?" Am shook his head, "I prefer to stay out of it." Diem smiled and said with a note of gentle persuasion, "We will have time to talk about your participation between now and January 26 of next year."

As she left the Palace, Hiep was troubled. Protected now as he was with several loyal units, Diem was safer now from being kidnapped or killed by the river pirates, when he stayed in his Palace. But she knew that the danger was not over. She knew that there were still more battles ahead for her brother, and that the future battles would be bloody. Hiep knew Diem was not an ordinary politician, an ordinary statesman. He had before everything else, a conscience. She said to herself, "That is his greatness, and it is also his vulnerability."

*

Three months had gone by since they had been with Diem in Saigon. Now Diem was back in Hue for the Lunar New Year. Hiep asked Am one final time, "Will you stay with us, after Mass?" Am declined the invitation, saying "I have told Brother Diem and you many times since we were in Saigon. No, I don't want to be involved in your political discussions."

Hiep knew by his tone, that he was unhappy. She asked, "Do you want me to stay out of the meeting too?" Am shook his head, "This is the thirtieth anniversary of your father's death. Brother Diem apparently wants to report not only to those still living, but also to the dead of the family, about what has been accomplished, and what remains to be done. As you are his sister, and as you were asked by your father on his deathbed, to speak to your brothers and sisters on his anniversaries, you must be there."

Hiep was surprised to hear Am's remarks, as if he had rehearsed his speech beforehand. She pressed on, "But apparently, you don't approve of the way these meetings are organized, do you?"

Am replied heatedly, "Normally, political debates like the ones you have with your brothers, should be held in the Cabinet. Unfortunately, we now have a coalition cabinet that includes many Ministers whose hostility toward Brother Diem is well known. The decision-making process had been displaced to the Palace, giving tremendous power to Brother Nhu and Le Xuan."

He hesitated a moment, then added, "Their minds, however, are too Europeanized, foreign to Brother Diem. He is not comfortable with the way they arrive at conclusions. He thinks that they are too logical and too Cartesian and consequently, they may miss the Vietnamese realities. But, no doubt about it, the three of them make the decisions. That is unhealthy if it continues. Brother Thuc, Brother Luyen and you are drawn in by Brother Diem to give him additional advice. But Brothers Thuc and Luyen were educated abroad. Their minds works almost exactly like the mind of

375

Brother Nhu. So, your presence is necessary as a counterweight. You represent your father's and the Duke of Phuoc Mon's way of thinking, which is more akin to that of Brother Diem. Don't you see the danger?"

Hiep asked, "Please, explain to me what the danger is." Though he knew he was treading on dangerous ground, Am almost burst laughing upon hearing Hiep's question. She sounded exactly like Ngo Dinh Kha and Diem. He took his wife's hand and told her, "You never really wanted to get involved in politics. Brother Diem apparently needs you by his side. If you are not careful, you will get involved in spite of yourself."

Hiep shook her head, but Am held her hand more tightly and forced her to look at him. He explained, "You are the daughter of your father. *That is your destiny*. You will have an influence on Brother Diem, without lifting a finger. You are not only his sister. You are his sister soul. That is why you have to be careful."

Hiep asked, "Have I done anything wrong, yet?" Am shook his head, "No, I have not seen you trying to influence Brother Diem's decisions, yet. All you have done is to help him see his own intentions more clearly, to clarify the issues for him. You leave him to make his own decisions. But the fact is *you can* influence him for good or for bad, even on major issues. That is tempting, and it is dangerous."

Hiep said, "I have felt the danger. The country owns us; we do not own the country. We do not have any mandate from Heaven to rule. Only Brother Diem has received an investiture from the Emperor. He should be able to recruit assistance from outside our family. Yet, for now, he is so lonely. In my mind, at times, I see him sitting by himself at his desk, while outside his Palace, the forces aligned against him howl and prepare themselves for the onslaught."

Am advised, "I do not think you should stay away from Brother Diem. But if you really want to stay out of politics, please make sure you never try to influence his decisions."

Hiep did not reply. A bird was singing outside of her window. Soon, she would have to go to her mother's house and meet with her brothers, and face the issues. For the moment, she closed her eyes and enjoyed the chilly air and the festive smell of early spring: a faint fragrance of fresh flowers and ripening fruit, of candies and cakes, new clothes and richly wrapped gifts. She said, "Let us forget about politics. I am so happy!"

*

Hiep came to the family reunion that year with understandable misgivings. Diem was charming. He was insightful, humorous, and analytical. He recounted the series of victories that had already been won, after only being in power for six months.

Even his brothers and sisters were surprised by the achievements. In July 1954, the whole world had expected South Vietnam to collapse quickly. By January 1955, the situation had been stabilized, in spite of the persistent threats of the Binh Xuyen and the sects. General Nguyen van Hinh, the rebel Army Chief of Staff, had been forced into exile and disavowed by Emperor Bao Dai. The French had not objected to the deadline set by Diem for the departure of all their troops from Vietnamese territory by March 1956.

Most of the important agencies controlled by the French had been transferred to the Vietnamese government, including the Public Works, the Treasury, the tribunals, the harbors, and the Military Academies.

The transfer of loyal battalions to the region around Saigon was complete. These battalions insured the safety and security of the Prime Minister, who in July 1954 had had no protection at all.

Diem did not gloat about the achievements. He recounted in more detail, his ongoing problems with General Ely and General Collins, and his frustration with Emperor Bao Dai. Finally he painted a clear picture of the upcoming confrontation with the Binh Xuyen and powerful elements of the sects.

Diem then projected that during 1955, he would have to eliminate the Binh Xuyen and bring the sects' military forces under control, integrating them into the National Armed Forces. He said that unless Emperor Bao Dai demonstrated more understanding and gave more support to his work, he would have to disassociate himself from the absentee Chief of State.

The mention of a possible disassociation from Bao Dai generated a heated debate. Luyen, who liked Bao Dai, whom he had known since his childhood, asked pointedly: "What would you do then with Bao Dai?" Diem tried to placate Luyen. "We would continue to recognize Bao Dai as Chief of State, but we would make it clear to him that he would be a nominal Chief of State."

Le Xuan said, "I do not think that halfway measures like that will help. Sooner or later, Bao Dai has to be deposed. If he stays on, under any kind of official title, the French and our enemies will use him against us."

Luyen was not at all pleased. He said, "Le Xuan, you have the Nguyen imperial blood in your veins. Your grandmother was a great princess. You were a close friend of Bao Dai, a cousin of his. Why do you want to see the end the Nguyen Dynasty?"

Le Xuan answered, "Nothing lasts forever, Luyen. I know how fond you are of Bao Dai. However, we are talking about national politics here, not about personal friendships."

Hiep, who had listened to the exchange with growing concern, finally intervened, "Look, we are considering dissociation from the Emperor only as a possibility. Many things would have to happen, before such a measure would be necessary. I propose that *if* and when Brother Diem is forced to consider that eventuality, you will meet again, to discuss this issue with updated information and points of view."

Diem said, "I vote for that; however, I wish to know why Sister Hiep said *'you'* instead of *'we.'* Aren't we all in this together?"

Hiep shook her head, "Father was very clear. When he died, he said that I should speak once a year to all of you, not twice a year, not three times a year. My husband is concerned that I could be drawn into politics. Please help me to stay out. You know I am with you. Your success is my success; your failure is my failure. I will pray for you every day, but I do not want to be in your Family Council anymore. I am married, and as a married woman; I belong to my husband's family. I am no longer a Ngo Dinh."

Diem burst out laughing. He said, "Your memory is very selective, Sister Hiep. I remember well what happened at your wedding. Mr. Nguyen van Dieu, your father-in-law, asked Am and you to prostrate yourselves in front of our mother and said to you, 'You are always a Ngo Dinh, I want you to remain a Ngo Dinh.'"

Hoang also insisted, "We are here because we live Father's dream. You were at the dead center of his dream. While we still were kids, he treated you like an adult. You cannot withdraw from the Family Council now."

Hiep felt Hoang and Le Xuan's eyes on her. If she withdrew from the Family Council, their membership in it would be tenuous indeed. She shrugged and said, "You may one day regret that you decided to keep me on the Family Council." They all laughed. She was the favorite sister of each one of them. Over the years, she had played her difficult role, pacifying them, reconciling them with one another. In age, she ranked third now, only after Thuc and Diem. For the rest of them, she was big sister.

Her intervention had succeeded in stopping the heated exchange between Luyen and Le Xuan. Diem took advantage of the truce to resume his interrupted briefing.

Diem explained that all of the seven objectives he had mentioned six months earlier ought to be achieved before June 1956, the date that had been announced for a referendum in view of reunifying the two zones. He stated that it was unlikely that such a referendum would take place, but he wanted the South to be strong and ready even for that remote possibility.

Diem then went on to discuss the problems of the private armies and warlords. He said that the river pirates, under General Le Van Vien should be eliminated first. He asked Nhu to continue the briefing. Nhu took over and explained that he expected the Binh Xuyen under General Le Van Vien to attack first.

Hoang interrupted him, "Why are we waiting for them to attack first? Isn't it true that those who attack first have the advantage of the element of surprise?" Nhu thought for a moment before answering, "I hold the same view; however, Brother Diem prefers to let the river bandits attack first, so that when we launch our counterattack, the people will more likely side with us."

Hoang persisted, "The people will side with the winner. They never side with the loser. If you want to obtain the favor of the people, be the winner, be the victor. A surprise attack will ensure that you are the victor."

Diem stood up and asked Nhu to sit down. He faced Hoang squarely, "So you have read what Father read. I have also read Sunzi. We are facing bandits. Those bandits have, however, been made friends of the Crown. Their leader, who has been made a general, has control of the national police. They provide the largest part of the Emperor's personal revenues. The Emperor has gone as far as making General Le van Vien his adoptive brother. How do we eliminate the bandits when they are covered by the imperial mantle?"

His sisters and brothers, including Nhu, looked at him, mesmerized. Diem went on, "Sister Hoang, wanted me to attack first. I did. I ordered the Great World Casino to be closed ten days before I came here. That was the bandits' most important source of revenues. I forced them to fight. I know they will have to attack within the next sixty days. I am ready for them."

He did not sit down. He looked at Hiep a long time before he said, "Sister Hiep, last year, in November, you came to Saigon. At the time, I was debating within myself whether I should resign. I was hesitant, and unsure of what I should do. You did not force the issue, but somehow during our conversation, while I listened to you, I realized that I had to stay and fulfill my duty. I have prepared myself for battle ever since. But to fight the Binh Xuyen means fighting the Emperor himself. I am not going to fire the first shot against the Emperor."

As Diem sat down, Nhu said, "After we closed down the Great World Casino in Cho Lon, the Binh Xuyen knew that their survival was at stake. They prepared their Assault Police units for a 'fight to the death', right in Saigon. If they succeed in motivating their troops, there will be a colossal battle in the Capital City; thousands of civilians would die as a consequence. We cannot allow this to happen.

"On the one hand, we will infiltrate the Binh Xuyen Assault Police units. Many members of those units are now ready to rally to us. On the other hand, we are in the process of organizing the Capital City Police, distinct from the National Police currently under the Binh Xuyen's control. Many members of the National Police have deserted, and Lansdale is doing a good job in promoting further desertion. Those who have deserted will be employed either in the Capital City Police, or in a Special Police force."

Diem said, "The objectives are to divide the Binh Xuyen, to isolate them from the other warlords and private armies, to make the French reluctant to side with them in the final battle, and to give the Emperor the time and the opportunity to dissociate himself from them."

Nhu added, "The ultimate goal is to win the battle while keeping the loss of innocent lives to the bare minimum."

*

In the afternoon, the discussion focused on the other private armies. Diem did not hide the fact that dealing with the sects and the Caodaist and Hao Hao armies would be far more difficult than dealing with the Binh Xuyen.

Nhu took over and gave a full briefing on the situation of the Caodaists, who held Tay Ninh province and a large part of the neighboring provinces. Nhu said that the Caodaist armies did not represent an immediate threat. Most of the Caodaist generals had negotiated the integration of their units under the command of the National Army. Prominent among them was Caodaist General Trinh Minh The, who had become a close friend of both Nhu and Diem.

The Hoa Hao leaders were members of Diem's government. The two major Hoa Hao armies, however, had close ties with the Binh Xuyen. There seemed to be an understanding that if Diem attacked the Binh Xuyen, their leaders would resign from the government, and their armies would move against Diem.

Diem added, "The Emperor himself has his own private army and his own fiefdom. His private army is composed of crack units of the Imperial Guards, and his fiefdom is the Imperial Domain of Central Vietnam, with Nguyen De as Viceroy."

Hoang exclaimed, "You may have to wage a civil war that could go on for thirty years."

Diem shook his head, "No, in fact I hope to have eliminated all the private armies by July of next year. With luck, we may even finish the job within this year. After my return to Saigon, I will immediately go to Tay Ninh and have a long talk with His Holiness Pham Cong Tac, the Caodaist Pope, and to meet again with General Trinh Minh The. I want to make sure that our alliance with the Caodaists is maintained. Within the next hundred days, we have to finish off the Binh Xuyen, and then quickly shift our attention to the Hoa Hao armies. I know they are also preparing for battle."

After the meeting was over, Diem asked Hiep what was bothering her. Hiep thought a long time before she answered, "In 1933, you became Prime Minister. But, it was merely a title without any real responsibilities. The French ruled. You had no need to make any decisions. Now, you have to make thousands of decisions every day. How can you be sure you do not make major mistakes every single day?"

Diem did not say anything for a long time. In the end he said softly, almost as if he was talking to himself, "That is for sure. I will make thousands of mistakes if I do not receive the best advice. I also need lots of prayers. Don't you see, Sister? Don't you see that, with all my optimistic talk, I know that everything could go wrong in the very next instant?"

As Hiep turned to go, Diem said, "Father asked you to pray for his soul and for us, every day. Have you forgotten me in your prayers?" Hiep looked at him but did not answer. Diem laughed, "Don't answer me then, but don't forget to pray for me." Hiep was gone; Diem stood there and laughed. "Of course, she still remembers father's advice. She never will answer rhetorical questions!"

CHAPTER TWENTY-ONE
THE END OF ALL THE PRIVATE ARMIES

On March 28, 1955, at midnight, the Binh Xuyen-led Police Assault Units launched their attack on the headquarters of the newly organized Capital City Police and the headquarters of the Joint General Staff. They also directed their mortar fire at the Independence Palace itself.

The Capital City Police and the paratroopers repulsed the attacks. Diem did not launch a counterattack. As the few mortar shells fell on the grounds of the Independence Palace, Diem called Hiep to tell her that he was all right.

Sensing the tension in Diem's voice, Hiep asked, "Have there been fatalities?" Diem answered solemnly, "Yes, on our side, two soldiers were killed; on their side, three assault policemen were also killed." Hiep asked pointedly, "Do you feel responsible for the dead and the injured?" Diem replied, "Yes, I feel responsible, yet, I know that casualties are inevitable." Hiep hesitated before she asked, "Any civilian casualties?" Diem sighed, "Five injured."

Hiep asked, "Why did you call?" When Diem didn't answer, she repeated her question. Finally Diem said, "Since we met, the Binh Xuyen has succeeded in creating a coalition with the Hoa Hao and the Caodaist armies. I cannot launch an all-out attack on the Binh Xuyen until that coalition is dissolved."

Hiep sensed Diem's need for her to question him further. He needed to speak to someone who wasn't afraid to face the serious issues at hand. She asked, "Do you think that our telephone line is secure?" Diem let out a derisive snort of laughter, "As secure as our people can make it, on both ends."

"You seem to expect their coalition to break," Hiep resumed. Diem replied, "Yes, their coalition will not last. I expect it to split within the next month."

"Then, what is your worry?" asked Hiep. Diem hesitated before he answered finally: "After the attack, all four of the Hoa Hao leaders in the cabinet resigned. They must have known ahead of time, because the resignation letters were certainly prepared before the attack."

Hiep asked, "Are you afraid that the Hoa Hao armies will combine their forces with those of the Binh Xuyen, and attack you on two fronts?" Diem sighed, "I cannot afford to fight on two fronts. I don't have enough troops for that."

Hiep was concerned now; she asked, "None of the Hoa Hao armies remains on your side?" Diem's voice sounded hopeful, "I think General Nguyen Giac Ngo still camps on our side." Hiep asked: "Then, you should not worry too much. What about the Cao Dai armies?"

Diem sounded more confident now, "All of them are with me. In a couple of days, by the order of His Holiness the Caodaist Pope, the generals will place their troops under my command."

Hiep asked, "If that happens, doesn't it follow that the Binh Xuyen-led coalition will cease to exist? "Diem said, "Not necessarily. All the alliances at this moment are tentative, parts of a game of wait-and-see. People who are on our side today may be with the Binh Xuyen in their hearts. Allies of the Binh Xuyen may be working for us."

Hiep laughed in spite of herself and in spite of the seriousness of the situation. She said, "So, you are living in confusion and deception, and you are feeling uncomfortable?" Diem acquiesced, "Precisely. The waiting is painful. Deception is not my *forte*. What should I do?"

Hiep laughed again, "Go and pray. You will feel better. Be sure you are one step ahead of the Binh Xuyen. That is all you need. Forget the Hoa Hao armies for the time being. Their alliance with the Binh Xuyen is not vital to them. They will not throw their troops at you to save the river bandits."

Diem was indignant. He said to his sister, "I'm surprised that you are laughing at my situation. Not only once, but twice, you have laughed at me!" Hiep said, "I laugh because you know you are winning, yet you dramatize your weakness. I laugh because you sound mournful just like you sounded as a child, when you were about to defeat Father in a game of chess." Now, it was Diem's turn to laugh.

*

The French had imposed a two-week truce. Thirty thousand French troops poured into Saigon under the pretext of protecting French residents in the Capital, but obviously, the actual reason they were there was to support the Binh Xuyen. Three hundred French armored vehicles were stationed at strategic points in the Saigon streets.

Diem cajoled, threatened, and negotiated, until finally the French withdrew their troops.

On April 24, 1955, Diem fired Lai van Sang, the Director General of the National Police, and right hand man of General Le Van Vien. That incident amounted to a declaration of war, as the National Police was the bastion of Binh Xuyen power.

By the same token, Diem dissolved the Assault Police Force, which recruited extremists and was led by the most fanatic Binh Xuyen officers.

Emperor Bao Dai sent a terse reprimand, telling Diem that he did not approve of the firing of Lai van Sang. The Emperor also demanded that Diem accept General Nguyen van Vy Commander of the Imperial Guards, as the new Army Chief of Staff, and ordered Diem to come to Cannes for a meeting.

Note: Very few Vietnamese at the time knew what the Imperial Domain (Hoang Trieu Cuong Tho) was about. But it was an independent fiefdom comprehending all the provinces of the Central Highlands, with an army (The Imperial Guards).

While Diem was considering his response to Bao Dai's cable, the Binh Xuyen broadcasted the cable's contents over their privately owned radio station, and began a generalized attack on government headquarters in Saigon.

The National Army reacted quickly, and pushed back the assaults. The fighting became increasingly fierce, as Binh Xuyen units holed up in heavily populated areas of the capital, and civilian casualties escalated. Army units succeeded, however, in pushing the Binh Xuyen back to Cho Lon, and then to the other side of the Saigon River.

In the middle of the emergency, a People's Revolutionary Council was organized with the participation of numerous political parties. It met continuously at the Saigon City Hall.

On April 29, General Nguyen van Vy went into the Independence Palace to force Diem to obey the Emperor's orders, while two battalions of the Imperial Guards, reinforced with armored vehicles, took position outside the Palace.

Leaders of the People's Revolutionary Council rushed to the Palace, and holding General Vy at gunpoint, forced him to declare his loyalty to Diem. The Council leaders announced the stripping of Bao Dai's power and his title of Chief of State, and the dissolution of the Ngo Dinh Diem Cabinet. They asked Diem to form a new cabinet, to pursue the elimination of the Binh Xuyen rebels, and to prepare for the election of a Constituent Assembly.

During the night of April 30, General Nguyen van Vy attempted to draw army leaders into a coup against Diem, but he failed. The next morning he hastily left Saigon with his battalions of Imperial Guards.

Note: The People's Revolutionary Council was not a creation of Ngo Dinh Diem. It included a vast coalition of parties, notables and leaders of military-religious sects. The role of Nhi Lang, a Caodaist in the Council steered the Council towards bold decisions that did not totally favor Diem.

*

Nobody dared approach Diem. He had returned to Hue, the victor who had crushed the Binh Xuyen. He had lost a true friend, however, in the last battle against the cornered river pirates. Cao Dai General *Trinh Minh The* had been killed while commanding his troops at the front.

General Trinh Minh The

*

Diem fainted when he heard that General The had been killed. The next day, as The's body lay in state, Diem went to pay his homage to his friend. He fainted again.

The Binh Xuyen rebellion had been crushed. The remnants of the Binh Xuyen armies fled into the swampy area of Rung Sat. They were aggressively pursued. The Imperial Guards were disbanded. A new cabinet was formed.

While in the entire country, mass demonstrations were calling for the dethronement of Bao Dai and asking Diem to take full power, Diem holed up in Hue, disconsolate. He did not even appear at the mass rally in Hue, when tens of thousands demonstrated in his favor.

Can sent for Hiep, but she refused to come to her mother's home, where Diem was staying. She knew Diem needed to be alone in his grief. In time, Diem called her on the phone, and asked her to come and visit him.

Though Hiep knew how devastating the death of General Trinh minh The was to Diem, she was unprepared for what she saw when she arrived. Diem was utterly disconsolate. His eyes were red and swollen; his lips and hands trembled.

He smiled weakly when Hiep came in, and he said, "I held my head up for two weeks, until everything was sorted out, until I came back to Hue." Hiep nodded, "Yes, you did." She came and sat down in front of him. Overwhelming grief was in his voice when he told her, "He is dead. They killed him." Hiep nodded again, but did not say anything. Diem said sadly, "He was the only friend I made since I took power. Now he is dead."

As Hiep did not seem to agree, Diem said, "Oh I know. Lansdale is a friend. But not like General The. Lansdale has given me good advice, helped assure my protection in the early days, he worries about my health, and he never tires of designing strategies and of discusses them with Nhu and me. If I die I will grieve for him a long, long time. But, The was so different. On the first day we met, he said that he would give his life for me. And he did!"

Hiep asked softly, "What about Mr. Nhi Lang?" Diem was startled, "How do you know about Nhi Lang?" Hiep shook her head to signify that the fact she knew about Nhi Lang was not important.

Diem mused a moment before he said, "Nhi Lang is General The's *alter ego*. He is the soul of the People's Revolutionary Council. He was the man that held General Nguyen van Vy at gunpoint, and saved me from being made prisoner at the Independence Palace. He later foiled General Nguyen van Vy's attempted coup d'état. He is a brave man and a philosopher. He and General The were the main reasons for the collapse of the Binh Xuyen-led coalition. He is a friend, the best kind of friend. If something happened to him I would suffer greatly, yet, I would not go to pieces like this."

Hiep asked Diem, simply to make him talk, "What about the other people who have toiled with you all these months?" Diem smiled bitterly, "What about them? General Le Van Ty, my hand-picked Chairman of the Joint

Chiefs of Staff, General Tran Van Don, my Army Chief of Staff? Both of them joined General Nguyen Van Vy to oust me on April 29. Without Nhi Lang, and without Trinh Minh The rushing his troops into Saigon, I would be rotting in jail right now."

Hiep laughed, "Yet, you promoted both of them the next morning. Why did you do that?" Diem also laughed, "Both General The and Nhi Lang advised me to do so. Neither Ty nor Don showed their hands too clearly during the crisis at the Independence Palace. I knew they were on General Vy's side. But they only gave him subtle support. I could break them, demote them, and end their military career, or I could keep them, and promote them, hoping that they would be impressed by my magnanimity and rally to support me."

Hiep said, "Do not count too much on that. Those who betray once will betray twice." Diem nodded and went on, "General The was gambling his life time and again. He had that in his blood. Nhi Lang, too. Their advice was strange. I followed it, by deference to them." Hiep interrupted him, "Why don't we go out in the garden to talk?" Diem said, "For the last two days, I have been wearing sun glasses even inside. But why not, sooner or later I will have to face the sun again."

They walked in silence for a while. Hiep picked a few fruits from a low-lying longane branch, peeled them and gave them one after another to Diem. Even in the shade, the sunlight was too bright for Diem. Hiep asked, "You came back to Hue, with the definite purpose of allowing yourself a few days of depression, is that not true?" Diem nodded, "Unless I let myself go, I would have exploded."

Hiep asked, "It is not your nature to question God's will. Why has General The's death affected you this way?" Diem sighed, "His youth first of all. He was much younger than I am. Why did he die and not I? He was the true revolutionary. He did not have a care in the world. He played with his life as if he constantly challenged fate. He was so full of life and fun. I do not question God's will. He fell as a hero. I should sing and not cry. Yet, with him gone, so many of the things we planned together have no meaning for me anymore."

Diem stopped, sensing that he had repeatedly contradicted himself. He shrugged and went on, "You know, when we started in July of last year, I had nothing. We kept winning victory after victory without even doing battle. When we engaged in battle a few weeks ago, we prayed that there would be no casualties. In order to wipe out the Binh Xuyen, we paid too high a price. Now I must face the war against the Hoa Hao armies *without* General The. What price will we have to pay this time? I am afraid the price will be even higher."

Hiep asked, "Have you exhausted all means to peacefully resolve the problem with the sects?" Diem shook his head, "No, not yet. I will try further negotiation, and I will continue to negotiate even after the battle has begun. But, I have the gut feeling that it will be a fight to the death."

Hiep said softly: "Before the Venerable Huynh Phu So, the founder of Hoa Hao Buddhism was killed by the Viet Minh, you met with him repeatedly. His patriotism, his passion and his vision impressed you. When you fight his followers, please remember him."

DUC HUỲNH GIÁO CHỦ PHẬT GIÁO HÒA HẢO

The Venerable Huynh Phu So, founder of Hoa Hao Buddhism

*

Diem sighed, "I don't want to fight them. They will have to fire the first shot. Once the fighting starts, however, I am afraid that the cauldron of passion in the Western Delta will start boiling over, until all the hatred is consumed. If only The Great Teacher were still here with us! I will remember him, no matter what happens. Yet, I am afraid, Sister. I am afraid that I will not be strong enough to face the consequences of the coming war."

*

It was early June 1955 when units of General Tran Van Soai's army fired the first shots in Cai Von, near Can Tho. The counterattack was swift. Colonel Duong Van Duc, of the National Army, led a lightning raid on Cai Von and seized General Soai's headquarters. The war against the Hoa Hao private armies had begun.

*

Diem looked at the big map in the situation room. He had looked at it a hundred times in past weeks and could not believe what he saw. The Western Region was largely covered by the four Hoa Hao fiefdoms:

General Lam Thanh Nguyen held Chau Doc and Cai Dau,

General Nguyen Giac Ngo held Cho Moi,

General Tran van Soai held Can Tho, Cai Von, Sadec, and Cai Vung;

General Le Quang Vinh held Thot Not, Long Xuyen, Rach Gia, Go Queo, and O Mon.

"Another era of the Twelve Warlords," Diem said to himself, referring to a different sad time in Vietnam history, the chaotic years in the middle of the Tenth Century.

General Le Quang Vinh was the most powerful among the warlords, and General Tran Van Soai, the most impulsive. Soai had been in Diem's Cabinet since September 1954. Temperamental, and inconsistent, Soai would not be a big problem.

Soai's troops were undisciplined, poorly trained and poorly led. His armies would dissolve in a matter of weeks. They offered some resistance when Soai's headquarters were attacked, but had consistently shied away from any engagement ever since.

Diem told Nhu, who had been watching him in silence, "Let's finish with General Soai quickly. I don't think he wants to face a real war. I don't think his troops are ready to die for him." Nhu nodded, "Of course. Within the last two weeks, more than two thousand of his troops have surrendered. The toughest battalion of his armies has joined General Le Quang Vinh in the O Mon, Thot Not area."

Diem advised, "Avoid pitched battles. Allow their troops to run." Nhu laughed, "That is what we have been doing. Strange tactics, though. If we continue like this, we may have to chase him until the year 2000. Today, our troops showed them what we were capable of; we fired one thousand cannon shells and one thousand mortar shells at General Vinh's and General Soai's troops, but not directly at them. Actually all the shells exploded a hundred meters behind their backs, as they ran."

Diem frowned, "That is no laughing matter. If they run, that is good. There will not be any casualties, and they will soon be exhausted." Nhu stopped laughing. He said, "I did not laugh at them. I laughed because your orders were so funny. This is not a real war. One cannot conduct a war this way. It takes a crazy guy like Colonel Duong van Duc to obey to the letter what you have commanded him to do."

Diem smiled for the first time. He asked, "Any casualties today?" Nhu shook his head, "None, on either side. By early afternoon, however, Duc reported that 800 rebels had surrendered, most of them from Soai's units." Diem looked happy for a moment, and then commented, "We have not succeeded yet in convincing a large number of soldiers to defect from General Vinh's armies." Nhu said, "Don't worry too much. There will be large scale defections from his armies soon."

Diem sighed, "Why do you give me only the good news? You did not report to me yesterday that there were fifteen dead, and fifty injured on the Hoa Hao side."

Nhu remained patient, "Look. We do everything we can to avoid casualties. So far we have been lucky. But there is a war going on out there. Some are going to be hurt. Every time we have had a major battle, you always go to the chapel and pray. Maybe that has helped to keep the casualties low, so far. But don't think that you will be lucky like that forever. In the final report on the war against the Binh Xuyen, when all was said and done, there were thirty-four dead on the Binh Xuyen side and fifteen on our side. In all only fifty dead on the battlefield in a big battle! It was purely and simply a miracle."

Diem shook his head, "That was not all, was it? The civilian casualties were high. The Binh Xuyen hid among the people, and then started burning the houses before they fled. Have you or anyone come up with a precise figure on the civilian casualties? Some journalists mentioned one thousand. Is it possible? We took all the necessary measures to try to ensure low casualties."

Nhu said, "I went there with you right after the fighting subsided. It was horrible, the sight and the smell of the burning slums. But people tend to exaggerate the figures. I would say about three hundred civilians may have died, but we have no way of knowing, for sure."

Diem was a little sarcastic, "So, please don't talk about miracles. Also, please remember we lost General Trinh Minh The."

Nhu hated himself now for having mentioned so lightly, the total casualties in the war against the Binh Xuyen. He would never forget the General. Before Diem knew the General, The had been Nhu's friend. The General had given Nhu a nickname, '*Thang Cuong*'. Nhu now used it frequently as *nom de plume* to sign his articles in the newspapers. He also used it sometimes as a code name for his confidential messages.

General The had explained the nickname to Nhu, "Your name is *Nhu*, which means 'soft'. '*Thang Cuong*' means 'defeats hard'. You are the man who uses flexibility to defeat naked force. The nickname stuck. Now that General The was dead, Nhu knew that he would continue to use the nickname in honor of its inventor. He would use it also to remind himself of the lesson The had wanted to give him as a true friend, "The soft will defeat the hard. Water is stronger than rock. Air is stronger than metal. The mind is stronger than matter. *Yin* is stronger than *yang!* "

*

The next morning, Diem called Hiep on the phone. He asked, "Are you observing the eclipse of the sun?" Hiep replied, "The sunlight has been getting dimmer. The air trembles. Did you call simply to tell me about the eclipse?"

Diem laughed, "Yes, simply to talk about the eclipse." Hiep said, "Fine, then talk to me about the eclipse." He replied quickly, as if he had rehearsed his answer: "Did you know that in ancient times, people believed that the sun was being eaten up by celestial dogs during an eclipse?" Hiep remained silent. Diem went on, "An eclipse of the sun always meant the end of an era, the end of a ruler, the end of peacetime, or the end of a war. What do you think is ending now?"

Hiep started to laugh. It was a guessing, game then. She said, "As you are not the ruler, the eclipse does not have anything to do with you. It may mean the end of the monarchy." Diem asked, "Why do you say so?"

Hiep sighed, "You cannot go on working with Bao Dai. The Emperor stabbed you in the back when you had to fight the Binh Xuyen. He was also at the origin of General Nguyen van Vy's failed coup. The People's Revolutionary Council has announced his dethronement and initiated mass demonstrations everywhere against him. Here in Hue, the Noon Gate has been opened wide, allowing the people to enter the Imperial Palace for the first time. The seals of the Chief of State have been confiscated. The Office of the Imperial Clan has ceased to recognize Bao Dai as a member of the Clan. Obviously, it is the end of the monarchy."

Diem asked, "The eclipse may mean the end of other things. What are they?" Hiep saw that the game went on, so she said, "The end of the warlords. They are still fighting, but you have almost finished with them. The outcome is no longer doubtful."

Diem pressed on, "What else?" Hiep laughed, "All right, the eclipse may mean the end of the French rule. Their intervention during the Binh Xuyen crisis seemed to have been the last act of interference."

Diem asked once more, "What else?" Hiep said, "The only other possibility I can see is the end of the American interference. General Lawton Collins, who had wanted to join forces with French General Ely to oust you is now gone, and the new American Ambassador, Frederick

Rheinardt, seems to have received clear instructions from his government to support you."

Diem then asked, "What is beginning?" Hiep replied, "Soon, you will begin to govern. There will be fantastic opportunities to create and rebuild. There will be the beginning of internal peace, and development. Unfortunately, there will also be the beginning of flatteries and lies around you. You will no longer be able to distinguish friend from foe, no longer be able to pay the debts you owe, or reward those who deserve." Diem said softly, "That is what I am afraid of." Hiep went on, "Because you will feel that the people closest to you may betray you one day, you will begin to feel very lonely. You will see that there is no cure for that loneliness."

Diem replied, "I will still have my family." Hiep said, "Brother Diem, I have always wanted to tell you this. Don't rely too much on your family, either. Your brothers and sisters love you, but we all have our serious shortcomings. We are not like you. You are the only one chosen by Father to continue his struggle. He never chose anyone else. He knew that even with all your imperfections, you were way above the rest of his children."

Diem sighed, "You started with good omens, and now you are predicting a very unpleasant future ahead of me." Hiep laughed, "Don't listen to soothsayers then. They can always be proven wrong, because you can always alter your own future."

Diem asked, "Is it pitch dark there in Hue?" Hiep said, "A minute ago, it was really dark. Now the darkness has begun to recede. Don't forget that in Hue we are a little ahead of Saigon, being farther east."

Diem laughed, "Don't be so provincial! Anyway, I want to tell you that I will be in Hue right after the Double Seven (July 7) to make a complete review of the past 365 days of my government. I want you to be prepared to make the strongest criticisms against the mistakes we have made."

Hiep sighed, "The critic easily loses his friends. You will soon stop talking to me." Diem laughed, "Very likely, indeed, very likely!" He hung up, still laughing.

*

It was only in late July that Diem, Nhu, Le Xuan and Luyen could finally arrange to travel to Hue. By then, the Hoa Hao armies were no longer a major threat to national security. Two of the three crack battalions under General Le Quang Vinh's command had surrendered, while the last one was surrounded. General Tran Van Soai was cornered and about to surrender.

General Le Quang Vinh when still a Colonel
in the Vietnamese National Forces

*

On another front, Diem had declared that the Geneva Agreements did not bind South Vietnam, as it had not signed them, and he refused to enter the preliminary talks with North Vietnam to prepare for the general elections prearranged by the Agreements.

As the family members met, it was clear that the primary subject for discussion was the Bao Dai issue. Nhu proposed that they should also focus on the attitude of the Americans during the yearlong crisis.

Luyen opened the discussion on Bao Dai by stating that although he had wanted Bao Dai to stay on as nominal Chief of State earlier, he now saw no possibility of keeping Bao Dai in any role, effective or nominal.

He said that the People's Revolutionary Council, which had held numerous demonstrations demanding the dethronement of the Emperor, had strong support among the people. He argued that Diem himself had made several irrevocable decisions, such as disbanding the Imperial Guards, abolishing the Imperial Domain, firing Nguyen De as Viceroy, and Baron Didelot, as Secretary-General for the Central Highlands.

Note: Baron Didelot married a sister of Empress Nam Phuong. Therefore he was Emperor Bao Dai's brother-in-law.

Diem explained, "We can no longer tolerate a state within a state, especially when the Imperial Domain was a French creation. It was a dangerous creation, because the French wanted to detach the tribal Vietnamese who inhabit the region from the rest of the Vietnamese population, and then use that region which saddles over the three states of former Indochina to influence policies in Laos, Cambodia and Vietnam."

Luyen sounded unhappy, "But you fired Nguyen De, who was most instrumental to your nomination as Prime Minister a year ago. I have never understood the weird friend-and-foe relationship you both entertain, but I have heard outsiders criticize you for firing him. Then, you fired Baron Didelot. Baroness Didelot is Empress Nam Phuong's sister. By firing Didelot you hurt the feelings of the Empress."

Diem agreed. He said, "Once the Imperial Domain no longer exists, the Regional Secretariat for the Central Highlands no longer exists. The jobs of Viceroy and Secretary-General become obsolete. I did not fire them without regret, but what else could I do? I have never understood Nguyen De. After he helped me become Prime Minister last year, he listened to French officials and bankers and again became my fiercest enemy. During the Binh Xuyen crisis, I sent former Governor Ton That Hoi to Cannes to meet with the Emperor. Nguyen De prevented the Governor from seeing the Emperor. Even more than Bao Dai, De wanted me out."

Hiep said, "What needs to be done has to be done. However, there have been unacceptable excesses in the media. They have been demolishing the

Emperor in a most outrageous way. Even the Empress has not been spared. Can't we do something about this?"

Nhu suggested, "We can stop all the gossip by imposing censorship. But then people would say that we no longer respect freedom of speech." Hiep was not satisfied with the answer, "Look, Brother Nhu, keep that kind of comment for the public. You work closely with the People's Revolutionary Council. The media respects the Council. If through the Council you make it known to the media that Brother Diem does not want to see anymore slander against the Emperor, many journalists will listen."

Nhu was pained by Hiep's remark. He explained himself, "We have given complete freedom to the media. If tomorrow we go back to censorship, the people are not going to like that. Journalists and many of them are less than professional, have found those titillating stories about the Emperor and his concubines and mistresses help to sell their newspapers. They are not going to desist so easily."

Hiep exclaimed, "Enough is enough! Today in the newspapers, I read this horrible story about the Empress. It said that she killed Mme Decoux. This has become ridiculous."

Diem was upset. He asked, "What did the story say? I have not seen today newspapers yet." Hiep replied, "It said that one day, in 1943, Empress Nam Phuong was outraged with one of the Emperor's new conquests in Dalat. She went to their love nest, carrying a revolver in her handbag. Informed about what was happening, Suzanne Decoux, the wife of the French Governor General, a close friend of the Empress, rushed to the scene with a view to avoid a tragedy. The Empress arrived on the scene, and caught Bao Dai and his new mistress in the act. She took the gun out of her handbag and fired, just as Mme Decoux burst in. It was Mme Decoux who got hit by the bullet. There was, according to the newspapers, a huge cover-up, to keep the lid on the scandal."

Diem was indisputably angry. He said, "Brother Nhu, you know as well as I do, that Mme Decoux was killed in a car accident near Dalat. You must insist that the newspapers stop inventing stupid stories like that one. Ask them to stop attacking the Emperor and the Empress."

Nhu shook his head, "I cannot stop the journalists. Freedom of speech is a dangerous privilege, when the journalists are not mature and educated enough. We opened a Pandora's box when we sought a free press. Now, if you want to try to stop the media from printing certain things, do it yourself, Brother Diem, and see whether you succeed."

Nhu was right of course. Diem sat, sullen and discouraged. Finally he said, "Is this the end of the dream? Do we have to accept this dirt in politics? I cannot disregard these mean-spirited attacks on the Emperor. Everybody will think that we encourage this filth. We have to come out now and say that we detest what is going on in the media." Nhu said, "An impartial spectator must notice that the *official* media has not slandered anybody, least of all the Empress."

Luyen said, "Before I left Paris to come back for this meeting, I went to Cannes to see the Emperor, Nguyen De and the Empress. The Emperor and Nguyen De had harsh words for you. I saw the Empress separately. She said, "Maybe there is no other way out. Maybe the Prime Minister has no other option.""

Diem looked up, the unhappiest man in the world. He asked, "What else did she say?" Luyen shrugged, "She said she would be retiring soon, to a farm. She has already started looking around for one. She said that maybe what you did would free her from any responsibilities in regards to Vietnam, and from her tenuous ties with the Emperor. She asked me to tell you that she would pray for you."

Nobody said anything for a while. Finally, with poignant resignation, Diem softly declared, "Let us put an end to the monarchy, then."

*

Hiep sat and watched Nhu and Diem arguing with each other and discussing General J. Lawton Collins. Hiep tried not to side with her brothers' view of the conflict which opposed them against the American Special Envoy.

She told herself that she had talked enough in the morning. She did not want to venture into the field of international politics. She promised herself that she would keep her mouth shut in the afternoon. She did not completely understand the genesis of the conflict, or why it could not be resolved to the satisfaction of both sides at different phases during the crisis. She was happy that the conflict had ended and that the General was gone. She had, however, the feeling that at any time, another similar conflict could arise, with even more harmful consequences.

She had the impression that Diem's and Nhu's briefings had not been complete. Luyen, Can and Thuc began the analysis of the situation. They all agreed that Diem should not condone Collins' arrogance. Can said: "We cannot agree to become an American colony. An American Envoy should not act as if he were a Governor General." Thuc, moderate as he was, thought the General's behavior scandalous, when he allied himself with French General Paul Ely, to put pressure on Diem to yield to the demands of the Binh Xuyen, and to disappear from the scene.

Le Xuan made running comments that tended to make Hiep feel uneasy about the whole process. Hoang who sat by Hiep's side pretended not to be interested. Hiep knew better than that. She knew that when Hoang had that absent-minded look, she was thinking furiously. Hiep knew that Hoang also felt uneasy.

With the men and Le Xuan talking one-sidedly, the *inquiry* was merely a summary of the words and deeds of General Collins, which had caused problems for Diem and Nhu when they had been engaged in a life-and-death struggle against the Binh Xuyen and the warlords.

The meeting was drawing to a close. Diem asked, "Sister Hoang do you have any questions or comments?" Hoang shook her head. Diem turned to Hiep, who faced him squarely, "Yes. I have a few questions. I want to know, what was the origin of the conflict? When and how did it begin?"

Diem and Nhu looked at each other. Nhu said, "You were in Saigon in November, last year. At that time we were already experiencing problems with General Collins. He showed his preference to work with the French, especially with General Paul Ely whom he had known during World War II. His attitude seemed to say, 'Ely has been my comrade-in-arms for years. Listen to him. He is a good man. He knows what is good for Vietnam.'"

Diem added, "He rarely came to see me by himself. He almost always arrived in the company of General Ely.

Hiep asked her brothers, "So, in the beginning, you did not like his attitude. You saw him as a supporter of French colonialism; therefore in your eyes, he seemed to represent a major danger to Vietnam." Diem nodded, "Something like that. Soon he started making demands, which were also French demands."

Hiep asked pointedly, "He requested that you expand your political base, that you take into your cabinet an ever increasing number of opposition leaders. Why did that demand bother you?"

Diem, recognizing the pattern of Hiep's questions, answered quickly, "Bao Dai asked me to take more warlords into the cabinet, because those were the people who paid his bills and contributed to his fortune. The French asked me to take the same people into my cabinet, because they had been loyal friends of France, and also because they would render my cabinet hopelessly impotent. Collins wanted me to take more warlords into my cabinet, because he saw the warlords as the only ones with loyal troops, while I did not have any troops. He also wanted opposition leaders to join my cabinet, because he believed in democracy."

Hiep pressed on, "So, with completely different objectives in mind, Emperor Bao Dai, the French and the Americans asked you several times to broaden your cabinet. Did you accept their demands?"

Diem nodded, "Yes, to a certain degree. I opened up the cabinet to Hoa Hao and Caodaist leaders, but I refused to accept any of the Binh Xuyen bandits. But even those few changes rendered the cabinet incapable of functioning properly. Major decisions had to be made outside the cabinet meetings. The decision-making process had to be taken away from the Cabinet, and transferred to a small unit in the Independence Palace."

Hiep asked, "That small unit includes the Prime Minister and his Advisor and Le Xuan. Are there other strong personalities in that unit, beside the three of you?" Diem shook his head, "No." Hiep commented, "That could be considered the beginning of a dictatorship." Diem smiled calmly, "Yes, it could; however, we knew that that state of affairs would not last for long. We expected that the coalition Cabinet would unravel quickly, and it did."

Hiep persisted, "But, during the time that this dysfunctional coalition cabinet was in place, and all the decisions were being made by yourself with the help of Brother and Sister Nhu, people were right when they said that you had dictatorial powers." Nhu frowned, but Diem agreed, "Yes. I had to utilize those extraordinary powers. But, I immediately shared them with the People's Revolutionary Council."

Hiep was not satisfied with the answer; she asked again, "The People's Revolutionary Council was not your creation. Yet, many people said it was. It authorized you to form a new Cabinet in May and you did. The Council was above you, because you received the mandate from it. So you cannot say that you shared power with it. Can you say that the new cabinet is functional, and that all the decisions are made using the correct democratic process?"

Diem said, "Yes. I no longer have extraordinary powers. All the decisions are now made by the cabinet, except for the decisions regarding the conduct of the war."

Hiep shook her head, "I am afraid that if I were General Collins I would act at least partly like he did. He was favorable to General Ely. I would be biased in favor of my friends. He wanted you to be surrounded by ministers with real following. I would want the same thing. He wanted democracy. How could I criticize him for practicing what he had learned from childhood? He hated to see you act alone, as a dictator. I don't see any problem with that."

While Hoang and Diem were smiling, having guessed what Hiep was driving at, the rest of them frowned. Hiep concluded, "What was wrong with General Collins' conduct was that he allowed his friendship with General Ely to act in a way contrary to the interests of his country. He was wrong when he saw strength where it did not exist, and when he did not see hidden strength. Again he was wrong when he believed the American concept of democracy to be the only brand of democracy on earth. Finally he was wrong when he did not see you were accepting extraordinary powers reluctantly, and that you were trying to get rid of them as fast as you could."

In the silence that followed one could have heard a pin drop. Diem asked after a while: "Where were we wrong?" Hiep said, "You were wrong when you did not try every possible means to make General Collins understand where he was wrong. You were lacking in the resources, or in the determination to make him understand you."

Diem took the criticism positively. He asked, "What are the consequences of our mistakes?" Hiep looked to Hoang. She said, "Why don't you ask Hoang?" Diem again turned to Hoang who said, "It is obvious that from now on, because you did not take the time to explain your views to General Collins, the Americans will continue to entertain the same criticisms that he has made. You will be seen as a lonely man who likes to have dictatorial power, unable to share it with your political opponents, unable to broaden your political base. Your success has made you their favorite, simply because Americans respect success. Unfortunately, they will think of your success as a matter of luck, a miracle, something given to you by God, not something planned by you or earned by you."

Diem asked Hiep, "Do you agree with her? Is that what you would say yourself?" Hiep nodded. Then she looked at the Nhu's and said, "I have also heard that General Collins objected to Le Xuan. That too will come back to haunt us, unless we are able to explain to people why she is so close to the center of power." Le Xuan looked at Hiep, waiting for her to continue. But Hiep just smiled at her, and did not add another word to what she had said.

CHAPTER TWENTY-TWO
THE BEST YEARS

Hiep was surprised by the invitation. This time the Nhu's had asked Am and her to come to Saigon on their wedding anniversary. Hiep said she would talk to Am to see whether they would be able to go.

A month earlier, on October 23, 1955, a national referendum had taken place. Bao Dai lost in that referendum and three days later, Diem became the President of the Republic of Vietnam.

President Ngo Dinh Diem

*

A few days before the referendum took place, Bao Dai sent a cable advising that Diem was fired. It was a futile gesture, which was the perfect end to a futile reign.

Hiep called Diem and asked him if she should accept the Nhu's' invitation. Diem said he did not know anything about the Nhu's scheme, but he would be delighted if Am and Hiep could come. Unexpectedly, Am was reluctant to go to Saigon. He said that he would be happier if he could just stay away from 'The President.'

Hiep had noticed Am avoiding Diem before. Now she wanted to know why, and Am had a very straightforward answer for her this time. He said, "I am a businessman, a successful one. I do not want people to think that my success is in any way due to your family." Hiep clearly understood what he had said, but she felt that Am had still not said it all. She pressed on, "What are the other reasons?"

Am walked away from her. He stood a long time in front of a window, looking out at the scenery while he pondered her question. Hiep waited patiently. Finally, Am said, "I am afraid that the President allows the Nhu's to have too much power in Saigon." Hiep asked, "What is wrong with that?" Am was becoming slightly annoyed with her questions. Then he realized that his wife was only asking questions out of habit. He calmed himself before he answered, "You know what is wrong with that. The President has only one passion in life: his country. Brother Nhu's greatest passion is his wife. Their goals in life do not match."

Hiep objected, "Nhu also loves his country." Am replied: "We all love our country. I would not, however, attempt to compare my sentiments for the country with those of the President."

Hiep asked, "What about Le Xuan?" Am sighed and walked out of the room without even giving a reply. Hiep felt hurt. She knew that Am had formed his opinion about Le Xuan a long time ago. It was a subject that Hiep had never tried to touch on. Yet, she knew that Am had heard plenty about Le Xuan from Khoi and Diem when he had gone on hunting trips with them.

Am was quite a good hunter, and he liked to go hunting with his brothers-in-law. Each time he came back from such a hunting trip, Hiep knew without even asking that Le Xuan had been a subject of conversation. She knew her men. She knew they would not gossip or say anything bad about her. But the message was clear: Le Xuan might cause trouble.

Now in the midst of Diem's triumph, Am indicated that he preferred to stay away from the President in order to avoid meeting with Le Xuan. Hiep knew that Am's reluctance to come close to Diem would also prevent her from seeing Diem as frequently as she had in the past. She was dismayed, but she understood her husband's position. She called Nhu and told him that for the moment, Am and she could not leave Hue. Hiep thought she heard disappointment in his voice, but also a little relief, as he said, "Then, we will see you again on the second day of the Lunar New Year, three months from now."

*

The annual meeting that took place in Hue in early 1956 was more practical than other meetings. Everybody was focused on the preparations for a wedding. Indeed, Tran Trung Dzung, Diem's Secretary for Defense and Nguyen Thi Hoang Anh, Hoang's daughter was to get married following the annual discussions. Diem was happy as one of his nieces was about to get married to one of his closest assistants in the Phu Cam Cathedral in Hue next to his father's home.

Nguyen Thi Hoang Anh 1956

Diem attending the wedding of Hoang's daughter, Nguyen Thi Hoang Anh and Tran Trung Dzung in Hue (1956)

*

Little did Diem and Nhu know that the two newlyweds would be the first ones allowed by the military junta to see their bodies in a hospital after they were murdered seven years later by the military junta. Ngo Dinh Can did not know either that seven years later Hoang Anh was asked by the military junta (believing nonsensically that the Ngo Dinh family had money stashed somewhere) to pay millions in ransom for his life. Little did they know that another obscure member of their family was to be brought to the front scene of their tragic saga at the end.

Note: Though some critics of the Ngo Dinh family suggested that Tran Trung Dzung was not loyal to President Diem, their arguments have no factual basis. Some also said that the military junta that overthrew Diem was afraid of Dzung and left him alone after the coup because he knew too

409

much-- as the Secretary for Defense—about the little secrets of the generals; but that also was never been proved.

*

Diem was on the phone, quite excited. It was April 26, 1956. The last units of the French Expeditionary Corps had paraded one last time in the streets of Saigon that morning, and then they were gone. The presence of the French troops that Diem had again and again claimed to be incompatible with total independence had become a thing of the past.

Diem said, "Please go and light a candle at Father's altar." Hiep was tempted to answer, "Tell Brother Can to do that." But, she controlled herself. She did not want to spoil Diem's perfect day. Now that General Tran van Soai had surrendered, the French were gone and the Constituent Assembly elected, Diem deserved some praise and encouragement. Yet, Hiep was dissatisfied with the whole situation.

First, Brother Luyen was now safely tucked away as the Ambassador at the Court of St. James. Those who had favored Luyen were now accusing the Nhu's of plotting to discard Luyen and to seize more power near Diem, as a result of Luyen's departure. Earlier, Luyen had been a Roving Ambassador who reported directly to Diem and came back to Saigon quite frequently. From now on, however, Luyen would have to act like a regular diplomat. He would have to live by the diplomatic code, and report to the Minister of Foreign Affairs. His access to Diem was reduced to a minimum.

Second, in Hue, although Diem had talked tough with Can during the previous Lunar New Year, Can had continued to assume more and more power, as nobody among the officials in Central Vietnam stood up against him.

Fortunately, everything was taking a turn for the better in the country. Diem's enemies were silent for the time being, not daring to challenge Diem's popularity.

Hiep asked Diem, "Are you happy?" Diem sounded cheerful, "Of course, I am happy. This is the happiest day of my life. The French troops are gone." Hiep said, "Everybody in Vietnam, in the South and in the North should be happy for that. But I was not asking about the country. I was asking about you."

Diem was silent. Hiep, sensing his pain, asked hurriedly, "What is the matter, Brother Diem?" Diem kept a dogged silence. Hiep pressed him, "What is bothering you? In God's name, tell me." Diem said, "It's too long to tell. There is too much bad blood among the factions in the western provinces. The war with the Hoa Hao private armies may end up with many more casualties than expected. I am afraid that some of the people close to me may use the war to settle old scores."

Hiep asked, "Could you not get rid of those particular people?" Diem replied, "I need them at the moment. They are the only ones who know the western provinces. I have given them full powers." Hiep exclaimed, "Brother Diem, get rid of them!" Diem sighed, "I can't."

Hiep persisted, "Remember the Venerable Huynh Phu So. He loved you. He introduced you to all his future generals. You should not allow anybody to kill them just to settle old scores."

Diem said, "The Venerable Great Teacher told me that he loved Nguyen Giac Ngo and Lam Thanh Nguyen. Both of these generals are safe. General Tran van Soai has surrendered; he is also safe. The Venerable told me, 'The one who is the most talented, yet the least virtuous is Le Quang Vinh.' Now, General Le Quang Vinh is still fighting a running war against our army. He is not safe. He has made lots of enemies."

Hiep commented, "Everybody is saying that either you, or members of your family are making all the decisions about everything in the country. Now I see that you are not so powerful after all. For once, though, I would like to see you use your power to get rid of those people who may take the control out of your hands."

Diem said, "Let us celebrate today. Problems can wait until to-morrow. Don't forget to light the candle."

*

Since coming to power, Diem had tried every means to find Khoi's remains. According to the last information before Khoi was killed, he had been near Hien Si, about twenty kilometers north of Hue.

The family knew that he had been killed somewhere near Hien Si and buried at the site of his execution. In late 1955, there was a breakthrough. The parents of two Viet Minh soldiers, who had been present at the execution, told local officials that their sons might know about the site. Unfortunately, their unit had been relocated to North Vietnam after the Geneva Agreements.

Can met with local officials and the parents of the soldiers. Two of the parents volunteered to go to North Vietnam to talk to their sons. A few months later, they came back from North Vietnam, with some rough maps. Thanks to these maps, the search area was narrowed down to a thin strip of woodland near the Black Panther Forest.

Digging started in May 1956, and soon enough, the remains of three bodies were found in a shallow grave. Preliminary identification was made on the spot. Pham Quynh's spectacles, and Ngo Dinh Khoi's gown and turban, as well as the rosary he had on him, helped determine that the remains were those of Khoi, his son, Huan, and Pham Quynh.

Hiep and Hoa, Khoi's widow, cried softly as the three coffins arrived in Hue. The three coffins were made of the same wood. They had the same shape and were decorated with the same carvings, painted in the same color. Diem had instructed that *there should not be any difference among the dead.*

Can stood motionless, tears streaming down his face. He turned to Hoa and said, "I want a national funeral for him." Hoa looked at Can, surprised. She said, "I will not allow it." There was so much determination in her voice that Hiep felt she should back Hoa up, "It will be a private funeral."

Hiep was stunned by what was happening. Why such a confrontation, on such an occasion? Yet, the confrontation was inevitable. For months, Can had talked to Hiep about how he would like the funeral to be, whenever Khoi's remains were found. For months, Hoa knowing that the remains would soon be found confided to Hiep that she would like to keep the funeral within the family.

So, the two persons who loved Khoi most in his life were challenging each other now over the way to bury him. Hiep felt so frustrated that she took Hoa's hand; and led her away from the coffins and the crowd of mourners.

In the garden of her mother's home, they sat down side by side. It was early May, but neither Hoa nor Hiep looked at the roses blossoming everywhere in the rose garden that Diem had first created years ago.

Hoa said, "From now on, I can bring fresh flowers and visit their graves every day." There was a note of triumph in her voice. Then she added, "My husband and my son were patriots. If they wanted to cover their coffins with the national flag, like any fallen soldier, I would not object. But they did not do anything spectacular for the country. Why does Can believe that my husband should have a national funeral?"

Hiep told Hoa, "You are the one who makes the decision. Brother Can should not interfere with your wishes." Hoa smiled bitterly, "Isn't he the Viceroy of Central Vietnam now? All his wishes must be obeyed, isn't that true?" Hoa's bitterness and vehemence appalled Hiep. She said, "He is no viceroy. He doesn't hold any office. He doesn't have any political responsibility." Hoa nodded, and then pleaded with her, "Then, please make sure that my husband and my son are buried in private."

Hoa had spoken as if she were praying. Hiep felt terribly angry. She said, " Brother Can has no right to hurt you. Please come with me. We will call Brother Diem." Hoa smiled weakly, and said, "Why should you talk to Brother Diem?" Hiep said, "In our family, after Brother Khoi was gone, whenever there has been a conflict, only Brother Diem has the authority to be the arbiter." Hoa said, "I thought you were the arbiter in the family quarrels."

They got Diem on the phone quickly. Hoa said without preamble, "Mr. President, Can wants a national funeral for my husband. I want to keep it private." Diem exclaimed, "You are the only one who will make the decisions on this matter, Sister Hoa. Brother Can must abide by your wishes."

Hoa gave the receiver to Hiep who said, "Then, will you please tell Can that, clearly. We cannot cover everything we do with your presidential mantle. This is a private matter. We need to keep it private."

Diem was a little surprised by the anger in Hiep's voice. He asked, "From what I have heard, it seems that both of you are angry. Is Can behaving badly?" Hoa shook her head, indicating to Hiep that Diem should not be bothered. Hiep replied, "He hasn't done anything wrong, so far, except trying to act as if we were an imperial family. Please put a stop to all his nonsense."

Hoa gently took the receiver from Hiep's hand. She told Diem, "I may have overreacted. What Hiep has just said may have originated from my own critical remarks about Can."

Diem was not convinced and he sounded very unhappy about his brother's behavior. "When Sister Hiep says something, she does not say it lightly. I'll have to look seriously into the matter. For the moment, please make all the necessary arrangements for the funeral. Nobody will interfere with your wishes."

As they walked out into the garden again, Hoa said, "Whatever I may do, there will be a crowd of officials at the funeral, I guess." There was more than a touch of sadness in Hiep's smile as she replied, "It's the inevitable price we have to pay."

Hoa was concerned; she asked Hiep, "You sound disenchanted. What's the matter?" Hiep said sadly, "I am drifting away from my brothers, one by one." Hoa exclaimed, "Oh, please don't do that. They need you now, more than ever before."

*

Khoi's and Huan's remains were buried in the family knoll, next to Ngo Dinh Kha's tomb in Phu Cam. Pham Quynh's children buried his remains in the grounds of the Van Phuoc Pagoda, in Ben Ngu. Hoa brought fresh flowers to the graves of her husband and her son every day until she died. The monks of Van Phuoc Pagoda, who had been recipients of Pham Quynh's largesse during his lifetime, took care of Pham Quynh's tomb.

*

It was midnight and General Le Quang Vinh was, as usual, in his small motorboat with four well-armed bodyguards. In spite of the defection of several battalions, and in spite of the presence of the national army troops in his fiefdom, Vinh was still the feared warlord of the swamps. Every night he traveled by boat, with a light escort, along the canals that he knew so well. The National Guards, hiding behind their fragile watchtowers, never dared stop him.

414

From time to time, from a watchtower, a National Guard would challenge the passing motorboat, "Who is there?" One of the bodyguards in the boat would curse and shout back, "Brother Ba is here." Le Quang Vinh was known as Ba Cut. Half of his nickname would suffice to silence the terrorized National Guard, and Vinh's motorboat would pass without any further problem.

General Vinh inspected his own positions every night, to show his troops that he wanted to be among them. He also made it a point to visit villages, see some of his mistresses, and make new conquests among the terrorized maidens. His nocturnal habits were not unknown to Nguyen Ngoc Tho, the Special Envoy of President Diem, and General Duong van Minh, commander of the army units operating in the western provinces.

On that fateful night, a National Guard challenged General Vinh as they came close to a small outpost on a canal bank at Chac Ca Dao. The youngster on the watchtower shouted, "Who is there?" One of Vinh's bodyguards shouted back, "Brother Ba is here." The voice from the watchtower said angrily, "Whoever he is, he must land over here for inspection."

What the youngster had said stunned the people in the motorboat. Vinh's bodyguards were ready to spray the watchtower with bullets, but General Vinh raised his hand and told them not to fire. Vinh ordered his escort to land. He jumped out of his boat and walked in front of his bodyguards, expecting that some older National Guards in the outpost would recognize him and apologize.

Seeing that Vinh marched in front of four armed bodyguards, the people in the outpost were scared. Had they challenged one of the high-ranking officers of the army? The poise and calm of the man in front of them did not leave any doubt. He must be *somebody,* if he had the right to be accompanied by armed guards.

The leader of the twelve-man squad ran to him and saluted. Vinh returned the salute. It was then that the squad leader of the National Guards noticed Vinh's hand with a missing finger. He realized, having heard about Vinh's missing finger, that he had the cruelest Hoa Hao warlord in front of him.

He cursed himself for having been transferred there just the night before, with his squad. He cursed fate, not knowing that Nguyen Ngoc Tho and

General Duong Van Minh had engineered the quick transfer the night before, intentionally. Now that he had recognized the Hoa Hao general, the squad leader had no choice at all. He had to arrest him or he would be killed.

His men also understood the situation. Upon a quick signal from him, they simultaneously jumped on the bodyguards and General Vinh and disarmed them. They tied them up and put through a call to the nearest army headquarters. On the same night, Special Envoy Nguyen Ngoc Tho, and General Duong van Minh arrived with a large number of troops. At dawn of the next morning, they had the Hoa Hao general driven to the provincial jail. The fierce Hoa Hao Tiger was finally in a cage.

*

After his friend, General Trinh Minh The, had died, Diem had gone to Hue, disconsolate. Now, a few days after the execution of General Le Quang Vinh, Diem was back in Hue, trying to recover his peace of mind.

General Le Quang Vinh had been condemned to death by a Criminal Court, had appealed, and lost. He was also condemned to death by a Military Court.

Diem spent days arguing with his aides on how to reduce the sentence while the pressures from Le Quang Vinh's enemies and former allies kept mounting: it would be dangerous for those who had helped the government, or defected to the government side in the war against General Vinh, if Diem showed leniency.

Diem still had the power of pardon. Yet, every account he had received assured him that nobody in the western provinces would live in peace if Vinh were pardoned. Nguyen Ngoc Tho and General Duong Van Minh told Diem he should not save the life of a rapist, a murderer, a man convicted of high treason. They reminded Diem that he had given them full powers to deal with the Hoa Hao armies.

On the eve of Vinh's execution, Diem could not sleep. He walked back and forth in his palace. During the preceding week, General Vinh had expressed his intention of becoming a Christian, and Diem did not know what to think of such a conversion. By midnight, his palace aides came to tell him that General Vinh had just been baptized and had asked the President not to feel responsible for his death.

Diem agonized all that night, and the next morning, at the time Vinh was executed in Can Tho, Diem was on his knees in his chapel, praying for the man he could not pardon.

Now, in Hue, Diem was still wondering what he could have done to save General Vinh's life. Another problem, a much bigger problem, was haunting him. He had seen, and felt raw, pure hatred oozing out of some of the people close to him. How could he go on working with them when he had seen their faces contorted with that kind of hatred?

Neither Nhu nor Can had been of any help. They told him, without hatred, but also without compassion, that General Le Quang Vinh deserved to die. He had turned to Thuc. But, Thuc rightly said that he refused to be Diem's confessor.

Diem knew he had come to Hue to meet with his sister. That knowledge made him shy. He picked up the phone a dozen times, each time replacing the receiver more hurriedly. He wondered what was going on. Hiep came to his mother's home every day. Why did she choose not to come when he was in town?

In the late afternoon, Hiep arrived. She did not show any surprise at seeing Diem there. She went inside and talked with Mrs. Kha. In the parlor, Diem waited for her patiently. Finally she came out.

Without preamble Hiep said, "So, *people close to you* have succeeded in killing General Le Quang Vinh?" Diem, scandalized, wanted to lash out at her, and then realized that he had never lashed out at her. He controlled his temper and replied, "He had to pay for his crimes. He committed all kinds of crimes. The Criminal Court and the Court of Appeals judged his case most impartially and condemned him to death. The Military Court also condemned him to death."

Hiep asked with some irony, "Of course, the Military Court was also impartial? Then, tell me why are you so troubled?" Diem did not say anything. Hiep watched him for a moment then, and all of a sudden, she realized that she should not be talking to him like that. She came and sat down quietly in front of him, waiting for him to talk.

Diem seemed to be lost in a painful dream. Finally he said, "You remember April 26? It was the happiest day of my life. I called you that day, in the evening, when the last French units had already embarked and were ready to leave Saigon. I called to ask you to go and light a candle on Father's altar. At least that was the original idea. But when you asked me whether I was happy, I felt that even on the happiest day of my life, I was also very troubled by the extreme hatred shown by some of the people close to me. Do you remember?"

Hiep nodded. Yes, she remembered vividly. What Diem felt, he had passed on to her, and after that telephone call, she had been watching the war against the Hoa Hao with increasing anxiety. She felt the hatred as she followed the trials of General Le Quang Vinh. She was tempted many times to pick up the phone and ask Diem to pardon the General, no matter what had happened, no matter what crimes he had committed. In the end, she did not do that. She knew that even if she called, Diem would not be able to pardon Vinh.

Diem exclaimed, "Hatred is an aberration. Hatred is an abomination. I cannot deal with hatred. I cannot deal with people who are consumed with hatred. It all goes back to the time when Nguyen Ngoc Tho was Province Chief of Long Xuyen, and the young warlord Le Quang Vinh only held the rank of a Major. Nguyen Ngoc Tho was a favorite of the French, while Major Vinh was a warlord whose periods of alliance with the French never lasted more than a few months."

Hiep asked, "How did the two first meet?" Diem replied, "The French assigned to Nguyen Ngoc Tho, the province of Long Xuyen which included the Hoa Hao Holy Land and also the area of operation of Major Le Quang Vinh. Tho thought that he had the total support of the French. He did not know that the French needed Major Vinh more than they needed him. Tho wanted to fight Major Vinh and the Major retaliated by setting up an ambush to kill Tho. Although Tho escaped unharmed, he was sick with fright. He went to the French and asked them to help him eliminate Major Vinh. The French, however, preferred to remove Tho from Long Xuyen."

Hiep asked, "That was how the enmity started? Are there other reasons?" Diem nodded, "When the Bao Dai solution was adopted by the French, Tho engineered the surrender of the Hoa Hao warlord, Nguyen Giac Ngo.

By obtaining Nguyen Giac Ngo's surrender, Tho ensured himself the favors of the Emperor. But the other Hoa Hao warlords, Nguyen Quang Vinh included, hated the man who had succeeded in splitting the Hoa Hao ranks." "Was that all?" Hiep asked.

Diem continued, "In March of this year, Hoa Hao warlords Tran van Soai and Le Quang Vinh, demanded the removal of four ministers from my Cabinet. Fighting for time, I had to let them go. As you know, one of them was Nguyen Ngoc Tho. I sent him to Japan as Ambassador, because apparently he had received death threats from General Le Quang Vinh. But Nguyen Ngoc Tho came back as soon as the war against the Hoa Hao armies started. He volunteered to work as advisor to General Duong van Minh. I appointed him Special Envoy, as he knew the region well. I did not know at the time that his motivation was revenge."

Hiep asked, "What about Duong van Minh?" Diem mused a while before answering, "Nobody knows him well. He is the son of Nguyen Ngoc Tho's best friend. That is why Minh called him 'Uncle.' He was in the French army, and then worked with the Japanese. When the French came back, he was arrested and tortured. Then he somehow got his officer commission back from the French. Nguyen Ngoc Tho introduced him to me. He served well in the war against the Binh Xuyen, though later on, we found out that he kept some of the Binh Xuyen treasury captured in Rung Sat for himself. Well liked by his troops, he hates the Hoa Hao's and they hate him."

Hiep commented, "During the Le Quang Vinh's trial, I recall that all the dossiers on General Le Quang Vinh's crimes came from the Nguyen Ngoc Tho group." Diem sighed, "They are most upset now, because I ordered our Embassy in Bangkok to give a passport and visa to General Vinh's wife, so that she could go to France. In my view, the lady has not committed any crime. We have no right to deny her a visa."

Diem shook his head and fell silent. Hiep asked, "Is there still something that you haven't told me?" Diem admitted, "Yes. I did not tell you that I acceded to General Le Quang Vinh's request to be buried on Mount Sam in Long Xuyen. A few days later, it was reported that his body was unearthed and cut to pieces. People suspect that an aide of General Duong van Minh was responsible for that barbarian profanation. People have been pointing at a man named Nguyen van Nhung, Duong Van Minh's bodyguard and adjutant."

Diem lapsed into another long silence. Hiep startled him by asking, "What are you going to do? You have surrounded yourself with too many people who have betrayed you, or who have acted in such a way that you have lost respect for them."

Diem said, "Yet if I get rid of them all, what will I have left, my brothers and sisters? Then, people would have good reason to say that our family dominates the government." Hiep looked at her brother. He had not lost the faith, but definitely he had lost some of his innocence.

*

On February 22, 1957, Hiep was chatting with Can when his military aide, Captain Nguyen van Minh rushed in, "A man has shot at the President." Hiep paled. Minh, out of breath, managed to report, "The President was not injured."

That was the first report Hiep received of the assassination attempt on Diem. Can got on the phone and found one of Diem's adjutants on the other end of the line.

Diem was in Ban Me Thuot, in the Central Highlands. He was there to open the Ban Me Thuot Fair. In the early morning, the tribal population of the region had assembled to welcome Diem. When Diem arrived and approached the podium, the crowd went into a frenzy of cheering. The tribal people knew how much importance Diem gave to them, how much he wanted to eliminate the social and economic differences that existed between the *highlanders* and the people of the lowlands.

While ovations and acclamations went on, a young man approached the podium, drew his sub-machine gun and fired. Diem turned around and found that the Minister of Land Reform who had been standing behind him was seriously wounded. He knelt down and talked to him.

In the meantime, the young attacker did not have the time to escape. The people around him had jumped on him, wrestled him down and disarmed him. Diem waved to the crowd. The cheers surged like thunder. The crowd wanted to lynch the young man. But the security force intervened and escorted him to a house nearby.

In spite of the worries of his escort, Diem went to the podium, delivered his speech, and came down to cut the ribbon at the gate of the Fair. He calmly visited many stands and after that, as usual, he walked into the crowd, stopping to ask a question here and there, while his aides tried ineffectively to surround him with a human shield.

Can asked, "How is he now?" Diem's adjutant hesitated, and then announced, "Here he is. He wants to talk to you."

Can told Hiep, "He is taking the receiver now." Hiep watched her brother as he listened and nodded, listened and nodded, tears streaming down his face. After a while he said hoarsely, "Sister Hiep is here. Do you want to talk to her, Mr. President?" He handed the receiver to her. Diem was jovial, "Did you pray for me this morning? You did? Then somebody was listening. Well, I am all right. Minister Cung was not so lucky. I will be going to see him at the hospital in a couple of hours."

Hiep asked, "Do you feel discouraged because somebody shot at you?" Diem laughed, "No, not at all. The young man did not try to kill me because he hates me, but because he received an order from the French, or from the Communists. We are trying to determine who issued the order."

Hiep asked Diem, "Are you making sure he is not being tortured or anything like that?" Diem laughed again. He said, "Nobody is torturing him. Nhu is questioning him personally right now. You know that Nhu cannot torture even a fly." Hiep asked, "What kind of sentence will a high court give to a man who has tried to kill you?" Diem reassured her, "Whatever the courts decide in the future, I promise you, Sister Hiep, the young man will not die."

Diem went on after a short silence, "From what we got out of him, the young man, whose name is Ha Minh Chi, he is an orphan, he lives alone, and has very few friends. A young man like that is very vulnerable psychologically, unstable emotionally. He may not even understand the enormity of his act. On the other hand, if I allowed him to be killed as punishment for his deed, I would be worse than him."

Hiep felt her heart go out to her brother. She said tearfully, "Take good care of yourself, Mr. President."

*

For months in 1957, Diem made official visits to Chiefs of State around the world. Encouraged by the United States Ambassador Eldridge Durbrow, Diem went to the United States in May, Thailand in August, Australia and South Korea in September and India in November. By mid November, Diem was back in Hue for the inauguration of the University of Hue, which he had established, with the help of Father Cao Van Luan.

*

Diem seemed to have enjoyed it all tremendously. Hiep smiled, wondering if all the superlatives that had been used by Chiefs of State and other international and national leaders to welcome him had gone to his head. The international media was extremely kind to him: Diem was the miracle man who had saved South Vietnam from Communism, the man who had defeated all the warlords in his dismantled country and unified all the private armies under the national banner.

There was not one single false note in the concert of praises. Now, Diem was back in Hue to inaugurate *his* University, to prove that he had faithfully followed the footsteps of his father who had founded in Hue, the National Institute (Quoc *Hoc*), under Emperor Thanh Thai.

Am came and greeted Diem, but did not stay. As Am left, Diem shook his head and said, "Am seems to disapprove of me." Hiep laughed, "If he did not like you, he would not set foot here. He has often told me about his hunting trips with you in his youth. He seems to miss those times."

Diem said, "I miss those times too. Now the only hunting trips I make are in Dalat, with Nhu. Now, Nhu is all right as a sharpshooter, but he is not a good hunting companion. At times, if he has a problem on his mind, he talks ceaselessly, scaring away the game. At other times, after a quarrel with Le Xuan, he is sullen and will not open his mouth for the whole day. With Am, it was different. He was a serious hunter. He knew when he could talk. Then he made me laugh with his jokes. In those days, I never knew he was in love with you. It was only when his father came and talked to Father that we knew."

422

Hiep was a little concerned. She knew Diem too well to believe that he had said all that without any purpose. She was right. Diem stopped a minute, and then commented, "He was slow in making his feelings known. It seems that he is feeling something very deeply today, too." He turned, and looking directly at Hiep, he asked, "What is it?"

Hiep shrugged, "You know what he feels. He feels that you have given too much power to Nhu and Can. He does not like to see Le Xuan too close to the center of power." Diem asked, "Has he said that?" Hiep shook her head; "I do not need him to say it in so many words."

Diem pressed on, "What about you? Do you feel the same way?" Hiep nodded but did not say anything. Diem sighed, "You are right, and Am is right. But what can I do?" Hiep said, "Now that both Nhu and Le Xuan have been elected as members of the National Assembly, their place is in the Parliament, not in the Independence Palace. They should take their role of lawmakers seriously and work with their constituencies effectively. You will have to surround yourself with other advisors, outside of your family. In Central Vietnam, you should allow the province chiefs, the Regional Delegate to have more power. Can's role will have to be reduced."

Diem agreed, "That is certainly what I should do. But you forget one thing: how many people in the country would talk to me like you have just done? I am looking for advisors outside my family. But I have found few people who could or would tell me the truth. I don't think this situation will go on forever. I have asked Luyen who is a good judge of people to be on the lookout for talented and sincere men and women."

Hiep nodded, "Luyen is the best man for the job. He is selfless. He does not want to build his own empire. He shies away from power. As you say, he is a good judge of men and women. But, you exiled him to London."

Diem was startled, "Exiled? By me? Or by the Nhu's? Is that what you, of all people, think? Look, Luyen wanted to get away. He told me, 'The atmosphere at the Independence Palace is too stifling for me. I need to get away from here.' That is why he was appointed Roving Ambassador, and that is why he is at the Court of St. James now. From London, or wherever he is, he is still is my best talent-scout, so far."

Hiep insisted, "It has been three years since you took power. It is time to have other advisors besides the Nhu's in Saigon, and Brother Can here in Hue." Diem said, "I would like that, too. Tell me Sister, whom do you see around you, who can replace the Nhu's at this moment? Then, tell me also how can I stiffen the backs of the province chiefs in Central Vietnam and in the Highlands, to make them work independently from Can?"

Hiep stood up. She said, "I have spent my life listening. I have listened to Father. I have listened to you. Now I want you to listen to me for once. Is it so hard for you to listen?" Diem was shaken. He tried to calm Hiep down, "Look, I was not angry with you or anything like that. I just want you to know that I have limited choices of personnel."

Hiep sat down again, but she pretended to listen only absent-mindedly. Knowing that she still was attentive, Diem went on, "I inherited people who had worked for the French. It is not a bad thing *per se*. I also worked during the colonial days. I do not want to be too critical of their passivity under the French and I give them the benefit of a doubt. They may be patriots disguised as collaborators. I have weeded out those who were too servile under the French, and those who harmed other Vietnamese in order to promote themselves."

As usual, when he pursued the thread of his thoughts, Diem lit one cigarette after another. Soon he spoke through a cloud of smoke. Hiep did not move a muscle, and that was encouragement enough for Diem. He said, "I weeded out those who were too corrupt, too cruel, too ignorant or too ineffective. But I cannot throw all of them out, first, because there are some good men among them, and second, because then, there would be no more government. To keep the majority of them presents a big problem, however: the French schooled them to be servants, to work under detailed order, to have no initiative. How can I change them now? How can I? How can I help them walk straight, talk straight, take risks to promote their own ideas? How can I help them to become all of a sudden bold, imaginative, and independent?"

Diem laughed sadly, "The French did such a good job that even now, many of my ministers would receive any European or American who comes knocking at their door, uninvited, but will not even let the lowest ranking officers in their ministry receive a Vietnamese talent. At official receptions, right at the Independence Palace, if a European or an

American shows up, he or she will be surrounded by a group of fawning listeners."

Becoming more confident that he had regained Hiep's full attention, Diem proceeded a little more leisurely, "The French heritage is poisoned. The most deadly poison is in the police and the army." Diem was immersed now in his own thoughts, "The policemen under the French had to work most of the time against their own fellow-countrymen. Agents who served in the Special Services learned the terrible art of torture. I have tried to weed them out. The war against the Binh Xuyen did not aid the process. The police force, as you must recall, was under Binh Xuyen control. I had to wrestle the control from the Binh Xuyen. Policemen, who were farsighted at the time, deserted the Binh Xuyen and rallied to me. Being farsighted is not, however, the monopoly of the virtuous. The worst elements in the police rallied to Colonel Lansdale at the beginning. They weakened the Binh Xuyen, but they are now in commanding positions. I am weeding them out now, but it will take time."

Hiep prompted, "What about the army?" Diem replied, "The army is much better than the police force. Yet, most of the highest-ranking officers today are handovers from the French. When I inherited them, they had been through an accelerated promotion process. Within a few years they had gone from non-commissioned officers, or mere second lieutenants to field officers, to general officers. Most of them had not joined the French army because they loved their country. We have to weed out most of them. It is easier for us here. To train and promote a new bunch of officers can be done rather rapidly. Still, it will take a few more years to clean up the army."

"What do you have in mind in terms of manpower then?" Hiep asked. Diem replied, "I will need a few more years to have capable people in the administration, in the army and the police. I am sure it will take at least three years to accomplish this."

Hiep shook her head, "Suppose you don't have three years." "Then I am doomed," he replied. "No, I should not say that. I understand your worry. Believe me, I am working on it. Since last October, I have given extensive powers to the Province Chiefs. If they would only stiffen their backs and their necks, Can will not be able to claim any power in Central Vietnam. As for the Nhu's, I have a terrible problem. I still need Nhu by my side.

But I know he and Le Xuan are not popular. He has agreed with me that he and his wife will need to take an assignment abroad, within the next couple of years."

To make Diem's promise more binding, Hiep said, "Father would certainly be happy to hear you say that." Diem said, as if to himself, "I cannot afford to fail. I must not fail. I cannot fail because of weakness or sentimentality. In August, I asked the Nhu's to hold a press conference to respond to gossip about them. They did a good job, didn't they?"

Hiep said, "Yes, they did a good job. Yet rumors are expressions of envy or hatred. As you said, Nhu and especially Le Xuan, are not very popular at this moment."

*

As usual, the Lunar New Year in 1958 was an occasion for celebration. The country was moving forward decisively, and the outside world was increasingly aware of South Vietnam's progress. Also, as usual, the family reunion, on the anniversary of Ngo Dinh Kha's death, was planned as an occasion for reviewing past activities and future plans as well as for criticism and self-criticism.

Two major issues were on the table: first, a letter from North Vietnam's Premier Pham Van Dong, and second, the recent decision of North Vietnam's Workers Party to adopt 'limited use of armed forces, to support political struggle,' against South Vietnam.

Diem said, "In July 1957, then again in April 1958, Premier Pham Van Dong wrote to me asking us to begin negotiations in view of reunifying our country. I sent you copies of the full text of his letters and my answers at the time. We need to discuss our long-term approach to reunification. I know that none of us wants to see our country partitioned this way. I also know that none of us wants to see Communist rule over a unified Vietnam. What then, are the alternatives?"

Nhu had prepared his response. He proposed that the process of reunification be linked with the obvious weakening of the Communist Bloc. He encouraged Diem to be patient, as the Communist Empire would soon unravel. He had seen signs of decay in the Soviet Union with the denunciations of Stalinism by Khrushchev and predicted a Chinese-

Russian conflict in the near future. He concluded by saying that if South Vietnam succeeded in building a stable and secure society, it could afford to wait until the Communists were overthrown in North Vietnam. He predicted that at that time, the country could be reunified under a non-Communist government.

Diem did not go into far-flung discussions about the future fall of Communism. He said, "In my letters to Premier Pham Van Dong, I stressed the need for democracy in both North and South Vietnam. Unless general elections are conducted freely and honestly, why even bother to organize them? I say that until there is freedom and democracy in North Vietnam, we cannot hold general elections in view of reunifying North and South."

Hoang asked Nhu, "Your remarks are very interesting. When do you think that the Communists will fall apart?" Nhu was happy that Hoang had returned to his remarks. He replied, "The Communist world still seems capable of further expansion. But the revolt in Hungary showed that it is vulnerable. It takes a long time to build an empire; it only takes a few months for it to collapse. I cannot predict with precision the collapse of the Communist Bloc. But I am sure that within one or two decades, it will fade away."

Hoang turned to Diem and addressed her question to him, "Suppose the Communist Bloc endures for another twenty years. What would happen in the meantime? Hanoi would not wait that long to launch a general offensive against the South to reunify the country by force."

Diem nodded, "That is precisely the decision that the Workers Party made only last month in a secret meeting of its Central Committee. It has decided to use military force against South Vietnam." Hoang wanted to know, "If it was a secret meeting, how do you know about it?" Diem smiled shyly. He told Hoang, "Except for these family reunions, which so far have not attracted the interest of the Communists, I have always assumed that the content of all my secret meetings with my staff, my Cabinet and my Vietnamese and foreign visitors is known by the enemy. Old friendships never die. I do have friends in the North."

Nhu said, "The Communist army units left a large number of weapons in caches all over the South, before they regrouped and were sent north according to the terms of the Geneva Agreements. We have found hundreds of them, but there are still hundreds more that we have not uncovered. Their cadres are still here. That is why we have launched campaign after campaign to find out whom they are, and where they are. Communist terrorists have killed thousands of hamlet and village leaders over the last five years. That is why we have made so much effort to track them down."

Hiep asked Diem, "What should we expect from now on? The Communists will do more than assassinate hamlet and village leaders. What do you foresee as their possible strategy?" Diem replied, "They cannot raise an army in the South. We will make sure that they will never be able to do that. Their only option then will be to send troops from the North into the South. In order to deny them even that option, we have to cut off all the infiltration routes."

Hoang exclaimed, "That would be impossible!" Diem shook his head, "Difficult, but not impossible. It would become impossible if the Communists were to control Laos. That is why we have to make sure that Laos is firmly in non-Communist hands. If Laos were lost to the Communists, we would then have to defeat whatever Vo Nguyen Giap might throw at us."

Hiep shivered, "Then, it will be a big war, with tens of thousands of deaths on both sides." Diem nodded sadly, "We have to work under that assumption. We are building army divisions to prepare for such an eventuality. But we have to make sure that we will not need to fight a war with units of divisional size. We have to make sure that non-Communist Laos survives."

Only now, Hiep understood why Diem had given Can such a broad mandate in Laos and why Can had secretly organized so many teams of agents working in Laos. Can said: "We have not talked about the option of launching our own agents into the North. I see it as a very viable option. We have so far, been able to maintain communications with people in Quang Binh, Ha Tinh, Nghe An and Thanh Hoa. We could give the Communists in the North a taste of their own medicine."

Diem was categorical, "We will continue to train teams for such an option. But I don't want to expand the war zones. Aren't our people miserable enough as it is?"

Can asked ironically, "Are you afraid that the Americans would not support such a strategy?" Diem was not amused; he said, "When it comes to the vital interests of our country, do you think that I will accept interdicts from any foreign power? No, Can, this is my conviction. *My* conviction! I do not want to take the war to the north, until I see that it is necessary."

Luyen, who had not said anything so far, finally observed, "These preparations for the war will give more importance to the military. I am concerned. It is never a good thing for a country to have a lot of military leaders. We have not finished building up new leadership in our armed forces. We still have too many old generals. Brothers Diem and Nhu, you should be careful."

Diem said, "Before we have recourse to the military, diplomats will be in the front line. Or rather, diplomatic activities and low-level military action in Laos should be our primary focus. Nhu and Luyen and Can, you have to make sure we do not lose Laos."

Hiep listened and her heart was filled with sadness. She looked at her brothers and realized that they seemed to have aged considerably. A terrible civil war was taking shape. She was there, in the small group of people who felt the first gusts of the coming storm.

During the lunch break Luyen told Diem and Hiep, who stood at the door looking out into the garden, "I visited Empress Nam Phuong last month at her farm in the Corrèze. She sent her greetings."

Hiep looked at Diem. His face flushed and he suddenly had that grave and melancholy look that Hiep knew so well, a particular look, which came over his features, whenever a name or a face emerged from the past, and tore at his heart.

He asked, "Was she well?" Luyen nodded, "She wanted you to know that she kept herself abreast of all the good things you have done for Vietnam and that she continues to pray for you."

Diem said as if only to himself, "In a certain way, I have betrayed her." Again Luyen nodded, but he reassured Diem, "The Empress said she knew you had no other option than to depose the Emperor in late 1955. As a matter of fact, in a recent phone conversation I had with Bao Dai, the Emperor himself recognized that you could not have done otherwise."

Hiep watched for Diem's reaction. But Diem seemed to be lost in contemplation of the butterflies that swarmed over the rose beds in the front yard. Diem had created the rose beds back in the thirties, after his resignation as a Prime Minister. Since 1944, when he left his mother's home, Can had made it a point to preserve them, as well as he could.

Hiep wondered why men like her father, Duke Nguyen Huu Bai, and Diem spent so much time watching butterflies. Was it because butterflies represented, in Vietnamese tradition, the symbol of dreams, the fragility of human endeavor and the transient character of life itself?

His promise to serve the Empress and her son was now tattered like the wings of a wounded butterfly. He had never wanted it to be that way.

Hiep looked at Luyen with reproach in her eyes. Luyen caught her look and lowered his head. He should not have mentioned the name of the Empress.

*

Burying her face in her cupped hands, Hiep cried softly. Thuan, who had rushed back from Rome, arrived only in time for the funeral of his aunt. He watched his mother's grief, helplessly. He knew how close his mother had been to Hoang. Now Hoang was gone.

The cancer was detected too late. Hiep had accompanied Hoang to Saigon for the tests, and when it was clear that Hoang had only a few months to live, Hiep had stayed in Saigon and visited her sister every day at the St. Paul's Hospital.

Almost every evening Diem came, casting aside the worries of the day to be with his sisters, praying with them, chatting with them. Together, they revisited scenes of their childhood. They talked about their childhood dreams. When they talked, Hoang seemed to forget that she was sick, and that she was going to die. She laughed and talked, talked and laughed, as if she did not have a care in the world.

Luyen, who managed to come back to Vietnam, often accompanied Diem. Sometimes Nhu also came. Luyen was delightful. He remembered the tricks he had played when Hoang was sixteen and he a little boy of nine. He was unstoppable. Hoang hit him playfully, like when he was a little kid. Nhu did not say much when he came. He seemed to be too immersed in what he had been doing during the day, and could not focus on the chatting around the sickbed.

From time to time, they would talk about politics. Hoang was still very curious about what was going on around the country and she read the newspapers more and more ravenously.

She was most interested in the negotiations between Laos and South Vietnam for economic cooperation, and the armed conflict between the Communist Pathet Lao forces and the Lao Royal armed forces. She asked Diem whether he still believed that North Vietnam would not be able to use the Laotian corridor to send troops into South Vietnam.

At times, Diem came early in the afternoon, and sat next to Hiep at the bedside talking to Hoang for hours. Diem talked about his dreams for the future. Hoang urged him on and Diem complied. He went on and on. His dreams sounded simple and feasible: a unified Vietnam, independent and democratic, its population prosperous and educated, its elite admired all over the world.

Hiep listened. She never offered a comment or posed a question. She was content to listen. For so many years, she had been deprived of this closeness with her brothers and sister. At St. Paul's Hospital, she experienced that feeling of timelessness. Apparently, neither she, nor Hoang, nor Diem, nor Nhu, nor Luyen was pressed for time. They could talk, and laugh, and reminisce forever.

No, it could not go on forever. For a while, they had hoped that a brilliant cancer expert from Paris would come to Saigon to treat Hoang. On the day of his departure from Paris, the professor was killed in a car accident.

Hoang accepted the inevitable with a rare courage. She assured her daughter, Hoang Anh, that there was no need to cry for her. In the evenings, when they all prayed aloud together, her voice was strong and clear almost to the end.

*

Hiep looked up and seeing Thuan by her side, she dried her tears and asked, "Has your father seen me crying?" Thuan shook his head. He asked himself, "Why does she need to hide even her tears?" But he knew the answer. He knew that the Ngo Dinh rarely allowed themselves to show their grief, even to those who loved them. Thuan could count on his fingers the times when he had seen his mother's tears. And then, most of the times, they were tears of joy.

CHAPTER TWENTY-THREE
FIRST SIGNS OF DANGER

On January 29, 1960, at 3:00 a.m. Communist units attacked and overran the headquarters of the Thirty-second Regiment, located at Trang Sup, six kilometers from Tay Ninh. Lieutenant-Colonel Tran Thanh Chieu commanded the Regiment.

The bad news had reached Diem when he was in Hue for the annual family reunion. The next day when Diem, his brothers, Le Xuan and Hiep met, Diem opened the reunion with a stony face. Diem explained the reasons for his disappointment: Lt. Colonel Chieu was one of the new generation of younger officers whom Diem really trusted. He was very fond of Chieu and was about to promote him once again.

What angered him was that the Vietcong would take advantage of the Lunar New Year to attack his troops, in spite of his strict orders regarding the observance of Tet celebrations. He had ordered all his troops to be on the alert, and advised his commanders to send out heavy patrols during the celebrations. He did not want his soldiers to go home on leave, and give the Communist guerrillas opportunities to attack.

The irony was that Colonel Chieu had obeyed his orders to the letter and fanned out his battalions. His soldiers were celebrating Tet by going into the jungles to look for the enemy. But Chieu was not protecting his base. All his troops were involved in a large-scale operation and almost none were left for the defense of his regiment headquarters.

The Communist attackers destroyed the communications post first, cutting communication between headquarters and Chieu. When Chieu's battalions, worried by the radio silence at Trang Sup, rushed back for the rescue, their regiment headquarters already lay in waste.

What concerned Diem most, however, was the capacity of the Vietcong to mount such an attack. He had doubted their ability to operate at battalion level. Now he knew that he had underestimated the enemy.

Sitting around the table, Diem and his brothers drew lessons from the stinging defeat. It was an isolated incident and taken in the context of the whole country, it was not very significant. Only a few days earlier, a Vietcong company had been destroyed in another province. But Trang Sup might galvanize the enemy, and boost the morale of the Vietcong troops. The Americans might start asking awkward questions about the qualifications of South Vietnamese officers, or they might even suggest the need for more American advisors.

Diem said, "Looking at the map, you see that the Vietcong are able to conduct company level operations in South Vietnam. They are unable to do so in Central Vietnam, where Can and his people have been more effective in detecting the stay-behind Communist units. This means that units sent from the North have met serious problems reaching the South."

Nhu nodded, then shrugged, "I wouldn't mind if Brother Can sent a few of his Mission Teams to the South to detect Vietcong units. In the meantime, we had better spend more resources in Laos and in the Central Highlands. We've got to stop the infiltration of North Vietnamese units."

Can did not understand why Nhu was so eager to praise his Mission Teams now. In the past Nhu had always protested against the work of the Mission Teams. According to Nhu, the teams were outside of any official chain of command and represented a threat to the discipline among intelligence services.

Diem seemed to understand why Can arched his eyebrows. He said, "There is no doubt that Central Vietnam has achieved the greatest success in isolating and capturing Communists. We recently captured a report to the Fifteenth Congress of the Workers Party. Oh, it is dated January 1959, that is a year ago; however, it is still most instructive. The report mentions that in Central Vietnam, or Zone V for them, forty percent of the Provincial committeemen were eliminated or captured between 1954 and 1958. At the same time, sixty percent of their district committee men and seventy percent of their Commune Committee men were captured, eliminated, or had rallied to the government."

Nhu followed up: "The report went on to say that in many provinces of Central Vietnam, only two to three Communist sections survived. It said that in Quang Tri and Thua Thien (Hue), out of 23,400 party members left behind in 1954, only 160 remained operational."

Diem said, "The report shows that we have taken the appropriate measures. In Central Vietnam, thanks to you, Brother Can, the situation is the best. But even in the Southern provinces only five thousand party members were reported to remain operational out of sixty thousand they left behind in 1954 after the Geneva Conference."

Can asked, "Brother Diem, now do you approve the use of Group 77?" Diem turned to the others and explained, "Group 77 is being trained under Brother Nhu's supervision, for infiltration in the North. Well, not yet. I do not want to expand the theater of operation, at this moment."

Nhu finally announced that he and his wife were ready to leave the country by year's end and that he had been busy wrapping up his affairs, and delegating more and more to his potential successors. That was not a surprise, as every year since 1957, they had been talking about that possibility.

Hiep sat and listened. It was unfortunate that the Year of the Rat had begun like that. She felt a premonition that the year would hold other unpleasant surprises. She was pleased, however, that Nhu and Le Xuan had decided to leave Vietnam for a while. That would help Diem tremendously. Their departure from Vietnam would certainly be viewed as a signal that there was no longer family *rule* in South Vietnam.

Hiep was concerned, however, that Nhu's departure would leave Diem all by himself in Saigon, in that immense Palace. Diem would feel lonely indeed.

*

It was Nhu who called. He announced laconically, "The cat and mouse game has started again." Hiep understood what he meant, so she said quickly, "Yes, I know what is going on."

Can had been telling her about this in the last two weeks. So, the American Ambassador had changed his tune. In the past weeks,

Ambassador Eldridge Durbrow repeatedly talked to Diem as if he were speaking to the head of a colony. He instructed Diem, admonished Diem, demanded this, demanded that and would not take no for an answer.

The change was quite sudden and dramatic. Until then, Durbrow had been the perfect diplomat and friend. Then, overnight everything changed. He had studied Diem, and knew in advance Diem's reactions. Now he moved against Diem. And he was deadly.

He was unlike J. Lawton Collins who wanted Diem out, but did not know how to make Diem walk into a trap. Durbrow was more like French Governor-General Pasquier who had played a deadly game of cat and mouse with Diem in 1933. Durbrow had decided to get rid of Diem, because he believed that Diem was ineffective and dictatorial.

His game consisted of making Diem lose his temper. As he knew that Diem was proud, he maneuvered in such a way to render Diem, out of pride, unable to make appropriate moves.

Learning that Diem was about to make Vice-President Nguyen Ngoc Tho concurrently his Minister of the Interior, Durbrow demanded that Diem appoint Tho to the Ministry of Interior. As a natural reaction, Diem refused to do the very thing he had planned to do.

The same thing happened with Nhu's departure. Having learned that Nhu was about to leave, Durbrow came to the Independence Palace and demanded his departure. Both Diem and Nhu then refused to comply.

Diem had wanted Nguyen Dinh Thuan to be his Minister of Defense. Again, Durbrow came to demand that Thuan be appointed. By then, however, Durbrow's game had become too obvious. Yet, Diem, out of his determination *to preserve the concept of national independence* had to postpone Thuan's appointment.

Hiep asked Nhu rather sharply, "Are you leaving Vietnam or not?" Nhu hesitated, "I don't know anymore. There are rumors of a coup d'état. The police turned up a dossier implicating some commanders of the Airborne. Brother Diem has asked me to stay on, for the moment. I myself don't want to go now. If I go now, people would say I was frightened away."

Hiep was worried. She said: "I understand your feelings; however, in a critical moment like this, both Brother Diem and you seem to allow people to play on your emotions. You are both so transparent. Isn't that dangerous?"

Nhu sounded both intrigued and irritated; he asked, "What do you want us to do?" Hiep laughed, "You should not ask for advice. You are the President's advisor. But I would suggest you do the exact opposite of what people expect you to do." Nhu said, laughing, "I will remember that and pass it on to the President."

*

On November 11, 1960, at 6:15 a.m. Thuan called and told Hiep about the coup. Thuan, since his return from Rome, was the Director of the Hoan Thien Seminary in Hue. By six o'clock that morning, Can had called Thuan to tell him that a military coup was unfolding and that he preferred to let Thuan announce the news to Hiep.

Hiep was stunned. The night before she had called Thuc in Vinh Long to wish him a happy birthday. Earlier that evening, Thuc had received phone calls from Diem and Nhu for the same reason. Nobody suspected anything.

While Hiep talked with Thuan, airborne units surrounded the Palace, and Diem's life was in danger. The more she listened to Thuan's report, the more disturbed she became. So airborne units were participating in the coup. Yet, Colonel Nguyen Chanh Thi, their commander, had been very close to Diem! Diem had been so fond of him that people had even said Thi was Diem's adopted son.

The Colonel was now commanding the troops that had lay siege to the Independence Palace? Hiep could not accept the fact. She refused to believe the information. Thi, of all people? It was Diem who had handpicked him for the command of the Airborne Brigade.

During the night, Thi and his troops arrived near the Palace and the first battle had taken place at 1:30 a.m. The fighting lasted for half an hour. Now, Thi's troops were surrounding the Palace but could not get into the Palace grounds, which were fiercely defended by the Presidential Guards.

Hiep went to her mother's home. She found Can sitting in the parlor, calmly sending out orders, and receiving information. Upon Hiep's arrival, Can went to her and reassured her, "Don't worry. We will be able to take care of this little rebellion."

He returned to his desk and came to talk to her only when he received news that was of interest to her. Hiep sat there for hours, pondering, nodding absent-mindedly to Can's aides who shuttled back and forth from his office building next door.

Hiep wondered why Can did not go to his office. There he would be closer to the sophisticated radio equipment, which had direct links to the Independence Palace. Then she realized that perhaps Can was drawing tremendous energy from the fact that he was *there,* in the house where everything had started. It was *there* that their father had started the dream. It was *there* that they came back almost every year to see how far the dream had become a reality. It was *there* that Can would do all that he could to allow the dream to go on.

At ten in the morning, Diem succeeded in broadcasting his proclamation on the radio. He asked the people to stay calm and called loyal troops to rush to Saigon to put down the rebellion. Can was perturbed. He said that Diem should not have done that, as loyal troops had already been converging on Saigon. He said that Diem should continue to negotiate with the coup leaders until the loyal troops arrived.

By noontime, all the fighting had stopped. Diem had apparently agreed to make major concessions to the coup leaders. Phan Quang Dan, one of the civilian leaders of the coup, was heard on the radio calling the people to support the Revolution.

What appeared to be bad news was hailed by Can as a great move. He said, "As long as Thi thinks he has won the day and does not lead an attack on the Palace, everything will be all right." Hiep did not know what to think. Of course, Can was feeding her only partial information, and she had to rely on his judgment and his reading of the situation. To her, the situation looked quite hopeless.

At three in the afternoon, she thought she was going to faint, when General Le Van Ty, Chief of the General Joint Staff read his announcement over the radio. "The President is giving the power to the generals to form a new government." Following the General, a Revolutionary Council member was heard encouraging the people of Saigon to participate in a demonstration the following day.

Can frowned but did not seem to be in despair. He sat down in front of Hiep and said, "Please go home now. Do not be discouraged. We are winning and they are losing, although they do not know it yet. Go home and pray. Tomorrow, there may be a big battle, if Thi does not recognize by then that he has lost. Please pray hard that there will not be any bloodshed."

Hiep went home and found Am waiting impatiently for her. Am, who had never wanted to get involved in her family affairs, had spent most of the day in the chapel praying. He asked, "What is the present situation?"

Hiep said, "The coup leaders seem to have won and the President seems to have given the power to the generals to form another government. Yet, according to Can, two divisions loyal to the President are converging on the Capital and have actually arrived in Saigon."

Am nodded. He said, "It must be the Seventh Division from My Tho, commanded by Colonel Tran Thien Khiem and the Twenty-first Division, from Bien Hoa, commanded by Colonel Nguyen van Thieu." Hiep exclaimed, "That is correct. But, how do you know?" Am laughed, as he said, "They are the nearest units. Both Thieu and Khiem are very close to the President. I wouldn't expect less from them."

Hiep went to the chapel and sat in the dark. She prayed hard for a peaceful end to the coup.

*

Two weeks after he had put down the coup, Diem returned to Hue. He found his mother quite shaken by the event. Mrs. Ngo Dinh Kha said, "It is your decision, Diem, but I would like to see you bow out of the race and not run for a second term. You have nothing to gain by staying. I am an old woman. I do not see far enough to make a good judgment. I only want to make sure that you do not end up dying tragically like your brother, Khoi."

Ngo Dinh Thi Hiep and Mrs. Ngo Dinh Kha in Hue, 1960

*

Hiep looked at Diem hoping that he would agree. Can looked neutral enough. He did not seem to care one way or the other. Diem had to make the decision whether to stay on or to quit. Can would accept Diem's decision without discussion.

Diem seemed to have thought it through before he had arrived in Hue. He stood his ground. "Mother, you know I do not attach any importance to being here or there, in power or without power. Father wanted an independent country. We now have independence for South Vietnam. Can I stop right now, and say to Father, 'I have done my best. Now I want to quit'? I don't think so. North Vietnam is not free, and the survival of the South is being seriously threatened, both by the Americans and by the Communists in Hanoi. I cannot walk away. I cannot desert now."

Mrs. Kha looked at her son and sighed, "Your father had a dream, however, he did not dream of putting all of his sons' lives in jeopardy. What happened two weeks ago shows that, as long as you stay in power, all of you are at risk. Do you want me to survive all of you? How terrible it will be for me, if some day, I have to cry at your funerals!"

Diem said, "Life and death are in God's hand. All we can do is to live and work according to our conscience." Mrs. Kha bent her head and said, "Don't ask for too many miracles from God, Diem."

Hiep looked at her mother. How much could she take? During the attempted coup d'état, she was kept informed by Can. She wanted to be told everything. She did not seem to have lost hope at any moment. Whenever Hiep popped in, her mother smiled and tried to reassure her. Yet now, it was clear that her mother had been to hell and back. She must have been expecting the worst.

Hiep said, "Brother Diem, please promise Mother that you will seriously reflect on what she has said." Diem promised, but Hiep knew that he had already made up his mind to continue with his work.

*

On Thuan An's deserted beach, Diem, Can and Hiep walked in silence. The waves were high, the water almost brown, and a chilly wind blew mercilessly, throwing wet sand in their faces. Can soon said, "I would rather go back inside." Diem looked at Hiep as if to challenge her, but she shook her head, rejecting the challenge. They walked back to Can's beach house.

Can called for tea and served Diem and Hiep, then served himself. He leaned towards Diem and said: "Mother is disturbed. We have to think of her."

"So this is the man who, according to everyone, is thirsting for power," Hiep thought. Diem did not answer him for a while. Hiep played with the teacup, turning it round and round on her fingertips. The scent of dried lotus drifted up to her nostrils, reminding her of so many cups of tea taken with her brothers and sisters.

Diem bent his head and said as if talking to himself, "I know Mother is perturbed. I am myself perturbed. The coup did not make any sense. We discover now that Thi did not lead the coup. Lieutenant-Colonel Vuong van Dong dragged him into it at the last minute. Dong came to see Thi that day and invited Thi to a party. Thi believed that he was actually going to a party while he was being driven to the coup headquarters. The coup simply did not make any sense."

Hiep asked, "Why do you keep saying that the coup did not make any sense?" Diem looked up, smiling, "I am trying to understand the leaders of the coup. There was Hoang Co Thuy, a protégé of the American Ambassador. He is an ambitious man, but has no talents to match. Lieutenant-Colonel Vuong van Dong is a good soldier, a good officer, but easily influenced by other people. All in all, the coup leaders convinced three airborne battalions to support them half-heartedly. When the coup leaders approached Colonel Soan, the commander of the Armored Brigade, after the coup had already started, he refused to participate, and they killed him. They had counted on the Armored Brigade, why I don't know."

Diem poured another cup of tea, lit another cigarette and went on, "It does not make sense to try to overthrow me with only three battalions. It does not make sense to hope that the coup would succeed when it was so poorly planned. It seems that the coup leaders believed they had more support than they actually had. Somebody convinced them that they had a great deal more military support than what they had ultimately."

Hiep waited for further explanation, but Diem lapsed into a long silence. She said impatiently, "Brother Diem, even with all its weakness and lack of organization, the coup had a chance of succeeding, didn't it?" Diem nodded, not knowing where Hiep was heading. Hiep explained, "They almost succeeded because you did not want any bloodshed. You knew they were amateurs. They did not occupy the radio station. They did not cut your telephone lines. Yet, if they had attacked the Independence Palace, you would have surrendered or you would have had to accept bloodshed."

Can told Diem, "You had better listen to her, Brother Diem." Hiep concluded, "That is why the coup makes sense to me. Either the Vietnamese behind the coup believed that even with three battalions they would succeed, because you would not fight your own troops or worse, behind the coup leaders, there were other people who wanted to test you, to see how you reacted. Now they know that you would negotiate, rather than fight. This coup may be merely the dress rehearsal for a better organized coup in the future."

Diem said, "We could have ended the coup very early in the morning of November 12. Our troops had by that time surrounded the airborne battalions. We waited, because the longer we waited, the more clearly it appeared to the coup leaders and their troops that they could not win. We thought that by waiting we would have a better chance of winning without fighting. We also waited for those who wanted to support the coup to show up. No one showed up, though."

Hiep looked up, "I hope that there will not be any witch hunt after this. I've heard that a dozen people were arrested." Diem shook his head, "A dozen had been called in to answer some questions; they were released immediately." Can added, "There will be no witch hunt. We have been fed a lot of names by various intelligence units. We have to be careful, though. It is not wise to suspect too many people. I guess brother Nhu has been given long lists of suspects. If he touches those people, we could create chaos within our own army and administration."

Diem nodded. He promised, "I will make sure that there will be no arrests and no secret files set up on the so-called suspects. I will, however, make public the evidence of the American participation in the coup."

Both Can and Hiep were aghast. Can said, "I know you have evidence against certain CIA agents and American Embassy officers. I suppose you can document their presence by the side of the coup leaders during the coup. Once you hold such information, why do you want to make it public?"

Diem argued doggedly, "They are supposed to be our allies. They are supposed to stand by our side. Yet, they were seen helping the coup leaders, even advising them on how to draft their address to be read over the radio. Isn't that betrayal? Isn't that deceit?"

Hiep asked, "What do you hope to gain by making public accusations against Ambassador Durbrow?" Diem said, "I want him to be recalled and replaced." Can followed with another question, "Don't you think that Ambassador Durbrow will be replaced anyway? The new President, John Kennedy, will certainly appoint another Ambassador to Vietnam. Why do you need to antagonize him even before he is sworn in?"

Again, Diem said, "The truth is the truth." Can, who was as hardheaded as his brother, replied, "Sooner or later the truth will come out anyway. So, why should it come out with your signature on it?"

Diem sat back. He looked at Hiep and saw that she seemed to agree with Can. He told them, "You may be right after all. General Lansdale is back. He may even be the next Ambassador. With him, this kind of nonsense will stop."

Can asked, "From here I heard all kinds of stories. Is it true that Brother Nhu threatened Mr. Carver?" Diem turned to Hiep and explained, "Carver was the American most involved in the coup." He told Can, "Nhu did not do anything of the kind. After the coup, I asked Bill Colby, the CIA Station Chief, to remove Carver. He procrastinated. Somebody who is working in our intelligence services put a threatening letter in Carver's mailbox. We escorted Mr. Carver to the airport when he left Vietnam."

Diem suddenly found that funny and laughed. Can also laughed, but Hiep did not join in. She thought, "While Brother Diem is doing so well in most everything, the Americans still stand behind a coup against him. What will they do if he begins to falter? What if he faces real problems?"

She remembered what her mother had told Diem. Diem had said, "Life and death are in God's hands." Was that an appropriate answer to a mother's anxiety? She would like to know.

*

It was Tet, and again it was time for the family reunion. But at the beginning of the Year of the Buffalo, for those present at the family meeting, all thoughts were on the creation of the National Liberation Front, which had occurred two months earlier, on December 20, 1960.

Diem said, "In itself, the establishment of the Front does not make any difference to the military and political situation. In Vietnam, everybody knows that a war is going on and that the Communists who receive direct instructions from Hanoi conduct the war.

"For foreigners, however, it is different. Journalists, politicians and scholars abroad are apparently seeing a difference between the Communists in the North, and the NLF in the South. Do they really believe there is such a difference? Or do they pretend to believe that myth? The more the myth grows, the greater is the propaganda success scored by the Communists."

Nhu showed his frustration, as the Communists were able to conduct battalion-level attacks in the Southern provinces. Diem told Nhu that everything possible should be done; including more raids into the 'safe areas' held by the Vietcong to ensure that the guerrilla units could not assemble to fight above company level.

Diem said, "Vietnam has always been at war. There have always been rebellions against the Kings and Emperors in the past. Most of those rebellions were limited in space and time; most of them caused few human losses. If we can prevent the Southern Communists from receiving reinforcements from the North, sooner or later, pitched battles at company level would stop and we would have a very minor civil war.

Nhu was asked to describe the situation of the infiltration from North to South, through Laos. According to Nhu, it was obvious that if Laos did not hold, it would be extremely difficult for South Vietnam to prevent the war from escalating in intensity. Yet everything pointed to the fact that Laos was falling apart. Intelligence reports showed that five battalions from North Vietnam had penetrated Laos while the three factions, leftist, rightist and neutralist, with their separate armies had begun waging violent combat against each other.

In spite of that, Hiep had the impression that both Diem and Nhu were optimistic about the prospects in Laos. As for the NLF, Nhu said he had been able to penetrate its highest structures. Hiep watched Nhu intently. Penetration was possible indeed. Hiep knew that Diem's government was heavily penetrated.

The rest of the day was spent on strategies for the final days of the electoral campaign. Though there seemed to be no serious contenders on the horizon, Diem wanted to be sure that he and Nguyen Ngoc Tho, the vice-presidential candidate had no surprises on April 9, the date of the elections.

*

Diem consented to celebrate Mrs. Ngo Dinh Kha's ninetieth birthday with the most solemn pomp, on September 18, 1961. The celebration rapidly became an affair of state. Every official in the country sent his or her long wishes to the matriarch of the Ngo Dinh. Nobody seemed to be aware of the incongruity, except Hiep who objected to public intrusion into a family affair.

After the Grand Mass and the lengthy ceremony that was rather too long for her, her children sat down for a chat.

Hiep took the opportunity to criticize her brothers for allowing the celebration to become a national event. She was angry, as flatterers had organized the celebration to make it similar to the Elevation of a Queen Mother. Newspapers called her *Thai Tu,* the Compassionate Highness, a title that sounded obviously imperial.

Surprisingly, her brothers did not respond to her criticisms. They understood her reservations, and saw now after the fact, how the event had gotten out of hand. Diem said, "I regret very much that I didn't listen to you earlier."

Hiep did not want to let Diem and the rest of her brothers off so easily. She had heard people say that her family assumed certain imperial prerogatives. People told her that because they knew that she would understand their good intentions. She asked Diem, "Have people told you those things?" Diem shook his head. Hiep said with a sad voice, "They cannot tell you things like that anymore, because they think you prefer to listen to flatteries."

Diem looked at her, a little bewildered. That was the first time she had launched a personal attack on him. Finally he defended himself, saying, "You know I don't like flatteries. Almost every year I have written official decrees telling people not to call me Excellency, only Mr. President. I have asked officials not to call me the *Venerable Gentleman*. But people who served the Emperors surround us. They think that to do less for me than what they did for the Emperors would mean they don't respect me enough."

Hiep sighed, "Because you do not have the courage to ask them to stop their nonsensical behavior toward you, they believe that only flatterers will find favors with you. Mr. President, do you want a republic or a monarchy?"

Only Luyen seemed to be on her side now. Thuc, Nhu and Can seemed to think that she was taunting Diem too much, and that Diem would soon explode. They started grumbling against her.

Diem sat with his hands covering his face during her last remark. He stood up and said, "When you are right, you are right, Sister. I do think that all of us (he looked at Thuc, Nhu and Can) will have to be more prudent in the future. Yes, Sister, we live in a republic, and I am an elected President, not the Emperor."

As they broke up for dinner, Diem approached Hiep. She thought that he would reproach her privately for her strong words. She burst out laughing when he pointed at a small tear on his gown and said, "Would you please mend this for me before I go back to Saigon?" In his eyes danced both amusement and affection. He said earnestly, "Don't hesitate to chastise us when we do wrong. Father gave you that responsibility."

That night, Hiep took the President's gown home with her. As she sat and mended it, she felt as if nothing had happened since the time when as children they had sat on the floor at the Grand Chamberlain's feet, listening to his words of wisdom.

Diem's gesture had filled her with amusement and pride. All the honors had not gone to his head, after all. He was still the innocent boy, running back to her when his shirt was torn, and she, though two years younger, would scold him and mend his shirt as best she could.

*

On February 7, 1962, they met again in Hue, at the beginning of the Year of the Tiger. The Tiger years always represented for Hiep a year of danger and challenges. She was prepared then for what Diem expounded: "President Kennedy has asked Ambassador Nolting to extract concessions from me that would, for all I know, make South Vietnam an American Protectorate."

Nhu said, "Apparently, the Ambassador received his marching orders from the White House sometime in November. He approached us in early December. He said that he had tried vainly to persuade President Kennedy's closest aides to change their views." Diem interrupted Nhu, "According to the message we received from Ambassador Nolting, I have to provide 'concrete demonstrations' that I will work to 'broaden the political base' of my government. I will also have to share with the Americans the responsibility of making decisions in all political, economic and military areas, as they affect the security of South Vietnam. There is no other interpretation possible. The closest aides of President Kennedy have demanded a joint United States - South Vietnamese administration." Can exclaimed angrily, "We would rather die than accept such a demand!"

Diem looked at his brothers, Hiep and Le Xuan and asked, "Did Brother Can express your own view, as well, on this?" One by one, they all raised their hand. Diem nodded gravely and went on, "We have not worked so hard to sell out our country, or at least part of our country to some arrogant bureaucrats in Washington. I have committed the terrible error of asking Brother Nhu to fight the American demands. He will be singled out for retaliation. Le Xuan, you too, will be in danger."

He smiled sadly and said, "From now on, I, personally, will be in charge of negotiations with the Americans. I don't want Brother Nhu and Le Xuan to be accused of being anti-American. They can blame me for being anti-American, if they want. But I will be the one who turns down unreasonable American demands, from now on."

Nhu objected, "In any chess game you can sacrifice the *horse* or the *cannon* but not the *chariot* or the *king*. Why do you want us to change tactics now? My wife and I are expendable; you are not."

Hiep was struck by Nhu's intensity. "So, this is the man whom some people describe as 'consumed by a thirst for power', a man who is ready to overthrow his own brother to satisfy his own ambition!"

She watched Le Xuan who frowned but did not object. Hiep felt at that moment more love than ever before for her sister-in-law.

Diem waved his hand, "Everybody is expendable, myself included. I would rather pay for my own mistakes. We now know that President Kennedy is impatient with the progress that is being made in Vietnam. We know that he and his entourage think that a guerrilla war can be won rapidly. We know that progress will be slow, the war against the Communists will take time, and we are not going to satisfy the young American President."

He lowered his head as he added; "I have, in a certain way, damaged South Vietnam's sovereignty by making my country too dependent on foreign aid. I will commit a more grievous sin: I will ask for more American aid. But this time, the aid money will not be used to expand our armed forces or build new industries. It will be used to build up Ten Thousand Strategic Hamlets. They will make it very difficult for the Communists to find shelter, food, supplies and new recruits. They will turn the Communist soldiers into 'fish out of water'."

He looked at Nhu a minute and said, "I will give you the task of overall supervision of the Strategic Hamlet Program."

*

Less than three weeks after their family reunion in Hue, two aircraft piloted by officers of the Vietnamese Air Force, bombed the Independence Palace. The entire left wing where the Nhu's lived was heavily damaged. Le Xuan was injured, and a Chinese amah who took care of Le Quyen, the Nhu's baby, was killed. Thuc was in the palace when the attack took place.

Thuc later told Hiep that for the first time since 1954, he had seen fear in Le Xuan's eyes. Hiep easily understood the fear. The bombing targeted the left wing of the Palace, exactly where the Nhu's lived. The pilots clearly wanted to eliminate the Nhu's. Though the entire attack only lasted ten minutes, from 7:15 to 7:25 that morning, to the Nhu's it seemed like an eternity.

The Navy in Nha Be shot down the plane piloted by Pham Phu Quoc, at 7:35, and Quoc who bailed out of his plane in time, was captured. The other plane, piloted by Nguyen van Cu, the son of a VNQDD (Vietnam People's Party) leader, escaped safely to Phnom Penh.

Diem decided to move to the Gia Long Palace. Smaller and more vulnerable, Gia Long Palace seemed to invite a coup. Hiep had the feeling that an immense trap was slowly closing on her brothers.

*

From July 2 to 23, 1962, the Geneva Conference on Laos took place. It was convened by the United Kingdom and the Soviet Union, and attended by four neutral states (Burma, India, Cambodia and Laos), five pro-Western States (The United States, South Vietnam, France, Thailand and Canada), and two Communist states (The People's Republic of China and the Democratic Republic of Vietnam).

The Agreements signed on July 23 made Laos a neutral country and allowed the Pathet Lao to participate in the government, which was to be a coalition government.

Nhu attended the Conference. He attempted to make the Americans understand that by allowing Laos to become neutral, the United States would be party to a rapid deterioration of the military posture of South Vietnam and endanger its security.

Averell Harriman, the artisan of the Geneva Agreements, found the South Vietnamese to be hostile to the United States' interests. He was to become the most ardent enemy of Ngo Dinh Diem, in the Kennedy Administration. Nhu and Diem, on separate occasions told Hiep that in spite of all American assurances, troops from North Vietnam would soon start pouring through Laos into South Vietnam, and the war would escalate.

*

They finished visiting the restored Tu Hieu Pagoda and, apologizing to the Abbot; Diem said that he wanted to walk around the Pagoda with

450

members of his family. The Abbot was a little worried about the security of the President, but Diem laughed and said the he was well protected. Indeed, though Diem had forbidden troops to be brought into the pagoda, a whole battalion was deployed around the site, while bodyguards discretely stood at regular intervals inside its walls.

Can said that he could not walk too much and that he would wait for them back at their mother's house. Diem, Hiep and Thuan walked leisurely along the paths they knew so well.

Tu Hieu Pagoda was where the names of the distant Ngo Dinh ancestors, down the line to his great-grand fathers, all of them Buddhists, were honored. The Pagoda, which had been built at the beginning of the Nineteenth Century, was renovated almost entirely under Emperor Thanh Thai, who visited it quite frequently. It was during one of the visits made by the Emperor, that Ngo Dinh Kha, who was accompanying him decided to have his ancestors honored at the Tu Hieu Pagoda.

From that time onwards, the family was a sustaining member of the pagoda and contributed every year for its maintenance. Diem and Hiep, in their childhood, as well as later, as adults, had visited the Pagoda many times.

Early in 1962, Can had reported to Diem that the whole wooden roof as well as the tall wooden pillars needed to be replaced. Diem immediately sent money to help. The rafters were replaced, the pillars were rebuilt, and Diem was appreciative of the care brought into the detail by the artisans who did the renovation work.

Now walking along the familiar paths around the Pagoda, Diem asked Hiep, "Do you remember the poem written by Prince Tung Thien in honor of the founder of this Pagoda?" Hiep told her son, Thuan, "It is the usual test, you see. The President has always asked me to say the poem, each time we come here. Smiling, Hiep recited:

"In the mountains, in the rainy and windy night,

He sat upright deep in serene meditation,

Whoever comes to this temple,

Will feel transported by the sounds of the bell

High into the blue sky."

Diem told Thuan, "This Pagoda has a lot to do with our family. The names of our ancestors are honored here. Emperor Thanh Thai was its sponsor. Minister Cao Xuan Duc, one of the closest friends of your grandfather, wrote the text on the marble stela behind the Pagoda in the cemetery of the Eunuchs."

Diem asked Hiep, "Do you find peace when we come here?" Hiep answered softly, "More than peace. This is a hidden jewel. It is so beautiful here. The half-moon shaped lake built under Emperor Khai Dinh, the Tombs of Prince Tung Thien, and the Consort of Prince Nguyen Phuoc Hoat, the stupas of the Abbots...I like the pine covered hill, the stream which runs among the pine trees..."

Diem sighed, "It is regrettable that we do not have time any more to come here and spend a whole day visiting the place, reading the steles, or simply walking around in this little universe filled with the history of our country."

Hiep said, "Then, let us enjoy this hour. I will show Thuan our favorite places where as children, we played hide and seek." But of course, they did not have an hour, and she could not show Thuan anything. Soon enough, an adjutant approached and told Diem that he had to see the Government Delegate at his mother's home within less than half an hour.

Little did they know that time was catching up with them, and that there would be no more tranquil days for them to spend together. They did not know that they were already at the entrance of the maelstrom that was soon to send them whirling into the final catastrophe.

PART FIVE

A TIME TO DIE

CHAPTER TWENTY-FOUR
THE YEAR OF THE CAT:
THE BEGINNING OF THE END

It was the *Year of the Cat*, Hiep's year of birth. As they met for the annual family reunion, her brothers and sisters and she did not know that it was to be the last.

The meeting opened on a sad note. Three weeks earlier, on January 2, 1963, a Vietcong battalion had soundly defeated the far superior South Vietnamese forces in the battle of Ap Bac, at the Plain of Reeds, near the Cambodian border.

The battle was an initiative from General Huynh Van Cao, recently made Corps Commander on the first of January, who wanted to offer to Diem, on the eve of his birthday, a 'Meaningful Present'. Ap Bac was where the Vietcong had installed a major radio center. Cao was so sure of scoring a big victory that he sent his people to Saigon to tell Diem of the upcoming present. The battle turned into a tragedy.

When the action was over, the body count was grim: sixty-five soldiers of the national army dead and one hundred more wounded. The Vietcong left 101 bodies on the battlefield.

Diem was disconsolate. He said, "The war is escalating. We have to find effective ways to stop this hemorrhage. Neither we nor the North can afford to fight a big war."

He turned to Hiep and said, "What also needs to be said is that the Vietnamese units were supported by American air support. Besides, accompanying our troops into the battle were fifty-one American advisors.

The Americans also sustained terrible losses: three advisors killed, six more wounded, five helicopters destroyed and eleven more damaged. This is our war. Why should those young men die? Our country has been at war since 1945, yet each death is devastating for a family. America is far away. It has no obvious interests here in Vietnam. If more and more Americans die, we will hear, in the United States, a vast clamor against continued American involvement. The families will want to get their children and their men back to safety, out of Vietnam. We have to find ways to reduce American casualties. Maybe, the Americans should no longer be active in combat situations."

Nobody said anything in response to his uneasiness. Diem sighed, "I am not only thinking of the political consequences. I am heartbroken when I visualize an American dying and not understanding the reason for his death."

He turned to Nhu and said, "Please tell the Americans that I want to take all the American soldiers and advisors out of combat situations. I want them to train our armed forces, not to fight our war."

He stopped speaking, but nobody wanted to say anything, because they knew that Diem was thinking about what he would say next. Hiep understood now what Am had told her much earlier in the game. He had told her to stay out of the family's political discussions. She had never thought that one day she would sit with her brothers and Le Xuan, talking about subjects with such enormous consequences.

She looked at Diem, seeing that his horizons had been expanding vertiginously since he had assumed power in 1954. He now carried upon his shoulders the responsibility of war and peace, victory and defeat, alliances and loss of alliances. He was responsible for all the deaths on the battlefield, both Vietnamese and non-Vietnamese.

Diem resumed, "We have to make the Communists decrease the level of the fighting. In order to achieve that, I will have our troops prevent the enemy from assembling large units in any one single area. We know how the enemy assembles troops at assembly points and where those points are. We have to be able to prevent their small units from converging to assembly points to attack us at battalion strength."

Nhu sounded meditative, "The French used artillery. Every evening, their cannon fired round after round at suspected assembly points. We remember the ritual *sunset salute*. Now we use infantry and Special Forces to go in and mess up their assembly points, more dangerous for our troops, but more effective. Our Strategic Hamlet Program will help liberate all our regular units from village defense duties. Our regular army will consequently become increasingly mobile. We are now carrying several operations into the enemy *'safe zones.'* Soon, there will be no more safe zones for them."

Le Xuan, who had been questioning the media's reporting of the Ap Bac battle, tried to prove that the battle of Ap Bac was, in fact, a victory and not a defeat. While she talked, Diem looked out of the open window, absent-mindedly. Obviously, he did not approve of Le Xuan's comments. He was a realistic man who disliked any efforts aimed at distorting the truth. Le Xuan's comments generated a heated debate. Can and Luyen were not at all in agreement with their sister-in-law.

Diem sat in silence, trying to control his temper. Finally, he waved his hand and asked everybody to stop and to listen to him. He said, "The Ap Bac battle was a test. That was the first time we had helicopters, artillery and armor combined with ground troops to encircle the enemy. Yet, after we sustained heavy casualties, the enemy managed to escape. During the battle, our units shot at each other. The test did not go the way General Cao expected, and obviously it was not a victory. Together with our generals, we will draw the appropriate lessons from it. I do not want us to spend time inventing an apology for Ap Bac." He looked at his brothers and sisters and said with emphasis, "It is more essential that we spend our time discussing the more important issues."

Can asked, "What do you propose as principal themes for discussion this year?" Diem smiled a little sadly as he listed the difficult agenda: "The eternal question of national independence, the approaches to improved relations with the United States, while preserving national sovereignty, and how to defeat the Communists without paying too high a price in human lives."

Diem's eyes were almost closed, as if he was trying to remember something from the past. He pursued, "As long as South Vietnam is independent, and as long as our sovereignty is preserved, we have a chance of defeating the Communists. Yet, the moment we lose our sovereignty, our struggle will be without a cause, and the people will abandon us."

Nhu frowned and demanded that Diem be a little more specific. Diem explained, "In my recent tours of the provinces, I have noticed the increasing power of the American advisors on our local government. As long as they are only advising, I have no complaints. It has been made clear to me, however, that the advisors are determining what level of U.S. assistance a province will get. That fact makes the advisors more powerful than our local officials.

Nhu asked sharply, "If that is what you see, what do you propose to do then?" Diem looked up at the picture of his father and said, "We have to ask the Americans to remove their advisors from the provinces. If we want our country to remain independent, we need to act quickly."

Hiep raised the obvious question, "Why did you allow the Americans to put advisors at the provincial levels, in the first place?" Diem was quick to answer, "At the time, I thought that the American advisors would only act as advisors. Now they are assuming increasing control of the provinces. Please remember that I never asked the Americans to bring so many advisors into South Vietnam."

Hiep continued with her questions, "Are you sure that the Americans really want to place themselves above your local officials? Or are the Vietnamese officials to be blamed? Aren't they the ones who, instead of making decisions themselves, prefer to let American advisors take the responsibility?"

Diem conceded that there were cases where incapable province chiefs had relied on American advisors and preferred not to be responsible for making decisions. He then said that he had seen too many cases where American advisors used U.S. assistance to wrestle decision-making power from the hands of the Vietnamese officials.

Hiep was not satisfied with the answer. She asked, "Do you think that American advisors do that because they are individuals who enjoy power, or because they are implementing a general policy?"

Diem nodded, "I like your question. It clarifies the situation for me. Let me say that at the beginning, when I started noticing this practice, I thought it was only some isolated incidents. But then, when I focused on the issue, I realized that the practice was widespread. It did not come from individuals, but rather, from a policy. Provincial advisors have obviously received instructions to use economic assistance as a weapon to take the control of the provinces away from our officials."

Hiep turned to all the others and remarked, "No treaty has been signed between the United States and Vietnam to allow this to happen. The question of advisors at the provincial level should be discussed as part and parcel of an alliance agreement with the United States."

Nhu shook his head; "We have tried to broach this subject with the Americans so many times already. The Americans have always said that they could not enter any kind of alliance with us, as that would constitute an infringement on the Geneva Agreements."

Hiep asked, "Then, the presence of the Americans, especially at the level it has reached now, is illegal?" Nhu nodded, "That is correct. According to the terms of the agreements of the Five-sided Protocol of 1950, signed by the United States, France, the State of Vietnam, Laos and Cambodia, the Americans could have a maximum of two hundred military and civilian personnel for all the three countries of Indochina. Today, here in Vietnam alone, there are more than two thousand advisors. The Protocol is completely outdated, yet, the Americans have repeatedly refused to sign any new protocol with us."

There was a long silence following Nhu's answer. Then Hiep asked again, "So, Brother Diem, you propose now to ask the Americans to remove their advisors from the provinces. What do you think their reaction will be to that demand?"

Nhu volunteered to answer, as Diem did not respond immediately, "The moment for this move is ill chosen. Certain high-ranking American officials at the State Department and at the White House did not like our attitude at the Geneva Conference on Laos. They may choose to see this demand of ours as another act of defiance." Diem added: "We have to act, even though we know that we have powerful enemies in the Kennedy Administration."

Hiep commented, "It seems that your objection to American policy goes beyond the matter of American advisors at the provincial level. Am I right?" Diem nodded. He lit a cigarette and drew on it for a moment, then started talking. His eyes became a little dreamy and his voice was softer than usual, "South Vietnam is independent. It became independent after a series of little wars.

"If we had not eliminated the warlords and abolished the Imperial Domain, South Vietnam would still be a feudal state under French rule. If we had not booted General Le van Vien out of Saigon and deposed Emperor Bao Dai, Vietnam would have fallen under Communist rule."

Diem crushed his half-consumed cigarette in an ashtray on the table, reached out and took up his cup of jasmine tea. He turned the cup on the tips of his fingers, "There are myth inventors out there who have created all kinds of myths about the role of the Americans in our success."

He smiled and went on, "My appointment by Emperor Bao Dai as Prime Minister in 1954 is now said to have been the result of American pressure. You all know how that appointment came about. Both Nguyen De and Bao Dai, who did not have any reason to like me, made that decision. They were the only ones responsible for that appointment. Why did they do it? Patriotism, I guess. The situation was desperate. They saw that nobody else would be able to reverse the situation."

Hiep listened and was struck by Diem's words. He was not an old man reminiscing. He was offering them the best interpretation he could come up with, of the events that had occurred since 1954.

She wondered, "Why now? Why does he have to do it now?" Then she realized that her father, Duke Nguyen Huu Bai, and her brother, Khoi, had always done that when they were about to do something important. She remembered how far back in the past they used to go in order to better understand what action they must take in the present. Hiep suddenly realized that Diem was about to fight the most decisive battle of his life.

Diem went on, "When I returned to Vietnam, the French troops were demoralized after their defeat at Dien Bien Phu. The Vietnamese citizens were preparing themselves for a Communist takeover. Did the Americans know much about Vietnam at that time? The answer is no. The Eisenhower Administration, who had not chosen to prevent the French humiliation at Dien Bien Phu, only understood vaguely where the American interests lay during the Geneva Conference."

Luyen nodded and added, "Neither Dulles, nor Bedell Smith offered any American initiative. Vietnam was partitioned. The initiative came from the Chinese and the French. I was there, I know."

Nhu interrupted his brothers, "In the first months of Brother Diem's rule, the Americans had no 'Vietnam Policy.' Dulles thought he had to do something quickly, to stop the expansion of Communists in Asia. He created SEATO or the South East Asia Treaty Organization, to protect South East Asia from Communist aggression. Strangely, the countries that needed the protection, South Vietnam, Cambodia and Laos, were not signatories of the Treaty. Actually, SEATO was a paper tiger."

Diem went on, "In South Vietnam, General Collins allied himself with French General Ely and repeatedly demanded my removal from office. The Americans provided military advisors to replace the French advisors. They gave us some economic assistance and, like the French, they were most generous in helping to transport refugees from North Vietnam to the South. Politically, the one American who really wanted to help us was Colonel Lansdale."

Nhu added, "After we unified the national army, eliminated the warlords, and got the last French military units to leave the country definitively, we were reasonably proud of what we had achieved. We had achieved independence for South Vietnam. But then, two major problems emerged: we had to fight the Communist terror, because the Communists had left cadres and party members in the South to cause trouble, and to use whatever means at their disposal to facilitate the final takeover of the South by Hanoi. In order to fight Communist terrorists effectively, we needed more American assistance. As we received more assistance from the Americans, their influence in South Vietnam increased. That has been our second major problem."

Diem broke in "At the end of the Eisenhower Administration, Ambassador Durbrow tried to force us to adopt the American model of democracy. I told him: "We cannot not afford to do that, first, because we are Vietnamese, not Americans, and second, because we are fighting a war." He did not like my answer. He encouraged Vietnamese officers to make a coup d'état. I think that he only wanted to give me a warning. He could have made a much larger coup. American agents had contacted several generals and colonels who at the last minute did not participate in the coup."

Luyen recalled: "Then Durbrow had to go, and Ambassador Nolting came in. President Kennedy wanted him to be friendly with Brother Diem. Yet, the first thing the Kennedy Administration did was to ask for joint decision-making, joint administration. In a certain sense, the Kennedy Administration was asking us to accept a *de facto* status of an American Protectorate"

Diem smiled a little sadly, "We successfully rejected that pretension at the time, and the Americans began to suggest a 'close partnership' instead of a joint administration. Today, three years later, the American President, who is young and intelligent, assisted as he is by several brilliant men, thinks that he knows everything about Vietnam and once again is trying to impose the concept of joint administration on us."

Hiep asked, "You say the young American President *thinks* he knows everything about Vietnam. Are you implying that he doesn't?" Diem did not dodge the question; he replied, "He doesn't, unfortunately. Reports he has been receiving from his aides are not reliable. People who barely know the location of our country have written some of them. Ambassador Nolting is a friend and an honorable man. But his voice has become more and more isolated."

Hiep asked, "Officially, what is the American general policy regarding Vietnam, at this moment?" Diem said, "Officially, President Kennedy and his aides want us to have a partnership in decision-making. I have tried to understand that concept, but alas it is beyond my understanding. For me, to surrender half of our decision-making power means to surrender half of our sovereignty. I simply cannot accept that demand."

Nhu told Diem, "It may be too late for us to pull back, though. We have already committed two major errors with the Americans. First, we have received more and more assistance from them: In 1960, aid amounted to only US$ 209 million; in 1961 it rose to US$ 287 million, and this year, it may rise over US$ 300 million. Second, we have accepted too many advisors: In 1951 we had 342 military advisors, and now we have almost two thousand of them. Since last year, we have launched the Strategic Hamlet Program that will cost us no less than two billion dollars to complete. The U.S. participation in that program would increase the level of assistance tremendously."

Diem shrugged, "I know it is rather late. That is why we have to roll back both the American aid and the American advisors."

Hiep looked at Diem, touched by the gentle, sad expression on his tired face. Years later, Hiep would remember that smile. Diem might have seen at that moment, on that day, a glimpse of what was to happen next and he had that sad smile because he knew he had no choice but to accept the coming disaster.

Around the table, Hiep saw her brothers and Le Xuan grow tense as they prepared themselves for the battle of their lives. Neither they, nor Hiep knew that it was the last time that they would have a family reunion together under the portrait of the Grand Chamberlain.

Rising to the occasion, when she was asked to give her thoughts towards the end of the meeting, Hiep said: "You have ruled this country for nine years. You have achieved many things. You have created a Republic out of a declining monarchy. You have united a country that was ravaged by warlords who preyed on their little fiefdoms and brought the nation to the brink of disaster. You have taken over a partitioned country, ravaged by years of war, burdened by a million refugees, and turned it into a prosperous land, with all the refugees decently resettled. You have built all the institutions of a modern and democratic country…. Yet, at this time, you should not look at your achievements. You should look at what you have left undone. My fear is that unlike when you assumed power in 1954, when you had nothing on your side and were faced with enemies, who had everything on their side, you now have many things you can count as your possessions.

"You have a powerful ally in the United States. You can also claim that most of the American allies are also your allies. Yet now, you cannot really count on the United States that does not seem to approve of you, and that may want to bring you down. You should not count on your other allies, because if the Americans withdraw, none of the other allies will remain on your side.

"You have a strong army. Yet, you constantly hear rumors that its leaders may be plotting for your overthrow, with the help of your 'ally'.

"You have plenty of financial resources now. Most of those financial resources depend on the good will of your great ally. Because you hold the keys to the treasury, the common people easily believe rumors of your graft and corruption.

"You hold all the political power in your hands, so people accuse you, with reason, that the regime is dictatorial. We know that you want to liberalize the regime as soon as you can do it safely. But the people don't know or don't want to believe your intentions.

"My concern is that you have forgotten Father's teachings that continue to be valuable. His strategies were based on meager resources, on poverty, on using weakness against strength. You are now planning your strategies like powerful men, rich men. Your strategies are based on power, on strength. Your power is unfortunately not yours entirely; your strengths are only strengths on the surface.

"You claim a hundred thousand Can Lao Party members. You have not talked privately with more than a dozen of them. You claim two million members in the National Revolutionary Movement, yet you have not really seen any of them except in mass demonstrations.

"I am afraid, that when time comes for you to call on your followers, there will be no response."

Nhu was about to answer her, when Diem shook his head. They sat in silence for a moment, and then Diem thanked her and ended the meeting.

*

None of them had guessed that a series of events was about to take place in Hue; in their native City, and that those events would have a determining effect on the survival of Diem's regime.

One day in March, Can stopped Hiep as she was about to leave their mother's home after her daily visit. He asked her to sit down and said he needed to talk to her.

He called for tea, and while they sipped a cup of fragrant jasmine tea, he seemed unsure of how to broach the subject. Hiep was amazed at times by the shyness of her brothers. They always seemed to have problems with beginning a conversation.

Finally, Can said, "I am worried. For many days I have kept this information to myself but I may have been wrong in doing so."

Hiep did not say anything. She sat back and waited for Can to tell her what was bothering him. Can did not look up. He seemed to be struggling with himself. He shook his head as if discouraged, "If I had stayed out of politics, everything would have been clear. A friend is a friend; an enemy is an enemy. Now, I don't know anymore. You see, the Venerable Thich Tri Quang has been a close friend of mine. I have also considered him as a comrade-in-arms, a trusted ally. Two weeks ago, Mr. Ung Trao dropped by to have a chat."

Ung Trao, great-grandson of Emperor Minh Mang, was Can's godfather. He lived in a house across the street, from Mrs. Ngo Dinh Kha's home. In the front yard of his house, stood the statue of the Blessed Tong Viet Buong, Officer of the Imperial Guards, Martyr. Tong Viet Buong was Ung Trao's great-grandfather on his mother's side.

Can asked Hiep, "Do you know Vinh Thao, his adopted grandson?" Hiep vaguely remembered the young boy. She nodded. Can said, "He is actually an illegitimate son of Judge Hoang Huu Khac. The Judge and Mr. Ung Trao have been the closest of friends. When the Judge had a son born out of wedlock, he asked his friend to adopt and raise him."

Hiep nodded, trying not to lose interest. She did not understand where Can was going with all of this apparently unrelated detail. Can went on, "Two weeks ago, Judge Hoang Huu Khac told Mr. Ung Trao that he was resigning from the Board of Directors of the Buddhist Studies Association of which the Venerable Thich Tri Quang is Secretary General. He said that he had to resign, because he had found a recent letter sent to Tri Quang by the Venerable Thich Tri Do from Hanoi urging Tri Quang to use every means in his power to bring down Brother Diem."

Hiep sat up. The last words Can said snapped her to attention She shivered. Somehow she had immediately believed in the truth of Khac's information. She said, "That means Hanoi will try to use Buddhism against Brother Diem. Isn't that a little far-fetched and ridiculous? Brother Diem has been known as a great sponsor of the Buddhist revival in Vietnam."

Can nodded, but he was not so sure, "People who know Brother Diem well are aware of his great respect for Buddhism. But the people, who do not know him well, only see him as a Catholic. Many Buddhists can be easily persuaded that South Vietnam, with a large non-Christian population, does not need a Catholic President."

Hiep could only agree with Can's reply. She asked him, "Do you think that the Venerable Tri Quang will obey his old teacher and start fighting the government now?"

Can hesitated, "Let us suppose that the letter to the Venerable Tri Quang does exist, then I am inclined to think that Tri Quang would certainly try to use Buddhists against the government. He would have to do that, because there exists in the Buddhist structure, plenty of underground Communists. If Tri Quang received a letter from Thich Tri Do, the underground Communists within the Buddhist structures must have also received the same instructions. Tri Quang cannot fight against his own structures."

Hiep asked, "Can you be more specific?" Can reminisced, "In the thirties, after he resigned as a Prime Minister, Brother Diem lived here in this house for eleven years. During that time, I watched him help Le Dinh Tham to reorganize the Buddhist structures. Tham was to become the most influential lay Buddhist, first in Central Vietnam and then nation-wide. Tham is now in Hanoi. He is directing all the Communist chapters among the Buddhist populations. The Venerable Thich Tri Do is merely a contact person, a leader of the second rank."

Hiep smiled within herself. Can had made a mistake there. She remembered that Diem had helped Le Dinh Tham even earlier than that. During the time he was in Binh Thuan as Chief of Province, Diem had come to Hue frequently. On one of those visits, he had taken Hiep and Thuan to various pagodas. On their way back, he sighed and said, "I may have made a big mistake in helping Le Dinh Tham. I want to see a real revival of Buddhism, but he seems to be more interested in transforming Buddhism into a political force."

Can's news worried her very much. She asked, "Do you know how strong the Communists are inside the Buddhist structures?"

Can shrugged, "In 1947, after the debacle following the Battle of Hue, Communist cadres from Hue disappeared into the Buddhist pagodas and temples all over the province, to escape the French dragnet. They survived the Indochina War. In 1954, not many of them were regrouped and sent to the North. They stayed behind. All these years, I have been careful not to touch them, even though I have destroyed most of the underground Communists elsewhere. I have not touched them because I don't want to be seen as anti-Buddhist."

Hiep asked, "In that case, the Venerable Tri Quang has at his disposal, a significant reserve of manpower if he taps into the Communist chapters."

Can looked at Hiep a moment and smiled, "Yes, if Tri Quang is himself a Communist. But let us suppose that he is not a Communist: he may think that by obeying the directive from Hanoi, he will become a national leader, a powerful man. He then will use the Buddhist structures, infiltrated as they are, for his own personal purpose. I would not want to be in his shoes, though. I have rarely seen anybody deceive or betray the Communists and survive."

Hiep asked, "What do you plan to do now?" Can replied, "I know that I have to report this matter to Brothers Diem and Nhu. Somehow I feel that if Tri Quang turns against us, we will have a very messy situation on our hands."

CHAPTER TWENTY-FIVE
HOW TO START A HOLY WAR

It was very early in the morning when Diem arrived in Hue. Hiep, knowing that her mother's house would be full of officials, decided not to make her usual daily visit. In the afternoon, Diem called Hiep on the phone.

Diem had come to Hue to celebrate the twenty-fifth anniversary of Thuc's Episcopal Ordination. Am and Hiep, though wishing Thuc a most happy anniversary, were feeling that once again a private family matter had become an official public celebration. They did not boycott Thuc's anniversary, but were not particularly enthused with the elaborate preparations either.

When Diem called, Hiep's mind was preoccupied with two concerns. First, Diem had told her at the Lunar New Year that he wanted to wrestle back sovereignty by asking the Americans to pull out their advisors at the provincial level. Hiep wanted to know what the American reaction had been.

Second, she was really worried about her recent conversation with Can when he told her that trouble might come from Thich Tri Quang. She wanted to know what Diem had done with the information.

Diem tried to reassure her. Yet, Hiep felt that Diem was quite tense. Nhu, who had called her on the phone the previous day, had told her that Diem knew the Americans would do something drastic to retaliate, in the near future.

Hiep said, "What you see and what the Americans see are two different things. Unless you spend the time to thoroughly explain your view about national independence, the Americans will interpret your efforts as unfriendly and hostile."

Diem said with a laugh, "Many of my American visitors have already complained about my long monologues. If I tried to talk any more, they would say that I am senile."

Yet, Diem did not want to put down the receiver. Hiep asked him, "What is the matter?" Diem told her, "The people who were behind the coup of 1960 are now being mobilized again. I told you that November 1960 was merely a dress rehearsal, or a warning. Now, if a coup takes place, it will succeed, unless I agree to suppress it in a blood bath."

Hiep sighed, "I know that you will never agree to have your defenders shoot at your own soldiers and officers." Diem agreed with Hiep's opinion. He replied, "Yes, I will not have different elements of our armed forces shooting at each other. The armed forces were created for the defense of the country, not for the defense of the President."

Hiep remembered that nine years earlier she had asked Diem to step down because she saw he would never use force to defend himself. She knew that someday, someone would see and take advantage of that weakness in Diem's armor.

Diem had stayed on. Now, somehow he had accepted the view that he himself was *dispensable*. He would never use loyal troops to defend himself against those who rebelled against him. Hiep wanted to scream. She knew that if a coup took place, Diem would first try to negotiate, and then would call loyal troops back to Saigon to show the rebel forces they were outnumbered. Hiep knew that if she understood that point, Diem's enemies had certainly understood it, too.

Choked by emotion, Hiep said, "There is another option, Mr. President. You may want to announce that you will not seek re-election and plan to retire after the end of this term of office."

Diem replied candidly, "I have thought of that option. But it is not really an option. I look around me trying to identify my replacement. I only see ambitious second-rate politicians, who have not done anything for the people, and whose only purpose is the pursuit of honors. I have even looked at the generals. What I see there is not encouraging either. Any one of my potential replacements would not have the courage to uphold national sovereignty, against American demands. As I have said before, once we lose sovereignty, we no longer have a *just cause*, and the Communists will win."

Hiep asked anxiously, "Does that mean that you will stay there until a coup kills you?" Diem did not hesitate a minute before he answered, "If that is what awaits me, fate will find me ready. I cannot desert my responsibilities now. If only we can last a little longer, we may win. I will have to do everything in my power to last until the Strategic Hamlet Program pays off, until the Communists see they have no way to win the war and desist from further attacking us."

What Diem said made sense, but Hiep knew that she should hang up before she started crying. She said, "Take good care of yourself, Mr. President. We will see you today and tomorrow at the jubilee celebrations." She did not know that the drama, which would soon engulf her family, would not begin in Saigon where Diem and Nhu lived, but right in Hue, only a mile from where she lived. She did not know that the plans for Diem's downfall were already in place the day she was celebrating her birthday that year, with her family.

*

On May 4, 1963, the twenty-fifth anniversary of Ngo Dinh Thuc's Episcopal ordination, his Silver Jubilee, Hiep attended the Mass he celebrated at the new Redeemer's Church, but she was not very happy with the way the event had been organized. There had been too much needless spending for such an event. In view of the situation, Hiep even resented Thuc's lack of sensitivity.

Yet, Thuc was the eldest brother, and she could not criticize him too much. She was also mollified by the seriousness of his medical condition. For years, he had been suffering from diabetes, and now his health was fast deteriorating.

Hiep had the impression that everything seemed to be spinning out of control. She wanted to scream and tell her brothers that the end was near, and that they should be careful in every little thing they did. She wanted to sit down and analyze with them what should be done and what should not be done, like they had done at the beginning of Diem's rule.

She knew, however, that they had no more time for analysis. She knew they were like exhausted people standing helplessly on a broken raft, moving swiftly through the dangerous rapids towards an unknown precipice.

Was that what had paralyzed Diem the year before, and made him agree to preside over the unreasonable celebration of their mother's ninetieth birthday? A sense of helplessness dictated by a vague awareness of inevitable doom? A premonition, which said that no matter what you did, however you did it, you were heading toward a crushing defeat, a final catastrophe?

She had watched Diem for the last couple of days. He seemed impervious to the danger that had been created by Thuc's celebrations. He seemed to think that it was normal that every official in the country had sent good wishes to Thuc, and that the celebrations were extravagant.

Now, Diem had left, and the well-wishers from out of town had left. Hiep got up and told Thuc that it was time for her to go home. As Thuc accompanied Hiep to the door, she told him, "A celebration like this will not benefit Brother Diem right now." Thuc smiled, exactly like Diem had, when she had criticized the extravaganza of their mother's ninetieth birthday. Thuc said apologetically, "I know. But all the bishops and the priests, the dioceses and officials said that they could not do less."

Hiep shook her head; "We are making more and more blunders, when we can no longer afford to make any. One of these days, all of this will come back to haunt us." Thuc looked at his sister. Only *she* dared criticize him. Only she could level criticisms against him without making him angry. She was right, of course. He swallowed hard and said, "I have asked people to make every trace of this celebration disappear by tomorrow."

Hiep nodded approval and left. At the gate, she looked back. Thuc was still standing at the door looking out, his tall, dark body framed by the light inside the house. How lonely her brother had been during his entire life. And now, he was so sick that he could die at any time. How could she be so heartless, to deny him a day of celebration for his silver jubilee? How could she, with her criticisms, spoil perhaps the last great day of his lonesome life?

Yet she knew that her Brother Diem's fate, and the fate of the First Republic, had been further endangered by the celebrations in Hue.

*

It was late in the evening. Thuc sat down heavily. He looked tired. He should not have come. Every year at Hiep's birthday he had called but never came. He knew that Hiep preferred to celebrate her birthdays with only her husband and her children. But Thuc had felt so lonely that he had to come.

In the afternoon, he had gone to visit Gia Hoi parish, on the left side of the Perfume River. On his way, he noticed a tremendous number of Buddhist flags on the streets. He felt angry, not because of Buddhists flying the Buddhist flags, but because in the past few years, the game of the flags had become progressively more annoying. Diem had decreed in 1962, that religious flags should not fly above the national flag and that they should not be used outside of religious sites.

The decree was not against the Buddhists, but against the Catholics, who had celebrated with too much enthusiasm, the Feast of the Immaculate Conception, which was also the Feast of Our Lady of La Vang. On that day, August 15,1962, Diem who had come to attend the pilgrimage in La Vang, sixty miles north of Hue, had noticed that the Vatican flags could be seen all along the highway.

Diem suspected the zeal of flatterers among local officials. How many times had he had seen the Vatican flags being waved by people who were not Catholics! Province chiefs, who had wanted to flatter him, had distributed those flags to non-Christian demonstrators. Each time he was subjected to that sort of spectacle, Diem had shown his anger. Sometimes he even refused to leave his plane if he saw too many Vatican flags at the airport.

When he had returned to Saigon after the celebration in La Vang, he sent out that decree, exhorting people to honor the national flag and asking the citizens to use some discipline in flying religious flags.

Understanding Diem's point of view, Thuc had been very careful with the Vatican flags. In late October 1962, Thuc was to inaugurate the new Redeemer's Church, next to the Monastery of the Redeemer. On the eve of the inauguration, Thuc rode past the Church. Noticing Vatican flags in the streets around the Monastery, Thuc stopped his car, went in to see the Superior of the Monastery and demanded that the flags in the streets be removed. He said that he would not come the next morning to bless the Church, if the Vatican flags displayed in the streets were not removed.

In the afternoon, when he saw the Buddhist flags in the streets he was frustrated. Neither the Catholics nor the Buddhists seemed to care about the decree that Diem had signed. He called the Government Delegate Ho Dac Khuong and talked to him about it.

They both realized that nothing could be done about it. Thuc said, "It may take years before the Catholics and Buddhists are willing to comply with the decree." Ho Dac Khuong agreed with him and they talked about other matters.

What irritated Thuc was that a few hours later, he received a phone call from Can. Can had spoken with Khuong, who told him about his earlier conversation with Thuc. On the phone, Can was angry. He rarely talked like that to Thuc. Usually, he talked to Thuc with the greatest respect as he observed the hierarchy in the family. Thuc was the eldest brother. Can was a distant junior and was expected to show respect.

This time, however, Can went straight to the heart of the matter. He said, "You have no right to speak to the Government Delegate. Whether the Buddhists are right or wrong in displaying the Buddhist flags in the streets, you should not meddle with that!"

Thuc was stunned with Can's vehemence. He acknowledged that he should not have told Ho Dac Khuong about the matter, and hung up.

Now, facing Hiep he did not know whether or not he should mention what had happened between him and Can. He was afraid that Hiep would side with Can. But, he had come to her to talk, and so he said, "I may have made a mistake. This afternoon, I noticed that Buddhists flags were being displayed everywhere. I told Ho Dac Khuong about it. This evening Can called me and remonstrated me quite sternly."

Hiep did not say anything. Thuc looked intently at his sister. Suddenly, he understood why Diem gave so much value to the little she said to him.

Although she sat calmly, he knew that her mind was working furiously. Thuc asked, "Did I make a big blunder?"

Again Hiep did not say anything. Thuc stood up and started pacing back and forth in the parlor. After a while, he stopped and asked, "Do you agree with Can that I made a mistake in calling Ho Dac Khuong about the flags?" Instead of answering him, Hiep asked, "What was your objective when you talked to the Government Delegate about the flags?" Thuc said, "I had no specific intention." He stopped short. Now he was really angry with himself. Calling Ho Dac Kuong, with no objective in mind, had not been an intelligent move.

Hiep was blunt; "You called the Government Delegate, without really thinking. You called him and complained about something the Buddhists had done. You called a Buddhist high-ranking official to complain about a Buddhist irregularity. Yet, you know you are an Archbishop, and people see you as the elder brother of the President. Now, you did not have any clear objective when you made the call. Father told us so many times, 'When you do something or say something, you have to know exactly the objective of your act or your words, and make it clear to the people around you.' He also told us, 'When you do or say things without a clear purpose, people will tend to think you are serving evil purposes.' I think Brother Can had every reason in the world to be angry with you."

Thuc did not know what to say. He sat down and faced Hiep, "What do you think I should do now?" Hiep shook her head, "You have done enough. I think it would be best if you kept quiet for the time being."

Thuc watched Hiep. There was more tension in her than what his little blunder could have caused. He asked, "You seem to be very upset, and not only because of me. What is the matter?" Hiep said, "Brother Diem is in trouble. He seems to believe that something big will surface soon. He thinks that those who were invited to plot against him but ended up watching the airborne coup in November 1960, have now been recruited to bring him down."

Thuc thought a moment, before he asked, "What do you mean by *ended up watching*?" Hiep replied, "In November 1960, besides a few operators, military and civilians who had stepped forward to make the coup, there was a second line of military leaders and politicians who were favorable to the coup but who did not get involved. They were not disturbed after the coup failed. Brother Diem had the feeling that the airborne coup was merely a dress rehearsal. He now believes that the real show is about to begin."

Thuc had heard Diem make the same kind of remarks. He asked, "Do you believe that yourself?" Hiep said, "This morning, a number of young men who said they were Buddhists were telling the people in the streets, here in Hue, that the Government was about to order the banning of the Buddhist flags. The young men encouraged the people to demonstrate against such discriminatory measures by the government."

Thuc was feeling very uncomfortable. Hiep pursued, "By noon time, Brother Can asked the Information Service in Hue to send out vans equipped with megaphones, to tell the people in the city that there would be no ban on the flying of Buddhist flags. By four o'clock, probably at the time you were talking to the government delegate, four Buddhist monks were seen in the Citadel stirring up people there, telling them that the authorities had pulled down Buddhist flags. Brother Can called several local agencies asking them to check and see whether there had been any such incidents. He found out that no Buddhists flags had been pulled down."

Thuc was not at all pleased with himself now. He complained, "Why didn't Brother Can tell me anything?" Hiep ignored his question and went on: "An hour ago, about one hundred civil servants demonstrated in front of the Provincial headquarters. Province Chief Nguyen van Dang went out to talk with them and explain to them that no Buddhist flags had been pulled down. The demonstrators went home peacefully."

Brother and sister sat in silence. They both felt a big danger lurking around them. Thuc said, "With all of this going on, did you still have a happy birthday?" Hiep smiled, "Why not? I am sixty and healthy. My mother is doing well All my brothers are in good health and each has an important role to play in the country, or in the Church. My husband and my children surround me with their love. Bless me, my Brother!"

Thuc gently placed his hand on his sister's head, and blessed her. He felt that even with all her worries, Hiep was still at peace with herself, and that she was sharing that peace with him. He was always amazed that without any definite role, Hiep was at the center of his family.

He said, "You should be the one who does the blessing." He walked out into the garden with her, sent his car away and started walking home. It was only half a mile from her home to his residence, but Thuc had never had the time or the desire to indulge in such a walk since becoming the Archbishop of Hue. Now that his diabetes had worsened, walking was no longer a pleasure.

Hiep followed Thuc with her eyes. Thuc waved his hand as if to say that he would be all right. As he walked on, he remembered a time when he had taken Luyen, his little brother, by the hand, right where he was now, and ran to the new railway tracks behind his father's home, to watch a heavy train pass by. It was a long time ago. Yet the memory was so fresh, so rich with detail, that he was overwhelmed with emotion.

He looked back. Hiep still was at the gate. He said to himself, "Yes, Sister, watch our backs for us. We have entered, without really knowing why, the center of a death ground."

*

It was the Feast of the Birth of Buddha. Hiep was surprised to find a small crowd at the gate of her mother's home. A quick look at them sufficed, for her to recognize that the small group included security agents and young Buddhists who accompanied senior Monks in their displacement.

Inside, Can was receiving Thich Tri Quang. As Hiep walked in, Can's aides steered her to the garden and started briefing her on what was going on. Though she had heard the story told by many other people, she knew that Captain Minh, Can's military adjutant, was probably the best source of information in town. She asked, "At the City Hall, what actually happened yesterday morning?"

Minh seemed to have every detail at his finger tips, "Yesterday, early in the morning, the Venerable Thich Tinh Khiet, Huyen Ton and Tri Quang went to the City Hall and demanded to be received immediately by the Province Chief. They were promptly ushered into the meeting room upstairs and welcomed by Province Chief Nguyen van Dang. You know that he is a very devout Buddhist and has been quite close to Thich Tri Quang. Without wasting time on civilities, the monks demanded that the authorities allow the Buddhist flags to be displayed anywhere in the city. Having received instructions from Uncle Can, the Province Chief told the monks that they were authorized to fly the Buddhist flags as they had always done in the past."

Hiep asked a little impatiently, "Were the monks satisfied?" Minh nodded, "Yes, they told the Province Chief that they were satisfied with his response. As they emerged from City Hall, they stopped to talk to the demonstrators who had been shouting anti-government slogans. The monks told the crowd that they had won a big victory and that the flying of the flags was no longer an issue. The demonstrators dispersed on their own."

Hiep said softly, "Yet, nothing was solved." Minh smiled, "No, nothing was solved. Uncle Can knew that. He invited Tri Quang to come here. Tri Quang accepted the invitation. They sat down yesterday afternoon to sip tea and talk about today's celebration. Tri Quang brought with him a tape of the sermon he is to give today and asked Uncle Can to listen to it. Uncle Can listened and agreed with the monk that the tape was fit for public broadcast and that he would like it to be aired by the Hue Radio Station. They parted like old friends and Tri Quang assured Uncle Can that he would make sure that no problems would crop up during this feast day."

Hiep exclaimed, "Yet, problems did crop up last night." Minh again smiled, a little ironically this time, "Last night and this morning. Last night, there was a procession. Buddhists marched from the Dieu De Pagoda to the Tu Dam Pagoda. They made a little detour and demonstrated in front of the Office of the Government Delegate. All of a sudden, anti-government banners were unfurled, and anti-government pamphlets were distributed."

Hiep prompted, "What happened next?" Minh shrugged, "Nothing much. The Government Delegate, Mr. Ho Dac Khuong, who is also a devout Buddhist, came out of his office and talked to the crowd. Soon enough the demonstrators calmed down and continued their march to Tu Dam Pagoda without any further problem."

Hiep shivered. The problems came up and disappeared, came up and disappeared. She felt as if there was a giant's hand pulling the strings on puppets.

Minh went on, "This morning, the ceremony at the Tu Dam Pagoda was attended by all the top ranking officials in Hue, including the Government Delegate Ho Dac Khuong, General Le Van Nghiem, Commander of the Military Region, and Province Chief Nguyen van Dang. In his sermon, Tri Quang was most insulting. From the beginning to the end, he accused the Government of dictatorship and of practicing discriminatory policies against Buddhism."

Hiep asked herself, "Is the Venerable the puppeteer, or is he himself a puppet?"

Minh commented: "The officials, all Buddhists, listened in silence and did not respond. After the ceremony, however, they went to see Uncle Can and reported to him the content of Tri Quang's sermon."

Hiep wanted to make sure she understood, "The sermon the Venerable gave this morning is different than from the taped text he gave to my brother yesterday?" Minh nodded, "Completely different!" Hiep noticed that Minh, who had always been very deferential to Thich Tri Quang, no longer called him the Venerable. Minh was a very courteous man. Looking at Minh, Hiep was aware of the fact that Minh had recognized the Buddhist monk as an enemy; a devious enemy and he no longer had any respect for him.

Hiep asked, "What is the Venerable doing with my brother inside?" Minh laughed a little sadly, "I am sure that he is giving Uncle Can assurances once more that there will be no further problems."

That was precisely what Can told Hiep after Thich Tri Quang had left, but Hiep saw in Can's eyes that he no longer believed in Tri Quang's assurances. Hiep asked, "What is going to happen?"

Can sighed, "We need to be prepared for anything. We have made too many mistakes lately. Both the Americans and the Communists will take advantage of those mistakes. They will use the Buddhists against us. If we are not careful, our country could be drawn into a hundred years of religious conflict."

*

Thanh, Hiep's younger son, who was a lieutenant in the national police, drove home to give Hiep a short account of the disaster; then he was gone. A little later, Can himself called and explained to her the events that had led to the tragic deaths of eight people in front of the Hue Radio Station.

Though it was quite late already, Hiep asked Am to accompany her to her mother's house to have a face-to-face talk with Can. As she and Am walked towards her mother's home, Hiep felt as if she were reliving the days before Emperor Thanh Thai was forced to abdicate in 1907, or the moment she was told that Ngo Dinh Khoi had been abducted in 1945. Her hands trembled and her whole body burned with fever.

Can was not surprised to see Am and Hiep arrive at that hour of the night. He kept muttering to himself, "God, how could such a thing happen?" What had happened was that there had been an explosion while thousands of Buddhists were demonstrating in front of the Radio Station, and eight people had been killed. And now the Buddhists believed that it was government troops who had killed them.

Hiep, trying to calm Can down, suggested, "Please go over the whole thing once more." Can nodded, realizing that he needed to examine every detail; until he could come to some understanding of had really happened. He said, "Why not? You were here at noontime, so you know what happened in the morning. Well, Tri Quang promised again that he would not attack the government any more, and again told me that the tape we had agreed to use for public broadcast would be the one to be broadcast tonight. Then he left."

Am said, "He did not tell you that demonstrators were organizing at the radio station?" Can shook his head, "The monks at the Tu Dam Pagoda simply told people to be there, because the floats would converge there in the evening. There were no floats converging anywhere. Tri Quang only wanted to have a crowd of bystanders on site. Only then did he send in his demonstrators. They demanded that the director broadcast the anti-government speech he had given this morning at Tu Dam Pagoda. Many monks were seen exciting the crowd and inciting them to take over the radio station."

Hiep pointed out the obvious, "There were no floats like in other years. Yet, the monks told people that the floats would converge towards the Square next to the Station. They have lied shamelessly to the people.

Since our childhood, we have believed that monks never lie. Those monks who openly lied to the people were no monks."

Can nodded, "Or monks who place politics far above religion. Anyway, seeing the crowd becoming angrier by the minute, the director of the radio station closed all the doors and windows and called for help. The Province Chief, Mr. Nguyen van Dang and his Deputy for Security, Major Dang Sy were talking at the Advisor's Office next door, when the call for help came in."

Can paused. He saw that Hiep was impatient to hear the rest of the story. He also knew that she would ask him pointed questions if he were not thorough enough. He sat back and calmly continued, "Mr. Dang ordered Major Dang Sy to take measures to disperse the crowd. The Major said he did not have any troops under his command. The only company he commanded was operating in the Nam Dong area."

Hiep asked eagerly, "What happened then?" Can tried to keep his composure, but in his voice, Hiep detected a trace of anguish. He continued, "Mr. Dang then told the Major that he was implementing President Decree 10-A, which gives full powers to Province Chiefs in case of emergencies. He ordered Sy to use all the forces available in the Military Area to disperse the crowd. Sy then called Major General Le van Nghiem, the Regional Military Commander to ask for manpower." Hiep inquired, "Such a Presidential Decree exists?" "Yes. General Nghiem directed Sy to the First Division and to the Phu Bai Training Center. The Chief of Staff of the First Division, Colonel Le Quang Hien, offered the Black Panther Company, a company famous for its experience in military intelligence and its courage under fire. The Commander of the Phu Bai Training Center, Major Vinh Bien, younger brother of Colonel Vinh Loc, took with him two companies of trainees to Hue and met with Major Sy at his headquarters, only two hundred meters from the radio station."

Can poured tea for Am and Hiep, and then went on, "At Sy's headquarters, he was now in command of three companies, as well as a number of policemen, military security, and military police personnel. Sy walked out of his headquarters and was joined by the Province Chief in the street. From where they stood, they saw a few thousand people in front of the Radio Station. Demonstrators had pulled the national flag down.

Thich Tri Quang, accompanied by Thich Thien Minh, went into the station through the back door to negotiate with the station director."

Hiep asked impatiently, "What happened next?" Can looked quite dismal now, his shoulders sagged visibly: "While Tri Quang was inside the station, Sy attempted to disperse the crowd. First he used water hoses on the demonstrators, without much success. Then he tried to approach the station with some troops. Their progress was slowed down, and then brought to a complete standstill, as young demonstrators built up barricades using bicycles. Then he ordered an armored vehicle to advance. As it moved in, accompanied by a platoon of troops, the young demonstrators rapidly retrieved their bicycles for fear of seeing them demolished. So the armored vehicle had no problem advancing toward the front door of the station."

Can paused a second, and then went on, "It was then that a deafening explosion was heard. It came from somewhere near the front door of the radio station. The crowd screamed and ran back. As if he were living in a nightmare, Sy approached the station. The sight of the dead there made him sick. He stooped down and observed the bodies. He knew that the powerful explosion had come from a devise containing high explosives. All the victims had been killed by the terrible shock of the explosion. Some of the bodies were beheaded. No fragments of bombs were found in the bodies or on the ground."

Hiep watched Can as he fell silent. Hiep asked, "Is there any way people could say that the explosion was caused by the security forces?"

Can sighed, "I swear on Mother's head, none of our people would dream of doing something like that. Yet, I know the Buddhist activists under Thich Tri Quang will point an accusing finger at us."

*

The 'Buddhist crisis' had begun. The eight victims of the explosion were said to have been killed by shots fired by soldiers under Dang Sy's command, or by a fragmentation bomb thrown by Dang Sy's men, or even crushed under the tracks of Dang Sy's armored vehicles. Foreign journalists never bothered to learn that the six armored cars used by security forces in Hue ran on *tires not tracks*. The one used by Dang Sy in front of the radio station was precisely one of these armored vehicles. No journalists bothered to find out that none of the soldiers under Sy's command carried fragmentation hand-grenades.

No journalists questioned what the government had to gain by killing Buddhists. The set-up was perfect. While the government firmly believed that it was either the work of the Communists or the CIA, the Buddhists and the foreign press immediately accused the regime of the 'massacre'. The Communists immediately joined in the chorus of accusations. The American Government sounded like they believed the regime had done it. False versions of the story began to circulate. Descriptions of soldiers firing on the crowd, machine-gunning down women and children were accepted as credible. The fact was that the troops had not fired one single shot at the people, and numerous investigations could not find a bullet, or even a bullet case in or around the area. The troops were also accused of throwing hand grenades at the crowd, killing and maiming dozens of people. It was later proven that the only grenades available, were training grenades that were brought on the scene by a company of boot camp trainees, and that could not have hurt anybody.

Then there was the gory story about the armored vehicles crushing people with their tracks. Unfortunately for the creator of that myth, the armored vehicles did not have tracks and ran on tires.

The lies went on. Hiep was surprised at the persistence and growth of the stories. Gorier detail was added to the narrative of that event in every new book published about the Vietnam War.

In 1966, a man acknowledged that he had detonated the plastic bomb in front of the Hue Radio Station. According to some Vietnamese officers who served in the same unit with him, Captain James Scott said he was the one who had placed the bomb and detonated it. It was three years after the incident in Hue. Captain James Scott served as a military advisor to the first Battalion, Third Regiment of the First Division of Infantry. It was during an operation in the A-Shao area, west of Hue that he recounted to the Battalion commander, Major Buu Binh and other officers in the same battalion, his involvement in the incident. He described the bomb as a very sophisticated time bomb. Reportedly, he was not bragging. He simply stated that by triggering the Buddhist struggle at that time, he had played a major role in the overthrow of President Diem.

In July 1975, Vietnamese refugees in the United States talked about reading an article in an American magazine signed by Captain James Scott. The article reportedly claimed that he was the one who had detonated the bomb that killed nine people in Hue.

By that time, however, Ngo Dinh Diem was dead and South Vietnam had been lost to the Communists.

*

Can was on the phone talking to Nhu, when Hiep came in. Can said, "Here is Sister Hiep. Do you want to talk to her?"

Hiep waved her hand in protest. She did not need to talk with Nhu. She went in to see her mother and returned to the parlor half an hour later. Can was still on the phone with Nhu.

Can turned to her and handed over the receiver. Hiep took it. Nhu's voice sounded a little hoarse, "I have made another blunder." Hiep pretended to take it lightly. She replied, "Everybody seems to be making plenty of blunders these days. What was yours?"

Nhu explained, "Brother Diem wanted to do it himself. He wanted to go to the American media and talk openly about American advisors. You know what my position has been. If there is an unpleasant thing that needs doing, I prefer to do it myself. So, I granted an interview to Warren Unna, an American reporter for the Washington Post. I told him that we had too many American advisors, and that we would like to see half of them sent home before year's end."

Hiep needed to collect her thoughts before she answered him. Finally, she said, "Since the Lunar New Year, everybody understands what Brother Diem wants. He wants to reduce the Americans' power in South Vietnam. But don't you think that, since May 8, we need to be a little more prudent? Can't we lie low for a while, and try to resolve these domestic problems first?"

Nhu sighed: "Our enemies will not give us the option of lying low. They will use the Buddhist activists to wreck our nerves, while they prepare for our downfall by other means."

Hiep, seized with anguish, asked "Do you consider the Americans now as our enemies?" Nhu replied quickly, "No, not at all. But I recognize that inside the American administration, both in Washington and here in Saigon, we have deadly enemies."

Before Hiep could say anything else, Nhu added, "Apparently, the 'Buddhist crisis' is a relief for both the Americans who don't like us, and the Communists. On May 14, the Central Committee of the National Liberation Front appealed to the people in Vietnam and the international community, to support the Buddhist struggle. Only yesterday, Chairman Ho Chi Minh condemned our government, saying that it is a crime 'which cannot be forgiven by Heaven and Earth', and he encouraged the Buddhists to be committed to the struggle against our government."

Hiep asked, "In Washington, can't your father-in-law do something? After all, he is our Ambassador to the United States. After nine years in Washington, he must have become acquainted with quite a large number of key people. Can't he make our points of view understood by the American elite and the American people?"

Nhu was rather cynical: "He is not the kind of friend who helps you when you are in trouble." Hiep insisted, "Yet, he is our Ambassador in Washington and he is Le Xuan's father."

Nhu sounded tired, "Since May 8, many good friends have turned into enemies. Many believe that we are not going to come out of this alive. There have been quite a number of desertions."

That was nothing new for Hiep, who had seen her father stand almost alone in 1907, Diem totally isolated in 1933, her brother Khoi fighting alone in 1945, and Diem and Nhu again in 1954 and again in 1960. Yet, in May 1963, Hiep knew that the danger Diem faced was much more deadly. She would have liked to see loyal friends rally around him.

On the other end of the line, Nhu seemed to feel her distress. He became more reassuring, "Look, we began our struggle with nothing in 1954, and we will manage with little this time too."

*

Hiep closed her eyes. But even with her eyes closed, she still saw the fire engulfing the Venerable Thich Quang Duc. "The question is not whether the monk immolated himself freely, or was pushed into the terrible act by others," Hiep thought. "The question is, why was this sacrifice that will mark the Vietnamese consciousness for decades, thought to be necessary?"

All of the foreign media had carried that photo of the monk surrounded by flames. Hiep knew that from now on everybody would believe that there was religious discrimination in Vietnam, and that Buddhists were being persecuted.

Hiep's mind had a hard time functioning. On one hand, she admired the monk for his courage. If he had immolated himself to protest against a regime hostile to Buddhism, his sacrifice was a noble act that would be recounted in Vietnam's history from now to eternity.

Yet Hiep knew that the accusations of religious discriminations did not date back very far. On the contrary, it dated back to only three months earlier. She even knew when and where it had all started. Then, if the monk had killed himself for an erroneous allegation, he had died in vain. Not only that, his death could possibly start a series of events that would bring Buddhists and Christians into a terrible and lasting conflict.

Hiep had heard how the monk had been brought to a public square, how two hundred monks had sat in the background to witness his self-immolation, how a young monk obligingly set fire to him, and how the foreign reporters had been invited to come and photograph his sacrifice.

Having been educated in the respect of martyrs, Hiep greatly admired the courage of the monk. She could not help but wonder about the cowardice of the people who were behind the self-immolation and who now exploited it in a professional and systematic way. That was not the act of one noble man. That was a drama arranged with virtuosity by political minds that knew how to use the weapons of propaganda.

In the history of Buddhism there had not been another example of a Buddhist monk immolating himself to defend the cause of the Buddha's teachings. Why now, why against her brother, Diem, who had given more to the Buddhists than he had given the Catholics during his nine years in power? Hiep wondered.

She wanted to call Diem and plead with him again to resign. She knew, however, that he would not listen to her if she did.

He was not focused on the Buddhist issue, because he had other problems to deal with. He had to preserve national sovereignty. He had to finish the construction of the Strategic Hamlets and improve their effectiveness, in order to reduce the level of fighting. At the same time, he had to watch his back and keep the generals at bay, tempted as they were by CIA agents to overthrow him. He had to do all those things before he could consider his work to be completed.

*

On June 24, the Feast of Saint John the Baptist, Diem's and Can's patron saint, Hiep called the President and wished him good luck. She was still shaken by the immolation by fire of the Venerable Thich Quang Duc, two weeks earlier.

Diem said, "Our enemies have used a terrible weapon that may help them to get rid of me effectively. But that weapon is even more terrible in the sense that it will divide our people for decades."

Hiep pleaded with Diem, "Please make all the necessary concessions. Make sure everybody knows you are not discriminating against the Buddhists."

There was a trace of defeat in Diem's voice, "If the behavior of all my life has not proven how much I care for Buddhism, then what else can I do? I will make all the reasonable concessions; however, the demands of the activist monks lay many traps for me. For example, they want me to compensate for those killed in front of the Hue Radio Station. If I acceded to that demand, they would tell the world that I acknowledged that our troops actually did kill Buddhists in Hue. I know, and you know, that no troops of ours killed those people!"

Hiep insisted, "We may know, but the people don't know. Either you have to prove quickly, and beyond any doubt that our troops did not do the killing; or you will have to accede to the demand of compensating the families of the victims."

Diem was as hardheaded as ever, "I have promised to talk about compensations after the investigations are over. I cannot agree to alter the truth, and the truth is: no troops of ours did the killing."

Hiep exclaimed, "Then do your best to bring to justice, the murderer or murderers!" Diem hesitated, and then said, "I may never be able to do that. Only three parties could benefit from such a wanton act: the Communists who would benefit from any trouble they can cause in our communities; the Buddhist activists who want to bring me down, and replace me with their henchmen; and finally, some Americans who need something to galvanize the half-hearted coup plotters they have been supporting. It will be difficult for me to catch a Communist terrorist who by now may have gone North, or a Buddhist terrorist who would kill his own people to defeat me. I cannot catch a CIA agent easily either."

Hiep commented, "You seem to no longer consider the Americans to be your allies." Diem sounded weary, "I would like Ambassador Nolting to be here. But he has decided to take an untimely vacation. I still trust General Hawkins, the American Commander, as well as Mr. Richardson, the CIA Station Chief here. I have much less confidence in Mr. Trueheart, the American chargé d'affaires."

Something struck a chord in Hiep's heart, and she shivered. It took her a minute before she realized that her sudden fright came from something her father had said one day when she was a little girl, "B*eware of chargés d'affaires*." He had been talking about a Mr. Levecque, chargé d'affaires at the Office of the Resident Superior in Hue at the time.

Before she could say anything, Diem laughed and said, "*Beware of chargés d'affaires*. Yes, I remember. In a certain measure, Mr. Trueheart represents a problem. He acts as if he does not know me at all. He does not allow any sentiment of respect or friendship to get in the way of his party line, or his uncompromising dedication to his job. I am afraid that I don't appreciate that way of doing business. Reason has to be tempered by the heart. Ambassador Nolting understands that. General Lansdale understands that, and Mr. Colby of the CIA understands that."

Hiep felt again the frustrations and anxiety of the days before Emperor Thanh Thai had been forced to abdicate. She asked, "What is the greatest danger for you now?" Without hesitation, Diem answered, "The division I perceive in the American Administration in Washington, and the ever-increasing dissent I see among the American officials here in Saigon."

Hiep asked, "Then, what do you propose to do?" Diem replied, "I think that if we can hang on for just a little longer, all of this will blow away." Diem added after a long silence, "You may say that this is wishful thinking."

Hiep knew that *all of that* would not go away. Hiep knew that Diem's hopes were indeed wishful thinking.

CHAPTER TWENTY-SIX
THE POINT OF NO RETURN

On August 29, 1963, the Commemorative Day of the Beheading of John the Baptist, Diem called Hiep again. He said, "You forget my Patron Saint's Day." Hiep replied, "That is not true. Your Patron Saint's Day was June 24; I called you on that day."

The fact that Diem was calling her on the day commemorating the beheading of John the Baptist really upset her. She said, "If this is a joke, Mr. President, then it is a bad joke." Diem did not make amends. He said, very seriously, "Life or death, glory or humiliation, crowning or beheading, are only expressions of *change*. Do not be disturbed. I called you to tell you that we have probably smothered the coup before it could take place."

Hiep said, "I hate myself for dousing your optimism, but have you read the newspapers lately? The raids on the pagodas nine days ago are still making the front page in America. Many journalists and commentators have said that your actions on August 20 marked a point of no return. They are pronouncing you dead and buried."

Diem laughed, "You can testify that I am alive. All the generals of the Joint General Staff and the Saigon Military Governor requested the raids. Military leaders told me that we had to do something quick to put the Buddhist crisis and the student demonstrations behind us. The anti-government student leaders are behind bars; the schools and universities are closed down, temporarily. There will be no more students' demonstrations for a while. Buddhist Pagodas of the An Quang faction were reported to have stored weapons and ammunition to stir up real troubles. Brother Nhu and I authorized the raids, with the generals' written request."

Hiep said, "The Voice of America has widely broadcast a retraction of its early reports. Right after the raids it announced the generals' participation in the raids, then it retracted, saying that only the mob police and the Special Forces under Brother Nhu's command were involved."

Diem sighed, "So, you noticed. Yes. Apparently, the Americans still want the coup to take place. They exonerate everything the generals do. The Voice of America incident clearly shows that some generals are still plotting. I hope, however, that the majority of military leaders have abandoned the coup plotters."

Hiep asked, "Have you met with the new American Ambassador?" Diem hesitated, but then he told her, "Yes, I met him two days ago when he came to the Palace to present his credentials. He asked me to send Brother Nhu away. I told him that Nhu wasn't any of his business. He told me that President Kennedy wished to see Nhu gone. Imagine how incredible it was! The first time we met! On the very day he presented to me his credentials! It is not a question of guts! It is simply the fact that he considered himself to be the proconsul of our country."

Hiep was concerned, "Do not declare war on him so soon." Diem said, "He declared war on me as soon as he arrived here. Thich Tri Quang is physically under his protection now. But with the students quieted, and the Buddhist activists without a leader, all I need to do now is to build bridges with the generals and colonels. I have seen the likes of Ambassador Lodge before, under the French. I will manage."

Hiep asked, "In 1954 and 1955, you survived because you had hidden forces. Now all your strengths are visible. If your strengths are visible, your enemy will find a way to use them against you. Have you built up a new hidden force, a force nobody knows you have?"

Diem seemed to be caught by surprise. In the end, he admitted, "I have no such hidden force." Hiep asked again, "Is it too late now, to organize such a force?" Diem sighed, "Not only it is too late to organize one, but it is also impossible to hide anything from the Americans now."

She pressed on, "Have you planned on a quick reassignment of all your military leaders, moving all the people you have now in Saigon, those you trust, and those you don't trust, to the provinces?" Diem said, "We have played with that possibility, Nhu and I. But we have right here in Saigon, the people I trust the most. Those I don't trust *don't* have troops under their command. Is that not enough?" Hiep said, "Why do you ask me? I am no military strategist. But remember Father's words: 'In a situation where you see you have all the advantages, yet, inside you feel disquiet, then something is wrong with your perception of the situation.'"

Diem asked, a little teasingly, "So you think I feel disquiet inside me?" Hiep ignored Diem's question; she repeated, "You should remember Father's teaching, at this critical moment." Diem asked, "What among Father's instructions, should I remember the most at this moment?"

Hiep sounded like she had long ago prepared her answer, "Father said you were an angry man. An angry man makes enemies during his bursts of anger. While he is angry he doesn't know how badly he behaves with people, so he doesn't know how he may have humiliated people. Because he doesn't know, he never apologizes; he never tries to make up with a lost friend. Among the people you trust today, how many have felt humiliated by you, when you were angry?"

There was a long silence. Was Diem angry now? Hiep continued, "Father said you were a hardheaded man. A hardheaded man makes a decision, and then finds himself bound by it. A more flexible man may find opportunities to make new decisions more appropriate to new circumstances." Diem admitted, "It seems that what Father said about me a long time ago, still holds true. Thank you for reminding me. What else do I need to be reminded of?"

Hiep took her courage in hand and said, "You were wrong when you told me that you were *dispensable*. You are *not dispensable*, but your family is. Nhu is dispensable, Le Xuan is dispensable, and Can is dispensable. It is time you separate yourself from those who have become liabilities to you and who may destroy all that you have built up. Separate yourself from all of us. You do not need us, but the country needs you."

Diem's silence this time was threatening. Hiep looked at the receiver and waited for an outburst. It never came. When Diem talked, his voice was soft and sad, "I know you are right. Yet, a man is born alone, and can die alone. But how can he live alone? I need Nhu to be right here with me."

Hiep held the receiver far from her so that Diem could not hear her sobbing. After a while Diem said, "Pray for me Sister. Life and death are not important for me, but your prayers are."

*

Thuc stood in the courtyard of the Archbishop's House. His eyes wandered from the flowerbeds to the gate, to the An Cuu River, to the other side of the river where his mother lived, and finally to the unfinished new Cathedral. He looked at his sister. She did not cry. She did not look sad. She told him, in her quiet voice, "In Rome, you will find a more peaceful environment. You will meet again with your old friends over there. You will see the Pope, your old classmate."

Thuc pointed at the unfinished Cathedral. He said, "I have ruined you and Am with that project. I know that you have advanced your entire fortune into the construction of the Cathedral. Now that I am leaving, who will pay you back?" Hiep shook her head, "Please do not worry about that. In 1946 we were all made bankrupt by the events, then we re-emerged more prosperous than ever a few years later. Do you remember how Am rebuilt the Flag Monument and the Palace of the Greater Peace after the war?"

Note: The unfinished cathedral is now finished.
Below is a recent photo of the cathedral.

Thuc nodded, and then said, "I feel as if I were deserting a sinking ship. I am afraid that my departure from Hue will encourage the President's enemies to think that even the Vatican is aligned against him." Hiep reassured him, "You are an Archbishop, but you are also a good foot soldier. Do you forget the motto on your Episcopal coat of arms? *Miles Christi*, 'Soldier of Christ'. You go where you are ordered to go. You don't question the Holy See's decisions."

Thuc was restless. He asked Hiep, "But what will happen to the President?" Hiep smiled, "His fate is in God's hand. Why do you worry?" Thuc cried out, "I worry because I don't have a faith half as strong as yours. That is why!"

Hiep hoped she could continue to smile convincingly. She knew that she would not be able to retain her poise while Thuc was showing his torment so openly. She said, "Brother Diem, like all of us, is trying to do the best he can to restore stability and confidence. He may succeed or he may fail. Only God is his judge. That knowledge makes him strong."

Thuc lowered his head and said, "But you and I know the hundred cracks in his armor. His enemies know them too. I am afraid that he will not be able to survive this crisis."

Having said that, Thuc watched Hiep to see how disturbed she was. He was surprised to see that Hiep did not pale with fright. She looked at him quietly and, only after a minute's silence, replied softly but distinctly, "Then he would have done his best and failed. He would die without regret."

Suddenly, Thuc realized that Hiep did not speak for herself. She had spoken to him on behalf of their father. Yes, the Grand Chamberlain would have said exactly what Hiep had said to him. Thuc raised his head sharply, resumed his poise and said, "Thank you very much, Sister. Take good care of yourself. I will be all right."

*

From the distant Corrèze came the sad news of the Empress' death. Hiep organized a Mass for the repose of her soul in her chapel.

Diem had called to say that he would be there in spirit with them. His voice was charged with emotion. He told Hiep once more, "She was quite a great lady!" Hiep hesitated, not knowing what to say. Diem sighed, "The only thing that stopped me from going back to the Crown Prince Bao Long solution, even in October 1955, was the fact that Vietnam was not ready for a Catholic Emperor. It looks now like Vietnam is not ready for a Catholic President, either."

Hiep asked, "Are you feeling lonely these days?" Diem admitted readily, "Yes, Le Xuan and Le Thuy went to Belgrade last week and Nhu went off this morning to join them in Europe. No, he is not going to leave for good. He wants to spend a few days with his wife and daughter in Paris, before they go off to the United States. Then he will return to Vietnam. Brother Thuc is also gone. I am alone here for a while."

Hiep asked again, "Is Le Xuan leaving for good?" Diem was quick to reply, "No, no. She and Le Thuy are going on a long trip to Europe and the United States. I wish to see her stop talking so viciously about the Buddhists. We have no quarrel with the Buddhists. I really don't understand her. She said she would go and offer our version of the events. But I see she is only making things worse for us." Hiep said, "Take care of yourself, Mr. President. We have never been able to solve that problem, and I don't think we can resolve it now."

Diem hesitated a while and said, "The Empress is now resting in peace. Nothing untoward can happen to her anymore. Indeed, life ends in death; human intentions are laid to rest, when man returns to the earth." A little embarrassed at sounding so dramatic, he laughed and said apologetically: "I am reading the Ecclesiastes too frequently these days."

Before Diem hung up, he said, "The Empress died on September 15, the Memorial feast of Our Lady of Sorrows. She had a wonderful childhood and youth. Then she married an Emperor and after only a few years of happiness, her sorrows began. They only ended two days ago."

*

In Hiep's chapel where wax candles burned brightly, there was next to the altar, a lacquered table covered with black velvet. On the table, flanked by a big wax candle decorated with a violet bow, stood a portrait of Empress Nam Phuong in its silvery frame.

Father Thuan in his ceremonial garb addressed a few words to the small group in the Chapel: his parents, his Uncle Can and his brothers and sisters. Thuan had never met with the Empress, though, like his mother, he had seen her entering his grandmother's home after Sunday masses from time to time.

The Mass for the repose of the Empress' soul was simple, with quiet dignity, the way Diem and his mother wanted it. Thuan evoked the life and virtues of the late Empress. As he spoke, he began to feel the unexpressed emotions that all of his family had felt for her over the years. He felt Diem's grief. Diem had always hoped that one day he would meet her again and have the chance to explain to her the inevitable decisions he made in 1955 to end the monarchy and to sever his political ties, not only with the Emperor, but also with her and the Crown Prince.

Hiep listened to her son's homily. She remembered the Empress walking through the gate of her mother's home. How graceful she was, how gentle! Hiep remembered her brother, Diem, talking to her about the Empress. Diem had felt comfortable only with a few women, and for some reason, he felt comfortable with the Empress. Was that because of her simplicity of manners and speech? Was it because he found in her a sister soul and because they did not need to talk much in order to understand each other?

For years, her interests were sacred to Diem. Now, she was gone and Diem was struggling for his own survival. Hiep suddenly shivered. She had the premonition that somehow the death of the Empress, at that particular time, was a bad omen for Diem. She looked at the portrait of the late Empress near the altar. With her melancholy smile, she seemed to be beckoning.

She felt the solitude of the Empress. Since 1957, she had lived on that farm of her's in the Corrèze, alone, without any social life. The Countess de La Besse, Emperor Ham Nghi's daughter, lived on the property next door. Yet, Luyen said that the two ladies rarely met. It had been a life of complete seclusion. Now, solitude had started weighing on her brother, Diem.

Thuc, under pressure from the Holy See, had left Hue and gone to Rome a week earlier. It appeared that he would be gone for a long time. Nhu and his wife, along with Le Thuy, their eldest daughter, were in Europe. Diem was all by himself.

Hiep said softly to the Empress, "Please look after my Brother Diem, you who have now reached the final haven. Protect him against his mighty enemies."

On the little table near the altar, the Empress, frail and young, in her phoenix brocaded gown, smiled sadly under the bright reflection of the candles.

CHAPTER TWENTY-SEVEN
THE LAST PREPARATIONS

On September 18, 1963, Joseph Alsop's article, *'Very Ugly Stuff'* appeared in *The Washington Post*. It revealed that Nhu had been meeting with representatives of the Communist regime in Hanoi, in view of negotiating a cease-fire.

Hiep knew the end of her brothers was near. The Apostolic Delegate, Monsignor Asta, who had *suggested* Thuc's departure, apparently had obtained from Nhu, a promise that he too would leave Vietnam. Knowing how Diem and Nhu felt at the moment, Hiep was sure that Nhu would never abandon Diem at that crucial moment.

Apparently Nhu had told Ambassador Cabot Lodge, in the presence of Monsignor Asta, that he was conducting delicate and secret negotiations with Hanoi representatives, and that his departure would disrupt the unique possibility of reaching a cease-fire agreement with the Communists. A few days later, the American Ambassador leaked the story to Joseph Alsop.

It was Can who told Hiep all about the latest story of woe. Hiep asked Can, "Do you think that Nhu has really contacted representatives of the other side?" Instead of answering her question, Can asked her rather emphatically, "Do you believe that we cannot talk with the other side?" When he noticed the expression of surprise on Hiep's face, he said quickly, answering his own question, "Of course, we can talk with the other side, if it is in the best interests of the country. Brother Diem is the President of a sovereign country. He is free to open any line of communications with the Communists."

He smiled and asked Hiep, "Do you remember the pictures that were taken at the Presidential Palace, on the Lunar New Year?" Hiep nodded, "Yes, if you are referring to the branch of pink cherry blossoms sent by President Ho Chi Minh to Brother Diem, I remember."

Can seemed to be in a good mood. He reminisced, "Brother Diem displayed the cherry branch in the Reception Hall at the Palace. Ambassadors who came to wish him a Happy and Prosperous New Year asked him where it came from, and smiling enigmatically, he told them, 'It is a gift from President Ho Chi Minh.'"

Hiep said, "Very romantic indeed! But is it true that contacts have been established with the Communists?" Can laughed, "Communists are everywhere. Whenever we talk, their agents hear us. Diplomats of various countries can always carry messages from one side to the other. The Americans have both direct and indirect contacts with the Communists. They even use double agents for the purpose. We receive messages from the Communists and they receive ours."

Hiep shrugged, "Stop talking in riddles. Has Brother Nhu contacted any high level Communists recently?" Can answered, "I don't think so. He is bluffing. Leaders in Hanoi are showing signs that they want to talk about a cease-fire, but I don't think Brother Diem is ready to negotiate at this moment. You see, he will not negotiate in a situation of weakness. He is weak at this moment." Hiep exclaimed, "Then the bluff has backfired. Now, the Americans can accuse us of shaking hands with Hanoi, behind their backs."

Can said, "On the surface, Brother Nhu has committed a real blunder, especially right at this moment. He wanted to make the Americans believe that we could turn around, make a pact with Hanoi and throw the Americans out. Apparently he wanted to blackmail the Americans, by telling them, "Back off, or we will join forces with Hanoi." Hiep shook her head, "You are still speaking in riddles. You use the words 'on the surface', and 'apparently'. So, presumably, Brother Nhu is not trying to blackmail the Americans. What is his real game plan then?"

Can seemed preoccupied. He said, "I have not talked to Brother Nhu since that article appeared in *The Washington Post*, but I suppose I understand what he has been up to. Consider these factors. *Item One*: We have received information that Hanoi wanted to hold direct negotiations with us, even before the 'Buddhist crisis'; therefore, it seems to us that this crisis was at least partly created to coax us 'gently' into accepting to negotiate. *Item Two*: If we sound like we are ready to negotiate with them now, the leaders in Hanoi will lay off for a while, and ask the Buddhist activists here to lay off as well. *Item Three*: If we have a temporary truce with the Buddhist activists and the students, our only remaining concern would the CIA and the generals the CIA has succeeded in buying."

Hiep shook her head energetically, "Brother Diem told me he thought the problems with the Buddhist activists and the students had been resolved, and that now he could devote his time to dealing with some potential coup leaders. But he did not mention the need to negotiate with Hanoi."

Can explained, "When he told you that, he was engaged in wishful thinking. The Buddhist activists can still create problems, and we cannot keep the universities and schools closed too long. We cannot detain student leaders too long either. I think that there are other valid reasons for Brother Nhu to state that we were conducting talks with Hanoi. First, as I said, we have the right to do so. The more the American Ambassador tries to show that he is the master, the more Brothers Diem and Nhu insist on showing him their independence. Second, in the long term, negotiation is the only way out of this war. Even if we win the war, we will still have to negotiate for peace. So, Brother Diem has started putting up antennas in Brussels, and Paris, as well as in New Delhi for such a purpose."

Hiep looked at Can. For the first time in a long while, Can was talking as if there was no dissension among him and Nhu and Diem. Now she had to be the dissenting voice. She said, "Please tell Brother Nhu, the next time you talk to him that I don't agree. Please tell him he should never bluff, that the American Ambassador has shown that he knows how to use Nhu's stratagem against him, and that the generals who are potential coup leaders now have a legitimate reason to make the coup."

Can did not say anything for a while. When he finally spoke, he seemed to spit out his words, "Listen Sister, the American leaders, one day, will want to see peace negotiations started. As for the generals ready to rebel, who will believe them when they accuse us of selling out the country to the Communists, or of being naïve about Communism?"

Hiep was not convinced; she said, "I understand the reasons for this maneuver. If it throws confusion among those who want Brother Diem to fall, then it's fine by me. But I am afraid the maneuver only gives his enemies another weapon to use against him."

They had said what they wanted to say. So, they smiled when they parted. Hiep was sick with foreboding. She remembered how the French had used every ruse invented by Emperor Thanh Thai, against him. She had the feeling that from now on everything and anything done by Diem and Nhu would be used against them.

As she sat in her chapel thinking about the situation, the only certainty she had was that, victors or vanquished, alive or dead, her brothers would not be abandoned by God, in whom they put all their hope. The only solace she found was that her brothers would not see victory where others saw it, and that they would embrace what others might call defeat.

In her heart, she knew that negotiation was the only way out of war. In her heart, she believed that the only way for the Vietnamese to live free of all foreign interference was for them to be reconciled and united.

*

That was the last time Diem put a call through to her. It was October 28, quite late in the evening. Rumors of coups were rampant, even in Hue. Hiep had spent most of the day praying. Now in the late evening, Diem's call seemed to answer both to her need to talk to him, and to her anxiety.

Diem sounded very calm. He said without preamble, "I spent a day and an evening with the American Ambassador and his wife in Dalat. We flew up to the Central Highlands in a helicopter and visited a Strategic Hamlet, and then I took them to a government guesthouse in Dalat."

Hiep asked, "Were you able to talk one on one with him?" There was some hesitation, and then Diem said, "Yes. We did have some time to talk one on one." Hiep, sensing his reticence, pressed him, "Did you two discuss anything substantive?" There was a long silence. Hiep heard Diem sigh. Finally, he said, "I did try. But I think he had already made up his mind about me and about Vietnam, even before he arrived in Saigon. For him, America is a big country, and Vietnam is a small country. We receive assistance from the United States and he feels that this gives the United States the right to dictate policies to us."

Hiep asked, "Did you quarrel with him?" Diem said, "He was my guest, how could I quarrel with him? I thought it would be an opportunity to have an honest discussion. But he was distant, absent-minded. He seemed to indicate that it was too late for him to re-write his script." Hiep tried to keep calm, but Diem's remarks made her exclaim, "So, you do not see a way out anymore. Is that what you are saying?' Diem tried to laugh off her concern. He told her, "There are always a few ways out, although right now all of them appear to be dishonorable ways out. If something happens to Nhu and me, then Can will not be safe either. Please take care of Mother."

Hiep helplessness made her want to scream. She controlled herself, however, and said simply, "I will take care of Mother if you take care of yourself. Do not give up so soon, Mr. President. Until the fight is over, nobody can claim victory, nobody should acknowledge defeat."

Diem said, "Do not think that I will not fight to the bitter end. Now, let me tell you that I have decided to release all the monks and the students who have been arrested in recent months. I will do that right away. That move will throw some confusion into the American game plan and some generals' designs."

Hiep shivered, as she countered, "I don't want to contradict you. Releasing them is a must; however, do not count on the beneficial effect of such a move. Coup plotters will only hasten to carry out their plans before the public appreciates the release of the detainees." Diem acquiesced, "That may be the case."

Hiep said, "How do you feel, Mr. President?" Diem said, "It feel like I have entered a dead calm. I know the big storm is coming. I have gone over what I have done in the last nine years, the achievements and the failures, the victories and the defeats, and I do not see what I could have done to alter the present course of events."

Hiep said, "So, you are without regrets." Diem again acquiesced, "I am without regrets." Three days later, the coup took place.

CHAPTER TWENTY-EIGHT
THE COUP D'ETAT

It was All Saints' Day, and Hiep went to church early. During the mass, Hiep was struck by the words of the offertory hymns from the Book of Wisdom, 'the souls of *the just* are in the hands of God, and the torment of death shall not touch them. In the sight of the unwise *they appeared to perish, but they are in peace,* alleluia.' All of a sudden, her eyes were filled with tears.

The premonition of an imminent and terrible disaster came to Hiep as she heard the verses read. She tried to calm her fears and she prayed hard for her brothers. She had almost regained her composure when she heard in the Communion hymn, 'Blessed are *the clean of heart* for they shall see God.' She shivered again. That was how she had always seen Diem: *the clean of heart*. She was terrified. She prayed in anguish, "Please God, take good care of my brother."

Hiep went to her mother's house right after the Mass. She wanted to wish Can a happy birthday before the local officials came. Can was his usual self, as they sat and talked a moment. Hiep suddenly asked, "Is the coup going to take place?" Can nodded, "Sooner or later, it will take place. But do not worry; we have taken all the necessary measures. Anyway, as long as a few key generals remain loyal, no coup will succeed." Hiep was not at all reassured by those words.

The fear lingered on. Then, at two o'clock in the afternoon, Can called her to tell her that a coup had started in Saigon. Her body felt as if it was weighed down with all the pains of the world. She did not listen to Can's reassuring words. She knew that it was the end.

Can said, "They would not dare to attack the Presidential Palace. The Presidential Guards are loyal and will fight to the end." Hiep disagreed, saying, "The President will not let them fight." Can exclaimed, "That would be foolish!" Hiep wept bitterly as she repeated, "He will not let his Guards fight the rebel troops." She put down the receiver and went into her chapel.

She was aware that her entire body ached, but her mind was calm. She sat down in her chair, knowing that she could not stay on her knees for long. She wanted to sit there for a long time, to wait in her sanctuary for news of the final outcome. She was aware that her husband had come in a little later and sat behind her. They did not make a single sound.

She lost the notion of time. Her children had come in, one by one, those who were in Hue. They were all there behind her, including Father Thuan, who had come from his seminary. No additional candles were lit. They sat together and prayed in silence.

Hiep knew that the situation was hopeless. If the coup leaders ordered their troops to attack, Diem would order his own troops to lay down their weapons; she knew that without any doubt. There might be a general, or a colonel who came at the head of his troops to save the President. But that was wishful thinking. American agents had approached all the generals and the colonels. There would be no counter-coup.

Hiep prayed that her two brothers' lives would be spared. But she knew *that* was again wishful thinking. The generals who directed the coup would never allow Diem and Nhu to survive. "The Americans may intervene to save their lives," she thought. Then even that hope appeared flimsy to her. "No, that would never happen, not with Ambassador Henry Cabot-Lodge," she thought.

*

By four o'clock in the afternoon, the radio in Saigon announced the coup. The list of generals and colonels who had rallied to the coup continued to grow. Each name announced was like a stab in her heart. Hiep listened to the men whom Diem had trusted and promoted and who were now affirming their adhesion to the coup and condemning Diem's dictatorial rule.

Finally, Am turned off the radio. He said, "Some of the people whose names are on the list may not have joined the junta." But Hiep knew that all those who were still loyal to Diem would have already been arrested or killed.

The Presidential Guards continued to put up a stubborn resistance. But Hiep knew that as soon as the coup leaders launched an all-out attack, Diem would order his troops to lay down their arms. Diem's voice still rang in her ears, "Our armed forces are responsible for the defense of our country. They are not responsible for my personal security." That was what Diem had told her only a few days ago.

*

Hiep was afraid to go to bed, to lie in the dark knowing that every minute that went by brought them closer to the final outcome. There was still the refuge of the chapel.

She went there and sat, remembering. It seemed like only yesterday when the Grand Chamberlain, on his deathbed, told Diem to strive for national independence. It seemed like only yesterday when Diem laughed as he gave her his torn gown to mend. She prayed, "My Lord, I do not understand your designs. But may your will be done."

CHAPTER TWENTY-NINE
THE DEATH OF A PRESIDENT

Thuan had gone to his grandmother's house after an early Mass. Can, sitting with Thuan in the garden, had not lost hope. He was telling Thuan how the situation could all of a sudden reverse itself, when Captain Minh, Can's military aide came in, unexpectedly.

Minh was choked with emotion. He finally managed to say, "They killed the President and Mr. Nhu." Can did not ask where Minh had obtained the information. Minh would not have reported to him without checking the veracity of the news first.

Can stood up and with a nod to Thuan, went inside the house. Thuan turned to Minh and quietly asked, "How did they die?" Minh said, "They were killed shortly after they were arrested in front of a church in Cho Lon. Apparently, they were escorted to the Joint General Staff Headquarters. They were killed before the convoy that escorted them arrived at the Headquarters. On the radio, the generals have been deceitfully reporting that the President and Mr. Nhu committed suicide. Nobody will believe that outrageous lie!"

Diem murdered

*

Minh watched Thuan. The young priest was calm, at least outwardly. Years of family training kept the man erect. Once again, Minh understood why he felt so strongly for the President, Nhu and Can and the whole family. They were a race apart. They reacted to tragedies that struck them, with a calm that was almost superhuman. He asked Thuan, "Should I tell your mother the bad news?" Thuan shook his head, "Thank you for the kind offer, but I will do it myself, presently."

Minh was gone; Thuan lingered on until Can emerged from the house. Thuan asked, "Did you tell grandmother?" Can shook his head, "She will know about it soon enough." Thuan told Can, "You are no longer safe here. Do you want to go into hiding for a while?" Can again shook his head, "The President is dead. Brother Nhu is dead. Why should I care so much about my own survival?" As Thuan turned to go, Can told him, "Take good care of your mother."

*

Thuan did not need to say anything to his parents. Am and Hiep had already heard the news on the radio. They did not believe the report, which said that Diem and Nhu had committed suicide. But they believed

510

that the President and Nhu were dead. Thuan said, "I have just left Uncle Can. He was told the bad news by Captain Minh."

Hiep, who might have cried earlier, was calm now. She sat quietly for a while, thinking about her brothers. Then, her voice echoing the pain in her heart, she said to Thuan, "Now that he is dead I can tell you a secret. In 1954, before he returned to Vietnam to assume his responsibilities as the Prime Minister, Brother Diem took the vows as an oblate of the Order of Saint Benedict. His religious name was Odilo. Saint Odilo was the one who established November 2 as All Saints' Day, to commemorate all the dead. It is God's design that my Brother Diem died today."

Thuan, shaken by what his mother had said, asked her, "Why haven't you told us about his being an oblate before?" Hiep went to her desk and brought out a bundle of letters. She took out Diem's letter that he had sent her in early 1954, with Diem's handwritten vows, and the poem he had written some time earlier. She gave them to Thuan and said, "When the President lived, I was held by my promise to keep his secret. But now that he is dead, please do whatever you wish with this information."

Thuan swallowed hard, "So, he was a religious, an oblate all these years, that is what you are saying, Mother?" Hiep nodded, "At my father's deathbed, he vowed to dedicate his life to the country. In 1954, he vowed at the Abbey of St. Andrew to dedicate his life to God. He never broke those two vows." Thuan thought in his heart, "Mother, what you have just said, is the best eulogy for the President's death."

Hiep led her family into the chapel. They recited the *De Profundis* together, and Hiep's voice rose clear and strong. Thuan watched his mother. He understood now why his mother had always been at the center of her family. At the most terrible moment of her life, she was on her knees in front of her God, unbroken, undefeated, almost without tears.

He tried to focus on the prayers being offered for the repose of the souls of his uncles. In his mind, he saw *La Pietà* that he had watched for hours in Rome. He felt the inhuman pain in his mother, yet on her face he could only see peace. The torment inside seemed to lend more gentleness, more softness to her features. He wanted to scream, "Cry, Mom, cry! Do not keep all that pain inside!"

Hiep looked up to the sanctuary. On a small table, set next to the altar, stood the pictures of Diem and Nhu. They both looked much happier in the pictures than they had been for years. She said, "For those who believe in you, my Lord, life is not destroyed; it is transformed, and when their sojourn on earth comes to an end, they already have an eternal dwelling in Heaven."

All of a sudden, a sob came out of her, and then another. She finally allowed the sea of pain within her to break through the barrier of pride, family convention and a life of self-discipline. Am said softly to her, "Let it go, Hiep, let it go."

Then the sea of pain subsided. Hiep found the courage to go on with her prayer, "Open, my Lord, to my beloved brothers, your house of light and peace, amen."

*

That night Hoang Anh, Hoang's daughter called. Her husband, Tran Trung Dzung, she, and Hiep's daughter, Niem, who lived in Saigon, had been asked by the generals to come to identify the bodies at St. Paul's Hospital. She confirmed that the President and Nhu were dead.

Hiep, who had not seen Hoang Anh since Hoang's funeral in August 1959, told her that she appreciated the call. Hoang Anh went on, "The President was shot in the head, Uncle Nhu too."

Tran Trung Dzung took the receiver from his wife. He said, "The generals lied when they claimed that the President and Mr. Nhu committed suicide. In the evening, pictures of the bodies of President and Mr. Nhu with their hands tied behind their backs, were being sold to foreign reporters. They certainly could not have killed themselves with their hands tied behind their backs."

Hiep noted the anger in Tran Trung Dzung's voice. Dzung, who had supported Diem since 1947, had thrown his lot in with Diem's party in 1953. He was appointed Minister from 1954 on, but later resigned from the government. Hiep was happy to see that Dzung was still loyal to the President.

She asked, "Who ordered the murder of the President?" Dzung replied, "Many generals wanted the President dead. All of them, collectively, are responsible for his death. I have the firm conviction that Generals Duong van Minh, Mai Huu Xuan and Tran van Don were those who directly gave the order to get rid of the President."

Hoang Anh was back on the phone, "We are worried about Uncle Nhu's children, who went to Dalat three days ago. Trac, Quynh and Quyen went to Dalat by themselves. We are also worried about Uncle Can. We hope that you and grandmother are safe."

Hiep told Hoang Anh not to be worried about Mrs. Ngo Dinh Kha and herself. She said that the United States Consulate had met with Can's aides and offered to send him to safety in Saigon. When Can insisted that he would go only in the company of his mother, the consulate staff said they needed to consult with Saigon first. Can had not heard anything more from them.

Hiep thought about Nhu's children. "How terrible it must have been for the children when they learned about their father's death. There they are, all by themselves in Dalat. They are so young to be alone; Trac, the oldest is fifteen, Quynh eleven and little Quyen is only four. What can we do now for them?" Hiep wondered. Hiep remembered the young children. Trac was a very precocious boy, with lots of leadership qualities. Quynh, his younger brother was already a good hunter like Trac. As for Quyen, the little tot, she was often seen wearing a camouflage uniform to attend public events with her mother.

She thought about Le Xuan, their mother and Le Thuy, their older sister, who were in Los Angeles. "How devastated they must be at this time. What will happen to them now?" Hiep wondered.

*

The next morning, the United States Consulate in Hue said that they had still not heard from Saigon. Hiep urged Can to go into hiding and let her take care of Mrs. Ngo Dinh Kha.

It dawned upon Hiep that, whatever promise was made by the Consulate, it was preordained that Can would be delivered into the hands of the generals as soon as he arrived in Saigon. Can had complicated the matter for the Consulate in Hue, by demanding that he should be able to leave in company of his mother. In a way, Can's pious demand, put Lodge in Saigon and Hebble, the American consul in Hue, in a situation of major political embarrassment.

Neither Lodge nor Hebble wanted to save Can's life. Lodge was intent on delivering him to the generals in Saigon. But he had no dark plans against the invalid, Mrs. Ngo Dinh Kha. Unwittingly, Can had messed up the preordained plans by insisting on having his mother with him. Those who had planned to deliver him to the generals were now faced with the problem of what should be done with Mrs. Ngo Dinh Kha.

Can took a little briefcase and went to the Monastery of the Redeemer. It was there that in 1946, Empress Nam Phuong had taken her refuge. Can stayed there in the greatest security.

Then, General Tran van Don arrived in Hue and signified to the Americans in the consulate that a solution had been found. The Vietnamese generals would transport Mrs. Ngo Dinh Kha, along with Hiep and her husband, in a Vietnamese military plane, while Can would go to the U.S. Consulate, and then be flown to Saigon on board an American plane. He would be promised a safe passage out of the country, escorted by consulate staff, but in Saigon he would, in fact, be immediately turned over to the generals.

*

When General Tran van Don asked Hiep to accompany her mother to Saigon, she knew that she could not object to his request. It was not a request but a demand, she knew. Leaving Hue was extremely painful for her, but how could she think of herself when both Diem and Nhu had just died so tragically? Yet, she was afraid that by taking her mother with her, she would make it easier for the Consulate officials in Hue to deliver Can into the hands of the junta, no matter what they promised.

Don, who tried to reassure Hiep, only succeeded in making her more certain that this was a trap. Don said, "We will take care of Uncle Can. We will meet him in Saigon and send him overseas." The 'we' Don used clearly meant the generals. Seeing Hiep's concern, Don repeated his promise, "I will make sure that he is safely sent abroad."

How many promises had been broken? How many lies had been told? Hiep knew that the only thing she could do was to look Don in the eyes and remind him, "The friendship between my brother, Can and you goes back to 1951. Before my Brother Diem came back to Vietnam, Can worked with you. Do not betray him, please."

Don, stung by her words, looked away and said, "Nobody will do anything against Uncle Can. We moved reluctantly against the President. None of us wanted him dead. I did not foresee his murder. It was almost an accident. One day you will find out who did it. You will see that I had nothing to do with it."

Hiep felt anger swell up in her. She had tried to be calm and dignified. Don's words triggered something in her and she turned her back on him, saying softly but firmly, "The President is dead. Who killed him? Who ordered him to be killed? These are questions that sooner or later will be fully answered. The parts that you or any of us played in his death, friends and foes alike will also be known. When everything is said and done, maybe none of us will be found innocent."

Don cleared his voice and said, "You may be right. My first concerns now are the safety of your mother, your own safety, then Uncle Can's. We will have ample time for all the other matters."

Hiep accompanied Don to the door. With dignity she said, "Thank you for your concern about our safety. I suggest, however, that the more important concern should be how to preserve what the President has done for the country."

Don seemed to be about to reply, but he hesitated, then finally, he said persuasively, "For the record, I want you to know that I did not want to kill the President. I had no part in his murder. I regret very much that such a crime took place. If you want to know who held the gun that killed him, I can tell you that right now. It was Captain Nguyen van Nhung, General Duong van Minh's adjutant. He was also the man who shot Mr. Nhu to death."

Hiep recoiled with disgust. She knew the name. In 1956, Diem had talked to her about Nguyen Ngoc Tho, Duong van Minh and Nguyen van Nhung after the Hoa Hao General, Le Quang Vinh was captured and condemned to death.

She asked, "Is this the same Nguyen van Nhung who desecrated General Le Quang Vinh's body?" Don nodded, "Yes. That is the man. He disinterred General Le Quang Vinh's body, cut it in pieces and threw them in a hundred locations so that the Hoa Hao's could not retrieve them. He is a man who has killed at least forty people."

After Don was gone, Hiep stood motionless for a long moment. She had not asked Don how the President died, who had killed him. She had not blamed him for being a leader in the coup. She had not shown any weakness. Yet, she knew that she would have to find out who had killed Diem. She knew that unless she found out who his murderers were, her mind would never find rest. She also knew that the finger pointing had already started among the coup leaders and their lesser cohorts. She knew that if she wanted to know the truth one day, she would have to be careful in detecting the lies that would inevitably be offered to her as facts.

Burning in her heart was her concern for the legacy that had been left behind by Diem She would find Diem's death a little more acceptable, if it did not mean the end of all his achievements. Discouraged, she felt that this was an idle wish, that sooner or later all of Diem's legacy would disappear. She clenched her fists as a long scream rose from her heart and echoed in every fiber of her being, "No! Not that! Please, not that! He died for what he tried to do for his country. Don't destroy all his work, as well!"

A gust of wind stirred the treetops. Hiep's anguish was swiftly replaced by a feeling of peace. From the devastated landscape of her soul surged soft vibrations, which brought back a beginning of peace and hope. No, Diem's work had not been all in vain. His legacy would survive, no matter what the immediate future looked like.

Hiep went back to her home and packed. Within less than an hour, she and Am were ready to leave everything behind and take the flight in a military plane to Saigon, in the company of her ailing mother.

*

Fortunately, Mrs. Ngo Dinh Kha was barely conscious of the tragedy that had struck her family. She was barely aware of what was happening, when they bundled her up and put her onboard the military plane that was to take her to Saigon, according to the orders of the generals. The noise of the plane bothered her. The altitude hurt her ears, but she looked up at Hiep as if she wanted to give her solace. Hiep held her tightly and prayed God not to let her understand the extent of the tragedy. But the matriarch had eyes that saw. Nothing could really escape those eyes.

Mrs. Ngo Dinh Kha had not seen Can around her for the last few days. Because she did not see Can, she knew that things were amiss. She looked at Hiep and her eyes were filled with tears. She tried to say something. But only Can could understand what she said. Hiep held her tightly. The plane plunged into rough weather and the turbulence seemed to go on forever. Hiep, holding her mother tightly in her arms, at moments felt that life was too long, too unendurable.

Then she remembered. Can was at that moment on another flight that was to deliver him to his friends of yesterday, his present enemies. No, she should not think about rest or death. She still had a fight ahead of her. She had to fight for Can's survival. Slowly during that flight, she began to accept the bitter reality that the generals and the Venerable Thich Tri Quang would never allow Can to survive.

*

Upon their arrival at Tan Son Nhat Airport, in Saigon, their son Nguyen van Tuyen, then a Captain in the army, their daughter, Niem, and Niem's husband, Brian Smith, welcomed them. During the long drive from the airport to his home, neither Tuyen, nor his sister Niem said much, but their parents felt that inside, they were seething.

At his home, Tuyen had arranged separate rooms for his grandmother and parents. After looking after the comfort of Mrs. Ngo Dinh Kha, they all came down to the small parlor to talk.

Niem began by saying that she, along with Tran Trung Dzung and Hoang Anh, had gone to St. Paul's Hospital on November 2 to identify Diem's and Nhu's bodies. She said, "I recognized them. Each was shot in the back of the head, one bullet for each of them. There were no other traces of injury or laceration or contusion. Many people are spreading rumors now that Uncle Nhu was stabbed. I did not see any trace of stabbing. Other people said that the President had contusions, that he had been beaten before he was shot. I saw no contusions."

Hiep asked, "Were they really recognizable? A head wound may seriously distort their features." Niem said without hesitation, "I recognized them easily. So did Hoang Anh and Tran Trung Dzung." Tuyen added, "I have seen where the generals buried the President and Uncle Nhu. I have gone there twice already. They did not allow me to lay wreaths on their graves, but I can go to the site any time I want."

Am asked, "Do you know anything about the coup d'état and the murder of the President, besides what has been reported by the media?" Niem and Tuyen looked at each other, then Tuyen said, "Yes. We have gathered quite a bit of information by talking to field officers who participated in the coup. Brian, on his part, had been talking to people from various Embassies, especially to American diplomats. Father Tran Tu Nhan and Father Thinh in the Monastery of the Redeemer also talked with generals and colonels. Hoang Anh and Tran Trung Dzung have made extensive contacts with diplomats and generals. I was able to talk with two adjutants of the President, before they were arrested."

Hiep said, "We do not need to go over all the details at this moment. I only want you to answer a few specific questions. First, who were the coup leaders, besides General Duong van Minh?"

Tuyen seemed to be surprised by the question. He said, "All the military commanders have quickly gone over to the side of coup leaders, except for those who were killed or detained from the very beginning. Captain Ho Tan Quyen, Commander of the Navy was killed by two of his closest aides, Lieutenant-Commander Luc, and Navy Lieutenant Giang."

Hiep stopped Tuyen and asked, "How did they kill him?" Tuyen was surprised by Hiep's desire to know all the details. He complied: "November 1 was Captain Quyen's birthday. Yes, I know, it is also Uncle Can's birthday. Early in the morning, Luc and Giang came in and invited the Captain to Thu Duc. They said they had arranged a lunch, to celebrate his birthday. Mrs. Quyen was abroad, and Captain Quyen did not see why he should not go with them. The two men drove their Commander to the Saigon-Bien Hoa Highway. On the way, they told the Captain about the upcoming coup and asked the Captain to join the coup leaders. Captain Quyen was very angry. He asked them to stop the car and started admonishing them."

Hiep said, "Navy Captain Quyen's loyalty was unquestionable. His Navy shot down one of the two planes that bombed the palace on February 27, 1962. I remember how the President spoke highly about Navy Captain Quyen!"

Tuyen resumed, "He told them the he would never betray the President. He asked them to return to reason and go with him to the headquarters, to help quash the coup. As he talked, he saw that his friends and closest aides exchanged looks. He knew that they were ready to kill him, so he jumped out of the car, and started running. Luc ran after him and shot him to death. He left the Captain's body by the side of the highway and drove back to Saigon to report what had happened to the coup leaders."

Hiep asked, "Didn't the coup leaders regret his death? He was one of their distinguished comrade-in-arms. Didn't they shed a tear for him?" Tuyen said, "All I know is that his murder, early in the morning of November 1, hastened the coup. The coup leaders were afraid that his death would soon be uncovered, and that was why they had to launch the coup before schedule."

Hiep pursued her questions, "Who else was killed?" Tuyen answered, "Colonel Le Quang Tung, Commander of the Special Forces and Major Le Quang Trieu, his brother were murdered by the order of the coup leaders, right outside the Joint General Staff Headquarters."

Hiep said, "The three of them will always be remembered along with the President and Uncle Nhu, at any commemorative services. Were there others?" Tuyen reluctantly told her, "Yes, while defending the Gia Long Palace and the Republic Fortress, many were killed." Hiep said, "Try to get all their names; they will be remembered in the same way by our family and our friends."

Hiep asked, "Who was detained during the coup?" Tuyen said, "From what I know, Colonel Nguyen Ngoc Khoi, Commander of the Brigade of the President Guards, Colonel Cao Van Vien, Major Tran Cuu Thien, Group Captain Huynh Huu Hien, Commander of the Air Force…"

Hiep asked, "Have they been ill-treated?" Tuyen said, "Except for Lt. Colonel Cao Van Vien who is a close friend of General Tran Thien Khiem, all the others were handcuffed." Am intervened, "We have all the time in the world to learn all about the coup, who were the real leaders, who did what during the coup, who gave the order to kill the President and Brother Nhu. We will find out who knew about the order before its execution, who pulled the trigger, who danced on their bodies, who cried on them. Let us rest now for a while."

Hiep nodded. The world before her was empty. Two concerns kept her going: her mother and Can's fate. She also wanted to know every minute detail of the coup and the murder of her brothers. She looked up and thought, "God, I have to know. Not to avenge their deaths. Revenge is in your hands, not mine. But I have to know if I am to fully recover my peace of mind."

Tuyen, Niem and Brian looked at her, waiting for her wish. Hiep said, "Your father is right. We have the rest of our lives to find out all about the coup, and the death of your uncles. We also have the rest of our lives to pray that their accomplishments survive their death."

*

Hoang Anh and Tran Trung Dzung were there the next morning to tell Hiep what they had learned about the coup and the murders. Hoang Anh first announced that Nhu's children were now safe in Rome. Two days earlier, on November 4, Hoang Anh was able to meet with Trac, Quynh and Le Quyen, Nhu's younger children at the Joint General Staff Headquarters in Tan Son Nhat. After that, she saw them off. They were to fly to Bangkok and then on to Rome to join Madame Nhu, who waited for them there. They left Saigon at 7:30 on November 4, on an Asia Pacific flight, with an American Consul for escort.

"So, Nhu's children are safe now," Hiep thought. Like her own children, like Hoang Anh, and Giao's children in Hue and Luyen's children in Europe. All of them were safe. Hiep said a silent prayer of thanksgiving while Hoang Anh went upstairs to see her grandmother.

Dzung's story about the coup was very detailed. He seemed to know the roles played by each coup leader at any time during the two fateful days. Hiep asked, "Why do the generals confide in you? After all, you are married to one of the President's nieces."

Dzung laughed, "I have certain leverage over General Duong van Minh." Hiep had heard about it. After General Duong van Minh entered the Binh

Xuyen headquarters in Rung Sat, there had been rumors that he had stolen part of the river pirates' captured funds. Later on, some of Minh's officers went with evidence, to the Ministry of Defense and testified against him. At that time, Minh was commanding Government troops in hot pursuit of Hoa Hao's rebel armies, and Diem asked Dzung, who was Secretary for Defense not to make a public scandal out of it. Hiep was told that Dzung had kept the dossier with him, even after he left the Ministry.

Dzung described the hesitation of key coup leaders such as Colonel Thieu, who had gone to see Nhu even on the morning of November 1, to warn him about a coup in the making. Dzung said, "By that time, Thieu had already brought his division to the outskirts of Saigon."

He recounted the bravery of the Presidential Guards. He said, "Major Due, who commanded them, in the absence of Colonel Khoi, taken prisoner at the Joint General Staff, asked the President to let him launch an attack on the Joint General Staff headquarters, and capture all the coup leaders there. But the President refused, saying that he did not want bloodshed."

Dzung recounted the moment when Diem and Nhu escaped from the Palace, under light escort, followed by Cao Xuan Vy, the faithful Deputy Head of the Republic Youth, and the moment when the generals learned of their escape. He laughed derisively, "The generals were panic-stricken. For a while, each one of them believed that they should flee. Then they pointed the finger at each other. There is no honor among thieves."

Hiep told Dzung, "I would certainly like to know everything that happened, both during and after the coup. I hope you will tell me everything you know about it, some day. But, right now, I need to go to church and pray for my brothers."

Dzung and Hoang Anh kept Hiep's spirits up. They were among the rare persons involved with the *old regime* that were not paralyzed by fear or anxiety in the aftermath of the coup. A campaign of terror had begun, aimed at anybody who had been loyal to Diem. A witch-hunt was started against *Can Lao* Party members and against the Catholics in general.

At the same time, a carefully orchestrated campaign to discredit Diem was conducted by foreign reporters, the local press and the An Quang Buddhist activists. Overnight, Diem became known as one of the worst dictators the world had ever known.

Hiep was not surprised by the viciousness of the attacks against Diem, her other brothers and Le Xuan, but the campaign of hatred gave her tremendous emotional pain.

*

Even Le Thuy, Nhu's eldest daughter was not spared. Colonel Do Mau had come into possession of her diary and immediately sent it to the local newspapers that published it in installments.

In view of the tremendous publicity surrounding the publication of Le Thuy's diary, and the promise of juicy stories that were to come out in future installments, Hiep was terribly worried for her niece. What could a young girl of nineteen have written in her diary?

In spite of the promises, in spite of the fact that the whole diary was printed, there was nothing indecent in the diary. Through her diary, one could only see a pure young girl, more attentive to what was happening to her country than to herself. Some of her views might be faulted as too conservative, or lacking in flexibility, but all in all, the diary did honor to the education she had received from her father and mother.

Hiep heard that Le Xuan's diary had fallen into General Nguyen Khanh's hands and that he often carried it with him. She heard that he sometimes would read out a sentence from the diary and comment on it with a friend. Through friends, she tried to convince Khanh to return the diary to her sister-in-law. She never succeeded in that endeavor. General Nguyen Khanh still carries the diary with him, and from time to time, reads a sentence out of the diary. Hiep appreciates the fact that Khanh has not allowed it to fall into evil hands and that he has never tried to use it against Le Xuan. She hopes that like Le Thuy's diary, Le Xuan's was written to record words of wisdom, interesting conversations, commentaries on books or movies, and viewpoints on current events.

The confiscation of the fortune of the Ngo Dinh did not turn up anything damaging to their reputation. Newspapers, hungry for sensational stories about the Ngo Dinh, and especially about Le Xuan, went to every place a member of the family had lived earlier, but could not find anything sensational to report to the public. Yet, foreign reporters, generals and colonels, as well as several Buddhist activists continued to slander them, while others using sly innuendoes and slogans, continued to drag their names through the mud.

*

Living in Saigon with her invalid mother, at her son's house, Hiep was soon reconciled with the new realities. Only a few people came to see her at first. Then more and more came. Most of her earlier visitors were grieving like her. Their husbands or their fathers had been with '*the old regime*', and had been held in jail since the coup, without trial. Most often, their principal crime was their loyalty to the late President.

Catholics were lumped together with *Can Lao* Party members, and were continually being attacked by certain newspapers. Certain Buddhist monks openly preached hatred against Christianity.

The circle of Hiep's visitors started expanding. Within two weeks' time, Hiep was seeing as many visitors a day as she had seen in Hue, during the time her brothers were in power.

Beside Colonel Dang van Quang who came to visit with Am and Hiep from the very first day they were in Saigon, more and more military officers came and paid their respects.

As for the politicians, besides Tran Trung Dzung, quite a number of the men and women who were in the new government also came to assure her of their friendship.

Hiep listened intently but did not say much. She wanted to know all about the last days of her brothers' lives. She wanted to piece together the threads of events great and small, which had led to the downfall of the First Republic. She also wanted to know what would survive of the social and political legacy that Diem had left behind.

*

Hiep stared at the radio. It was only seven o'clock in the morning in Saigon. Am had turned the radio on just a minute earlier. The President of the United States had been shot earlier and was now believed to be dead.

Hiep turned to look at her husband. Am, staring blankly, kept murmuring to himself, "Impossible! Impossible!" Hiep ran back to her room, threw herself on her knees and tried to pray. She did not know why she felt such acute despair. Had she hoped that President Kennedy would live to tell the world more about the coup against Diem? Had she hoped that President Kennedy would intervene for Can? Had she refused to believe that President Kennedy had a direct hand in the coup, overthrowing Diem?

Since her brothers' deaths, she had thought about President Kennedy only in passing. "Now he is dead," she thought sadly. Diem, the first Catholic President of South Vietnam, had died only three weeks earlier, a bullet to his head. Now, Kennedy the first Catholic President of the United States was dead, also with a bullet to his head. "Was there a parallel here?" Hiep wondered. President Kennedy's eldest brother had also been killed during the war.

As she prayed for Kennedy, she felt anger surge within her. Her mind tormented her with heart rending unanswerable questions, "Why, why all these dreams, why all these struggles? Why all these ambitions, plans, efforts, victories and acclamations, triumphs and defeats? Why all this despair in the end? Diem was dead. Now Kennedy was dead. How much of their dreams and their achievements would survive? How much would their examples help to guide future generations?"

Her telephone was ringing off the hook. Hiep knew that Am would take care of the calls. She hid her face against a pillow and remained on her knees at the side of her bed. Her head swam as she tried to cope with this fresh tragedy and exhausted, she dozed off.

She woke up feeling Am's hand shaking her shoulders gently. Am said, "People keep calling. They seem to see a link between Brother Diem's and President Kennedy's deaths. Some talk about God's justice. What nonsense!"

Hiep stood up but had to lean on Am. She shook her head, "It is pure nonsense. How dare people think of God like that?" She knew that some people would continue to think that way. "It's blasphemy," Hiep muttered.

Am said, "A caller told me that three weeks ago, right after she learned about our President's and Brother Nhu's deaths, Le Xuan told the newspapers in Los Angeles, 'The blood of our President and my husband has been shed; it will stain the White House.' The caller claimed that Le

Xuan was prophetic." Again Le Xuan! Hiep was angry. Le Xuan, a prophetess?

Hiep shuddered, "Le Xuan was distraught. She did not know what she was saying. I hope she keeps quiet at this moment."

She called Thuc in Naples. She did not care what time it was in Italy. She had to talk. Thuc was not in bed. For hours he had been listening to the radio. He said, "This morning, I will say a Mass for the peace of President Kennedy's soul. I will ask Trac, Nhu's eldest son, to serve as altar boy." Neither of them thought that saying a mass for the repose of President Kennedy was incongruous. Neither of them saw anything wrong in having Trac serve as altar boy for the mass.

Hiep asked, "Why this death, Brother Thuc, why?" Thuc sounded very tired when he said, "I don't know, Sister Hiep. I don't know. Only God knows why the just, the innocent, the young have to die. Only God knows why violent deaths take place. I will pray for him and our two brothers. You know, I have promised myself to say masses every morning for our Brothers Diem and Nhu for a month. I have not finished a month yet. Only three weeks after their deaths, I will now say Masses for the three of them."

Hiep said, "Here in Vietnam we have not heard much detail about what happened. How is Mrs. Jacqueline Kennedy?" Thuc told her, "I saw her on the television. It was awful. All his blood was on her dress. Pray for her, Sister, pray for her."

Hiep asked, "How did Le Xuan react to President Kennedy's death?" There was a hesitation, and then Thuc replied, "Since our President and her husband died, Le Xuan has been in despair. Though her children surround her now, she is not well. She sent Mrs. Kennedy a terrible cable. She offered her condolences of course, but ended the cable by saying that Mrs. Kennedy must be feeling now what *she* had felt when her President and her husband were murdered."

Hiep, choked with tears, cried, "How could she write such a cable! She cannot send a cable like that in the name of our family!" Thuc reassured Hiep, "No, she wrote her cable for herself. When I heard about it, I sent a cable myself to Mrs. Kennedy, on behalf of our family." After a moment Thuc asked, "How is Mother? How is everybody over there?"

Though Mrs. Ngo Dinh Kha was entering what appeared to be the final coma, Hiep said, "Everybody is doing as well as possible, considering the circumstances. Mother becomes weaker and weaker. My daughter, Niem, gave birth a few hours ago to a beautiful girl, and her name is Kim Lan (Golden Orchid)."

Thuc exclaimed, "There you are! Grandmother! The miracle of life and death! The day the world is shocked with President Kennedy's death, a child is born to our family."

CHAPTER THIRTY
SOUTH VIETNAM SUBJUGATED

In January 1964, Ambassador Lodge told reporters that he was working hard to develop the Vietnamese generals into successful politicians and military men. Photos of the Ambassador appeared almost every day in the Saigon newspapers.

Without comment, the newspapers reported that the Ambassador had instructed the generals to arm and train Hoa Hao's and Cao Dai units. They reported that the generals had no objection to doing this. Now, after so much hard work to eliminate them, and after such a tremendous loss of lives in 1955, the sects' armies were back. Ironically, Duong van Minh, who had helped get rid of the private armies, now presided over their re-emergence.

On January 30, General Nguyen Khanh overthrew General Duong van Minh in a bloodless coup, and assumed power. But the authority of the South Vietnamese government continued to be eroded.

In February 1964, American advisors were positioned not only at the provincial level but also at district and village levels. Even General Khanh and his colleagues knew that such a move would make them 'look like lackeys', as Khanh said, but they acquiesced. Hiep cried as she remembered how Diem and Nhu had tried to remove the American advisors at the provincial level.

Duong van Minh, soon restored as Chief of State, together with Khanh, asked for an 'American brain trust' to help them govern South Vietnam. Hiep angrily shoved the newspaper over to Am, and declared, "The Americans are governing South Vietnam. We are living in an American protectorate."

Hiep only had to open a local newspaper, to read about one betrayal after another, of national sovereignty on the part of the generals. She was alarmed with the speed at which the American Ambassador was encroaching on South Vietnam's independence.

Diem's legacy was being destroyed systematically. In the end, South Vietnam was no longer an independent country.

*

Tran Trung Dzung said, "He is dead, the man who killed the President and Uncle Nhu." Am looked at his wife and noticed that she shivered. She bent her head in an attitude of prayer. Am wanted to know more, but Dzung did not know much. It seemed that Major Nguyen van Nhung, the man who had shot and killed Diem and Nhu, had hanged himself with his bootlaces in his prison cell. Dzung added that General Nguyen Khanh had ordered his arrest after the coup of January 30 and that Nhung had been sent to a prison cell where he was interrogated about his participation in the murder of the President. It was reported that he had hanged himself a few nights later. His death had been kept secret for a while, but soon there had been leaks and speculations."

Dzung commented, "There has been too much speculation. Some have said Colonel Nguyen Chanh Thi ordered his 'suicide', because he wanted to avenge the death of the President." Hiep exclaimed, "No, the President would never want to be avenged that way." Dzung, a little surprised by Hiep's vehemence, went on, "Thi has said to many people since his return from Cambodia after the November coup, that though he himself had participated in a coup against the President, he cursed the people who had murdered him."

Hiep sighed, "The President always had a soft spot for Colonel Thi. People called him 'the adopted son of the President' before the coup of November 1960. Even after the coup, the President still believed that the Colonel was innocent and hoped that he would return to stand trial and be exonerated. "

Dzung said, "Others speculate that it was General Khanh himself who wanted to avenge the President's death." Hiep shook her head in disagreement, but did not say anything. Dzung continued, "I have talked to field officers who knew Major Nhung well. They told me that Nhung had been having nightmares and had sometimes been seized with visions that made him shake like a leaf. They told me that he thought he was going to be killed by the people who had ordered him to murder the President."

Hiep again bent her head. There were so many lies, so many secrets, since the confusion had set in. She listened to Dzung who concluded sadly, "The truth may never be known." Hiep wanted to agree; yet she knew that no secret was safe forever.

Major Nhung was dead. Nobody believed that he had committed 'suicide.' Who had killed him, and for what reasons Hiep did not know. What she knew was that the President's death seemed to be having endless violent ramifications.

Quite recently, somebody had suggested to her, "The most terrible crime is the killing of a *just* man, because God himself will avenge his death." What a terrible prediction! What a terrible thought! Hiep listened and heard a scream of protest within herself, "My God, is it not enough? Is it not enough that my brothers died?"

Within her surged a vision: the horses of the Apocalypse rushing wildly and aimlessly in a nightmarish landscape of fire, and pestilence and death. Dzung and Am looked at her as she shivered. Then the vision was gone and Hiep smiled apologetically, "It is nothing, I assure you. There is a terrible draft in this house at times."

*

Thuc cried over the phone. That was the first time Hiep had ever heard him cry. Hiep said, "Mother did not suffer. She passed away very peacefully. We buried her decently, and simply. There was no big crowd walking behind her coffin. I'm sure she must be much happier where she is now. Yes, she did receive the Extreme Unction before she passed away."

Thuc said remorsefully, "I am an ungrateful son. I was not even there when she passed away." Hiep tried to reason with him, "What could you have done if you were here? Right now there are people who swear they would kill you or put you in jail, if you were here. Please do not torture yourself like that."

Thuc did not seem to hear her. He went on, "I was not there when father died. I was not there when mother died. What kind of a son am I?"

Hiep was concerned. Thuc sounded so distraught that she could barely recognize him. How he suffered! Would he have the strength to go on living? Would he have the strength to continue in his service to the Church? Would he and Luyen help each other in their forced exile?

Luyen had been calmer on the phone. He had started working in a Catholic Secretariat helping to develop a new approach to private education in France. He talked about the possibility of returning to Vietnam. His mention of that possibility filled Hiep with hope.

Now holding the receiver, she felt so very tired. Then, unexpectedly, Thuc was speaking to her again. With a voice that was almost normal he said, "Forgive me for my moment of weakness. I will be all right. But please, Sister Hiep, continue to be strong for all of us."

*

Hiep looked at the headlines and saw that the generals had decided to abolish the committees in charge of the Strategic Hamlets. She carefully folded the newspaper and put it back on the table.

Am who was watching her closely told her, "The generals will soon regret that decision." Hiep looked up and asked, "What decision?" Am smiled, "The only decision that could make you angry enough to stop reading the newspaper, the decision about the Strategic Hamlet Program. But don't you worry. In no time, our generals will have to change their strategy again."

Hiep was not in a talkative mood, and Am was trying to cajole her into saying something. He pursued, "The generals are doing exactly what the Vietcong were hoping for. The Strategic Hamlets were strangling them and they were losing the war."

Hiep nodded, "The Hamlets that my brothers had already built up were not perfect, but at least they were able to assume the defensive role, and allowed the regular army units to be on the offensive. Brother Nhu predicted that within another couple of years the Strategic Hamlets would be perfected and the Communists would have to stop waging war against us, or they would be defeated."

Am sighed, "Unfortunately, the President and Brother Nhu did not have another couple of years. Now, what will the generals do after the Hamlets are dismantled?"

Hiep replied without hesitation, "The generals have learned a lot from the President. Unfortunately they have not learned the essentials. What will happen is that they will have to use regular army units for the defense of the hamlets and they do not have enough troops to do that properly."

Am asked again, "Then, you predict that sooner or later the generals will have to return to the Strategic Hamlet Program, or something similar?"

Hiep shook her head, "The generals do not believe in the people like the President did. They would set up hamlets to be defended by paramilitary units or semi-military units instead of hamlet people. They will be considered inferior to regular army troops even though they may be more exposed to danger than regular soldiers. Their rate of desertion will be very high and they will not fight. Any such program will fail."

Watching Hiep, Am wondered. How many lessons were buried within her? How many treasures of reflection were to be found in her and her surviving brothers? He understood now why Hiep never believed that the generals and the Venerable Thich Tri Quang would allow Ngo Dinh Can to live.

Hiep saw Am's sudden sadness. She was moved by his steadfastness. Throughout their marriage, he had never complained. Every tragedy suffered by her family became his own tragedy. He allowed her to live a full life as a Ngo Dinh. He surrounded her with discreet care, and never bothered her with his own anxiety.

He had followed her to Saigon without asking a question. He had ended his active life as a businessman and allowed her to take care of her mother day and night. Hiep felt a moment of great peace within her. Among the ruins of her family, she still had Am, and her children. She looked away to hide her tears of gratitude.

*

In the midst of all her worry about Can, Hiep felt devastated when General Nguyen Khanh reported to the press in Saigon what he had told the American Ambassador; "We Vietnamese want the Americans to be responsible with us as partners, and not merely as advisors."

In the end, Khanh was now offering on a silver platter what the Kennedy Administration had pursued from the very beginning, and had constantly been denied by President Diem. The Americans had been given the responsibility for Vietnam. Khanh made no secret of the fact that his government had surrendered national sovereignty to the Americans.

What Diem had ultimately died for, his country's independence, had been relinquished without regret by the Chairman of the Revolutionary Military Council.

*

Colonel Dang van Quang kept his face in the darkness. It was better that way. Hiep did not turn on the lights. Am and she sat there and absorbed the bad news. Hiep did not cry, but deep inside her surged wave after wave of pain and anger.

So they had condemned Can to death, and the man who came to announce the bad news was Colonel Dang van Quang, the President of the Revolutionary Tribunal and Am's godson.

The fact that Dang van Quang was there in their home showed his courage and sincerity. He had tried hard to save Can from capital punishment. He had done all that he could. But in the end, he was alone to defend Can. The other members of the Tribunal knew his links with the Ngo Dinh family and barely listened to him. They were under strong pressure to get the trial over with quickly. They were under severe pressure to condemn Can to death. Hiep lowered her head and accepted the inevitable.

The Venerable Thich Tri Quang and his Buddhist activists in Hue and in Saigon would never allow Can to live. Though Can was very sick and would soon die in prison, he might talk. There was so much in his memory. He had to be destroyed.

Few on the Buddhist side dared now to talk about compassion. The teachings of the Buddha were relegated to a few obscure pagodas where genuine believers came and prayed. Such pagodas stood as small islands of peace in a sea of hatred. In one of her visits to Can in prison, Can had told her, "For sure, they will condemn me to death. When I die, I want to be buried in a Buddhist pagoda ground." Hiep had exclaimed, "You are not going to die. The Pope himself has intervened for you. Ambassador Cabot Lodge gave his word to the Pope that your life would be spared."

Can had looked at her with tenderness and said, "Do not take Ambassador Lodge's word, like you took Brother Diem's word. The Pope is far away. I need his prayers and blessings more than his intervention. Anyway, I will die, in prison or facing a firing squad. But please promise me that you will bury me in a Buddhist pagoda ground."

Hiep shook her head. She still wanted to hope, even though she knew there was no more room for hope. What Can asked her to do was impossible. She told him, "How can we do that? You are a Catholic. You must be buried in a Catholic cemetery, on blessed ground."

Can smiled sadly, "Neither Brother Diem, nor Brother Nhu are buried in a Catholic cemetery. Like Brother Khoi and our nephew Huan before them, they were buried hastily in unmarked graves. Sister Hiep, I want to be buried near a pagoda. During my lifetime, I have not been successful in preserving the harmony between the Christians and the Buddhists. Let me in my death remind all the Vietnamese that we, the Ngo Dinh, have always had a tremendous respect for the Buddha, and that we have never had any quarrel with Buddhism."

Hiep sobbed uncontrollably. She asked Can, "Have you talked to your confessor, Father Thinh, about this decision?" Can smiled: "He was shocked at first, but then he understood."

Hiep asked, "What pagoda is ready now to receive you? Aren't all the Buddhists against you?" Can looked at Hiep a long time before he answered, "There are more Buddhists than you realize, who understood Brother Diem. They are silenced now by the hatred around them. But you will find courageous people among them. They also want to do something to atone for this terrible hatred. You will find many Buddhist monks here in Saigon who will be pleased to give my remains a dignified burial after I die."

*

Hoang Anh stared at the colonel in astonishment as he waited for her answer impatiently. He firmly believed that she would soon say, "We will raise the money."

Soon enough, however, what he heard was, "You are wrong to believe that we have lots of money. We have nothing. I will talk with my aunt, but I already know the situation before I talk to her. We cannot raise even half a million, and you are asking for six million? That is a ridiculous demand!"

The colonel shrugged, "General K. is not asking this for himself. If I mention money, it is because I know that other people will not help without being paid. General Minh is still the Chief of State. Only he has the power to pardon Uncle Can, but he cannot pardon him without spreading money to make other people more flexible."

Hoang Anh said, with a point of irony in her voice, "Colonel, please tell General K. that I know he would like to help. He loved the President and is fond of Uncle Can. I know that he would like to save Uncle Can's life. But when he asks for that kind of money from us, we will have to say thank you, but we cannot afford to pay."

The colonel said, "It will be most difficult to save Uncle Can's life. Even with money, it would be difficult for us to persuade General Minh and others to pardon him, against the wishes of the Venerable Thich Tri Quang. Without money, it is next to impossible."

He looked at his watch, "I have to get back to my office. Talk to your Uncle Can. He must have some money stashed away somewhere. Talk to your Aunt Hiep, she must know the family's secret caches, too. I need to warn you that we are running out of time. They want to execute him on the anniversary of the *incident* in Hue, that is May 8."

He got to his feet. Hoang Anh stood up. The colonel saw that anger had replaced grief in her eyes. Defiantly, she said, "Then, go and kill him. Does General K., of all people, believe my uncles to be corrupt officials?"

The colonel stood his ground, "No, the General does not believe that the late President was corrupt. He does not think that the late Advisor Mr. Ngo Dinh Nhu was corrupt either. But, yes, your Uncle Can is thought to be corrupt."

Again the colonel recoiled as the anger in Hoang Anh's eyes lashed at him, "Your Revolutionary Committees have already confiscated everything that you claimed was owned by my family. Yet, none of the assets, none of the cash the Committees have put their hands on, belonged to my family. Clearly, it was all property belonging to government operations and public associations. You, more than anybody else should know that my Uncle Can lived in his mother's house and did not have a dime he could call his own."

The colonel walked to the door. He turned to say again, "His life depends on your capability to raise six million. Please act quickly or there will be another death in your family."

Hoang Anh stood there a moment thinking about the ridiculous and impossible demand. A sudden and sharp pain shot across her body and she grabbed a corner of the table to steady herself. Her eyes blurred and were blinded. She closed them and clenched her teeth. She waited for the pain to subside, then picked up her phone and called her Aunt Hiep, and told her about General K.'s demand.

Hiep knew immediately that Hoang Anh was suffering. She asked, "What is wrong? You are having problems breathing, and your voice trembles. What is the matter?" Hoang Anh tried to reassure her, "It is nothing. I apparently have a stomach ulcer or something like that. It does not bother me too often. Let us talk about General K.'s demand."

Hiep said, "Take a rest first. When you are rested, take a taxi and come over to my house and we will talk. Telephone lines here are not to be trusted."

*

All the money Hiep and Am had was tied up in the construction of the new Cathedral of Hue. They had advanced money for the construction until all they had were debts. Now, the Archbishop of Hue was gone, and nobody would be able to pay back to them the earnings of a lifetime.

Hiep told Hoang Anh that she had nothing left, except her home in Hue. She would like to sell it and raise some money. But houses in Hue were cheap and would take time to sell. Anyway, the sale of her house would not bring them anywhere near the amount demanded. As for Hoang Anh, she had inherited a large house in Hue from her mother. The sale of that house would not help much either.

Hoang Anh said with bitter anger, "Had they been corrupt, we would now have a chance to save Uncle Can's life." Hiep shook her head, "No, even if we had the money, we would not be able to save his life. General Duong van Minh would not dare pardon him. The man who decides his fate is the Venerable Thich Tri Quang. He is determined to have your uncle executed. I would like to have the money and give it to General K. That would not save your Uncle Can, but then I could say I had done everything I possibly could for him. But be sure of this, my poor niece, your Uncle Can will be executed, no matter what we do."

*

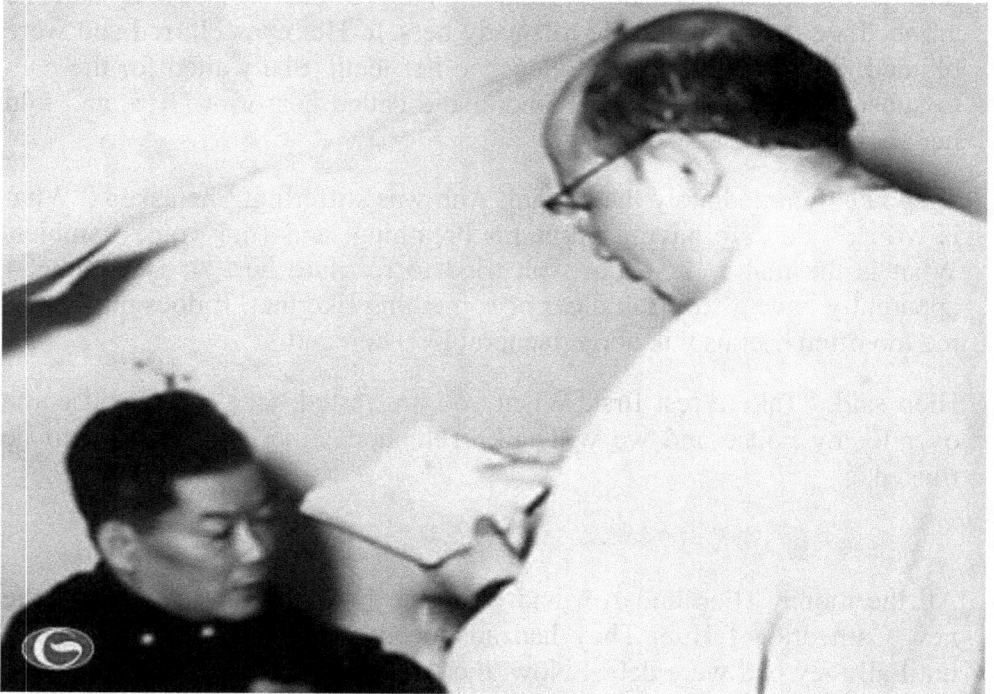

Ngo Dinh Can the day before his execution

*

On May 8, 1964, Can was shot in front of a small group of people, including a Buddhist abbot and a Vietnamese priest. The priest happened to be Can's godson. Newspapers later described Can as being unable to walk; actually he deported himself with calm dignity until the last minute.

Walking down the steps to the courtyard where he was to be shot, Can refused to be helped. He also refused to be blindfolded and agreed to let the executioners blindfold him only when they pleaded that they had to obey the regulations.

The priest approached Can for the last time, and gave him his blessings. Can thanked everybody present and asked those who could, to recite an *Our Father* with him, He then said that he was ready.

*

Hiep and Am, in the company of Father Thuan and Tuyen, together with Niem and Brian Smith, sat at Tuyen's home, waiting. The generals had forbidden their presence at the execution. The generals promised, however, to send a car to pick them up after the execution was over. They would be allowed to claim his body, and take care of his burial.

It seemed like an eternity until finally a military police van arrived. Everybody climbed into the van. They were taken to the Chi Hoa Prison, and shown to the room where Can's body had been brought after the execution.

Hiep's vision blurred as she saw the pool of blood on the floor. Am tried to shield her from Can's bruised body, but Hiep stepped forward and put her hand on her brother's forehead. In a trance, she remembered fragments of prayers. In a kind of waking dream, she looked at her brother's face and remembered his face as a child.

Tuyen and Thuan tried to support her, but she struggled to stand erect by herself. She turned to ask the Buddhist Abbot, "Sir, have you made all the necessary preparations?" The Abbot nodded, "Dear Madam, we are honored to give the Advisor a most decent burial. He will find peace on the grounds of our Pagoda, according to his wishes."

*

So, on that same day, the Buddhist Abbot took the body back to the Mutuality Pagoda in a simple coffin, and buried him on the grounds of the pagoda.

A long commemorative ceremony assembled Buddhists and Christians the next day. Hiep watched the faces around her. On all the faces she read sadness and pride. They were the people who came to pay their respects and to pray for the man who had been condemned to death and executed for crimes he had never committed. His request to be buried among Buddhists, on Buddhist ground, illustrated clearly the fact that he had never hated Buddhism.

The fact that a Buddhist monk stood by his side with a Catholic priest at the execution, and received his body in his pagoda, showed that many Buddhists believed in his innocence and respected him.

Hiep whispered to Can, "Rest in peace my brother. Somehow, we will find a way to get Diem's and Nhu's remains out of the Joint General Staff grounds and give them an appropriate burial. We want them to rest in peace. Will you help us?"

*

After Can was killed, Hiep's mind went numb. Apparently, the human mind knows when pain has gone past the threshold of endurance. Hiep was still capable of conducting a long conversation with a visitor, but she declined to meet with anyone who was not a relative or a long time friend.

She listened to the radio. She read newspapers. She commented on events with members of her family. But she would not venture out of her house unless it was absolutely necessary.

She noticed with sadness the *triumphalism* of Buddhist activists. She knew that *triumphalism* in any religion would lead to disaster.

On May 26,1964, the Feast of the Birth of Buddha was celebrated with great fervor, while the final preparations were made for the dramatic trial of Major Dang Sy, the man who had allegedly ordered his troops to fire on innocent Buddhists on May 8, the previous year.

Dang Sy told the Revolutionary Tribunal that he had been approached in his cell by the new authorities who promised to release him if he accused

Archbishop Thuc of being responsible for the deaths in front of the Hue Radio Station. His presentation of the events was clear and concise and he did not show any fear of the prosecution.

Hiep, coming out of her inaction, had asked some relatives to go and attend the trial. What they reported filled her with horror. Major Dang Sy, throwing all caution to the wind, gave the Court and the public a detailed narrative of his encounter with General Do Mau on November 22, 1963.

The Major said, "On November 20, I received the order from the Military Council to go to Saigon and report to the Chairman of the Council, General Duong Van Minh. Before that date, my Regional Commander, General Do Cao Tri in Da Nang had assured me that I would have no problems with the generals. He had told me that I had done everything by the book on May 8, at the Radio Station in Hue. As I arrived in Tan Son Nhat Airport, however, I was accosted by two Military Security officers and taken to the Military Security jail."

The presiding judge inquired, "Were you told the reason for your arrest? Dang Sy replied: "No, Sir. Two days later, General Do Mau came to my cell and said, 'Sorry to see you here, Major, but we can settle this quickly. I know you are good material for a command at regiment level. After we settle this little matter, you can have a regiment, any regiment. If you want to see other countries, we are also ready to send you as a military attaché to any embassy of your choice. Now all we want you to do is to tell us the truth about the incident on May 8. Tell us all about Archbishop Thuc's role in that matter. Then you are free, and your future is assured.'"

The presiding judge asked, "Did you tell General Do Mau the truth?" Dang Sy answered, "I told him the truth. I told him what actually happened. I told him I had received the orders from Province Chief Nguyen van Dang and General Le van Nghiem."

The presiding judge questioned him, "You denied having received the order to kill the Buddhist demonstrators from Archbishop Thuc?" Dang Sy insisted, "I did not kill any Buddhist demonstrators and I neither received my orders from, nor discussed any orders with the Archbishop. That was what I told General Do Mau. He said, 'You can repeat your story from now to eternity, but that will not help your career. What we want to hear from you is the truth, that Archbishop Thuc ordered you to go in and kill Buddhist demonstrators.' I told him what he wanted from me was not the truth, but a lie. I am not going to lie. Never!"

Hiep knew how the trial would end. The Revolutionary Court condemned him and gave him a life sentence at hard labor.

While the army started grumbling, Catholics demonstrated to demand that the authorities stop their witch hunts of former *Can Lao* Party members. The trial of Major Dang Sy marked a turning point in South Vietnam's politics. All of a sudden, a Catholic political movement of re-assertion came to light. That movement soon pitched Catholics into a head-to-head confrontation with An Quang Buddhist activists.

On June 7, 1964, one day before the Revolutionary Court was to deliver the verdict against Sy, forty thousand Catholics held a demonstration at Lam Son Square in Saigon to demand an end to the harassment and persecution of Catholics.

Yet, after Major Dang Sy's trial, came the trials of Colonel Nguyen van Y, Commander of the former Special Commission of National Intelligence, and thirteen others. With neither proof of any wrongdoing, nor any credible witnesses to the allegations of misuse of power, four of the accused were given life sentences at hard labor.

A real campaign of terror continued to be conducted by Buddhist activists against the Catholics.

*

Hiep heard with sadness that General Paul Harkins, the American Commander who had not wanted to see Diem betrayed, had left Vietnam and retired from the army.

Then she saw the pictures of Ambassador Henry Cabot Lodge in a Vietnamese brocade grown, leaving Vietnam among a crowd of grieving generals, monks and student activists who had come to the airport to say farewell to him. Lodge had accomplished his mission and was going home.

After that, Hiep had the feeling that everything had stopped. The outside world stopped at the threshold of her door. Nothing outside her home seemed to deserve her attention anymore. She was in that frame of mind when the Americans moved massively into Vietnam, and started *the American War*.

PART SIX

THE AGONY OF SOUTH VIETNAM

CHAPTER THIRTY-ONE
SOUTH VIETNAM DRIFTING

The Buddhist activists did not understand at first that the Americans had had a change of heart. They thought that with President Diem gone, they would rule, and that the generals would obey their orders. They thought that the Americans would accept all their demands. They were soon to learn that they did not weigh much in any political equation and that their role as a political tool was over.

After the coup d'état of 1963, they acted as if they owned the country. They intimidated the generals and started a campaign of harassment against Catholics, labeled as *Can Lao* Party members. Less than a year later, however, Catholics reasserted themselves and fought back. Street fights, demonstrations and counter-demonstrations, threatened to poison forever the relations between the two religious communities.

The leaders of the An Quang Pagoda group succeeded in placing some of their people in the national organizations. They carved for themselves a large fief in Central Vietnam. Their People's Council for National Salvation, based at the University of Hue, with the support of the Tu Dam Pagoda in Hue, carried out a campaign of terror aimed at silencing anyone not friendly to their views.

In early 1966, with General Nguyen Chanh Thi, the Regional Commander, on their side, Buddhist activists and the People's Council for National Salvation openly challenged the central government. When they found only lukewarm support from Lodge, who had come back for a second term as Ambassador to South Vietnam, they turned furiously against the Americans. Demonstrators shouted anti-American slogans while students burned down the American Library in Hue.

The Americans allowed General Nguyen Cao Ky to crush them pitilessly. Thich Tri Quang, who had been led to believe that he could 'make America tremble', found himself defenseless. His hunger strikes made no headlines, his pagodas were searched and his chief assistants sent to prison. Even self-immolation by fire did not make the headlines. Buddha's altars that he ordered to be brought into the streets to slow the advance of security forces did not succeed in slowing them down at all. Soldiers simply threw them aside into the gutters.

Hiep was stunned by the reversal of the tide of fortune for those who had believed they could use the Buddha, and take advantage of the Buddhists, to advance their worldly ambitions.

It took the Buddhist activists of the An Quang persuasion less than three years to lose everything. Having relied on an American Ambassador who flattered them into thinking of themselves as *the* new force in Vietnam, they quickly disappeared into oblivion as soon as he no longer needed them.

*

In September 1965, officers of the Joint General Staff approached Captain Tuyen. They told him that the generals wanted the remains of his uncles to be removed from where they were buried and taken to Mac Dinh Chi Cemetery where they would be re-interred. Tuyen asked for the reason why such a decision had been made. He was told that the generals had been talking among themselves. There had been too many major civil strives and military disturbances since November 1963, and they wondered why. Some of them had voiced the opinion that all the troubles, the coups, the counter-coups, the exhibitions of forces, the half-coups, came from the fact that the President was buried in the wrong place and that his spirit was angry.

With the approval of his colleagues, General Do Mau had gone to consult a soothsayer. The verdict was clear: As long as the remains of President Diem and Mr. Nhu stayed on Joint General Staff ground, the generals would not know a day of peace.

Tuyen asked what was expected from his family. His contacts said that the generals would take care of everything and pay all the costs. All they wanted was the agreement of Tuyen's family.

Tuyen smiled at the ironic turn of events, as he said, "The generals can do anything they want now. Why do they need our agreement?" The contact men did not answer. Tuyen guessed that the soothsayer had certainly told the generals to seek the agreement of President Diem's family. Tuyen sighed. It was the time for false prophets, card readers, horoscope readers, and *feng shui* experts.

He went home and told his mother. Hiep nodded, as she said, "The time has come then." She told Tuyen to stay out of it entirely. She said, "Tell the generals that I cannot represent the family. Your Uncles Thuc and Luyen are the ones they should contact about the President. As for the remains of your Uncle Nhu, the generals should contact his wife in Italy."

Hiep knew that with, or without her consent, the generals would move the remains of her brothers out of the way. So, one rainy evening, a squad of soldiers excavated Diem's and Nhu's graves. The soldiers had been told to be extremely respectful. They had been warned to be careful not to touch the coffins with their spades. It took them quite a while to reach the coffins, and then they brought them up carefully, by hand.

Two graves had already been dug at the Mac Dinh Chi Cemetery. They arrived there near midnight, and quickly finished re-interring the coffins. The thunder threatened and the rain began to fall heavily; the uneasy soldiers left the scene quickly as if in flight.

The next evening, a colonel of the Joint General Staff came to visit Hiep. He presented an envelope to her. She broke the seal and removed the contents. It was a map of the Mac Dinh Chi Cemetery, with the new tombs of President Diem and his Advisor clearly marked.

The colonel offered to drive Am and Hiep to the cemetery, and they accepted the offer eagerly. Once again it was a rainy night. The darkness in the cemetery lifted up here and there by the thunder and lightning, was quite threatening. Yet, Hiep, dripping wet in her raincoat, felt only peace and joy.

Somehow, Hiep had felt that as long as her brothers' remains were kept on the Joint General Staff grounds, they were still the generals' prisoners. Now, the President and Nhu were free at last.

Hiep knelt down and touched the tombs with her hands. Am knelt down in the mud beside her. They prayed for peace and quiet to come back to their war-ravaged country, for the repose of Diem's and Nhu's souls and for reconciliation.

The storm, however, raged on. A large branch fell, crashing down nearby. The colonel called out impatiently, "Let us go now. You can come back to pray any time, from now on."

Hiep got up and said, "Please tell the generals that I appreciate what they have done." She did not use the collective 'we'. She knew that Le Xuan and Luyen would not stand for her thanking any general at that moment.

Ngo Dinh Thi Hiep in Saigon, 1965

*

For a moment, she thought about Le Xuan. She had so many talents and so short a time to display them. She remembered the day when she heard that Le Xuan had made a last ditch effort to have Can pardoned. She had written to the Pope and to President Johnson, asking them to intervene for Can. Only the Pope had answered her. Only the Pope tried, through his Apostolic Delegate in Saigon, to remind Lodge of his promise to save Can's life. Even the Pope did not succeed in overcoming Thich Tri Quang's desire to see Can dead. Even the Pope had not succeeded in making Lodge keep his promise.

During all the years that her family was in power, there had been continual bickering between Le Xuan and Can. After Can's death, people talked about Can as if he were a most brutal man. Hiep had seen Can back down time and again, from Le Xuan's attacks. Can knew that unless the issue was extremely important, he would not fight the wife of his older brother.

To know that Le Xuan had repeatedly fought for Can's life was a relief to Hiep. She was reconciled with Le Xuan, even though family members and friends had told her so many times after Diem's fall, that Le Xuan's aggressive behavior and her strong words had contributed in a major way to the final tragedy.

Hiep had made it a habit to say a prayer every night for Le Xuan and her children, especially after an unfortunate car accident killed Le Thuy, one dark night near Paris.

She smiled, remembering the letters that had been sent by Luyen a few years back. Apparently, soon after Diem's fall, Luyen was invited by the royal family of Morocco to go and spend a few weeks of vacation there. Luyen was surprised when the King's aides came to him with all kinds of investment possibilities, asking for his evaluation. After a while, it dawned on Luyen that the King wanted him to invest in those schemes. Luyen was forced to admit that, contrary to rumors, his clan did not have any funds stashed away in foreign banks, and that he was as poor as Job.

Hiep was both amused and saddened by the story. The relative poverty of her clan was a reality, and yet, foreign writers continued to describe her brothers' corruption, even though they could see how the surviving members of her clan lived.

She remembered a particular letter from Luyen in which he quoted some verses from *Jeremiah:*

> *Weep not for him, who is dead,*
>
> *Mourn not for him!*
>
> *Weep rather for him who is going away;*
>
> *Never again he will see*
>
> *The land of his birth.*

It had been quite a long time ago, but each time she remembered the letter she could not contain her tears. Luyen and Thuc, like Le Xuan, were suffering tremendously from their forced exile, and wanted to return to Vietnam. But they knew and Hiep knew that it was not safe for them to come back yet. She did not know that soon she would also be on her way to a long and painful exile herself.

*

It took a lot of prodding from Am to convince Hiep to take the short trip to Vung Tau. The two-hour ride was safe. Only seventy miles separated Saigon from Vung Tau, but on the way, the car was halted a dozen times at security control stops. At each stop, former Colonel Thong, who drove the car and who seemed to know all of the guards at the stops, talked with them about the security of the section of highway ahead of them, before he drove away again.

Hiep asked, "You said the highway is perfectly safe. Why do you ask so frequently about the security of the highway?" Colonel Thong laughed, "It is a habit of mine. Anyway, the guards so far have told me that there has been no incident on the highway today." Am smiled and said, "Security is never absolute these days. The highway is as safe as can be expected."

For the first time, Hiep saw scores of American military trucks and jeeps and sedans. All of them drove very fast and did not stop at the control stops. The barriers were raised quickly as they passed. Hiep also noticed Australian military trucks, with the drivers sitting on the wrong side of the cab. From Long Binh to Vung Tau, there seemed to be five times more American troops than there were Vietnamese.

When they arrived at Vung Tau, Colonel Thong drove around the peninsula and showed Am and Hiep the various beaches. On the way, Hiep noticed the bars, chock full of Americans dressed in colorful shirts. Colonel Thong told her that they were soldiers who came to Vung Tau for Rest and Recreation, as Vung Tau had been selected as an R & R station.

Loud music was blaring from the bars. Inside the bars, Hiep could see bargirls in mini-skirts gathered in small groups chatting, or drinking with American soldiers. In Saigon, on her rare outings, Hiep had seen bars and bargirls. In Vung Tau, however the bars spilled out onto the main streets. After a complete tour of the peninsula, Hiep told Colonel Thong that she preferred the more secluded Rocky Beach. They went there, and sat at a French restaurant looking out at the sea.

Hiep, like her brothers, had always loved the sea. As she sat and talked, Am noticed her joy, and wondered why he had not taken her to Vung Tau before. The sea breeze was quite strong that day. High waves launched themselves against the dark rocks, sending white foam and sparkling sheets of water high into the air.

Am chatted with Colonel Thong so that Hiep could sit back and enjoy the sea. Hiep's mind wandered back into the past where she saw other beaches and other faces. The seagulls hovering above the dark rocks reminded her of other seagulls screaming and diving near her Brother Khoi's beach house.

Suddenly, a familiar face came into her field of vision. Cuong was standing next to her inquiring about her health. Am and she had known Cuong since he was a young boy. He had gone to France, received his doctorate, and then returned to teach at Hue University. Recently, she heard, he had joined General Nguyen Duc Thang's team that had created and implemented a national program of rural development. Cuong introduced his American friend who accompanied him, as Dick Burnham, one of his advisors.

Cuong said, "We come here all the time. Our national training center is only fifteen kilometers from here, and on Saturdays, what can you do in a training center? Is this the first time you have come to Vung Tau?" Am nodded and invited them to sit down and have lunch with them. Colonel Thong also knew Cuong, so the invitation was quite natural. Hiep was uncomfortable with Dick Burnham's presence at first. He tried a few sentences in Vietnamese. Hiep had heard worse, but she could not help laughing at Burnham's awkward attempts.

Seeing a disaster in the making, Cuong said, "Why don't we all speak French?" Dick Burnham was quite happy with the suggestion, as he was most fluent in French. Soon, Hiep was glad she had the opportunity to see an American up close. She was also glad she had met Cuong again. She knew how close Cuong was to her son, Thuan.

Suddenly, with a quizzical smile, Cuong addressed Hiep; "Dick and I, are working in a program that you know very well. It was called *The Strategic Hamlets Program,* but now it is called the New Life Hamlets Program."

Narrowing her eyes, Hiep looked at Cuong, unwilling to take the bait. Unaware of whom Hiep was, Dick Burnham said, "After the coup d'état of 1963, the generals made a stupid blunder. They demolished the Strategic Hamlets. With the Strategic Hamlets gone, security in the rural area was gone. The Vietcong were free to roam everywhere in the countryside. We had to bring the American troops in to save South Vietnam from complete collapse."

Wincing at Burnham's mention of the coup d'état, Cuong prodded him, "Please, tell my friends here about the initial concept of the New Life Hamlets." Dick Burnham shook his head, "I don't want to bore your friends." When Cuong insisted, Burnham said, "You can tell them all about it better than I can. Anyway, we have gone back to Ngo Dinh Nhu's concept of the Strategic Hamlets, and borrowed heavily from it."

Hiep looked thoughtfully at the two young men. Different as they were physically, they seemed to talk, act, and think in the same way. They had the same way of protecting themselves to others. Was that the results of their studies in France? Or was it because, ultimately there was no real difference between races? Burnham said, "Diem and Nhu knew what they were doing. The generals killed the only leaders they ever had." He stopped short, as he noticed that Hiep was in tears. He turned to Cuong, who told him, "You are talking to President Diem's sister."

Burnham apologized but Hiep said quickly, "Why do you apologize? You are the only American that I've heard praise my brothers since the coup d'état." Burnham said softly, "Dear Madam, many of us regret what happened, believe me. I, for my part, cannot forgive the Americans who brought us into this situation, where hundreds of American boys have to die every day in Vietnam. With your brothers in power, you may have won or you may have lost the war, but few Americans would have lost their lives."

He was a little angry with Cuong for not telling him who Hiep was from the very beginning, but he didn't stay angry for long. Burnham began to feel more comfortable with his new friends. He told them about his family, his studies, and his long stay in the Mekong Delta where, after the coup of 1963, he had seen the rapid deterioration of security in the countryside.

Hiep asked: "Are you opposed to the presence of American troops in South Vietnam?" Burnham laughed, "Mrs. Am, let me tell you my exact feelings about this situation. I hate to see American lives lost in Vietnam. I want to see the Vietnamese fight their own war. Right now, however, there is no other choice than to continue pouring more American troops into Vietnam. South Vietnam is still on the brink of defeat. Without the American presence now, South Vietnam would collapse within three months."

Just then a group of Americans came into the restaurant. Hiep gasped as she recognized one of them. She had seen hundreds of photos of him: it was General Lansdale. Recognizing Cuong and Dick Burnham, Lansdale left his group and came to their table. Cuong said in French, "General Lansdale, please meet Colonel Thong, and Mr. and Mrs. Am. Mrs. Am is the late President Diem's sister." Lansdale looked at Hiep a long moment before he said also in French, "We have never met Madam, yet we are very close. In a way, President Diem and Presidential Advisor Nhu were my brothers, too."

Hiep said, "My brothers sincerely loved you." Lansdale replied quietly, "I know." Neither Lansdale nor Hiep thought they needed to say anything else. The moment was charged with emotion, yet silence seemed to be the best expression for what they felt.

After a moment, Lansdale told Cuong with a little reproach in his voice, "You've never told me about your ties with the family of President Diem. We should meet tonight over a drink. I will tell you all about my previous life with the President."

He turned to Hiep again, and struggling to control his deep emotions, he said, "People like Cuong, Dick and myself are reviving parts of your brothers' legacy. Pray for us, Madam." He bowed and left to rejoin his group.

After he left, there was a long silence at Hiep's table. Hiep pretended to look out at the sea, but her eyes were blurred with tears. So, Diem and Nhu were not dead after all. As long as there were people like Lansdale, Cuong and Colonel Thong, they were not dead.

They barely touched their food. Instead, they sat sipping the scalding hot tea that was served. Am said, "I did not expect that this outing would turn out to be like this." Turning to Cuong and Dick Burnham he explained, "We only wanted to offer my wife some sea breeze and sunshine. I did not foresee that we would meet both of you here and then General Lansdale, as well."

Dick Burnham proposed they should drive to the Back Beach and take a walk on the sands there. His suggestion seemed reasonable as the sky had become very cloudy and the sun was no longer as scorching as it had been a little earlier. As Hiep got up from her seat to leave, she saw Lansdale hurrying toward them. He said, "Meeting you reminds me of a promise I made to myself upon learning about your brothers' deaths. I have written, on and off, a book about my experience in Southeast Asia. Most of the book is about your brothers. I promise you that I will finish it someday."

*

On Back Beach, as the sky was overcast, there were not very many swimmers. Am and Hiep sat on the sand, while the others strolled along the beach nearby.

After a while, they came and sat down with Hiep and Am. A little group of American soldiers who were on leave was swimming a short distance away. They were laughing loudly and seemed to enjoy jumping the waves. Burnham asked Hiep, "Are you annoyed at seeing so many American soldiers around?" Hiep said, "I am glad that they can have a break from their dreadful duties once in awhile."

Burnham nodded, "It is good to see them happy. At times, eighteen, nineteen year old kids come to me on this beach asking me to explain to them why they have had to come to Vietnam. It is awful to see their confusion. I wish we spent more time explaining things to them before they were sent here. In fact, we have no good explanation to give them, except to use slogans like 'we come here to defend freedom', or 'we are here to help South Vietnamese defend themselves.'"

After some hesitation, Cuong said, "The massive presence of Americans here in South Vietnam robs us of our cause. It is difficult to see how we can prevail. When President Diem started the Strategic Hamlets, South Vietnam was independent. Now, while we start the New Life Hamlets, South Vietnam has become an American Protectorate." Hiep was surprised that Burnham did not object at all to what Cuong had said. They sat side by side, watching the sea, as if looking for a sign.

A young American soldier passed in front of them with his Vietnamese girl friend. She seemed to be from a good family. They joined the group of soldiers who were swimming.

Hiep was listening absent-mindedly to Am and Colonel Thong who were talking about fishing or hunting, when all of sudden, there was an alarming silence. Hiep looked and saw that the whole group of American soldiers had been caught in a strong current. The silence was shattered with their screams for help. Vung Tau beaches are known for their sudden and deadly cross currents. They come from nowhere, without warning, drown a few swimmers and are gone again within minutes.

As Hiep watched, the Americans were dragged this way and that, struggling helplessly against the current. A hand, a foot, or a head would emerge, and then disappear again in the whirling waters. Then the current left them, and they were standing again on firm ground, except for the young Vietnamese girl. The Americans dived repeatedly for her until one of them found her and dragged her to the beach. They desperately tried to save her, but it was too late.

Hiep who had approached the scene with her small group, stood devastated. The young American who had passed in front of Hiep a moment earlier with the young girl, was now sobbing uncontrollably. Hiep saw his despair. Hiep was herself hurt beyond words by the unexpected death, its suddenness, and its apparent absurdity. Silently, she prayed for the young girl and the American boy, and their bereaved companions.

Am had to force her to leave the scene. Having said goodbye to Cuong and Dick Burnham, they took the highway back to Saigon in silence. Hiep was shaken by the tragic incident. That morning, when she had left home for Vung Tau she had not bargained for such a dramatic trip. She said to herself, "Let me go back to my cocoon. Let me be content with my peaceful life, forgotten by all, forgetting all."

She knew, however, having met Lansdale and Cuong and Burnham, that the world still remembered her family and her brothers. She would not forget the Americans she had met, neither Lansdale, nor Burnham, nor the young soldier who lost his girl friend, or their companions.

*

Hiep cut the photo from the magazine and framed it. The photo showed the tall and handsome American Ambassador, Henry Cabot Lodge, stooping down and offering Tran Van Do, the Minister of Foreign Affairs of the Second Republic, a copy of the Constitution of Vietnam.

Hiep felt shame each time she looked at the picture, but she displayed it in a prominent place, so that she looked at it at least a dozen times a day. She understood why her brothers had refused to yield to American pressures. The Americans used to press Diem to take this politician and that politician from the noisy and ambitious crowd of 'salon politicians', into his government.

Diem had told her, "They do not have the interests of the country at heart. They only want power and prestige for themselves. They shamelessly use American influence to get what they want. I am not going to yield."

Tran Van Do was a special case. He had belonged to the *Tinh Than* Group, a think tank that, under Nhu's leadership, promoted Diem's return to power in 1954. He was made Foreign Minister, as soon as Diem took over. He led the South Vietnamese delegation at the Geneva Conference and denounced with eloquence the partition of Vietnam, and the abandonment of a considerable segment of the population to Communist rule. He gained the admiration of many, and not only in Vietnam.

Now, without Diem's guidance, Tran van Do allowed himself to be photographed as he received a copy of the Constitution from the hand of a foreign ambassador.

Am called the picture, 'Moses receiving the Ten Commandments from God.' Hiep, steering clear from the sarcasm, tried to draw some useful conclusions from the photo. She said, "This is a perfect symbol of subjugation. The Constitution was handed down to our government. Our Minister of Foreign Affairs smiled gratefully as he received it. *The President*, preferred to die rather than to live under such a condition. He was right."

Am looked at his wife. She was suffering from severe insomnia; yet, her face was as calm as usual. She controlled her anger perfectly and spoke without departing one iota from decorum.

He would like to see her meet with Tran Van Do now. Tran van Do, brother of Tran van Chuong, uncle of Le Xuan. He imagined Hiep staring at the Foreign Minister until he shrank, saying in the most matter-of- fact way, "You should be ashamed of yourself, Mr. Minister."

Yet, somehow Am knew that Hiep would never act like that. She would greet Tran van Do with calm and not a single muscle of her body would betray her disapproval for what he had done. He had never seen Hiep fail to be courteous to the person in front of her. The only blunt words she had ever spoken were for her brothers whom she loved.

CHAPTER THIRTY-TWO
FIGHTING AND DYING IN A DISTANT LAND

Hiep looked out of the window as the car sped away from Lien Khuong Airport. Dalat City was about twenty miles from the airport and Hiep did not see why they should be in such a hurry to arrive there. She asked the driver to slow down. All around her the lush vegetation covered dark red volcanic soil. She gazed at the plantations on the slopes of the hills and down in the narrow valleys. The soil was so rich that it made Hiep wonder what the people of Hue would be able to achieve if they had lands equally fertile.

With the fertile land and the clement weather, the farmers of the Central Highlands, at least those near Dalat, ought to be able to reap much larger harvests with much less work, than their counterparts in Hue.

It was here in Dalat where Nhu had started his political apprenticeship in the late Forties. It was here where Diem and Nhu, once they were in power, returned frequently to rest and to hunt. Diem and Nhu had even passed on their passion for hunting to Nhu's young children. Hiep smiled as she remembered how Nhu described to her his discovery of *Personalism*, the doctrine of Diem's regime, and the ideology of the *Can Lao* Party.

It was here in Dalat that Nhu had studied with a French priest by the name of Parrell, the social teachings of the Catholic Church. It was here that Nhu had become greatly enthused by the achievements of the labor movements around the world. In Nhu's mind two key words became inseparable: *human dignity* and *labor*. Nhu became an ardent advocate for labor unions. Later on, giants in the labor movements, such as the Belgian

557

Auguste Vanistandael, helped Nhu organize the largest confederation of workers in Vietnam, which Nhu eventually placed under the leadership of Tran Quoc Buu in 1953.

Once Nhu told Hiep, "People explain *personalism* in overly complicated terms. They relate it to Emanuel Mounier and other Christian existentialists. They should look only at the genesis of the labor movement in the world, and at the social doctrine of the Catholic Church for a proper explanation."

Her brothers would have liked to explain so many things. They did not have enough time. And now, they were gone.

Sitting back comfortably in the car, Hiep remembered how distraught Diem had been when the Central Highlands were given to Bao Dai as an Imperial Domain, by the French authorities. Within the boundaries of his personal fief, Bao Dai, who had abdicated in 1946, once again became an Emperor, thanks to that subterfuge.

Diem was distraught not because Bao Dai had resumed his imperial mantle, but because he saw that the country had become further divided by the creation of a new fief. He suspected the French of using the fief to keep a permanent sway over the three countries that the Central Highlands dominated: Vietnam, Cambodia and Laos.

She remembered how Diem described the danger to her, how he saw the Highlands as the strategic high ground from which military forces could launch victorious offensives against disadvantageous defenses in the lowlands.

She knew that the Communists were now trying hard to conquer the Central Highlands. They had conducted large-scale attacks against the American forces, which were spread out all over the Highlands. Like Diem, both the Communist and the American Commands were well aware of the strategic value of the Highlands.

Diem said, "If this war goes on, some day we will wage the biggest battle in the Central Highlands. Whoever holds them, holds the key to victory." Quoting Sunzi, Diem said, " *'Fight downhill, do not ascend to attack'*. The day we allow the Communists to take the Central Highlands, we have lost the war."

Diem was interested in the Highlands not only because of their strategic significance. He loved the highland minorities with a love bordering on obsession and was afraid, when they were transformed into an Imperial Domain, that those minorities would be persuaded by the French to turn against their Vietnamese brothers in the lowlands.

One of the major moves Diem made in 1955, right after he decided to do away with the monarchy, was to reincorporate the Highlands into the national territory. He dismissed the Viceroy of the Imperial Domain, his friend-and-foe Nguyen De, dismissed the Secretary General of the Domain, Count Didelot, the Empress' brother-in-law, and dissolved the Imperial Guards.

Hiep was daydreaming about the past, when an American jeep that had passed her car a moment earlier, ran into an ambush.

*

The deafening explosion stunned Hiep. Her driver slowed the car, and then brought it to a stop on the roadside, unsure of what he should do. Now they could hear rapid bursts of automatic rifle fire.

There was the option of turning the car around and heading back to the Lien Khuong Airport. The driver, however, told them he did not know how the ambush was set. By turning back, they risked the possibility of running into another pincer of the ambush. So, they sat in the car and waited fearfully. It was useless to run for cover. On both sides of the highway the slopes were too steep. Anyway, they did not know where and how the ambush was set. For all they knew, guerrillas could be waiting at the bottom of the hills.

The driver rolled down his window and a strong burning smell came to them from the battle. The winding highway, and the tall reeds and weeds did not allow them to see very far ahead; they could only guess the distance that separated them from the battle scene.

They sat there and prayed. Am wondered now why he had accepted the invitation from Father Lap, the President of Da Lat University. He had thought a change of scene would be good for Hiep. He had thought that the sight of the University founded by Archbishop Thuc would raise her spirits. He had never thought he would be putting her life in danger.

There were a few explosions that sounded like hand grenades. Then, the firing was over. The driver said, "Either the Vietcong have fled, or they have finished off all the Americans."

Hiep was shaken by the driver's comments. Indeed, a little earlier, a jeep with five or six American soldiers in it had passed them. It was that jeep that had been ambushed then. She remembered their young faces. When they passed, they had waved at Hiep and Am, and smiled. Hiep clutched at the beads of her rosary, praying earnestly, "God, please let them be safe."

Hiep was suspended in time, agonizing over the fate of the young men. "So young, so cheerful just a few minutes ago! Yet, now they may be lying lifeless over there. God! Why do these things have to happen?"

A second passed, and then Hiep remembered the other party, the Vietcong. Were there dead among their party too? How should she feel? *How should she?* Hiep agonized. "The Vietcong are Vietnamese too," she thought, unable to analyze her own anguish.

In a whirlwind, her mind worked furiously, "They may also have come from the north, from far away. They may have trekked through a thousand miles of jungle. They may have been bitten by insects and tortured by malaria. They may have staggered on their feet as their minds and their bodies were drained of strength by hunger, thirst and the fear of B-52 bombings."

"Then again," she thought, "they may have come from a village nearby. Last night they may have been laughing with their wives and their children, who are now waiting and trembling for them."

Hiep clutched at the rosary beads. Americans or Vietnamese, those who had engaged in battle only a few hundred meters from where she was, had never thought in their innocent childhood that one day, they would find themselves here, a gun in their hand, ready to kill or be killed.

*

Now large numbers of military vehicles were arriving. American and Vietnamese soldiers jumped down from their vehicles and waved to Hiep's driver. He was ordered to get out of there immediately. He started the car and moved forward.

At the battle scene, Hiep saw a big hole in the asphalt and the smashed jeep, turned upside down. It still was burning, giving off black smoke and an acrid smell. Near the jeep were two corpses, and three injured men who were still holding their rifles. The small group was covered in blood. Sirens wailed all over the hills around her, echoing through the narrow valleys. The sirens announced that help was on the way, but they also seemed to announce death.

By now, her car had gone far past the battle scene. Hiep wanted to say something to Am, but through her tears and agony, her voice was strangled, and Am could only guess what she was trying to tell him. He thought that she said: "Why should they die like that, so far from home?"

A black sedan was coming fast toward them from the direction of Dalat. The driver recognized the car and stopped. Father Lap stepped from his car and with relief in his voice, he said, "Knowing your time of arrival, I was dreadfully worried when I heard there had been an ambush right outside of Lien Khuong Airport. I took my car and rushed here as fast as I could. Thank God, you are all right."

They were transferred to Father Lap's sedan. The University President was apologetic. He said a little reproachfully, "I asked you to allow me to welcome you at the airport, but you kept telling me not to come. My God, if something had happened to you, I would have died with remorse."

Hiep replied, her voice still trembling a little, "If our car had been going a little faster, we would have been right in the middle of the ambush."

Father Lap commented, "There has never been an ambush on this section of the highway, until today. Oh, in a guerrilla war, there is no safety anywhere. Did you see anything, after the battle was over?"

Am told him, "I saw two Americans killed and three injured." Hiep shivered. Yes, it was done that way in bulletins: two killed and three wounded in action. Hiep thought. "Who will report that three minutes before they were ambushed, they had lifted their young smiling faces at us and waved?"

*

In the cell offered to them by the University President for their stay in Dalat, Am and Hiep sat and looked at the vaulted ceiling and the stained glass windows. Every little thing suggested the loving care of Archbishop Thuc, the founder and Chancellor of the University.

The cell that had been assigned to Hiep and Am looked exactly like the other cells, which were occupied by visiting professors. Hiep opened the window. Spread before her eyes were lush green lawns under pine trees. In the afternoon, Hiep chanced to see the names of a building on the campus, *Thu Nhan* or *Shu ren, which* meant, 'to grow a man'. It was in reference to a Confucian thought, '*It takes ten years to grow a tree and a hundred years to grow a man.*'

Like Diem, who had founded the University of Hue four years earlier, Thuc had created Dalat University in 1961 with the same love and dedication. Thuc had worked diligently on every detail, from the time the first blue prints were drafted. He worked with the architects, landscapers, engineers, masons and carpenters. He was there to see each one of the buildings go up.

When everything was completed, Diem came to inaugurate the University, on February 11, 1961. Hiep remembered the date because it fell on the Feast of Our Lady of Lourdes. All her brothers had been there for the occasion. They had invited her, but she declined, using a persistent cold as her excuse.

Looking out of the window now, Hiep said to herself, "Even if nobody remembers my family anymore, as long as this University stands here, as long as the University of Hue and the National Institute stand in Hue, the work of my father and my brothers will endure."

*

On June 24, 1967, Hiep and Am were back in Hue. Almost four years separated that day from the moment she had fled her native city hastily, after the coup d'état.

Father Thuan and her relatives had taken care of her house during her absence. Many pieces of furniture had disappeared. Thieves had broken in from time to time. But the house still smelled good. Old fragrances still lingered, old fragrances and old memories.

Am watched her as she walked about in the garden. He knew she wanted to shout for joy. In two days time, Father Thuan would celebrate his Episcopal ordination. Am remembered his wife describing one day, a long time ago, how her family had risen from the ashes of the Grand Chamberlain's ruin, like a Phoenix. Now, the Phoenix was about to soar again.

As soon as they arrived in Hue, visitors began pouring in. Am was glad that there was a truce in effect, and that Hiep could walk in the garden by herself for a while. In the garden, Am had seen Hiep walk leisurely with Khoi, Thuc and Diem. Each one of them had come here to find strength, peace of mind, or insight into a problem. Each time, Hiep had listened to them, answering them more with her silence than her words, and then they went away appeased, strengthened, or enlightened.

In that garden, she had tended to Thuan, after Xuan's death, the *mater dolorosa*, hovering over her new great hope bending on her great hope. How many years had she spent hovering over him, not quite believing that he would grow to manhood? How many years had she held his hand, with the fear inspired by Xuan's death gnawing at her heart?

Thuan had grown into a man. He had become an ordained priest. Now, in two days he would become an ordained Bishop.

Am remembered well Mrs. Ngo Dinh Kha's joy and pride when Thuc had become a Bishop. It was almost thirty years ago. Now, it was Hiep's turn to feel the same joy and the same pride.

In the garden, unaware of Am's gaze, Hiep started humming. A couple of large 'peacock butterflies' hovered over her for a moment, and then resumed their flight in the direction of the river. It seemed to her that many lives had gone past since the time she and Diem had coined that name for the blue-green butterflies with large round eyes on their wings.

Hiep remembered the annual rituals after Diem's return to power in 1954. Every year, on Lunar New Year's Day, Diem would receive the members of the Diplomatic Corps and the Cabinet early in the morning. Then he, his brothers Thuc, Nhu and Luyen, and Le Xuan would take the plane to Hue, arriving close to noontime. Can, Hoang and Hiep would then join the Saigon party to present their wishes to Mrs. Ngo Dinh Kha.

On the third day of the Lunar New Year, they would attend a Mass for the repose of their father's soul, visit his tomb, and then participate in the annual family council meeting. Late in the afternoon, Thuc and Diem would lead a ritual visit to Hiep's home, and then to Hoang's home.

It was a long time ago, but now, standing in the bright sunlight, Hiep could still see her brothers and sisters walking past her gate, laughing and chatting noisily, then upon seeing Am and Hiep at the door of their house, shout merrily, "Happy New Year!"

*

Bishop Thuan placed the flowers on the tomb. His mother, with a Hue conic hat on her head, had knelt in front of his grandfather's tomb, and was now deep in prayer. Somehow Thuan guessed that it was to be the last time his mother would be able to do that.

His Episcopal ordination had gone beautifully and now he was ready to leave for his diocese in Nha Trang. He was glad that Am and Hiep had been able to return to Hue, though many things they saw there might re-open old wounds.

Am and Hiep had taken a short walk from their home. They had seen that their mother's house was guarded. The revolutionary courts had confiscated it. They had seen the Cathedral half-finished. That had been Am's last major project; a project that was left unfinished when Archbishop Thuc had gone away, and Am himself was forced to leave for Saigon with Hiep and Mrs. Ngo Dinh Kha.

They went to the Archbishop's House where Thuc had resided. Archbishop Nguyen Kim Dien, his successor, had received them with kindness, but they did not stay long. Their wish was simply to have a look at the residence and the gardens that they had known so well. It dated back to the days of Bishop Allys, then Bishop Lemasle, Bishop Urutia and then Archbishop Thuc.

Among the pervasive memories of Archbishop Thuc, Hiep turned to her husband and said, "My father was an *Assistant to the Throne* under Emperor Thanh Thai. Bishop Allys, on his Silver Jubilee, was given the title of Assistant to the Pontifical Throne. Then my brother Thuc, after 1964 was also made Assistant to the Pontifical Throne by his friend, Pope

Paul VI." Am nodded, "I have often wondered why our life has been so full of strange coincidences."

They had come to Thuan's seminary, where he had been the director for many years. They had attended his Episcopal ordination there, in the front courtyard. The ceremonies had been conducted in the open with thousands of people attending. Thuan saw his mother's joy and pride. He saw renewed hope in her eyes. He prayed hard, asking God to let him not disappoint her.

Now in front of his grandfather tomb, his mother prayed, peace radiating from her face, protected from the hard sunrays by the traditional conic hat. In Thuan's heart, he knew that to be *the concluding rites*. He knew that the Communists would soon be there in Hue, and that his mother would never be able to come back there again.

Not far from there was Tu Dam Pagoda. In the calm afternoon, the sounds of its large bell could be heard. There was more than sadness in the sounds of the bell. They seemed to be full of regrets and nostalgia. They carried in them the broken dreams of An Quang Buddhism They announced dark days ahead for everyone, Buddhists and Christians alike, who huddled now around the walls of Hue, with their days of glory, their dreams and their innocence gone.

He told his parents, "It is time to go."

*

Nha Trang diocese covered quite a large territory. At that time, three large American installations had been established in the diocese, the Cam Ranh Bay Base, the Nha Trang Base and the Thap Cham Base.

Thuan was soon invited to the bases to give the Sacrament of Confirmation to the American soldiers. Thuan took that pastoral responsibility very seriously, and his memory was soon crowded with names of American soldiers and officers with whom he had been in contact.

As he opened his door and his heart to young Americans, more and more of them came to him and he began to understand their torment. Most of them had been drafted into the army and knew nothing about the reasons for their presence in Vietnam. A young soldier asked him one day, "Why do the Vietnamese shoot at us? We are supposed to be here to help you." How could one answer to such a basic question? Thuan looked at the young man with sadness in his eyes; he was unable to find a reasonable answer to his question.

A more mature sergeant had once asked Thuan, "You all look alike to us. How can we tell a Vietcong from a friendly Vietnamese?" Thuan understood the sergeant's confusion. He could tell him that for him, too, there was no way to know. Thuan had come to the conclusion that, for many of his fellow South Vietnamese, being for the Vietcong or against them was a matter of the moment and a matter of degree. At times, they were more for the Communists than for the regime in Saigon. At other times the popularity was reversed, depending on who had been seen committing what evil acts most recently. What could he answer to such basic questions as these?

Groups meeting with Thuan under the tents, in American bases, asked more personal questions, "Why can't we make the acquaintance of women of good Vietnamese families? Why are we only allowed to know bar girls and cab drivers?"

In the midst of a war without fronts, American soldiers found it difficult to keep their morale high. Seeing their friends killed or maimed was intolerable to many of them. Seeing the war drag on without any sign of abating was another reason for despair. But the worst torment for most American soldiers was not being able to understand what was going on. They were not fighting on American soil; they were not defending American territory. They did not see where there were American interests in the plains and mountains of South Vietnam. They wanted to go home.

Thuan saw their need to pray and to believe. He spent endless hours talking to groups of soldiers, preparing them for Confirmation. He prayed with them and tried his best to bring comfort and solace to them. Seeing their confusion and fear took a toll on him. After each visit to an American base, Thuan would come back broken-hearted.

He saw that the tragedy of his country was becoming the tragedy of the United States as well. He knew that the Americans would not stay long in South Vietnam, but he also knew that they would be there long enough to write a few tragic pages in the history of their country. He remembered what Diem had tried to do earlier. He had tried to keep the Americans out of the war, as much as possible. He had tried so hard to avoid the escalation of the war.

*

Thuan looked at his audience. The American chaplains knew who he was. The words had been passed around. *"He is the nephew of late President Ngo Dinh Diem."* They expected him to speak his mind about the American involvement in the coup of 1963, and the murder of his uncles. They expected him to criticize the American policies that had led to the need to send half a million American soldiers into the jungles and the swamps of South Vietnam.

Thuan did not do anything of the kind. He had come there to help the American chaplains with their retreat and he intended to talk with them only about the hardship of the American soldiers on the battlefield and at the bases.

The American chaplains looked almost as young as the soldiers they served. Thuan knew how hard their daily work was. They were the ones who knelt down next to the dying soldiers to hear their last confessions. Night after night, they sat in military hospitals, at the bedside of injured soldiers. They accompanied their companies or platoons during their deadly patrols.

They never asked Thuan simple, basic questions. They wanted to know the historic background of the American involvement in Vietnam. They wanted Thuan to help them understand why the United States and South Vietnam were now engaged in what appeared to be an endless war.

They wanted him to talk about his uncle, President Diem. No, they did not want to trap him in any way. They only wanted to know. But Thuan, still wrapped in his terrible pain, refused to comply.

He talked to them about the Nha Trang diocese, about the three American bases set up there. He talked about American soldiers and officers he had met, and their simple yet unanswerable questions. He talked about hope, and faith and human strength, and the power of God.

Listening to him, the chaplains nodded approval. Thuan was not a guest at their retreats. He was one of them. He was a pastor dealing with the despair, suffering and confusion of the men and women who were his charges, as well as theirs.

They would have liked to see men like him all over South Vietnam. But the South Vietnamese whom they met were rarely like him. South Vietnam was in full degeneration, and the Vietnamese friends they made talked about their personal ambitions, their personal needs and their fears. Some of them often met with the Vietnamese who were in positions of power. They were quite perturbed by the pusillanimity and selfishness, which seemed to characterize the behavior of this influential group; greed and vanity seemed to be their greatest driving force.

The chaplains listened to Thuan and applauded, but they would rather have heard him talk about Diem and the beginnings of the American mistakes that had led to its military involvement in Vietnam.

Thuan had chosen not to talk about President Diem because there was not enough time to be able to tell the chaplains everything about Diem's efforts to prevent them from being there in South Vietnam.

Soon enough, they would hear about Vietnamization. Their commanders and the politicians who had sent them there would be telling them that Vietnamese were responsible for the war, that it was a Vietnam War. It was exactly what Thuan's uncles had tried to tell the Americans from the very beginning.

Thuan could not tell them that it was because Diem had refused to let Cam Ranh become an American base, or to let hundreds of thousands of American soldiers come to fight and die in a distant land, that he himself had to die.

Thuan was pastorally concerned about the men serving in Vietnam. He distanced himself from what he personally thought about their presence in South Vietnam's territory. He wanted only to listen to each individual story of the American youths that came to see him, and to let each one of them know that he cared.

After being a very popular bishop with the Vietnamese in his diocese, Thuan also became quite popular with the American troops stationed in Nha Trang, Cam Ranh Bay and Thap Cham.

*

Cardinal Terence Cook faced Thuan under a tent in Cam Ranh Bay Base. He said, "I have never been so distressed in my entire life." As the General Chaplain of the United States Armed Forces, the Cardinal was touring the major American bases in Vietnam. He shook his head, "These young men are as brave as the American soldiers of any previous wars, I guess. But in any previous war, the soldiers were told, or understood implicitly why they fought and died."

The Cardinal scrutinized Thuan's face, trying to gauge his feelings about the war. Thuan was young, tall and handsome. He did not seem to show any scar of the great tragedies that had struck his family. The American prelate asked, "Do you resent the presence of American troops in Vietnam?"

The question could not have been more direct than that. The Cardinal had wanted to throw Thuan off balance, but Thuan did not seem to be surprised or bothered by the question.

He lowered his head a little and said rather pensively, "A chain of events has brought us to this juncture. Who is the most at fault? My uncles who did not succeed in making the Americans they dealt with understand their views? Or the Americans who did not want to listen to my uncles? At this very moment, we have more than half a million American troops on our soil. We know that sooner or later we will lose this war. Who will have to pay the heaviest price, the South Vietnamese or the Americans?"

Cardinal Cooke asked, "Do you believe that the Vietcong will defeat the American might?" Thuan answered candidly, "Not on the battlefield. But some day not too far in the future, the Americans will begin to see that they are paying too high a price for this venture, and they will try to find a way out. Then the Vietcong will prevail."

The Cardinal said, "I am not as strong or as patriotic as Cardinal Spellman. I cannot bless American soldiers and tell them to go to battle in the name of Christ." Thuan smiled: "Medieval Christianity was simpler.

We can no longer be crusaders. My uncles, Diem and Nhu, are sometimes described as stubborn nationalists who always believed in what they did. Actually, they were always struggling with self-doubt. I prefer to see them as they were, men who had to deal with situations a little too complicated for them. They hoped that they were doing the right thing, but often, they were afraid that they were unable to find the best solutions."

The Cardinal waited for an answer to his own painful question. Thuan said, "I would not hesitate to bless a soldier going into battle. He has to be in God's hand, whether what he does makes sense or not in the end."

Cardinal Terrence Cook hesitated a minute, but then asked all the same, "Did your uncles hate the Americans?"

Thuan did not say anything for a moment. He looked out at the Base, an immense military installation, perhaps the largest in the world. Cam Ranh Bay Base was built in the image of America. Everything was big and new. He had no intention of dodging the question.

He said, "My Uncle Diem's heart was molded in such a way that there was no space for hatred. He remembered every kindness ever done to him during his entire lifetime. There were too many Americans who had loved him and helped him, for him to be able to feel hostility towards the American people, or the United States. My Uncle Nhu was not as perfect as his brother, but I know he took pride in emulating his brother. In the end, there was no real difference between them." The Cardinal nodded, "It is so tragic that they are no longer with us."

Officers rushed in. The helicopter was ready, and it was time for the Cardinal to go. He turned to Thuan; "I guess we will see each other at least once a year from now on, until the end of this war. So, goodbye for now, my friend. Take good care of the souls of my soldiers. As you said, they need to be in God's hand when they go into battle, and I would like to add, when they come out of the war as well."

It never failed, Terrence, Cardinal Cook managed to visit with Bishop Thuan at least once a year, until the U.S. troops were pulled out of South Vietnam.

CHAPTER THIRTY-THREE
TOO HIGH A PRICE

Gunfire could be heard coming from many parts of the city. Hiep's first reaction was to exclaim anxiously, "Here we are with another coup d'état." But this was no coup d'état. Soon it was clear that Saigon was under attack and that part of the city was already under Communist control.

Am turned on the radio and listened to the sketchy accounts of the fighting. President Thieu reported that the Communists had launched a general offensive and that more than twenty cities in Central Vietnam and in the Central Highlands and the South were under attack. The Mau Than Tet Offensive of 1968 had begun.

Hiep remembered how cautious and alert Diem had been during the Lunar New Year periods. Hiep remembered the year when Lieutenant-Colonel Chieu's troops had been attacked during the Tet and his regiment headquarters taken by the Communists. How angry Diem had been. It wasn't as if the poor colonel had been relaxing or celebrating Tet. He was, in fact, out in the jungle when the attack came. It had been a mistake on his part, but it certainly hadn't happened because he wanted to rest during Tet.

Now, the whole country had been taken by surprise, by the Communist Offensive. Hiep wondered how that could be possible. Especially now that the Americans had more than half a million troops stationed in South Vietnam, how could this have happened?

For the first time, Hiep began to question the capabilities of American intelligence. Am said: "Sooner or later some in South Vietnam will come out and accuse the Americans of collusion with the Vietcong."

Hiep knew that Am was right. One had to believe that either the American intelligence was unable to identify the signs of a general offensive, or that the Americans knew about the general offensive, but had callously allowed it to take place without giving any warning to the Vietnamese Government.

As the news soon reported that Hue was under the heaviest attack and that large parts of the city were under Communist control, Am and Hiep began to fear for the lives of all their relatives and friends in the old capital.

The situation in Saigon was not very bright either. Apparently the Communists had been able to penetrate the walls of the United States Embassy, assault the Presidential Palace and they now held several key points in the middle of Saigon.

Hiep was never in real danger during the entire offensive. She was unbearably worried about her relatives and friends in Hue, and about Bishop Thuan in Nha Trang. The inter-city telephone lines were all cut off. Radio services were sporadic.

Soon enough, all the cities that had been captured by the Communists in the first hours of the Offensive were liberated one by one, except for Hue. The battle for Hue lasted more than a month. Watching the American military television reports, Hiep was horrified by the heart-breaking devastation. Soon, Hue was only a huge mass of smoldering ruins.

Eventually, the Communists were driven away from the Citadel of Hue. As soon as they left, it was discovered that the enemy had executed thousands of civilians and buried them in shallow graves all over the province around Hue.

*

Hiep's friends and relatives who survived the Battle of Hue in 1968, found their way to Saigon in droves. Hiep could see the suffering in their eyes, and she could read the death of her city in that sorrow. It would take decades to rebuild the city of brick and mortar. It would take hundreds of years to recover Hue's cultural treasures. The soul of Hue might never be found again.

Am told Hiep: "I will never let you go back to Hue, even for a short visit." She thought he might be right, but her father's tomb was still there. Am said: "We will mourn for our beloved city. But it's gone, Hiep. It's gone for good. There is nothing left to see."

The disappearance of her birthplace was a notion that Hiep could not conceive of at first. Friends, who moved from Hue to Saigon, after the Mau Than Tet Offensive, told Hiep repeatedly, "The soul of Hue is gone." Hiep simply could not comprehend the loss. Hue, for her, was its sky, its mountains and rivers, the somber ramparts of the Citadel, the honest poverty of the people. Of course the Imperial Palace was gone, parts of the ramparts were gone, but how could the soul of Hue disappear?

Slowly, she began to understand what the repeated message meant.

Hue had undergone many vicissitudes. In 1885, when it fell to the French, and then again in 1946 when the Vietminh troops burnt parts of the Imperial Palace before they fled, the people in Hue had seen their city diminished, humiliated and downhearted. In 1968, with the City in ruins, with its native population evaporated, even its mountains and rivers seemed to have lost some of their beauty.

Yet, what really took away much of the pride of the citizens in Hue, was the treatment they received at the hands of the Communists when they captured the City. Many inhabitants of the rebellious City that had challenged Saigon from 1964 to 1966, initially expected that the Communist commanders and their troops would show them respect and sympathy. The Communists did not. Buddhist activists were harassed, arrested and many were slaughtered. Only a few Communist agents who had been appointed as provisional administrators showed any sign of decency toward the people.

After the Mau Than Tet Offensive, the people of Hue knew that eventually their city would fall under Communist rule for good. The bitter taste of the Mau Than days did not allow them to imagine that their new rulers would bring them paradise on earth.

*

Hiep would never forget the image she saw of President Johnson on the television screen. Pale, with the deep wrinkles on his face more visible than ever, the American President had announced his decision not to seek another mandate.

Was this an admission of defeat? Was he simply acknowledging that he had made some wrong assumptions about the war? Hiep said to herself: "No, it is simply the realization that the price is too high, and the only reasonable option is to try to get out, hopefully with a little dignity."

While reporters and generals were debating the question of whether it was the Vietcong, or the South Vietnamese army and the Americans who had won the decisive victory during the Mau Than Tet Offensive, the American President had realized that the costs were too high for the Americans.

It was immaterial to the Vietcong that they had lost a tremendous number of troops, and that most of their major units had literally evaporated; *their objective had been achieved*. They had attacked the psychology of the Americans, and had succeeded in breaking the American will.

*

On June 5, 1968, Senator Robert Kennedy was shot in Los Angeles. The U.S. military TV in Vietnam announced it immediately. But Hiep and Am only heard about it the next morning when they were about to go to church.

It was reported that the Senator had been seriously wounded in the head. Hiep felt so weak that she asked Am to wait a moment until her weakness passed. After a while, Hiep seemed to be ready for the short walk to the church. She walked in silence. Am saw that she was crying, but he did not dare hold her hand in public.

It was very early in the morning, but Ky Dong Street in front of the Redeemer's Church was full of people who had come to look at the headlines in the newsstands. Hiep said, "Why did this have to happen?" Am shook his head. He remembered the effect the assassination of President John Kennedy had had on his wife.

As it was a Thursday morning, the early morning Mass was sparsely attended. Hiep opened her missal and prayed. The Gospel that morning told the parable about the master who entrusted his servants with silver pieces. The master said to the deserving servants: "Come, share your master's joy!" Am noticed that Hiep's lips moved audibly. "Come; share your master's joy!" Tears were streaking down her cheeks. Am tried to focus on the Mass but his wife's sorrow distracted him. Strange indeed was his wife's affinity to the American family that had been at least partly responsible for the death of her brothers.

*

Less than two months later, the third Kennedy brother, Edward, was involved in a car accident that caused the death of one of his beautiful young friends, Mary Jo Kopechne at Chappaquiddick.

As the political fortune of the Kennedy's was at its lowest point, Hiep felt herself sinking into a new period of depression characterized by insomnia. She saw in her own family and in the Kennedy's, terrible lessons to be learned about the risks of power. The parable about the silver pieces that she had read on the day of Robert Kennedy's assassination came back as a reminder to her. To her family and to the Kennedy's, God had given perhaps a little too much, and that in itself, was not always a blessing. In return, too much had been expected from them.

*

Ho Chi Minh died on September 3, 1969, leaving a questionable legacy. The radio announcement was terse and abrupt. There were no immediate comments regarding his achievements or failures.

Hiep sat for hours, trying to remember all the things that Diem and her other brothers had said about Ho. She remembered that they had never said anything disparaging about Ho, even during the most intensive Communist propaganda campaign against them. In a certain way, Diem had been fond of Ho.

Her brother, however, was strongly opposed to Communism, which Ho wanted to impose on all of Indochina. Diem constantly told the people of South Vietnam, "Communism is not socialism. It is not a philosophy. It is not an economic system. It is a mechanism to take power and to retain power."

She did not know how much Diem had been in touch with Ho over the years. Knowing Diem, Hiep would have been surprised if he did not have intermediaries capable of assuring communication at the highest level with Hanoi. Over the years, Diem had certainly tried to convert Ho to the need for peaceful coexistence between the two zones of partitioned Vietnam.

At certain times, she had heard Diem mention the name of Nguyen Luong Bang, the trusted friend of Ho Chi Minh, who occupied a discreet yet most important role in the Communist Party's Politburo. Was it through Nguyen Luong Bang, or Vo Nguyen Giap, that Diem had kept a channel open with Ho?

In the last year of his life, before the Lunar New Year of 1963, Ho had sent Diem a beautiful branch of pink cherry blossoms, with a note attached, wishing Diem and the people of South Vietnam a happy and prosperous year. Diem had proudly displayed the branch in the Gia Long Palace.

What had gone through the minds of the two men? Had they seen that the war too costly for both sides, the Americans too demanding and the escalation of the war inevitable?

While Nhu went about noisily, making references to his meetings with Pham Hung, a member of the Politburo and an overseer of all the operations in the South, Diem had discreetly built up his antennas in Paris, Brussels and New Delhi to keep communication channels open with Hanoi.

Hiep believed that at the time, neither Diem nor Ho had considered a rapid unification of the country. They apparently had come to the conclusion that Vietnam should not be sacrificed in the confrontation of international interests between the Western powers and the Communist Bloc. They had apparently decided that both North and South Vietnam would be better off if the Vietnamese leaders could resolve Vietnamese differences among themselves.

Hiep closed her eyes. Their intentions could not be carried out. Their peace talks had never materialized. Yet now that they were both gone, the Paris Peace Talks were about to begin.

*

As more and more Americans began to demonstrate against the Vietnam War in the United States, Hiep could see the writing on the wall. Without the will to fight, no victory could be won. She knew that the war would soon end with the Americans trying to get out, leaving their South Vietnamese allies behind.

On January 18, 1969, the first session of the Paris Peace talks began, with the South Vietnamese government dragging its feet. There was nothing South Vietnamese leaders could do, however, to prevent the opening of the Peace Talks, or their progress towards eventually ending the war, and allowing the Americans to withdraw in safety and dignity.

Hiep remembered a time when Diem had problems participating in another peace talk. It was in 1962, and the peace negotiations did not concern South Vietnam directly. The delegations in Geneva at that time were discussing peace and neutrality in Laos. Diem and Nhu were adamant in their conviction that by selling out Laos to the Pathet Lao and Hanoi, the Americans would be dealing a fatal blow to South Vietnam. President Kennedy's chief negotiator there, Averell Harriman would not listen to Diem and Nhu, and he became Diem's enemy ever after.

Now, in 1969, Nguyen van Thieu was in a worse quandary. It was not Laos, but South Vietnam itself that was to be sacrificed and Thieu had no desire to make enemies in the Nixon administration.

The outcome was clear. Thieu would survive, at least for a few more years. But, South Vietnam would have to accept any conditions that were required to protect the American withdrawal, to retrieve the American POW's and to allow the Americans to walk out of Vietnam without too much loss of face.

Hiep remembered one of the last things Diem had told her before he was overthrown and murdered, "The United States is a big nation. It can make major mistakes and survive. South Vietnam is a small country; any major mistake we allow the Americans to make for *us*, will finish us off. That is why we should never allow the Americans to make policy decisions for us."

CHAPTER THIRTY-FOUR
A TIME TO LEAVE

On October 23, 1969, President Nixon confirmed the withdrawal of a considerable number of American troops from Vietnam. For the first time since early 1967, American military strength in Vietnam fell below the five hundred thousand mark.

Hiep was certain that the American withdrawal would be totally safe. The Communist High Command would never commit the mistake of trying *to thwart an enemy returning homeward.* Communist generals and Politburo members would not waste the lives of their troops simply to humiliate the Americans, by launching attacks on the weakened American forces.

Yet, Hiep saw that the Americans had begun a series of self-inflicted wounds during their retreat.

In November 1969, *The New York Times* published its story of the My Lai Massacre. The tragedy of My Lai took place at a crucial time, when people in America had had enough of the war. Mass demonstrations against the Vietnam War were organized in Washington. On November 13 and 14, and again on November 20, up to a quarter million of demonstrators swarmed over the capital, angrily demanding an end to the war. The people of America understood that there was no need to confirm criminal recklessness in the war. *The Vietnam War was worse than a crime. It was a mistake.*

Hiep understood the American people's fervent desire to withdraw from the war. Her only cause for bitterness was that there had been no good reason for Americans to be directly involved in the war in the first place.

*

In the meantime, a large movement to restore President Diem's political honor was underway. Since their remains had been moved to the Mac Dinh Chi Cemetery, groups of people arrived daily to pray over Diem's and Nhu's tombs. A political Party, the *Nhan Xa* (Personalist Socialist Party), which claimed loyalty to Diem's name, was created and began to thrive. Many newspapers, wanting to show respect for Diem, derided the awkward imitations of his words and deeds among the new breed of politicians and military leaders. He was again known as the *Venerable Gentleman*, or more popularly the *Late President*.

Diem's people were finally honoring him again. A solemn Mass was said for the repose of his soul in the Saigon Basilica on November 2, 1970. Nhu's and the President's loyal comrades-in-arms who had fallen during and after the coup d'état of 1963, were not forgotten either. A commemorative service at the North Vietnam Mutuality Pagoda in honor of Diem, Nhu and Can attracted both Christians and Buddhists. After the Mass at the Basilica and the ceremony at the pagoda, the participants moved to the Mac Dinh Chi Cemetery. Inside the Cemetery, they bowed their heads and prayed, and afterwards lined up in front of Diem's and Nhu's tombs to pay their respects to the fallen heroes.

At the Basilica, Hiep and Am were asked to sit in the front pew. Am watched Hiep as she prayed. The huge crowds, both inside and outside the Basilica, did not seem to affect her inner peace. Isolated in a world of her own, she was praying, asking for God's reassurance that her brothers had not died in vain.

Former dignitaries of Diem's regime, generals and colonels, ostentatiously showed themselves at the ceremony. President Thieu's wife was among those present. The Commemorative Mass marked the end of an underground cult for Diem and Nhu. It marked the public vindication of what Diem, Nhu, Can and their fallen comrades-in-arms had achieved in their lifetime.

Hiep did not seem to see the pomp and the outpouring of emotions around her. What she saw in her mind's eyes was an ageless rotund man, in immaculate white sharkskin, who looked at her with calm and said, "Do not worry, Sister. Someday the heart will prevail over reason, wisdom over politics, justice over oppression, and truth over lies. Our country has outlived more than two thousand years of written history. It will overcome all these momentary setbacks someday. God will have the last word."

*

In April 1971, half a million Americans demonstrated in Washington for 'Peace Now!' Hiep knew that faced with that great longing for peace, the American government would soon have to abandon the battlefield.

She was glad for the American youths. Their continued unnecessary deaths in Vietnam would not resolve anything. She remembered the ambush in Dalat. She remembered what Bishop Thuan had told her about his encounters with American soldiers in his diocese. Hiep only had a prayer, "Please God, stop this madness, this useless, purposeless loss of lives."

Two months later, *The New York Times* published the first installments of the *Pentagon Papers*. It was indeed a horrible experience for Hiep to read the translations of the Pentagon Papers, offered to her by Colonel Thong. He had a pool of translators who performed translation jobs for foreign firms in Saigon. His translators had found the time to do this extra work for the Colonel.

As Hiep read on, the roles of the Americans in the overthrow of President Diem became more and more obvious through reading the classified cables and memoranda. At times, Hiep stared at the text, unable to go on, "So, this is how the highest ranking leaders of a great nation spent months plotting to overthrow a long time ally, an elected President of a small allied nation?" Page after page of documents showed the arrogance, the duplicity, the inhumanity of so many of the politicians who had been called *the best and the brightest* and who had served under President Kennedy. Page after page revealed the courage and the wisdom of so many American officials who unfortunately, were not listened to.

Her bitterness grew to such a point that for days she stopped reading the translated text. It was too painful for her to read the callous commands from the White House and the State Department that ordered the overthrow of Diem. Over the years since 1963, Hiep had heard enough about the American involvement in the coup. Now, in black and white, the Pentagon Papers gave the official confirmation of what she had heard.

As the cast of characters during the drama of 1963 became public knowledge, certain Vietnamese generals saw their unsavory role on display. Hiep, who had forgiven all of them a long time ago, felt shame and humiliation for them.

After a while, the *Pentagon Papers* were no longer a threat to her inner peace. She accepted the tormenting pain, rejoicing only in the fact that at least part of the truth had been restored.

*

On March 31, 1972, the Communists launched a major offensive, which came to be known as the Good Friday Offensive. Why was it so painful for Hiep this time? Neither the scale nor the duration of this Offensive was comparable to the Mau Than Tet Offensive. The body count was not as terrible, either. Yet, Hiep knew that it spelled the beginning of the end.

During this Offensive, the American troops sat back and watched. They only intervened with a little air support. The South Vietnamese launched desperate counter-attacks and succeeded in recovering all the lost cities, but all their points of vulnerability were displayed.

Soon enough, Hiep knew, the Communists would launch the final Offensive, but they would wait until the Americans were gone. With the American air cover gone, with no more American air strikes to make a difference, the South Vietnamese troops would be completely outgunned. The Communists would be able to fight the South Vietnamese troops either by swarming over the coastal plain north of Hue, or better, as Diem had predicted, by conquering the Central Highlands and then, launching their divisions from there down to the lowlands to finish off the Saigon regime.

Hiep felt only sadness, not bitterness. Diem had seen the ineluctable end a long time ago. As soon as South Vietnam became subjugated to the United States, as soon as it had lost its independence, and therefore lost its *just cause*, defeat was only a question of time.

There were South Vietnamese and Americans who thought that the war could be won by the United States, arguing that if the United States had bombed North Vietnam back to the Stone Age, the war could have been won. Hiep was not of that opinion. Even if the Americans had used unfettered, unrestrained force against North Vietnam, Hiep knew, they could not have won the war. That would have united the Vietnamese, North and South, faster than it actually had, against the Americans.

Such a strategy would have very quickly provoked a vast opposition movement in the United States, against American involvement in the war.

The Offensive had started on Good Friday. It was the first time in her life that she did not wake up on Easter morning with a feeling of resurrection. The joyous sounds of the bells of the Redeemer's Church on the morning of Easter did not erase from her consciousness the sad tolls of the bells on Good Friday.

Weeks and then months passed. The bells of Good Friday still tolled in her mind. The relief came from out of the past. It came when she needed it most.

*

In 1972, Hiep heard about General Edward Lansdale's book, *'In The Midst of Wars'*. This time, Hiep called Colonel Thong for help. The translation was magnificent. Apparently the Colonel had put his star translators on the job.

General Lansdale had kept his promise. She remembered their chance meeting in Vung Tau. That day, he had said that he would finish the book. She read the complete book in translation. The parts where Lansdale wrote about his experience with Magsaysay, the Filipino President, intrigued her.

Hiep remembered how Diem had admired Magsaysay, and how he grieved when the Filipino leader met his death in a plane crash in Cebu, on March 17, 1957.

Lansdale's book was full of anecdotes about Diem. Throughout the book, Diem was vindicated for his role in the difficult years of 1954-1955. What struck Hiep the most was Lansdale's sincere admiration for Diem, even though he recognized all of Diem's weaknesses and shortcomings.

It was so refreshing for Hiep to read Lansdale's book after her painful struggle through the documents of the *Pentagon Papers*. Hiep said to herself, "I really need to read and re-read this book. It reveals so many things about Diem and Nhu that I was never aware of previously. Yet, even those parts unknown to me carry in their descriptions by the general, an authenticity that is striking. They confirm the parts I know of them." For months, Hiep read and re-read the translated pages and gathered peace from what was written there.

Lansdale's friendship never ended. Later on, when Hiep lived in exile, every year, around November 2, she heard that he had written yet another beautiful note to Vietnamese Communities abroad that got together and commemorated the anniversary of Diem's death.

*

Lansdale's book brought relief to her mind. Yet, Hiep knew that South Vietnam was moving closer and closer to the abyss.

General Dang Van Quang, Am's godson, then Presidential Advisor for National Security, came to see Am and Hiep quite frequently. One day he said, "The Good Friday Offensive did not shake President Thieu as much as the draft agreement given him by Alexander Haig last week."

It was October 1972. Saigon was full of rumors. People discussed the Paris Peace talks and imaginary draft agreements in cafés, in the newspapers, even at parish meetings. This was the first time Hiep had heard about the existence of a genuine draft agreement.

Am asked: "Is the draft agreement *that* bad?" Quang nodded, "Bad enough. We will not even be able to hold on to the territory we still control, if we sign this agreement. You see, according to the draft, Communist troops now in the South are not required to withdraw to the North, and they are allowed to retain the northern area they have occupied since the Good Friday Offensive. The Americans, on the other hand, will have to withdraw from South Vietnam within ninety days after the agreement is signed."

Hiep did not say anything. So, both the Americans and the Communists had got what they wanted. The South Vietnamese people would be the ones to pay the price.

Am asked: "What is President Thieu's strategy now?" Quang answered, "Assurances from Ambassador Bunker will not be enough. Assurances from Alexander Haig and Kissinger will not be enough. Thieu wants assurances from President Nixon himself. He wants to be sure that the Americans will react forcefully if Hanoi launches another major offensive."

Intervening in the conversation for the first time, Hiep asked, "When President Thieu receives such assurances from President Nixon, will he sign the agreement then?" Quang nodded. He was startled by the look he saw in Hiep's eyes. She was not simply asking a question. She seemed to know already the consequences of such an agreement, no matter what assurances were given, by whatever authorities.

Quang felt uncomfortable under her gaze. Thieu had told him how people had felt defenseless in front of Nhu and Diem. Thieu had said: "They seemed to see right through you. They seemed to see through your subterfuges, your half-truths. Their eyes seemed to pin you to the wall."

Quang wanted to tell them everything. He wanted to tell Am and Hiep all of his frustrations, worries and nightmares. He looked at the pictures on the walls and on the desks. Diem, Nhu, Can, and Luyen fixed him with their eyes. He sighed and said, "We can only do what we can."

Was it a faint echo of what Diem had said in the last days of the First Republic? Hiep wondered, yet she knew that Diem had really done everything he could. Would Thieu do the same?

*

On January 27, 1973, the Cease-Fire Agreement was signed in Paris. The fate of South Vietnam was sealed.

But there was no cease-fire. While Kissinger and Le Duc Tho, the main negotiators of the Agreement, were awarded the Nobel Peace Prize, the war went on. Now both sides kept count of the other side's violations of the agreement, until finally, it all became a farce. The war continued and the rural areas became less safe than ever before. Four million people from the villages and hamlets of South Vietnam who found themselves in contested areas, flooded to the cities and their suburbs in search of better security.

The Catholic Bishops decided that it was time to play a role in assisting those displaced persons.

*

With the approval of the Holy See, the Vietnamese Bishops organized the Cooperation for the Reconstruction of Vietnam or COREV, as a humanitarian organization that coordinated all the Catholic assistance to the displaced.

Bishop Thuan was elected as the executive vice-president to oversee all COREV activities. His selection to head that major undertaking of the Catholic Church in Vietnam met with enthusiastic approval from both foreign funding sources and the displaced persons in South Vietnam.

Thuan himself saw in his appointment an opportunity to emulate Diem's care for refugees in his lifetime. He drafted a general plan for the assistance of displaced persons, and then went to work for the funding and the implementation of that plan.

Within the framework of the general plan, local entities, parishes, villages, and Buddhist communities presented their specific projects. Thuan, along with his Committee, screened the projects, approved many of them and released the money required for their implementation.

Having to work on thousands of requests every month for funding from every province in South Vietnam, and also to meet with international donors, Bishop Thuan now spent a great deal of time in Saigon.

Thanks to that arrangement, Hiep saw Thuan on a regular basis. She was interested in all the different aspects of his assistance work. She constantly reminded Thuan, that ultimately, his general plan and even the specific projects did not matter as much as the individuals involved. She constantly reminded him to spend time with the displaced people and to avoid intermediaries whenever possible.

When Thuan felt tired with his work, he only had to look at his mother and draw strength from her love and enthusiasm. Invigorated, he would go back to his work again.

*

Everything that happened in the United States had repercussions in South Vietnam. That was natural, considering that South Vietnam depended so much on America for its survival.

For months the Watergate scandal was at the top of everybody's mind in Saigon. Every new revelation, every new twist and turn unfavorable to Nixon appeared to Thieu to be another nail driven into the coffin of his regime.

He had depended on Nixon. He had signed the Paris Peace agreement on the faith of assurances given to him personally by the U.S. President. Now, in all probability, Nixon was about to fall.

The last Americans troops had left South Vietnam by March 29,1973. There was not a chance in a million that a new U.S. President would honor Nixon's secret assurances that had been given to Thieu, and order American troops back into South Vietnam if the North sent all of its divisions into the South for a final offensive.

The agony of Nixon was finally over. On August 8, 1974, he resigned. Thieu knew then that the wait would not be long. Very soon, the North Vietnamese would launch the decisive attack.

CHAPTER THIRTY-FIVE
ANOTHER YEAR OF THE CAT:
THE FINAL AGONY

After the disaster in the Year of the Cat in 1963, Hiep felt quite nervous about the approach of another Year of the Cat in 1975. Hiep knew what was going on. She knew that the final preparations were being made by the Communists to finish off the South Vietnamese regime.

On January 3, 1975, when the Communists launched their attack on Phuoc Long City and captured it within three days, even the man in the street knew that it was the beginning of the end.

On March 11, several North Vietnamese divisions took the City of Ban Me Thuot, the capital of the Central Highlands. Instead of launching a vigorous counter-attack to dislodge the North Vietnamese from Ban Me Thuot, or to prevent the takeover of other cities in that strategic region, Thieu ordered his troops to withdraw completely from all the Central Highlands.

The evacuation of the troops from the Central Highlands turned into a nightmare. The huge column of retreating soldiers and fleeing civilians took the old Highway 7, a mountainous highway that was in terrible disrepair, and interrupted by many broken bridges. The Communists relentlessly attacked the column day and night, swooping over it mercilessly. Nothing could prevent the massacre. Because there was no food, the fleeing refugees began to starve as they traveled along the treacherous trail.

Bishop Thuan, with the approval of his Committee and the Apostolic Delegate, rented planes and dropped tons of food on the column; meanwhile the Communists continued the carnage.

Hiep knew that Thuan was fully aware of the consequences of his act of mercy. It was clear now that Communist rule was about to begin. Thuan's intervention would certainly not help him gain the favor of the new masters. Thuan had to do it, Hiep knew, because he could not stand to see the people starve. But before long, he would have to pay the price for his action.

When the remnants of the column arrived in the plain ten days later, the will of the South Vietnamese forces had been irremediably broken. The Communists no longer had to fight a war. They could begin their triumphant march from the north to the south.

The debacle began with the spontaneous abandonment of Quang Tri City, north of Hue on March 19. Hue itself was abandoned on March 24. Then on March 29, Danang, South Vietnam's second largest city, a hundred miles south of Hue, was captured.

On April 2, Communist troops entered Nha Trang, and all communication with Thuan became impossible. On April 3, the immense base of Cam Ranh was in Communist hands and by April 18, Phan Rang, Thieu's native town, fell to the advancing Communist troops.

*

Ham Tieu, Hiep's daughter who lived in Australia, had been constantly on the phone, begging Am and Hiep to leave Saigon before it was too late.

Am knew that there was no other option, but he waited until Hiep was willing to go. Hiep was not sure whether she should go, when Thuan's life seemed to hang by a thread. Amid rumors of his being elevated to the rank of Archbishop Coadjutor of Saigon, Hiep knew that the next regime in Saigon would give him no peace.

The lives of her daughters finally convinced her to leave. She agreed to go with Am and her daughters to Australia. In the back of her mind, she remembered what her father had told her about Elizabeth of Portugal, her patron saint. Apparently Elizabeth, Queen of Portugal, had also known years of exile in her momentous life.

*

On Friday, April 25, 1975, Am, and Hiep and their younger daughters left Saigon on a Qantas flight. It was time to leave. Four days earlier President Nguyen van Thieu had resigned under American pressure. President Tran van Huong, who took over, was in the dark about the intentions of both the Americans and the Communists.

The Communist forces were now at the gates of Saigon and were about to launch the final attack.

As the Qantas plane left Saigon behind, Hiep turned to Am. For the first time in their married life, Hiep saw that Am was crying. Beside him sat Thuy Tien and Thu Hong, their daughters. They too, had tears in their eyes.

*

It was in Australia that she learned about the final agony of South Vietnam. It was in Australia that she watched on television, the Communist tank rolling over the grounds of the Independence Palace and the surrender of the South Vietnamese President to an officer of the North Vietnamese army.

April 30, 1975 was a date she would never forget. General Duong Van Minh who, with the support of the Americans, had overthrown Diem and had given orders to kill him and Nhu, surrendered shamefully to the Communists, in front of his hastily assembled Cabinet.

For Hiep, the final agony of Vietnam was a lesson for all countries that relied on powerful allies. The powerful allies might one day leave them in their hour of direst need.

For her, the blame for the disastrous series of defeats suffered by the Vietnamese armed forces in 1975 should have been placed squarely on the military and civil leadership who were in power at that time.

Hiep said to her daughters, "South Vietnamese should not blame the Americans for their final defeat. Even if they were abandoned by

591

Americans, the final drama would not have been so tragic, if South Vietnam had the right kind of leadership."

In her new home on Maroubra Beach, she kept saying, "They had two years of reprieve. They had a strong army. They had planes and aircraft, and they had tanks. Diem, in 1954, did not have one percent of the resources that Thieu had in 1975. But the will to fight, and the leadership was no longer there."

At another moment, she wondered, "If Thieu saw that the will to fight was no longer there, why did he hesitate to really negotiate with Hanoi? Why didn't he come to terms with Hanoi to save the lives of soldiers and innocent civilians?"

For quite a while, she was unable to forgive General Duong van Minh, who betrayed Diem and put an end to Diem's rule twelve years earlier, and who was President for forty hours in late April 1975. She said, "He betrayed the First Republic in 1963, and now he has betrayed the Second Republic and put an end to the freedom of the South by surrendering to the North Vietnamese."

After a while, Hiep was reconciled with the thought that not only Duong van Minh, but all the South Vietnamese including herself had, each in his or her own capacity, contributed to the final tragedy.

She contemplated with an immense sadness, from afar, the ongoing devastation, a thousand times more terrible than what had taken place in 1963 at the end of the First Republic, when only the Ngo Dinh Brothers had died with a handful of loyal friends.

She saw the obviousness of the relationship between the two devastating tragedies. The fall of the Second Republic and the loss of South Vietnam were, in her eyes, the direct consequences of the betrayals that had led to the fall of the First Republic.

Her mind held on to those simple convictions. Then, even those convictions became blurred and for the first time in her life, she came close to despair, despite her steadfast faith in God. Dimly, confusedly, deep in her mind, she heard a voice saying to her, "Rest now. Rest, Hiep."

PART SEVEN

THE YEARS OF EXILE

CHAPTER THIRTY-SIX
WAITING FOR NEWS FROM HOME

In the beginning, Hiep felt only a certain numbness. Initially, it was a mere sensation of dull pain in her chest and a slight heaviness in her limbs. She wondered if she was coming down with a cold. Soon enough, however, she realized that the pain was coming from deep within her mind.

Sydney was a proud and beautiful city, and Australia a country free of war. Yet, feeling her way amid the natural and man-made beauty, absorbing through her skin the absence of war, Hiep lived in world filled with unreality.

The only realities she still seemed to recognize were Am and her daughters. Mentally, she clutched at them: they were the only certitude, the only voices she understood, and the only refuge she had against the searing pain.

Even the sun seemed unreal when, imitating the sun she had known in her own country, it reclined on an immense bed of red clouds above a purple sea, behind Harbor Bridge. The streets were unreal, full of strange voices, sounds and noises, crowded with alien faces and signs, exhaling unidentified odors, flowing with a river of unfamiliar ambitions, desires, joys and sorrows.

Time had no meaning to her. This unreal feeling was imbedded in her soul and in her mind. Only the instinct of self-preservation made her struggle to return to the real world. Something inside her kept repeating, in a dull refrain, "Wake up, Hiep, wake up! Wake up, Hiep, wake up!"

She, who had stood firm in the face of so many tragedies, now found herself incapable of even waking up. For a while, all her strength evaporated, all her pride faded away and her consciousness seemed to seek nothingness.

Yet, even in the absence of hope, she still prayed. At first, the prayers did not bring solace. They were, however, a link to her past. They were the tenuous communications with a silent God. They were diaphanous sparks of light in the darkest night of her soul. Painfully, she asked herself: "How can faith survive without hope? If I believe in God, I must have hope. Yet, where is hope?"

There was a strange progression in her prayers.

Soon enough when she prayed she saw herself walking in a desert at night, climbing endless sand dunes, no longer in total darkness, but now under the pale reflection of cold and distant stars.

Then, the prayers brought her to desolate landscapes of rocky hills, dried up marshes in the twilight.

After a few months, she began to make serious and conscious attempts to come out of that strange lethargy. Slowly, in the unreal world around her, she began to glimpse reality. Groping at anything that lent an air of authenticity, she began to feel herself among the living again.

She tried to relearn how to feel. She kept repeating to herself: "I must feel joy when I watch the sun rise. I must feel happiness when I hear a bird sing. I must love to walk on the beach and watch a seagull dive into the hollow between two waves. I should get up early in the morning, and sitting on the edge of my bed, fill my nostrils with wisps of fragrances, fill my ears with tiny sounds of wood cracking, air moving, misty echoes of whispers... I should feel my fingers recoil at the touch of a rose thorn."

In the streets, people did not speak Vietnamese. Cars were driven on the wrong side of the road. Most of the street signs had no meaning, at least to her. Most restaurants did not offer rice on their menu and the stores did not carry the spices needed for the preparation of a decent meal.

Neither Hiep nor her husband could say a word in English. When her daughters turned on the television, she watched but did not understand anything at all. All guesswork was dangerous here.

She compared what she thought she understood to what Ham Tieu, her daughter heard, and was embarrassed to find out that she had guessed the opposite of what had been said. Ham Tieu, who had lived in Australia since 1961, and who now played hostess to her, said, "Mom, don't worry! You will understand everything soon."

Hiep was not so sure that someday she would understand everything. There was a time when she had watched the U.S. military TV channel in South Vietnam. She had come to understand most of the shows offered by the channel. But that was another time, another place. It was a time when she was still ready to learn. Hiep told herself a little bitterly, "I was safe. I was moving among familiar things, so at that time, a strange language did not scare me." Now, familiar things no longer surrounded her, and that made all the difference. She thought that unless she moved around constantly, she would become totally depressed. So, she kept herself busy. She went to the beaches, and she traveled to other cities near Sydney. But the change of scenes only added to the sense of profound alienation.

*

She started looking homeward. The universe in which she had lived for more than seventy years was no longer there. The return to another scene of desolation did not bring Hiep any relief.

Home was not a dreamland. It was, in fact, the complete opposite of a dreamland. Pictures taken after the Communist takeover showed in black and white a melancholy Saigon, now re-baptized Ho Chi Minh City, and still drowning in its humiliation.

Two of her children had stayed in Vietnam and both had been arrested by the new regime. Thanh had been a captain in the South Vietnamese Police before the fall of Saigon. He was soon picked up and sent to one of the reeducation centers. Bishop Thuan, who had been appointed Archbishop Coadjutor of Saigon, a few days before President Duong van Minh surrendered to the Communists, had disappeared.

Confusing news reached Hiep concerning his fate. Apparently, the Communists refused to acknowledge his appointment as Archbishop Coadjutor, claiming that it was a dirty trick played by the Vatican. Apparently, he had been arrested, interrogated, released, then arrested again, and then, there was an information blackout.

Where was he? What had they done to him? Was he still alive? The uncertainty caused her as much pain as when her brother, Khoi, had been arrested and carried away by the Vietminh in 1946, along with his eldest son. "Uncertainty is sometimes harder to bear than the worst calamity," Hiep thought. She, who had experienced so many times this agony of waiting when tragedy struck, felt she was about to snap.

Hiep was indeed ill prepared for the new tragedy. For years, she had steeled herself to accept family tragedies. She had survived the devastation of the murder of Khoi and Huan, in 1946. She managed to survive the tragedies that took place in 1963 and 1964. She was trying to come to terms with spending the rest of her life in exile. Thuan's disappearance seemed about to wipe out any progress of that effort.

Of course, Hiep had expected that Thuan would have problems with the new regime. She knew that the regime would not be pleased to see him appointed as Archbishop Coadjutor of Saigon.

She had not foreseen, however, that the regime would move so quickly and so drastically against him. "His cassock has not protected him, in the least. His elevation to the rank of Archbishop has not prevented the new regime from arresting him. It has not prevented him from disappearing into thin air", Hiep thought bitterly.

Her depression kept her from being able to finish even one single book. She kept trying to read the various accounts of the fall of Saigon, written by several different French journalists. *L'adieu a Saigon* by Larteguy was such a book. She read bits and pieces of his account, feeling her anger swell. His journalistic insensibility, his superficial outlook, his complete lack of respect for the Vietnamese made her shudder.

She thought, "If this is the way the Vietnamese are seen by every foreigner, then there will be no salvation for us. There will be no salvation for Vietnam as a country, and no salvation for Vietnamese as a nation."

The dirges for Saigon were not all of that kind. She read *Chant Funèbre pour Phnom Penh et Saigon* (Funeral Song for Phnom Penh and Saigon) with more relief. A medley of reminiscences and emotional outpourings, the pages filled her with sadness and shame. It did not matter to her that the book contained only French authors and gave expression only to French perspectives. The deep emotion of the writers compensated for their lack of knowledge about Vietnam and its people.

Overseas, Vietnamese also started writing. Soon enough, she had on her desk every week, at least a dozen Vietnamese magazines. While she understood the anger of Vietnamese writers, she often felt at odds with them. She hoped that some day they would write more kindly about themselves, and that they would be able to overcome their anger and their hatred.

She recognized that national reconciliation was not yet at work, either in Vietnam or abroad, and that war still ravaged the Vietnamese psyche.

*

She began to try to find out what had happened to her friends and relatives. She talked to the many Vietnamese refugees who came to see her, or Am, or their daughters. Many others, having found a safe haven in Australia, America or elsewhere, wrote to her. Slowly, she began to piece together a picture of the tragedy that befell all those she had known in South Vietnam.

There was an advantage to being in Australia. Like Ham Tieu, President Diem and Thuan had made many friends and political allies here over the years. Australian friends came to visit Hiep, and bring her the latest news about Vietnam, about the Church and about the world in general.

Officials in the Australian Government and the Australian Bishops prodded by great friends of President Diem, such as Robert Santa-Maria, and by Ham Tieu herself, made continual representations to the Communist regime in Vietnam, asking for the release of Archbishop Thuan.

Hiep had become more aware of the beauty of Sydney and Australia. She took long strolls on Maroubra Beach with her husband. Sometimes, Ham

Tieu drove her to Manley Beach, where she could watch the glorious sunsets. She admired the forests and grasslands, and deserts around her.

Two painful sorrows remained in her heart: in Europe, the uncertain fate of Archbishop Thuc, and in Vietnam, the long ordeal of Archbishop Thuan.

*

She was aware of the passing of Zhou-Enlai and Mao ZeDong in 1976. She was aware of U.S. President Jimmy Carter's intention to engage in negotiations with Vietnam in 1977, in view of normalizing relations between the Socialist Republic of Vietnam and the United States.

As President Carter pardoned most of the ten thousand Vietnam draft evaders right on the day of his inauguration, Hiep understood his intention was to close a sad chapter of American history and to really start the healing process in America. Yet, a part of her mind rebelled against such a move. She still wondered, "Has everything ended? Has anything ended?"

Something had ended. The Vietnam she knew had ended! It was a terrible feeling for her to realize that she had grown up and fought a lifetime alongside her father and her brothers and sisters, for a country that suddenly was no longer there.

Oh, she readily admitted that Vietnam was still there physically. It was still a country, now with a population of seventy million. It had a stable government. It had the same flag with a yellow star on a red background. There were still the same mountains, the same rivers, the same jungles and marshlands. Yet, she believed that the soul of the country, as she had known it, was gone. The Vietnam she had loved, the universe that had formed not only an environment for her life, but also the texture of her soul, was gone forever.

*

The miracle of life is that at any time, without warning, a spark of real interest can pull a mind out of its lethargy, and infuse warmth and light into the darkest despair.

Sometime in 1977, Ham Tieu, Hiep's daughter, read and translated for her part of Oriana Fallaci's *Interview with History*. The Italian Fallaci was

600

interviewing President Thieu in 1973. Listening to Ham Tieu's translation and running comments, Hiep closed her eyes and pictured Thieu, forlorn in the Independence Palace, expressing his fears, his anger and his sense of helplessness. "Fallaci must have been amused to witness Thieu's torment," Hiep said to herself. For a moment, she felt reconciled with Thieu.

She startled Ham Tieu by saying, "The President often told me that Colonel Thieu was a very intelligent man. Your Uncle Nhu said the same thing about him." That was the first time since Hiep's arrival in Australia that Ham Tieu had heard her mother talk about President Diem. Usually, even when an Australian friend mentioned Diem's name in her presence, Hiep had closed her eyes and changed the subject.

Ham Tieu closed her book and waited for more to come. Hiep drew a deep breath and went on, "Colonel Thieu never really wanted to overthrow the President. Yet, he was the one who brought a whole division to the side of the coup leaders and gave the generals the courage to start the coup. Without his Fifth Division, the generals would not have even considered launching their insignificant units against the Brigade of Presidential Guards."

Ham Tieu watched her mother closely. Hiep did not seem to notice her daughter's insistent gaze. She said, "You have just read what President Thieu said. In Ms. Fallaci's words, 'The name of Diem evoked in him an unexpected sadness.' He told Ms. Fallaci, 'They promised me they would not kill him. I told them all right, I'll join you on condition that he's not killed. Instead, they killed him, those idiots! Irresponsible madness!'"

Ham Tieu objected, "But, Mother, Oriana Fallaci did not believe in President Thieu's sincerity." Hiep did not seem to hear her daughter's objection. She asked, "What else did he say? Oh yes, "It gave me a pain that I still have, here between my head and my heart. Each anniversary of his death, I have a Mass said, here in my chapel. And I always pray for him, for his soul."

Again Ham Tieu protested, "Mother, the journalist did not believe in his sincerity. She imputed his words to his 'diabolical shrewdness'. Don't you think that she was right?"

Hiep drew herself up, "The words may be insincere, but the facts talk louder. It is a fact that Mr. Thieu had learned many things from the President and from your Uncle Nhu. He was extremely reluctant to commit his troops to the attack of the Presidential Palace in November 1963, although he brought his whole division into Saigon. Like the President, he could not decide if he should launch his own troops against their comrades-in-arms. I call *that* sincerity. In November 1970, he sent his wife to the first public Commemorative Mass for the President at the Saigon Basilica. I call *that* sincerity."

Suddenly Ham Tieu realized that she was witnessing a miracle. Her mother was back. She had gone through hell and back. But she was definitely back, with all her faculties intact. She lowered her head and asked, "Tell me more about the President, Mother."

In the darkening room, Hiep began to talk. As she talked, the dates, the names came back to her more and more readily. Faces and words long forgotten emerged from the past. Ham Tieu sat listening devotedly. She believed that the things she had heard that afternoon would become parts of a story that would one day be told.

*

Hiep now began to take stock of what had happened to her, to her family, and to the Indochina refugees all over the world. She began to understand that the exodus of Vietnamese refugees had become an historical phenomenon of unprecedented magnitude. Throughout its history, Vietnam in troubled times had seen small groups of its people flee to neighboring countries such as China, Cambodia, Laos or Thailand. The largest groups that had ever left Vietnam before were Christians who were fleeing persecution in the last century. They all ended up in Cambodia or Thailand.

This time, however, the Vietnamese had gone beyond the neighboring countries. Like ants streaming out in all directions after the anthill has been destroyed, Vietnamese refugees left their native land in successive waves.

The first wave of refugees who left South Vietnam in April and May 1975, about a quarter million of them, had readjusted to their new lives, by the time Hiep had regained interest in the world around her. More than a hundred thousand had gone to the United States. The rest had resettled in France, Canada, Australia, New Zealand and other European countries.

Besides a few fishermen and private soldiers who were evacuated along with others in the prevailing chaos in Saigon and Vung Tau, most of Vietnamese refugees of the first wave were professionals, civil servants or military officers who had little difficulty in resettling in a foreign country.

Following the fall of Phnom Penh on April 17, 1975, thirty thousand Cambodians fled across the tightly controlled border between Cambodia and Thailand, while more than a hundred thousand found their way into Vietnam. The Cambodian refugees who arrived in Thailand were the fortunate survivors among a much large number of fleeing refugees who gambled their lives through Khmer Rouge minefields and crossfire. As Laos was gliding under Communist control thousands of Lao and H'mong refugees crossed the Mekong River into Thailand, in May and June 1975.

Hiep was surprised by the incredible generosity of the foreign communities who took care of her fellow-refugees. It was as if, all of a sudden, selfishness and racism had disappeared from the nations. Hastily written laws were promulgated and implemented to protect and assist the Indochina refugees. Parliaments voted for humanitarian budgets, Ministries and Departments came up with human resources and programs. Private citizens and local communities opened their doors and their hearts to Indochina refugees. It was as if suddenly, the springtime of human generosity was back.

Hiep was mesmerized by what she saw. Coming out of the winter that had numbed her soul, she marveled at the new miracle. She remembered how Diem had cared for the refugees. The million of refugees who fled from North Vietnam to the South had been Diem's chief concern day and night. Not only were they his responsibility, they were also his obsession.

Diem, the Oblate of the Order of St. Benedict, had appropriately taken the name, Odilo, as his religious name. He had faithfully followed the model of the Abbot of Cluny, his patron saint. Like Saint Odilo, who had opened the French churches and monasteries as sanctuaries to refugees of his time, Diem opened South Vietnam to refugees from the North. He also opened his heart to them.

Hiep remembered how Diem had carried in his arms, babies of refugee families, how he touched the heads of refugee children with his hand, as if to bless them. With the limited resources he obtained from the United States, France and other allies of South Vietnam, he was never able to give refugees anything fanciful. A roof over their heads, food for three to six months, farming implements and a plot of land that was all he could do for most of them. That was all.

But Diem had gone to work for the refugees with his faith, and with the example of his patron saint, Odilo. During all nine years he was in power, Diem spent time trying to improve the resettlement of refugees, learning from mistakes, inventing new approaches. He never considered that his partnership with them was ended. It was a long time ago, yet it seemed as if it had only happened yesterday.

After the Paris Peace Agreement of 1973, her son, then Bishop Thuan, the Executive Vice President of Cooperation for the Reconstruction of Vietnam, with the help of hundreds of Catholic organizations around the world, had resettled hundreds of thousands of displaced persons with the same zeal.

In the darkest days of the agony of South Vietnam, in March 1975, when an interminable column of refugees trekked the impracticable highways and roads to reach the coastline from the Central Highlands, Bishop Thuan intervened energetically. To ease their desperate hunger, Thuan had organized mercy flights and dropped tons of bread and food on the column. Thuan told her, "Mother, it is terrible. The Communists constantly fire on the column of retreating troops and refugees. The highway is impracticable. We have to drop food on the river. The column is wading now in the river. The whole river is full of wading people."

Now, Hiep could only pray for the Vietnamese refugees overseas. She dreamed that one day Archbishop Thuan would be released from prison, and would be able to leave Vietnam to help his fellow countrymen abroad.

Australian friends asked her why so many Vietnamese had left their country. Hiep suggested that they simply read the newspapers. Numerous foreign correspondents and reporters were showing the sad picture of North and South Vietnam. Hundreds of thousands were being detained in re-education centers or in prisons all over Vietnam. Most of the former members of the armed forces and administration of South Vietnam were detained, many of them for long periods of time.

New economic zones had sprouted up here and there, supposedly to increase agricultural production, but actually to help absorb the displaced people who had created slum areas around the cities during the thirty years of war. As those who were sent to new economic zones did not receive much help from the government, their lives were very bleak.

Most of the Vietnamese who became refugees knew that they would never have a normal life, if they stayed in Vietnam. In Cambodia, the Khmers Rouges caused the death of at least 1,200,000 people. In Laos, the H'mong tribesmen were targets of massacres even before the Communist takeover in December 1975. For the majority of the Indochina refugees, the option to stay on in their native countries did not really exist.

*

By April 1978 another wave of refugees fled South Vietnam, this time, by boat. They came to be known as *the boat people*. The *immediate* cause for that exodus was probably the order that was issued in March 1978, by the Socialist Republic of Vietnam, which effectively eliminated all private businesses in South Vietnam.

The measure seemed to be aimed directly at the ethnic Chinese living in Cho Lon, the Chinatown of Saigon. More than thirty thousand businesses were confiscated. By April 1978, even the smallest businesses had been eliminated.

In North Vietnam, there were increasing conflicts between the government and the ethnic Chinese, and by July 1978, a total of a hundred sixty thousand Vietnamese of Chinese descent had crossed the border into China. Later on, another seventy-five thousand escaped to China by sea.

The plight of the Chinese moved Hiep to tears. Under Diem, they were not very happy with his various decrees that had tried to assimilate them. No more Chinese schools without classes of Vietnamese. No more Chinese sounding names for Vietnamese citizens. All Chinese were allowed to become Vietnamese citizens; those who refused citizenship could no longer practice certain professions in South Vietnam.

Yet, even with all those decrees, Diem remained in the eyes of the Chinese, an honorable man, a patriot. Diem and Nhu spent their last night in the home of a Chinese leader in Cholon. Ma Tuyen, the Chinese leader, did not care about the consequences of harboring the overthrown President. He considered it an honor that Diem had come to his house after he had fled from the Palace.

Ma Tuyen would have to pay a heavy price for that honor. He was put in jail by the generals, after 1963. It appeared that the Communists again put him in jail after 1975.

Hiep, remembering the debt, was broken-hearted as the Chinese who had been driven out of Vietnam, were reported to have drown by the thousands in the South China Sea, when their small, un-seaworthy boats sank. Boat people escaped from every port, heading towards every destination imaginable. The monthly total of boat people continued to swell until it reached sixty thousand per month by mid 1979.

The plight of the boat people became the focus of world attention, when leaky boats began to arrive in Thailand, Hong Kong, the Philippines, Indonesia, Singapore, Taiwan, Korea and Japan, landing more than half a million refugees on every beach and in every harbor of South East and East Asia.

During that same time, the Laotians, H'mong and Thaidam who escaped from Laos into Thailand reached a total of three hundred thousand.

The invasion of Cambodia by Vietnamese troops in December 1978, forced the Khmers Rouges to loosen up their control of the Khmer-Thai border and resulted in an exodus of two hundred thousand refugees far into Thai territory, while another five hundred thousand obtained precarious asylum right on the Thai border.

*

Only a few months later, Hiep watched helplessly as countries of first asylum, such as Malaysia, Thailand and Indonesia, started to consider the boat people as a threat to national security. She trembled, as those countries no longer recognized the refugees as desperate human beings in need of help and compassion.

The springtime of goodwill was over. The nightmare of the boat people began. Hiep woke up at night screaming. The drowning of tens of thousands boat people in the South China Sea, and the escalating barbaric attacks of Thai pirates preying on defenseless refugees, haunted her day and night. Her prayers became cries of despair.

In July 1979, an International Conference on Indochina Refugees was convened in Geneva. First asylum countries, as well as resettlement countries suffering from compassion fatigue, were beginning to think about ways to put an end to the exodus of boat people from Vietnam.

Having believed that the fall of South Vietnam was the natural outcome of the overthrow of President Diem, Hiep saw in the plight of the boat people the terrible consequence of the American decision to do away with the First Republic in Vietnam.

She visited refugees in the Sydney area, and liked to talk to those who had newly arrived. She listened to their long odysseys. Their ordeals made her wonder why God permitted so much misery. In the back of her mind, she wondered what her son, Thuan, could have done for these unfortunate boat people, if he had been there.

*

It was only much later, that Hiep became reconciled with the plight of the Vietnamese refugees. It took time for her to realize that the Vietnamese Diaspora, spread out all over the world, might be a blessing after all.

She began to hear the leaders of the Church in Europe and in America praise the Vietnamese Christians for their faith, their courage and fortitude. Young Vietnamese Christians joined seminaries in droves and constituted a major new source of religious vocations. She heard bishops and priests tell her that the Vietnamese Catholics renewed and strengthened their faith.

In Australia, in Europe, in America, in most collective ordination ceremonies, there were more and more Vietnamese among the ordained.

Buddhist temples built by the Vietnamese now outgrew the number of Buddhist temples built by Chinese and Japanese, outside of Asia. Catholic churches and Buddhist temples built by Vietnamese thrived side by side.

In the meantime, she also saw that the Vietnamese, because of their hard work, had acquired everywhere the reputation of people with good work ethics, dedicated to education, disciplined and patient.

Slowly, Hiep began to see a miracle in the flight of the Vietnamese. Vietnam would never have had the resources to send so many overseas for studies and for work in such a short period of time, had it not been for the cataclysm that had made them refugees.

She saw that most of the Vietnamese overseas had learned something new and that their collective knowledge was extremely vast. Hiep thought that someday, all that knowledge accumulated and acquired overseas could contribute to make her country richer and more tolerant.

Instead of crying over the past ordeals of the boat people, she began to dream about the potentialities of all the experience acquired by the Vietnamese living overseas. She hoped that someday the people who remained in Vietnam, and the people who had left, would join forces. That day, she thought, would come in her lifetime.

*

In 1978, the shadow of the past revisited her. Hiep listened to Ham Tieu's slow and laborious translation of page after page of General Tran Van Don's *The Endless War*. Though Don was at times polite, though at times he was full of praise for the Ngo Dinh, Hiep felt the truth had been betrayed again and again.

She remembered Don quite well. He was one of the most assiduous courtiers in Can's small retinue in Hue. He knew how to please Can, and how to flatter him. He was with Generals Duong Van Minh, Tran Thien Khiem and Ton That Dinh, the principal artisans of the coup that overthrew Diem. In his book, Don flatly denied any participation in the murder of the President. Yet, he was the architect of the plot. He was also the main contact between the coup leaders and the Americans. Had he wanted to spare the life of the President, he would have made the necessary arrangements to fly him out of Vietnam.

Hiep remembered having said to Diem one day, in 1955: "Be careful, those who betray you once will probably betray you twice." It was right after Don had sided with General Nguyen van Vy, when Vy went to the

Independence Palace and tried to force Diem to leave Saigon and go to Cannes for consultation with Bao Dai. Instead of firing Don, Diem preferred to promote him. Though many reports pointed to Don's ambiguous attitude in the November 11, 1960, coup Diem preferred to ignore the reports.

Yet, Diem should have known better. Don's father had volunteered for the French army during World War I. He came back to Vietnam as a medical doctor, honored by the French colonial administration. Made Mayor of Saigon then Ambassador to London, under Prime Minister Tran Van Huu, Don's father so frequently betrayed Vietnamese Government secrets to Massigli, the French Ambassador that even his old friend Tran Van Huu had to transfer him. Don's father officially renounced the French nationality that he had acquired in 1956, when Don himself, who had been educated, trained and promoted by the French, burned in an *autodafé* all his French insignia and medals.

Hiep knew that Diem did not have the benefit of her hindsight. After betraying Diem, Don went on to betray Duong van Minh for Nguyen Cao Ky, and then he betrayed Ky for Nguyen van Thieu. Diem did not live to see how Don gave his promise to send Can abroad, but instead delivered him to the generals who put him to death.

Hiep listened absent-mindedly to what Ham Tieu translated. She tried to find some reason to reconcile herself with Don. "Is betrayal in the nature of man?" she wondered. "No, no. There have been too many men and women who would rather die than to betray." She remembered how calmly Diem predicted betrayals, how easily he forgave those who betrayed him. She lowered her head and silently prayed, "Brother, teach me. Teach me how to reconcile myself with those who betrayed you."

Sensing Hiep's anguish, Ham Tieu closed the book. Hiep looked at the book on the desk. She wished her mind could be closed and opened at will like the book. Day and night, memories rolled like an endless movie through her mind. She understood why Don had to write a book. She expected to see other books of the same kind appear in the future. Don's book was an act of exorcism. Whether it helped him get rid of painful memories or not, Hiep had no way of knowing.

Looking out of the window, feeling the ripening of a beautiful autumn day, Hiep told Ham Tieu, "Someday, I would like to read a story by a

Vietnamese, written without shame and without anger, without self-conceit and without guilt."

Ham Tieu said, "We have not recovered inner peace yet, Mother. It will take some time for us, as a people, to rediscover our lost innocence." She asked her mother, "Why don't you write such a book?"

Playfully, Hiep began, "In the beginning there was a man, a proud and angry man. He was the Grand Chamberlain who served an Emperor he literally worshipped...." She stopped and laughed. Then she said, "You are right, we have not recovered our inner peace yet. It is premature to write about that painful period now."

Outside of the window, the autumn sun shone on jade green blades of grass. Hiep wished Don could see the delicate beauty of the grass, the palpable movements of sunrays on the lawn. She wanted to say, forgetting all the bitterness she had felt only a few moments earlier, "It is all right. Everything is all right including pain and guilt, shame and pride. Let the past bury the past. Only the future of our people matters. Only future generations matter. And they will be all right, you will see."

*

She had lived under only four Emperors, but she, who was born in the last months of the reign of Pope Leo XIII, had outlived seven Popes. Pope Paul VI, who had been a classmate of her brother, Archbishop Thuc, died on August 6, 1978.

Pope Paul VI

*

Since 1945, Hiep had taken August 6 as a private day of mourning, in memory of those killed by a nuclear bomb in Hiroshima. Now she had another reason to keep that commemoration. Contrary to the rumors, which had been circulated in the United States and in Vietnam by the enemies of the Ngo Dinh, Pope Paul VI in 1963, never turned his back on Archbishop Thuc. After the coup d'état, the Pope had intervened most actively with the United States, and personally with Cabot Lodge in Can's favor.

Afterwards, he assigned to Archbishop Thuc the title of Assistant to the Throne, exactly the title Ngo Dinh Kha had under Emperor Thanh Thai. The Pope was patient and generous with his former classmate, even after Archbishop Thuc had been taken advantage of by fringe elements in the Church who attempted to create a schism.

The death of Paul VI was followed closely by that of his successor, Pope John Paul I, whose reign lasted less than a month.

Hiep was surprised and encouraged by the advent of Pope John Paul II. He came from a country that was under Communist rule. He understood Communism and he had valiantly resisted the Communist authorities in Poland.

His election marked a new departure within the Church. It was, in Hiep's eyes, gravid with prophecy. The day he was elected, Hiep went down on her knees and prayed. She prayed God to bless him, and his country. She also prayed God to bless all the countries still under Communist rule.

*

In the end, it happened. Hanoi decided to invade Cambodia. For months tension had been escalating between the two Communist governments. Skirmishes at the borders were almost daily occurrences. Mutual accusations of atrocities had been exchanged with ever-increasing vehemence. Then, draping themselves with the mantle of liberators, Vietnamese troops invaded Cambodia. Within two weeks, Phnom Penh fell to the 'liberators', while the Khmers Rouges initiated a virulent guerrilla war against the 'invaders'. It did not take long for the Vietnamese occupiers to find themselves in a quagmire.

Hiep told Ham Tieu, "Maybe I have lived too long. I have seen it all. These days, Vietnamese mothers must cry for their children fallen in a foreign land, just like the American and the French mothers before them."

Ham Tieu asked: "Don't you think that the Vietnamese troops will soon eliminate all of Pol Pot's guerrilla fighters? After all, the Vietnamese generals have been the masters in guerrilla warfare."

Hiep shook her head in disagreement, as she said, "The President said, 'Terrorism and guerrilla warfare are weapons of the poor and the weak. Anybody can conduct terrorism and guerrilla warfare, and it takes tremendous resources to eliminate them. The success of terrorism depends on the will to show the utmost cruelty in killing and the utmost indifference to the consequences. The success of guerrilla warfare depends on the anger of the fighters, and the fear of the people who feed them.'"

Ham Tieu waited for the conclusion that never came. In the end, she had to ask her mother, "So, you expect the Vietnamese expeditionary corps to be defeated?" Hiep nodded, "If they have the folly to stay, they will be defeated."

*

Their folly was to have entered Cambodia in the first place. On February 17, 1979, Chinese troops invaded Vietnam, 'to teach Vietnamese a lesson'.

Hiep was not interested in the war bulletins. She knew that both sides sustained heavy casualties. She knew that the Chinese had limited objectives for their invasion. They achieved those and withdrew. Both sides could then claim victory.

What worried Hiep was the isolation of Vietnam, even in the Communist world. She worried, because she knew that an isolated and weakened government, with a full-fledged war in Cambodia, and a border war with China, would not be kind to its own people, in its internal policies. She knew that it would turn against many among its own people.

Vietnam's isolation was complete when the Soviet Union invaded Afghanistan and was mired in a costly and lengthy war against Afghan guerrilla fighters.

After the French and the Americans had defeated themselves in the Vietnam War, it was the turn for the Vietnamese and their Russians allies to slip into the quagmire of their own 'Vietnam War', in Cambodia and in Afghanistan.

Hiep was horrified when she saw the glee with which the enemies of the Communist world described those wars. She understood their reason for rejoicing in the weakening of the Communist countries, but could not understand their indifference to the sufferings of Cambodian, Vietnamese, Chinese, Afghan and Russian mothers at home and their sons on the battlefield. She told Ham Tieu, "After all, what makes a big difference between us and the Communists is our heart."

*

One day in 1980, Cardinal Rossi, Prefect of the Congregation of Propaganda Fidae, showed up at Hiep's doorstep. The powerful clergyman had been visiting various countries in South and Southeast Asia, and had decided to visit Am and Hiep to show the solicitude of the Vatican towards Archbishop Thuan and his family.

Hiep sat and watched Am and the Cardinal. They spoke in French and she had no problem following their conversation.

At a certain moment the Cardinal said, "Do not believe even for a minute that we have forgotten about Archbishop Thuan. The Holy Father has allowed me to say that he often prays for the Archbishop. We have managed to send visitors into Vietnam to bring our encouragement to him." Then he asked, "When the next emissary goes in, what do you want him to tell the Archbishop?"

Am looked at Hiep as if asking for her advice, then resolutely he said, "Please let the next emissary tell our son that our message to him is this: Stand firm and show courage. Be loyal to the Church and faithful to God."

The Cardinal looked at Am, then at Hiep. He understood why the Nuncio in Australia had told him that he should absolutely pay them a visit. He understood why the cardinals and bishops in Australia never failed to visit them, whenever they came to Sydney.

He got up and said; "Now I have a beautiful story to tell the Holy Father when I am back in Rome."

*

One day in 1980, Ham Tieu brought her mother a copy of Emperor Bao Dai's 'The Dragon of Annam'. It was written in French. She said, "I sat up all night reading the book. The Emperor does not seem to hate the President."

Hiep took the book and started turning the pages; "The Emperor understood that there was no other way, in 1955. The President had to depose him, because the Emperor was the prisoner of French interests, and was too easily manipulated by a small group of Vietnamese with pro-French sentiments."

Ham Tieu said, "So many authors have written about the Emperor and the President. What was the real story behind the façade? What were their true feelings about each other?"

Hiep closed her eyes and reminisced. For a moment, Ham Tieu thought that her mother had dozed off. Sitting near the window, Hiep's face was bathed in a shaft of sunlight that came through the white muslin curtain. Ham Tieu had rarely seen her so serene in recent years.

As if awakening from a pleasant dream, Hiep opened her eyes and smiled, "Before 1932, the President, like most of the Vietnamese, had only had a glimpse of the ten year old Child-Emperor, when Bao Dai returned from France, at Emperor Khai Dinh's death, to ascend to the throne. That was in 1925. The President was Head of Hai Lang Prefecture. I think he was invited to the Inauguration of the new Emperor, but he had no opportunity to talk with Bao Dai. You know what happened next?" Ham Tieu replied, "Yes, the Emperor went back to France to complete his studies. He stayed there for years."

Bao Dai the Child Emperor

*

Hiep said, "It took him seven more years to complete his studies. During that time, the President only had three sources of information about Bao Dai. First, there were the occasional newspaper articles written about the Emperor and his activities in France. Photos of the Emperor were often shown in those articles. He liked sports, cars, and he loved the French lifestyle. The second source was your Uncle Luyen who also studied in Paris and became a close friend of the Emperor. Though your Uncle Luyen wrote enthusiastically about Bao Dai, praising his intelligence and his simplicity, his letters made your grandmother nervous. She asked your Uncle Khoi and the President to write to him and warn him against having too close a relationship with the Emperor."

Ham Tieu asked, "Why? Did the Emperor already have the reputation of a playboy at that time?" Hiep shook her head, "No, but even from your Uncle Luyen's letters, one could see that the Emperor didn't want to return to Vietnam, that he was only interested in horses and fast cars, comfort and fashion. Your grandmother was afraid that your Uncle Luyen would model himself on the Emperor."

Ham Tieu asked, "What was the third source of information about the Emperor?" Hiep said, "Prime Minister Nguyen Huu Bai. The Prime Minister was in constant touch with the Emperor and with the French. You have to understand that the Prime Minister had not been happy with Emperor Khai Dinh. He had expected the Emperor to show more backbone in dealing with the French. As it turned out, Emperor Khai Dinh was too submissive. The Prime Minister regretted his role in placing Khai Dinh on the throne. His reservations about Emperor Bao Dai were in a way, excessive. He found fault in the young Emperor too readily. He did not approve the Emperor's long stay in France, under the influence of Mr. Jean Charles, whom many Vietnamese called *the most dangerous colonialist.*

Ham Tieu pressed on, "So, the President already had a bad opinion of the Emperor before 1932." Hiep shook her head, "People who didn't know the President thought that he was a man with many prejudices. That's not true at all. Even with all the unflattering information he received about the young Emperor, the President wasn't at all sure what he should think of Bao Dai. The first real test was when the Emperor asked him to be Prime Minister."

Elderly Emperor Bao Dai

*

Ham Tieu asked, "What was the verdict?" Hiep smiled. She remembered it all as if everything had happened only the day before; "You know that the President accepted the post of Prime Minister with the definite plan to resign and create an embarrassment to the French colonial administration. So, neither his acceptance of the position nor his resignation reflected a judgment on the Emperor. But during that period of over seventy days, he had many opportunities to observe the Emperor. After his resignation, he went back to live in Phu Cam for eleven years. He often talked to me about the Emperor."

Ham Tieu knew that now her mother would drag her feet. Hiep hated to criticize people. If she heard critical comments, she rarely repeated them. So now, Ham Tieu sat back, armed herself with patience and waited.

Finally, Hiep said, "The President found the Emperor to be one of the most intelligent persons he had ever known. He told me one day, 'If the Emperor used only one tenth of his intelligence, people would call him a genius.' He saw great qualities in the Emperor: self-confidence, poise, and

617

serenity. The greatest weakness of the monarch, according to him, was his *ennui*, his boredom. That boredom prevented the Emperor from persevering in his undertakings, from proving his patriotism and his real concern for his people."

Ham Tieu was not satisfied. She exclaimed, "That's all? What about his well-known selfishness and his demonstrated lack of will?" Hiep smiled sadly, "Not in 1933. It was much later, when his boredom, aided by his long depression caused by the reclusive life in the Imperial Palace, led him to find solace in women and gambling."

Hiep shrugged, "After he abdicated and went to Hanoi, then to China, another Bao Dai emerged. One can be crueler in one's judgment about him since then. When the French brought him back to power, the people who led him astray surrounded him. Yet, at no time, did he intentionally hurt the interests of his country and his people."

Ham Tieu reminded her, "What about his ties with the Binh Xuyen pirates?" Hiep's voice now sounded sadder than ever, "The French also had ties with the Binh Xuyen pirates. The Emperor made many mistakes in his life. It is fashionable to label him as a womanizer, a cynical playboy, and an inveterate gambler. His original sin was his boredom. Maybe he wanted to be a great ruler, but knew from the very beginning that he would never be allowed to rule. His boredom may have come from that awareness of his situation." Ham Tieu asked, "That's how you want us to see him?"

Hiep nodded, "Maybe with time, history will be kinder to him than it has been up to now." Hiep took her small reading glasses out from a lacquered wooden case lined with velvet. She started to leaf through the pages of Bao Dai's memoirs. She said, "Here come many sleepless nights."

*

Since Diem's assassination, Hiep recoiled at any news of an assassination attempt. In March 1981, she was horrified when she learned about the attempt on President Reagan's life, in Washington.

Less than two months later, she was even more horrified when she saw on television the haunting images of the attempted assassination committed against the Pope. While the world waited to know his fate, while the surgeons worked on him, Hiep prayed.

For hours she prayed for him. She said, "Dear God, I am past my eightieth birthday already. May I die in his place?" It was not the first time she had prayed that way. She had said almost the same prayer when Khoi was arrested and taken away by the Viet Minh. She had prayed God to let her die instead of her brothers when the Presidential Palace was surrounded by rebel troops in 1960, and again in 1963. She had wanted to die in Can's place in 1964. The Pope did not die.

Having now turned eighty, Hiep had only one major hope left: she wanted to see her son, Thuan, before she died. She did not know that it would take seven more years of waiting and praying before she would see him again.

*

It took some time for the information to reach Hiep. In late 1983, when she finally knew, her feelings were quite ambivalent. The authorities in Saigon had decided to clear the Mac Dinh Chi cemetery, and relatives of hers were ordered to move her mother's, Diem's, and Nhu's remains to Lai Thieu, thirty kilometers east of Saigon. As the Abbot of the North Vietnam Mutuality Pagoda had died in the meantime, her relatives also decided to move Can's remains to the same site.

With the information she also received a few photographs of the new graves. The pictures showed her mother's grave in the middle with an epitaph marked simply 'Pham Thi Than, deceased on February 1, 1964'. Diem's and Nhu's graves flanked their mother's; Diem's epitaph carried the words 'John the Baptist, the elder, deceased on November 2, 1963', and Nhu's epitaph read 'James, the junior, deceased on November 2, 1963.' Near the group, the pictures showed Can's grave. His epitaph read 'John the Baptist Can, died in 1964'.

Giao's daughter, Sister Truong Dinh Ly, stood in the background of most of the pictures. She was reported to have been the driving force behind the move. Hiep told Am, "You see, my Sister Giao, who was so detached from the Ngo Dinh family concerns when she was alive, has now through the hands of her daughter, insured the repose of my mother and my three martyred brothers."

She spent days reminiscing about Giao, the 'free spirit'. She was the only one of Ngo Dinh Kha's children who had not felt bound by her father's dream. Hiep remembered her standing in her orchard, watching Luyen and her son, Ban, climbing from branch to branch, high in the litchi trees. Hiep remembered Giao standing at her gate, after she had sent Luyen and Ban to school with their lunch bags that she prepared with care every morning.

Giao had been there to mourn Khoi's death. She was not there to celebrate Diem's triumphal return to power. She adamantly refused to participate in any major decisions of the family, and refused its help, even when she needed it.

Now that all her brothers and sisters were either dead or in exile, it was Giao's daughter who had taken the remains of Mrs. Ngo Dinh Kha and her three sons to their permanent resting place.

She added after a while, "We, the women in the family, Mother and my sisters and I, were the ones who agonized as the men in the family struggled for their ideals. We cried when they fell, buried them when they died and went on protecting their rest long after they returned to the ashes."

The tombs were built gracefully. "Here in this distant cemetery, they will never be disturbed again", Hiep thought. On one hand, she was glad that all those of her family who had died in Saigon could be together now, but on the other hand, she regretted that Can's remains had been moved from the grounds of the Buddhist pagoda. She was told that there was no other way. But she still regretted that one of Can's last wishes could no longer be satisfied.

She remembered the day when in prison, Can had requested that his remains be permanently buried on the grounds of a pagoda, to emphasize his family's ties with Buddhism.

Andre Nguyen Van Chau

CHAPTER THIRTY-SEVEN
SUNLIGHT AFTER DARKNESS

On July 11, 1984, Archbishop Thuc sent a humble letter to Pope John Paul II, from Washington D.C., expressing his regrets over his past errors and asking for forgiveness from the Holy See. The Holy See forgave him and five months later he died in Springfield, Missouri.

Archbishop Ngo Dinh Thuc

*

Hiep was glad that her Brother Thuc had died peacefully, after a long life. He had died at the age of eighty-four, and was given a beautiful funeral by the priests of the Congregation of Mary, the Co-Redeemer, in Carthage nearby. Attending the funeral were her brother, Luyen, and her son, Tuyen, as well as numerous Vietnamese friends who had come from all over the United States.

Among the mourners, was Father Cao Van Luan, who was a long time friend of the family and who had ended up fighting her brothers at the most critical moment in 1963. Father. Luan shed tears at the funeral Mass.

The priests who had been instrumental in the release of her elderly brother from the schismatic monks, who had kept him captive for years, promised Luyen that they would care perpetually for the Archbishop's grave.

Hiep did not cry. She no longer found the passing from life to death, to resurrection a fearful process. She prayed for the repose of her brother's soul and hoped that God would readily forgive him the many errors and weaknesses that had marked his life. She hoped that his long and painful years of exile had compensated for his sins. She prayed that people who had known him for what he was, would remember him as a man conscious of all his failings, but endowed with a big heart and a burning desire to serve his God.

*

In February 1987, Luyen arrived in Sydney. He was to spend the next two months in Australia. Am and Hiep had welcomed him at the airport, and taken him home. Luyen had asked immediately if they could all go out to the beach and take a walk. Though Maroubra Beach was next door, Ham Tieu suggested that they drive to Manly Beach, a little to the north.

As they walked, Hiep watched her brother. Luyen was as elegant as always. At the age of seventy-three, he was still agile and looked quite young. Luyen had brought news with him about the United States and Europe. Hiep watched Luyen as he talked. Apparently he had been overwhelmed by what he saw in the United States, when he had arrived there in late 1984 during the final days of Archbishop Thuc's life.

He said, "I first went to Carthage and Springfield, Missouri, to see Brother Thuc. He was weak and barely conscious. I knew he was conscious because when I talked to him about our childhood, he smiled happily. But he kept his eyes closed and made only slight signs of recognition when I was around."

Hiep imagined the scene. It was like it had been during the last days of her mother's life. She knew how hard it was to watch somebody you loved slipping slowly into a coma. Luyen continued, "In Missouri, Tuyen and a group of his friends came. At night, I sat talking to them. How fervent they were! How eager they were to learn everything I knew about the President."

Luyen's words put salve on Hiep's wounds. He said, "One of them asked me, 'If you had to choose one among the lessons we have to learn from the President, which one you would pick?' It was a hard question. I asked him to wait for a while. I had to think it over." Hiep smiled, "Which one did you pick?"

Luyen watched his sister intently as he answered, "I told him that it would be the way the President used his own weaknesses as advantages." Luyen saw that his sister was satisfied. She asked, "Did you clarify that lesson for him?" Luyen answered, "Yes, I described to him the circumstances in which the President assumed power, how he had to start with nothing, how he had to pitch his faith and his will against mighty enemies." Hiep smiled, "As long as there are people who still want to learn from the President's example, all our sacrifices have not been in vain."

Luyen nodded acquiescence. He went on, "After a few days in Missouri, I decided to go to California, where a large number of our loyal friends live. There, on November 2, I attended the Commemorative Service for the President, Brother Nhu and Can, and their comrades-in-arms who died during and after the coup."

Luyen bent down, picked up a round pebble and threw it into the waves. He said, "There were thousands of people at the Christian ceremony and also thousands attending the Buddhist commemorative service. You should go there someday and see it for yourself. During the ceremonies I sat thinking, 'The President is vindicated.' After more than twenty years, people still remember him. From what I saw, there will be even more people who remember him in the future."

Hiep asked, "Did you address the crowd?" Luyen laughed, "I have never learned to speak to a large audience, you know. Yet, the organizers insisted. So, controlling my emotions, I said a few words. I was a big success. The people did not need an eloquent orator. They simply wanted to see the brother of their heroes."

Hiep looked out at the open sea. The same seagulls came out of her memories, emitted sharp screams and plunged between two waves. The meaning of Diem's life and death appeared to Hiep as evanescent as the solitary fleck of red cloud on the horizon, yet as enduring as the ocean. She startled Luyen when she said, "Everything is well, then."

*

Ngo Dinh Luyen

*

Luyen died on April 23, 1988. Hiep came to treasure even more, the memories of Luyen's visit the previous year. She remembered Lucie, his first wife, at the age of sixteen, when Hoang and she saw her for the first time in Cho Lon, in 1938.

She remembered Marie, with her simplicity and her perpetual smile, married to Luyen two years after Lucie, her own sister had died. She knew that Marie had stood up to Le Xuan on more than one occasion. She had the courage to come back to Vietnam and stand by Luyen's side during the darkest hours of 1955. She had come to Hue twice for the family reunions. Her silent gaze sometimes sufficed to change the direction of the discussions. Diem listened intently to her few words.

After the coup of 1963, Luyen and she were behind all the commemorative ceremonies for Diem and Nhu, organized in Paris on

November 2, every year. Now Luyen was dead. Hiep did not feel pain, only sadness.

Ngo Dinh Thi Hiep and Nguyen Van Am in Sydney

With Luyen gone *she* remained the last of the brood. She wondered if she had been spared for a purpose. She wondered whether she should be the one to tell the story of her once mighty clan.

*

On June 19, 1988, despite all the protests raised by the Communist regime in Vietnam, Pope John Paul II solemnly canonized one hundred and seventeen Vietnam Martyrs. The controversy risked complicating recent understandings between the Church of Vietnam and the government. It put a strain on the relations between the Vatican and the Socialist Republic of Vietnam.

Hiep, who had seen signs of rapprochement and hoped that thanks to improved relations with Vietnam, the Holy See would soon be successful in having Archbishop Thuan released, now feared that his release would be put on the back burner.

Hiep believed, however, that the Vietnam Martyrs should be canonized, no matter what happened to her son. She believed that by honoring the martyrs, the universal Church honored Vietnamese Christians, and the entire Vietnamese nation. Over three centuries of persecution, more than one hundred thousand Vietnamese Catholics had been killed because of their fidelity to their faith. Hiep and her family, born of martyrs, drew tremendous pride from the fact. The day Pope John Paul II announced the canonization of the Vietnam martyrs; Hiep could barely contain her joy. She asked Ham Tieu to go and attend the ceremony on behalf of her family.

Ham Tieu made the trip to Rome. She wrote back, enthused by the great event, and by the crowds of Vietnamese who had come from all parts of the world. It was during the meetings with Vietnamese communities from all of the continents that she was able to measure the extent of President Diem's influence on the Vietnamese overseas and the respect they professed for Archbishop Thuan. Everybody seemed to be of one mind. They all prayed for Thuan to be released and allowed to fill his leadership role within the Church of Vietnam.

*

628

On November 21, 1988, the Feast of the Presentation of Mary at the Temple, and the sixty-third anniversary of his parents' wedding, Thuan was released from prison and allowed to stay at the Archbishop's House in Hanoi. On his document of release, there was no mention of his ever been in jail. It simply stated that he was allowed to leave his residence in Giang Xa and move to the Archbishop's House in Hanoi.

Thuan's release was announced by a great many news agencies, and soon enough, Hiep was receiving dozens of telephone calls every day, from friends and acquaintances who wanted to know more about Thuan's physical condition and whereabouts. Hiep did not mind answering the calls. Her joy was so great that nothing could diminish it. Officially, Church sources had informed her that Thuan would soon be allowed to go to Australia and visit his parents.

At night, Hiep saw Thuan in her dreams. She saw him arriving at the airport and she and her husband wanting to run to him but not being able to move. Oppressive as the dreams were, she woke up feeling happy for having caught a glimpse of him.

She was afraid that he would find her too old, too weak, and too frail. She was afraid that instead of joy he would feel pain on seeing her. She spent hours powdering her face, combing her long hair, and changing her gowns. She said to herself, "No, I will not let him guess how much his long captivity has aged me. I will not let him know how many sleepless nights I have spent praying God to spare him, to make him well, to give him strength."

Then she thought that Thuan might have suffered so much that he would look really terrible. She braced herself, "I will not cry, even if looks like a ghost. No, I will not cry, no matter how he looks. Probably it would help if I cry now, before he arrives."

*

She did not know that there had been a plot in the making. One day, her daughter, Ham Tieu, took a flight to Bangkok, without telling her or Am. The Australian authorities told her that Thuan had one day walked into the Australian Embassy in Hanoi and asked for a visa.

Apparently, the Australian Embassy officials were stunned to see Thuan. All bureaucratic procedures were waived, and the visa delivered immediately. Now, the Australian authorities were told that Thuan was scheduled to depart for Sydney on March 28, 1988, but they advised Ham Tieu not to put too much faith in it. They said a scheduled departure from Vietnam did not mean a confirmed departure.

Ham Tieu flew to Bangkok on the day Thuan was to take an Air Vietnam flight out of Hanoi. He was to meet with her at the Krung Thep airport, if everything went as planned. For Ham Tieu, everything could go wrong. She was praying hard, on her flight to Bangkok and while she waited for him there. Meeting with him in Bangkok seemed to her both so near and yet so uncertain.

Ham Tieu could barely refrain from crying when she saw her brother. He was still gaunt and tall. His shoulders were as straight as those of his grandfather, the late Grand Chamberlain. She remembered that her grandmother had always said that Thuan was the only one with straight shoulders, as her sons all stooped a little.

They flew to Sydney together and were welcomed at the airport by the Nuncio upon their arrival. On their way from the airport to Ham Tieu's house, there was so much traffic that day that the Nuncio said, "There's so much pollution, so much traffic here. I am sorry that we have to drive at snail's pace like this in this city." Thuan smiled and said, "Your Excellency, you know that I have just come out of jail. After thirteen years of hell, everything smells, sounds and looks like heaven to me now."

After a few hours of rest, Ham Tieu called her father and told him, "A monsignor who knows Brother Thuan would like to see you this afternoon. Is it possible?" Her father was more than a little excited, as he said, "Tell the monsignor he may come at any time. Your mother and I will be waiting impatiently for his visit."

Over the years, how many times had a cardinal, a bishop, a priest come to see them and give them the latest news about Thuan. Both her parents had drawn strength from those visits. Ham Tieu felt a lump in her throat when she heard the excitement in her father's voice.

She said quickly, "I will be there with him at three." And then she hung up.

*

Am and Hiep were all dressed up. At the first ring of the doorbell, Am opened the door. Am was elegantly dressed in his blue gown, while Hiep had gone to the extra length of putting on one of her best brocaded robes. They looked at Thuan and Ham Tieu. There was a second of hesitation, then Am exclaimed with a little laugh, "Monseigneur!"

Hiep stood one step behind Am. She said softly, "Thuan, you are here. You are alive." Feeling and not feeling, she had dreamt about that minute for so long. She had imagined it in so many ways. Yet, she had never thought it would be as simple and as satisfying as that.

Hiep repeated, and her own voice seemed to her to come from very far away, "Here you are, alive." There were so many things she would like to say, but then, she knew that they could also be left unsaid. Thirteen years in jail and Thuan still had the same smile, the same voice, and the same pensive way of bending his head when listening.

Am turned to Ham Tieu and said in mock accusation, "So you knew about your brother's arrival and did not tell us!" Both Thuan and Ham Tieu smiled. Thuan said, "I called her from Hanoi, and asked her to come and join me in Bangkok. We flew together from there to Sydney this morning." Hiep asked, "Why did you think that was necessary? Were you afraid that your father and I would have a heart attack if you showed up all of a sudden at our doorstep?"

Ham Tieu interrupted, "I was told by the Australian Government people not to tell you anything. They were afraid that at the last minute, the authorities in Vietnam might change their minds and prevent Brother Thuan from boarding the plane. That was why I did not tell you." Thuan nodded and said, "Ham Tieu told me in Bangkok, that she was trembling the whole time she was waiting for me there. She was afraid that I would not make it to Bangkok."

He looked intently at his mother, then at his father. "They have not changed a bit," he thought. His mother was still the same woman he had seen after President Diem's death, strong and unbending. His father entered the game without missing a beat, *"Monseigneur"*, he had said, as Ham Tieu had announced the visit of a monsignor.

For the first time Thuan understood why the current rulers in Vietnam felt that they had to arrest him and drag him from one prison to another for thirteen years. They, like so many others, feared that indomitable spirit in his blood. They had to break him in order to submit the Church in Vietnam to their will.

Yet, nothing broke him, just as nothing had cowed his grandfather, Ngo Dinh Kha; as nothing had broken the spirit of his uncles, Khoi, Diem, Nhu and Can; as nothing had sapped his mother's strength.

For the first time, Thuan understood his father's sacrifice. His father had perhaps even more pride and more strength than his mother. Despite that, he had chosen to stand behind her, given her his unconditional support, suffered with her all the tragedies of her family, and never complained. He had allowed her to play an active part in the politics of her family. He had stood by her when everything collapsed around her, when everything built up by her brothers turned to ashes.

Thuan laughed at himself now for having entertained the naïve fear of giving his parents a heart attack, when he showed up on their doorstep. He had told himself that he would not recount his ordeal to his parents until much later. Now, he saw that they were ready to hear his story. It was he who now had problems revisiting the thirteen-year odyssey that brought him from prison to prison, from interrogation to interrogation.

Am told him, "We want to hear your story, but take your time. We are not going to die before we hear all about the things that have happened to you since we last met in Saigon." Hiep nodded. She sat at a distance from him. Joy and contentment shone on her face. She had prayed for the last thirteen years, day and night, and now he was there. Alive! Once again, God had listened to her prayers.

*

Archbishop Thuan did not tell the story of his captivity in one afternoon. Nor was he eager to tell it. Hiep saw his reluctance. She respected her son's wish to reflect more on his ordeal before he said too much about it. Bit by bit, the story came out. Thuan tempered everything with his smile and his humor. He was never melodramatic. At no time did he paint himself as a martyr. He seemed to have made his peace with his former captors. He seemed to have forgiven his former tormentors.

Listening to him, Am and Hiep had to guess how he had been humiliated, how he had suffered, how he had seen himself approaching the threshold of despair.

*

Archbishop FX Nguyen Van Thuan

*

On August 18, 1975, the feast of Assumption, Thuan, newly appointed the Archbishop Coadjutor of Saigon, had been taken to the Independence Palace for questioning. It was inevitable. For days, 'patriotic' priests had been organizing demonstrations against Thuan and Archbishop Henri Lemaitre, the Nuncio whom they denounced as the instigator of his promotion.

After several hours of questioning, the officials told him that he was under arrest and that they were taking him back to Nha Trang, his former diocese. They signified that they were not about to recognize his new position of Archbishop Coadjutor of Ho Chi Minh City. The authorities viewed his appointment as Coadjutor, with the right to succeed, as the greatest threat against the new regime. Aging Archbishop Nguyen van Binh could die at any moment, and the new regime had no desire to deal with Thuan as the new Archbishop.

In Nha Trang, Thuan was not allowed to stay at the Bishop's House. The authorities kept him under house arrest at the Cay Vong Parish, located five miles outside of Nha Trang City, in the direction of the mountains. It was there, that Thuan jotted down a few thoughts every day, on small bits of paper. Smuggled out of his place of captivity, one small piece at a time, it was printed in Vietnam and then brought out overseas. *The Road to Hope*, a book unique in its genre, has inspired thousands of people and has been translated into seven languages.

Thuan used the simplest language to deliver his most sophisticated thoughts about life, death, and the relationship between God and people. It is a devotional book that goes far beyond simple devotion. It is a message of hope written by a man who was forbidden to hope. Most of his readers keep his book within reach and read parts of it every day.

*

Cay Vong Parish was judged to be too close to where Thuan had administered his diocese with kindness and dedication, for more than seven years. The authorities decided, in the end, to put him in a real prison. On March 18, 1976, the Feast of St. Joseph, he was sent to Phu Khanh Prison Camp.

Here, Thuan recognized many familiar faces among his prison mates. They gathered around him in the evenings and listened to his advice and encouragement. Thuan listened to their stories of woe: they were military officers or civil servants of the old regime, and they knew neither what crimes they were accused of nor for how long they would be detained.

Not many of them were Christians, but they respected him because of his manners, because he volunteered for the most unpleasant chores, and because often, pretending he could not eat too much, he gave most of his daily portions to others.

For many months, Thuan was put into solitary confinement. In his isolation cell, Thuan was told to write his life story, over and over again. It was a blessing that he had been told on the first day of his detention, how to write his 'Confession'. The one who had given him the advice was an old warden. He had told him to write as little as possible, to keep it as simple as possible, and to keep a copy of what he wrote. He was told never to deviate from the first version.

Thuan was grateful for the advice. He never deviated from the first version of his 'life story'. But the periods of isolation took a terrible toll on him. He yearned each time for the return to the company of his fellow inmates.

Phu Khanh Prison Camp still was too close to Nha Trang. It was clear that he was gaining more and more ascendance over the other inmates. It was decided that he should be sent away from his diocese.

Thuan did not know what awaited him. On November 29, 1976, he was brought back to the South. He was held in Thu Duc, fifteen miles outside of Saigon for a few days. He did not even bother to ask what his destination would be. His wardens would not have told him anything, anyway.

On December 1, 1976, he found himself on board a ship, which left the South the next day for Hai Phong, where Thuan arrived ten days later. It was the first time Thuan had set foot in North Vietnam. At first, he was overwhelmed with emotion. This was the part of Vietnam he did not know. Since childhood, the North had been for him shrouded in mystery. He had listened to stories told by his Uncles Diem and Nhu, and had imagined himself in the midst of North Vietnamese landscapes. Now he was there. He guessed, correctly, that he would not be allowed to see much of North Vietnam's beauty.

That same day in the afternoon, he was brought to the Vinh Quy Prison Camp near the Tam Dao Mountains, not far from the Temple of Kings Hung (the first legendary kings and founders of Vietnam). He found solace in the fact. The Prison Camp was far from every trace of civilization. Yet, being close to the Temple of Kings Hung was for Thuan an exhilarating experience.

Every day, the inmates had to work hard in the fields, but Thuan did not mind the hard labor. He saw the inmates help each other. He saw dignity in the worst deprivation. He saw his faith in humanity grow.

On rainy days, when work in the fields was impossible, Thuan worked inside as a carpenter. He managed to keep two little sticks of wood. They were so small that they escaped routine inspections. He decided to use the wood to make a wooden cross. He told himself, "This wood was collected near the Temple of the Kings Hung, the founders of the Vietnamese nation. For me, it will have a spiritual value."

Working on the tiny pieces of hard wood with a little knife was not easy, but Thuan managed to make a decent cross. Hiding the cross from the prison wardens was even more difficult. Thuan molded soap around the cross. And so the hidden cross passed all future inspections undetected.

*

Thuan was not allowed to stay in Vinh Quy Prison Camp very long, for fear that he would create a legend. On February 5, 1977, he was taken to Thanh Liet Prison Camp in the suburbs of Hanoi. The camp had been used during the war as one of the detention centers for American POW's. Thuan stopped at times to imagine the ordeal of the American inmates there. Traces of their passage still remained: inscriptions on the walls, names scribbled with charcoal, dates marked on wood with nails.

The air of the camp still seemed to reek with sweat and despair. At times, conversations at the far end of the Camp seemed to sound like English. Some of the wardens had stayed on since the end of the war. They told stories about American prisoners.

Sometimes, Thuan thought that the high authorities in Hanoi had forgotten all about him. Indeed, he was left alone in that camp for more than a year. As usual, he was ordered to write and re-write the story of his life. He was interrogated about his alleged anti-revolutionary activities. Neither he nor his captors really cared about the story he wrote. For him, the story had been rewritten so many times, that he now knew it by heart. For them, the story he wrote only demonstrated his stubbornness. They did not care about it anymore. They said, "It runs in the family."

*

636

The place where he was detained for the longest time was Giang Xa. He was taken there on May 13, 1978, and was kept there until November 5, 1982. In Giang Xa, he lived in relative comfort. He was assigned a dilapidated pastor's residence, and a couple of security agents as guards. He lived next to a parish church, yet he was not allowed to say mass or tend to any type of pastoral duties. The guards did not allow him to go anywhere beyond the little garden that surrounded the vicarage.

Thuan enjoyed working around the house and in the garden. He enjoyed talking to his guards. He had a grudging admiration for them, in spite of their incredible ignorance and their presumptions.

They seemed to care for him. When he was sick, they tried to get a doctor to come over and look at him as soon as possible. But they were not powerful cadres and sometimes a doctor and medicines took time to reach him. Thuan's illnesses which were initially mild, often turned deadly because of this lack of medical care

Thuan was past worrying. He knew that the Holy See and many governments were intervening continuously in his favor. In late 1978, he received a crucifix sent to him by the Holy See, through the care of Archbishop Nguyen Kim Dien, Thuc's successor. As the Archbishop of Hue, Dien had been allowed to go to Rome and he managed to bring back the crucifix and send it to Thuan. The gift encouraged Thuan for a long time.

Then visitors from foreign countries came to visit him, always accompanied by security officers disguised as interpreters. Thuan learned to speak with double entendre, and tried to end as quickly as possible, his conversations with innocent visitors who did not observe the rules of discretion.

Giang Xa was a far better place to live than the prison camps he had known previously. Being placed there made him wonder if perhaps he was not too far from the day of his release.

*

He did not realize yet, that there was no logic in Communist prison life. He did not foresee that after Giang Xa, his real ordeal would begin. On November 21, 1982, Thuan was taken away from his almost friendly guards in Giang Xa and sent into solitary confinement. He could not identify all the places where he was held. He remembered that he was transferred from one cell to another, from one location to another, all of them in the suburbs of Hanoi.

Solitary confinement can easily break a man. Thuan missed the contact with fellow human beings. Some of the isolation cells were so dark, that Thuan could not tell night from day. Sometimes not one single sound reached his ears. Sometimes a cell was so hermetic that Thuan had to lie on the floor with his nose to the little crack under the door, in order to breathe. At times, the silence and the isolation drove Thuan to the brink of mental breakdown.

One day in his dark cell, Thuan tried over and over again to say the words of the *Hail Mary*, but he could no longer remember them. That was the first time he cried.

Years later, Thuan still could not understand why his tormentors, towards the end, had put him through six years of solitary confinement. He did not understand why they had gone out of their way to destroy him. Little by little, however, Thuan learned to live even in solitary confinement. His prayers, no matter how he said them, gave him the strength to survive one hour at a time.

On November 21, 1988, without rhyme or reason, the authorities released him. He was brought in to meet with top Communist leaders who had been keeping track of him throughout his detention. There were no apologies, only a statement of fact, "We had to do it. It was not personal. The fact that you are *who* you are and *what* you are, made your detention inevitable."

Thuan did not recriminate. He went and lived in the Archbishop's House in Hanoi.

*

For Hiep, Thuan's release coincided with some significant changes in Vietnam. *Doi Moi* (Renovation) policies were creating new opportunities for Vietnam to develop economically, if not socially and politically. Hiep welcomed the changes and hoped that other reform policies would soon follow them. To her, it seemed that Vietnam had embarked on a course of liberalization. The Socialist Republic of Vietnam was promoting foreign investments, and authorizing businesses to flourish.

The collapse of the Communist world soon left Vietnam, Laos, China, North Korea and Cuba as the only remaining Communist countries in the world. Hiep remembered that Diem had predicted in 1955 the collapse of the Communist regimes.

It had taken a little more than thirty years for his prophecy to become a reality. "Indeed, it has taken thirty years and a Polish Pope!" She corrected herself, "No, it has taken more than that. It has taken the realization of people living under communism that the Communist system has never really worked."

Hiep rejoiced at the changes that had were taking place in Vietnam. One of the things she dreamed for now was religious freedom in her country, where both Buddhists and Christians were persecuted and continued to suffer. She yearned to see the end of religious persecution.

Since 1988, Vietnam had allowed many of those who had been in reeducation centers, to go to the United States and other countries. She had the pleasure of meeting with old friends she had thought dead, people she never thought she would see again.

*

Soon her son, Archbishop Thuan could no longer stay in Vietnam. The authorities gave him an exit visa and told him he should not return. He went to Rome where Pope John Paul II made him Vice President of the Pontifical Council of Justice and Peace.

A few years later, Hiep and Am left their home in Maroubra Beach and went to live in a nursing home, the Village St. Joan of Arc. There she planted two small trees, a fig tree and a cypress. She bent them into the shape of a dragon, the shape of Vietnam. She spent a great deal of time and energy on the trees. Every day, when she stood in front of the trees, she was again reconciled with the world.

Andre Nguyen Van Chau

CHAPTER THIRTY-EIGHT
BEYOND THE SUNSET

On June 30, 1993, Am woke up with a pain in his chest. He did not complain but he was unable to finish his breakfast. He smiled and said that the breakfast was fine, but he was unable to swallow anything. Hiep was alarmed and called the doctor. By the time the doctor arrived, Am had started breathing painfully, laboriously and the doctor asked the nurses to bring in an oxygen tank.

Hiep asked the doctor if Am should be taken to the hospital. The doctor looked at her, and she saw in his eyes that the end was near for Am. She went outside with the doctor, and he told her that taking Am to the hospital would only cause him more pain and discomfort. He suggested that Hiep should call a priest.

Father Hoach came in and shook hands with Am. He winced as Am playfully applied more strength than necessary to the handshake. As he had done several times recently, the priest gave Am the Extreme Unction. All of Hiep's daughters had arrived, and one by one, they winced as Am squeezed their hands really hard. When he did that, his eyes shone maliciously like when he told a joke or played a little prank.

His spirits were high all morning. Then in the afternoon, he began to pray intensely. By evening, his eyes were closed most of the time. He opened them occasionally for a few short minutes, but he did not seem to see much. By nightfall, his breathing had become erratic and he sunk slowly into a coma.

Hiep did not feel pain inside her. She looked at him dying and only remembered the best moments they had shared. Am was dying so peacefully. Hiep knew that Am was about to pass away, but nothing in her wanted to pull him back to life. At midnight, June 30, he was gone. In steadfast faith, she recited the prayer for the dying.

Huddled together, she and her daughters prayed for him. They thanked God for his peaceful death, his passing from this worldly life to his life near God. Hiep was glad that she had her daughters to comfort her. She knew that it would have been terrible if she had to face Am's death alone.

Her sons were arriving, Thuan from Rome, and Tuyen from Houston. They would arrive in Sydney in time for the funeral. For now, the presence of her daughters forced Hiep to be strong, and gave her time to sort out her feelings before she had to face the emptiness within.

She was amazed to see how her daughters overcame their grief and talked about times they had spent with their father. Together they discussed dates and details and recalled so many memories about their father. They talked and laughed, talked and cried, and Hiep was once again surprised by the closeness of pain and joy, suffering and happiness. She was glad that none of her daughters thought that death was the end of everything, and that they all believed that they would someday see their father again.

Hiep listened to their soft voices and sank into a state of semi-consciousness. Softly, as if not wanting to disturb her husband's rest, she whispered, "I commend you, my beloved, to Almighty God who created you, so that when by your death you have paid your debt to which every man is subject, you may return to God your Maker who formed you from the dust of the earth."

Mother and Son

*

The funeral took place four days later. In the meantime, both Thuan and Tuyen had arrived. The Mass for the Dead was officiated by Archbishop Thuan, concelebrating with two other bishops. Hiep's daughters wanted her to deliver the readings during the Mass, but they were afraid that she would not be up to it. It would be disastrous if Hiep broke down and could not finish the reading. Hiep herself had some doubt about her own strength. But she went through the Reading and the Responsorial Psalm without stumbling once.

After the Concluding Rites, Thuan, in full Episcopal vestments, prostrated himself three times in front of his father's body, in recognition of what his family owed his father in life and in death. He bowed three times before his concelebrants and again three times before the congregation to thank them all for their presence. All the members of his family prostrated themselves, and bowed with him.

The rituals he observed brought Hiep back to a time and a place far from the present, far from Sydney, to a time and place where rituals reflected the inner need of one's deep respect for others, and where children's piety was a mixture of love, gratefulness, admiration and respect.

*

Still praying

*

Hiep had made up her mind to travel to Lourdes. Kneeling in front of the grotto where Bernadette had witnessed the apparitions of the Blessed Mary, Hiep found it so easy to pray. She had not come to Lourdes to pray for herself. On November 2, 1963, a minute before her brothers, Diem and Nhu, gave themselves up to those who murdered them, they had come out of the St. Francis' Church in Cho Lon, and stopped to pray at a replica of the grotto of Lourdes, which had been built in front of the church. When Hiep reminisced about her brothers, the vision of them standing and praying in front of the grotto of Lourdes was always the final image.

Lourdes had been identified in her mind since childhood with miracles and miraculous healing. It had not been her intent, however, to go to Lourdes to ask for the alleviation of her own ailments. She wanted to go there to thank the Madonna for all the wonders that had visited her family, to pray for the repose of her brothers' souls, and also for the healing of all the wounds caused by the war in Vietnam.

Thuan, who accompanied Hiep on that trip, was surprised by his mother's strength. She was on her knees for hours, her face radiating her inner peace and joy.

Then she was in Rome, the heart of the old Christian world. She had longed for so many years to see the gardens of the Vatican, and the Catacombs where the Christians of the Primitive Church had lived. Having heard so much about the Roman ruins and Roman architecture, she dearly wanted to see all the wonders of Rome before she died.

Archbishop Thuan served as her guide. He took her to the Piazza of St. Peter one evening and she stood there in the moonlight, listening to the faint rumble under her feet. For a moment she thought she could hear the heart beats of the Universal Church.

Then there was the memorable audience with the Pope at Castel Gandolfo, his summer residence. She was worried about her appearance, her gown and her veil until the last instant. But the meeting was very tranquil, and from the first minute, John Paul II's manners reassured her. His kindness and the love he professed for Vietnam and the Vietnamese impressed her. He conversed with Thuan in Italian, but spoke to her in French. He obviously knew her son well and that made her proud. The little he said to her directly filled her with contentment.

Rome seemed so familiar to her! All the books brought back from Rome by Thuc and Thuan, all the postcards they had sent her over the years during their stays in Rome, had made of Rome one of her favorite cities. Now, staying in Rome, looking at the wonders of the Eternal City, Hiep relived moments of the past when she had first seen them, at first in black and white, and then in color photographs.

She suddenly realized that in fact, at the most difficult moments of her life in Vietnam, she had opened those picture books, and revisited those postcards and she had drawn solace and encouragement from their beauty.

*

The success of her first long trip inspired her children to organize a second trip for her. She visited the United States and Canada, and there she met and thanked all those who had had an interest in her family, those who still honored the memory of Ngo Dinh Diem.

In California, she found thriving Vietnamese communities that made her proud. She was more convinced that ever that the exodus of Vietnamese during the Seventies and the Eighties had definitely been a wonderful opportunity, in spite of the tragic circumstances in which it had taken place.

She was amazed at the achievements of the Vietnamese Americans who in a very short time, had almost caught up with other Asian immigrant groups that had been resettled in the United States long before them.

At commemorative Masses said for her husband or at those said for her brothers, she met three generations of Vietnamese who wanted to know more about Diem, his deeds and his thoughts. She was asked to speak about him and even to write about him. "Diem has become a legend," she thought.

In Carthage, she visited the tomb of Archbishop Thuc. The calm and peace of the environment there was temporarily shattered by the arrival of thousands upon thousands of Vietnamese Christians who had come for the annual pilgrimage to Our Lady, the Co-Redeemer. She mingled with the crowd and marveled at the number of old friends she met there.

After the travels, the visits, the new faces and the old, Hiep longed to be back in the quiet of her home near Maroubra Beach. She decided that it was time for her to sit down and enjoy the sunset.

*

On August 1, 1997, former Emperor Bao Dai died in Paris of a cancer in the brain, at the Val de Grace Hospital. On August 6, a funeral service was held for the repose of his soul at the St. Pierre de Chaillot, near the Place de l'Etoile.

Hiep prayed for the Emperor, with Ham Tieu in her small room at the Village Joan of Arc. She was told that he had been baptized nine years earlier, in 1988, and had taken John-Robert as his Christian name. She was also told that the Emperor spent hours praying in his parish church. It was further reported to her that on a Good Friday, the elderly Emperor carried a heavy wooden cross down the Champs Elysees in the midst of his fellow-parishioners.

"How men change," Hiep thought. "How incredible the path taken by Bao Dai! Only God knows how a life will end." With Bao Dai gone, the ranks of major living witnesses of the century seemed to her to be fast fading away.

She has felt that she still has another voyage to look forward to. Looking out into the sea at Maroubra Beach, she felt the need to sum up her life in a nutshell. How will she say it? Should she borrow the words from *Dao Ze Jing?*

Reward bitterness with care.

See simplicity in the complicated.

Achieve greatness in little things.

In the universe the difficult things are done as if they are easy.

In the universe great acts are made of small deeds.

Outside her room, the cypress and the fig tree both bent into the shape of a dragon, which is also the shape of Vietnam, are the ultimate expression of her soul. She has spent years coaxing them into the desired shape. She has nurtured them, day after day, even while her own health is failing.

She longs to see her country again, but maybe not in this life. She wants to see it happy and prosperous, her people reconciled and united.

The trees are the only things she would leave as a heritage for her children and grandchildren: they are the symbols of her country and her people. The trees will tell her children and grandchildren to remember to forgive everything and never to forget their country.

Archbishop Thuan and his sister, Nguyen Thi Thu Hong in Rome

*

In January 2001, her son was made a Cardinal. When he asked her on the phone what that meant for her, her answer was quite unexpected: "You are a priest; when you became Bishop, you were still a priest with some more responsibilities. Now you are made Cardinal: you still are a priest with much more responsibility."

She was not overwhelmed by the news. She went on her knees and prayed for her son, who now was a prince of the Church.

After that she became more and more fragile and began to forget things. She was not fully aware that Cardinal Thuan passed away in September 2002.

Geneva, February 28, 1999

By showing up close the various players in the Ngo Dinh saga, the author brings out the strengths and the weaknesses of key members of the Ngo Dinh family. In the dialogues and discussions of the Ngo Dinh brothers and sisters found in the book, the readers may see how they were the harshest critics of their own mistakes and shortcomings. Those dialogues and discussions are, contrary to some critics-not imagined by the author-but the products of serious reminiscences and great efforts aiming at remembering word by word, sentence by sentence what the Ngo Dinh siblings have uttered during special family reunions by surviving members of the clan many years after Diem, Nhu and Can were killed so tragically.

Ngo Dinh Thi Hiep appears larger than life in this book. Because even as a little girl she was already the young confident of Ngo Dinh Kha and Nguyen Huu Bai, and later on, the confident of President Ngo Dinh Diem, she deserves to be seen at the center of the Ngo Dinh family.

Ngo Dinh Thi Hiep passed away on January 27, 2005 in Sydney Australia, three years after Cardinal F.X. Nguyen Van Thuan, her son, died in Rome.

Headstone of Ngo Dinh Thi Hiep's grave in Sydney, Australia

Austin, December 2014

About Andre Nguyen Van Chau

Andre Nguyen Van Chau was born in the Citadel of Hue, the old capital of Imperial Vietnam. He grew up with classmates who have become known writers, poets, composers and painters.

After obtaining a doctorate degree in the humanities at the Sorbonne, Paris, he taught English and creative writing at various universities in Viet Nam for twelve years.

In 1975 he began twenty-five years of work for migrants and refugees around the world, ten of which were spent at the head of the International Catholic Migrations Commissions with 84 national affiliates and with headquarters in Geneva, Switzerland.

He has traveled and worked in over 90 countries.

Back to the United States after Geneva he was for ten years the Director, Language and Accent Training at ACS, then Xerox before retiring in Austin, Texas and beginning a new career as a full-time writer.

One of his published works, *The Miracle of Hope,* has been translated into nine different languages.

The New Vietnamese-English Dictionary, on which he spent an inordinate number of hours in the last twenty years, was finally published in 2014.

He and his wife, Sagrario, have four children: Andrew, married to Jodie Scales, Boi-Lan, married to Rodolphe Lemoine, Michael, married to Rachel La Fleur and Xavier. They have seven grand-children: Katleyn, Géraldine, Alix, Drew, Noah, Isabelle and Luke.

www.ingramcontent.com/pod-product-compliance
Lightning Source LLC
Chambersburg PA
CBHW050401110426
42812CB00006BA/1761